HISTORY OF THE CONCEPT OF MIND

'This book is essential reading for those who want to know how our current understanding of the human psyche evolved. Why does it now sound quaint, pious or ironic to speak, not of a person's mind, but of their soul and spirit? Paul MacDonald's magisterial history of these concepts helps to provide answers. The reader is guided on a journey from ancient Hebrew and Greek visions through all the main landmarks in the history of philosophical psychology, as well as less familiar territory from literature and theology. The sweep of his book is immense; [it undertakes] a monumental task whose results are very impressive'.
David E. Cooper, Professor of Philosophy, University of Durham, UK

'The wide differences between the ways in which people of the past have understood themselves and our own ways show that the content of so-called folk psychology is utterly contingent, and this might bear on widely discussed issues in contemporary philosophy of mind. In this book, MacDonald shows himself to be a learned and acute scholar who provides an original and illuminating perspective even on previously familiar material'.
Stewart Candlish, Professor of Philosophy, University of Western Australia

In the twentieth century theorists were almost exclusively concerned with various versions of the materialist thesis, but prior to the current debates accounts of soul and mind reveal an extraordinary richness and complexity which bear careful and impartial investigation. This book is the first comprehensive, single-authored work to examine the historical, linguistic and conceptual issues involved in exploring the basic features of the human mind – from its most remote origins, to the beginning of the modern period. Paul MacDonald traces the development of an armature of psychical concepts from the Old Testament and Homer's works to the eighteenth-century advocacy of an empirical science of the mind. Students and readers of philosophy, psychology, literature and theology will find this accessible, comprehensive text an invaluable resource.

History of the Concept of Mind
Speculations about Soul, Mind and Spirit from Homer to Hume

PAUL S. MACDONALD

ASHGATE

© Paul S. MacDonald 2003

All rights reserved. No part of this publication may be reproduced, stored in a retrieval system, or transmitted in any form or by any means, electronic, mechanical, photocopying, recording, or otherwise without the prior permission of the publisher.

Published by
Ashgate Publishing Limited
Gower House, Croft Road
Aldershot, Hants
GU11 3HR
England

Ashgate Publishing Company
Suite 420
101 Cherry Street
Burlington, VT 05401–4405
USA

Ashgate website: http://www.ashgate.com

British Library Cataloguing in Publication Data
MacDonald, Paul S., 1951–
  History of the concept of mind: speculations about soul,
  mind and spirit from Homer to Hume
  1. Philosophy of mind – History 2. Mind and body
  I. Title
  128.2' 09

Library of Congress Control Number: 2002100873

ISBN 0 7546 1364 X (Hbk)
ISBN 0 7546 1365 8 (Pbk)

This book is printed on acid-free paper.

Typeset in Times by Manton Typesetters, Louth, Lincolnshire, UK.

Printed and bound in Great Britain by MPG Books Ltd, Bodmin, Cornwall.

Contents

Acknowledgements …………………………………………………………… vii

Abbreviations ………………………………………………………………… ix

Chapter 1 **Ancient Hebrew and Homeric Greek Life-Force** …… 1
    1. Hebrew Old Testament ideas about life and breath
    2. Homeric Greek ideas about life and breath
    3. The pre-Socratic soul as property-like thing

Chapter 2 **Plato, Aristotle and Hellenistic Thought** …… 37
    1. Plato's twofold and threefold account of soul
    2. Aristotle on soul as form and body as matter
    3. The Stoics, Epicurus and Lucretius on material spirit

Chapter 3 **From the New Testament to St. Augustine** …… 89
    1. The New Testament and St. Paul's new vision
    2. Neo-Platonic teachings and Plotinus' One-Mind-Soul
    3. The Greek and Latin Church Fathers
    4. Augustine's Christian–Platonist synthesis

Chapter 4 **Medieval Islamic and Christian Ideas** …… 161
    1. Islamic concepts: Alfārābī, Avicenna and Averroes
    2. Theological summation: Albert the Great and Thomas Aquinas
    3. Dante's soul in the service of love

Chapter 5 **Renaissance Platonism, Hermeticism and Other Heterodoxies** …… 205
    1. The centrality and dignity of human being
    2. The rediscovery of Plato, Plotinus and the Hermetica
    3. Magic and occultism in the service of science

Chapter 6 **Mind and Soul in English from Chaucer to Shakespeare** …… 245
    1. The various senses of 'soul' from 1200 to 1500
    2. The various senses of 'mind' from 1200 to 1500
    3. The natural shape of 'soul' and 'mind' in Shakespeare

Chapter 7	**The Triumph of Rationalist Concepts of Mind and Intellect**	279
	1. Descartes: mind as simple, immaterial thinking thing	
	2. Spinoza: mind as the idea the body has of itself	
	3. Leibniz: soul as an infinitely small incorporeal automaton	
Chapter 8	**The Empiricists' Advocacy of Matter Designed for Thought**	315
	1. Early attempts at a mechanical account of matter in motion	
	2. Locke, Berkeley and Hume for and against the materialist thesis	
	3. Summary overview and general conclusions	

Bibliography	363
Index of Names	387
Index of Subjects	391

Acknowledgements

For comments and suggestions on particular sections my thanks to: Dr. Loren Stuckenbruck, Theology Department, University of Durham, for reading the section on the Old Testament; Prof. C. J. Rowe, Classics Department, University of Durham, for reading the section on Plato; Dr. Nicholas Southgate for reading the section on Locke, Berkeley and Hume, and Dr. Nancy Victorin-Vangerud, Theology Department, Murdoch University (Australia) for reading the section on St. Augustine. My special thanks also to Robert Victorin-Vangerud for many insightful comments and suggestions on the first thirteen sections.

My gratitude also to Sarah Lloyd, Philosophy Editor at Ashgate Publishers, who, right from the start, made an unswerving commitment to a large and wide-ranging undertaking such as this book. My copy-editor, Jeanne Brady, did an excellent job in helping me to sort out hundreds of small but significant inconsistencies in the text, notes and bibliography.

To Duquesne University Press for permission to use the diagram by Robert Wood from the Introduction to Stephan Strasser's *The Phenomenology of Feeling*, Pittsburgh: Duquesne University Press, 1977, reproduced in Chapter 8, section 3.

My greatest thanks are attended with love, as always, for my wife, Fiona. For patience and good humor in listening to endless unsolicited remarks about *nepesh* for three years, this book is dedicated to her.

1

Abbreviations

ANRW	*Aufstieg und Niedergang der Römischen Welt*. Berlin: de Gruyter, 1972–date.
BICS	*Bulletin of the Institute of Classical Studies*.
Bremmer	J. M. Bremmer & others (eds) *Hidden Futures: Death and Immortality in Ancient Egypt, Anatolia, the Classical, Biblical and Arabic-Islamic World*. Amsterdam: Amsterdam University Press, 1994.
CCL	*Corpus Christianorum, Series Latina*.
CHB	*Cambridge History of the Bible*. P. R. Ackroyd, G. W. Lampe & S. L. Greenslade (eds) 3 vols. Cambridge: Cambridge University Press, 1963–70.
CHHP	*Cambridge History of Hellenic Philosophy*. Keimpe Alga et al. (eds) Cambridge: Cambridge University Press, 1999.
CHLGEMP	*Cambridge History of Later Greek and Early Medieval Philosophy*. A. H. Armstrong (ed.) Cambridge: Cambridge University Press, 1970.
CHLMP	*Cambridge History of Later Medieval Philosophy*. Norman Kretzmann & others (eds) Cambridge: Cambridge University Press, 1982.
CHRP	*Cambridge History of Renaissance Philosophy*. Charles Schmitt et al. (eds) Cambridge: Cambridge University Press, 1988.
CH17CP	*Cambridge History of Seventeenth Century Philosophy*. Daniel Garber & Michael Ayers (eds) Cambridge: Cambridge University Press, 1998.
CTC	*Catalogus Translationum et Commentariorum*. P. O. Kristeller (ed.) 7 vols. Washington, D.C.: Catholic University of America, 1960–92.
DMA	*Dictionary of the Middle Ages*. J. R. Strayer (ed.) 13 vols. New York: Scribner, 1982–89.
EER	*Encyclopedia of Religion*. Mircea Eliade (ed.) 16 vols. New York: Macmillan, 1987.
EEP	*Encyclopedia of Philosophy*. Paul Edwards (ed.) 8 vols. London: Macmillan, 1967.
EHPhR	*Etudes de l'Histoire de Philosophie et Religion* (journal).
EI2	*Encyclopedia of Islam*. New edn. H. A. R. Gibb (gen. ed.) 7 vols. Leiden: E. J. Brill.
ERE	*Encyclopedia of Religion and Ethics*. James Hastings (ed.) 12 vols. Edinburgh: T & T Clark, 1913.

Hist Rel	*History of Religions* (journal).
JHI	*Journal of the History of Ideas.*
JHP	*Journal of the History of Philosophy.*
JTS	*Journal of Theological Studies.*
Lampe PGL	*Patristic Greek Lexicon.* G. W. H. Lampe (ed.) Oxford: Clarendon Press, 1976.
LSJ	Liddel, Scott & Jones (eds) *Greek-English Lexicon.* 9th ed. rev. Oxford: Oxford University Press, 1968.
LXX	Septuagint (Greek Old Testament).
LCL	Loeb Classical Library.
MED	*Middle English Dictionary.* 15 vols. Ann Arbor, MI: University of Michigan Press, 1970–85.
NIDNT	*New International Dictionary of the New Testament.* 3 vols. Colin Brown (ed.) Exeter, UK: Paternoster Press, 1975–78.
NCBS	*Novae Concordantiae Bibliorum Sacrorum.* 5 vols. Stuttgart: Frommann, 1977.
NCE	*New Catholic Encyclopedia.* 16 vols. New York: McGraw-Hill, 1967–74.
NEJ	*Encyclopedia of Judaism.* Jacob Neusner et al. (eds) Leiden: E. J. Brill, 2000.
Nov Test	*Novum Testamentum* (journal).
NRSV	New Revised Standard Version.
NRT	*Nouvelle Revue Théologique* (journal).
NTS	*New Testament Studies* (journal).
OCB	*Oxford Companion to the Bible.* Bruce Metzger & Michael Coogan (eds) Oxford: Oxford University Press, 1993.
OCD	*Oxford Classical Dictionary.* 3rd edn. Simon Hornblower & Anthony Spawforth (eds) Oxford: Oxford University Press, 1996.
ODCC	*Oxford Dictionary of the Christian Church.* 2nd edn. F. L. Cross & E. A. Livingstone (eds) Oxford: Oxford University Press, 1990.
OED	*Oxford English Dictionary.* New edn. 13 vols. New York & Oxford: Oxford University Press, 1985.
OLD	P. G. W. Glare (ed.) *Oxford Latin Dictionary.* New York & Oxford: Oxford University Press, 1968–72.
Onians	R. B. Onians. *The Origins of European Thought.* 2nd edn. Cambridge: Cambridge University Press, 1951.
PL	*Patrologiae Latina, cursus completus.* J. P. Migne (ed.).
PG	*Patrologiae Graeca, cursus completus.* J. P. Migne (ed.).
RAC	*Reallexikon für Antike und Christentum.* 18 vols. Stuttgart: Hiersemann, 1950–98.
REP	*Routledge Encyclopedia of Philosophy.* Edward Craig (gen. ed.) 10 vols. New York: Routledge, 1998.
RE	*Real-Encyclopdie der Classischen Altertumwissenschaft.* Paulys, Wissowa & Kroll (eds).
RHPR	*Revue d'Histoire et de Philosophie Religieuses.*
RTAM	*Recherches de theologie ancienne et medievale.*

TDOT	*Theological Dictionary of the Old Testament.* G. J. Botterweck & H. Ringgren (eds) 10 vols. Grand Rapids, MI: Eerdmans, 1974–90.
TLOT	*Theological Lexicon of the Old Testament.* Ernst Jenni & Claus Westermann (eds) 3 vols. Peabody, MA: Hendrickson, 1997.
TLNT	*Theological Lexicon of the New Testament.* Cselas Spicq (ed.) 3 vols. Peabody, MA: Hendrickson, 1994.
TDNT	*Theological Dictionary of the New Testament.* G. Kittel & G. Friedrich (eds) 10 vols. Grand Rapids, MI: Eerdmans, 1964–76.
Thorndyke	Lynn Thorndyke. *History of Magic and Experimental Science.* 8 vols. New York: Macmillan, 1923–58.
TRE	*Theologische Realenzyklopädie.* 30 vols. Berlin: de Gruyter, 1984–date.
Vulgate	Latin Old and New Testament.
Wright & Potter	John Wright & Paul Potter (eds) *Psyche and Sōma: Physicians and Metaphysicians on the Mind-Body Problem from Antiquity to the Enlightenment.* Oxford: Clarendon Press, 2000.
ZAW	*Zeitschrift für die Alttestamentliche Wissenschaft* (journal).
ZNW	*Zeitschrift für die Neutestamentliche Wissenschaft* (journal).
Note:	Greek and Latin texts are cited according to the standard abbreviations in OCD, 3rd edn.

What then did I formerly think I was? A human; but what is a human? Shall I say a rational animal? No, for then I should have to inquire what an animal is, what rationality is, and in this way one question would lead me down the slope to other harder ones ... Instead I propose to concentrate on what came into my thoughts spontaneously and quite naturally whenever I *used* to consider what I was ... As to the nature of this soul, either I did not think about this, or else I imagined it to be something tenuous, like a wind or fire or ether, which permeated my more solid parts.

But what shall I *now* say that I am ...? I am then in the strict sense only a thing that thinks; that is, I am a mind or intelligence or intellect or reason – words whose meaning I have been ignorant of until now.

Descartes, *Second Meditation*

Chapter 1

Ancient Hebrew and Homeric Greek Life-Force

The history of the concepts of mind and soul is a complex and twisted network of many paths, each path strewn with obstacles, dead ends, false or hidden beginnings, relapses into old ways of thinking and forward leaps of imaginative projection. One of the principal problems is to sort out exactly which issue is being addressed when one holds up for scrutiny any one of the numerous terms involved in the ancestry of the modern concept of mind or soul. The obverse side of this same problem is to think that, in starting one's inquiry with the concept of *mind*, for example, instead of *soul* or *spirit*, and then making an effort to discern its earliest lineaments, one has a sure grasp of a clearly defined, well-marked out concept. In other words, if there is no consensus on what the concept of *mind* picks out or what it makes reference to, if the historian cannot appeal to a readily identifiable conceptual item, then how can any effort to trace its ancestry ever be confident that discussions of an earlier version are indeed versions of the same thing? One can imagine an aptitude test in which the subject is asked to match each of three or four original geometrical shapes with a plethora of target shapes, each of which is blurred or even vague. One then discovers that in the process of shifting one's attention from the source shape to its potential targets, the original shape has changed, and more than that, its shape is continually fluid.

The enormous number of books and articles on the mind–body problem (as one facet of this issue has come to be called) give the overwhelming impression that every aspect of human nature falls under one or the other concept. Although there is serious disagreement over the boundaries, whatever aspect is physical or material falls under 'body' and whatever aspect is non-physical or immaterial falls under 'mind'; though this bipartisan picture does not take account of those disputants who think that every aspect of human nature, including conscious episodes and intentions, is physical or material. Those who maintain some version of dualism are sometimes stuck with difficult cases, but these are resolved by assigning them to an admixture or permixture of mind and body. Thus one question posed by this debate for the historian of ideas concerns the fact that only one concept (mind) in the rich and complex ancestry of discussions of human nature has come to dominate the field. One would be hard pressed to make a coherent statement about the relative positions of the concepts of 'mind', 'soul', 'spirit' and 'psyche' in the framework of an all-inclusive understanding of human being. And it does not serve to clarify the issue by peremptorily claiming that 'soul', 'spirit' and 'psyche' have all been subsumed under, or eliminated in favor of, the concept of mind. It is very common, even routine, for example, to hear a scholar of Descartes' works remark that 'soul' and 'mind' mean the same thing, that these concepts can be interchanged without loss of meaning – but that is patently false. Descartes was well aware of the difference between 'soul' and 'mind' and was the first philosopher to explicitly abandon all of the conceptual baggage associated with the word 'soul' in favor of a radically new term, 'mind' and its principal attributes.

(1) Hebrew Old Testament ideas about life and breath

The present chapter begins the task of tracing the ancestry of the many ideas that composed our earliest understanding of those aspects of human 'nature' which escaped description in terms of outward appearance and physical attributes. The Hebrew authors of the Old Testament and the Homeric author of the *Iliad* and the *Odyssey* repeatedly call attention to cognitive and affective aspects of human nature which indicate an inner, personal dimension, something which is hidden from others but open to one's own awareness. The English word 'mind' is from the Latin root *mens*, itself an evolved form of the Greek word *menos*, 'life-force', whose verbal form is *menomai*, 'to desire or crave'; the word *mens* served the earliest Latin translators of Homer, Plato and Aristotle for the Greek word *nous*. But the word *mens* also did service for the Greek word *kardia,* 'heart', and the Hebrew word *leb* (plural *lebab*), 'heart or bosom'. The English word 'spirit' is from the Latin root *spiritus*, 'breath', whose original connotations survive in words like re-*spiration*, in-*spiration*, per-*spiration*, and so forth. The word *spiritus* served to translate the Greek word *pneuma* in the Vulgate or Latin Bible (St. Jerome, *c.* 400 CE) and editions of Plato and Aristotle (though not Homer); the original connotations of *pneuma* survive in words like pneumatic drill, pneumatic trough and pneumonia, that is, about the in and out cycle of air. The Greek Version of the Old Testament, the Septuagint or LXX (*c.* 250 BCE), uses *pneuma* in 75 per cent of the cases to translate the Hebrew word *ruach*, 'breath or force'. The English word 'soul' does not have a Latin or Greek root, but instead derives from an Old English and Old High German root (for example, *sawol, seel, seol*); 'soul' was used in the Geneva Bible (1560–1650) and the King James Version (1611 onward) to translate the Latin *anima* and the Greek *psychē*. In the LXX the Greek *psychē* is used in almost 90 per cent of the cases to translate the Hebrew *nepesh*, which means either 'desire' or 'vitality' or 'life-force'.

In Ancient Hebrew, each of these words has many nuances which subtly alter its meaning, nuances that depend on whether the word is the subject or object of an action, whether it is predicated of an animal or a human or God, and with which verbs of action it is linked. In addition, each word has undergone an evolution, or at least an attenuation in its total reference field. The most primitive meaning of *nepesh* is concrete and site-specific, the 'throat or gullet'; a further meaning is 'desire or longing', that is, to satisfy the need for food, drink and air taken in through the throat. The more abstract meaning 'life or vital force' refers to that which sustains or supports desire and longing; it can also refer to one who is alive, an individual; and finally in the later OT books, it can refer to the self, such that 'my *nepesh*' can be translated 'me' or 'I'. The most primitive meaning of *ruach* is also concrete and site-specific, it is the 'wind'; in so far as each living thing has God's wind within, it is the 'breath' or the organ of breathing. But, like *nepesh*, it can also refer to one who breathes, the individual; and further in the later OT books, 'my *ruach*' can be translated 'me' or 'I'. The Hebrew word *leb* follows a similar pattern, so that first it means 'heart', then 'will' or 'intention', next 'conscious' or 'conscience', and finally the self in the sense of 'me' or 'I'. In an approximate and tentative manner we could outline the evolution or progression of these various meanings according to the following scheme:

$$(\text{concrete} + \text{outward}) \rightarrow (\text{concrete} + \text{inward}) \rightarrow (\text{abstract} + \text{inward}) \rightarrow$$
$$(\text{self-referring or reflexive})$$

This is only one vector of development, however, since it will become apparent that various ambiguous meanings of both (concrete + inward) and (abstract + inward) can reciprocally influence each other:

$$(\text{concrete} + \text{inward})_1 \leftrightarrow (\text{abstract} + \text{inward})_1 \rightarrow (\text{concrete} + \text{inward})_2 \leftrightarrow$$
$$(\text{abstract} + \text{inward})_2$$

And hence each antecedent meaning can become detached from its initial consequent meaning and destabilize the process in several different directions, becoming more closely associated with other lines:

$$(\text{concrete} + \text{inward})_1 \rightarrow (\text{abstract} + \text{inward})_2 \leftrightarrow (\text{concrete} + \text{inward})_2 \rightarrow$$
$$(\text{abstract} + \text{inward})_3$$

It is important, however, to consider the details hidden within the various shadings of these key Hebrew terms, since the details provide a framework into which much later conceptual precipitates will fit. Aubrey Johnson offers a succinct statement of his meticulous analyses of the OT use of the word *nepesh*:

> At one extreme [*nepesh*] may be used to denote that common vital principle in man or beast which reveals itself in the form of conscious life ... It is the thought of a common life vouchsafed by Yahweh and identifiable with the blood (for the blood is said to be or contain the *nepesh*) which requires that all blood shall be sacred to Yahweh and taboo for man, and so is made the basis for the grim ritual of sacrifice. From this standpoint, therefore, the *nepesh* may be distinguished from its bodily vehicle, the *basar* or 'flesh'. Accordingly at death it is described as being breathed or poured out; so that normally man is then like water which has been spilt on the ground and cannot be gathered up again. In other words, when a person dies, the *nepesh* is said to 'depart'; and if in special circumstances life should be restored to the corpse, it is then said to 'return'. Nevertheless, as we proceed, we shall note the recognition of a strong ebb and flow between these two poles, corresponding to the degree of vitality manifested by the *nepesh* at any given time; and ... this corresponds to the fact that the Israelite did not always think in terms of a clear-cut distinction between 'life' and 'death'.[1]

The concrete and specific meaning of *nepesh* is clear in several passages: 'the underworld wrenches wide its *nepesh* and opens its mouth beyond measure' (Isa.

---

[1] Johnson, 1964, p. 9; see Wolff, 1974, pp. 10–25.

5:14), one speaker says of the greedy person that 'he opens his *nepesh* wide as the underworld and is like death and never has enough' (Hab. 2:5); thus *nepesh* is the throat or gullet which takes in food or drink. The poet of Psalms says, 'the hungry and thirsty whose *nepesh* fainted within them' (Ps. 107:5) and further that one ought to thank Yahweh, 'for he satisfies the thirsty *nepesh* and the hungry *nepesh* he fills with good things.' The context in which *nepesh* is used mentions hunger and thirst, being faint or satisfied, its dryness and the sense of being filled, and this shows quite unambiguously that in these passages *nepesh* should not be translated 'soul', but 'throat': 'All the toil of man is for his mouth, and yet his *nepesh* is not satisfied' (Eccles. 6:7). Although these contexts show that the throat is meant, at the same time it shows that the needy person as such is indicated.

But the *nepesh* is not just the organ for taking in food and drink, it is also the organ or the site of breathing. In some of these cases it is also quite evident that animals have their *nepesh*; thus in the case of the female camel, 'in the lust of her *nepesh* she pants for breath' (Jer. 2:24). The action of the *nepesh*, especially in its outward manifestation, is to blow or breathe out. For example, the throat of the fainting mother pants heavily (Jer. 15:9); the hope of the godless is to breathe out their *nepesh* (Job 11:20); and the crocodile's *nepesh* can kindle coals into fire (Job 41:21). When the flood-waters rise to the level of the *nepesh* one is in danger of drowning (Jonah 2:5; and Ps. 69:1). Although *neshama* in ancient Hebrew also signifies 'breath', the chronicler in Kings understands some sort of conceptual separation between the two terms when he says that the child's *nepesh* returns to the widow of Zarephath although there had been no *neshama* left in him (I Kings 17:21). In addition, although Hebrew also uses another word for neck, in the Psalms it is clear that the throat as the organ of life is designated: 'they forced his feet into fetters, his *nepesh* was put into iron' (Ps. 105:18); the witch of Endor asks King Saul, 'why do you want to lay a noose for my *nepesh* to bring about my death?' (I Sam. 28:9).

The part-for-whole shift from concrete and outward to concrete and inward, and from concrete and inward to abstract and inward is common in most languages. One readily understands the remark that someone 'has a big mouth' means that so-and-so talks too much, that someone 'has a big head' means that so-and-so has an overly large picture of their own importance. In similar fashion, 'to fill his shoes' means to take his place, to act in his role, and to 'feel the long arm of the law' is to find no escape from lawful punishment. The Latin phrase *per capita* is most often used in statistics or enumeration to indicate a single individual, much as journalists used to report that so many 'souls' were lost at sea; the poll tax (in its many nasty forms) uses the medieval English term for the top of a person's head. The isomorphism with *per capita* is evident when *nepesh* is used as a count-noun, for example, in lists of numbers of slaves, descendants, or inhabitants (Ex. 12:24; Ezek. 18:4; Gen. 46:15; Num. 31:28; Josh. 10:28).[2] The part-for-whole meaning of *nepesh* is evident in statements like the proverb which reads 'a worker's *nepesh* works for him, his mouth urges him on' (Prov. 16:26), or 'when you go into your neighbor's vineyard, you may eat your fill of grapes according to your *nepesh*'

---

[2] Seabass, in TDOT, vol. IX, p. 515; Westermann, in TLOT, p. 755.

(Deut. 23:24). In these contexts, *nepesh* indicates 'desire' or 'longing' in a straightforward manner, though it can also signify more than the physical desire for food and drink; the desire to remain free or to follow one's free will. For example, when a man wants to leave a woman who has once been his prisoner, he is only allowed to dismiss her in accordance with her *nepesh* (Deut. 21:14); in the same way, slaves should be set free according to their *nepesh*, that is, their freely chosen desire (Jer. 34:16).

The further part-for-whole conceptual shift is profound since it signifies not just a greater whole of which an organ or power is a lesser whole but the *kind of being* that has (or more properly *is*) the control or investment of this vital power. Thus the shift to the abstract and inward moves the concept of *nepesh* beyond the outwardly observable, into the individual's inner depths, and here the Hebrew word approaches the meaning of *anima* or soul. The prophet exhorts the nation of Israel, 'you shall not oppress a stranger; you know the *nepesh* of a stranger, for you were strangers in the land of Egypt' (Ex. 23:9). Here the writer is thinking not only of the stranger's needs and desires, but of the whole range of his feelings, feelings that arise from leaving his own land and the threat of slavery.

Many passages can be attested in which *nepesh* is used as a bridging concept between the desire or longing of a living being and a living being's soul as the 'seat' or 'inward place' of such desire or longing. Westermann concludes one portion of his analysis with the remark that 'only the group of passages that speak of the misery and sorrow (less often the joy and comfort) of the *nepesh* may be unequivocally and always appropriately translated "soul" in accord with Eng[lish] usage.' There are about 15 passages in which the fixed pair *nepesh* and *merr* ('bitter') occur; thus 'the healthy and whole *nepesh* can be altered when God makes it bitter. The person has become bitter at the center, at the core', and so forth. The bitter soul 'indicates a typical element of the OT understanding of *nepesh*: melancholy, desperation, and bitterness demonstrate the humanity of the individual with particular clarity; these very elements constitute the "uniqueness" (M. Heidegger) of humanity.'[3] The large and varied group of passages that depict the *nepesh* as bitter and troubled has no comparable counterpart that depicts the *nepesh* as joyful or delighted.

However, the desire or longing of the *nepesh* can be oriented towards something less concrete than the thing which would satisfy its physical craving. Thus, an individual's *nepesh* can be turned towards Yahweh or deliverance from bondage or an individual whom one loves: 'Jonathan's *nepesh* was bound to David's *nepesh*, and Jonathan loved him like his own *nepesh*' (1 Sam. 18:1). On several occasions the Song of Songs employs *nepesh* as the subject of love between man and woman: 'This category is especially characteristic of *nepesh*. The translation "soul (or heart)" is entirely appropriate here; but it is also clear at the same time that *nepesh* in these passages is not something existent [or] present, but a movement towards some thing; *nepesh* here corresponds totally to the meaning "desire".'[4] However, the few fixed pairs in which *nepesh* is coupled with *leb* ('heart') are later, secondary

---

[3] Westermann, in TLOT, pp. 748–9.
[4] Westermann, in TLOT, p. 750.

constructions; when the OT writer speaks of loving 'with one's whole soul and whole heart', it is the *nepesh*, not the *leb*, which is the proper subject of this affection. OT scholars point out that passages such as these are purely formulaic; 'and I (God) will plant them in this land with the whole heart and the whole soul' (Jer. 32:41); or 'write these my words in the heart and soul' (Deut. 11:18). The most common English usage of this pair actually inverts the Hebrew usage: the heart is the subject of thought, memory and reflection, and the soul is the subject of love and emotional bonding. The association of blood (*dām*) with *nepesh* is an additional secondary accretion which derives from another, *non*-Hebrew tradition. These same scholars astutely point out that the apparent identification of blood and soul occurs only in priestly prohibitions and edicts; 'for the blood is the *nepesh*' (Deut. 12:23); 'for the *nepesh* of all flesh is its blood' (Lev. 17:14). The correct interpretation of these and other passages is that the life of a living being is manifest or evident through its containing or pouring out blood. Hence, the figure of speech, 'the soul (as blood) poured out' means that the life-force drains away when the breath expires or the blood runs out. With our current medical techniques for monitoring and intervening in basic life functions, the terms that now describe the end of an animal being's life make reference to other manifest indications. Profuse bleeding, serious trauma, and even the cessation of heartbeat are no longer sufficient conditions for death; thus the doctor now might say that the person is dead when the EEG monitor has 'flat-lined'. One recent heated debate in medical ethics concerns the relative weight that should be assigned to the termination of either heart functions or brain functions; to further complicate matters, artificial techniques and devices can be used to temporarily circumvent even these terminal states.

Westermann's extraordinary exegetical precision allows him to tease out 'a surprising circumstance' with regard to the latter use of *nepesh*; it does not mean 'life' as such, nor is it used in the general, very broad sense in which we might now say 'city life', 'course of life', 'lifestyle', or 'alien life-forms' and so forth: 'Instead usage is strictly confined to the limits of life; *nepesh* is life in contrast to death. Consequently, occurrences of *nepesh* in this meaning divide naturally into two major categories: one concerns deliverance or preservation, the other, threat or destruction of life.'[5] An individual does not **have** a *nepesh* in the sense of a separate or separable possession, rather, an individual **is** a *nepesh*; the human life is coterminous and coextensive with its *nepesh*: 'Just as *nepesh* does not mean simply "life", but rather the individuation of life, as which it effectively appears, so too *nepesh* does not denote the soul as one nuance among others – it refers rather to psychic power, abounding personality, energy that exorcises all gloominess.'[6] According to the holistic Hebrew concept of the person, the *nepesh* is not a distinct aspect or part of human being; instead it refers to the distinct human being, or perhaps, the human being in its distinctness. One can readily understand how *nepesh* can be translated 'living being' in several texts, but then also 'person', 'individual', or 'self' in a more general and abstract fashion. It can even have a clearly pronominal sense and thus refer to one's self or ego.

---

[5] Westermann, in TLOT, p. 754.
[6] Seabass, in TDOT, vol. IX, p. 510.

Although the phrase *nepesh yahweh* does not occur in the OT, a number of passages associate *nepesh* with God and with events that transpire through God and his people. Yahweh cannot be said to have desire, longing or craving, since these are uniquely human characteristics. The principal relations in which God stands to humans' *nepesh* is to save their life, to bless them, or to punish them. Due to constant threats and dangers to human life in the Biblical epoch, one turns to God and beseeches him 'to redeem my *nepesh* from every distress' (2 Sam. 4:9). Where the human *nepesh* is the subject and God is the object, several texts speak of the *nepesh's* hope, yearning and prayer for God's saving presence. Westermann comments on

> a remarkable and suggestive circumstance: in reference to God's activity with the human *nepesh* [it] refers exclusively to 'life'; the behavior of the human *nepesh* directed toward God, always in the sense of 'soul' … The life that God saves and protects, as well as the desire of the soul for God, is life in intentionality. The soul desires life. Both groups occur in the language of the Psalms. God's inclination corresponds to human devotion; *nepesh* is human selfhood in its reciprocal event.[7]

Another important Hebrew term connected with human being is *ruach*, translated in 75 per cent of the cases in the LXX by *pneuma* and in Latin by *spiritus*. Its concrete outward meaning is 'wind'; variants of *ruach* occur at least 420 times in the OT. Although *nepesh* sometimes refers to breathing as an indicator of life, and *neshama* means the breath of an animal being, *ruach* refers to the power or force behind the wind or breath:

> In this sense it may denote at one extreme no more than what we should call a 'whiff' (or 'breath') of air, in particular a gentle, refreshing breeze of the kind which sometimes springs up in the East toward sundown, and so encourages one to walk abroad after the oppressive heat of mid-day. On the other hand, of course, it may be far more vigorous and much less gentle, blowing hot from the East to scorch one's vineyards, driving before it the straw and chaff, the dust and leaves, which lie in its path, or bending to its will (as it were) the very trees of the forest which stand in its way, or even darkening the sky with a portentous cloud of locusts. Indeed, it may reach such a pitch of violence as to sweep down upon one's dwelling and bring the walls about one's ears or lash the waves of the sea into a fury of storm and ship wreck.[8]

The wind not only itself moves across the land and sea, it also sets other things in motion. The mysterious power at work behind the scenes (so to speak) becomes visible and tangible only in this fashion. No human can control the wind, only the divine force of Yahweh can do so; thus, by analogy, it is the breath of God which instills or *inspires* the life-force in living things, though *this* breath (not the animal's breathing) is only observable through its effects. The wind is God's creation and a sign of his majesty as creator of the world: God created the wind (Amos 4:13), he has free access to it (Jer. 10:13), they are his messengers (Ps. 104:4), the wind performs God's word in creation (Ps. 148:8), and God's breath exercises dominion

---

[7] Westermann, in TLOT, pp. 758–9; see Childs, 1992, pp. 571–3.
[8] Johnson, 1964, p. 24.

over all things (Ps. 147:18). In several passages *ruach* signifies an intermediate stage between wind and breath, especially when connected with the rapture and transport of a prophet (1 Kings 18:12; Ezek. 3:12, 8:3, 11:1, 43:5). The second basic meaning of *ruach* as breath does not refer to a constant phenomenon, but to the force or power expressed through respiration. This force, or rather the play of this force, occurs both within and without, inside and outside, the person, that is, it proceeds from the inside and its effects occur outside. According to Westermann, '*ruach* does not indicate "normal" breathing, a component of human life (*neshama*) ... but the particular process of breathing that expresses the human being's dynamic vitality.' Its tempo increases in fear or anger, and decreases in weakness or illness; 'it is the elan, the psychic tension, the will to live, which can be revived ... by good news or diminished ... by "fatal" anger.'[9] Ruth Padel makes the same point about Greek medical ideas: they did not think that perpetual motion within was normal; inner surges and violent flux caused the soul itself to move.[10]

Walter Eichrodt makes a confident assertion regarding the relation between *nepesh* and *ruach*:

> If *nepesh* is the individual life in association with a body, *ruach* is the life-force present everywhere and existing independently over against the single individual. We might say that the same force is considered from different points of view. The vital element considered as *principium*, effective power, is called *ruach*; the same thing as realized in the creature and active, that is as *principatum*, is called *nepesh*. If *nepesh* is individual, and comes to an end with the death of the individual, *ruach* is universal, and independent of the death of the creature; it does not die.[11]

But this does not mean that there is any kind of life *after* death; rather, as Ezekiel says, God has the power to *restore* life to a dead person: 'in his lament the prophet cries that the breath of life blows over the dead and enlivens them.'

The concept of *ruach* is often closely associated with that of *leb* (or *lebab*), 'heart'; along with the concept of *nepesh*, these three terms divide the inward work of describing the human being as God's special creation. The word *leb* or *lebab* occurs about 850 times in the OT, especially prevalent in Psalms, Proverbs, and several of the prophetic books. Its earliest concrete and external meaning is 'breast' or 'chest'; it denotes a part of the body that can be seriously injured, even pierced by arrows (2 Sam. 18:14), without causing death. Thus, in the strict sense, it refers to the walls of the heart or the thoracic cage, rather than the heart as an internal organ. References to a non-human animal's heart are almost completely unknown; though there are a rare few uses in connection with animals, they are entirely metaphorical. The OT authors' use of *leb* and *lebab* for humans alone is in stark contrast to *nepesh* and *ruach*, both of which are used about animals' life-force and behavior. The heart functions in all aspects of human existence and brings to the fore emotional, cognitive and volitional elements. The early teachings of Proverbs show the central importance of the heart: 'keep your *leb* with all vigilance, for from

---

[9] Westermann, in TLOT, pp. 1207–8.
[10] Padel, 1992, pp. 67–8, 88–98.
[11] Eichrodt, 1967, II, p. 136.

it flows the springs of life' (Prov. 4:23, 25:13). The vital physical nature of an individual is concentrated in the heart; if one wants to continue living, the heart must be refreshed and nourished, especially with bread and wine.

The notion of the heart as the seat or focus of human emotions emerged gradually from that of the heart as the chest or bosom, the container or enclosure of breath and vitality; as we will see, this is closely paralleled in the Homeric usage of *phrenes* and *kardia*. The transition to concrete and internal meaning is evident in some of the standard imagery of the Biblical laments which often employ the vital bodily functions to describe emotional reactions; when the heart pounds, flutters or convulses it conveys the ideas of excitement, worry and fear. The basic emotional states are rooted in the heart: despair, grief and sadness are mentioned more than eighty times; this usage outweighs the positive emotions of joy and delight which are mentioned about fifty times.[12] The negative emotions or moods (as one might now refer to them) are especially destructive for the heart which is most vulnerable when it feels fear. The heart's frailty shows the creature's weakness and finitude in contrast with God's omnipotence and infinitude. Nevertheless, the positive emotions, in the main love and sympathy, also have their source in the heart. The deep emotional bond between husband and wife, parent and child, and Yahweh and his creatures is 'vested' in the heart. (Notice that the word 'vest' and 'invest' refer to the garment worn over the chest or bosom.) In the *locus classicus* about Yahweh's love for Israel (Hos. 2:16), Yahweh will entice Israel, bring her back, and there speak to her heart: 'This approach, aiming to restore the unbroken bond between Israel and Yahweh, demonstrates that Yahweh's unconditional love is the only requirement for the healing of faithlessness and shows his punishment to be an act of love.'[13]

In terms of the earliest historical documents concerning the concept of mind, the most important Hebrew usage of 'heart' is in passages that clearly indicate intellectual, cognitive and reflective operations.[14] While the sense organs engage in sense perception, it is within the heart that thought, memory, understanding, attention and reflection take place. The heart's cognitive activity is prior to seeing with the eyes or hearing with the ears, since it initiates the sensory operations. Following this internal activity, the heart internalizes and preserves the content of sensory percepts for the purpose of making judgements and decisions. The opposite of the heart's cognitive action is not sensory failure but lack of attention and confusion in making judgements. Perceptive and cognitive operations are initially directed at concrete, particular things, but then, as the main OT texts advance this concept, the heart can be directed toward instructions, signs and wonders. In prophetic contexts, the object may be an individual's vision, the word of God, or his grace and mercy. In the Wisdom Literature, the heart knows wisdom, love, faith and human fate. In addition, the heart is the seat or storehouse of memory, used to recall a previous situation in order to find a motive for a certain action. Remembrance in the heart can be construed as internal advice, one's own rule of thumb, or the ethical 'call' of

---

[12] Fabry, in TDOT, vol. VII, p. 414; see also Eichrodt, 1967, II, pp. 142–4.
[13] Fabry, in TDOT, vol. VII, p. 418.
[14] Wolff, 1974, pp. 40–58; Fabry, in TDOT, vol. VII, pp. 419–25; Johnson, 1964, pp. 75–87.

conscience, where the context indicates moral precepts or rules. The concept of 'wisdom' (Greek *sophia*) is especially characteristic of the heart's nature and action. The books of Job, Sirach and Proverbs refer to the wisdom and sage counsel of those who know best. On the other hand, if the heart lacks wisdom it is subject to a kind of folly which can show itself as heedlessness, willfulness and failure to see the larger picture. The heart can be deluded by wine, sex, worldly goods, material gain, temptations, idolatry, wicked words and corruption. The boundary between the cognitive functions of the heart and the activity of the will is often blurred; perhaps this is due to a conceptual (and hence semantic) oscillation between referents that are concrete and internal and those that are abstract and internal. In any case, the heart functions as the driving force behind an individual's voluntary actions, and engages in conceiving and planning.[15]

One of the most important gradations in the later abstract meaning of *leb* for mind occurs in its use for inner-directed thought (reflection), for example, in the phrase 'speak within one's heart', or 'words written on the heart'. There are perhaps thirty or forty passages in the OT, many in Zephaniah, which employ the phrase 'speaking to (or in) one's heart'. An entire strategy or course of action can be thought through when a person speaks to his/her heart (Gen. 24:45, 27:41; 1 Kings 12:26f); for example, according to Genesis, 'Abraham fell on his face and laughed, for he said in his heart, "Shall a child be born to a man who is one hundred years old?"' (Gen. 17:17). It is possible – and this is a highly tentative and unverifiable hypothesis – that the speech which occurs in speaking to one's heart indicates some sort of reflection or meditation because it is an internalized form of the word. There is one passage that might provide a clue to this hypothesis: when Hannah was praying silently near the temple, 'only her lips moved, but her voice was not heard.' The priest thought she was drunk and demanded that Hannah put away her wine, to which she replied that she was not drunk but had been pouring out her heart before the Lord (1 Sam. 1:13–15).

Wolff concludes his analysis of the notion of *leb* as inner-directed thought with these words: 'The "heart" in Hebrew describes the seat and function of the reason. It includes everything that we ascribe to the head and the brain – power of perception, reason, understanding, insight, consciousness, memory, knowledge, reflection, judgment, sense of direction [and] discernment.'[16] Westermann astutely remarks that *leb* is sometimes assimilated to *ruach* to refer to the center of human thought and planned action due to the fact that the entire OT picture of human being is dynamic. Thus, although each of the three key terms – *nepesh, ruach* and *leb* – originate in separate and distinct concrete parts of the human body, they all signify, at an intermediate level, the vital desire of humans as living beings. This occurs before each term precipitates further into more abstract meanings which refer, not to concrete independent parts (pieces) of the human body (as flesh and bone do), but to dependent parts (aspects) of the interior, hidden dimension.

A. R. Johnson summarizes his study of the Hebrew concept of heart in these words:

---

[15] Fabry, in TDOT, vol. VII, pp. 419–24.
[16] Wolff, 1974, p. 51.

However, for all that the heart is thus brought so often into relation with man's psychical life at the emotional level ... it is as the seat or instrument of his intellectual and volitional activity that it figures most prominently in Israelite thinking. Thus the term for 'heart', besides being used with a force which approximates to what we should call 'mind' or 'intellect', is frequently employed by metonymy to denote one's thought and therefore, on occasion, one's wish, purpose, or resolve; for one's thought or wish is essentially 'that which is in the heart', or, as we should say, 'what one has in mind'.[17]

Granted that the numerous semantic forms and qualifiers directly connected with *leb* or *lebab* clearly indicate the product of comparison and association of sense percepts and memories, it is still the case that the use of 'heart' as part-for-whole with the meaning 'intellect' or 'mind' obscures the distinction between cognitive agent and cognitive content. As we will see in Homer's archaic use of psychical terms for heart, desire and will, an ambiguity remains at the 'heart' (center) of the Hebrew concept of heart; where one's thoughts can mean either the power or agency of thought, on one hand, or the content of an occurrent thought, on the other.

With great unanimity, OT scholars ... regard the translation of *nepesh* with *psychē* insufficient or even misleading because it introduces the 'Greek doctrine of the soul' or Greek spiritualism or dualism. If one begins with the pre-Platonic usage of *psychē*, however, this judgment does not hold, as Bratsiotis demonstrates. The basic meaning of *psychē* is 'breath'; it often occurs in the meaning 'life' and can indicate the seat of desire, of emotions, and the 'center of religious expression'; it can also stand for 'person' or in place of a pronoun. Bratsiotis reaches the conclusion 'that there is an astonishing correspondence between the Hebrew term *nepesh* and the Greek term *psychē*'.[18]

When Daniel Lys investigated the Greek translations of *nepesh* in the LXX he discovered that for 754 passages in the OT that use *nepesh*, the Greek text used *psychē* in 680 cases. Despite the fact that various divergences in translation result from the LXX writers' use of 'person' or 'self' more often than the Hebrew writers, Lys remarked that 'the LXX never goes in the direction in which "soul" would be understood as opposite to "body" (as in Platonic dualism).'[19]

Let us attempt to capture some of our more important findings in the table below.

term	meaning	degree*	object-taking	action	said of God	said of animals
nepesh	throat	no	yes	consumes	never	often
nepesh	desire	yes	yes	intends	rarely	often
nepesh	life-force	no	no	sustains	rarely	often
ruach	wind	yes	yes	blows/moves	ruled by	never
ruach	breath	yes	no	inspires	often	sometimes
leb	heart	no	no	beats	never	rarely
leb	mind	yes	yes	intends	rarely	never

* **degree:** yes = occurs in degrees; no = either fully present or fully absent.

---

[17] Johnson, 1964, pp. 77–8.
[18] Westermann, in TLOT, p. 759.
[19] Lys, 1959, p. 227.

The transition in meaning from (concrete + internal) to (abstract + internal) for all three central Hebrew psychical terms is paralleled by an equivalent triform transition in archaic pre-Platonic Greek usage (as we shall see below). Remnants of this threefold concept formation survive in contemporary English (and cognate Romance) language expression, though the 'seat' or internal location has sometimes shifted. Thus, one says of a deeply held conviction, 'with heart and mind and soul' and this conveys more than just three words standing for one thing. Thus, Hebrew *leb* is both the thoracic cage that holds the heart and the organ that 'holds' thoughts and memories, the *ruach* is the breath that fills the lungs and carries the life-force through the whole body, the *nepesh* is the desire manifest in an animal being whose life-force is instilled by God's creative action. The human being as an animal is a living thing (*hayyim*) composed of flesh (*basar*) or soft tissue, and bones and sinews; like an animal, a human has (or is) *nepesh*, a vital force responsible for self-moved action, whose essential properties are characterized by breath and blood flow, which can increase or decrease (in sleep or anger). Although Yahweh has instilled *ruach* in all animals including humans, *ruach* assumes a different function and brings about distinctive effects in humans alone due to the presence of the *leb*, heart. Human as an animal has a heart as an inner fleshy organ, but only humans have a heart as the seat of memory and intellect; through the loss of *nepesh* in his animal being humans also lose both *ruach* and *leb*, and thus in no sense is the OT soul immortal.

(2) Homeric Greek ideas about life and breath

Scholarly study of the early Greek idea of the soul really begins with Erwin Rohde, Nietzsche's close friend, in his groundbreaking work *Psyche: The Cult of Souls and Belief in Immortality Among the Greeks* (1890–94). Rohde's intention was to show that the Platonic description of the *psychē* could be derived for the most part from the introduction of ascetic religious values into Greece in the period after Homer's epics. This religious infiltration took place through the expansion of the Orphic cult and the alleged philosophical speculations of the Pythagoreans. These religious beliefs Rohde derived in turn from an earlier practice of ecstatic Dionysian rituals; in this he may have been influenced by Nietzsche's comments on Apollonian and Dionysian polarities in *The Birth of Tragedy*. 'But Rohde never successfully explained how the one truly indispensable piece of evidence for any theory of change in the idea of the soul in Greece, namely the surviving occurrences of the word *psychē*, could be made to support his thesis.'[20]

In the mid-twentieth century, another great step forward was made by Bruno Snell in his classic work *The Discovery of the Mind*; still much discussed, it is a turning-point in the interdisciplinary approach to archaic mentalities. In addition, valuable comparative linguistic studies were done by R. B. Onians in *The Origins of European Thought*; though Claus later questioned Onians' determination to find an organic and concrete source for each 'soul' word. An approach which integrated

---

[20] Claus, 1981, p. 2, see also p. 92, note 1.

linguistic analysis, classical philology and archaeology was first undertaken by the Swedish Sanskrit scholar Ernst Arbman, one of the touch-stones for Jan Bremmer's recent work, *The Early Greek Concept of Soul*. Arbman found that the Indo-European concept of soul (*atman* or *purusa*) was preceded by some sort of dualistic picture where the eschatological and psychological attributes of the soul had not yet merged. He distinguishes between 'body-souls' which endow the body with life and sentience, and the 'free-soul', an unencumbered soul which represents the individual at the personal level. The free-soul is active during periods of unconsciousness, and passive during periods of consciousness when the conscious individual replaces it. It is not exactly clear where the passive free-soul resides in the person's body. On the other hand, the body-souls are active during the waking life of the individual; in contrast with the free-soul, the body-soul is often divided into several components. According to Arbman's analysis, the components of the body-soul fall into two categories: one is the 'life-soul', usually identified with the breath or vital agency; the other is the 'ego-soul'. The body-soul, or several of its parts, represents the individual's inner self or person. In an early stage in the development of the Archaic and Vedic belief in the soul, the free-soul and the body-soul did not yet constitute a unity. Later the Vedic concept of the free-soul (*atman*) subsumed the psychological attributes of the body-soul, and this concept is shared amongst many primitive mentalities.

Bremmer's study applies the model of 'primitive' soul belief with the distinction between a free-soul which represents a person's individuality, and the body-soul which endows a person with life and sentience. The Homeric idea of *psychē* is identified with the free-soul, whereas terms connected with a person's inner life, such as *thymos, nous* and *menos*, are seen as aspects of the body-soul. Although the concept of *psychē* developed into the modern idea of the unitary soul, its 'primitive' character can be discerned in so-called shamanistic traditions and the archaic descriptions of dreams. For the Archaic Greeks of Homer's time, the free-soul of the living continued as the soul of the dead, although other manifestations of the dead were also thought to exist. There was no uniform picture of the dead in an afterlife and neither did all of the dead have the same status.

The use of the idea of *psychē* in Homer can be best identified with the loose concept of free-soul; it is only used in contexts where the living person is in crisis. Passages in the *Iliad* and the *Odyssey* reveal that without *psychē* the person cannot survive. When the embassy of the Greek army implores Achilles to suppress his anger and resume fighting, he complains that he continues to risk losing his *psychē* (Il. ix.322); when Agenor summons up his courage to face Achilles who is routing the Trojans, he reflects that his opponent has only one *psychē* (Il. xxi.569); and when Achilles pursues Hector around Troy, the poet comments that the prize will be Hector's *psychē* (Il. xxii.161). When someone swoons or passes out their *psychē* leaves the body; one of the inexplicable features of Homer's stories is that *psychē's* return is never mentioned, though presumably if the person lives on, it must have returned. The later post-Platonic myth of Eros and Psychē, which includes an important motif of return (or recession), draws its narrative power from an entirely new concept of *psychē*. But for Homer, when someone dies their *psychē* leaves forever and departs for Hades, the land of the dead. In these cases, *psychē* is sometimes closely associated with the *aion* or vital force; but unlike *psychē*, in

Homer one does not find *aion* ascribed to older persons, it is only the young which possess its full power.

It has been argued that for Homer the *psychē* was located in the head, since the terms *psychē* and head are sometimes used in an interchangeable manner.[21] This might explain the ancient Greek custom of holding the head of the deceased during mourning (Il. xxiv.712, 724), the primal offering (Il. iii.273) and the importance attached to sneezing which expels the breath. But the fact that *psychē* and head are used in an interchangeable manner may only mean that they both represent the same thing, that is, the whole person. The little that is known about Homer's references to the location of the *psychē* is that it flew away from the limbs (Il. xvi.856; xxii.362), or left the body through the mouth (Il. ix.409), the chest (Il. xvi.505), or through a wound in the flank (Il. xiv.518).

According to Bremmer, this picture of Homeric *psychē* shows that it is very similar to Arbman's notion of free-soul, which is always active outside the body and is not bound to it like the body-soul. However, because the free-soul functions outside the body, its place inside the body is rather obscure, for when its owner is conscious the person's body represents the individual and only its activities are of any interest. In this state the free-soul is only present in a passive sense and is rarely mentioned. Arbman found that in North Eurasian belief systems, the free-soul was thought to be located either in the whole body, or in the heart, the lungs or the kidneys. In any case, the free-soul does not seem to have any identifiable attributes aside from its representation of the individual. In addition, it is impossible for the free-soul to continue its worldly existence when its body is dead, even though it is only active outside the body. This soul cannot remain behind in the dead body but must go in search of an afterlife. But this is a mutual dependence since when the free-soul disappears the body dies through illness or injury.

Nevertheless, one feature of the free-soul is clearly absent from the Homeric *psychē*, for the *psychē* does not represent the individual person in dreams or any other dimension of the unconscious. But this conclusion cannot be final because Homer employs dream stories almost exclusively to advance the narrative action. In this sense, they cannot be relied upon to provide a complete picture of actual dream experience for the Archaic Greeks. Homer's dream stories follow a very strict pattern in four stages: the circumstance before the dream; the dream image moves towards the sleeper and stands over his head; the dream image's speech, and the dream's aftermath. Bremmer concludes that, although we do not find in Homer any of the activities of the dream soul, its absence does not necessarily presuppose its non-existence. In sum, the comparison of Arbman's concept of free-soul and Homer's actual usage of *psychē* reveals several parallels: both (1) are located in an unspecified part of the body; (2) are inactive when the body is active; (3) leave the body during a swoon; (4) have no physical or psychological connections; (5) are preconditions for life's continuation, and (6) represent the individual after death. In Arbman's more complex analysis of the twofold concept of body-soul, he used the idea of ego-soul to denote individual living humans, in contrast with the free-soul and the life-soul, but did not describe the various psychological aspects of the soul linked to the individual.

---

[21] Onians, pp. 107–17, 123–31, 141–50; esp. p. 115, note 7.

One of Arbman's pupils, Hultkrantz, was more aware of these multiple aspects and offered his definition of ego-souls as 'potencies behind the various acts and phases of the life of consciousness'. Yet Bremmer comments that this sort of analysis still fails to suggest the psychological richness of the Archaic Greek concepts.

In the Homeric and Epic Greek traditions, there is a cluster of words closely associated with the beliefs and actions of human beings, a cluster that falls unequally into two groups: on one hand, *psychē, thymos, nous* and *menos*; on the other, *kēr* (in Epic form, *kradiē*), *phrenes* and *hēpar*. (The two groups' criteria of distinction will be discussed later.) The most common Homeric term connected with the behavior of ensouled beings is *thymos* which, unlike *psychē*, is only active when the body is awake. When Achilles is wreaking havoc among the Trojans and he confronts Aeneas, 'his brave *thymos* roused him' (Il. xx.174). Sometimes *thymos* expresses hope, but always hope toward action, not to receive some thing. After Patroclus had been killed, the poet said of the Trojans that, 'their *thymos* strongly hoped to pull away Patroclus' body from under Ajax' (Il. xvii.234). In the Homeric texts, *thymos* is the pre-eminent source of the emotions; friendship and revenge, grief and joy, anger and fear all spring from the *thymos*. Homer's use of this term is comparable to the Hebrew use of *nepesh* when it signifies desire or longing, especially in its vigorous externalization. Other examples extend our comprehension of Homer's sometimes ambiguous and often under-determined use of psychical terms. Deiphobus 'feared in his *thymos* the spear of the fiery Meriones' (Il. xiii.163); Hector reproaches Paris when he does not join the battle, 'fool, wrongly you stored up bitter anger in your *thymos*' (Il. vi.326). However, the action of *thymos* is not always restricted to emotional outbursts, for it sometimes serves an intellectual purpose. But the ruminations and deliberations of the Greek heroes are not those of a detached spectator, rather their intellectual reflections always take place in an atmosphere charged with emotions. When Odysseus is left alone by the Greeks during one of the battles, 'he spoke to his proud *thymos*' (Il. xi.403), and having realized there were only two options open to him, he ends his reflection by asking himself, 'but why does my *thymos* consider that?' (Il. xi.407).

This Homeric usage is in contrast to its parallel in Hebrew where it is the *leb* or heart to which one speaks in reflection. It seems fairly clear from a number of passages that the *thymos* was thought to reside in the chest, which was the main seat of the *phrenes* (or lungs). The *thymos* normally stays in its proper place and does not move around, but it is affected by a swoon. In some cases, *thymos* seems to be closely linked with *psychē* in the sense of 'breath', so that the breath can leave the chest but without really going anywhere else. Claus' detailed analysis shows that in many cases the Homeric use of *thymos* obviously implies 'strength', a value contiguous with that of other words connected with eating and drinking, as well as recovery after a swoon. When described as a concrete physical entity *thymos* is breath-like, blood-like, or even heart-like. The majority of uses either directly support a concept of life-force or indirectly substitute for this concept by means of an archaic tendency to explain every human activity as a personified exchange of some kind.[22] Several Indo-European linguists, such as R. B. Onians and Georges

---

[22] Claus, 1981, pp. 21–3, 37–41; Padel, 1992, pp. 27–30.

Dumezil, have suggested that *thymos* must once have been thought of as some kind of substance that could be brought into movement. One hypothesis is that *thymos* is connected with the root term which in Latin became *fumus* or smoke; thus *thymos* was conceived as a thin or diffuse vapor.[23]

Of the three terms used by Homer in descriptions of individual souls, the term most closely associated with what we now think of as higher-order cognitive functions was *nous* (in Homeric Greek, *noos*), which we might perhaps render as 'intellect'. 'It is the mind or an act of mind, a thought or a purpose', remarks Bremmer; but that is a grand assumption which imbues far greater unity to the concept than is warranted by any of the passages which he cites. Whatever action Patroclus may carry out, 'the *nous* of Zeus is always more powerful than that of men' (Il. xvi.688). The OT parallel for this sense of mind is found in the use of *ruach* in connection with Yahweh's power. The *nous* is always located in the chest (Il. iv.309) but it is never thought of as something material the way *thymos* is often conceived. It cannot be struck or pierced or blown out of the body and there is nothing that even hints at its origin in the body. Bremmer thinks that *nous* is ambiguous in some uses, since he claims that it signifies an emotional state when Agamemnon rejoiced in his *nous* at Achilles' and Odysseus' quarrel as to which was the best man. But Snell's interpretation is far more consistent: 'Agamemnon's delight does not spring from the altercation of the two most valiant heroes – that would be absurd – but from his recollection of Apollo's prophecy that Troy would fall when the best heroes contended with one another. The basis of his joy, therefore, is reflection.'[24] Snell goes on to consider other passages which support this concept of *nous*: Nestor says, 'let us take counsel ... if the *nous* may accomplish anything' (Il. xiv.61). In this context *thymos* would have been inaccurate since Nestor asks them to consider whether 'counsel', that is, expert reflection on the circumstances, may achieve anything. Snell suggests that *nous* is probably connected with the verb *noein* which means 'to know' or 'to realize'.

The verb *noein* is often conjoined with *idein* 'to see clearly', and here it means not just visual perception but also the mental act which goes along with that vision, and this puts *noein* close to *gignoskein*, 'to recognize'. Thus, at the same passage cited by Bremmer above, Snell comments, 'it is the mind as a recipient of clear images, or more briefly, the organ of clear images.' However, this summary identification occludes a crucial distinction of which Bremmer was aware, though he makes the same imputation for different reasons, namely that the mind can be equated with a bodily organ, the brain. Again, Claus' linguistic analysis shows that *noos*, like *phrēn* or *phrenes*, can regularly be considered as that in which a thought is conceived or even the thought itself, that is, its occurrence. It can be a distinct plan or intention, but diverges from other psychical terms in that, as a pure function devoid of all ambiguity, it undergoes specialization into something like 'reason' and can occupy the subject position, like *thymos* or *psychē*. The word *noos* must be treated as an agent noun of the same type as *logos* 'and cannot

---

[23] Dodds, 1951, pp. 16–18; see Caswell, 1990, for further speculation on meanings of *thymos*.

[24] Snell, 1953, p. 12.

possibly have its Homeric character accounted for by reference to some original physical identity'.[25]

The third Homeric term *menos* does not refer to a bodily organ but signifies the momentary impulse of one or several mental and/or physical activities mainly directed toward a specific action. The character may be intellectually aware of this impulse but can only influence its expression to a limited extent. When Odysseus' father rejoiced in the fight against the suitors, 'Pallas Athena breathed a great *menos* into him ... and whirling back he swung his long-shafted spear' (Od. xxiv.520); after the wounded Glaucus has prayed to Apollo, the god 'immediately eased his pains ... and put *menos* into his *thymos*' (Il. xvi.529); when Nestor tries to resolve the dispute between Achilles and Agamemnon, Nestor appeals to the king, 'son of Atreus, stop your *menos*' (Il. i.282). The general sense concerns the warrior's fury or ardor, but *menos* can be located either in the chest (Il. xix.202), the *thymos* (Il. xvi.529), or even in the *phrenes* (Od. i.89). Onians suggested that *menos* was conceived as something gaseous, since the Abantes are described as 'breathing forth *menos*' (Il. ii.536), and during a night raid, 'the owl-eyed Athena breathed *menos* into Diomedes' (Il. x.482), but Bremmer comments that this may be a strictly poetic expression; 'just as one breathes into the fire and fans it, so one breathes into persons spiritual powers and fans them.'[26] But if *menos* as breath is merely a metaphor for some actual relation which holds between the person's soul and divine 'inspiration' then we want to know (or at least have an educated guess) about what this relation was. Onians goes further than Bremmer gives him credit for: 'At the stage of thought when those beliefs emerged there was difficulty in conceiving anything except material entities. *menos* is apparently not an abstraction or a mere state of something else, but conceived as itself something, fluid or gaseous, which for convenience we may translate "energy", and which was felt inwardly much as we feel what we so name.'[27] Let us resist the temptation to render *menos* with the English word 'energy', since this word has its own history in Aristotelian *energeia* (in contrast with *dynamis*).

Onians has struck on an important point, however, the salience of which does not have to do with whether *menos* is gaseous or not, but with the notion that such concepts make reference not to a state or mode of some thing, but to some thing itself, whatever that thing may be. Claus argues that *menos* is the easiest of all Homeric words to identify as life-force; unique among all soul words it is routinely used of non-human, even inanimate items. Thus *menos* conveys an impersonal characteristic that explains why it is not described in personalized terms like 'love' or 'desire'. When Ares speaks of himself as lucky to escape being one of the *zōs amenenos*, it cannot mean 'life without life', but rather 'living without life-force'. Occurrences of *menos* compatible with this interpretation show that this concept

---

[25] Claus, 1981, pp. 19–21; see Padel, 1992, pp. 32–3; Claus' catalog of passages in note 40, with the various connotations of *noos* specified in these contexts, is remarkably similar to Fabry's catalogue of connotations for *leb*, see Fabry, in TDOT, vol. VII, pp. 419–23.
[26] Bremmer, 1983, p. 60.
[27] Onians, pp. 51–2.

was 'in Homeric speech a self-contained category of thought about the person, able to unify inherently all physical, psychical and "life" uses of these words'.[28] This *substance-based* conception of the soul is one of the undercurrents in Descartes' radical new vision of the soul and mind, one which carefully (and perhaps permanently) separates the essential features of soul from the essential features of mind.

With respect to the Homeric use of *phrenes*, von Fritz observed the strong tendency to refer to this feature when the results of the mental activity in question are immediately discernible.[29] Claus says that this means that it is often impossible to decide whether either *phrenes* or *noos* denotes an autonomous psychical agent, that which thinks, or the function of such an agent, the thought: 'This strong ambiguity between agent and function must be seen, therefore, as decisively weakening the ability of *phrēn* [or] *phrenes* to be perceived as an autonomous *source* of thought and emotion, and thus as something denoting the self of man as a whole.' In contrast with *noos*, which regularly takes the subject position, *phrenes* does not usually do so, and unlike *noos*, which can usually be construed as a long-lasting disposition, *phrenes* does not have this dimension. Claus argues against the view that Homer's usage of *noos* and *phrenes* in certain contexts commits him to thinking of them as physical and autonomous entities; instead 'it can be suggested that they are so treated because something not originally concrete in nature has undergone personification.'[30] The best candidate for organic location is the lungs (or diaphragm), which enclosed or contained (on the current anatomical understanding) the heart and source of breath. Ruth Padel summarizes some of the key ideas:

> *Phrenes* contain emotion, practical ideas and knowledge ... *Phrenes* are containers; they fill with *menos*, 'anger', or *thumos*, 'passion'. They are essentially mobile, too, and they 'tremble within'. They are the holding center, holding the heart, holding the liver. A thunderbolt striking 'in the very *phrenes*' is an image of annihilation. You are struck, you know, understand, tremble, feel, or ponder in that responsive, compact, containing center.[31]

The last key term is *kēr* (Epic form, *kradiē*), usually translated 'heart', and clearly in all cases referring to the heart as an organ in the animal body. Claus' careful analysis shows that

> in the great majority of instances ... the uses of *kēr* conform to the thesis that it can be one of two things: (1) a man's 'life-force' itself, directly acting in contexts where palpable waxing and waning of physical strength, consciousness, energy, endurance, and the like replace what we would call emotions in such contexts as grief for the dead, syncope, excitement in battle, and the like; (2) the 'life-force' personified ... but still generally restricted to contexts appropriate to the 'life-force'.[32]

---

[28] Claus, 1981, p. 26; see Padel, 1992, pp. 24–6.
[29] Quoted in Claus, 1981, p. 16.
[30] Claus, 1981, p. 21; against Onians' ingenious speculations, 1951, pp. 23–31.
[31] Padel, 1992, p. 21.
[32] Claus, 1981, p. 32.

Ruth Padel agrees with the emotional elements in this synopsis, though balking at the equation with life-force; the heart suffers, endures, and is full of hope and love. In some sense, it is 'moved' in that it rejoices, grieves, fears and becomes angry.[33]

There is some consensus amongst Bremmer, Onians and Snell in that they agree that there is no unified concept of the soul in Homeric thought; the notions of *psychē, thymos, menos,* and other subsidiary terms are aspects or dimensions of something unknown. It may be the case that Homer simply could not decide between competing 'pictures' of *nous*; his texts reflect the partly incongruous usage of this term amongst the Greek heroes. On the other hand, there may be a systematic ambiguity in the concept of *nous*, such that different uses reflect overlapping 'pictures'. One way to characterize this entire view of Homer's pictures of human nature is 'unity in multiplicity'; no cohesive emotional and personal identity; the human in its psychical being is as disjointed and fragmented as the human body is in its physical (organic) being. Ruth Padel objects to this view: 'If we add multiple innard-words to internal dialogue, we reach, not the absence of any consistent idea of self, but something far more positive: Homeric "insight into the disunity" of mental and emotional experience; a unified vision of an inconsistent thing.' In favor of this view, she instances Homer's careful descriptions of Achilles' and Hector's internal and external struggles, about which she says, 'the narrative shows us one man over a short time, not as a bunch of separate voices, but as someone experiencing disorientation, self-conflict. Disunity and multiplicity are part of the coherence with which Homer presents a human being. They are essential to Homer's concretely multiple vision of persons and life, of body and its innards.'[34]

The principal orientation of Claus' superb linguistic analyses of the Homeric and Early Classical usage of soul-words has been to demonstrate their tendency to coalesce around the concept of life-force, its various intrinsic properties, and the manifold ways in which the life-force is exhibited by human agents. He resolutely opposes the arguments made famous by Snell, Onians and Burnet to discern the original notion of *psychē* in breath, the power or internal seat of breathing, the organic functions involved with respiration, inspiration, and so forth. Against this predominant interpretation, Claus argues that, whatever its origins, *psychē* has already been largely absorbed in the archaic period into the life-force category of words, such as *thymos, menos* and *phrenes*, and thus shares with these other words 'a natural ability to act as a psychical agent of the life-force type'. In favor of this he advances five main points: (1) it seems an inherent ability of such words other than *psychē* to function as psychical agents, that is, used in expressions where emotion is treated as a function of life-force. (2) In lyric poetry of the same period *psychē* has a similar semantic role, but restricted to pleasurable and erotic contexts. (3) In other contexts that employ life-force words, *psychē* becomes comparable to heart and blood, that is, it can assume all vital functions except strength. (4) Aside from its use for 'shade' or 'double', *psychē* clearly indicates life-force in death contexts, since it is what is destroyed, lost, or poured out; it is breath-*like,* blood-*like*, but only in so far as breath and blood carry or transmit the life-force. (5) After

---

[33] Padel, 1992, pp. 18–19.
[34] Padel, 1992, pp. 46, 47.

the Homeric texts, *psychē* appears in contexts conjoined with *philos*, that is, 'to love life', one who loves his soul is one who holds life dear. 'From these comparisons there can be no doubt that *psychē* has a relatively consistent "life-force" identity from Homer on in popular usage and that this identity cannot readily be explained by post-Homeric analogy to any one of the related words.'[35] Clause extends this linguistic schema to the tragic texts, especially Euripides as its most mature exponent, and feels confident in asserting that, 'all words that do not have a connection with "life" or "life-force" expand in some way, and all words except for *psychē* that do have such a connection ... are eliminated or diminished in importance.' Behind the tragic and poetic expressions lies 'the gradual adoption into popular speech of *psychē* as the word of choice to designate the natural animator of the body'. All of the evidence that he has advanced underscores the emphasis placed on 'life-force' in explanation of the various soul-words; 'if the success of *psychē* as the archaic "life-force" is what accounts for its expansion of usages in the fifth century, it is very likely the same meaning, unaffected by afterlife speculation, that accounts for its development into a psychological agent after Homer'.[36]

There is one facet of the Homeric picture of *psychē* that does not fit well with this view of soul as life-force, inextricably linked with the individual's bodily existence and hence mortal or death-bound – and that is the idea of the 'shade' or 'double' of the dead person. Filled with regret at the death of his friend Patroklos, Achilles stays awake all night, recalling the brave warrior's appearance and deeds, his heart choked with loss. Just as he is about to fall asleep the *eidolon* (image or simulacrum) of Patroklos comes to stand above Achilles' head: 'And here is the *psychē* of the unhappy Patroklos who comes to him, totally like the hero in his stature, his beautiful eyes, his voice, and his body clothed with the same garments' (Il. xxiii.65); 'his *psychē* resembled him very much' (Il. xxiii.107). When Achilles attempts to touch the *eidolon* there is nothing to grasp; it is no more than a thin vapor that vanishes beneath the earth with a tiny cry like a bat (Il. xxiii.100). The same scenario is played out when Odysseus confronts the *psychē* of his dead mother Antikleia who has returned from Hades to drink blood from the victim Odysseus has just sacrificed; in doing so she hopes to recover some of the knowledge death made her lose. Odysseus converses with his mother's *psychē*, but when he attempts to embrace her, she flits away like a shadow or a dream. When he asks her if this is a trick played on him by the infernal deities, she says, 'It is the law of our mortal nature when we come to die. We no longer have sinews keeping the bones and flesh together; once life has departed from our white bones, all is consumed by the fierce heat of the blazing fire, and the soul slips away like a dream and goes flitting on its way' (Od. xi.205–22).

Granted that Homer uses the same word *psychē* to denominate the mortal life-force of each individual human *and* the appearance of the dead human, there seem to be basically incompatible beliefs at work here, or at least an unresolved tension. How can the soul cease to exist with the person's bodily death and then reappear

---

35 Claus, 1981, p. 97.

36 Claus, 1981, pp. 101, 102; Ruth Padel has mixed feelings about Claus' findings; she says 'he identifies a core meaning "life-force" in most "soul-words", which in my view weakens his clear-headed, skeptical approach' an identity achieved at the expense of discounting 'anomalous instances', 1992, p. 29, note 66.

from the depths of the underworld? The answer to this dilemma lies with Homer's archaic use of *eidolon* (image) and *phasma* (phantom); the dead Patroklos' *psychē* and the dead Antikleia's *psychē* are exact replicas or simulacra of the living person's corporeal appearance. Homer says that Apollo fabricated a *phasma* of Aeneas in his armor, placing him in the thick of battle, although the real Aeneas is sheltered in the citadel (Il. v.450–3); it is an *eoikon* (semblance) of Nestor who comes as Zeus' messenger in a dream to Agamemnon (Il. ii.56), and an *eidolon* (image) fabricated by Athena of the daughter of Ikarios made to stand guard over the sleeping Penelope (Od. iv.796–8). Thus the *psychē* of the dead share the same characteristics as these phantoms, replicas and simulacra – they are not the actual *psychai* of living beings, but the mere similitude of the being who is now or has been ensouled. There is no survival of the human soul after the individual's bodily death, no other form of human life beyond or after the extinction of humans' life-force. It is not true that the Homeric texts betray an internal inconsistency or that they depict some sort of conflict between different sets of beliefs; rather, the 'double' or 'shade' does not have the ontological status of an autonomous, self-founding being, the human individual's soul minus its host's body.

Jean-Pierre Vernant makes this crucial point in a forceful and persuasive fashion:

[The doubles'] unity comes from the fact that in the cultural context of archaic Greece, they are all perceived by the mind in the same way and all bear an analogous meaning. It is also correct to understand them all as a true psychological category – the category of the double – that presumes a different mental organization than our own. A double is a wholly different thing from an image. It is not a 'natural' object, but it is also not a product of the imagination: neither an imitation of a real object, not an illusion of the mind, nor a creation of thought. The double is a reality external to the subject and is inscribed in the visible world. Yet even in its conformity with what it simulates, its unusual character ensures its substantial difference from familiar objects and the ordinary setting of daily life. The double plays on two contrasting levels at the same time: at the moment when it shows itself to be present, it also reveals itself as not being of this world but rather as belonging to an inaccessible elsewhere.[38]

Let us attempt to draw together all of the strands in the fabric of Homer's concept of human nature by marking the criteria of distinction between two sets of central psychical terms. One group is comprised of *psychē, thymos, menos* and *nous*, each of which is a soul-related (psychical) function necessarily dependent on an animal body (its host), though its 'seat' or internal site is indefinite and underdetermined, and as a component of the whole being (an ensouled animal) has a complex array of properties. The other group comprises *kēr* (or *kradiē*), *phrenes*, sometimes *hēpar*, and later *kephalē*[37], each of which is an organic internal component of the

---

[37] Vernant, 1991, p. 187; see Redfield, 1985; Onians, pp. 39–40; Claus, 1981, pp. 98–9; Padel offers similar premises in her analysis of the double but draws rather confused implications from this, Padel, 1992, pp. 31–2. Burkert, 1985, pp. 194–9, points out that even in Homer there are 'certain motifs which contain the germs of a radical transformation in beliefs concerning the afterlife.' Helen herself had been replicated, as Calasso reminds the modern reader, 1993, pp. 130, 133.

[38] The noblest part, LSJ 9th rev., p. 945, sec. 2.

animal body, occupies a definite, determinate internal site, and upon which the first set of psychical functions has a necessarily dependent relation, but whose properties are ambiguous and over-determined. Regarding the question of the inherent (or intrinsic) unity of the kind of being that can most properly be described with this exact cluster of terms, perhaps a more cautious statement would be that our modern post-Cartesian concept of mind has its *closest ancestor* in Archaic Greek thought in Homer's *nous*. But where Descartes and his descendants will equate the mind with the faculty of reason, Homer characterizes *noos* (mind or intellect) as one dimension of the human being. The closest ancestor in Archaic Greek to the medieval and pre-Cartesian concept of soul or *anima* is *psychē*, but only in so far as Homeric *psychē* characterizes the uniquely human life-force or vitality which does not survive bodily death.

The inescapable conclusion that one must draw with regard to the Hebrew psychical terms, such as *nepesh, ruach* and *leb*, is the consequence of a cumulative elimination of feasible candidates to explain the distinctive 'nature' of living beings with soul. Due to the superbly detailed linguistic excavations of OT scholars in recent years, it is possible to identify the best candidate for *nepesh* as 'life-force' or vitality. This concept does not mean the condition of being alive, or the status of living thing, for which the Hebrew writers used the word *hayyim* (much as Greek writers used *zōon*); nor for the breath as such, for which the Hebrews used *neshama* (much as the Greeks used *pnoē* or *pneuma*), which is the overt manifestation or exteriorization of the life-force. This core concept helps to make sense of the numerous passages in the OT where *nepesh* can increase or decrease, where it is present in degree, and especially in cases where *nepesh* is poured out or breathed out, though the individual is not yet dead. However, when the living human dies the *nepesh* is gone forever; only the living have the power to bring back – restore or augment – life-force or vitality. This is virtually the same conclusion that Homeric scholars have reached regarding the archaic concept of *psychē* (though Onians is more tempted to organicize the life-force in one of several internal organs) – the best candidate for *psychē* is 'life-force' or vitality. Neither *psychē* nor *nous* is ever properly applied to non-human animals, with the exception of the snake, whose ascription of *psychē* may reflect a unique encoding of Orphic ritual doctrine.[39] Other Homeric soul-words are routinely used of animals, for example, *thymos, menos, phrenes, ētor* and *kēr*, but not that which distinctively individuates humans' life-force from the mere animal status of living being. The part-for-whole expressive force of other soul-words used in conjunction with *psychē* can also work in reverse, that is, whole-for-part, where the individual is said to be 'full of life' when he is vibrant or passionate, or 'to have a great soul' when he is generous or expansive. It is thus *psychē* that uniquely differentiates human beings from other living, animate beings, through or by means of vital attributes such as self-moved action, desire for what is absent, and the noetic powers, those attributable to *nous*, of imagination, memory and reflection.

---

[39] On the snake-*psychē*, see Bremmer, 1983, pp. 126–8; Claus, 1981, pp. 61–3; Onians, pp. 206–8.

(3) The pre-Socratic soul as property-like thing

The centuries from the Homeric age to the Classical age of Greek thought are a transitional period in the development of philosophical speculation and, more specifically, of overt thematic concern with the nature, source and functions of the soul. There are many ways in which priority is assigned to one or another figure between the eighth and the fourth centuries BCE; different criteria are used to assert that someone is the *first* in saying something. Thus, Pherecydes and Pythagoras (who lived at about the same time) were the first to import into popular culture the 'foreign', shamanistic ideas about an immortal soul, going-under, ecstatic foresight, and so forth.[40] But Pherecydes, like Hesiod, is also assigned a secondary, lesser status in philosophical genealogy[41] (or perhaps, the birth of ideas) since he took part in speculation about the birth of the cosmos (cosmogony) and the birth of the gods (theogony), that is, regarding the origin and powers of divine agents. Aristotle referred to Pherecydes and the Magi (Near-Eastern mystics)[42] as 'mixed theologians, those who do not say everything in mythical form', as did Homer and Hesiod, for example, and who claimed that 'the first generator is the best' (Meta. 1091b8). Kirk and Raven, in the opening lines of the First Chapter on 'Forerunners', said that these transitional ideas were not concerned with pure mythology, 'but with concepts which, although expressed in the language and through the personages of myth, are not mythopoeic in kind but are the result of direct, empirical, non-symbolical ways of thinking.' To claim that the concepts of Birth, Night, Chaos, and so forth, and the four roots or elements of all things are the result of 'direct, empirical' thought is strange indeed, though Thales and his successors' attention to water and fire could be said to be non-symbolic: 'These quasi-rationalistic views of the world are most frequently concerned with its earliest history, starting from its actual birth or creation; for this way of thinking was incidental to the attempt ... to systematize the manifold deities of legend by deriving them from a common ancestor or pair of ancestors at the beginning of the world.'[43] Centuries later, however, Pherecydes was routinely recognized by Latin writers as the first author to hold that the human soul was immortal.[44] The one almost certain historical link between Greek speculative thinking and the remote lands of the Magi and shamans is the first-hand account made by Aristeas of Proconnesus (*c.* 630–20 BCE) of his travels to the land at the Back of the North Wind (Hyperborea), beyond the Black Sea, where he encountered the Scythians, the Arimaspi and other extraordinary peoples, returning many years

---

[40] On Pherecydes' views about the soul, or at least views which can be derived from the testimonia, the fullest account is in Schibli, 1990, pp. 104–27.

[41] See Kirk & Raven, 1960, pp. 48–72; West, 1971, Chaps 1 & 2; and Schibli, 1990, pp. 11–13, 132–4.

[42] The gifts of the Magi are interpreted along cosmological lines by West, 1971, pp. 213–42.

[43] Kirk & Raven, 1960, p. 8; on Thales' connection with Eastern thought, see West, 1971, pp. 208–14.

[44] See esp. Cicero, Tusc. Disp. 1.38; Lactantius, Div. Inst. 7.7.12; Augustine, Contra Acad. 3.37, and Letters 137.12; all testimonia and fragments excerpted by Schibli, 1990, Appendix 2, pp. 140–75.

later with an astonishing narrative,[45] rehearsed by Herodotus (Hist. iv.12–16). Bolton argued quite convincingly that many features of Aristeas' account, filtered through Heraclides Ponticus' reworkings, show up again in Empedocles' writings and stories about his life. Aristeas clearly reported the results of shamanistic extrasomatic experience, as well as preaching some version of the immortal soul doctrine.[46]

On the other hand, Thales is usually ascribed the status of first person to speculate about principles and first causes in a distinctively philosophical manner. Aristotle granted Thales this primordial role more than once, in one case separating Thales' attitude from that of his predecessors: 'the very ancient and indeed first speculators about the gods, long before the present age, made the same supposition about nature' (Meta. 983b27). In Simplicius' commentary on Aristotle he said that 'Thales is traditionally the first to have revealed the investigation of nature (*peri phuseōs historian*) to the Greeks' (KR fr.83). However, given the very small number of Thalean documents, the evidence is under-determined and the priority claim itself is highly contentious. Pythagoras' 'giant shadow' falls on many thinkers after him, but his sayings and deeds are devoted almost exclusively to ritual actions about personal preparation and purification. It is not feasible in this section to enter fully into the complex (even torturous) discussion about Pythagoras' contribution to Greek thinking about the soul; his influence on Platonic doctrines will become more apparent in the next section. Heraclitus is unanimously accorded the position of the first to make *psychē* a thematic issue in his logos-inspired discourse; but the riddling, ambiguous character of his extant fragments leaves irresolvable the general framework into which his claims could be fitted. And in the final priority assignment, Socrates is (almost) always said to be the first to self-consciously articulate the basic scheme of dialectic, a theory of knowledge, an ethical theory, and an account of the nature and functions of the soul. So many firsts, so many ways to make a beginning; it will be our task in much of what follows to keep track of which way an idea is said to start.

Thales of Miletus lived in the first part of the sixth century BCE and is commonly accorded the title of the first Greek philosopher, that is, an inquirer who made explicit some questions that later came to be associated with a distinctly philosophical attitude. As with many other early thinkers, some of our knowledge of his teachings is derived from Aristotle's summary of his predecessors' opinions about the nature of the soul. Amongst the few sayings attributed to him (beyond various anecdotal comments about his life) are the following: 'Thales too supposed the soul (*psychē*) was a mover (*kinētikon*), given that he said that the [magnetic] stone has a soul because it moves iron' (Aristotle, de An. 405a19; KRS fr. 89). This report from Aristotle is restated by Diogenes Laertius when he says that Thales 'gave a share of soul even to soulless objects, taking his evidence from the magnetic stone and from

---

[45] Bolton's meticulous and ingenious reconstruction, 1962, pp. 74–118, has been confirmed at many points by recent archaeological investigations in Central Asia; see esp. J. P. Mallory & Victor Mair, *The Tarim Mummies*, London: Thames & Hudson, 2000, Chapter 3, retracing Aristeas' route.

[46] On indications in Aristeas about the 'flight of the soul' and his influence on Pythagorean doctrines, see Bolton, 1962, pp. 146–57, 164–5; summary statement, pp. 172–5.

amber' (Lives 1.24; KRS fr. 90). Aristotle adds to his picture of Thales' view of soul a claim regarding the more general context in which Thales might have made this remark: 'And some say that it [soul] is intermingled in the universe, which is perhaps the reason why Thales also thought that all things are full of gods' (Aristotle, de An. 411a7; KRS fr. 91). The Aetius source, following Theophrastus' summary, appears to add further detail to this claim: 'Thales said that the mind of the world is god (*noun tou kosmou ton theon*), and that the sum of things is ensouled and full of daemons; through the elemental moisture there penetrates a divine power that moves it' (KRS fr. 95). But this paraphrase interpolates the idea of mind (*nous*) into Thales' original claim, and despite Thales' obvious preference for moistness or moisture (*hugros*) as the principle of all things, shows later Stoic interpretation in assigning divine power to the source of this movement.[47]

It is true that for Aristotle the 'cause' of movement, especially of self-directed movement, is the linchpin in his *physical* explanation of the ensouled status of living beings. He also devotes a great deal of attention in his *psychical* explanation of the integration and coordination of cognitive and perceptual powers to the kind of soul that must be responsible for these operations. Although Thales apparently thought there was something significant about the magnet's 'power' to move pieces of iron, significant in that it indicated the presence of some kind of soul, this does not imply that Thales thought that this took place because the soul was some kind of mover. When Aristotle reviews his predecessors' efforts to establish the material principles of all things coming-into-being and passing-away in *Metaphysics* Book Alpha, he reports Thales' precedent-setting supposition as follows: 'Thales, the founder of this type of philosophy, says that it [the principle] is water (*hudōr*) ... perhaps making this supposition from seeing the nurture of all things to be moist (*hugran*) ... Both from this and from the seeds of all things having a moist nature (*spermata tēn phusin hugran*), water being the natural principle of moist things' (Meta. 983b6). The third clause could be construed as saying either that all things have naturally moist seeds and their (the seeds') principle is water (an element), or that *some* things have moist seeds as their nature, and their (those things') principle is water. The second clause claims that Thales observed that (presumably) living things depend for their growth (and movement) on the presence of moist seeds, whose principle of action is derived from water. This point is reinforced by other attributed statements where Thales thought that there were indeed *four* elements (KRS fr.88); the other three (air, fire and earth) did not contribute to an explanation of the living (that is, ensouled) nature of certain kinds of things. Perhaps it is an unwarranted inference to claim that Thales thought that magnet or amber (which exhibits magnetic properties when rubbed) was ensouled because its principal element was water; rather it exhibited some features of an ensouled thing in so far as it had the power to move things other than itself. Despite this, Schofield says that one may infer that 'Thales was well on the way to conceiving of *psuchē* ... as the central essence which connects our various faculties. In animals the power of movement is intimately related to cognitive powers, to the extent that is hard to imagine Thales

---

[47] West, 1971, pp. 208–13 for an attempted reconstruction.

not ascribing cognition also to *psuchē*, had the question occurred to him. Unfortunately we have no information as to whether he considered it or not.'[48]

It seems that Aristotle thought that Thales' statement that all things are full of gods and the statement that soul pervades the whole world are connected. The purported link then is between the souls of moist things and the presence of gods, perhaps along the lines that the gods' divine power institutes the generative and nutritive properties of moist things through the material presence of water, and that one outstanding instance of this is the magnet's perceived action on external objects. McKirahan offers this summary of Thales' contribution:

> Water is primary since it is prominent in the physical makeup of the world ... and it is needed for the generation and maintenance of living things and of some apparently non-living things. Thales conceives of water not as a chemically pure substance, but as the moist element quite generally – in the sea, in rain, in sperm ... If everything is made of water or ultimately arises from water, the life force of water pervades the whole world, showing up in some things more than others (just as some things are wetter than others). Moreover, as a living thing with no beginning in time (everything else owes its beginning to *it*), and apparently no end in time either, water is divine (since for the Greeks the primary characteristics of the divine are immortality and power independent of human will). Hence all things, being composed of or arising from water, are full of the divine.[49]

Anaximander, also from Miletus, was called the pupil and successor of Thales: his most notable achievements, according to the earliest historians, were the discovery of the *gnōmon* (set-square) and sundial, the first written treatise 'On Nature', the first world map, and the central cosmological concept of the boundless (*apeiron*).[50] It does not seem likely that he actually invented these instruments, but rather that he introduced them from Babylon where astronomical measurements had been conducted for some time. There is an immense scholarly debate about the meaning of his key principle, *to apeiron*, either the boundless, the indefinite, or the infinite, from which all things are derived. He said that it was neither water nor any of the other elements, but some other boundless nature, which is eternal and unchanging and surrounds the world (KR fr.103). The four elements were separated out from this substratum and differentiated into the various opposites, such as hot and cold, wet and dry (KR fr.120–2). His doctrine of cosmic creation is that a fiery sphere formed around the air (or dark mist) about the earth, like bark round a tree, and when broken off and enclosed in circles, formed the heavenly bodies (KR fr.123). This appears to be paralleled at the level of organic things: 'the first living things were born in moisture, enclosed in thorny barks (*phloios*),[51] and as their age increased they came out onto the drier part, their bark broke off, and they lived a different kind of life a short time' (KR fr.136).

But it is with the sixth-century Milesian writer Anaximenes, himself probably the pupil of Anaximander, that the concept of soul (*psychē*) makes its first definite appearance. The most important document is the reconstructed argument from the

---

[48] Schofield, in Everson, 1991, p. 23.
[49] McKirahan, 1994, p. 31.
[50] Kirk & Raven, 1960, pp. 102–5.
[51] On the bark-image, see West, 1971, pp. 95–6.

Aetius source (KR fr.163): Anaximenes declared that 'air is the principle of existing things; for from it all things come-to-be and into it they are dissolved. As our soul, he says, being air (*aer*) holds-together-and controls (*sugkratei*) us, so does wind (or breath, *pneuma*) and air enclose the whole world – air and wind are synonymous – But [added Aetius] he is in error to think that living things consist of simple and single-form air and wind' (KR fr.163). The unusual word *sugkratien* is composed of two more standard archaic words, *sunechein* ('holds together') and *kratein* ('controls'), perhaps interpolated backwards from a much later redaction.[52] Kirk and Raven commented that the comparison between one and the other is not very clear, since it seems to say that breath and air enclose the whole world in the way that our soul, being air and breath, holds together and controls us (or our bodies). They proposed four possible versions of this statement: (i) 'air holds us together, from inside, and the world together, from outside, <and therefore human and the world are more alike than at first appears>, *or* <and therefore air is operative in the most diverse kinds of object>'; (ii) 'as our soul holds the body together and so controls it, so the originative substance ... holds the world together and so controls it'; (iii) 'the soul, which is breath, holds together and controls man; therefore, what holds together and controls the world must also be breath or air, because the world is like a large-scale man or animal'; (iv) 'the life-principle and motive force of man is, traditionally, *pneuma* or the breath-soul; <*pneuma* is seen in the outside world as wind>; therefore, the life-principle of the outside world is *pneuma*; <therefore, wind, breath, or air is the life and substance of all things>.'

Kirk and Raven remarked that the idea of the soul holding together the body has no other parallel in pre-socratic thought; that Anaximenes could have meant by *sugkratein* that the soul possesses the body, that is, it permeates the whole body, and thus controls it; and that this is the first extant use of the world *pneuma*, 'breath', which would later become such a pivotal psychical term. The analogy drawn between the world-whole (*kosmos*) and the soul is also very early; it only became common later in the fifth century, under the influence of medical theories, to compare the human microcosm to the world macrocosm: 'The mention of soul is important itself apart from [Thales' dictum] it is the first Presocratic psychological statement to survive – though the actual structure of the soul envisaged, as breath, belonged to an age-old popular tradition.'[53] But, against this view, there is no mention in the text of the *body*; it is just as sensible to read this to mean that soul as air holds together an individual being, one which is embodied. Claus agrees about the signal importance of this document: first, that 'it would allow the analogy of nature and man to be focused specifically in the *psyche* so that the nature and activity of the *psyche* could be explored through the nature and activity of the *arche*, and vice versa.' Second, 'the use of *sugkratein* in the fragment could imply extension of the functions of soul already at the outset of Presocratic thought beyond those of simple animation.'[54] One might also add that Anaximenes' claim shows a clear connection with Homeric usage of soul as the breath of life, since it makes a comparable equation of external air as wind with internal air as breath. The

---

[52] Kirk & Raven, p. 159, note 1.
[53] Kirk & Raven, pp. 160–61.
[54] Claus, 1981, p. 123.

importance of this extension of the concrete reference of soul-related ideas, only marginally differentiated along the external–internal axis, will be seen again in Heraclitus and Empedocles.

However, the fullest credit must surely be given to Heraclitus of Ephesus (c.540–480 BCE) for making the human soul a theme (though not a theory) in his reflections. There are just enough instances in the surviving fragments (ten explicit uses and three or four implicit uses) to make scholarly investigation worthwhile, but not enough to resolve some of the more perplexing problems. Claus helpfully summarizes some of the central points, first made by Zeller more than a century ago:

> First, that the *psychē* is itself fire and undergoes changes of state analogous to those of fire in the cosmic system. Second, it is distributed throughout the body and is unmeasurable. Third, its changes of state are manifested by waking, sleeping, and death. These conditions depend on the ratio of moisture to fire in the soul … Fourth, like cosmic fire, soul fire is in some ways nourished by moisture, although how this happens is not explicitly described. Finally, … it seems likely that Heraclitus envisions two kinds of 'death' for the *psychē*: one by fire for those cut down by violence in the prime of life [whose *psychai* are fiery] … the other by water for those whose *psychai* gradually become moist through disease and degeneration.[55]

Heraclitus was known as the riddler, the obscure, and other epithets that signified the puzzling character of his philosophical reflections. It is not possible to circumvent his deliberate obfuscation and puzzle-setting, since he thought this mode of discourse most suitable to the kind of issues he was addressing, as well as being most in accord with his personal relation to the *logos*. Nor is it feasible in this section to enter into the complex and heavily contested arena of Heraclitean exegesis. It will be sufficient for our purposes to elucidate *some* of the important conceptual innovations that he made in his thematic attention to the subject of the human soul. One outstanding example of this riddling format ('a marvelous specimen', as Schofield says) asks the reader (or hearer) to consider the way in which sleep and dreams are connected to the soul: 'A man in the night kindles a light for himself when his vision is extinguished; living he is in contact with the dead when asleep, and in contact with the sleeper when awake' (KR fr.236) – the word *haptetai* means both 'kindle' and 'touch' or 'contact'.

Numerous interpretations of this statement have been offered,[56] not counting those who throw up their hands in frustration, when dealing with either the overt or the hidden level. Schofield offers the most intelligent and ingenious explanation by making good sense of this statement on three different levels of meaning. He says that on the superficial, riddle-solving level the metaphor of lamp-lighting (taken up again in Empedocles' poem) describes an ordinary phenomenon. Although his eyes are closed in sleep, the dreamer creates an illuminated scene where the departed 'appear', and at the same time the waking man is in contact with the sleeper in as much as he remembers his dreams. At the second level the universal logos is disclosed: through kindling the light of his dream, the living man kindles himself,

---

[55] Claus, 1981, p. 126; see another comparable summary in McKirahan, 1994, pp. 146–7.
[56] Kirk & Raven, pp. 208–9; Kahn, 1979, pp. 214–17; Robinson, 1987, pp. 93–100.

even though he is 'dead to the world' in his dreams; and the waking self kindles the sleeping self, for dreams are a sort of wakeful sleep. The third level is the level of physical truth, supported by another fragment regarding ever-living fire, kindling and going out in measures (KR fr.220). And thus the fragment as a whole means that although the fire of the sleeper's soul is quenched in some measure, he rekindles it in another measure in his dreams. Since Heraclitus identified the *archē* of soul with fire, when the soul sleeps the internal fire is diminished; this also confirms his belief that when a man is drunk his soul becomes moist, and thus falls away toward death.[57]

The latter claim is most strikingly made in another fragment (KR fr.232): 'for souls it is death to become water, for water it is death to become earth; from earth water comes-to-be, and from water, soul', such that 'a dry soul is wisest and best' (KR fr.233). An interpretation which supports the notion of a spectrum of physical states of the soul between the extremes of wateriness and fieriness fits well with his further assertion that 'a man when he is drunk is led by an unfledged boy, stumbling and not knowing where he goes, having his soul moist' (KR fr.234). Being drunk deprives a human of the use of his active powers, such that he is led about (that is, controlled) as if by a child whose powers are not fully mature but equal to the task of getting the drunken adult home. Again, this remark makes more than just the trivial and obvious claim that a drunken man has doused himself with liquid. The highly pertinent word *hugros* ('moist') also means supple and loose, and was used in conjunction with *sarx* and other words to indicate soft tissue, but also to signify the slackness shown when someone stumbles.[58] Onians reminds us that for the early Greeks the young were said to abound in liquid, their limbs' looseness and suppleness was explained by an abundance of moistness, thus setting this physical feature in contrast to hard or rigid (*sklēros*). The analogical relations between moist and dry, young and old, hard bones and soft flesh shows through in such common expressions as 'drying up' or 'withering' in old age.[59] This traditional, common sense of opposition between hard bones and gristle, on one hand, and soft tissue or flesh on the other derives form an archaic view about *psychē* as life-force in Homer, as well as the ancient Hebrew *basar* in contrast with *nepesh*.

The most puzzling saying about soul, the one that reaches the deepest into the mysterious logos, is the following: 'immortals mortals, mortals immortals, living their death and dying their life' (KR fr.242). Charles Kahn said of this fragment (from Hippolytus' *Refutation of All Heresies*) that 'this is in point of form Heraclitus' masterpiece, the most perfectly symmetrical of all the fragments.'[60] There have been many, many attempts to make sense of this profound riddle; again let us follow Schofield's analysis for one plausible and coherent interpretation:

> Our life as mortals depends on the temporary extinction of the physical elements from which it comes to be and into which it is destroyed. And the processes of living and

---

[57] Schofield, 1991, pp. 27–9.
[58] Schofield, in Everson, 1991, p. 21; see LSJ, 9th Edn,1968, s.v. '*hugros*', p. 1843.
[59] Onians, pp. 213–5; Claus, 1981, pp. 129–31.
[60] Kahn, 1979, p. 218; for several different ways to render this in English, see Kirk & Raven, 1960, p. 210 and Nussbaum, 1972, p. 163–4.

dying will be not only ... the same in form but numerically identical: the birth of the soul *is* the death of water, and vice versa ... The very concepts of mortality and immortality, life and death, collapse into each other. The resonances of this implication reach further than the confines of an interpretation in terms of physical truth. It threatens both traditional religion, with its confident separation of mortals and immortals, and Pythagoreanism, with its consoling promise that there is really no such thing as mortality – it is merely a form of immortality.[61]

It remains to make some determination with regard to the vexed question about whether Heraclitus thought the human soul to be itself immortal, whatever its metaphorical connection to the immortal souls of gods.

Claus concludes his very cautious exegesis of the Heraclitean soul fragments with these words: they 'unquestionably constitute the most complicated and elusive body of material that must be dealt with in this study, and the one least amenable to a semantic investigation ... [These] in some sense discover the psychological value of *psychē* for Greek thought. At the least, *psychē* is, as all commentators have seen, an entity responsive to a systematic scheme of changes, and on these changes intelligence and the emotional life depend.'[62] Perhaps it is wise not to make a definitive claim about Heraclitus' view of the soul's mortal or immortal status. However, such abstention from judgment makes it more difficult to understand how Heraclitus' thought is transitional between the influx of mystical, non-Greek ideas and the more explicit (albeit agnostic) thesis of Socrates in the early dialogues. Martha Nussbaum attempted to strike a highly nuanced balance between two equally tenable inferences:

> [T]he Heraclitean doctrine of *psychē* amounts to a radical and profoundly creative critique of traditional ideas about man's faculties, his language, and his death. For the first time, apparently, in the history of Greek thought, man is seen explicitly as having a central 'self': a single, vital faculty in terms of which sense-perception, language, ethical behavior, and ultimately death, must be understood. As the cosmos, articulated into a plurality of species, is, nonetheless, one through the all-connecting *logos* of fire, so a man, though he has many faculties, is one by virtue of the central, connecting faculty of *psychē*.

Nussbaum concludes that, 'Heraclitus' *psychē* theory recognizes death as necessary and denies posthumous survival. And yet it accords to man the possibility of the kinetic immortality of *kleos* [glory], which even the immortal gods cannot attain.'[63] McKirihan is less cautious and opts for a more decisive conclusion: 'Heraclitus believed in an afterlife depending on the soul's state at the moment of death.' Although he tempers this claim by pointing out that Heraclitus seems to offer hope for only *some,* more noble souls, the sense of everlasting glory pertains not just to the memory of their deeds, but to their post-mortem souls absorbed into the cosmic fire.[64]

---

[61] Schofield, in Everson, 1991, p. 32.
[62] Claus, 1981, p. 138.
[63] Nussbaum, 1972, p. 169.
[64] McKirihan, 1994, p. 146.

Anaxagoras of Clazomenae (*c*.500–428 BCE) made mind (*nous*) as important a theme in his cosmic speculation as Heraclitus had made *psychē*. Large portions of Anaxagoras' verses survive, partly due to the high regard accorded them by Simplicius in his commentary on Aristotle's *Physics*. One of Anaxagoras' main concerns had been to refute the views of Pythagoras and Heraclitus that the world was the scene of incessant warfare between opposites. He asserted that physical matter was infinitely divisible, that it composed all sensible bodies, and that the principles of all things were infinite in number. But Mind, he said, is itself infinite in extent, self-ruled, and mixed with nothing, alone by itself. It is the finest and purest of all things, it has knowledge about and power over all things, and its power is manifest through its control of movement in living things (KR fr.503). Kirk and Raven comment that in these and other passages, Anaxagoras struggles to imagine and describe an infinite incorporeal entity, but whose infinite extent must mean occupation of space like other finite bodies. In doing so he sets up a vast cosmic dualism, between mind unmixed with anything else, and all other bodies in which mind is absent: 'But both members of this dualism are peculiar. Mind, like matter, is corporeal and owes its power over matter to its fineness and purity. Matter itself, so far from being pure, is originally at least an infinitely divisible mixture of every form of substance that the world is ultimately to contain.' In the original mixture all things were together, including the seeds of all things that would come to be, but now everything contains some portion of every other thing except Mind itself: 'If there are some things in which Mind is present, there are obviously other things in which it is not. Mind is presumably therefore to be imagined as discontinuously distributed throughout the world in living things.'[65]

In Empedocles of Acragas (in Sicily), in the early to mid-fifth century, several other principal features of the pre-Socratic account of soul began to take shape. In his one long poem in two parts (or, his two poems),[66] Empedocles makes unambiguous references to an immortal soul, some of its basic functions, its physical composition, and ritual operations to purify its bodily host. Near the start he refers to himself as 'an immortal god, no longer mortal, honored among all'; an unusual assertion, to say the least, for no other figure ever claims *to be* a god in addition to being immortal. He was reputed to have been a skilled medical doctor, an ardent democrat, and to have leapt to his death (or fiery life) in the Mt. Etna volcano.[67] There are many details in both his life-story and his sayings that have clear parallels with the sorts of shamanistic beliefs and rituals evident in Pherecydes, Pythagoras, Aristeas and others. His mysterious tattoos, his skin after death (or murder) used in some ritual fashion, the extra-somatic travel and prophecy, legends of rebirth and bilocation – all point toward the magically inspired idea of an immortal soul.[68] But in addition to this, he made several significant contributions to philosophical speculation. First, he argued against Parmenides' assertion that there was no real

---

[65] Kirk & Raven, 1960, pp. 374–6.

[66] On this point see *inter alia*, Kirk & Raven, 1960, pp. 321–3; Kingsley, 1995, pp. 363–70; Kahn, 1973, pp. 428–34; reconstructed in its most likely proper order by McKirihan, 1994, pp. 232–54.

[67] On the significance of his leap into fire, see Kingsley, 1995, pp. 250–55.

[68] For more details on these topics, see Kingsley, 1995, pp. 233–8, 251–9.

change or movement in things by putting forth the notion that there were four roots (*stoikheia*), which moved under the influence of Love (*Philia*) and Strife (*Neikeos*). Second, the influence of Love and Strife alternated over time such that the world went through innumerable cycles. Third, he argued that there were four basic material forms, the elements, from which all particular things were composed. Fourth, he made an early effort at establishing the mechanisms of respiration through the postulation of very fine pores and hidden tubules[69] (repeated in some detail in Aristotle, KR fr.453). And finally, he made an explicit statement that the human soul is immortal, that it can be trained through discipline, and that (at least some) souls can move between individual animal bodies after their hosts' death.

With regard to the last theme, he appears to have made an innovation in attempting to explain how some souls can both survive their hosts' bodily death *and* move between separate host-bodies in terms of a *double* birth and death: 'Double is the coming-to-be of mortal things, and double is their failing; for the coming together of all things produces one birth and destruction, and the other is nurtured and flies apart when they grow apart again' (KR fr.423). This story is twofold since it follows accounts of two births and two deaths: in terms of the particular material thing, its birth and death coincide with the initial mixture and terminal decomposition; but in terms of the divine, immortal element, its birth is the formation of those elements and its 'death' is just the name for its dispersal into the original matrix. The concept of double birth and double death is taken up much later in an astonishing synthesis of Christian and Neo-Platonist doctrines by St. Augustine. Where Epicurus will later conclude that the material composition of the living individual is sufficient evidence to demonstrate that the soul is in fact *mortal*, Empedocles uses similar premises to show that the soul must be *immortal*: 'There is coming-to-be of not one single thing of mortal things, nor is there any end of deadly death, but only mixture, and separation of what is mixed, and nature (*phusis*) is the name given to them by humans' (Plutarch Adv. Col. 1111f).

The nature specific to human beings, in virtue of which they are living, thinking beings, is manifest in (or explained by) the presence of blood; an idea that relates thought (*noema*) to the vital-force conveyed by blood as fluid.[70] 'The heart nurtured in the sea of blood surging back and forth, where most especially is what is called thought by humans, for the blood around the heart in humans is called thought' (KR fr.458). Theophrastus reported that Empedocles, in asserting the thesis that like is known by like, and that wisdom is perception of something identical or equivalent, offered this account: 'out of these things are all things fitted together and constructed, and by these do they think (*phroneousi*) and feel pleasure or pain. So it is especially with the blood that they think (*phronein*), for in the blood above all other parts the elements are blended (*stoikheia tōn merōn*)' (KR fr.459). Nevertheless, the fluid blood is not identical with the human soul, but rather its temporary vehicle, and the body its dwelling or 'garb'. The source of the human soul is 'outside' its carrier, the soul visits or sojourns in the body,

---

[69] On the verbal imagery surrounding the soul's connection with pores, channels and tubes, see Padel, 1992, pp. 41–2.

[70] On the imagery of surging, liquid forces of soul, see Padel, 1992, pp. 88–91; Onians relates this concept to the Latin terms *sapiens, sapere*, etc.: Onians, pp. 61–3.

and, as a wanderer or traveler in the material realm, it can indeed visit within *other* bodies, after death: 'It is not our blood, he says, nor the blending of our breath that produced the essential principle of the soul; rather from these [things] the body is molded, earth-born and mortal. Since the soul has come hither from elsewhere (*hēkousēs deuro*) he calls birth a sojourn abroad – the most comforting of all names – but in truth the soul is a fugitive and a wanderer, banished by the decrees and laws of the gods' (KR fr.486). And thus he can utter what is perhaps his best-known saying regarding the transmigration of his own soul from one bodily 'garb' to another: 'For already I have once been a boy and a girl, a bush and a bird and a [dumb] fish from the sea' (KR fr.476). E. R. Dodds argued that the non-Greek belief about the soul's transmigration from body to body, the belief that some dreams are 'psychic excursions', and the special technique of extra-somatic projection probably derived about the same time, from the same exogenous source.[71]

The seemingly incongruous juxtaposition of Empedocles' poem on nature and the 'mystical' poem on purification led Jaeger to describe him as 'a philosophical centaur, so to speak – a prodigious union of Ionian elemental physics and Orphic theology'. Vlastos remarked that 'prodigy' (that is, monstrous offspring) is indeed the right word to use here for 'the union of physics and theology, as it is for the junction of immortal god and mortal flesh. The one is as much of a miracle as the other, and Empedocles doubtless devoutly believed it to be such. He left us no explanation of either, and it would be futile to try to supply it by rationalizing the theology of the mystic or mystifying the logic of the cosmologist.'[72] One important dimension in Empedocles' thought about the immortal soul is the different weight he attaches to *daimon* in distinction from *psychē* when he attempts to account for the 'fallen state' of some human souls. Kahn is surely right in calling attention to this when he synopsizes Empedocles' contribution to the pre-Socratic, transitional understanding of the nature and destiny of the soul:

> The terms he uses suggest the continued, harmonious coexistence of discrete individuals, very much like the celestial cavalcade of gods and spirits in the *Phaedrus* ... [He] express[es] the inner conviction of all mystics, that there dwells within us a fallen spirit or portion of deity whose rightful place is elsewhere, in a realm of pure harmony and peace. Empedocles' physical doctrine of Love is an attempt to integrate this conviction within a systematic explanation of the natural world ... What real connection there was between this unity [of the sphere] and the company of the blessed daimons, we simply do not know.[73]

Claus draws together his own tracing of life-force uses of *psychē* with respect to Pythagoras and Empedocles in these terms: 'Although the new ideas of survival and of occult existence undoubtedly helped to create an environment in which the connotations of *psychē* could be greatly enriched as against earlier beliefs, deeply ingrained traditional attitudes had first to be overcome for such influences to be

---

[71] Dodds, 1951, p. 172 note 97
[72] Jaeger and Vlastos quoted in Kahn, 1973, pp. 428–9 note 4.
[73] Kahn, 1973, pp. 449–50; agreed to by Claus, 1981, pp. 114, 119.

felt, and this process may simply not have occurred in the century after Pythagoras.'[74]

It is difficult to form a coherent picture of what the pre-Socratic thinkers understood the soul to be and that is (at least in part) because it was difficult for those thinkers to understand what the soul could be – perhaps we now are in no better position. Sometimes, in their fragmentary texts, the soul is referred to as a thing or a substance with a nature or essence, whose functions are explained in terms of the predominance of one element, or the outgrowth of a mixture of elements with a predominant 'profile'. At other times, psychical powers seem to be the properties of one specific element which, when combined in a highly determinate manner, produces a living thing manifesting such underlying functions (or properties). Granger argues that when the soul is said to be the same as, or made out of, the hot or the cold, it is an ambiguous kind of entity which perhaps one could refer to as 'quality-thing'. In other words:

> [T]hey are entities in their own right, and they are not the qualities or properties of an object that provides them with a subject and the basis of their existence. Nonetheless, they were not typically thought to exist independently or in isolation from other contrary qualities and the objects they compose. Quality-things in their thing-like nature also exercise causal agency upon one another. They act directly upon their contraries after their own nature, the hot heating and the cold cooling, unless they are impeded in their own action by the qualities contrary to them, and cooled or heated in turn. The 'quality-thing' of these presocratic natural philosophers perhaps provides an ancestor of the 'property-thing' that is Aristotle's soul or form of organisms.[75]

Explanation on this issue moves in two or more directions: (1) the principle (*archē*) of soul is the presence of life-forces in the material composition of a living body; (2) the principle of all things is one or more primordial entity (including the boundless) which bestows or informs part of itself on particular kinds of things, making them living, ensouled entities. Positing the principle as the conceptual first stage in an explanation of the nature of anything, however, can follow more than one explanatory scheme: (3) it is a definite kind of underlying substance or element; (4) it is a quasi-substance, like a higher-order property or relation, for example, hot and cold, love and strife; (5) it persists into Socratic schemes, since he makes equal and unequal, opposite and the same into ideal forms. These different forces or vectors in explanation converge (or at least appear to converge) in the early seventh or sixth century under the impact of strange and alien ideas from eastern sources. The so-called 'Orientalizing Influence' has long been recognized by Classical scholars, especially after the publication of ancient Near Eastern texts in the 1950s, and the dissemination of the Russian research on shamanism about the time of Karl Meuli's ground-breaking 1935 paper.[76] The idea that the human soul is immortal was initially deeply interlinked with ecstatic foresight and magical practices. The

---

[74] Claus, 1981, p. 120.
[75] Granger, 1996, pp. 149–50.
[76] Karl Meuli, 'Scythica', in *Hermes,* vol. 70, 1935, pp. 121–76; E. R. Dodds lucidly and succinctly expressed this insight some time ago, 1951, pp. 146–7.

problem for these transitional thinkers was to map the non-Greek concept onto the popular, accepted usage of *psychē*, linguistic usage embedded in the long-standing Homeric framework which understood the soul to be a cluster of life-forces and thus, in its nature, mortal and death-bound.

Chapter 2
Plato, Aristotle and Hellenistic Thought

(1) Plato's twofold and threefold account of soul

Although there is some general consensus about the development of Platonic doctrines from the Early Socratic dialogues to Plato's late work in the *Laws*, there is some disagreement about where to draw the lines between early, middle and late works. There is even more controversy about the development, or at least internal modification, of the Platonic doctrine of the soul (*psychē*). Whether the soul is mortal or immortal, material or immaterial, bipartite or tripartite, and so forth, depends to some degree on which dialogue is under examination. T. M. Robinson chooses to interpret the very idea of Plato's multiform doctrines in a uniform manner: 'As far as the doctrine of "personal" psychē is concerned, the dialogues ... suggest no particular development on Plato's part. On the contrary, he appears to use particular "models" of psychē to suit particular contexts, and seems to be peculiarly unbound by dogmatism in this regard till the end of his life.'[1] As we will discover, however, although Plato's mature view of the concept of soul may leave unresolved some crucial issues about the 'nature' of *psychē*, it was surely one of his main dialectical concerns to adjudicate between competing models, and attempt to account for one overall concept in which, or under which, these other models would find their place. One might well pause in some concern (if not incredulity) when considering what Robinson says about discussion appropriate to the nature and function of the soul: 'For the term "soul" to most people (including those who reject it as nonsense) suggests an "inner person" or "ghost in the machine" (to use Ryle's phrase), that is, *in my opinion*, very close to Plato's usual view on the matter.'[2] This certainly advocates an eccentric, contentious philosophical point of view by the same author who has only just castigated previous Platonic scholars for allowing their own philosophical prejudices to color their interpretation of Plato's concept of soul.

I. M. Crombie once argued that Plato's doctrine of *psychē* is unstable due to strains exerted on some of the key terms by divergent, incompatible pictures of life, soul, immortality and other issues, especially where Socrates sometimes seems to be under the influence of the 'mystics' (about which more later). According to many scholars the Platonic doctrine of reincarnation and transmigration of souls enters at some stage of his development through the Orphic and Pythagorean secret teachings. Through this mystical infiltration, the concept of soul comes into conflict with the more common, popular understanding, one which appears to have retained many of the characteristics of Homeric *psychē*. Crombie asserted:

---

[1] Robinson, 1970, pp. vii–viii.
[2] Robinson, 1970, p. viii, emphasis added.

There are at least four forces which pull upon the word *psuchē* as Plato employs it. The one force draws it towards the meaning 'life', so that it is possible to speak of the *psuchē* of a plant. The next force draws it towards the meaning 'rationality' and this perhaps makes it easier to attribute *psuchē* to so orderly and punctual an object as a heavenly body; the third force tries to keep the word anchored to what Plato deems to be immortal in a human person ... the fourth force finally tries to make the word *psuchē* serve as a name for everything mortal.[3]

Nearly one hundred years ago, the great Oxford classics scholar John Burnet held that the core doctrine of Socrates' view of the soul could be found in the *Apology*, where Socrates' argument before the tribunal lays great stress on the care of the soul, and how to make the soul as good as possible.[4] Socrates repeatedly gives voice to an injunction about care of the soul and considers this care of one's own soul to be the goal of wisdom and truth. He considered it his moral duty to pursue the love of truth, to examine himself and others in the hope of removing ignorance. When he enjoined someone to not care more for one's possessions than for one's self in order that one may become as good and wise as possible, he seems to equate the soul with the self. He appears to argue that the soul is that upon which everything else depends. Over and above the unavoidable desire for life, there is a further desire for the moral good. On one hand, the physical good is the best for one's body, but on the other, the moral good is best for one's soul. In the *Apology*, the soul is not conceived as a principle sufficient for life in the Homeric sense, but it is thought to be a necessary condition for the body's life. Faced with the prospect of death himself, Socrates is composed, confident and agnostic about the outcome. He poses an intellectual dilemma to the tribunal in an attempt to convince them that either of only two alternative outcomes is welcome: 'Death is one of two things: either it is annihilation and the dead have no sensation (*aisthēsis*) of anything, or as we are told, it is really a change, a migration of the soul from this place to another. Now if there is no sensation, but only a dreamless sleep, death must be a marvelous gain' (40b). If the whole of time after one's death were like a dreamless sleep in an endless night, then there is nothing to fear. 'If, on the other hand, death is a removal from here to some other place, and if what we are told is true, that all the dead are there [including the true judges], what greater blessing could there be than this?' (40c–e). At least in the *Apology*, it is not Socrates' concern to argue for the soul's immortality, nor whether its putative immortal status is the result of its 'nature'. Rather, he is quite explicit about one belief that he holds to be certain: 'that nothing can harm a good person either in life or after death, and his fortunes are not a matter of indifference to the gods.' He says that his trial has not come about by accident, and since his 'inner voice' (*daimon*) has not counseled him against the event, it is quite clear that his time to die has come. He asserts that Socrates must go to die and the judges to live, 'but which of us has the happier prospect is unknown to anyone but the gods' (42a).

Although the *Crito* does not overtly mention the soul, Socrates questions his friends about that part of a person that can be harmed by wrong actions and

---

[3] Crombie, 1962, I, p. 301.
[4] Burnet, 1916, pp. 237–40.

benefited by good ones. Life is not worth living if that part has been damaged beyond repair; surely one cannot think that part is less important than the body (47e). The *Charmides*, in contrast, contains an important though obscure story about one of the sources that Socrates considers in his scrutiny of the nature of soul. From an unnamed Thracian physician Socrates heard a story about their king Zalmoxis, who said that, 'as you ought not to attempt to cure the eyes without the head, or the head without the body, so neither ought you to attempt to cure the body without the soul.' Those medical doctors who disregard the whole can never cure the person, since the part can never be well unless the whole of which it is a part is well: 'For all good and evil, whether in the body or in the whole person, originates in the soul and overflows from there as if from the head into the eyes' (156e). The whole person, therefore, consists of a body and a soul, but the two are not equal in nature or value. The analogy at work in this passage is that soul is to body as head is to eyes or body is to head. This is a strange and baffling notion, since the lesson should be that the soul is the whole of which its body is a part.

Now it is true that the eye and the head can be considered two substances, but the eye has a meaning or function only *in terms of* the head, and the same can be said of the two substances, head and body. An eye cannot exist as a proper eye except in a head, and the body cannot exist as a proper (animal) body unless it is animated, that is, brought to life, by a soul. But in each case, the whole of which the items are parts is not a summative or aggregate whole; one cannot add up a head and an eye, a head and a body, and so forth, and then arrive at a whole person. This would be to commit a category mistake (as it came to be called); each item may indeed be a thing or a substance with identity conditions, but they are things of different kinds. Robinson says that, 'We seem to be precluded from taking the soul as some sort of ghost or duplicate enjoying substantial existence in addition to the body; one cannot cut away the body, it seems, and find oneself left with a complete psychic substance qualifying for the name of the person or the "real self".'[5] Ostenfeld argues in almost the opposite direction when he infers from these passages that Socrates thinks that both body and soul are material substances, even though the relation of the soul to the body is rather unlike the relation of the body to its parts. To some extent the body *qua* body is logically and causally dependent on its parts in a way that the soul is not casually dependent on the body. He concludes that disembodiment would be logically and causally possible, whereas the body would be causally and logically dependent on the soul.[6] However, there is simply no textual evidence in the *Charmides*, a dialogue devoted to the virtue of temperance, to support either a substance dualist interpretation or the doctrine of an immortal soul.

The lesson that Socrates does derive from the report about King Zalmoxis is that the cure of the soul, harmed by immoral and dishonorable deeds, is prior to the cure of the body. The psychical cure is brought about by certain charms or incantations; Charmides wants to make a charm or amulet to ward off headaches. Socrates refers to these charms as 'noble words' (*kaloi logoi*); through the use of these words,

---

[5] Robinson, 1970, p. 6.
[6] Ostenfeld, 1982, pp. 161–2.

'temperance is implanted in the soul, and where temperance comes and stays, there health is more easily imparted, not only to the head, but to the whole body' (157a). Ordinary Greeks of this era did commonly employ magical amulets or charms (*epōdē*), which often contained written incantations. But Socrates stresses that the 'noble words' are addressed to the soul, words which the soul then learns; it is thus an intellectual, rational process of persuasion towards the good. Robinson thinks the introduction of Zalmoxis' message is highly significant; regarding earlier ideas of *psychē*, he says:

> Nowhere had it been affirmed that the soul is both the principle of cognition and the 'total self', a being entailed in any affirmation that such-and-such is a living body ... This is clear from the fact that that no one had ever said that the body was an integral part of the self. For the Homeric warrior on the one hand, the body *was* the self; for the Orphic the self was the incarnated soul. [Here] the self is apparently the *whole man*, of which body is an integral and inalienable part.[7]

The Zalmoxis tradition has been re-examined in great detail by Walter Burkert who showed its intimate connection with shamanism and its confusion with the Pythagorean legends.[8] Claus relies on these findings when he claims that

> Socrates' transformation of this figure into a physician of souls shows as much as any Platonic text the deliberate use to which historical antecedents of *psychē* can be put. For the Greek of the Fourth Century this passage entails contextual associations with both the immortal *psychē* of Pythagorean legend and the *psychē* as an object of medical therapy. When these have in effect canceled each other, Socrates introduces the notion of *psychē* as the moral self.[9]

Claus considers the Zalmoxis passages to be the most important text in the early dialogues for an understanding of the Socratic idea of the soul:

> Whatever else Plato may intend, the passage as it stands offers a profound rebuttal of any naïve psycho-somaticism centering on the *psychē* ... The soul matters primarily because it is the locus of generalized good and evil. To such physicians, therefore, the health of the body cannot really be the object of soul therapy but merely an epiphenomenon, accompanying the health of the soul, which is a good in its own right, and since all else depends upon it, the only good with which we need concern ourselves.[10]

Since Burkert and Claus build very strong arguments in favor of the signal importance of the Zalmoxis story for an understanding of both the early Platonic position *and* evidence of an incursion of non-Greek soul-belief, let us look more closely at some details of this story. The Zalmoxis legend is derived from Hellanicus' *Barbarian Customs*, itself the source of the widely known account in Herodotus (Hist. iv. 94–6).

---

[7] Robinson, 1970, p. 8.
[8] Burkert, 1972, pp. 157–65; on the state of Pythagorean studies after Burkert's work, see Huffman, in Long 1999, pp. 66–87.
[9] Claus, 1981, p. 170, note 44.
[10] Claus, 1981, p. 171.

Zalmoxis was the deified king of the Getae tribe, 'those who live without death', and he may have been a disciple of Pythagoras. Every four years the Getae send their god a messenger by means of a human sacrifice. Zalmoxis the King had built a banquet hall where he entertained his guests, and promised them that they and their descendants would not die, but would live forever enjoying all good things. He also built an underground chamber where he withdrew for three years and was mourned as dead; but in the fourth year he returned to the surface and was acclaimed for his conquest of death. Burkert considers it doubtful that this underground chamber really belongs to the Zalmoxis tradition; it is more likely that Zalmoxis dwelt in high places, where religious beliefs normally accord the holiest setting.[11] Other features of the story also support the view that it has become amalgamated with the Pythagorean legends, especially his 'going-under' (*katabasis*). Both Zalmoxis and Pythagoras exhibit ritual techniques and issue sayings (*acusmata*) that pertain to shamanistic practices, ecstatic travel to other places, overcoming death, bringing back health to the sick, and conducting souls of the dead to their new home: 'The significance of the idea of shamanism for the history of philosophy lies in the conjecture that the new conception of the soul, which was to become the dominant one through the influence of Plato, is to be traced to this source. The independence of the soul from the body is immediately experienced and depicted in the shaman's ecstasy.'[12]

In the *Protagoras*, Socrates advises Hippocrates, an aspirant to the study of wisdom, when the young man demands to see Protagoras, the famous sophist-teacher, about the greater importance of soul over body. Socrates poses the hypothesis that if you were to entrust your body (*soma*) to a stranger for treatment then you would ponder deeply about whether this was a good or a bad thing, whether you had good reason to trust the stranger with your body. But if you were to entrust your soul to a stranger, as Hippocrates seems to want now, then you have consulted with your friends about whether it is a good thing to put your soul in the care of a stranger. Socrates shows some surprise and annoyance that the young man has not discussed whether or not to entrust 'your self' to Protagoras (313b). Having carefully segregated soul from body, Socrates now clearly identifies soul and self; entrusting the soul (*psychē*) is the same thing as entrusting oneself. To reinforce his point about the folly of eagerly trusting in a sophist as trainer of the soul, he draws an analogy between merchants who supply food for the body and the sophists who supply food for the soul. Unlike bodily foods which the buyer can take away to examine before consuming, pieces of knowledge cannot be taken away without being already taken in, that is, in the process of learning knowledge is received in the soul. Socrates draws the further lesson that the soul can be either righteous (*khrēston*) or depraved (*ponēron*) as the result of the benefit or harm it receives from such knowledge. However, the nature of the relation between soul and body is left unexplored till another dialogue that features another great teacher, Gorgias.

---

[11] Burkert 1972, pp. 100–102.
[12] Burkert, 1972, p. 163; see also Cornford, 1965, pp. 88–106; Dodds, 1951, pp. 135–78; and Mircea Eliade, *Shamanism: Archaic Techniques of Ecstasy*, trans. by W. R. Trask. New York: Pantheon Press, 1964, pp. 103–10.

In the *Gorgias*, Socrates argues that there is a specific art or technique for the maintenance of health in the body and another for health (or well-being) in the soul. For the body the appropriate techniques are gymnastics and medicine; with regard to the soul, it is politics, including knowledge of the law and justice. He refers to 'the pair, body and soul' (*duoi pragmatoin*) which suggests that here he considers body and soul to be on an equal footing, though the soul is in charge of (*epistatein*) the body. In the extended analogy between medicine and cookery, Socrates argues that the former is concerned with the good of the soul (and thus the whole person), whereas the latter has only the goal of pleasure for the body. Claus claims that in this passage the relation of soul and body is 'decisively transformed' from the earlier crude analogy of therapy for body and therapy for soul. In the prior analogy, 'those things that were once regarded as practical treatments for the psycho-somatic soul are relegated to the role of cookery in treating the body. The various extended analogies in the *Gorgias* finish any practical or technical interest in the body-soul analogy and exploit the comparison with medicine as a means for inquiry into more abstract ideas of soul … [This is] the first unmistakable antithesis in Plato of soul as master and body as subject.'[13]

With regard to Socrates' alleged acceptance or rejection of common, everyday Greek notions of *psychē*, Claus argues that, 'the main point of interest is that the antithesis has come about not by separating soul and body on religious or ontological grounds … but by constructing an extended discussion which assumes, in contrast to earlier ideas, that body and soul are served by utterly different therapies, not by a common, or nearly common, therapy addressed to a psycho-somatic mixture of body and soul.' The Socratic or early Platonic view of the nature of human being is clearly some sort of dualism, but what sort of dualism is not yet decided; whether the soul is mortal or immortal, material or immaterial, is left in the air. The distinctive stand Socrates takes in the *Gorgias* shows 'the soul's capacity for *self-regulation*, through its own achievement of internal regularity and order, that gives it the capacity to achieve *sophrosynē*, and this self-regulation is compared at once to the regularity supposed for the body's constituent parts by scientific medicine.'[14] The *Gorgias* dialogue seems to occupy a crucial place in Plato's constantly elaborated description of the soul, for it decisively establishes the essential congruity of the soul with the individual human person. Claus concludes his examination of this text with these words: 'The chief accomplishment of the *Gorgias* then is to establish unequivocally … the identity of soul as a comprehensive personal self and to use that doctrine as a way of clearing the air of what are by comparison the shallow and morally unacceptable versions of both the animative [life-force] and afterlife soul that Plato had inherited from others.'[15]

In an effort to persuade Callicles of his rather uncommon point of view about the nature of soul Socrates makes use of a mythical story whose seriousness and literalness have been the subject of much controversy. It concerns an alleged comment made by the tragic writer Euripides, 'who knows then if life be death and death be life?' To which Socrates responds with these reflections:

---

[13] Claus, 1981, pp. 176–80; see Robinson, 2000, pp. 40–45.
[14] Claus, 1981, p. 179.
[15] Claus, 1981, p. 180.

And perhaps we are actually dead, for I once heard one of our wise men say that we are now dead, and that our body is a tomb, and that that part of the soul in which dwell the desires is of a nature to be swayed and to shift to and fro. And so some clever fellow, an Italian or Sicilian, writing in an allegory, by a slight perversion of language named this part of the soul a 'jar', because it can be swayed and easily persuaded; the foolish he called the uninitiated, and that part of the soul in foolish people where the desires reside, the uncontrolled and unretentive part, he likened to a leaky jar, because it can never be filled ... He shows that some of those in Hades, by which he means the unseen world, the uninitiated, must be the most unhappy, for they will carry water to pour into a perforated jar in a similar perforated sieve. And by the sieve, my informant told me, he means the soul, and the soul of the foolish he compared to a sieve, because it is perforated and through lack of belief and forgetfulness is unable to hold anything. These ideas may naturally seem somewhat absurd, but they reveal what I want to put before you ... (493a–c)

Walter Burkert reports that an early scholiast on this text named the Pythagoreans, particularly Empedocles, as the 'wise ones' who held this view, but also remarks that Socrates is prone to call several others by the name *sophos*.[16] In addition, he says that the sophist must be distinguished from the mythologer, either Sicilian or Italian, who recounts the myth of the water-carrier, an image known in the Delphic mysteries and which may have been an element in an Orphic *katabasis*.[17] In his use of this myth, for whatever didactic purposes, Socrates refers to two important motifs: the image of the soul as a vessel and its contents as liquid, and the image of the body as a tomb or prison. On his use of these pivotal ideas in such an early dialogue, E. R. Dodds comments that Plato makes continual efforts 'to transpose his religious beliefs from the mythical to the philosophical level, thus transforming them into truths of reason. This has the curious result that his conclusions often emerge earlier than the philosophical arguments by which they are established; thus his doctrine of the soul appears in mythical guise in the Gorgias before it is presented as a truth of reason in the Phaedo.'[18]

In the *Phaedo*, Plato presents a reconstruction of the last days of his beloved master Socrates. Condemned to death by the Athenian tribunal, Socrates spends his final days in prison with his close friends, discussing the nature of death, the soul and wisdom. Here he declares that the soul and the body are two separate and separable things, that the soul survives bodily death, and moreover that the soul is immortal. Here he asserts that the core property of the soul is intellect (*nous*), and the body is a tomb or prison. His two principal disputants are Simmias and Kebes, two Pythagoreans from Thebes, who belonged to the school of Philoläus, one of Pythagoras' chief exponents and interpreters.[19] With regard to the vexed question of Pythagorean influence on Platonic doctrines, Burkert comments:

> The true problem of the Pythagorean tradition lies in Platonism, for Platonizing interpretation took the place of historical reality. One can only guess at the reason why

---

[16] Burkert, 1972, p. 78, note 157.
[17] Burkert, 1972, p. 248, note 48.
[18] Dodds, 1945, p. 24.
[19] Crombie, 1962, vol. I, p. 305.

Plato and his pupils saw themselves as continuators of Pythagoreanism. Personal contacts were certainly important; they were already present in the Socratic circle. Simmias and Cebes of Thebes, 'hearers' of Philoläus, appear even in Xenophon as pupils of Socrates and we may believe that, as the Phaedo has it, the Pythagorean Echecrates of Philius had some connection with Socrates.

He also adduces the connected point that Timaeus claimed to have received from him some information about the Locrians: 'Plato's friendship with Archytas is attested by the Seventh Letter, and the later biographers of Plato agree that a principal motive of his first journey to Magna Graecia was to establish contact with the Pythagoreans there.'[20]

The correct view of philosophy is to conduct one's life as a preparation for dying and death, Socrates tells his distraught friends, and thus there is no reason for the lover of wisdom to fear death (64a). A proper understanding of the nature of soul will lead to a better grasp of what death means. If you think that the soul is like smoke or vapor dissipated on the wind when the body dies, then you would have a childish fear of death (70a, 77d). But if you come to understand that the soul is incorporeal, intellectual and immortal then death is seen as a release (or return) to its original, pure state. Death, he says, is 'the separate condition of the body *by itself* when it is released from the soul, and the separate condition *by itself* of the soul when released from the body' (64c). Socrates advances arguments to demonstrate the immortality of the soul, arguments that are of interest for our purposes only in so far as they show what he takes the soul to be.[21] He also adduces various 'stories' (or myths) to illustrate either incorrect accounts of the soul or to further support some specific feature of his own account of the soul. Sometimes it is difficult for his readers to determine which alternative the illustration is meant to support.[22]

The soul, he says, 'can best reflect when it is free of all distractions, such as hearing or seeing or pain or pleasure of any kind, that is, when it ignores the body and becomes as far as possible independent ... in its search for reality' (65c). He refers to the function or power of the soul as 'unaided intellect' and 'pure and unadulterated thought' (66a). The use of the term 'intellect' (*nous*) indicates one key aspect of the soul, and the use of 'purity of soul' another. The influence of Orphic-style conceptions on Socrates' account in the *Phaedo* is clearly evidenced in his remarks about the body as a nuisance, a positive evil and a hindrance to the soul's grasp of the truth. Much of the first half of the dialogue employs ascetic language in keeping with Orphic mystery rituals: inner purification, cultic initiation and despising one's body. The concept of sin or moral evil as pollution is itself derived from the archaic notion, in both Hebrew and Greek thought, that the soul as an internal and concrete thing can be stained.[23] Socrates summarizes his main line of argument thus: 'No soul which has not practiced philosophy and is not absolutely

---

[20] Burkert, 1972, p. 92; Kingsley, 1995, pp. 110–15.

[21] Several scholars have pointed out the fallacies in these arguments, see for example, Crombie, 1962, vol. I, pp. 307, 318–20; these need not concern us here.

[22] Robinson, 2000, pp. 45–8.

[23] For the archaic idea of sin as an inner stain, see Paul Ricoeur, *The Symbolism of Evil*. Boston: Beacon Press, 1970, Chapter One.

pure when it leaves the body may attain to the divine nature; that is for the lover of wisdom' (82b).

There is an old story that the souls of the dead exist in another world, Socrates continues, that they return again to this world, and come into being from the dead (70c). The argument that follows attempts to show that everything comes to be from its opposite, the living from the dead, the dead from the living; that a living being has soul, and that the dead are without life but not without soul. Socrates imports the doctrine of recollection (*anamnesis*) from the *Meno* to show that truths of reason, grasped by the intellect alone (*nous*) could only be achieved if the person's soul had once been in contact with the Forms, before its birth (that is, entrapment or imprisonment) in the body, whose sense organs provide diminished images of these forms: 'Our souls had a previous existence, Simmias, before they took on this human shape. They were independent of our bodies and they possessed intelligence' (76c). Another argument proceeds from the liability of composite or compound objects to dissipate or break up into their component parts, and of simple pure things to remain as they are. Since the person's sense organs convey images of composite things and since percepts are prone to error, confusion and obscurity, the body *qua* composite of organic natural parts is liable to decompose and break apart; but since the soul has existed in a prior state and can be trained to grasp the timeless and unchanging forms, it too must be timeless and unchanging. When the soul reflects 'it passes into the realm of the pure and everlasting and immortal and changeless, and since it is of a kindred nature, when it is once independent and free from interference, it consorts with it always and strays no longer, but remains … and this condition of the soul we call wisdom' (79d).

In response to one of Cebes' objections, Socrates refers to the Egyptian practice of embalming dead bodies (80c), where the physical parts remain for some time after death. However, Socrates continues, the soul as an invisible part goes away to an unseen world (Hades), 'into the presence of the good and wise god'. Those humans whose souls are pure upon their arrival are rewarded with happiness, release from uncertainty and folly, fears and uncontrolled desires and all other human evils, and where, 'as they say of the initiates in the mysteries, it really spends the rest of the time with god' (81a). It is no accident that this doctrine appears in the context of the Orphic mysteries and Egyptian mortuary practices. One of the most contentious scholarly hypotheses concerns the so-called Orientalizing Influence[24] on Classical Greek thinking, and here this might take the shape of Oriental beliefs about the soul's immortality. Pythagoras' two pupils, Philoläus and Echechrates, clearly demonstrate the connection between Plato's philosophical ancestry and Oriental mystery religions. One of the mystery's main tenets concerns the idea of reincarnation, in this context, the belief that impure souls are compelled to wander the earth until imprisoned in another body. But it is Cebes who says that the soul 'has such natural vitality that it persists through

---

[24] See M. L. West, 1971, Introduction; Walter Burkert, *The Orientalizing Influence*, Harvard University Press, 1992, Chapter 1; Dodds, 1951, pp. 146–7; the influence in this period is clearly evident in plastic arts and ceramics, see R. M. Cook, *Greek Art*, Penguin Books (1972) 1991, pp. 37–41.

successive incarnations' (88a), and this is not possible on Crombie's interpretation that Socrates argues for the idea of *psychē* as an animating or life-force principle.

One version of the mature Platonic account of the soul emerges in the *Phaedrus*; in this famous text (245ff) Plato presents one of his great 'myths', using its archetypal imagery to arrive at truths of reason about the nature and powers of soul.[25] He opens the myth by saying that his story applies to 'soul in all its forms', that is, to the very Form (*eidos*) of the human soul itself. His story revolves around the principal image of the human being as a chariot ensemble: the chariot, its driver, and two horses, one noble and one base. Like all other animals, the human has (a) a chariot (the body) which is dragged along with the whole, inanimate and not self-moving; (b) a noble horse, that which inspires to higher emotions, and (c) a base horse, that which craves desirable things.[26] But unlike other animals, a human alone has a driver, that which thinks and reasons; the driver or driving force provides the whole with direction. In one of the passages describing the whole soul Plato asserts that it is eternally moving (*aeikinētos*) and self-moving (*autokinētos*) (245c). Robinson comments that 'this view of soul as a principle of movement is a milestone in Plato's thought, and the direct ancestor of the cosmological argument from motion first outlined by Aristotle and followed by Aquinas.'[27] Robinson goes on to assert that the driver and the noble horse always act in union, that together the pair comprise the good, moral and just form of the soul, whereas the base horse, wanton and lustful, is in conflict with the human–noble horse pair, and that this segregation indicates *bipartition*, that is, the soul has two parts. But, as we shall see below, this is an unwarranted conclusion which rests on a confusion between real division into parts and conceptual distinction between powers.

Socrates carefully unpacks the details of this story: 'Any body that has an external source of motion is soulless, but a body deriving its motion from a source within itself is animate or ensouled' (245e). He concludes that souls of all kinds are immortal, and since *psychē* is the principle (*archē*) and cause (*aitia*) of life, this is an accurate indication of the nature (*ousia*) of *psychē*. However, the complete nature of soul would require a long story that only a god could tell. Thus he proposes an analogy with a winged chariot, driver and two horses. 'The composite structure of soul and body is called a living being and is further called mortal' (246c); though it is true that an individual living being is composed of two things, body and soul, the soul itself is composite. The ontological status of the soul's constituents is non-determinate according to the *Phaedrus* account: 'All soul [or every form of soul] has the care of all that is inanimate and traverses the whole universe though in ever-changing forms.' The further imagery of the soul's ascent

---

[25] See Cornford, 1952, pp. 67–70.

[26] My grasp of these Phaedrean 'powers' was greatly clarified by C. J. Rowe, who remarked to me that 'the white horse seems to represent the higher emotions, i.e. those not associated with food, drink, and sex; esp. emotions connected with power, ambition, and self-esteem. Not without reason, as they say, is *thumos* in this context translated as "spirit" (but not "vital spirit"), [rather] as in "a spirited horse".'

[27] Robinson, 1970, p. 116; he also argues that the later *Timaeus* account endorses a basic bipartition into mortal and immortal parts, although he admits that the soul is further subdivided, pp. 122–4.

and traversal of the eternal unchanging heavens is taken up and adumbrated more fully in the *Timaeus* and, centuries later, by Plotinus in the *Enneads*. In other dialogues Plato uses the word 'chariot' for star (Timaeus 41e, Laws 899a, Epinomis 986b), by which he may have meant that the gods move through their orbits like chariots round a circuit in fixed patterns forever. But humans are confined to this mutable world; a living being is compounded or blended from soul *and* body, though the soul itself is not a composite or compound, even though it has three functions or forms.

The driver possesses reason, insight and foresight, and directs the two horses (247c); one horse is basically good, loves glory, and is temperate and modest (253d); the other horse is crooked, hot-blooded, wanton and lustful (253e).[28] As we shall see later, this threefold structure is entirely compatible with the three forms of the soul in the *Republic: logistikon, thumoeides* and *epithumētikon*. In the *Phaedrus* account, according to Ostenfeld, 'the soul is viewed as *desire for knowledge*, but has *other bodily interests* as well, and this applies to gods no less than to men. Tripartition, therefore, seems to involve three tendencies of an organism rather than three parts of an immaterial substance ... The innovation in Plato's psychology, if we are right, is therefore better stated by saying that from now on the soul is essentially embodied and therefore tripartite.'[29] The use of 'wings' in 'winged chariot' and 'winged soul' relies on a commonly accepted psychical picture, itself reaching back into archaic thought. Homer said that the *thumos* could fly (Il. xvi.469, xxiii.880), speeches that issue from the *thumos* are winged like birds (*epea pteroenta*), unspoken thoughts kept in the *phrenes* are not winged (Od. xvii.57). These archaic, ordinary figures of speech might have suggested Plato's image of the soul as a cage full of birds,[30] though it does not employ the chariot-horse analogy (Thaetetus 197c). Homer also uses horse imagery when he talks about the winds (Il. xvi.149; xx.223) and the winds are manifestations of the god's ruling breath, itself closely associated with *psychē* as breath.[31]

The well-known doctrine of the so-called tripartition or three-part soul occurs in *Republic* Books Four and Ten; some traces of this doctrine also appear in the *Timaeus* and the *Laws*. Socrates' exposition of the nature and function of the individual soul follows after and is designed to support his elaborate and multi-faceted argument about the three classes or kinds of citizen in the ideal *polis*. One of the very first problems which any student of Plato's teachings on the soul has to deal with is the heavy emphasis on parts in the innumerable commentaries on the *Republic*. It is difficult to find a translation or exegesis which does *not* use part-terms, for example, ruling part, spirited part, desiring part, and tripartite, bipartite, and so forth. An explicit instance of this presumption about the validity of part-terms in the middle Platonic concept of soul is found in a recent work on St. Paul: 'While Greek thought tended to regard the human being as made up of *distinct parts*, Hebrew thought saw the human being more as a whole person existing on different dimensions. As we might say, it was more characteristically

---

[28] For which see Ostenfeld, 1982, p. 324, note 132.
[29] Ostenfeld, 1982, p. 232.
[30] For the use of birds in soul imagery, see Onians, p. 67, note 4.
[31] Onians, p. 120, note 6.

Greek to conceive of the human person "*partitively*", whereas it was more characteristically Hebrew to conceive of the human person "aspectively"'[32] – but this claim is simply not supported by textual evidence. Julia Annas judiciously comments on this issue: 'Talk of "parts" of the soul has also been found a problem. But Plato never says that they are spatial or temporal parts, and in fact does not use the language of "parts" himself very much. Plato keeps his vocabulary here perhaps deliberately vague; he is insisting that there is complexity in a single person without saying too much about how that complexity might be realized.'[33] It is crucial that one understands the reasons for our reluctance here to use part-terms to interpret and reconcile Plato's elaborate description of the nature of human being, especially with respect to its soul. This long and intricate argument (from 436a to 448e) is devoted to the dialectical discovery of three distinct 'items' in the human *psychē* (though animals share two of the same 'items'). He refers to these three 'items' in these terms: (a) *logos* = reason, or *logistikon* = the reasoning, or that-which-reasons; (b) *thumos* = spirit, or *thumoeides* = the spirited, or that-which-inspires; and (c) *epithumos* = desire or appetite, or *epithumētikon* = the desiring, or that-which-desires.

Although Plato refers to these three items, either together or one by one, at least one hundred times, he only uses the word *meros* ('part') twice – this hardly licenses the regular translation of each instance in part-terms. The most common word by which he refers to the three groups of citizens is *genē* (kinds or classes), and the most common word by which he refers to the three soul 'items' is *eidē* (plural of *eidos*), usually translated in other Platonic texts as 'form', in fact, it is the suffix for the second item – *thumo-eides*. There are several occasions when he uses the term *onta* ('entity' – very neutral) or *ousia* ('nature' or 'essence'); sometimes he simply says, 'the first', 'the second' or 'the third'. The most important lesson to be drawn from this philological examination is that *no* conclusion can be made about the part-like or tripartite division of the soul. As we shall see in the third section below, it is largely due to Cicero's rather haphazard translation and exposition four centuries later that the term *pars* (plural, *partes*) is imposed on the Platonic texts, and from these Latin versions the part-vocabulary enters the philosophical canon. In his meticulous examination of the various ways in which later Platonists, Neo-Platonists, and Patristic writers used Plato's so-called 'tripartite' schema, David Bell remarked on the uncritical adoption of part-like terms to explain Plato's position: 'Much of the problem ... devolves upon the meaning of the word "part", for if it is taken in a crude and obvious sense (which Plato never intended), it is clearly at variance with any idea of an indivisible soul.' To which he adds in an attached note, quoting an article by J. L. Stocks: 'Plato himself clearly means "trifunctional", and uses a series of terms, not just *merē*, to describe the three modes of the soul's operation: *eidē, genē, tropoi, ēthē*. But "in English the word part suggests a crudity of which Plato was incapable." The continual agitation of later writers over the term is

---

[32] James Dunn, *Theology of Paul the Apostle*, Eerdmans, 1998, p. 54; emphasis added.

[33] Annas, 1981, p. 124; 'Plato uses ... most often the term *eidos*, only occasionally the more committing term *meros*. This shows that Plato is understandably cautious in speaking of the parts of something non-bodily.' Ostenfeld, 1982, pp. 215–16. In their commentary on the Republic, Cross and Woozley clearly indicate that the translation 'part' is inadequate

therefore less a reflection of a real difficulty in Plato's teaching than the power of the slogan [three-part].'[34]

The 'power' of reason is also referred to as that which loves wisdom (*philosophon*) and learning (*philomathes*); its two functions are first, searching for the truth and increase in knowledge; in addition, it derives pleasure from this pursuit. Its second function is to rule the whole soul, since it is the only soul-form that cares for the interests of the whole soul and not just itself, whereas the other two soul-forms care only for their own interests; *to logistikon* corresponds closely to the driver in the *Phaedrus* myth. The second form, *thumos* ('spirit') is also referred to as that which loves honor (*philotimon*) and victory (*philonikon*). *Thumos* had been a prominent soul-term in Homer, but then declined in importance in poetic and tragic literature until the fourth century, where it recurs in more specific psychic contexts.[35] Perhaps 'spirited force' might be a more accurate rendition of *thumos*, since 'spirit' in the NT and later Hellenistic texts translates *pneuma*. The term *to thumoeides* means that which shows aggressive, assertive and forceful tendencies, more overtly seen in children and animals; it can be rough and harsh unless properly trained, and corresponds closely to the noble horse. The third 'power' is desire or appetite, *epithumētikon*; it loves money (*philochrēmaton*) and gain (*philokerdes*); it corresponds most closely to the base horse. Socrates is hard pressed to make the same correlation as in the other two cases: 'because of its manifold aspects we had no special name to give it, but we have named it after the biggest and strongest thing in it, and have called it the appetitive because of the violence of the appetites for food, drink, sex and other things which follow from these.'

In Book Ten of the *Republic*, Plato returns to his teaching about the *psychē* in order to draw further insights about reason and desire. Reason, he says, enables humans to correct visual impressions by appeal to the objective procedures of counting, weighing and measuring (602c–603b); it also enables humans to achieve some distance from immediate misfortunes by situating them in a wider context. Desire appears as the psychic form that accepts visual appearances without reflection and indulges or gives way to emotional discharges. The whole soul when turned toward objects illuminated by truth and reality appears to have reason; as the sun 'causes' vision and light, so the Good 'causes' knowledge and truth. Ostenfeld comments that, 'The soul is viewed as an organ possessing *dynamis* [power] for knowledge, just as its objects have *dynamis* for being known; both are activated or triggered off by the Good ... So *ergon* [function] is related to *dynamis*, not exactly as effect to cause, but rather as actualization to disposition. Hence it would seem that *ergon* may be viewed either as actualization of a disposition or ... as a function of a thing.'[36] The passage in Book Ten which introduces the argument regarding the immortality of the soul carries forward the sight-seeing-sun metaphor in its treatment of the natural good and its opposite in terms of the eye as an organ of sight; this extension brings out the force of *disposition* versus *function*. The soul, he says in this later text, has only one natural evil (injustice),

---

and misleading in most cases, but then fall back on metaphorical, as opposed to literal, use of part-whole terminology, Cross & Woozley, 1964, p. 127.

[34] David Bell, 1980, p. 18 and note 8 (from sec. 3 below).
[35] Claus, 1981, pp. 49–50.
[36] Ostenfeld, 1982, p. 212.

but it is not destroyed by injustice, rather the soul is provoked to overcome it and become good; from this, Plato is willing to conclude that the soul must be immortal (608d–611a). Book Ten seems to ignore the threefold division of the soul advanced in Book Four, and instead focuses exclusively on various dualities: the good (or highest) versus the base (or lowest), rational versus irrational, mortal versus immortal, body versus soul. However, it is difficult, if not impossible, to reconcile Plato's threefold division in the *Phaedrus* and *Republic* Book Four with the twofold division in *Republic* Book Ten. The myth of Er in Book Ten confuses the issue even further. According to this story, a warrior caught between life and death is permitted to view the workings of the cosmic spheres and the movement of human souls from the underworld to the heavens, their selection of lots in earthly lives, and the punishments and rewards they receive in their various after-lives.[37]

However, three important cautions should be registered here. First, the twofold analysis in Book Ten concerns the substances involved in human 'nature': soul *qua* substance is incorporeal and immortal, subject to rebirth in many forms, basically good though corruptible, basically rational though susceptible to irrational desires. Whereas body *qua* substance, on the other hand, is corporeal and mortal, the temporary prison of the soul, the seat of irrational and immoral desires, and basically bad (*aschron*, perhaps better translated 'shameful'), though it can be trained. The threefold division of the soul in terms of the living being whose body is its vehicle is generally compatible with the substance dualist account. Although it is true that *some* implications of Plato's separate analyses of connections between reason, 'spirit' and desire are in conflict with wisdom, justice and temperance. Moreover, Plato admits that our poor, frail human intellect cannot grasp the real nature of the soul; its condition, he says

> ... resembles that of the sea god Glaucus.[38] His first nature can hardly be made out by those who catch glimpses of him, because the original members of his body are broken off and mutilated and crushed and in every way marred by the waves; other parts have attached themselves to him, accretions of shells and seaweed and rocks, so that he is more like any wild creature than what he was *by nature* – even such is our vision of the soul marred by countless evils (611d).

In other words, given Plato's clear commitment to a divinely crafted, immortal soul, temporarily housed in an organic body, an individual's intuition (insight into pure forms) will be dimmed and confused by sensible appearances. In this case, the sensible aspects of a living being obscure the hidden, inner power (*dynamis*) that animates the whole organism. It is also generally agreed that Book Ten is something like a set of appendices or supplements added to the previous nine books, in response to specific requirements made by the Socratic characters and later students in the Academy.

---

[37] Annas carefully teases out a number of serious problems and errors in the Er account, 1981, pp. 345–53.

[38] Glaucus from *glaukōs*, 'gray' or 'sea-gray' color, a deified mortal with prophetic powers, according to Aeschylus' *Glaucus Pontius*, TGF 3. 142–8, and Euripides' *Oresteia*, 362–5.

The late dialogue *Timaeus* presents one of the most influential and monumental Platonic systems. It involves the cosmogony of the Demiurge and the World Soul; the cosmology and astronomy of the celestial spheres; the psychogony of the creation of all souls; the cycles of birth, death and rebirth, and many other themes. It is difficult to situate the historical character Timaeus, and equally difficult to situate the *Timaeus*-doctrines within the Platonic corpus. Exegetes in the next few centuries, such as Xenocrates, Speusippus and Posidonius, interpreted Plato's *Timaeus* as Pythagorean, and this particular exegesis is partly responsible for the dialogue being considered a source of genuine Pythagorean teaching. Plato's pupils, especially Aristotle, considered the *Timaeus'* exposition of ideal numbers to be distinctively Pythagorean.[39] However, Plato clearly wanted to characterize Timaeus as one of the Pythagoreans, and indicated this affiliation in several ways: by saying that he was from Italy, that he studied the nature of all things (*peri phuseōs tou pantos*), that he was politically active, and so forth.[40] It is not feasible, nor strictly relevant to our purposes, to delve into the many fascinating aspects of this dialogue; let us focus our attention on its account of the human soul.[41]

The cosmos was created by a divine craftsman (*demiourgos*) using the model of a compound form, described as the perfect and eternal living being. The sensible world is thus a living being (30d), which receives a soul through its composition in a celestial mixing bowl. The craftsman also creates the divine portion of human souls, though this portion has an inferior nature. In addition, he is the creator of the gods themselves and to these he delegates the formation of non-human animal souls, and the non-divine portions of human souls. It is the gods' task to complete the making of the world, filled with living beings, an imperfect imitation of the archetypal living being. Human souls have an intermediate status (*meson*) between the eternal and indivisible, and the limited and divisible. The soul is a double mixture (*krasis*) of the divisible and indivisible (in three versions), and a mixture of being, difference and sameness. Part of the being, sameness and difference that comprises the soul is characterized as constant and indivisible (*ameristos*), and thus is similar to the timeless and perfect Forms or Ideas. The other part is variable (*gignomenē*) and divisible (*meristē*) and is in these respects similar to copies (*mimēmata*) of the Forms which enter and leave parts of space (51b). According to Ostenfeld's synopsis of these main points:

> [T]he soul's affinity to matter means: first, it is in time ...; second, it is in space, i.e. it inhabits an individual body; third, it moves in some sense, i.e. it can act and be acted on; fourth, it is generated in terms of its intermediate status. The soul's affinity to the Forms means that: (1) it is everlasting; (2) invisible; (3) bound together by proportion; (4) moves in uniform circles; (5) it is the best of generated things. In sum, the soul is a harmonious compound which is only dissoluble in theory, i.e. its parts (or forms) are not normally separable.[42]

---

[39] See Physics 209b, De Anima 404b; Burkert, 1972, p. 65.
[40] Burkert, 1972, pp. 84–6; Cornford, 1965, pp. 117–20.
[41] On the concepts of soul, mind and reason in the *Timaeus*, see esp. Frede 1996, pp. 34–58.
[42] Ostenfeld, 1982, p. 245.

Stripped of its mythical overtones, the *Timaeus* account says that the soul is by nature *similar to*, not the same as, the conjunction of both form (*eidos*) and matter (*hulē*). On first glance, the soul seems an improbable and monstrous compound made up from an incorporeal, indivisible portion, and a corporeal, divisible portion – but not in light of Plato's theory of opposites and composites: 'White and not-white, for instance, are logically uncombinable, but factually they combine well. Only, white is no longer white when blended with not-white. Soul is like gray [*glaukos*], a genuine third entity with qualities of its own. It is neither absolutely self-consistent and indivisible, nor ever changing and divisible, but it is ever thinking the same about the same and it is a harmonic mixture.'[43]

The soul stuff is divided into as many souls as there are stars and each soul receives a star from whose position it learns the nature and laws of the cosmos and its own destiny. When the gods fabricated the human body, they fastened the orbits of the immortal soul to that living being's vehicle. The organism's dependence on food, sensation and other external things upsets the orbits, bringing the same to a halt, robbing it of power and motion, while difference is disordered. The harmoniously divided circles are indissoluble except by their maker, but they are twisted in all directions so that their movements are irregular (43d). Sensations and bodily needs impinge on the soul so that it cannot tell, that is, give an account, of the same and the different (41d). In addition to the form of sensation (*aisthēsis*), humans have desire mixed with pleasure and pain, and fear and anger (42a). While 'spirit' (*thumos*) is located in the chest (70a), bodily desire (*epithumos*) is bound like a wild beast to the stomach (70d); reason (*logos*) is located in the head, because it is spherical and thus an imitation of the perfect cosmos.

Onians claimed that Alcmaeon of Croton was the first thinker to suggest the importance of the brain (*enkephalos*) in an account of the soul: 'He held that the seed came from the brain; but against an existing view that this came exclusively from the marrow, he tried to show that the flesh, more particularly the fat, was also drawn upon. But even this was not new. He discovered passages leading from the eyes to the brain and urged that the latter received the perceptions of sight, sound and smell, and was the seat of thought. This is a very real advance.'[44] Timaeus, then, had something like an Alcmaeon-style empirical view when he described the internal movements (*kinēseis*) that pass through the body to the soul (45d). In a later passage, the marrow[45] (*muelos*) is considered to be the life-bearing substance at the root or basis of the soul (75b); some marrow has more soul and genius than other varieties, even the bones are ensouled. The soul is planted or fastened in the marrow; it is the seed (*sperma*) or *in* the seed, and the seed is stored in the skull and spine; it is further transmitted through the genitals for procreation (91b). But beyond this organic picture, reason in the *Timaeus* is closely allied to the principle of self-motion and thus to the life-giving force of organisms. It is in control and directs the lower psychic forms, desire and appetite, tied to both the body *through* the blood, marrow and breath, and towards food,

---

[43] Ostenfeld, 1982, p. 245.

[44] Onians, p. 115; on various medical studies of the brain as seat of thought, see Gundert, in Wright & Potter, 2000, pp. 13–36.

[45] On the importance of marrow, see Onians, pp. 110, 119–20, 149–50.

drink and sustenance, but still taking part in the divine through its affinity with the Forms.

In summary, whatever the merits of the *general* argument about different, sometimes incompatible stages in the maturation of Plato's thought from early to middle to late period, it is clearly evident that Plato's account of soul undergoes profound modifications. When Plato turns toward questions about the soul it is almost always in an ethical context, or with an ethical point of view, either with regard to the good of an individual or the good of society, according to Claus. He is rarely concerned with strictly metaphysical questions about the nature, composition and functions of the soul, unless such abstract issues touch upon the ethically prior question of the soul's good in this life, care for the soul, justice amongst ensouled agents, the immortal soul's rewards and punishments, and so forth. In the early dialogues Socrates is decidedly agnostic about both the nature of the soul and its immortality; to some degree his attitude and arguments reflect the carry-over of Homeric ideas into common usage. In this sense the Socratic picture of the human soul is an ambiguous substance monism; that is, *psychē* is the life-force, the principle of self-motion, the bodily endowment of an animal being, manifest in its breath, blood and desire. As such the *psychē* is more noble in humans than in other animals, with greater aspirations for the good (worthy) and greater temptations for the crass (unworthy). It is this moralization and revaluation of the distinctively human dimension of the human soul that sets Socrates' analyses apart from more traditional conceptions; the soul set over against the body is a strictly pedagogical division which permits the notion of a psychical therapy.[46]

At some later date Plato's dialogues reveal some knowledge (perhaps personal experience) of so-called 'mystical' doctrines, whether they are Orphic, Pythagorean, or derived from some other shamanistic set of beliefs. The exposition of Plato's views, whether voiced by Socrates or by one of his visitors, is either under the influence of, or attempts to take account of, various teachings about the immortality and immateriality of the human soul. It becomes an important, even necessary concern for him to demonstrate that the soul is a separate and separable substance, intimately linked with the animal body and dependent for some of its functions on the whole being, an ensouled body. But with regard to its highest (most noble) functions, rational insight into the Forms, pursuit of the good, and return to its divine source, the soul can exist on its own, independently of the existence of its host. The *Phaedrus, Parmenides* and especially the *Timaeus* show Plato grappling with the difficulties attendant on the merger of the previous Socratic picture and this new mystical vision. Conceptual schemata that superimpose on these texts either part-like terms, such as bipartition or tripartition, or section-like terms, such as bisection or trisection, are unwarranted later accretions that obscure Plato's significant achievement. Other awkward efforts to determine whether or not some stage of Plato's account, or even an allegedly uniform Platonic account, is either dualist or monist or pluralist often fail to discriminate what it is there are said to be two or more of. It is one thing to assert that Plato said that there are two separate things, soul and body, or two 'parts' of

---

[46] See Claus, 1981, pp. 181–3.

one whole, the individual; it is another thing to claim that he said that the soul has two (or three) things as 'parts' of the whole soul. And it is still another thing to claim that each part *qua* part has relative dependence or independence as a psychical, in contrast to a physical, constituent of a greater whole of which it is a part.

In his efforts to blend the best of both pictures, and provide an account of an immortal soul attuned to the good, Plato presents various arguments about the composition of the whole being in terms of soul as an entity and body as an entity. He also presents arguments about the composition of the soul itself as a whole entity whose formal aspects are either two or three discriminable functions or powers. In one version of the latter psychical account, in both the *Phaedrus* and the *Republic*, the soul has three powers: reason, 'spirit' and desire. Reason is the only one cognitively dependent on sensory reports supplied by the bodily organs and vitally dependent on the other two powers for the continuance of its host *qua* whole individual. But reason is not dependent in its own nature, that is, for the exercise of the power itself, on any bodily organic entity. In another version, the soul has two kinds of power, where 'kind' (*eidē* or *genē*) itself is differentiated with respect to the criterion of reason (*logos*). The relevant difference is between rational and non-rational, though the rational power or faculty of the whole human has to 'take account of' the needs and desires made known to it through the human non-rational power. Nevertheless, the rational power of the soul (*nous*) is itself an autonomous whole in so far as it is taken account of in terms of the cosmic plan of an order of beings. In this order that-which-reasons is not a power or function of some *thing*, but an agent or entity whose basic nature (*phusis*) is *expressed through* human beings' rational governance of their beliefs and actions, especially actions directed towards moral goods.

(2) Aristotle on soul as form and body as matter

Aristotle's conception of the physical or the natural is much different than our contemporary understanding informed by scientific advances since the seventeenth century. Aristotle thinks that it is true of natural objects and their behavior that they cannot be fully understood in terms of their material constituents and their properties, but have to be explained in terms of their *essence* or *nature*. Aristotle's introduction of essences or natures reflects the fact that he takes an anti-reductionist view; he insists that natural objects, including human beings, are not just configurations of more basic material constituents and hence should not be conceived of just in this way, since essences or natures enter in a non-causal way into an explanation of their status and behavior. His understanding of the 'causal', principled character of soul is pivotal in making sense of his sometimes incongruous statements regarding soul as substance and soul as property. Ancient and modern interpreters have placed greater or lesser weight on textual evidence for one position at the expense of the other; recently, several radical interpreters have held forth a tentative third way, that the soul is a 'property-thing', a hybrid of the two standard views. In the last resort, Miles Burnyeat has argued that Aristotle's view of the nature of soul, that is, its ontological status in terms of the categorical template, is 'totally alien' to our way of thinking and 'deeply mysterious'.[47]

Aristotle's account (*logos*) of soul (*psychē*) makes excellent use of several conceptual templates: substance and attribute, matter and form, and explanatory factors (*aitia*).[48] He uses the apparatus of matter (*hulē*) and form (*eidos* or *morphē*) to explain the nature of every kind of object, whether living or non-living, natural or artificial. The matter of an object is the stuff that either it or its parts are made out of; in the simple case of an artifact, for example, a bronze sphere or a house, its matter would be the bronze stuff or the bricks and timber. The form of an object is its specific shape or profile; the form of a bronze sphere is its spherical shape, the form of a house is a complex arrangement of its material parts. Aristotle has a unified theory of living things, and hence the human soul, since his account of soul is another variation on his matter–form analysis, and since every living thing is explicable in terms of matter and form *qua* material and formal 'causes' (*aitia*). In his distinction between matter and form Aristotle intends the notion of form to be immaterial (in some sense yet to be specified) when, for example, he says that natural objects may be defined through the definition of their form alone, without the inclusion of matter in that definition (Meta. Z.11, 1037a). The immaterial status of form is further indicated when he maintains that not everything has matter, but only those objects that are generated or destroyed. These perishable things are distinct from other things, including the form of an object, which 'are or are not' without undergoing any change (Meta. H.1044b). Matter is physical in an ordinary sense in most contexts within his matter–form analysis of objects. It is often the case that his idea of materiality may be roughly equated with our contemporary idea of physicality, yet one should be cautious, especially with regard to his strange doctrine of 'intelligible matter'. It is fairly clear what he means by 'perceptible matter', such as bronze or wood, since their material constituent parts are graspable by the sense organs. But intelligible matter belongs to intelligible objects alone, such as an abstract circle or triangle; it follows that such 'objects' can be grasped by the intellect (*nous*) alone. Perceptible matter is always changeable and allows for the full range of possible types of change (generation and destruction, alteration, movement, and so forth) which an object composed of such matter can suffer. On the other hand, intelligible matter constitutes imperceptible, changeless 'objects'. Still another use of the idea of matter appears in his analysis of the 'subject' which underlies and persists through substantial changes, that is, the coming to be and passing away of composite substances (Phys. 192a); it is whatever provides the subject for any of the other sorts of changes (GC 320a).

According to H. Granger, there are two main lines of interpretation regarding the ontological status of soul (*psychē*) as the form of living things: one that considers the soul to be the property or attribute of some thing, and the other that considers the soul to be a substance, a thing that has properties or attributes. According to Aristotle's logical template, things or objects are the types of entities that provide the values of variables in first-order predicate logic; they comprise the reference

---

[47] Burnyeat, in Nussbaum & Rorty, 1992, pp. 15–26.
[48] On his matter–form and substance–attribute accounts, see Barnes, in Barnes, 1995, pp. 90–101.

division of count nouns or sortal expressions, and can serve as the 'subject' of first-order properties. They are usually characterized as independent entities that can exist in their own right. As the subjects of properties 'things' exemplify properties; they are the things that can *be* white or bronze or wooden. The nature of properties is harder to pin down, but basically properties cannot exist on their own, without some thing they are the property *of*; they are common to all the instances of things that exemplify them. Properties are dependent entities that rely for their existence upon the things that provide them with their subject.[49]

Aristotle also speaks in general terms about matter as 'subject' and form as 'predicate'; form is a predicate in that it is predicated or 'said-of' its subject or underlying thing which is its matter. Properties and kinds (genus and species) provide paradigm examples of predicates that are 'said-of' things; the subject stands for what properties and kinds are 'said-of'. Thus Aristotle's application of predicate and similar expressions to form and his application of subject to matter are good evidence for the view that form as a predicate of matter is a property of matter.[50] In more modern terms, the word 'sub-stance' does good service for *hypostasis* as that-which-stands-under, the 'subject-matter' of some discourse indicates that the independent thing that bears properties is its matter, and of course (most enigmatic of all) that any kind of object can be the 'subject' of inquiry or investigation. There is also some indication that Aristotle views form as universal,[51] that is, that property or feature which is common to a number of different things. In other words, properties are common to many different things, each of which exemplifies that property, though perhaps in different ways and through different relations. He associates the universal with what he calls a common predicate, which he describes as 'such' (*toionde*), in contrast with what he calls 'this' (*tode ti*), an expression that he often uses to describe concrete particular things. In one passage Aristotle seems to say that form is 'this' and not 'such' (Meta. Z.8, 1033b); but he maintains that things of the same kind differ through the difference in their matter, and that they are the same in their form, since it is indivisible (Meta. Z.11, 1036a).

In the opening of the second book of *De Anima*, Aristotle draws the distinction between body and soul in matter–form terms, and situates this distinction in his prior distinction of subject and predicate: 'Since it [the body] is also a body of a certain sort, for it possesses life, the soul would not be body; for the body is not some thing predicated of a subject, rather it exists as subject and matter. Therefore, it is necessary that the soul be substance as the form of a natural body possessed of life potentially' (DA 412a). The body serves as a subject or thing that has a soul, but the soul is not another thing in addition to its body, or some part of the body, but a property the body possesses as a living thing. Later he says that the soul is not without a body, yet it is not 'a certain kind of body'; rather, it is something that belongs to a body. Still another formulation is that the soul is something *about* the body, which would appear to be a property of the body through its dependence on

---

[49] Granger, 1996, pp. 8–14; see also van der Eijk, 2000, pp. 57–60.

[50] On this topic, see Barnes, in Barnes, 1995, pp. 86–90.

[51] On the relevance of universals to his account of soul, see Granger, 1996, p. 9, note 16, and pp. 60–62.

the body's existence. The soul is not a thing that can exist in its own right. He contrasted his view with the Pythagorean notion that the human soul was independent of an individual's body. He complained that the mystics expound only upon the nature of the soul itself and not on the nature of the body that is needed to receive or house the soul. For the mystics, the body might be anything, and thus it would really be irrelevant to its having a soul; in principle the soul might be taken into or housed in any kind of body. Aristotle thinks this view is absurd, since *inter alia* it ignores the account-force of explanatory factors, that is, it makes nonsense of the connections between substance (*ousia*) and 'causes' (*aitia*). The mystics treated the soul as an independent entity that might be attached at random to any sort of body. In contrast, since Aristotle's idea of the soul is property-like, the soul is dependent upon its body, but not as another bodily part upon the whole body, since the soul is not any kind of body at all.

Aristotle stresses the difference between matter and form in order to reinforce the notion that they are different in type; they cannot be compared because they do not share any thing. It would be a category mistake to employ terms from one type to explain anything about another type. He argues that things compounded out of material parts, in so far as they form a whole and not a heap, must possess some aspect (but not a thing) other than their material parts to account for the unification of their material parts into just that whole.[52] If this were not the case, its parts would comprise some other whole, and make it a different particular thing. If one attempts to explain the unity of the parts through an appeal to another material part (that is, an item of the same sort) no account has been achieved, since something *else* must be appealed to in order to explain the unification of both the original parts and the new part. If an appeal is made only to further material parts, then an infinite regress enters the account. Thus something entirely other than the material parts, namely the form of the object, must be resorted to in order to account for the unity of all the parts in the one whole. Aristotle calls the parts that compose the whole its elements and the form of the whole its principle: 'When this observation on the difference between matter and form is added to the observations already made about the difference between them as "subject" and "predicate", and about the nature of the dependence of form or soul upon matter, the evidence mounts up significantly in favor of the view that the difference between matter and form, or body and soul, amounts to an asymmetry that is different in type ... the form or soul as an attribute of matter or of the body.'[53]

Sometimes it seems that Aristotle does indeed refer to the soul *qua* form as a substance, but this should be taken under advisement, since he clearly says that the word 'substance' is ambiguous (DA 412a); that it can signify 'primary substance', 'matter', 'form' or the 'composite' of matter and form. Perhaps one can disambiguate this remark by thinking that 'substance' in the broadest sense means no more than *an entity* of an as yet unspecified categorical type. He clearly indicates that in his analysis of the principal properties of soul the term 'substance' can be taken three ways: as its constituent matter, as its proper form, and as the composite of its matter

---

[52] For a detailed analysis of this argument, see Granger, 1996, pp. 116–18.
[53] Granger, 1996, p. 18–19; see also Irwin, 1988, pp. 280–95.

and form: 'Now we speak of one particular kind of existent thing as substance, and under this heading we thus speak of one thing *qua* matter, which in itself is not a particular; another *qua* shape and form, in virtue of which it is then spoken of as a particular; and a third *qua* the product of these two' (DA 412a6–8).[54]

The other main feature of his discussion of soul in matter–form terms regards the soul as the 'first actuality' (*entelecheia*) of the natural body in its living state. He goes on to say that 'actuality' has two senses, only one of which is appropriate to the idea of soul:

> [O]n the one hand, it is the possession of knowledge, on the other hand, it is the exercise of knowledge. Hence it is evident that the soul is like the possession of knowledge, for both sleep and waking exist in the presence of soul, and waking is analogous to the exercise of knowledge, and sleep to the possession and not the exercise of knowledge. Now the possession of knowledge is prior in being in the same individual. On which account, soul is the first actuality of a natural body having life in potentiality. [DA 412a]

Here he indicates that the first 'actuality' is what one would now think of as a disposition or dispositional property; the capacity that something has for exercising or manifesting a certain activity in certain circumstances. For example, solubility in water is a paradigm case of a dispositional property of sugar; it dissolves when placed in an adequate amount of water. The dissolution of sugar is the manifestation of its disposition towards solubility and sugar possesses this property even when it is not manifesting it through active dissolution. Aristotle's own example of first actuality as disposition involves the condition of someone who has undergone instruction in some subject-matter. After instruction, the person has mastered the knowledge of the subject-matter, because he has the capacity for exercising that knowledge under appropriate circumstances. This capacity is comparable to the dormant condition of sleep, in contrast with the active state of being awake, in which an animal exercises its various faculties. This capacity is a disposition as a property of the particular thing, and is the first actuality of the soul.

He also compares the actuality of the soul to that of an axe or an eye. If an axe were a natural body (but it is not), then its soul would be axe-like insofar as it cuts things; if the eye were an animal, then its soul would be sight, insofar as it sees things. The activity of the axe's cutting and the eye's seeing are actualities, comparable to the state of being awake, but not the first actuality. Rather, the first actuality is the disposition that makes sight possible in the eye; this is what Aristotle calls power or potentiality (*dynamis*). He thus draws a parallel between the soul and the *dynamis* of the axe for cutting and the eye for seeing. In another section of the same book, he describes a person who knows grammar but is not at the moment exercising it as having *dynamis* for the exercise of that knowledge, which he may exercise when he chooses (DA 417a). The first actuality of the living body is its being the substance (*ousia*) in accord with the definition (*logos*), its being the essence of a certain sort of body, the ensouled body of a human being.

Aristotle was patently dissatisfied with his predecessors' accounts of *psychē*, which he thought directed inquiry away from the real question, namely what it is

---

[54] But see Irwin in Everson, 1991, pp. 61–3, where he argues for two senses of substance.

about the 'nature' of living things that permits them alone to have 'soul'. He said that there had been too many futile attempts to proffer definitions of the 'nature' of soul without equal efforts to account for how ensouled things could be actual entities in the natural world. Most of Book One of *De Anima* is taken up with his criticisms of previous concepts of *psychē*; there is much scholarly debate today about the accuracy of his assessments of his predecessors' views, but that will not concern us here. Many of his specific criticisms are epitomized in his remarks about Plato's view, when he says that, 'along with most theories of the soul, [it] involves the following absurdity: they join the soul to a body, or place it in a body, without giving any specification of the cause [*aitia*] – that is, of the bodily conditions' (DA. 407b12). Such theories made an error in thinking that it is sufficient to merely describe the features of *psychē*, while failing to discuss the relation between *psychē* and the bodies within which *psychē* can properly be said to reside. More specifically, he attributes their failure to discover any satisfactory explanation of the 'nature' of soul to their neglect of the notion of essence and the definition of substance, as Everson explains: 'Rather than treating substances as conceptually autonomous, they thought that substances could be treated simply as functions of their constituent material components. Aristotle's claim is that it is only by treating the substance as conceptually prior to its matter that one will be able to achieve a properly integrated explanation of what the matter and its properties contribute to the substance it instantiates.'[55]

In contrast with previous attempts, Aristotle's concept of the soul is situated in terms of living things; *psychē* is that in virtue of which some kinds of bodies are *living* bodies: 'Soul is the substance, in the sense of form, of a natural body which has life potentially' (DA 412a). Substance in this restricted sense does not mean an entity that can exist independently of the existence of other entities. The phrase 'in the sense of form' refers to the definite level of complexity which ensouled substances have. The animal *psychē* is an excellent example of an entity that has an enormously complex form. It comprises the capacity to be nourished, to take in sensory information about the environment, to move under its own volition, and (for humans alone) to have thoughts. It is in terms of *psychē* and its actions that one can explain these characteristic human activities and account for the bodily parts and organs on which they depend. In most cases, Aristotle argues, such an account will offer an explanation in terms of goals that are aimed at, rather than in terms of mechanical motions that the organs which support such features carry out.[56]

On Aristotle's view of the twofold account offered of natural things, the physicist who studies the human *psychē* must specify both the physical conditions and the psychical properties that characterize those living beings that possess soul.[57] The passions or affections of the soul (*pathē tēs psychēs*) are enmattered accounts (*ta pathē logoi enhuloi eisin*) since they involve both thoughts and bodily states. To explain the passions of the soul requires the joint efforts of the physicist who gives an analysis of the physical conditions of the living body, and the dialectician who

---

[55] Everson, 1995, p. 183.
[56] See Irwin, 1991, pp. 63–6.
[57] On the twofold account, physical and psychical, see Everson, 1995, pp. 182–4.

gives an analysis of the principal psychical aspects that are associated with each passion. A. O. Rorty clearly expresses this insight in these words:

> In one sense, the physical and the cognitive accounts are separable from one another, and in another sense they are not. That they are separable in thought is evident from the fact that they are the subject of two distinct types of inquiry ... That they are not separable in being or in fact is evident from Aristotle's claim that explanations of such affections of the soul as anger are incomplete unless they include both accounts (DA 403a25ff). Anger involves the boiling of the blood around the heart *and* the person must think himself unjustly injured, to the extent of having a desire for revenge along with the pleasurable expectation of revenge (DA 403a31; Rh 1378a31ff). If the boiling of the blood around his heart had simply been caused by a feverish illness, without his having the accompanying thoughts, the person would not be angry.[58]

There is an underlying tension, however, at the very start of Aristotle's twofold account of an animal as ensouled matter. His commitment to the view that an animal or human is *in essence* an ensouled body seems to conflict with his further claim that the primary concept of matter is potentiality (*dynamis*), namely to embody different forms; and hence that it is the substance which persists through generation and corruption. If matter is conceived to be whatever persists through substantial change and alteration, and thus whatever acquires and loses form, then in the case of living things, they would acquire and lose their soul. But if a particular body is ensouled in essence (*ousia*) then that particular concrete thing can*not* acquire and lose its soul. Thus, on one hand, the tension between the two accounts would lead to the implication that a person's body survives his death, that is, in the corpse-matter, and that a person's soul becomes separated from its enmattered form through death, and 'lives on'. The first consequence does not pose serious problems since it endorses the notion that natural objects can lose specific forms, but the second consequence contradicts the common-sense notion that the soul is dependent for its existence on the living body whose soul it is.

There have been several attempts to rescue Aristotle's position from this impasse. One persuasive interpretation[59] argues that there are two distinct things that Aristotle calls an animal's matter: one is the organic body and is essentially ensouled, while the other is the organic body's compound of elements. Whiting argues that the relation between the form or soul and the elements of the organic body is contingent in a manner in which the relation between the form or soul and the organic body as a whole is not. This divergence in ontological dependence allows for contingent connections on the functionalist view of *psychē* without requiring one to reject a commitment to the existence of essentially ensouled bodies. Aristotle asserts not only that the *psychē* is the essence (*to ti ēn einai*) of a certain kind of body, namely animal bodies, but also that this body is organic (*organikon*), that is, composed of organs. An animal or human body is composed of organs that are defined by their functions; moreover, an animal body cannot exist in the absence of *psychē*, without

---

[58] A. O. Rorty in Nussbaum & Rorty, 1992, p. 8.
[59] Whiting, in Nussbaum & Rorty, 1992, pp. 75–91; Irwin separates 'proximate' from 'remote matter' in this context, Irwin, 1991, pp. 62–3.

which those organs could not perform their functions. He compares the function of an organ with the form of the whole of which the organ is a part:

> If the eye were an animal [note, that it is *not*], sight would be its soul. For this is the essence (*ousia*) of an eye according to its account (*logos*). But the eye is the matter of sight, such that when sight leaves it is no longer an eye, except in a homonymous sense [per the same name], like the one made of stone or painted. And it is necessary to take what is said of the part to apply to the whole living body ... It is not that body having lost its soul, which is potentially such as to live, but the one having soul. [DA 412b18]

This passage has been interpreted in several different ways, but the underlying point is that there is some matter that once was, but no longer is, an eye when sight leaves through death of the animal. But it also suggests that some thing 'having lost its soul' survives the loss of that soul, though it is not the *same* thing as the being whose soul has departed.[60]

Some material parts of the animal body clearly do survive their owner's death; the corpse is not just an uncanny simulacrum or duplicate of its previously living version. Aristotle admits that flesh and blood have functions *and* survive in the corpse-matter, but unlike the hand or the eye, it is not always possible to account for their functions, or what conditions must be met for them to exercise their functions:

> The function of [the flesh] is less clear than that of the tongue ... For all these [fire, bronze, silver] are what they are by some potentiality to act or be affected, just like flesh and sinew. But the accounts of these are not precise; so it is not easy to discern when they exist and when they do not, unless a thing is very far gone and the shapes alone remain, as when the bodies of very old corpses suddenly turn to ashes in their coffins. [Meta. 390a14ff]

According to Whiting, this passage suggests that he takes the uniform parts of animals, like flesh and blood, to differ from non-uniform parts, like hands and eyes, insofar as uniform parts do not perish at the same time as the animal itself expires. He seems to think that it is an unresolved issue when such uniform parts perish; it is clear in the case of very old corpses' changing into ashes, but not clear in the case of 'fresh' corpses where such change has not taken place.[61] In the latter example, the flesh (and perhaps the blood) survives for some time after the animal's death. This interpretation cogently supports the view that Aristotle discriminates between two senses of 'matter' in the definition of soul as an enmattered account.[62]

The ability of flesh to carry out its function depends on its being related in certain ways to the other functionally defined parts of the organism as a whole. Since the flesh is intimately connected to the animal heart, once the heart stops beating the flesh can no longer perform its proper function, as Whiting explains: 'The important point here is that the ability of a part ... to perform its function

---

[60] See Everson, 1995, pp. 172–4.
[61] Whiting, in Nussbaum & Rorty, 1992, pp. 78–80.
[62] This is not quite the same explanation that Everson offers of the autonomous levels of material description, Everson, 1995, p. 186.

depends on its standing in the right relations to the other functionally defined parts of the organism as a whole.' However, it is also cogent to speak of the uniform parts in terms of their differential features, namely the relative ratios of their *elemental* constituents, earth, air, fire and water. When the animal dies the corpse-matter continues to be made up of those contraries, in roughly the ratios that would be causally necessary, though not sufficient, for the existence of flesh and blood in the previous sense: 'Flesh, bone and each of the parts like these are twofold ... for both the matter and the form are called flesh or bone' (GC 321b19f). This assertion is strong evidence in favor of the view that Aristotle is giving an account of two things, the form and the matter, each of which is called 'flesh', and not accounts of one thing that can be considered or described in two different ways: 'Aristotle's view seems to be that functional flesh (the form) and compositional flesh (the matter) are homonymous; they share the same name, but the accounts of their being or essence are different. Compositional flesh is only homonymous with functional flesh and so can survive the loss of soul. But that doesn't mean that compositional flesh can't *constitute* functional flesh.' Aristotle often appeals to the elements in order to explain the features of animal parts; they grow old and perish because they are composed of materials that differ with respect to their natural places in the scheme of things, and because the elements in living things are not *in* their natural places: 'The idea is that living bodies age and corpses decay because the elements which constitute them tend to move toward their natural places – fire up and earth down – with the result that the elements gradually become separated from one another and cease to be present in the proportions necessary for the existence of the [non-uniform] parts.'[63]

It is in Aristotle's detailed biological treatises that one can find his account of the functions and properties of the uniform parts: blood, marrow, semen, bile, milk, flesh, bone and sinew. Not only is his conceptual analysis of these parts' contribution to the bodily whole important for his own twofold account of *psychē*, it is also important for our historical survey in tracing some of the Homeric and pre-Socratic terms used to describe the human soul. In his discussion of the roles that various organs play in their contribution to psychical activity, Aristotle underlines the intimate connections between the forms of integral parts and the matter of which they are composed. With respect to the passions or affections of the living body, there are material states which are sufficient for their occurrence. Under ordinary circumstances, these material states occur only when the organism perceives something through one of the sense organs. The central sense organ is the heart (*kardia*) and when the specific sense organs are affected by their objects, the affections pass through the blood to the heart.[64] Although each sense is defined by reference to its specific capacity, 'there is a common capacity which accompanies them all, by which one perceives that one sees and hears; for it is not by sight that one sees that one sees ... but by a part which is common to all the organs; for there is one sense and one master sense organ' (De Som. 455a15–21).

---

[63] Whiting, in Nussbaum & Rorty, p. 80, 82, 83 – altogether an ingenious interpretation; see also Everson, 1995, pp. 185–6.

[64] See Everson, 1995, pp. 187–8; Onians, pp. 40–43.

The heart is not only the central sense organ, but it is also the center of all psychical capacities; 'the capacities of perception, nutrition, and for moving the animal are all in the same part of the body' (PA 647a25). This common center or locus of control is crucial if the animal's perceptions and affections are to give rise to action: 'If the region of the origin [the heart] is altered through perception and thus changes, the adjacent parts change with it and they too are extended or contracted, and in this way the movement of the animal necessarily follows' (MA 702b21–5). In fact, there are occasions when Aristotle speaks as though the heart (or the brain) is the location of the *psychē* itself.[65] On one occasion he goes so far as to speculate that *psychē* is not present in equal measure in all parts of the body: 'It is in some governing origin of the body, and the other parts have life because they are naturally connected to this' (MA 703a37). In *Metaphysics*, Book Z, he says that, 'since the soul of animals (for this is the substance of living things) is their substance according to the account, i.e. the form and essence of a body of a certain kind ... therefore, the parts of soul are prior, either all or some of them, to the concrete animal, and similarly in each case of a concrete whole; and the body and its parts are posterior to this substance, and it is not the substance but the concrete thing that is divided into these parts as its matter.' However, the order of priority varies according to which of the two accounts one follows: 'Some parts are neither prior nor posterior to the whole, i.e. those which are most important in which the account, i.e. the substance, is *immediately present*, e.g. perhaps the heart or brain' (Meta. 1035b14–27).

The uniform parts such as blood and flesh are especially important for his account of the nutritive function of the soul. It is the flesh that serves as the primary organ or medium of the sense of touch. But in addition to its tactile role, flesh also serves a distinctive cognitive role. He says that every other part exists for the sake of flesh (PA 653b30) and specifies 'bones and skin and tendons and blood-vessels, and again hair and all kinds of nails and so on'. His arguments about the fleshy, soft tissues as the primary medium of contact with external objects have been the topic of much scholarly debate, but whatever the exact status of flesh as perceptual medium, it is an intrinsic and proprietary property of animal bodies. While he claims that flesh is an *archē* or principle for the body as a whole, blood is described as, in some sense, the matter for the whole of the body (PA 668a5). Blood definitely serves an end or *telos* for the *psychē*, since its final cause is nutrition; in addition, it is the body or flesh in potential. Moreover, blood contributes directly to a large range of other psychical functions. In one section of the *Parts of Animals*, he presents his case that various distinctive characteristics of different animal species, such as intelligence, courage, timidity and so forth, can be attributed to the quality of their blood; its heat, purity, thinness, fibrousness and so forth. G. E. R. Lloyd explains how the material constituents are intrinsic components of ensouled matter:

> The two cases we have considered, flesh and blood, illustrate how, even at the level of the fundamental uniform parts that form the material of the living body, his account is concerned with far more than just their role as stuff ... The primary simple bodies in

---

[65] See Everson, 1995, p. 188, note 26; on the brain as organic site, see Granger, 1996, p. 123.

Aristotle's element theory are, of course, earth, water, air, and fire, considered as combinations of the primary pairs of opposites, hot and cold, wet and dry. But when he comes to consider those opposites in PA 2 he leaves us in no doubt that it is not just as inert material that they are important. The very reason why it is essential to get clear about hot and cold, wet and dry ... is that 'it seems clear that these are responsible practically for death and life, and again for sleep and waking, for maturity and old age, and disease and health' ... Thus, of the pair wet and dry he tells us [at GA 733a11f] that wet is particularly associated with, or productive of, life (*zotikon*), while the dry is furthest from the soul. More strikingly still, the kind of heat that he refers to repeatedly in his explanation of generation is explicitly described not just as what is appropriate to living creatures, their proper or own heat, but as the vital (*psuchikon*) heat.[66]

On the other hand, *psychē* as 'breath' or 'spirit', in the earlier Homeric sense, receives scant treatment in his biological works, and deserves a mention only when he discusses *pneuma*, which he sometimes refers to as the material instrument of psychic activities. He criticized the crude notion that the soul of an animal is force or some other *dynamis*, though he does allow that it might subsist in some such body. When he discusses how animals and plants are formed of the earthly and the moist, he says that there is water in the earth, and *pneuma* in water, vital heat in all *pneuma*, and concludes that in some way (*tropon tina*), everything is full of soul.[67] In Granger's words: 'Whether the *pneuma* is purified heat or intensely hot air or some extraordinary additional element, it is still material, and presumably like any sort of material, it must be subject to the agency of the soul if it is to issue in living things.'[68]

Whiting continues this line of thought in her exposition of the basic features of an ensouled matter:

> Aristotle can consistently claim *both* that the matter of an animal is essentially ensouled *and* that the matter of an animal is only accidentally or contingently ensouled. For Aristotle is talking about different things, each with different criteria of identity and persistence – one, the organic body and its functionally defined parts (including the [uniform] ones); the other, the elements constituting [uniform] parts. And the organic body and its functionally defined parts (both uniform and non-uniform) are essentially ensouled but constituted by portions of the elements which (when they constitute an organic body) are (in virtue of constituting that body) accidentally ensouled.

The conclusion follows with respect to the compatibility between an essential and an accidental relation of the soul as form and the body as matter. There is 'a sense in which the matter of an animal *is* only contingently related to its form or soul, but not ... one which Aristotle takes to be incompatible with the sense in which the matter of an animal is essentially ensouled.'[69] For example, when an individual comes to be or ceases to be, a compound that is an intrinsic unity of form and matter comes to be or ceases to be. This compound is the form (or soul) of *its* (not

---

[66] Lloyd, in Nussbaum & Rorty, 1992, pp. 152–3.
[67] Lloyd, in Nussbaum & Rorty, 1992, p. 153, note 23.
[68] Granger, 1996, p. 122, note 16.
[69] Whiting, in Nussbaum & Rorty, 1992, pp. 84–5.

another's) body, and the body of which *its* (not another's) soul is the form and the essence:

> The compound which comes (and ceases) to be when Socrates comes (and ceases) to be is a compound of his individual form or soul and his organic body. And although the organic body must be constituted by *some* compositional matter at any time at which it exists, it can, insofar as it is functionally defined, be constituted by different portions of compositional matter at different times. But insofar as it is functionally defined, the organic body (unlike its constituent matter) cannot exist apart from the soul which is the set of capacities in virtue of which the organic body is capable of performing its defining functions; this body is *essentially* ensouled and so comes and ceases to exist simultaneously with the soul, which is its form and essence.[70]

Aristotle characterizes *psychē* as the first actuality (*entelecheia*) of a natural body capable of sustaining life (*sōma phusikon metechon zōēs*), that is, an organism composed of organs. It expresses the living thing's defining essence (*ousia*), its 'cause' (*aition*), principle (*archē*) and goal or end-state (*telos*). In the common English phrase, the *psychē* is 'the life and soul' of an organism, engaged in its natural activities of eating, drinking, moving about and reproducing. It is not the case, on Aristotle's view, that an organism has life as one of its properties the way it has a certain size, shape or power. Rather, the soul of a certain kind of living body consists in its being active in a definite manner, pursuing those actions and goals that constitute its being the kind of thing it is. Life is not a precondition of activity; rather, to be alive is to be engaged in outwardly directed activities that constitute one's nature (*phusis*): 'Aristotle does not draw a sharp distinction between those vital activities which, like self-nourishment, just keep an organism alive, and those that express the nature of the thing, that constitute a way of living. The view is severe: an organism that can survive but not engage in its "higher" activities is only equivocally (homonymous) a member of its species.'[71]

Amongst all the functions that characterize human beings in their animal 'nature', one function sets human beings apart, and that is the capacity for 'insight' or reflection. Aristotle indicates the changed focus of his account in his use of the term *nous*, which has a special status within the psychical organization of human being. Here Aristotle moves away from, and even seems to contradict, his overall holistic view of *psychē* as dependent on the organism. He says that *nous* is simple and unaffected; it is a substance that cannot perish; it is a different form of soul that can exist separately from its body, in the same way that what is eternal and unchanging can exist separate from what is changing and perishable. Unlike perception, memory and phantasy, *noesis* can take place in pure *theoria* and does not involve the actualization or fulfillment of any particular part or aspect of the body. Rather, it is the whole person that is perfected or actualized by his thoughts (*dianoia*). He further argues that there is nothing of which the mind is incapable of thinking (DA 429a17); that *nous* does not exist as an independent entity before it

---

[70] Whiting, in Nussbaum & Rorty, 1992, pp. 86–7; Irwin argues that Socrates ceases to exist, but his 'ex-spirit' lives on, 1991, p. 72.
[71] A. O. Rorty, in Nussbaum & Rorty, 1992, p. 10.

begins to think; that it is in its first actuality as active in thought, and thus identical with its objects and the forms of images.

The passages in *De Anima* Book Three, Chapter Five, devoted to *nous* (intellect or mind), and especially to *nous poetikos* ('maker's mind') are generally regarded as an embarrassment by many commentators.[72] No attempt will be made in this section to offer a resolution of these difficulties; rather, let it suffice for us to simply set forth what Aristotle has to say about that aspect of human nature. Aristotle claims that *nous* has no bodily organ and hence that the cognitive faculty or power (*to nōetikon*) is not only logically distinct, but actually separable from the body (*sōma*) and the rest of the *psychē*. This seems to commit him to some version of substance dualism and to contravene the very basis upon which he rests his definition and account of human nature. In an earlier passage, he describes *nous* entering the soul as a complete substance (*ousia tis ousia*) and says that this is imperishable. The compound of body and soul is perishable, 'but *nous* is probably something more divine and impassive' (DA 408b29). When he introduces his matter–form definition of *psychē*, he immediately qualifies the *definiens* with this comment about *nous*: 'it is clear that the soul is not separable from the body, or that parts of it are not separable if it is divisible into parts ... But nothing prevents some parts from being separable, because they are not the actualization of any body' (DA 413a4).

He thereby asserts that his definition of *psychē* does not apply to one part of the whole being, namely *nous*: 'Concerning *nous* and the power of contemplation nothing is clear as yet, but this seems to be a different kind of soul (*psychēs genos heteron*), and this alone cannot be separated, as the eternal [is] from the perishable' (DA 413b24). Thus, he escapes from the charge that the 'nature' or character of *nous* contravenes his definition of the 'nature' of *psychē*, but at the expense of seeming to claim that the 'nature' of the whole compound may comprise *two* kinds of *psychē*. In other words, if *nous* is radically different from the other parts, how is it connected to the other parts of the soul which are the actualization of an organic body as a living being? Humans and animals have souls, the former differing from the latter in terms of greater complexity in their form (amongst other factors); but now it seems that humans have *two* souls, one in virtue of which we are animals, and the other in virtue of which we are humans.

Charles Kahn has proposed an ingenious reading of these texts which offers a plausible compromise between the original definition of the essence of *psychē* in

---

[72] K. V. Wilkes, in the postscript to her excellent paper on '*Psuchē* versus the Mind', confesses, 'I cannot understand this chapter, and none of the secondary literature has so far helped me to do so. Thus I will end this paper with one or two comments which may help to mitigate this difficulty; all the same I have to say that I wish he had never written this chapter', in Nussbaum & Rorty, 1992, p. 125. Michael Frede comments that there are 'a formidable array of remarks' in the texts that throw all of his (Frede's) previous exposition of Aristotle's concept of soul into doubt; they are 'very confusing, so confusing that they have been the subject of debate since antiquity' and have generated an enormous variety of interpretations, ibid., p. 104–5. Everson's plaint is similar: 'it is sad, though, that his discussion of *nous* ... is quite remarkably obscure', in Barnes, 1995, p. 191, note 31; Franz Brentano provided a thorough overview and critical analysis of the many historical positions adopted on *nous poetikos* in *The Psychology of Aristotle*, 1977, pp. 4–24, 182–97.

terms of the matter–form template and the qualified statements regarding the essence of *nous*. He says that two conditions must be satisfied by a human being in order for thinking to take place: (a) empirical consciousness or sentience, which humans share with animals, comprising sensation and perception; and (b) access to the noetic domain via the faculty of *nous*. One must further distinguish between *nous* as the capacity for thinking and *noeisthai* or *dianoeisthai* as conscious acts or acts of thought (*dianoia* is his word for thoughts). What Aristotle does not spell out, but which Kahn argues for, is implied by his remarks about sensation, perception and embodied living, that is, that acts of thought will usually, perhaps always, involve the sensory faculty as well, since these are in fact the conscious acts of the whole human being, the concrete individual:

(i) For the *psuchē* as a whole Aristotle wants to deny that, as a form, it is properly subject to local motion or change; it is only moved incidentally when the body is moved, whose form it is ... Such changes can be traced to, but do not occur in, the soul, for the *psuchē* is localized only by its relation to the body which it informs.
(ii) The point concerning *nous* is quite different, but connected with the previous point by reference to the hylomorphic or bodily aspect of thinking. When the heart (or brain) decays, such hylomorphic activities are impeded, just as in sleep. When the whole human being perishes, no activities of the complex *psuchē* can survive. Thus consciousness in the ordinary sense, as percipient awareness comes to an end. But the principle of *nous* itself, which never really formed part of the hylomorphic *entelecheia*, survives intact.[73]

The reason why it is the principle (*archē*) of *nous* that allows it to survive intact the death of the individual is that, according to Aristotle's theistic doctrines in *Metaphysics* Book Lambda, it is the seed or spark of the divine intellect, itself eternal and immutable.[74] Kahn says that in knowing itself, in grasping its essence as noetic activity, *nous* simply is 'the formal structure of the universe *becoming aware of itself*. This is partially realized in us to the extent that we live the life of *theōria*, fully realized in the divine intellect.'[75] With this insight about the origin and nature of *nous* as it is realized in human beings, the finite limited intellect (*nous pathetikos*), one can understand how this concept is related to Aristotle's further doctrine about the divine intellect's relation to the *nous poetikos*.

The specific office of the maker's mind is the maturation of material mind into its overt practice, in the sense that it is the actualization of our innate ability to think into the acquired skill of actual thought. In this vein, Aristotle spoke of maker's mind as akin to the office of light, insofar as light 'causes' colors that are potentially visible to become actually visible. Light makes colors actual in bringing colors into a state of first actuality in the same way that mind makes things thinkable, not actually thought, that is, it brings into being the still potential acquired intellect. In these terms, Kosman offers the Standard View about the 'nature' of the *nous poetikos*, one view, he says, 'chosen from the Talmudic matrix of possibilities', that is, possible interpretations of this obscure doctrine: 'The maker mind makes

---

[73] Kahn, in Nussbaum & Rorty, 1992, p. 374.
[74] On the 'quasi-dualism' implied by this stance, see Irwin, 1991, pp. 72–3.
[75] Kahn, in Nussbaum & Rorty, 1992, p. 375.

both potential intellect and what is potentially thinkable in the sense of first potentiality, into actual intellect and what is actually thinkable in the sense of first actuality: that is, into what is actually *able* to think and what is actually think*able*.'[76] However, in order to fully appreciate the analogy between maker's mind and light, one needs to understand that Aristotle thought not that light creates visibility, but that it creates vision; he does not say that light makes the visible visible, but that light brings into existence the full actuality of being seen. Kosman suggests that one interpret Aristotle's doctrine about light in terms of three necessary conditions: (1) the object's visibility, (2) the eye's visual capacity, and (3) light itself. Light, he argues, is the third state (*hexis*) needed to bring about vision as an intellectual activity *and* the visibility of visible objects: 'For while light could be said to make the object of sight visible if the seeing eye is not yet at hand, it could be said *either* to make it visible *or* actually envisioned if it is.'

Along the lines of this extensive parallel, Aristotle's theory of perception and cognition is grounded on an agreement with Plato's discussion of light and vision in *Republic* Book Six. Here Socrates says that, 'When sight is in the eye, and the person who has it tries to use it, and color is in the things he is trying to see, then if there is not present a third sort of thing which is specifically and naturally directed to just this purpose, you know that the sight will see nothing, and that the colors will be unseen.' This third sort of thing is light, and it is thus 'in no small way true that the perceptual faculty of seeing and the power of being seen are linked together by a link more worthy than that linking other pairs, if indeed light is not without worth' (507d11f). Since light is what makes possible seeing, and since being able to see is defined by reference to seeing, light is said to make visibility itself actual. Plato extends this analysis to the operations of the thinking soul, that is, the intellectual or rational 'part' or power: 'The same is true of the eye by which the soul thinks. When it fixes upon that on which shines truth and being, it thinks and knows and seems to possess intellect (*nous*). But when it is fixed on what is diluted with darkness, on coming to be and passing away, it opines and is dimmed, changing its opinions back and forth, and then seems not to possess intellect' (508d4f). Kosman links this conceptual unpacking of the threefold operation of light directly to Aristotle's declarations about the 'nature' and functions of the maker's mind:

> It is because *nous poietikos* effects the actualization of *nous* in the actual activity of thinking, that is, because it brings about the realization of second-actuality thought, that we are able to describe it with equal facility as actualizing *nous* and *noeton*. Thus we can save the consistency of our two earlier answers by stressing the primacy of second actuality to first actuality, and the consequent primacy of the actualization from first actuality to second actuality ... [It] is actual *thinking*, that is, second-actuality thinking, that the maker mind brings into being.

Kosman draws these conclusions about the maker's mind from Aristotle's scattered remarks. (i) It is important to remember that *nous* is not simply a principle of intelligibility, but a principle of active consciousness. (ii) This active consciousness

---

[76] Kosman, in Nussbaum & Rorty, 1992, p. 347, 349.

is (an admittedly intermittent) capacity of human *psuchē*. (iii) The paradigm of this activity of mind is that divine mind whose substance is *energeia*, and specifically the *energeia* of *theōria* ... It is finally ... that active thinking, thinking as *theōria*, which the maker mind makes, a thinking most fully exemplified in the unremitting active thinking of the divine mind.[77] Given the fact that Aristotle himself was prone to employ common words in new and unexpected senses, that many of his key concepts are ambiguous between several senses, it is not surprising to claim that *nous* also has more than one sense. Thus, in one sense, *nous* is the human capacity or faculty to think; that is, beyond having animal sensation and perception, humans alone have thoughts about many things. But in another sense, it is the principle of that capacity, especially as it is realized in the human activity of building logically connected systems of knowledge (*epistemē*), that is, the human genius to offer accounts of such things as soul, mind, world and god:

> The activities of life are activities which depend upon the separability of form from matter. Thus the reproductive faculty is the ability to recreate the form of the animal in another individual, that is, in different matter, and the threptic is the ability to take the nutritive power of food and make it one's own. Similarly, the activities of consciousness are activities of taking on form ... Behind this general power of *psuchē* to grasp, as it were, the qua of being, to separate, distinguish, and discriminate, is the power of *nous*, the capacity to separate out being and, as it were, to dematerialize it; so it is that *hē nou energeia zoē* – life is the activity of the mind. *Nous* is also therefore divine being and therefore the *archē* of that principle which orders the world in its fundamental order, that of intelligibility.[78]

In closing our analysis of Aristotle's account of soul, its nature, functions and operations, we return to the difficult question raised at the start. Whatever the status of the maker's mind, is the soul (*psychē*) a substance, the bearer of properties, or a property (even if a very special one) of a living thing *qua* substance? If the soul-form of a compound thing gives that thing its distinctive, essential 'nature', and the soul is itself a substance-like thing, how does Aristotle's matter–form theory differ from other contemporary two-kinds-of-substance theories? Every conscientious commentator on Aristotle's complex, often baffling, account of soul, in advocating one or the other interpretation, has to concede that there are central (not peripheral) passages where he makes claims that run counter to their favored view. Nevertheless, as Granger astutely points out, 'a better case can be made for substantialism, at the cost of attributivism, by considering passages ... in which soul or form is treated as an actor that effects changes in the execution of its causal efficacy, than can be made for substantialism by appealing to the particularity of form or the uncertain evidence for its subjecthood.' Numerous textual examples show

> Aristotle's crediting form or soul with some variety of causal agency [that] could not be dismissed as just the result of sloppiness of expression on his part. They occur throughout his work, and many of them show up in important accounts of the 'causality' of the soul. It is reasonable to suppose that these passages reflect a genuine substantialist dimension

---

[77] Kosman, in Nussbaum & Rorty, 1992, p. 356.
[78] Kosman, in Nussbaum & Rorty, 1992, pp. 357–8.

within Aristotle's conception of form, in which he conceives of form in a non-attributivist way as an *agent* acting upon matter and the bodily parts of organisms.[79]

But against this preponderant orientation, there are other equally central passages where Aristotle argues for the notion of soul-form as the predicate of its material subject, and other contexts in which he defines the soul as the first actuality of a material living body. Much of the current revival of interest in his psychical theory argues for an early, only partially worked out version of functionalism, where the soul is construed as the most distinctive, defining *disposition* of living beings. But this theoretical interest still has to accommodate the very peculiar character of this dispositional power, since it often displays the features of an agent in its involvement with the generation, unification and maintenance of the organism. The most balanced and cautious assessment faces an intractable dilemma – the soul *qua* form does not accord neatly with any single ontological category: 'Hence soul or form gives the impression of being *a hybrid sort of entity*, or a confused combination of thing and property, as if it were a kind of "property-thing" or "power-thing" – for want of better descriptions – which shares essential features with both the nature of a property and of a thing.' Having made such a serious and far-reaching concession, Granger proffers an explanation of how two such versions could rest side by side, by setting out an etiological diagnosis that traces the attribute picture to his matter–form doctrine, and the substance picture to his concept of efficient causality as a kind of causal agency.[80] There seems to be some consensus that rejects an earlier view according to which Aristotle's thought about these issues went through three identifiable phases. But a good case can still be made that he began with a substance-based idea, similar to that found in the middle Platonic dialogues, and then attempted to retain some aspects of this doctrine under the pressure of his later matter–form theory.

If one does not want to concede to either the substantialist or the attributivist thesis, and in so doing insist that textual passages incompatible with one's preferred view either be dismissed or redacted, then few options are left. One is to claim, as Miles Burnyeat does, that Aristotle's concept of form is 'totally alien' to our way of thinking today, an archaic, mysterious concept that only the conjoined ideas of thing *and* property can approximate.[81] On the other hand, one might want to consider the possibility that Aristotle has an eccentric, anomalous idea of property (in contrast with an anomalous idea of soul or mind), namely, that some properties are causal agents, and in this sense behave with a thing-like character. Granger concludes his admirable summary of some of these main points with these sober words: 'It seems more helpful to acknowledge that Aristotle does not distinguish sharply between "property" and "thing" when he comes to his conception of the

---

[79] Granger, 1996, pp. 129–30.

[80] Granger, 1996, p. 134, emphasis added; this also seems to be one sense that underlies Irwin's notion of 'quasi-dualism', in Everson, 1991, pp. 72–3; Furth also holds another version of this radical thesis, and assigns the causal features of the causal powers that unite material elements to shared specific forms, identified with the eternally existent forms of species, Furth, 1988, pp. 241–5.

[81] Burnyeat, in Nussbaum & Rorty, 1992, pp. 15–26.

soul or form of natural objects, and that, as a result, he credits form with features that rightfully belong to the categorically distinct entities of thing and property.'[82] The student of the history of the concepts of soul and mind can take this valedictory comment either as something to be really discouraged about or as a challenge to rethink some of our most basic ontological vocabulary. The studies in this chapter (and in upcoming chapters) are not discouraged or disheartened by Aristotle's account of soul not falling neatly into an established taxonomy of plausible positions. On the other hand, it is beyond the scope of this book to attempt to meet the challenge posed by his remarkable 'likely story'.

(3) The Stoics, Epicurus and Lucretius on material spirit

It is standard in the history of Greek philosophical 'schools' to distinguish three main periods in the maturation of Stoic doctrine: the Early Stoa took shape under the guidance of Zeno of Citium (*c*.336–264 BCE), ably assisted by his younger disciples, Cleanthes of Assos (*c*.330–232 BCE) and Chrysippus of Soli (*c*.280–206 BCE); more than any other, Chrysippus was responsible for developing Stoicism into a systematic philosophy. The transitional Middle Stoa flourished in the next two centuries; its most reputable proponents were Panaetius of Rhodes (*c*.185–110 BCE), who brought Greek Stoic thought to the attention of the Roman intelligentsia,[83] and Posidonius of Apamea (*c*.135–31 BCE). The Late Stoa flourished and expired during the Roman period in the first and second centuries CE; its most prominent exponents were the powerful patrician counselor Seneca, the freed slave Epictetus, and the Emperor Marcus Aurelius.[84] Cicero (*c*.106–43 BCE) plays an unusual role in the history of philosophical ideas; he was an immensely learned scholar of Greek thinkers, whose highly eclectic attitude meant that many of the principal Platonic, Skeptic and Stoic theories received their first definitive expression in his superb Latin rendition. Most of his philosophical writings antedate the publication of Lucretius' *De Rerum Natura* (*c*.55 BCE) which advances an Epicurean physics of the natural world and psychics of the soul and body. Other prominent Latin writers of the next generation promoted Stoic views about morality, providence, the just state and the soul. Epicurean doctrines, though much debated by these writers in popular forums, had little influence on Neo-Platonic, Patristic and medieval philosophy.[85]

The Stoics adopted a position on the nature of *psychē* that was resolutely materialist; when they asserted that the soul was material they situated the soul entirely within the physical world. However, one should bear in mind that their concept of matter was itself quite different from our modern, scientifically robust concept of matter. Diogenes Laertius reported that for the Stoics, 'the soul is a nature (*phusis*) which can perceive; this is the "spirit" (*pneuma*) connate with us, and thus it is body (*sōma*)' (Lives 7.156; SVF 2.774). For them to claim that the

---

[82] Granger, 1996, pp. 155–7.
[83] For a detailed account of this influence, see E. V. Arnold, 1911, pp. 243–310.
[84] Philip Hallie, in EEP, vol. 8, pp. 19–20.
[85] Kristeller, 1993, p. 6.

soul is connate means that *pneuma* is of the same nature as the physical body, born with the individual's birth, dying at the individual's death. One dimension of the Stoics' view about the materiality of soul is attendant on their concept of causality. Given the fact that ensouled beings act on and are acted on by bodies, and that only bodies can interact, soul too must be some kind of body. But much like their strange view of matter, the Stoics' view of the *world* of bodies (the cosmos) is also different from our modern view. Diogenes Laertius remarked that the Stoics believed that the world itself is a living being – rational, animate and intelligent (Lives 7.142). Thus, human and animal souls are not the only things in the cosmos that can rightly be called souls, for souls are everywhere; they penetrate through the whole cosmos and humans share in this as ensouled parts (SVF 1.495). Both the world soul and the human soul are the same in being composed of *pneuma*, but human souls differ in several important respects from the world-soul.

Over the centuries, various Stoic thinkers proposed alternate accounts of the basic concept of *pneuma*: that it was heated matter or warm air or fire itself. These candidates for *pneuma*-status seem to converge on the central doctrinal claim that *pneuma* functions by way of, or in terms of, the heat contained within it. Cleanthes held that the 'ruling part' of *pneuma* itself was the sun's heat, and situated the world-soul within his conceptual scheme in its pervasive function as cosmic heat. Chrysippus took advantage of his expert knowledge of the most advanced medical studies by using their findings to explain the functions of *pneuma* in animal bodies. He claimed that *pneuma* is the single explanatory factor (*aition*) that makes the best sense of the observable properties and behavior of living things. Living and non-living things, he said, are differentiated in terms of the tension (*tonos*) of the *pneuma* present in their bodies. In this picture there is no ontological diremption between physical and psychical being, since physical and psychical properties are manifestations of a greater or lesser degree of pneumatic tension.

The Stoics did not avoid the issue of how the two kinds of physical 'nature', body and soul, are connected. In Stoic physics there are three ways in which kinds of stuff can be conjoined: first, through juxtaposition, for example, beans and wheat grains, which do not blend completely but retain their original properties. Second, through fusion, for example, eggs, flour and water, which combined together create a new stuff with new properties, such that the original ingredients do not retain their original properties. Third, through blending or mixture (*krasis di holon*), for example, water and wine, such that no part of the new stuff does not consist in both original ingredients, yet each of these retains its own properties and can in principle be reconstituted. The Stoics claimed that the soul and body are mixed or blended in the living being, and the point of this assertion was to permit descriptions of human nature in terms of discriminable properties.[86]

One of the most striking features of Greek medical theory, and the Stoics' use of this theory, is the prominence accorded to the concept of *pneuma*. One facet of the popular or common view taken up by the medical theorists was the imputation of a specific vital element in living beings. When an animal dies its breath and warmth disappear, and *pneuma* was posited as the element whose workings were manifest

---

[86] For more details, see Long, in CHHP, 1999, pp. 560–65.

in breathing and bodily warmth. Aristotle made only scattered and somewhat confusing references to *pneuma*, but he did assert that it is *pneuma*, and not heat, that is required for the psychical operations of movement, reproduction and sensation. Heat, however, is associated with *pneuma* since heat is a specific property of *pneuma qua* substance; thus, for example, he speaks of vital heat (*thermotēs zōtikē*) and soul heat (*thermotēs psuchikē*) (GA 739b20–6, a9–12), but breath, on the other hand, serves a cooling function. He also claims that *pneuma* is not a special substance, but just warm air (GA 736a), though it differs from ordinary air in being connate (*sumphuton*) through its function in animal metabolism whereby it acquires no new properties (Som. 456a11, PA 659b13–18, 669a1–2). It is able to bring about movement, it provides animals with their strength, and it plays some role in sensation. In the strange passage in 'Generation of Animals' cited above (736b30) the *pneuma* contains some thing important for all psychical functions, perhaps related to the fifth element of which the stars are composed. Aristotle does not have a coherent account of the nature and functions of *pneuma*, and it is not integrated into his general theory about the soul as the form of an individual body.[87]

For the Greek medical theorists *pneuma* is not a peculiar substance found only in living beings, but rather ordinary air that is transformed within the vital organs and there takes on new properties. Some of the earlier medical researchers argued that the heart distributes blood through the veins to nourish the body and distributes *pneuma* through the arteries to energize and sensitize the body. One ingenious modification of this thesis was to hypothesize that the heart and the brain distribute different kinds of *pneuma*. Air breathed in through the lungs goes to the heart where it is dispersed as *vital pneuma*; some of this goes to the brain where it is transformed into *psychic pneuma*. The former accounts for lower non-rational functions and processes, the latter for higher, rational ones. The Stoics retained the earlier medical model of a single kind of *pneuma* which differs according to different metabolic processes. They failed to appreciate the more correct later model of dual *pneuma*, but made a definite scientific advance by postulating a centralized mechanistic system, through which the *psychē* drives the organic body.[88]

According to the Stoics there is a scale of beings in the cosmos, a scale whose measure is the degree to which things are unified in themselves. The lowest level of unified function is the state (*hexis*) of an inanimate thing whose parts simply cohere together; their unity consists in a determinate composite of stuff. At the next level, plants grow and reproduce, being held together through an internal principle of unity that provides them with their 'nature'. At the next level, animals perceive their surroundings, and move about (as well as grow and reproduce), being unified through the presence of soul (*psychē*). Whereas at the highest level on the scale of being, humans, in addition to the functions gained at the lower levels, are further unified through the presence of intellect (*nous*) (SVF 2.988). On this view, *psychē* is not just the presence of *pneuma*, but a specific level of *pneuma*, whose degree of

---

[87] See Lloyd, in Nussbaum & Rorty, 1992, pp. 153, 166 note; Granger, 1996, p. 122, note 16.
[88] See Gundert, in Wright & Potter, 2000, pp. 13–36; Hankinson, in Everson, 1991, pp. 194–217.

tension permits it to function as the *pneuma* of *psychē*, unifying its body and enabling it to perceive and move in certain ways. The body with which the *psychē* is mixed or blended is not inert matter, since it is a body already held together and enabled to function in plant-like ways by *pneuma* in the form of its *phusis*. So the *psychē* interacts with an already living body, itself unified at a lower level by an already cohesive body, held together by its physical state (*hexis*); in this manner, the intellect interacts with an already ensouled body.[89] Sextus Empiricus, the great compiler of skeptical arguments, made an additional important assertion regarding *psychē* identity criteria when he said that the Stoics often used the word *psychē* in two different senses. One sense applies to the *psychē* as the animating principle of the whole compound, and another sense applies to the *psychē* as the 'ruling part' (*hēgemonikon*) of the whole, that is, the rational soul or intellect (thus equivalent to *nous*). Where the soul as such is blended with the whole body and makes it an animal (=animate) body, the intellect is located in one part of the body, even though it controls or dominates the whole body (Sextus Adv. Math. 7.234–40).

With regard to the soul as such, the Stoics classified various aspects, each of which has an identifiable function. Perhaps the definitive expression of this doctrine is found in Chrysippus:

> The soul is *pneuma* connate with us, extending as a continuum through the whole body as long as the free flowing breath of life is present in the body. Now, of the parts of the soul that have been assigned to the several parts, that which extends to the trachea is the voice, that to the eyes, sight; that to the ears, hearing; that to the nostrils, smell; that to the tongue, taste; that to the entire flesh, touch; and that which extends to the testicles, having another such account (*logos*), is seminal. That part where all these meet is in the heart, being the ruling part of the soul. This being so, there is agreement about all other parts, but about the ruling part of the soul there is disagreement, some placing it in one region, others in another ... Thus the place seems to elude us, since we have neither a clear perception [of it] as we had with the others, nor sure signs through which this matter might be inferred; otherwise, disagreement among physicians and philosophers would not have grown so great. [Galen, de Lacy ed., PHP 170]

The soul's parts do not differ in terms of their material composition, since the soul is entirely composed of *pneuma*. But the parts do differ in their proper location, since each extends through different bodily parts (members and organs), and each part also has its proper function. The ruling part exercises centralized control over the other psychical parts; in the Stoics' own imagery, it is like an octopus whose tentacles extrude the *pneuma* to the sense organs (SVF 2.836), or like a spider in the middle of a web sensitive to movements in specific places (SVF 2.879). Whatever occurs in or at the sense organs is transmitted to the ruling part which itself perceives what the organ has received.

Julia Annas, in her admirable exposition of Stoic texts on the soul, draws three important lessons from these assertions about the nature of *psychē*. First, although the Stoics distinguished between two senses of soul, they tended to take the second, strict sense to refer, not to the entire organic mechanism, but just to the ruling part. Since it

---

[89] Annas, 1992, pp. 53–4; Long, in CHHP, 1999, pp. 570–72.

is in the *hēgemonikon* that what happens to the rest of the soul is registered and organized, the human soul really *is* the intellect: 'Plutarch complains that the Stoics cram all the events of our psychological life into the tiny space of the *hēgemonikon*; this has some analogies with modern objections to taking all our mental life to occur in the brain.' Second, the Stoic concept of mind is deeply influenced by the insight that the soul is 'a communication mechanism'. Since the ruling part receives sensory input, registers, unifies and makes sense, the Stoics thought that what it receives are messages, that it transmits information, and operates in language. The Stoic account of perception characterizes psychical processes in terms of their content and not their phenomenal qualities: 'This is perhaps the most distinctive and original feature of Stoic philosophy of mind; its distance in this respect from Aristotle can to some extent be explained by the differences between their underlying models.'

Third, the Stoics stressed the unity of the soul far more than Aristotle did; beings that are capable of perception and reaction are unified selves; in these terms animals, as well as humans, are unified selves. But where animals unify their psychical processes in an automatic and instinctual manner, humans are rational, and their intellect allows them to interpret meaningful contents in a rational manner: 'Hence the Stoics denied to animals not only reasoning but emotions and even desires; since animals cannot articulate and interpret in language the content of their experience, they have only quasi forms of what in humans are desires, emotions, and so on.' From these three lessons, Annas draws the following succinct conclusion: 'the *hēgemonikon* can be thought of, not too misleadingly, as the mind, and the Stoic theory of the soul as a theory of our mental life.'[90]

In addition to this classification in terms of parts and their mixtures, the soul can also be sorted in terms of its faculties or powers (*dunameis*). The Stoics defined *dunamis* as that which brings about events and controls the subordinate activities (SVF 3.203). Although scholars disagree about how the Stoics explained the ontological status of such powers, it seems that their reference to dispositional powers relies on underlying differentiated physical structures. Iamblichus claimed that Zeno and Chrysippus posited the soul as a substance that existed before the powers existed, that is, the soul was ontically and logically prior to its powers (SVF 2.86, 2.831); the soul's powers then are properties of the subject whose soul it is. The best-known image the Stoics employed to illustrate the relation of psychical qualities to the bodily subject was that of the scent of a fruit to the fruit itself. For example, Iamblichus said that, 'just as the apple has in the same body its sweetness and its scent, so the ruling part has put together in the same [body] appearance (*phantasia*), assent (*sunkatathesis*), impulse (*hormē*), and reason (*logos*).' Annas comments on this passage: 'The functioning of the mind, or *hēgemonikon*, can thus be classified as the manifestation of four different powers. Appearance is manifested in our reception of information through the senses ... Assent is manifested in our interpretation of the information we receive. Impulse is manifested in our acting on it. Reason is manifested in the fact that humans do all these things in a rational way, one that is articulable in language.'[91] Against this view, some critics accused the

---

[90] These three lessons from Annas, 1992, pp. 63–4.
[91] Annas, 1992, p. 66; see Long, in CHHP, 1999, pp. 572–5.

Stoics of placing too great an emphasis on reason, reducing the other non-rational parts to deviations from the true nature of the human soul.

However, although the soul is a simple thing in virtue of its composition out of uniform *pneuma*-stuff, its description is complex, involving eight parts and four powers. The ground for their claim that the human soul is basically or strictly rational is itself based on their prior claim that the rational soul is the *pneuma* at a higher degree of tension than the rest of the *pneuma*-soul. In other words, not only will the soul as such be more cohesive than the physical body, the rational soul will be more cohesive than the non-rational soul. It is this doctrine that supports the well-attested Stoic claim that the soul will survive an individual's death, and the more rationally developed souls will last the longest. Cleanthes believed that all souls will survive bodily death, though Chrysippus believed that only the souls of the wise will do so (DL Lives 7.157; SVF 2.811). But two important provisos should be noted: souls last longer than bodies, but they are not immortal, they do not endure forever; further, there is no personal survival after death, since the soul is not identical with the individual. There are thus no rewards or punishments in the Stoic afterlife; the person whose good or evil actions would have incurred such consequences no longer exists, and hence as Epicurus and Lucretius vehemently stated, 'death means nothing to me.'

Epicurus' life (*c*.340–270 BCE) was roughly contemporary with the Early Stoa; an Athenian educated by Platonists, he established his school in the garden (instead of the agora or stoa), an open school which had the distinction of welcoming slaves and women. Much of his original work has been lost, partly due to the infamous reputation his school acquired for teaching that human souls were mortal, that pleasure was a moral good, and that the gods should be abandoned.[92] The Stoic and Epicurean pictures of *psychē* are similar in structure and in some details about psychical parts and functions.[93] But the two pictures are based on radically different metaphysical assumptions: the Stoics held a continuum theory of matter and claimed that the cosmos is animate, governed by laws that disclose divine providence; whereas the Epicureans held an atomic theory of matter, and rejected all appeals to providence and purpose in the workings of the cosmos. With regard to their more specific theories about the nature of *psychē*, the Stoics were heavily influenced by current medical and scientific discoveries, whereas the Epicureans were less impressed by such technical claims and relied more on common sense and conceptual analysis.[94] Epicurus' atomistic physics led him to a rather crude argument about the physical nature of *psychē*. The motion of atoms in the void, he said, gives rise to compounds among which some are animate, sentient beings. Epicurus rejected the panpsychist assertion that *psychē* as life is present everywhere, that is, at the level of the ultimate constituents, and thus he asserted that atoms are inanimate – without *psychē*. Living beings, he thought, do *not* display the workings of a life-force which operates in the whole cosmos.

---

[92] OCD 3rd edn, pp. 532–4; the standard scholarly collection was established by H. Usener in 1887; the current authoritative collection, including new fragments, is by G. Arrighetti, 2nd edn, 1973.

[93] See Everson, in CHHP, 1999, pp. 542–59.

[94] Von Staden, in Wright and Potter, 2000, pp. 79–116.

Against the Stoics and their allies, Epicurus argued that there is no scale of beings, that the world is not an ordered whole, and thus that humans do not have a pre-assigned, special place in the whole. Against the Stoics he also argued that there is nothing like reason (*logos*) that permeates the world and gives its parts and their relations meaning or significance. Lacking an inbuilt or intrinsic significance the world also lacks providence and purpose. Humans do not possess reasoning (*logismos*) or mind (*nous*), characteristics that separate them from other animals. In one passage, from the fragmentary text *On Nature*, Epicurus remarks that tame animals' actions depend on an inner cause, and Lucretius later makes the seemingly outrageous claim that horses and deer have minds (RN2.265, 2.270, 3.299). However, animals have only some, not all, rational capacities; from the Epicurean point of view, reason is not a single thing, not a separable part, but a particular cluster of capacities.

According to Epicurus, the soul (*psychē*) consists of the smoothest and roundest atoms greatly superior in these respects to the atoms of fire. Diogenes of Oenoanda[95] added yet further detail to this picture: 'The soul provides nature with the reason for the [presence or absence of] life. For even though it does not possess the same number of atoms as the body, being placed in it with its rational and non-rational elements, still it encompasses the whole body and, being bound by it, binds it in its turn, just as the shortest dash of acid juice curdles a vast quantity of milk.'[96] Although the relevant passage from Epicurus' letter to Herodotus is not entirely clear, other sources about Epicurus' doctrine permit a more complete picture.[97] The soul is composed of four kinds of atom; each kind is similar to, or just like, fire, air, *pneuma* and an unnamed fourth kind.[98] Annas comments on the important qualifying phrase 'just like': 'the soul does not contain just the kind of fire that we find in fireplaces, but something which is like that in basic respects, but more refined ... The idea we have of it comes from our idea of fire ... Thus our concept of it is simply something fire-*like*, since we have no direct access to it in experience; all we can do is simply extend the experiential conception that we do have.'[99]

The nameless fourth element has a special status and function: it exceeds the other three in the fineness of its parts (*leptomereia*), and is more sensitive to (*sumpathēs*) the entire assemblage. According to Plutarch, it is from this fourth nature that there comes about 'that by which the agent judges and remembers and loves and hates, and in general the intellect and reason' (Adv. Col. 1118e). According to Aetius, this element is the only one that can produce sensation; in sum, it seems to be responsible for sensation, thought, emotion and memory. The fact that Epicurus cannot give it a name drawn from his Greek lexicon is rather trivial; if he had given

---

[95] Diogenes carved an enormous inscription in the Lycian Stoa recording important Epicurean doctrines in the second century CE; in 1884–95, approx. 88 fragments were discovered and published, increased by another 124 fragments, compiled and edited by M. F. Smith in 1970–84; see Clay, in ANRW, 1990, vol. 36.4.
[96] Quoted in Annas, 1992, p. 137.
[97] Long & Sedley, 1987, 14A, pp. 65–6.
[98] Long & Sedley, 1987, 14C, p. 67.
[99] Annas, 1992, p. 138.

it an invented name, the more serious problem would still remain. The problem is that, given his commitment to an entirely physicalist account of everything and his doctrine that all our knowledge is derived from experience, there must be some thing in our experience of material objects that would justify positing another element beyond the three already adduced. The functional role of the fourth element emerges only in Lucretius' exposition of the components of *anima* and *animus*, to which we shall turn shortly.

Diogenes of Oenoanda also attests to the Epicurean view that the soul is not uniform; the rational part is located in the chest, while the non-rational parts are diffused through the whole body. (In Lucretius' Latin version this distinction is made by calling the former *animus* and the latter *anima*.) Like the Stoics' claim that the ruling part is in the chest and not the head, Epicurus located the seat of the emotions in the heart (*kardia*). But unlike the Stoics, who were reluctant to divide the soul, he clearly demarcates the rational part by way of functional criteria; the rational soul dominates the whole soul and organizes the whole soul's activities. In many ways the rational soul can carry out its functions independently of the activities of the whole soul, but not vice-versa; at least in humans anyway, the whole soul's functions depend on the governance of its ruling part. Since the whole soul is composed of all four elements, and since the ruling part is an actual, material part of the whole soul, then some cluster or aggregate of the four must determine the workings of the ruling part *qua* ruler or governor. One plausible candidate for this role is the *ratio* of component elements: in some fashion unspecified by Epicurus the fourth element must dominate the elemental composition of the ruling part. The fourth element is either present throughout the whole soul, though denser in the ruling part, thus impugning the assertion that the ruling part can sometimes operate in complete autonomy, or the fourth element is only present in the ruling part, thus impugning the notion that this part unifies the whole soul in terms of its overall functions.

On many occasions Epicurus refers to the body as the container or vessel of the soul. It is the body that holds together and enables the unified workings of the living being. This brings about a reversal of the Stoic notion that what makes an agent living and moving is the soul's holding the body together:[100]

> While the soul is indwelling it never lacks sensation through the removal of any other part – whatever of the soul itself is destroyed too when all or part of the container disintegrates, will so long as it remains, have sensation. But the rest of the aggregate, when either all or part of it remains, does not have sensation after the separation of however many atoms it takes to make up the nature of the soul. Moreover, when the whole aggregate disintegrates, the soul is dispersed and no longer has the same powers or its motions. Hence, it does not possess sensation either. For it is impossible to think it perceiving while not in this composite, and moving with these motions when what contains and surrounds it are not of the same kind as those in which it now has these motions ... Thus, those who say that the soul is incorporeal are talking nonsense.[101]

---

[100] Annas' judicious comment, 1992, p. 148.
[101] Long & Sedley, 1987, 14A, p. 66.

It is not the case, Epicurus asserts, that the soul requires the body for the living thing to have sensation, nor even that sensation is the product of the interaction of soul and body. His position is more extreme than either Platonic substance dualism or Aristotelian hylomorphism, as Julia Annas explains:

> Epicurean soul and body need each other to exist and to function *as soul and as body*. Without the body, the soul no longer exists or functions as soul, but is just scattered atoms; without the soul, the body no longer exists or functions as body, but is a mere corpse. Sentience brings this out; it is the product of the mutually dependent soul and body, for the soul needs the body to exist as the soul of a sentient agent, and the body needs the soul to exist as the body of a sentient agent.[102]

The co-determination of soul as soul and body as body within the whole living being is the *sine qua non* condition for Epicurus' (and later Lucretius') declaration of the soul's mortality. Although neither Epicurus nor Lucretius claim that the soul's survival is a logical impossibility, they do argue that without the containment of the bodily vessel, the component elements of the soul would be dispersed in the air and thus, having lost their unity, the individual's soul as a functional whole would disappear. Further, since the individual's memory, emotion and volition are identified by the presence of the co-dependent soul *and* body, the dispersed or scattered soul would not be continuous with the original individual anyway.

It is fairly standard scholarly practice to treat Lucretius side by side with Epicurus and, more than that, to supplement lacunae and aporiae in Epicurus' texts with quotations or periphrases from Lucretius. Given Lucretius' explicit declarations of affiliation and homage to Epicurus, this is hardly surprising. But it is worth considering some special circumstances in Lucretius' case, in light of which his exposition of the nature, functions and mortal status of the soul will be treated separately. First, his detailed arguments in *On the Nature of Things*, Book Three, are not mere supplements or expansions of his Greek mentor's account of the soul; they are moments of a coherent whole, devised as a comprehensive theory in its own right, whatever its flaws. Second, in contrast with the eclecticism of other first-century Latin writers, each of whom wrote about philosophical issues as stock topics among other literary endeavors, Lucretius' work is perhaps the first systematic philosophical treatise in Latin, though organized around standard Greek topics. Third, Lucretius' employment of Latin terms for *psychē, nous, pneuma,* and so forth – in conjunction with Cicero's translations and summaries – decisively shaped the later Latinate philosophical vocabulary. Lucretius and Cicero molded their own native language in such a distinct and clear manner that key psychical terms, such as *animus, anima, mens* and *spiritus*, take on their original meanings here.

Lucretius' *On the Nature of Things* Book Three stands as one of the first systematic treatises in the Latin language on the nature and functions of the soul and mind. Almost nothing is known about Lucretius' life (*c*.95–51 BCE) aside from the fact that his 'great poem' was published about 55 BCE (when Cicero excitedly mentioned it in a letter to a close friend) and the highly unlikely story that he died from an

---

[102] Annas, 1992, p. 149; Long & Sedley refer here to 'the extreme functional interdependence of soul and body', 1987, p. 71.

overdose of a love potion given to him by his wife.[103] Lucretius' explicit allegiance to Epicurus' philosophy is evident from the very beginning of Book One; at a time, he says, when human belief was crushed under the weight of superstition, one person alone (Epicurus) raised his eyes in defiance and challenged the stories about the gods. Zeus' thunder and lightning did not frighten him, but provoked his courage and his wisdom 'to smash the constraining locks of nature's doors'. Epicurus' mind journeyed beyond this world and through infinite reaches,[104] returning with the victorious knowledge about 'what can be and what cannot; how the power of each thing is limited, and its boundary-stone sticks buried deep'. Through the benefit of his unique insights, humans have defeated superstition and have attained, if not in power, at least in thought, to the level of the gods (I. 63–78).

One of the locks that Epicurus' insights opened was that guarding the soul; its chambers are component parts in their specific structural relations, and its hasp is the intimate blending of soul and body in the mortal living being. Almost the entire content of Book Three is devoted to an analysis of these topics: first, the basic nature (*natura*) of soul (*anima*) and mind (*animus*); second, the four component elements of the *anima*; third, the connection between body (*corpus*) and *anima* in the living being; and finally, the demonstration of the soul's mortality, something that he argues for in thirty separate proofs. Where the Greek writers usually employed *psychē* for soul and linguistically unrelated (non-cognate) terms for mind or intellect (*nous*), Cicero and Lucretius make use of an obviously close connection between *anima* (feminine ending) and *animus* (masculine ending). The origin of this morphemic splitting is obscure and is not helped by Cicero's gnomic utterance that 'it is said that *animus* itself is from *anima*' (Tusc. Disp. 1. 9, 19).[105] Although Lucretius often seems to use *animus* and *anima* as synonyms, he also discriminates the mind's mental functions (using *mens, mentis*, and so on as the base) from the soul's emotional functions.

R. B. Onians readily admits that the problem of the original meanings of *animus* and *anima* is one of great difficulty. Though the two words are obviously cognate, the fact that they are differentiated after the second century BCE probably indicates that at an earlier date there was only one more inclusive word, *anima*. He observes that for the Romans, the vital principle was located in the head and, before its Greek-inspired identification with *anima*, it was more common to refer to this as the *genius*.[106] Where Latin writers had used *animus*, it almost always meant the principle of consciousness, that is, thought or intellect. Onians quotes the early tragedian Accius' maxim, *sapimus animo, fruimur anima*; when the later grammarian Nonus quotes this maxim he says *animus est quo sapimus anima qua vivimus*. Onians summarizes the Latin pre-philosophical usage in these words:

---

103 According to the OCD, 3rd edn, pp. 888–90.

104 Comments about his extra-somatic projection and ecstatic insight ally him with shamanistic thinkers such as Pherecydes, Pythagoras and Empedocles.

105 On Cicero's philosophical orientation in the *Tusculan Disputations*, see OCD 3rd edn, pp. 1562–3; Philip Merlan, in CHLGEMP, 1970, pp. 57–8.

106 For Onians' discussion of *genius, numen* and *caput*, an immense topic in its own right, see Onians, pp. 123–52; compare G. Dumezil, *Archaic Roman Religion*, University of Chicago Press, 1970, pp. 356–69.

To contemplate some action is to have it in one's *animus*; to turn one's attention to something, an idea within or an object in space, is 'to turn the *animus* toward it'; courage, despair, etc. are matters of *animus*; to feel faint, to be on the way to losing consciousness, was in the Plautine phrase, 'it goes ill with one's *animus*'; when a man loses consciousness 'his *animus* leaves him'; to collect one's faculties and spirits is 'to collect one's *animus*' ... Animus is concerned with consciousness and *anima* has nothing to do with consciousness. So much is clear.

He goes on to argue, citing numerous examples from Latin texts, that *anima* was pictured in physical terms associated with wind, breath, vapor, and so forth, located in the chest.[107] But this vital breath could also be employed by the *animus* in more highly directed and guided actions, for example, in the production of speech, the expression of affective states, and other actions that indicated the presence of rational soul. Onians supposes that this sense of *animus* tied it most closely with the pre-Platonic Greek word *thumos*, but his most ingenious supposition is that the *animus* as the overt, outward exteriorization of the indwelling rational soul *by means of breath* associates it very closely with *spiritus*, and its cognate forms, such as *inspiro, conspiro*, and so forth.[108]

In the opening argument of Book Three Lucretius' first premise is that the soul (*animus*), often called the mind, is a genuine part of the whole living being, and that the soul (*anima*) is also a genuine part, but with different functions: *Primum animum dico, mentem quam saepe vocamus, in quo consilium vitae regimenque locatum est, esse hominis partem nilo minus ac manus et pes atque oculi partes animantis totius exstant* (6. 94–7). Much hinges on whether one thinks that the author identifies *animus* and *mens*, using the words interchangeably without loss of meaning, or whether, at this first stage, although the two are usually distinct, the predicate that follows (*in quo consilium vitae regimenque locatum est*) is equally true of either of them. Several translators render *animus* 'mind' and *mens* 'intellect' and *consilium* 'understanding', thus reading 'first I say that the mind, which we often call the intellect, in which is located the understanding and guidance of life, is a part of the human, no less than the hand or foot or eyes are parts of the whole living being', that is, ensouled being (from *anima*). He then rejects the view that the intellect's sentience (*sensum animi*) is not located in a certain part, but is a true (real) habit of the vital body, which makes humans live with (or as) sensing beings. However, he carefully qualifies this by saying that in no part does the intellect exist (*nulla cum in parte siet mens*).

Lucretius observes as a matter of fact that 'life often lingers in our limbs (*membris*) after a large part of the body (e.g. an arm or leg) has been cut off. On the other hand, when a few particles of heat (*corpora pauca caloris*) have dispersed abroad and some air has been let out through the mouth, life deserts the veins and leaves the bones' (3. 119–23). He then draws an inference from this observation that foreshadows his decidedly materialist conclusion: 'You can know from this that not all particles (*corpora*) have an equal part, nor support life equally, but it is mainly in those that are seeds of wind and heated vapor (*ventiquae sunt calidique vaporis*

---

[107] See OLD, 1968–72, s.v. *anima*, p. 132, s.v. *animus*, pp. 134–5.
[108] Onians, pp. 168–73.

semina) lingering in the members that life remains. There is then heat and vital wind in the body itself which deserts our dying limbs (or frame)' (3. 124–9). Cyril Bailey notes that in this context Lucretius speaks of *ventus* and *vapor*, whereas earlier he had spoken of *calor* and *aer*; *calor* and *vapor* certainly have the same meaning and, although he later distinguishes between *aer* and *ventus* as constituents of the soul-particles, here they are synonymous.[109]

In Book Six of Vergil's *Aeneid*, the elderly Anchises explains some of the mysteries of the cosmos to his son. Vergil's sympathies with Stoic philosophy are clearly evident in this passage,[110] and he may have had this section from *De Rerum Natura* in mind when he wrote these lines:

> In the beginning, Mind fed all things from within ... It was Mind that set all this matter in motion; infused through all the limbs, it mingled with that great body, and from the union there sprang [all living things] ... The living force within them is [made] of fire and its seeds have their source in heaven, but their guilt-ridden bodies make them slow and they are dulled by earthly limbs and dying flesh. It is this that gives them their fears and desires, their griefs and joys. Closed in the blind darkness of this prison they do not see out to the winds of air. Even when life leaves them on their last day of light, they are not wholly freed from all the many ills and miseries of the body which must harden in them over the long years and become ingrained in ways we cannot understand. [Aen. 6. 724–40, trans. by David West]

Following the lines about wind and vapor, Lucretius asserts that the *animus* and the *anima* are conjoined, and between them compose a single nature (*unam naturam*). But the head is, as it were (*quasi*), the ruler (*dominus*) of the whole body, that is, the understanding, which we call the *animus* or mind. This is seated in the middle region of the chest, and thus the heart is the locus of fear, terror and joy. But the rest of the *anima* is spread through the whole body; it obeys the mind and is moved by the will (3. 140–4). The mind alone, by itself, understands itself, rejoices in (or for) itself, when nothing moves the *anima* or body. Although the mind or *animus* can think or feel emotions on its own, when it is moved by some stronger feeling the whole *anima* feels-with (*consentire*) the mind through the members. From this observation one can learn that the *anima* is conjoined with the *animus*, since when the *animus* strikes (*percussat*) the *anima* it propels the body and pushes it (3. 158–60). By the same reason, the nature of both *animus* and *anima* is corporeal; although each is distinct in function and composition, they are the same in being material entities.

Lucretius now turns his attention to what differentiates *animus* from *anima*, specifically with respect to their composition out of small bodies (*corpora*, used in the technical Epicurean sense).[111] The *animus* or mind is a very subtle thing, made out of very small particles (*esse aio persubtilem atque minutis perquam corporibus factum constare*) (3. 179–80). It is formed from exceedingly round and small seeds, so that it is moved when struck by even a slight impulse. He adduces as proof of

---

[109] Bailey, vol. II, p. 1009; on the poetic resonance of this imagery, see Segal, 1990, Chapter 4.

[110] On the philosophical influences in Vergil's work, see OCD 3rd edn, pp. 1605–7.

[111] For this technical sense, see Bailey, vol. II, pp. 1026–8.

this supposition the rapidity of thought, that is, the 'movement' from idea to idea. The cliché 'as quick as thought' was common in Greek verbal imagery: Homer spoke of 'ships swift as a bird's wing or thought' (Od. vii. 36); Thales said that, 'the mind is the swiftest of things for it runs through everything' (DL, Lives 1. 35); Cicero said that, 'nothing is speedier than the mind' (Tusc. Disp. 1. 19.43). In more summary fashion, Varro affirmed that, 'the mind is such that it flies in an instant of time wherever it wishes' (Ling. Lat. 6. 47).[112] In what follows Lucretius draws upon and extends the Epicurean doctrine of four kinds of atomic particles; each kind is of the same basic material, but differentiated by shape and texture; later the internal factor of resistance was added to these criteria. His explanation of the motion and action of other kinds of natural objects is couched in terms of the fluidity, motility and cohesiveness of these component particle features.

Lucretius employed two analogies to illustrate his point: the contrast in motility between water and honey, and that between a heap of poppy seeds and a heap of stones or corn ears (3. 180–205). There are two factors (not just one, as some scholars assume) that result in greater non-motility in things: first, the weight which ultimately depends on the size of the atoms, and the concomitant scarcity of void or empty space; second, the roughness (*asperitas*) of the atoms, which causes interlacing (or interlocking) and makes it difficult for things to separate. The heap of stones is difficult to separate by the wind's force because of their weight, the corn ears because of their roughness. The mass of honey clings together because its particles are not smooth and round. But soul-particles are at the other extreme for both factors: its particles are extremely small and thus very light in weight, and they are smooth and round, and thus not impeded in their motion. It is crucial in following Lucretius' argument from this point onward to realize that *corpora* and *semina* do not mean 'atoms', but 'particles' or 'seeds', since he goes on to claim that the soul-particles themselves are compounds of the four atomic elements: heat, air, wind and the fourth nature.

The nature of the *anima*, in contrast with the *animus*, consists in these properties: it has a thin texture, and it is contained in a small space. As soon as death occurs, there is no noticeable loss of body weight, only a loss of heat and breath, as well as loss of the proper feeling of life (*vitalem praeter sensum*). The whole *anima* is necessarily pervaded by small seeds, linked through the veins, marrow and nerves, such that when life departs the outer contour of the members (or limbs) is preserved unbroken (3. 208–20). He compares the departure of the soul from the body upon death to the dispersal of scent from a flower: the scent vanishes but the flower-body remains. The analogy of a scent to a flower with a soul-breath to an animal body was also a common Greek figure of speech.

The next long section of *De Rerum Natura* deals with the composition of both the *animus* and the *anima* from the four elements: wind, heat, air and the fourth. Before considering the details of this demonstration, let us bring out four salient issues. (1) Heat is anomalous alongside wind and air, since wind and air are substances (perhaps even the same substance), whereas heat is a property or quality;

---

[112] Cited in Bailey, vol. II, p. 1018; for this image in the tragedians, see Padel, 1992, pp. 96–8.

there has to be some *thing* in order for heat to be present or absent. (2) Wind (*ventus*) and air (*aer*) seem to be two forms or species of one thing; surely, one wants to say that wind is simply air in motion.[113] (3) Perhaps the ratio between the four elements, that is, the identity criteria of the various *anima-animus* functions, could be correlated with the degree of warm air in motion, in terms of a constant (air) with two variable factors (heat and motility). (4) Aside from this initial list of elements, Lucretius nowhere else refers to the fourth nature, and thus it is not clear what function this concept has in his scheme.

Up to this point, he has employed two pairs of element terms – heat (*calor* or *vapor*) and wind (*ventus* or *aura*) – but now he introduces air (*aer*). Much later he admits that 'wind is produced when air is agitated by motion' (6. 685), but in this particular context 'air' seems to take on a technical sense, as in Epicurus' 'air-*like* atoms'. When the air element is in motion it undergoes some sort of atomic metabolisis which transforms it into something similar, but subtly different. Such a hidden change might also lie beneath Lucretius' strange and obscure statement about the connection between air and heat:[114] 'It is a certain thin breath (*aura*) that deserts the dying, mingled with heat (*mixta vapore*), and heat draws the air with it. Nor is there any heat that has not air mixed with it. For since its nature is rare, it needs be that many first-beginnings of air move about in it' (*aeris inter eum primordia multa moveri*) (3. 232–6). Although his description of the intrinsic properties of these three elements may be vague, his later analysis of their componential functions in the operation of the whole soul is better worked out. Regarding the fourth unnamed nature, his account fares no better than his master Epicurus. Plutarch ridiculed the very notion of a fourth nature, and said that 'it is a confession of shamefaced ignorance to be unable to name what they cannot grasp' (Adv. Col. 20. 1118d).

Lucretius' concern with the process and structure of sensation is focused on the *anima*, and not the *animus*, as Cyril Bailey carefully explains:

> When an object impinges on the body, provided it is not so small as to fall between the nuclei [particles] of *anima* in the body, it comes in contact with a portion of the *anima* distributed through the limbs. At this point then, the 'nameless element' is first set in motion ... it then communicates the motion to the other elements of the *anima* in the ascending order of their grossness; first to heat, then to wind, then to air; air, the grossest element in the soul and therefore nearest akin to the composition of the body, sets the body in motion. It moves first the blood and the flesh, which are nearest to it, and also, being soft, the most sensitive parts. If the sensation, whether pleasurable or painful, is very acute and the motion therefore very violent, it may penetrate to the harder parts of the body, the bones, and even to the marrow. If the disturbance reaches as far as that ... then the result is fatal and the soul escapes through the pores of the body. But normally the painful movement is stopped or assuaged 'on the surface of the

---

[113] On the complex history of the elemental concepts of air and wind, see Kingsley, 1995, pp. 24–35; on wind images in connection with the human soul in the tragedians, see Padel, 1992, pp. 88–93.

[114] Perhaps this subtle shift in meaning between the two terms for 'air' lies behind the occult tradition that ascribes some significance to an individual's 'aura', above and beyond the airy breath in the soul.

body' (*in summo corpore*), so that the soul is retained within the body and life is preserved.[115]

Lucretius then moves on to describe the internal relations of the elements to one another and their effects (3. 258–322). The four elements together form a whole and act as a whole, such that no one element has either an independent existence or effect. The fourth element, he says, 'is the most hidden and beneath the others'; but by this phrase he does not mean that it is deeper within the body, rather, since it is composed of the very smallest particles, it is beneath or below our sensory perceptions. He has to use local or spatial terms to suggest what is in fact an epistemic relation between the three coarser elements and this fourth one. In Bailey's striking phrase, it is to the soul what the soul as a whole is to the body.[116] Lucretius inserts a word of caution here: the ratio of elements differs in each individual, such that every ensouled body manifests its own four-term coefficient. The doctrine of the four elements in various combinations producing the various humors or temperaments was common in Greek thought, especially Galenic and Stoic schemes, but with respect to their effect on the *animus* or *mens*, Lucretius is the only extant source.

In another passage he struggles to express a metaphysical insight into this hidden motive force. Here he says that *inter enim cursant primordia principorum motibus inter se, nil ut seceriner unum possit nec spatio fieri divisa potestas*. In our literal translation: 'for the first-beginnings course to and fro among themselves with the motions of principles, so that no single element can be set apart, nor can its powers be set in play divided from others by empty space; but they are, as it were, the many forces belonging to a single body' (3. 262–4).[117] Bailey offers his interpretation of this obscure statement:

> In the soul the atoms which compose each of the four elements are yet all mixed up with one another in their atomic movements. In consequence, the elements in the soul are not spatially separated: it would be impossible to say that *one* part of the soul is the air, another the heat, another the wind, another the *quarta natura*. Nor is their action thus spatially separated, heat acting in one part of the soul, wind in another, and so on. Just as their component atoms intermingle, so the effects of the four elements are the effects of the whole soul.[118]

Deep within the soul this nature lies hidden, nor is there anything deeper or further away than this in our bodies; it is, he says, the very soul of the whole soul (*anima est animae proporro totius ipsa*). Whereas, within our whole body and each of its members, the force of the mind and the power of the soul are secretly mixed (*latens mixta*), because it is formed of small and rare particles.[119] In such fashion the vital

---

[115] Bailey, vol. II, p. 1028.
[116] Bailey, vol. II, p. 1034.
[117] Note that the R. E. Latham & John Godwin translation of this passage completely obscures the references to *primordia* and *principia* and thus distorts the sense of the whole statement; Penguin Books, 1994, p. 73
[118] Bailey, vol. II, p. 1037.
[119] See Kerferd, 1971, for Lucretius' interpretation of the Greek concept of blending.

force lies concealed, and the soul is, as it were, the whole itself of the soul properly, and rules over (*dominatur*) the whole body. The three coarse elements are mingled together, but in different proportions depending on the individual's constitution and the circumstances that give rise to various sensations, perceptions and actions. For Lucretius, all particles are below the level where our senses could penetrate; even the combination of three (or four) kinds of atoms into a small cluster of *anima*-stuff is invisible and intangible. But as these clusters grow larger and larger (like dense smoke coalescing in one spot), the effects become more and more forceful to the extent that they 'emerge' into a conscious event, and are discernible to others in their outward bodily manifestations.

Lucretius argues that the *anima* and the body are intimately linked; the soul is totally blended with the animal body, such that the whole body has sensation. This faculty or power of sensation does not belong to the body in its own right (*proprium*), but is infused within it by the *anima* that possesses this power in itself. He follows Epicurean teaching in claiming that when the soul leaves the body at death the corpse does not have the power to feel or move.[120] He first makes this claim with regard to the sense of touch, but expands his inference to include all the sense organs, and then to include the *animus* or mind. Just as with simpler sensations, it is not the body that feels but the soul within and by means of the body, so also it is not the ears that hear and the eyes that see, but the soul within. The *anima* does so through the portals of the sense organs and the passages that connect them with the innermost 'dominant' *animus* or mind. He actually compares the eyes to windows or doorways through which the soul peers into the outer world.[121] In arguing in this fashion he directly confutes Stoic theory, a view clearly expressed by Cicero: 'For we do not even now perceive the things we see by our eyes; for there is no sensation in the body ... But there are, as it were, passages to the eyes and ears and nose, bored through from the seat of the mind (*sede animi*) ... so that it can easily be understood that it is the mind which sees and hears, and not those parts which are, as it were, the windows of the mind' (Tusc. Disp. 1. 20, 46).

In the opening stage of his first discussion about the nature of *anima* and *animus* Lucretius posited some relation between the two; at the close of this mini-treatise within Book Three he returns to this theme in considering the connections that *anima* and *animus* have with the animal body. The loss of *animus* causes immediate loss of life in the animal, but large parts of the *anima* may be lost while life remains. Strictly speaking, he means that, in the loss of a limb, the body-part with which a portion of *anima* is blended is separated from the whole. Here again Lucretius moves beyond his master Epicurus, or at least beyond what scholars can deduce from the extant fragments: 'So long as the soul (*psychē*) remains in the body, even though some other part of the body is lost, it will never lose sensation.' Lucretius, on the other hand, emphasizes the role of the mind (*animus*), which itself cannot be lost either whole or in part without loss of life: 'The mind is more the keeper of the bounds of life (*animus vitai claustra coercens*), more the ruler of life than the power of the soul (*anima*). For without the mind and understanding (*mente*

---

[120] Epicurus, in Long & Sedley, 1987, A14.
[121] Architectonic imagery made famous in the thirteenth century by Dante, in *Convivio*, 3.8. 9–10.

animoque) no part of the soul can hold out in the frame (*artus*) for a small [moment] of time, but follows in its train easily and scatters into air, and deserts the chill frame in the frost of death' (3. 395–401). He compares this loss of first principle within the soul to the loss of function in the pupil of the eye, such that, even if the rest of the eye (its orb) is undamaged, light sets and darkness enters. Thus, in such an intimate compact are the soul and the mind bound together forever (*hoc anima atque animus vincti sunt foedere semper*).

With these words Lucretius returns the reader's swift-winged thoughts to the opening where he spoke with such rhetorical force about the loss of life observed in a dying soldier's final moments. Cold pallor sets in, the breath stops, and motion ceases. All these first-hand reports and the detailed account of the material composition of the soul and mind are overwhelming evidence for his principal conclusion – that the soul of all living things is mortal, and that claims for immortality are baseless superstition. In the remainder of Book Three, itself twice the length of the accounts above, Lucretius parades thirty separate arguments to demonstrate the soul's mortal status. Some of these are little more than précis of more elaborate arguments in the first part, others are (apparently) derived from an unknown Epicurean source, and still others rely on dubious empirical evidence and faulty premises.[122] Still, the salutary lesson of this over-packed catalogue was unavoidable as early as the close of the first part. You may live on for many, many years, but death waits for you anyway; those who die later than earlier will not, because of that delay, have less time in everlasting non-existence.

---

[122] Bailey, vol. II, pp. 1089–94.

Chapter 3

From the New Testament to St. Augustine

(1) The New Testament and St. Paul's new vision

An amalgamation of Hebrew and Greek ideas about human nature slowly gathered momentum over several centuries, from the third century BCE to the first century CE; several writers attempted an overt syncretism in an effort to reconcile apparent inconsistencies in diverse 'schools' of thought. This conceptual and linguistic mingling took place in different regions at varying paces; a gradual verbal mapping of one set of terms onto another set of terms. At least three broad currents can be discerned during this period. First, the translation into Greek of the seventy main texts of the Hebrew Scriptures, the Septuagint (or LXX). This was produced in Lower Egypt in the early third century BCE, possibly on the instructions of the Pharaoh Ptolemy II; according to legend, this immense task was accomplished by 72 elders in 72 days in Alexandria. The Greek text of the Hebrew books quickly achieved an authoritative status, although it included some non-canonical texts whose Hebrew originals had been lost (the Apocrypha); some Jewish groups rejected the LXX and attempted to produce their own ultraliteral Greek translation.[1] Second, the incorporation into the Hebrew and Greek canon of non-Hebrew, alien texts, usually referred to as Wisdom Literature: the books of Proverbs, Job and Ecclesiastes, as well as Sirach and the Wisdom of Solomon from the Apocrypha.[2] These texts are unusual in that they present instructions regarding the correct conduct of life in various settings, especially the court, the school and the family. Greek concepts of human nature in the wisdom texts sometimes bridge the distance between Hebrew OT vocabulary and Greek NT vocabulary

Third, the obvious need observed by the Evangelists and St. Paul to reach the largest and most receptive contemporary audience. St. Paul's public exhortations and letters are addressed to specific Greek communities, for example, in Corinth, Thessalonia or Phillipi. As the result of Alexander the Great's sweeping invasion of the Near East and Middle East regions, numerous enduring Greek colonies became established in urban centers. Immigration, trade and communication between the Greek city states and the colonies in Magna Graecia brought a steady influx of medical, philosophical and popular ideas, including contemporary teachings about human nature. The diffusion of Platonic, Stoic, medical and magical ideas surrounding speculation about *psychē*, *nous* and *kardia* was gradual and patchy but pervasive.

Greek psychical terms are present to a greater or lesser degree in different clusters of Biblical texts: the LXX, Wisdom, the Four Gospels, St. Paul, Qumran

---

[1] OCB, 1993, p. 752.
[2] OCB, 1993, pp. 801–3.

(the Dead Sea Scrolls), Rabbinic and Gnostic literature. The Greek language of the NT is very similar to the *koinē* (common) dialect, but preserves its native Semitic tone and modes of speech; it diverges from Hellenistic *koinē* in coining new words to express OT-specific ideas and uses older words with newer Christian and Jewish connotations. In connection with the diffusion of new words, different texts present greater or lesser agreement with accepted Hellenistic usage of psychical terms. Near one extreme one finds Philo's erudite attempts to bring about an accommodation or compromise between basic Hebrew concepts and Greek philosophical usage, and at the other, St. Paul's idiosyncratic and (nearly) unprecedented doctrines about *sōma* and *sarx*, the psychical body and the spiritual body.

In the LXX, including the Apocrypha, *psychē* occurs more than 900 times, occurrences distributed fairly evenly among the various books. It is most often the Greek translation for the Hebrew *nepesh*, but also 25 times for *leb* (heart). This preponderance in favor of *nepesh* indicates that *psychē* renders *nepesh* where *nepesh* had been used to signify the living element or principle in human or animal being. It also more specifically indicates the affective and volitional aspect of human being, the seat of the emotions, love, longing and gladness:

> The 'soul' reveals its life in movement and the most various expressions of the emotions. It is the uniting factor for the inner powers of man: hence the phrase 'with all your soul'. (Deut 12:20) Within the soul dwell the desire for food, the lust of the flesh, and the thirst for murder and revenge. The soul expresses its feelings: it weeps, is poured out in tears, is 'made long' in patient endurance. But knowledge and understanding, thought and memory have their seat in the soul as well.[3]

The usage of the Greek term *psychē* to render *nepesh*, however, does not bring with it any of the dualist connotations associated with the Greek *concept*, for example, in Plato's middle works or Hippocratic medicine: 'A clear indication of how unfamiliar the OT is with the concept of a soul separate from the body, or a soul which becomes separated from the body at death, is the fact that it can speak of a dead person as the *soul* of that person, and mean by this phrase the dead person in his corporeality.'[4] With regard to the distinction between *psychē* as life-force and *psychē* as spirit or mind, Schweizer comments: 'in classical and post-classical Greek, both meanings are connected with the common idea of the soul as an immaterial, or at least invisible, essential core of man that can be thought of as distinct from the body. It gives worth and duration to the human self beyond the limits of physical existence. This idea is in every way alien to the OT.'[5]

On the other hand, the conceptual distinction between soul and body common to Greek thought in the third century appears more often in non-canonical writings, whether originally composed in Greek or merely preserved in a Greek version from a non-Hebrew source, sometimes Egyptian: 'In Wisdom, the ideas connected with *psychē* are wholly Greek. The body/soul antithesis dominates religious and moral thinking. The body is a burden for the soul or its noblest part, the *nous* or *logismos*

---

[3] Brown, 1978a, p. 680; see esp. D. Lys, 1966.
[4] Brown, 1978a, p. 680.
[5] Schweizer et al., 1975c, p. 632.

... yet unlike Gnostic texts, Wisdom never says that soul is or contains a truly divine constituent. The whole man is God's creature, even though he is destined for immortality as the image of his creator.'[6] There are several passages in the Wisdom of Solomon that strongly exhibit a dualistic picture of *sōma* and *psychē*: 'wisdom will not enter a deceitful soul, nor dwell in a body enslaved to sin' (Wisd. 1:4). The immortality of the soul is clearly indicated in the passage, 'the souls of the righteous are in the hand of God and no torment will ever touch them'; the wise have renounced or foresworn sin, and can expect another life beyond their earthly life, whereas the foolish think that bodily death is the end, and cannot themselves hope for another better life. Where the opening verse of Chapter 7 refers to the molding of the human body in the mother's womb prior to birth, another parallel verse in Chapter 8 seems to refer to the pre-existence of the human soul *before* its 'capture' by the embryo: 'and a good soul fell to my lot; or rather, being good, I entered an undefiled body' (Wisd. 8:19–20). 'Though undefiled at first, the body is perishable (*phthartos*), corruptible not in the sense of sinful by nature but in the sense of liable to sin and decay – and as such "weighs down the soul". The duality is plain, but even here we have not reached the full dualism of Hellenistic thought, in which evil is more closely allied with the body.'[7] At death the body returns to the earth and the soul to God who lent the person its soul (Wisd. 15:8).

In the Book of Baruch, 'the dead are those who are in Hades, whose spirit (*pneuma*) has been taken from their bodies' (Baruch 2:17); in the Second Apocalypse of Baruch, the speaker refers to the existence of souls before and after their earthly life, and further the reuniting of the souls and bodies of the righteous (that is, the wise) at the second coming, and the grief-laden continuation of bodiless existence for the souls of the wicked (that is, the foolish). Job describes the final state of the righteous person in terms of death for the body and blessed immortality for the spirit: 'and their bones shall rest in the earth and their spirits shall have much joy' (Job 23:31). According to Enoch, the souls of righteous martyrs make suit to God (Enoch 9:3); later Enoch tells the reader that certain 'hollow places have been created for this very purpose, that the spirits of the souls of the dead should assemble therein' (Enoch 22:3) – spirit *of* the soul *of* the dead sounds like a strange pleonasm. It is not clear how a spirit can be predicated of a soul, even the soul of a dead person. Many other verses[8] discuss the different post-mortem results of a righteous versus a wicked life; in some cases the punishment for the wicked is a diseased and degraded *bodily life*, in others it is a burning and miserable *spiritual life* in the afterworld; though for the righteous, it brings healing of bodily infirmities and spiritual bliss in the afterlife (Enoch 51:1; 67:8–9; 98:3; 103:3–8).

Hellenistic ideas about the nature of *psychē* and its relation to the human body are also clearly discernible in late Judaic texts of this period, especially the apocryphal books of Maccabees, which several times explicitly demonstrates body–soul dualism in so far as the immortal soul separates itself from the body in death. According to the speaker, death is the right way to immortality, the victor's prize for virtue is an everlasting life for the soul; at the hour of death the soul of the righteous is received

---

[6] Schweizer et al., 1975c, p. 632.
[7] Gundry, 1976, p. 88.
[8] See also Schweizer et al., 1975c, p. 633; Brown, 1978a, p. 682.

by the patriarchs. According to Colin Brown, the late Judaic concept of psychic afterlife is in the immediate background of two passages from the NT in Luke: when Lazarus is taken into Abraham's bosom (Luke 16:23) and in the phrase, 'Today you will be with me in paradise' (Luke 23:43). On the other hand, he argues, we do not find the notion that there are two separate judgments for body and soul:

> Rather we have the picture of a resurrection, where God will bring the soul and the body together and judges them both. There is thus no room for the notion of the soul as the location of ideas, thoughts, and moral conviction, with the body as the seat of the passions. Despite Hellenistic ideas about the soul, the typical Jewish hope remains of a resurrection, and thus of the righteousness of God, which can only then come into play.[9]

Philo Judaeus (Alexandria) (*c*.20 BC–40 CE) occupies a special place in this history, mainly because of his highly informed knowledge about both Greek philosophical discussions *and* Hebrew rituals and traditions. The son of a wealthy and prominent family in Alexandria, little is known about his life; although he made a pilgrimage to Jerusalem, he need not have had much contact with Palestine. In his old age, the Egyptian Jewish community sent him as the head of their delegation to Rome to seek redress from the Emperor for the wrongs that the Romans had inflicted on the Jews. Many of his extensive writings survive intact, preserved in the library of Caesarea built by Origen and catalogued by Eusebius. Three-fourths of the corpus consists of exposition of the Pentateuch in three series. The bulk of his work is devoted to an interpretation of the scriptural teachings in terms of Greek philosophical concepts, and an effort to revise Greek philosophical argument in light of these scriptural teachings. Of the various concepts of God in Greek thought, Philo considered the one most compatible with Biblical teaching to be Plato's concept of God in the *Timaeus*: a divine being who had existed from eternity without a world, and then after he had brought the world into being, continued to exist as an incorporeal being beyond or outside the corporeal world. Using a new method to harmonize inconsistencies in the diverse and multiform Biblical texts, Philo attempted to reconcile the *Timaeus* with Hebrew thought by endowing the divine ideas with two stages of existence: first, from eternity the ideas existed as the thoughts of God; and then prior to the world's creation, they were created by God as real beings.

Philo's interpretation of the Platonic ideas, whose original domain had been a timeless, other-worldly realm, integrated them into an *intelligible* world, an expression that does not occur in Greek philosophic speculation before him, as Wolfson points out.[10] He adopted Aristotle's claim that the thinking or rational soul (*nous*) is the 'place of forms' and then asserted that the intelligible world had its place in Nous, which under the influence of LXX terminology, he also named Logos. Just as he could not accept that the ideas themselves were eternal, so also Philo could not accept that the pre-existent matter out of which the world was created was eternal. He solved this difficulty by arguing that there had been two creations: the creation of pre-existent matter out of nothing, and the creation of the

---

[9] Brown, 1978a, p. 682; see Neusner, 2000, pp. 1342–6.
[10] Wolfson, 1967, pp. 151–2 for this short biography.

world out of that matter. God, he said, was an all-powerful free agent, who did not have to create this world (or any other world) and who could, if he chose, de-create the world through its destruction. God exercised governance over this world through direct supervision and, where need arose, through suspension of natural laws; he governed human beings through providence exercised over each individual.

Philo's understanding of the human soul is derived in large part from his attempts to harmonize Plato's doctrines; given the sometimes disparate and even incompatible statements made by Plato about the soul, from the early to the late dialogues, this would have been a complex task. Philo distinguished between irrational souls, created together with the bodies of humans and animals, and rational souls created at the creation of the world, prior to their 'capture' in bodies. From the plenitude of pre-existent rational souls, some remain bodiless whereas others become invested with bodies. Philo reconciled this doctrine with both the Biblical references to angels and the Greek references to demons and semi-divine heroes. In one passage he writes of higher beings that join themselves with mortal bodies for a specific length of time and then leave them again. He further claims that the pre-existent rational souls that become embodied are equal in number to the celestial spheres; they are placed in newly born humans whose bodies are already endowed with irrational souls. Whereas the rational souls are immortal, the irrational souls die with their bodies. But where for Plato, say in the *Phaedrus* or the *Timaeus*, the soul is immortal in its nature (*phusis*) and thus cannot be destroyed, for Philo the soul's immortality is the result of God's grace, endowed through his will and power, and thus *can* be destroyed if the individual proves itself unworthy of this gift.[11]

Philo is familiar with the Platonic division of the soul into three parts (or forms) and Aristotle's distinction of three kinds of soul, as well as its eight functions. Following Stoic and medical theories, he identified the inferior or irrational part with the blood and the superior or rational part with *nous* or mind, which he calls the 'soul of the soul' (*psychē tis psychēs*). The nature (*phusis*) of the rational soul (the *logismos*) is the divine spirit (*pneuma*); but Philo also connects *logos* and *nous* in the Gnostic fashion, namely, that the *logos* is the receptacle or vehicle of *nous*.[12] In general, the soul is the seat of the emotions, especially the virtues, through whose practice it achieves eternal life; whereas *nous* is expressed in thinking, willing, reproduction and perception. In symmetry with its pre-existent state before birth in bodily form, after death the soul returns to the world of imperishable and incorruptible things. The soul is really only at home in the divine world, and is imprisoned or entombed during its bodily existence. Since the soul is in constant motion, it belongs to God who is himself the all-encompassing world-soul, and thus is in constant, eternal motion.[13]

Henry Chadwick offers a tidy summary of the principal features which connect Philo's doctrine of soul with mainstream Greek ideas of his day. He says that the dualist tendency becomes quite pronounced when Philo comes to expound his ethical point-of-view. The 'coat of skins' that clothed Adam and Eve after the fall

---

[11] Wolfson, 1967, pp. 151–2; derived from his earlier work, Wolfson, 1962, vol. I, pp. 360–423.
[12] Schweizer et al., 1975a, p. 635.
[13] Brown, 1978a, p. 681.

from grace referred to their bodies. The soul dwells in the body as in a tomb and carries it around like a corpse. He approves of Aristotle's notion that the good can include external, physical things, not just the moral good of the soul; although he sometimes adopts the more austere Stoic view that the only true good is what is good for the soul. In general, Philo's ethics inclines towards 'a world-denying asceticism', even though he disapproves of needless bodily mortification and self-degradation. During the term of an individual's earthly life, the soul is a pilgrim and visitor, 'like Abraham when he migrated from the astral religion of Ur to the true religion of the promised land, or the Israelites wandering in the wilderness'. But Philo's attitude to the body–soul relation implies more than just detachment from the earthly sphere: 'in the course of spiritual self-discipline the soul comes increasingly to realize that the body is a major obstacle to perfection'.[14]

Josephus is another important source for our understanding of Greek-Hebrew syncretistic doctrines about soul and *psyche*. A native of Palestine (*c*.37–100 CE), from a priestly family, he received a thorough training in the Jewish Law, lived for three years in the desert as the disciple of a hermit, and went to Rome to plead for the release of Jews held as prisoners. He became one of the leading Jewish commanders in their struggle against Roman oppression, and though his actions in two famous sieges inspired the suspicion that he might have betrayed his comrades, no evidence for this has ever been adduced. Still, he was an admirer of Roman civilization and spent much of the last thirty years of his life at the Roman court, where he composed *The Jewish War*, the *Antiquities of the Jews*, an autobiography, and a defense against current anti-Jewish sentiments.[15] According to Josephus, for the Essenes soul and body together comprise the whole person; they resign their souls confident in the hope of receiving them again. They believe that their bodies are perishable because of the impermanence of matter, but that their souls are immortal; the soul emanates from very fine ether, becomes entangled in the bodily prison, and thus dragged down to earth. The souls of the righteous are borne aloft to enjoy bliss in paradise, whereas the souls of the wicked plunge into a dungeon full of torments. He favorably compares some of these Hebrew notions with Greek ideas; *psyche* refers to the inner person, whose various powers and functions include thought, perception and memory; the *psyche* is the locus of the will and the emotions.

Josephus reports that the Pharisees believe that every soul is immortal, that good souls enjoy reward and evil souls receive punishment, and that only good souls can enter into other bodies. He also reports that Eleazar (leader of the rebels at Masada) claimed that death liberates the soul from its bodily prison to depart for its own pure abode, and that sleep provides a temporary liberation of the same sort;[16] this accords more or less with one of the Stoic doctrines about temporary loss of soul. Josephus sometimes seems to express his own personal views on these questions, for example, when he admires a soldier whose body had been wasted but whose soul was heroic. When he urges his close friends not to commit suicide in resistance to the Romans, he says, 'why separate the very fond friends body and soul? (or

---
[14] Chadwick, in CHLGEMP, 1970, pp. 146–7.
[15] ODCC, 1990, p. 759.
[16] Crossan, 1998, pp. xxii–iv.

body from soul)'. He writes that souls are planted in bodies at conception and separated at death, the immortal soul ascends to heaven to await its resurrected body.[17] In one passage of the *Antiquities*, he attempts to explain the Jewish ritual of animal slaughter by equating blood with *psychē* in the Mosaic Law. However, his use of *pneuma* in other passages does not show any clear differentiation from *psychē*, nor any reflection on how these two concepts are unified in late Judaic and Christian thought.[18]

In the NT, the sense of *psychē* expands its range and becomes more determinate; *psychē* indicates something distinctive about human being as the carrier of life-force; *psychē* sets off identity-criteria for what gives (or keeps) life in human nature, both life in this world and the world to come. In Matthew, *psychē* is the life of the child Jesus which his enemies are seeking (Matt. 2:20); in Luke, it is the rich farmer's *psychē* which is required by God (Luke 12:20). There is an implicit criticism here of an idea of life-in-this-world, since a person's life is on loan from God, according to Schweizer:

> The earthly life is taken so seriously that in sickness it is not worth calling real life at all. The mere movement of the heart or drawing of breath is not enough. Life has content here as the full life which God intended at creation. It is not just a formal concept. We can easily see why in the last resort life can properly be called this only when it is lived in God's service and to God's praise, so that the question of greater or smaller physical powers or the degree of health is a subsidiary one.[19]

Insofar as *psychē* primarily indicates the physical life of human being, it can be the agent of the slaying, giving, hating and persecuting of souls; the soul is limited and constrained by the fact of death. Yet the soul cannot be separated from human or animal being; many NT passages strongly suggest that what is at issue is not the phenomenon of life in general, but the life that is manifest in the individual human.

Matthew, for example, lays heavy emphasis on the new interpretation of Mosaic Law and the coming judgment; thus *psychē* for him means the individual self that lives its life 'before God' (that is, in God's full view) and will one day have to give an account to him at the last judgment. John refers to the *psychē* in the sense of the inner 'place', the center of the inner person, who can decide for or against Jesus: 'how long do you hold our soul in suspense?' (John 10:24). In Luke also, the soul is addressed in an inner soliloquy; it has its own goods, it can take its ease, eating, drinking and making merry (Luke 12:19) – an interesting passage since it refers to both physical and psychical activities.[20] In many collateral passages, *psychē* is mentioned along with *pneuma*: 'stress is thereby laid on the fact that such activity of the *psychē* is ultimately the gift and work of God.'[21] In this usage, *psychē* is contrasted with *pneuma*, since *psychē* marks out the individual human as such, the one who can be moved inwardly through reflection, who can be influenced by

---

[17] Gundry, 1976, pp. 90–91.
[18] Brown, 1978a, p. 681.
[19] Schweizer et al., 1975c, pp. 638–9.
[20] See Brown, 1978a, pp. 684–5.
[21] Schweizer et al., 1975c, p. 641.

others, who can suffer and undergo passions and affections. It is thus closely related to the Greek concept conveyed by the term *kardia*, though it is related to the Hebrew *leb* or *lebab* only when OT formulae are adopted by the NT speakers.

Jesus himself often employs *psychē* in a manner that clearly indicates its connection (if not identification) with life; one of the best-known examples is his synoptic statement: 'For those who want to save their life (*psychē*) will lose it, and those who lose their life (*psychē*) for my sake will save (or find) it. What does it profit them if they gain the whole world, but forfeit themselves?' (Luke 9:24; Matt. 16:25; Mark 8:35). The original form of this saying may have been, 'he who would save his soul will lose it, and he who loses his soul will save it.'[22] Both the reference to preserving the soul as life and the losing of soul as life show that Jesus is telling humans that they will achieve *full* or *true* life only when they no longer cling to it, but find it through loss or sacrifice. Thus, as before, soul as life is the kind of thing that can be risked by one's actions. Jesus' sacrifice of *his* life leads to his disciples' willingness to risk their own souls; but it is said only of Jesus that he has the power to take up his life again. In saying this of himself he intends that *psychē* be taken to mean an individual life possible after death, and not merely the vehicle that carries life in this world. Moreover, the inescapable fact of death is not stronger than this life, since a human will find his life (that is, soul) only in giving it up; the soul will be preserved by God in spite of the loss of physical life. In Luke also, it seems likely that the active sense of the verb 'to win' or 'to gain' points toward the primary meaning of *psychē* as eternal life, one's life in the afterworld. The connection between Luke 17:20 and the later passage in 17:32 shows that he loses his true life who looks back on his life like Lot's wife and cannot detach himself from it; whereas he wins true life who gives it up.

Schweizer comments on this interpretation of soul *qua* life in terms of the more real life to come: 'The awakening to eternal life is not a magical change, for the believer already has *psychē*. Again, the *psychē* is not an immortal soul, for otherwise we should not be called upon to hate it. *Psychē* is the life which is given to man by God and which through man's attitude towards God receives its character as either mortal or eternal.' The parallel passage in John says, 'Those who love their life lose it, and those who hate their life in this world will keep it for eternal life' (John 12:25). Schweizer writes, 'In John there can be no question of possession [of one's own life]. Life is kept by God for eternity only in the lasting sacrifice of life and in permanently living by the gift of God.'[23] One can draw the conclusion that in all variants of this saying, the soul is the life given by God, none other than this physical life; but the emphasis should be on life as the *gift* of God and lived in his sight. It is the life lived in one's physical body (*sōma*) which can lose itself or find itself, and which will be brought to fullness at the Last Judgment. The human soul then is not a substance that survives bodily death; it is life under God's gift or decision.

Matthew refers to God's power to destroy the soul *and* the body in Hades (or Sheol) (Matt. 10:28), and this idea is clearly opposed to the idea that the soul itself is immortal, as Schweizer points out:

---

[22] Schweizer et al., 1975c, p. 642 note 156.
[23] Schweizer et al., 1975c, p. 644; see Brown, 1978a, p. 682.

God alone controls the whole man, *psychē* as well as *sōma*. It can hardly be contested that Greek ideas have influenced the formulation. Nevertheless, the saying is to be understood in terms of the development indicated and its point is that man can end only the life which is in some way limited by the earthly *sōma* and which is not, then, life in the true sense. As man does not really control his life, since sickness and sin already threaten it, and it is thus death rather then life, so it is not in the power of men to end it.[24]

Luke in the Acts of the Apostles (Acts 2:31) interprets *psychē* in the Psalms as person and places the stress on flesh (*sarx*) instead of body (*sōma*); in this fashion he can claim that Jesus' flesh did not undergo corruption after his death. Further, he also seems to presuppose that after death the person as a whole will either undergo the torments of Hell or the pleasures of Paradise. When he describes Jesus' resurrection on the third day, Luke portrays Christ's wounds and scars with great physical realism and distinguishes his appearance from that of a shade or double (Luke 16:22, 23:43). At only one place does Luke refer to the flesh and bones (in the Hebrew sense) that accompany the soul after bodily death (Luke 24:39) – this is an enigmatic and difficult passage to understand. Schweizer comments on Luke's unusual claims about the future state of the soul and its attendant properties: 'the *psychē* is now something that one only attains to. If it might be inferred from the other sayings that true life is simply given when it is orientated to God and does not seek itself, *psychē* here is plainly understood as eternal life. On the other hand, this saying, too, steers clear of the idea that Luke rejects, namely, that of an immortal soul which man does not attain to only in the future.'[25] In an analogous context, Matthew reports Jesus' saying, 'Do not fear those who kill the body but cannot kill the soul; rather fear him who can destroy both soul and body in Gehenna' (Matt. 10:28). Gundry interprets this passage to harmonize with Luke: 'The distinction between body and soul is clear. So also is their separability in that man can kill the body but not the soul. We might reason in the opposite direction that the destruction is of both soul *and* body.'[26]

St. Paul's picture of human nature is different in subtle ways than the other evangelists' portrayal.[27] Although Paul was quite clearly aware of both Hellenistic and Late Judaic soul concepts he either chose to ignore or bypass them on most occasions. Schweizer's succinct statement of Paul's point of view can stand as the motto for this section: 'Paul does not think in such strongly Greek terms that he can adopt the Hellenistic idea of the soul, nor in such strongly non-Greek terms that he can ignore the fact that in Greek culture *psuchē* means something different than *nepesh*.'[28] In his careful and impartial manner, James Dunn makes a similar preliminary assessment: 'Still more confusing has been the long-running debate on whether Paul's anthropology was influenced more by Hellenistic or by Jewish categories and to apportion Paul's ideas accordingly.'[29] Dunn goes on to caution

---

[24] Schweizer et al., 1975c, p. 646; see Brown, 1978a, p. 686.
[25] Schweizer et al., 1975c, p. 647.
[26] Gundry, 1976, pp. 114–15.
[27] Childs, 1992, pp. 580–85.
[28] Schweizer et al., 1975c, p. 648; see Chamblin's summary, 1993, p. 766.
[29] Dunn, 1998, p. 54; see also Heckel, in Wright & Potter, 2000, pp. 117–20.

any interpreter who attempts to read Paul's meaning for psychical and human-nature terms 'straight from the diverse Hebrew and Greek use of these terms'; it is the special way that he makes use of these terms that lends Paul's view its distinctive character. But Dunn also wisely points out that Bultmann's extremely influential interpretation of Paul's doctrines – the human being infused with Christ's spirit can be *identified* with his body (*sōma*) – accords the Hebrew influence greater weight over the Greek.[30] In response to the predominant viewpoint, Robert Gundry has devoted much effort to carefully marshalling arguments *against* Bultmann's highly biased interpretation (which we cannot pass in review here).[31] Although it may seem to be stating the obvious, it is worth pointing out that Paul was not engaged in any kind of philosophical discussion; rather, he was addressing common people, bringing Christ's message about the true relation of human beings to God, their moral duties to one another, and their hopes for salvation.

The overwhelming importance of the term *sōma* for St. Paul can be readily discerned in his body-oriented language, but on this basis alone it is not possible to make the kind of definitive assertion that Bultmann does. Paul says that given over to the desires of the heart, fallen human beings dishonor their bodies (Rom. 1:24). Husband and wife have authority over each other's bodies (1Cor. 7:4): Paul will be present in the spirit, though absent in the body (1Cor. 5:3); and he recalls an out-of-the-body experience (2Cor. 12:2). Dunn argues that these and many other uses of *sōma* primarily indicate that Paul's concept of body, beyond the normal, everyday sense of physical body, is 'a corporate whole or corporation' (surely an ironical phrase seeing that *corpus* renders *sōma* in Latinate vocabulary), that is, individuals in their bodies 'working together in harmony for a common purpose'.[32] Robinson has made a comparable assessment: 'the flesh-body was not what partitioned a man off from his neighbor; it was rather what bound him in the bundle of life with all men and nature.'[33] Paul's most distinctive use of the concept of body, one which clearly differentiates his picture of human nature from both the Greek and the Hebrew, is the diremption between the present living body and the resurrected body in First Corinthians (1Cor. 15), to which we shall return after the ground has been better laid.

Dunn summarizes his analyses of the diverse and sometimes perplexing references to body as a psychical agent in Paul's letters in these lucid terms:

> ... *sōma* expresses for Paul the character of created humankind – that is, as embodied existence. It is precisely as embodied, and by means of this embodiment, that the person participates in creation and functions as part of creation. The body, the body corporeal and not just the body corporate, is what makes possible a social dimension to life, [it] is what enables the individual to participate in human society, or ... what prevents the individual from opting out of this world, or constructing a religion which denies social interdependence and responsibility.[34]

---

[30] Dunn, 1998, p. 55.
[31] Gundry, 1976, pp. 135–56.
[32] Dunn, 1998, p. 57.
[33] Robinson, 1952, p. 15.
[34] Dunn, 1998, p. 61; see Motyer, 1978, pp. 238–41.

Despite Dunn's initial qualms to the contrary, this (frankly modernist) attitude is surprisingly similar to the Heidegger-inspired existential orientation of Bultmann, with his emphasis on the lived-body, sociality, inter-subjectivity, and so forth. As mentioned earlier, Robert Gundry, in his valiant efforts to counter this prevalent interpretation, compels each of Bultmann's arguments, and each of the texts cited, to pass muster. His fine-grained, decidedly more impartial linguistic investigations demolish the complex edifice built around several fundamental assumptions about the reference of key terms such as *sōma* and *sarx*:

> We conclude that in neither the Pauline epistles, nor the literature of the NT outside these epistles, nor the LXX, nor the extra-Biblical ancient Greek literature does the definition [for *sōma*] 'whole person' find convincing support ... Aside from its use for a corpse, *sōma* refers to the physical body in its proper and intended union with the soul/spirit. But *sōma* does not *mean* 'whole person', because its use is designed to call attention to the physical object which is the body of the person, rather than to the whole personality. Where used of whole people, *sōma* directs attention to their bodies, not to the wholeness of their being.[35]

Another important psychical term for Paul is *sarx*, usually translated 'flesh'; the Apostle used this very often in contrast with *sōma*. The Hebrew OT and the LXX translators had only one word at their disposal (*basar*), which can mean either an animal's body or its flesh, that is, its soft tissue. Paul uses *sarx* almost 100 times, and 26 times in Romans alone, about three times more than all the other Gospels together; no Pauline term has generated more controversy than *sarx*. Scholarly disagreement is reflected in the more up-to-date English versions of the NT where *sarx* has been rendered by at least a dozen different English words and phrases.[36] R. Jewett and James Dunn have sifted through all the passages in which *sarx* occurs and have managed to construct a spectrum or continuum of meanings, all of whose nuances lie on one axis. The spectrum of shades of meanings ranges over the following contexts: *sarx* is weak and cannot inherit the kingdom of God; it is perishable and mortal, subject to affliction and weariness; its weakness has moral overtones, such that no person *qua* flesh can ever be justified before God. Further, *sarx* is the sphere or domain of sin, or at least the tendency to sin; it is wayward, fickle and deviant, whereas the spirit (*pneuma*) follows the right path; it can be the source of corruption and even hostility to God.

Regarding this wide range of meanings, Dunn comments:

> There is a common link throughout, namely, *sarx* denoting what we might describe as human mortality. It is the continuum of human mortality, the person characterized and conditioned by human frailty, which gives *sarx* its spectrum of meanings and which provides the link between Paul's different uses of the term. The spectrum runs from human relations and needs, through human weaknesses and desires, through human

---

[35] Gundry, 1976, pp. 79–80; Chamblin says, 'terms for a corporeal or incorporeal function (such as *sōma* or *pneuma*) may be applied by synecdoche to the whole person, but what represents the whole is not equated with the whole', Chamblin, in Hawthorne & Martin, 1993, p. 767.

[36] Thiselton, 1978, pp. 680–82.

imperfection and corruption, to the fully deprecatory and condemnatory tone of the *sarx-pneuma* antithesis.[37]

But the distinction repeatedly drawn by Paul between *sōma* and *sarx* does not show any kind of substance or thing-like duality, at least not without the additional concepts of *psychē* and *pneuma*. They are not separate or separable things or entities; rather, they refer to modes of human existence. Thus, Paul draws our attention to the important difference between the life lived *in* the flesh (*en sarki*), an inescapable condition of humans as bodily beings, and life lived *by* the flesh (*kata sarki*), a morally culpable manner of living, one which must be abandoned in order to attain the kingdom of God and the chance for resurrection.

One plausible conjecture about the ambiguity and perplexity of Paul's usage is that there was no clear distinction between a neutral and a moral sense of flesh. One of the definitive passages on this score is from First Corinthians: 'flesh and blood cannot inherit the kingdom of God, it is the body which will' (1Cor. 15:35). The doctrines that the *body* will attain redemption (Rom. 8:23), that the flesh will be dissolved and destroyed (1Cor. 5:5), and that the body will be regained at resurrection comprise an enigmatic and difficult teaching (to which we shall return later). Dunn queries the source of Paul's distinction between flesh and body and argues that

> ... he was combining elements of Hebrew and Greek anthropology into a new synthesis. On the one hand he affirmed the more holistic Hebrew understanding of human embodiment, with what that meant for the corporeality and corporateness of human existence as integral to being human. At the same time he recognized something of importance in the more negative Greek attitude to existence 'in the flesh', which he also wanted to affirm. For Paul, however, the negative factor was not simply bodily existence itself but the ephemeral character of human existence as existence in desiring, decaying flesh which, as it is focused on and clung to, subverts that existence as existence before and for God.[38]

This statement about Paul's efforts to reconcile opposing views of the 'nature' of flesh and its relation to bodily salvation is surely correct, but imputes to Paul and his audience an understanding of *existence* as a primordial dimension of human being, an existential dimension the concept of which was simply not articulable by either the philosophical or religious mentality of that epoch.

Although *sōma* and *sarx* are obviously the most significant concepts in Paul's picture of human nature, our presentation must include some reference to other salient psychical terms, such as *nous* and *kardia*, *psychē* and *pneuma*, in order to gain a better and fuller understanding. One of the key features of Paul's thoughts on the subject regards the body's renewal at resurrection, and this strange and puzzling teaching is not graspable without the distinction between *psychē* and *pneuma*. The word *nous* occurs only 21 times in Paul's letters, most of them in Romans; it was

---

[37] Dunn, 1998, p. 66; see Schnelle, 1996, pp. 59–63; Robinson, 1952, p. 25.
[38] Dunn, 1998, p. 72; in close harmony with Robinson on this point, Robinson, 1952, p. 31.

also infrequent and irregular in the LXX and in the other gospels. In Romans, Paul says that the human mind (*nous*) perceives the being and nature of God (Rom. 1:20); it is with his mind that he approves God's law (Rom. 7:23); the transformation of Christian existence takes place through renewal of the mind (Rom. 12:2; Eph. 4:23); it was of great importance that his mind conformed to that of Christ (1Cor. 2:16). In several passages Paul refers to the mind in contention with, or set over against, flesh or spirit:[39] 'With my mind I am a slave to the law of God, but with my flesh I am a slave to the law of sin' (Rom. 7:25), and 'I will pray with the spirit (*pneuma*), but I will pray with the mind (*nous*) also; I will sing praise with the spirit, but I will sing praise with the mind also' (1Cor. 14:15). Paul's occasional employment of *nous* may simply indicate his acknowledgment of his non-Jewish audience, one more accustomed to normal Greek usage.

The word *kardia*, 'heart', occurs 52 times in Paul's letters (one-third of all NT usage), 15 times in Romans alone; it can equally well reflect Hebrew or Greek usage. In Paul's letters, it generally refers to the innermost 'part' (or aspect) of the person, the seat of emotions, thought, and volition.[40] God is the one who searches the heart (Rom. 8:27); God's law must penetrate to the heart (Rom. 2:15); obedience and belief come from the heart (Rom. 6:17); love, anguish and desire are said to arise within the heart. This usage accords well with common Greek usage in this period in denoting the organ or locus of decisions and reflections (1Cor. 7:37; 2Cor. 9:7): 'It was important for Paul that the experience of God's grace penetrated to the innermost depths of a person and that the corresponding faith was an expression of deeply felt commitment.'[41] That brings the NT concept of *kardia* very close to the OT concept of *leb*, the seat or source of cognition and reflection.

In the entire New Testament, the word *psychē* occurs only about 100 times, and Paul follows this general pattern in using *psychē* only 13 times, thus making it his least common psychical term. Paul is aware of the importance of the concept of *psychē* for his Greek audience and attempts to correlate some of his remarks with this presumed usage. On the basis of such a small sample, it is difficult to offer a conjecture about the precise place of this concept in his overall picture, but one can readily observe that Paul never speaks of *psychē* in a negative tone. His use of *psychē* is rather neutral, carefully balanced between one side and another; *pneuma* is always the opposite of *sarx* or *nous* in the unbeliever, never the opposite of *psychē*. In the main he uses it in a fairly conventional NT sense to refer to the whole person, the seat of life or even life itself, but with the patent restriction to life in this world, life lived 'in the face of God'. Schweizer astutely points out that there is one place where it is surprising that Paul does *not* have a doctrine of soul, namely, in his Letter to the Colossians: 'The absence of a doctrine of the soul is all the more astonishing in view of the fact that the Colossian heretics taught a Jewish brand of Neo-Pythagoreanism in which the purification of the soul from everything earthly and its ascent to the highest element where Christ dwells occupies a central place.'[42]

---

[39] For detailed analysis, see Gundry, 1976, pp. 90–5; Jewett, 1971, pp. 378–80.
[40] J. Behm, in TDNT, vol. III, pp. 606–10; Schnelle, 1996, pp. 102–7.
[41] Dunn, 1998, p. 75.
[42] Schweizer et al., 1975c, p. 650.

In Alexander Polyhistor (fl. after 105 BCE) all the terms of the Letter to the Colossians, Chapter 2, occur in a fragment of an anonymous Pythagorean document.[43]

The most difficult passage to interpret is from the Letter to the Hebrews, where the author says that the word of God penetrates to the inner 'part' or aspect of the person:[44] 'Indeed, the word of God is living and active, sharper than any two-edged sword, piercing until it divides soul from spirit, joints from marrow; it is able to judge the thoughts and intentions of the heart. And before him no creature is hidden, but all are naked and laid bare to the eyes of one to whom we must render an account' (Heb. 4:12). This statement is equivocal about whether God's word separates *pneuma* from *psychē* or pierces through them both. Since it is hard to imagine the separation of bones (or joints) from marrow, the text probably claims that God's word has penetrated the *pneuma* and *psychē* in the same way (or to the same degree) that it has penetrated the bones and marrow. Schweizer again offers an ingenious parallel, this time from Philo Judaeus: God's word is the divine reason which can make logical distinctions. Philo calls this divine power the *tomeus*, 'cutter', as in 'wood-cutter'. It can pierce and dissect not only corporeal things, even down to atomic constituents, but also *psychē* and that which is perceived by the *pneuma*.[45] This power or 'character' in Philo's ontogeny plays an archetypal role, something like the personified forces in Hesiod's theogony: God is the all-powerful being who can cut things into parts such that we finite created beings can only *conceptually* separate them. Here we encounter the very being or 'nature' of *tomē*, as in dicho-*tomy*, tricho-*tomy*, and so forth. These are key terms in the ancient and modern debate regarding the 'division' of the soul. Can the soul be cut into parts or functions or elements? What is the ontological status of such cut items; are they substances, properties, or powers? One also needs to ask comparable questions regarding the various claims that such-and-such is the *seat* of the emotions, of thoughts, of the life-force. In other words, what does it mean to claim that some thing is a seat?

The soul, unlike the spirit, can be hated and killed; the soul is God's gift and a human receives it by living his life in the natural, ordinary sense. The *psychē* is always an individual's own life, but not in the sense of the phenomenon of life; *psychē* and *pneuma* can equally well denote an individual in a reflexive, pronomial manner. However, *pneuma* is never used of non-Christians or for impulses and desires that are morally wrong. Certainly *psychē*, in its close relation to *kardia* with its emphasis on the will and personal commitment, can be the locus of faith. Although *psychē* can never be sundered from the purely physical life, it is not identical to that life; one may find life or miss life as God intended: 'The difficulty with *pneuma* is not to let God's Spirit working in man become an inner spiritual life that is given to man ... With *psychē*, however, the difficulty is the opposite one of not restricting the God-given life to the purely physical sphere which is threatened by death, but also embracing therein the gift of God which transcends death.'[46]

---

[43] On this testament, see DL Lives 8.1; Zeller, vol. 3, part 2, pp. 103–8; Kirk & Raven, 1960, p. 447.

[44] On the concept of 'inner human being', see H. D. Betz, 2000, esp. pp. 339–41; and Burkert, 1998.

[45] Schweizer et al., 1975c, p. 651.

[46] Schweizer et al., 1975c, p. 655.

With regard to Christian teaching about the soul's immortality, it seems that both *psychē* and *pneuma* can refer to the departed person, that is, the individual's continued existence after bodily death. An important insight on this score is expressed in John's Revelation, where *psychē* denotes the soul's intermediate status prior to resurrection. The *psychē* that has survived its host body's death has self-awareness, awaits God's righteous judgment, and is protected by God under the heavenly altar. Even so, the departed souls are not entirely incorporeal[47] since God can see them and they are clothed in white garments (Rev. 6:9). Since the totality of human being is given by God alone and lived out in his full view, and since the extent (or domain) of this totalizing benefaction is in and through the body (*sōma*), the body reappears under a new guise: 'Paul speaks only of the *pneuma* which is to be saved through death ... after Paul *psychē* can be used to describe an existence which will reach its goal only *after death*. It thus becomes identical with the soul as the Greeks understood it, although this is never thought to be pre-existent.'[48]

One might turn to Colin Brown for a summary expression of the relation between the NT Christian concept of soul and the contemporary Greek concept:

> Although the Hellenistic term *psychē* appears more frequently in the later epistles of the NT than in other parts, it must not be imagined that this implies the concept of the soul as the real and valuable part of man, the eternal and permanent element. That would be a misunderstanding ... this is just what the NT does not teach. The soul is simply that area in which decisions are made concerning life and death, salvation and destruction. Moreover, every statement about the *psychē* in the NT is linked in [its] context with eschatological statements about renewal and resurrection.[49]

Whatever the undoubted merits of this capsule description, to designate the central meaning of the NT concept of soul as an *area* where rational choice and reflection take place leaves the ontological or categorical status of *psychē* undefined.

The essential properties of *pneuma* can be derived from a comparably close analysis of its usage in NT and Pauline contexts. The most frequent use of spirit in the NT is in reference to the Holy Spirit of God, but it is also used in a coherent fashion to refer to human spirit, or perhaps, to refer to humans insofar as they belong to the spiritual realm. The human spirit is that aspect through which God most directly encounters his creatures (Rom. 8:16, etc.); that aspect wherein humans are most responsive to God's will (Matt. 5:3; Luke 1:47, etc.). Numerous passages are ambiguous with respect to the source and autonomy of *pneuma*: whether its origin is within the human being or, as a power or force from without, it is merely experienced as coming from within. Several other passages suggest that the Hebrew idea of *ruach* as the breath of God lies just under the Greek writers' use of *pneuma*. However, Brown claims that there are some criteria that allow one to discriminate Paul's use of *pneuma* from the rest of the NT writers. In the NT before Paul's letters

---

[47] Brown, 1978b, p. 686.
[48] Schweizer et al., 1975c, p. 656.
[49] Brown, 1978b, p. 686.

... at death man ceases to exist *both* in the realm of the physical *and* in the realm of the spiritual, and continues existing *only* in the spiritual; and the physical body, ceasing to be the embodiment of the whole man in the observable world, becomes merely a corpse (Jas. 2:26). Whereas, in Paul's terms, the danger confronting man in the world is that he lives *solely* on the level of the world of sense and soul ... and not also and predominantly on the level of the spirit ... so that when the body dies, the whole man dies in the destruction of the flesh.[50]

Perhaps the best-known and most enduring Pauline statement which intertwines the many strands in the fabric of his account of human nature is the valediction of the First Letter to the Thessalonians: 'May the God of peace himself sanctify you entirely; and may your spirit and soul and body be kept sound and blameless at the coming of our Lord Jesus Christ' (1Thess. 5:23–4). Although the expression of this threefold blessing may indeed be formulaic, it still indicates an overtly Christian attitude toward the three fundamental 'components' of human being, or rather, the multifaceted character of those who have accepted Christ as their savior. There are numerous passages that contrast flesh and body, spirit and flesh, the new body and the old body, the earthly life with eternal life, and so forth. These can most plausibly be construed as endorsing some version of dualism; in point of fact, some sort of *substance* dualism seems to be entailed by the repeated assertion that the person's soul survives bodily death and even gains another, more perfect body at the world's end with the Second Coming.

In his thorough assessment of the many texts where one 'side' of human nature is contrasted with an other 'side', Gundry concludes that, although it is true that for Paul *psychē* does not hold as much significance as it does for Plato, one ought not to take the verbal difference as an indication of total divergence between the thinking of Paul and Plato:

> Paul along with most Jews and other early Christians habitually thought of man as a duality of two parts, corporeal and incorporeal, meant to function in unity but distinct and capable of separation ... In a veritable host of other passages a certain and frequent emphatic duality pervades the thought. There is no single formula by which Paul expresses his dualist view of human nature, but terms such as 'inner man', 'spirit', 'soul', 'mind', and 'heart' all refer to the incorporeal aspect or part, and terms such as 'outer man', 'flesh', 'body', 'members', and so forth all refer to the corporeal aspect or part.[51]

The scholarly question of whether Paul's position on human nature is some form of dualism or not for *some* commentators hinges on two prior questions: whether the dominant Greek philosophical position (exemplified in the Platonic school) endorsed a dualist picture of some sort, and to what degree Paul was influenced by this accepted view of the Greek position. Depending on several (usually unstated) assumptions about what constitutes substance dualism, and then depending on the many ways in which the two previous questions have been answered, a bewildering variety of assertions have been made about Paul's acceptance or rejection of some vaguely defined notion of dualism. In attempting to come to grips with this impacted

---

[50] Brown, 1978b, pp. 693–4.
[51] Gundry, 1976, pp. 154–5.

issue, E. R. Dodds' irritable comments about sorting out the competing theories regarding the Greek concept of immortality seem equally applicable to the concept of the dualism of soul and body: 'I shall have to traverse ground which has been churned to deep and slippery mud by the heavy feet of contending scholars; ground, also, where those in a hurry are liable to trip over the partially decayed remains of dead theories that have not yet been decently interred. We shall be wise, then, to move slowly, and to pick our steps rather carefully among the litter.'[52]

It seems that every New Testament scholar, when confronted with the details of Paul's picture of human nature, and this picture's relation to Greek philosophical concepts, feels compelled to take a stand on the grand topic of human duality. Chamblin synopsizes several current interpretations of this issue: Bultmann argues that Paul's moral dualism can be segregated from his anthropic monism; Gundry argues for an anthropic (or ontological) duality and functional pluralism, but not monadic unity; whereas Cooper contrasts Pauline and Biblical views in terms of functional *versus* ontological holism and holistic dualism *versus* holistic monism. Chamblin himself seems to prefer holistic dualism, which he says is utterly opposed to other kinds of dualism in the ancient world.[53] Crossan repudiates 'human dualism in any shape or form' and embraces what he calls 'monism of enfleshed spirit'.[54] The editors of the TDNT entries under *psychē* incline towards a complex view that the various Greek divisions of human nature into various portions or sides are overcome in the NT by an emergent concept of spiritual monism. Berkouwer's protracted discussion[55] of the relative merits of dualism and trialism, dichotomy and trichotomy, bipartition and tripartition (and so forth), and his attempts to adjudicate between various scholars' positions on the NT concept of human nature ultimately founders on ontological and categorical problems. In most of the torturous debate on this subject there is rarely any clarity about *what* is being divided, cut or parted; the status of the resultant parts or items cut; the conditions that some item has to satisfy in order for it to be cut, rather than parted; whether the conceptual separability of two or more entities implies anything at all about their real separateness, and so forth. Since there is little agreement on these questions with regard to Plato's account of human nature *and* little agreement on the extent of Plato's account informing Paul's account, it is hardly surprising that there is no common ground amongst the contending theories.

In many contexts previously mentioned, for example, the Late Plato, the Stoics and Lucretius, assertions about the soul's mortality or immortality provide a very helpful indicator (though not, it must be admitted, a sufficient condition) about the oneness or twoness of human nature. Thus, on first glance, without other premises to the contrary being advanced, to claim that the soul survives the bodily death of the person whose soul it was would seem to indicate both a real and a conceptual separability between two entities, body and soul, excluding claims about whatever comprises the parts or aspects of the soul itself. However, on the issue of the soul's immortal status, Paul's stated position is very peculiar indeed; it is difficult if not

---

[52] Dodds, 1951, p. 136.
[53] Chamblin, 1993, p. 767.
[54] Crossan, 1998, pp. xxii–xxvii.
[55] Berkouwer, 1962, pp. 203–20.

impossible to reconcile his claims about this with *any* of the prior Greek or Judaic doctrines.

Confronted with incredulity by his Corinthian audience about the true character of personal resurrection at the final judgment, Paul responds by rebuking them for lack of imagination in thinking that the only body one could have is the earthly body: 'What you sow does not come to life unless it dies; and what you sow is not the body which is to be, but bare seed ... But God gives it a body as he has chosen, and to each kind of seed its own body' (1Cor. 15:36–8). He then distinguishes heavenly bodies from earthly bodies, using the word *sōma* to refer to the bodies of sun, moon and stars; the former, he says, are incorruptible and imperishable, the latter are corruptible and perishable.[56] He then proceeds to draw an analogous contrast with the person's present earthly body and the same person's future body after the resurrection: 'It is sown an ensouled body[57] (*sōma psychikon*), and it is raised a spiritual body (*sōma pneumatikon*). If there is an ensouled body there is also a spiritual body. Thus it is written, "the first man Adam became a living being" (or ensouled life, *psychēn zōsan*); the last Adam became a life-giving spirit. But it is not the spiritual (*to pneumatikon*) which is first, but the soulful (*to psychikon*) and then the spiritual' (1Cor. 15:44–5). James Dunn comments on this enigmatic passage: 'The soulish body takes after Adam, of the earth, made of dust; the spiritual body will be patterned after Christ's resurrection body. Evidently, the soulish body, the present body as such, cannot share in the kingdom of God; it is also corruptible flesh and blood, and only the incorruptible, the spiritual body, is capable of inheriting God's kingdom.' After trying out several possible interpretations of this crucial Pauline text, Dunn quietly confesses, 'quite what Paul envisaged we can hardly begin to say.'[58] Four centuries would pass before St. Augustine offered a coherent and integrated interpretation of Paul's astonishing declaration.

It is worth mentioning an unusual and curious connection once made by Reizenstein, who drew a parallel between Paul's doctrine of the pneumatic post-resurrection body and certain elements of the Mithras liturgy, best understood through Manichean and Mandaen texts. In this liturgy the initiate speaks of an ascent of the soul to the celestial realm, where he wishes to be reborn and become the son of god. He addresses his own celestial body, which God himself has formed for him in the world of light. He must put on this body (like clothes) and leave behind the earthly body, but he assumes the latter again after the divine activity is finished. The author also connects this teaching, via a common source, to Gnostic doctrines: a person is psychical who does not have gnosis, and is thus made of earthly material: 'In contrast with *pneumatikos*, a person who is *pneuma* or who has *pneuma*, *psychikos* can only mean a person who is *psyche* or who has *psyche*, but it can never mean a person who, besides his *psyche*, does not *also* have a

---

[56] The first clause resembles one of Socrates' early arguments about the coming-to-be from opposites; the second clause is resonant with the Stoic imagery of seeds scattered by the divine mind; and the reference to two kinds of body in heaven and on earth to the *Timaeus* and other mystical claims about corruptible and incorruptible composite matter.

[57] It is no help at all if this is translated as 'physical body', fairly common in many English versions.

[58] Dunn, 1998, pp. 60–61; see also Martin, 1995, pp. 123–9; Gundry, 1976, pp. 161–5.

pneuma; in that case, in these sharp contrasts an *apneumatos* [un-spirit] would have been set in opposition to the *pneumatikos* [spiritual].'[59]

In conclusion, let us summarize some of the main points about St. Paul's account of human nature. First, Paul's point of view about the nature and function of the human soul is under-determined; there are too many equivocal passages, which without disambiguation, cannot indicate anything along the lines of sufficient conditions for identity criteria. Second, his conceptual vocabulary is too small; it is mostly inadequate for making the number of important distinctions that he wants to draw our attention to. Third, some of the serious problems attempting to reconcile Greek and Christian views on the immortal status of the human soul (or spirit) hinge on incommensurable doctrines about the nature of body. Fourth, the NT and Pauline exposition of human nature is complicated further by efforts to build in the idea of the flesh having an intrinsic tendency toward sin (or evil). The Stoic and Platonic notion that the body is the soul's prison supports the idea that the body is ethically neutral; in other words, Christian flesh (*sarx*) plays a much different role in accounts of human-embodied nature than the Greek *sōma*. And finally, the NT discussion of human nature outside St. Paul is simply incomplete or open-ended; in addition to their use of *psychē*, one of the distinct features of the NT concept is the equal weight the authors placed on the idea of *pneuma*. Where Aristotle subordinated *pneuma* to the role of a lesser functional component of humans' organic matter, and where the Stoics elevated *pneuma* to the status of principal 'cause' in their explanation of the life-force of living things, the NT authors balanced the role of *psychē* with the role of *pneuma*. In Paul's Letters an even more complex, and perhaps ultimately mysterious, pedagogical scheme is at work – and this scheme is clearly indicated in his exhortations that believers in Christ must believe 'with body, soul, and spirit'.

(2) Neo-Platonic teachings and Plotinus' One-Mind-Soul

The Platonic Academy, established in the fourth century BCE, reached its zenith in the person and teaching of Plotinus (*c.*205–270 CE), an imposing figure who brought clarity and solidity to the rather foggy thinking that characterized the third-century schools.[60] Plotinus was born in Upper Egypt, and he may have been a Hellenized Egyptian, not an immigrant Greek. According to Porphyry, his biographer and distinguished pupil, Plotinus turned to the study of philosophy when he was twenty-eight; disappointed by several local tutors, he went to study with Ammonius Saccas. Almost nothing is known about Ammonius or his teaching, partly because he enjoined his pupils to keep his doctrines secret. Much to the disgruntlement of many later scholars, Ammonius' students kept their word to their master, and this included Plotinus himself, Origen the Christian (who will enter our story later), Origen the Pagan and Longinus. After studying with Ammonius for eleven years, he joined the army of the Emperor Gordian III in his expedition against Persia; according to Porphyry, Plotinus said that he wanted to gain first-hand knowledge of

---

[59] Reitzenstein, 1926, pp. 46, 69, see also pp. 435–42.
[60] On his life, see Merlan in EEP, vol. 6, p. 352; OCD 3rd edn, p. 1199; Rist, 1967, pp. 2–20; and Armstrong, in CHLGEMP, 1970, pp. 195–210.

Persian and Indian wisdom. But, in any case, everything went badly wrong when the Emperor was murdered and Plotinus (thinking he might be suspected) fled first to Antioch and then to Rome.

Some scholars have speculated that Plotinus may have had highly placed friends or family in the Roman Senate; certainly the circle that formed around him contained some Very Important Persons. From 244 to 253 he gave open public lectures, held private tutorials with his select pupils, and played an important role, sometimes as an arbitrator, in Roman social circles. He began writing various topical treatises sometime about the beginning of the reign of Emperor Gallienus in 253, and continued to work on these at a fairly steady pace, often composing his thoughts 'as if he were copying from a book'. Porphyry came to join him about ten years later and stayed close to his master, acting something like a personal assistant, for the next six years. Porphyry later remarked that Plotinus had the uncanny ability to 'read' a person's soul, and Porphyry himself must have been stunned when his master told him that he (Porphyry) must not think of suicide, but instead go on a long holiday. Porphyry's holiday brought him for a long rest cure to Sicily, and it was there two years later that he learned of Plotinus' death. The master had been attended in his last months only by his faithful physician friend, Eustochius. Sometime shortly before his death Plotinus had expressed to the Emperor the rather wild scheme to found a philosophers' city (called Platonopolis), and even proposed a site in Campania to build it. As Plotinus' foremost expositor, Porphyry was entrusted with the task of sorting out his master's various treatises and bringing them to publication. He rearranged all of Plotinus' texts under six main headings, each containing nine tracts (hence the name given to the whole work, *The Enneads*).

Plotinus was an extraordinary thinker with a peculiar and often baffling expository style. J. M. Rist once said that

> ... perhaps no philosopher has been accorded more respect and less understanding than Plotinus. The reasons for this are manifold: the desire to over-emphasize the originality of other thinkers by playing down Plotinus' achievement; the misunderstandings engendered by a too literal-minded interpretation of key phrases; a false theory of the 'atmosphere' of ancient philosophy, particularly Platonism; and the simple fact that Plotinus' Greek is at times almost untranslatable in our present state of knowledge.[61]

Although Plotinus himself readily acknowledged his indebtedness to Platonic theories and formulae, it is not always clear in his treatises *which* lines of Platonic thought are being carried forward; and this incurs the difficult and painstaking task of critical exegesis. Armstrong encapsulates this dynamic tension between the private and the public, the esoteric and exoteric, in his opening remarks about Plotinus' stature:

> He was an original philosophical genius, the only philosopher in the history of later Greek thought who can be ranked with Plato and Aristotle, and was impelled by a personal mystical experience of a kind and quality unique in Greek philosophical religion. So the result of his critical rethinking of the long and complex tradition which he

---

[61] Rist, 1967, p. 21.

inherited was a really original philosophy with far greater coherence and vitality than Middle Platonism, and one which had a wide and deep influence on later European thought.[62]

In his recent work on the deep and abiding connections between Augustine and Descartes, and Augustine's debt to Plotinus for an account of the ascent of the soul, Stephen Menn characterizes the peculiarly ambivalent nature of Plotinus' originality:

> Plotinus is sometimes considered as an essentially independent thinker, a mystic, a man with his own experiences, who wished to construct a picture of the universe as he had experienced it ... On this understanding, Plotinus' Platonism would consist, not in [any] affiliation to an established school, but simply in a personal appreciation of Plato. This interpretation is found to varying degrees in a great many writers, but it is entirely false. Plotinus was a Platonist, and to be a Platonist in the third century AD meant something definite: it meant to be a member of a certain school or *hairesis*.[63]

There are at least three main concerns which Plotinus shared with his contemporaries; being aware of these concerns allows the attentive modern reader to situate Plotinus' exposition of central themes within previous and concurrent philosophical discussions. These concerns are his reflective and respectful appropriation of the more 'mystical' Platonic dialogues, his employment of Aristotelian arguments to sort out difficulties and lacunae in Platonic theories, and his constant efforts to combat some of the main tenets of Gnosticism.

Armstrong has carefully worked out which Platonic dialogues Plotinus drew on most heavily; he commented that Plotinus never really makes any use of the early Socratic dialogues, and although there are many references to the so-called middle dialogues (and others), his use of their verbal imagery and paraphrases are often little more than as supportive and illustrative texts. The principal dialogues which Plotinus relied on again and again in his creative transformation of Platonic doctrine were the *Phaedo, Phaedrus, Symposium, Timaeus* and *Republic* Books Six and Seven: 'He uses texts from Plato, in fact, rather as Christian preachers or scholastic theologians use texts from the Bible, and not as a scholar would use them.'[64] Of course, this analogy implies that for Plotinus the Platonic texts are beyond doubt the authentic words of the master. In order to properly understand Plotinus' Platonism then, and for our purposes, to accurately situate Plotinus' concept of soul and mind, it is crucial to grasp just which aspects of Plato's mystical teachings he found most appealing and thus what he did with what he had.

It is not essential, however, that we here identify all of the Platonic doctrines that Plotinus adopted, but only those that pertain directly to his account of mind in its relation to the cosmos, and the soul as it descends into the material world. First, Platonic doctrine is quite distinct from other philosophical positions regarding the diremption of the cosmos into two realms. The Stoics argued that nothing existed beyond the material world, and that everything is done by (or through) bodies. The

---

[62] Armstrong, 1970, p. 195.
[63] Menn, 1998, p. 83.
[64] Armstrong, 1970, p. 214.

Aristotelians accounted for change, motion and the soul in terms of form instanced in bodies (or perhaps, forms manifest through bodies), but these forms did not comprise a separate, intelligible domain, since there could be no form as such which was not a form *of* some body. Augustine succinctly captured this special character of the Platonic two-tiered cosmos when he said that the Platonists 'believe that there are two worlds, an intelligible world in which truth itself resides, and this sensible world which it is plain that we perceive by sight and touch; so that the former is true, and the latter is like the true and made in its image' (Contra Acad. 3.17.37). Second, Plato offers several accounts of the relations between these two worlds; according to the *Timaeus* (which had an exemplary influence on Plotinus), sensible objects are distinguished from intelligible forms in that the former exist in matter, whereas the latter do not. The material realm is 'the receptacle and nurse of all becoming'; it is entirely without qualities in itself, neither an intelligible form nor a sensible body, but it provides a location to all things that become, since it can receive the likenesses (or semblances) of all things intelligible and eternal (49a–52b). Third, Plato accounts for the cause of the intelligible form 'impressing itself', like a seal in many pieces of wax, by positing the governance of the cosmos in a rational divine power, which is itself the source of the rational order discernible in the material world. Where some earlier thinker might have said that this highest governing principle was *logos*, Plato followed Anaxagoras in calling it *nous*; one should be wary, however, of translating this as 'mind' or 'intellect', as we soon shall see.

When Plato holds forth *nous* as the concept of the supreme ruling principle it should be clear that he does not mean *nous* as mind, but rather as the virtue of rationality or reason. In the *Philebus*, he said that 'all the wise agree that *nous* is the king of heaven and earth'; and that 'the sum of things, the universe, is ruled by reason and a wondrous regular intelligence' (28c,d); later that this presiding cause is wisdom (*sophia*) and reason (*nous*) (30c). In the *Timaeus*, he identified this world-governing power as the demiurge, the divine crafter and world-maker. Through rational reflection the demiurge discovers that 'it is impossible for *nous* to come to be in something without soul, and he thus makes the world-whole itself an ensouled, mindful living thing' (*zōon empsuchon ennoun*), that is, an animate being with soul in its body and *nous* in its soul. Fourth, the thesis of the world-soul is Plato's answer to the question about how rational order can be transmitted from the intelligible to the sensible realm. The supreme *nous* does not impose order on the material world by an external dictate, rather it creates the world-soul as an instrument of rational governance.

Where non-living bodies could only be ordered by an external physical compulsion, souls can be made to perceive the truths of reason, and thus can be made rational in their very nature.[65] When the demiurge has created the world-soul, its rational soul is interwoven with the world-body and thus communicates its rational order to the bodies which it animates. Since the essence and definition of soul is to be self-moved, every body moved from without is soul-less and every

---

[65] In Stephen Menn's admirable argument, 1998, pp. 88–9; for another version of Plotinus' argument about the creation of the world according to reason, see Rist, 1967, pp. 84–102.

body moved from within is ensouled (in concord with *Phaedrus* 245e). And finally, since the soul is the medium through which order is transmitted from the intelligible to the sensible realm, it is not itself an 'element' or entity in either realm, but rather occupies an intermediate place. Plato speculated that the demiurge blended together portions of the eternal, immutable realm and the transient, mutable realm, and that this third form of substance is the 'stuff' of the soul itself.

Irrespective of their physical or non-physical persuasion, ancient Greek thinkers were obsessed with the concept and mechanics of blending (*krasis*) and mixture (*mixis*). Without the benefit of scientific information about chemical bonds and exchanges, their only recourse in explaining the existence of composite things, including human beings, in terms of their constituent ingredients, was through one or another variation on the theme of mixture. Not only was there disagreement about what counted as a mixture as such, but there was at least as much controversy about the various types of mixture. It was still another question where the embodied soul had its place in the mixture scheme. On this issue, Plotinus shared some of his most basic tenets with the Stoics, such as the claim that the whole world is an ensouled and rational animal. But he would have balked at the Stoics' qualification of this thesis such that aether is its ruling principle.[66] According to Chrysippus and Posidonius, 'the world is governed according to *nous* (mind) and *pronoia* (providence), where *nous* pervades every part of it as the soul does in us' (DL. Lives 7.1.139). But there is no claim in this passage that *nous* exists outside (or beyond) the world, or that the soul has been informed or imposed onto bodies by the action of god. The Stoics did not think that the presence of soul in certain bodies was the result of an informing process at all. From their point of view, it is not due to form (*eidos*) but to the admixture of a subtle material element (*pneuma*), blended with matter as wine is blended with water. Plotinus would have severely censured the view that 'some bodies are governed by cohesion, some by nature, some by irrational soul, and some by soul having reason and thought' (SVF II. 460). Plotinus himself was a master blender; in his skillful hands the elements of Stoic, Platonic and Aristotelian arguments about the relation of souls to bodies, forms to matter, and mind to soul, are deftly combined into a seamless whole.

Plotinus was concerned with more than just an attempt to confute the Stoics' materialist ontology, he was also strongly opposed to the Gnostics' view of the earthly, sensible world as an inferior, imperfect world which tended toward evil. 'Plotinus resembled someone ashamed of being in a body', are the strange words with which Porphyry opens the biography of his master. But in this respect he would not have been much different than many other thoughtful individuals in the third century. As Pierre Hadot put this point:

> The first three centuries of the Christian era witnessed a flourishing of Gnosticism and mystery religions. Man felt himself to be a stranger in this lower world, as if he had been banished into his body and the sensible world. The popularization of Platonism was, in part, responsible for this collective mentality: the body was considered a tomb and a prison; the soul was to separate herself from it because she was akin to the eternal Ideas;

---

[66] See the thorough summary of this argument in Emilsson, 1994, ANRW 36.7, pp. 5342–3.

our true self was held to be purely spiritual. Astral theologies too must be taken into account: according to these, the soul is of celestial origin, and has come down here via a stellar voyage, during the course of which she has become encased in ever-thicker envelopes, the last of which is the terrestrial body.[67]

One might accept this synoptic statement provided two important qualifications are made: first, that the soul is a tomb, implying a psychical death for the duration of bodily existence, is definitely not the same as saying that the soul is a prison, implying a continued psychical life under restricted conditions. And second, that the notion of 'ever-thicker envelopes' recalls Empedocles' poem and other pre-Socratic texts about the corporeal body as an enclosing bark or rind which forms around the soul during the multi-stage process of generation.

But against the Gnostic view Plotinus affirmed that the true realm of the human soul can be discovered within oneself. Plotinus abjured reliance on the sensory organs and teachings of our bodily nature because they distracted our rational insight away from what was divine in each person. Augustine, and much later Descartes, were to follow Plotinus' lead in this ascetic inward contemplation – the ascent of the soul towards its true home began with the inner vision of the purified soul. But it was not just the self that would be transfigured by the soul's 'wondrous majestic beauty'; rather the whole world would be suffused with divine light: 'Although the spiritual world is within us, it is also outside us. Just as it was enough to learn to look within our selves in order to discover this world, so it is enough to learn how to look outside our selves in order to perceive the spiritual world behind the world of appearances. The metamorphosis of inner vision thus has as its counterpart the metamorphosis of physical vision.'[68]

There is an ambivalence in Plotinus' attitude toward the human body as a prison for the soul, and this is matched by a tension in his anti-Gnostic attitude toward the material realm as the product of a perfect creator. J. M. Rist expresses this underlying tension in these words:

> ... on the one hand he believes with Plato's *Phaedo* that the soul is a prisoner in the body and that the material world is an inferior version of the intelligible; on the other, he holds with Plato's *Timaeus* that the material world is a product of God and the best possible world of its kind, that it is the work of Providence, and that it is full of the glory of its maker. When thinking of the return of the soul to its source ... Plotinus thinks of a flight from the world and of souls living in the world as fallen and being punished for their fall by bodily life.

But Plotinus' thinking is pulled in another direction also: 'when opposing the extreme dualism of the Gnostics, for whom the creator of the material universe is evil and his productions monstrous, Plotinus takes the contrary position and is almost Franciscan in his praises of the excellence of the cosmos and his talk of the importance of the soul as its maker and organizer. The two positions may be

---

[67] Hadot, 1993, p. 23.
[68] Hadot, 1993, p. 35.

incompatible, the result of conflicting pressures which Plotinus was never able to resolve.'[69]

There are further issues that underlie (or even cause) these 'serious tensions' and make it very difficult to identify any 'doctrinal unity in ancient pagan Neo-Platonism', in Richard Wallis' words. At least three factors can be mentioned in this context, though it is not feasible to go into details here.[70] First, as Wallis argues, despite his overt condemnation and ridicule of Gnostic doctrines, Plotinus has 'a love–hate relation' with Gnostic tendencies, such that his account of the soul's ascent is remarkably similar to the account of the Zostrianos text. Second, he follows Albinus' orthodox Platonic interpretation of the first god and the nature of soul, but diverges in his refusal to identify the Good with the First Nous, and instead falls back on an Aristotelian-inspired adjustment. Third, he must carefully segregate his adherence to specific late-Platonic doctrines from the Gnostics' appropriation of certain tenets in Platonic philosophy, which they had fallaciously derived from a distorted reading of these texts. According to Chadwick:

> The Gnostic heretics had appealed to the principles of Platonism to provide a philosophical justification for their doctrine that the elect soul must be liberated from the evil inherent in the material realm to escape to its true home and to enjoy the beatific vision. Their deep pessimism about this created order *was not fairly deduced* from the texts of Plato, but there was a sufficient plausibility about the argument to make it look impressive. The Gnostic appeal to pagan philosophy did not tend to encourage the study of philosophy among those who feared Gnosticism as a corrupter of the truth.[71]

Wallis draws these salient parallels between Plotinus and the Gnostic Gospel:

> It is the *Zostrianos*, whose hero ascends through a series of 'True Earths' corresponding to the several levels of the Intelligible Cosmos, that presents the closest parallels to Plotinus ... In addition to both authors' vitalistic conception of the elements of the Intelligible world, and their clear common dependence on past tradition, including the True Earth of the *Phaedo* myth, the Aristotelian doctrine of Nous, and the vitalism of the Stoics, we may observe that *Zostrianos* describes his ascent as a 'vision', and both sources, in my view, rest on a common experience. Doctrinally we may note their agreement on six points: (a) the membership of souls in the Intelligible world, (b) the existence of Forms of individuals, (c) the Aristotelian doctrine of the identity of Nous and its objects, which leads *Zostrianos*, like Plotinus, to describe the members of the Intelligible world as 'thoughts', (d) the notion of Intelligible Matter ... (e) the identity-in-diversity among the members of the Intelligible order, and (f) the doctrine ... that incorporeal beings are free from spatial limitations and hence present everywhere in their entirety.[72]

The extraordinary and widespread disagreements about the central tenets of Platonic philosophy, how these tenets were interconnected, and what (if any) relation they

---

[69] Rist, 1967, p. 112.
[70] Discussion of the Gnostic and Hermetic accounts of soul might form chapters in a second volume of the *History of the Concept of Mind*.
[71] Chadwick, 1993, p. 74.
[72] Wallis, 1992, p. 465.

bore to Christian doctrine are hardly surprising, given the diverse and unstable views laid out in the Platonic dialogues. There was no single, univocal and isolable Platonic doctrine about *anything* it seemed, since Plato's position varied from the early Socratic discourses to the middle period and the last works (especially the *Laws*). In addition, it was not always completely transparent what attitude Plato himself had toward his main 'guest speakers', such as Protagoras, Timaeus and the Eleatic Stranger. But Plotinus thought that he had discovered an exceptionally good path through this doctrinal maze in an important and mysterious remark that Plato made in the Second Letter (whether or not the letter is genuine is another issue).

In writing to the tyrant Dionysius of Syracuse, Plato responded to an earlier message which conveyed the report that Dionysius had not been satisfied with Plato's previous account of the first principle. Plato said that he would transmit 'a secret teaching' that must be written in riddles in case someone might read the letter while en route. The true doctrine, he said,

> ... is like this: it is in relation to the king of all things and on his account that everything exists, and that fact is the cause of all that is beautiful. In relation to a second, the second kind of thing exists, and in relation to a third, the third kind. Now the human mind, when it is concerned with them, endeavors to gain knowledge of their qualities, fixing its attention on the things with which it has itself some affinity; these, however, are in no case adequate. In regard to the king and the things said there is nothing like this. Then the soul says, 'but what are they like?'. This question ... is the cause of all the trouble, and if it is not expelled from a person, he shall never genuinely find the truth. [312e–313a]

Plotinus focused his profound exegetical talents upon this text and proceeded to identify the first, second and third principles with the One (*hen*), Intellect (*nous*), and Soul (*psychē*); these same three were later identified by the Church Fathers with the Father, the Son, and the Holy Spirit. Armstrong explains:

> Soul is, of Plotinus' three hypostases, the most wide-ranging and various in its activities. At the top of its range it lives on the highest level, in the world of Intellect, and with Intellect can rise in self-transcendence to union with the One. At the bottom, it is responsible for the formation of bodies in the visible world ... Its proper and most characteristic activity is discursive thinking, reasoning from premises to conclusions; but it possesses the whole range of lower forms of consciousness, with the external activities appropriate to them ... The initiative in this self-transcendence, as always in Plotinus, comes from above. It is Intellect which, by illuminating Soul, raises it to its own level. The relationship between the three hypostases in Plotinus is one of hierarchical distinction in unity. They are not cut off from each other. The One and Intellect are always present to Soul and acting on it, and this eternal presence and action is the most important thing which we (who are Soul) discover in philosophical reflection.[73]

The things that the mind fixes its attention upon through affinity are the properties of the king of all things (*nous*); its affinity with the highest principle is due to its

---

[73] Armstrong, 1970, p. 250; see also Blumenthal, 1993, II, pp. 203–19; Schwyzer argues that, in the intelligible world, soul is not different from Nous, RE xxi (i), 1951, p. 563.

being made in, and having the nature of, the divine mind. Plotinus repeatedly claims that it is through an art or discipline or practice that the soul leads the whole person to where he should go (Enn 1.3). Unlike the Stoics or the Aristotelians, Plotinus accepts Plato's injunctions in the *Symposium* and the *Phaedrus*, that the soul must be trained to follow the steps in an ascent to its original source. Our souls, he says, 'have forgotten their father god, and though they are portions from the intelligible world (*ekeithen*) and are entirely of it (*ekeinou*), they are ignorant both of themselves and of it.' Once souls have deserted the intelligible world, 'they are ignorant even that they come from there (*ekeithen*), as children who have been immediately torn away from their fathers and grow up for a long time far away are ignorant both of themselves and of their fathers' (ibid.). The Plotinian notion that created humans are infants in the sight of god is one that will be made much of by the Church Fathers, especially Origen. Those who remain ignorant, who think ignorance is their natural state, do not honor themselves in the right way, and prefer body over soul, worldly goods over the good of the soul. Therefore, he says, 'one must give a double account to those who are thus disposed, if indeed one is to turn them toward the opposite things and toward the first principles, and would lead them up to the highest and the one and the first' (ibid.). The first account will show the shame or lack of worth (*atimia*) of bodily things currently honored, and the second will teach the soul about its own kind (*genos*) and value. Thus, Plotinus' position is not merely the holding-forth of a rationally grounded doctrine about soul, but also the articulation of a discipline or education (in the literal sense of leading-out-from) by means of which the soul can actually reachieve its genuine nature ('genuine' in terms of its own *genos*).[74]

The first step on this path is to turn one's attention away from the body and toward the soul. Plotinus thought that the Stoics had caught a glimpse of the soul's beauty and aspired to be guided by the soul rather than the body, but also thought they had not understood the true nature of soul, falling back on an account of soul in material, pneumatic terms. He argued against the materialist thesis that living things do not have their life within, or through their own being, but from some prior ordering and animating principle. He admitted that the Stoics, guided by the truth, 'bear witness that there must be some form of soul prior to bodies and better than them' (Enn. 4.7.4), but located this *archē* within the world. In contrast, Plotinus argued that this first principle must be 'outside and beyond nature'. The Stoics realized that not every body had *pneuma*, or rather that not every *pneuma*-endowed body had *psychē*. Since they could not appeal to incorporeal principles, they accounted for ensouled beings by postulating that their bodies were specially disposed (*pōs echon*) to become living things. Plotinus thought that the Stoics' refusal to invoke Platonist incorporeal principles in an account of soul led to intractable difficulties and reversed the true order of dependence among things, making the derivative into the principle from which it should be derived. On Plotinus' view, the Stoics' invocation of the idea of special disposition is their way of evading the question of whether or not the principles acting on bodies are real things existing beyond the bodies. On one hand, it is clearly the case that living

---

[74] On *genos,* genius, genuine, etc., see Onians, 1951, pp. 175–82.

things contain some sort of *pneuma*, and further that this *pneuma* will be disposed differently than *pneuma* in non-living things; but this fails to deal with the issue about what causes the special disposition in only some things.

This line of argument echoes one of the complaints made by Aristotle against his predecessors in *De Anima*, Book 2, section 2, that they had not explained how it is the case that some things are so disposed that they receive a soul. Plotinus believed that the special disposition of certain things to be ensouled could proceed only from an incorporeal principle. This belief is just a pre-eminent instance of a more pervasive, higher-order belief that all active principles in bodies are incorporeal. In the special case of soul, Plotinus wanted to offer an account of its unique psychical activities: thinking, sensing, reasoning, desiring and governing. In Stephen Menn's words:

> The effects we attribute to soul are rational thought and the rational government of bodies, effects which require one single principle coordinating diverse operations, and which therefore cannot be produced even by the incorporeal powers dispersed in bodies, much less by the bodies themselves. Even if we condone the Stoics' confusion between bodies and their incorporeal qualities, their conception of soul remains inadequate: in order to conceive soul as a body somehow disposed, they have degraded it to the level of an irrational power, since this is all that bodies (or more properly, their qualities) could be imagined to produce. To understand soul in a way that is suitable to it ... we must conceive it as an incorporeal substance which, without subsisting in the separate parts of a body like the irrational powers, is able to control the parts of the body and their powers, and to subordinate them to a single rational order.[75]

When the soul turns away from its contemplation of bodily things and towards its own being, it shows the power of an incorporeal rational agency directed toward an incorporeal rational being. Plotinus thought that this twofold, bidirectional power made the best sense because every individual soul has an affinity with the world-soul, since each soul is, in some sense, a part of the world-soul. The Stoics regarded the soul as something dispersed through the parts of the living body, such that the souls of animals and humans are parts *qua* organs of the world-soul. Our souls are in accord with divine purposes when they properly carry out their subordinate functions in the world-soul's governance or ministrance of the world-body. For Plotinus, the nature of the individual soul does not reside in the extended parts of the body the soul governs. In other words, the soul that administers a more extensive body need not contain, or be superior to, the souls that govern its constituent parts: 'The world-soul has the same task in governing its body that our souls have in their bodies, namely to think rationally, and to impose its internal rationality on its body as far as possible.' But on the other hand, in Menn's words,

> ... the world-soul cannot be entirely identical to ours, since it administers a different body; but this applies only to the soul once it has descended into the body. In the intelligible world, souls are the same not only in essence but also in activity, being purely rational and not yet related to any particular body. Plotinus says that souls in the intelligible world are in some way all one, but also in some way many, since they are

---

[75] Menn, 1998, p. 109; this sub-section owes much to Menn's astute account, pp. 110–20.

capable of descending separately into bodies. A human soul thus discovers its relation to the world-soul, not by going through the world, but by returning into itself and discovering the intelligible origin that it and the world-soul share.[76]

One of the crucial points at issue in Plotinus' dispute with the Gnostics is about the moral status of the world-soul and the implications of this status with respect to the moral character of worldly material beings. According to his interpretation, the Gnostics believed that the world-soul and wisdom (*sophia*) declined from their perfect realm and entered the material world. But for Plotinus, the world-soul is a hypostasis of true being and hence cannot enter the sensible, mutable realm; rather, it produces and creates the world from above or beyond. The Gnostics claimed that the world-soul made the world after its 'wings failed', clearly echoing Plato's words in the *Phaedrus* myth. But Plotinus argued that the world-soul cannot suffer or undergo anything; the world-soul is entirely creative and thus inclines upward toward what is superior, and does not decline toward what is inferior. The Gnostics spoke of the soul as coming down or descending, and in so doing illuminating or casting light upon the darkness (or dark matter). Plotinus suggests that the reverse is the case: the world-soul remains above and illuminates the material world without having any physical contact with dark things. It is only after particular souls abandon the world-soul in the intelligible realm that their wings fail, they descend to earth, and thus fall into evil ways: 'The so-called world-soul has never taken part in lower activity but, unaffected by evils and in a state of contemplation, oversees what is below it and at the same time stays fixed in what is above' (Enn. 4.8.7).

Although every soul, in so far as it is a soul, is concerned both with the intelligible and the sensible realm, the way in which the world-soul operates is distinguished by its purity: 'The world-soul as an entirety governs the universe through that part of it which leans to the body side, but since it does not exercise a will based on calculation as we do, but proceeds by a purely intellective act, as in the execution of an artistic idea, its ministrance is that of a laborless over-powering' (Enn. 4.8.8). Both the production and the governance of the material world are the fulfillments of the world-soul's functions, but ones to which no impurity or stain attaches. This argument helps to show how the activities of the world-soul and individual souls can be discriminated, in J. M. Rist's words:

> The world-soul governs a body, the material universe, which will be maintained forever in fundamentally the same state, for in Plotinus' view the four elements will never pass away, nor will the various species of living creature that inhabit the earth's surface. The individual body, however, is a temporary and fragile lodgement for a soul which may from time to time pass through a whole string of such bodies without necessarily forming an intimate connection with any of them. This different status of the body of the world and of individual bodies helps to indicate the different effects they will have on their governing souls. The individual soul governs what is short-lived and therefore partial; the world-soul governs something that will endure in some sense in its completeness and perfection.[77]

---

[76] Menn, 1998, p. 111.
[77] Rist, 1967, pp. 115–16.

In contrast with the Stoics, for Plotinus the inmost essence of *psychē* is that it is rational (*logistikē*). In its origin in the intelligible realm every soul is rational; it is only through its descent into the host body that soul becomes irrational. As Stephen Menn asserts, 'Plotinus is apparently the earliest philosopher to make rationality essential to soul, and therefore to conceive soul through the "first-person" reflection which will be most prominently found, divorced from Platonist vitalism, in Augustine and Descartes.'[78] Menn also speculates that there are hints of the notion of the soul's original, pure rationality in Plato's texts; for example, this seems to be one of the points of comparison between the human soul and the sea-god Glaucus in *Republic*, Book Ten. In the *Timaeus*, the human soul produced by the demiurge is purely rational before the 'young gods' attach the irrational parts, and the motions of the infant body disrupt its rational activities. In any case, the soul's reflection on itself is the necessary condition for achieving a higher concept of soul, and through this acquisition to a higher understanding of god as *nous*. Through his meditative practice Plotinus leads his pupils' thoughts from their individual souls to the world-soul and then to *Nous*.

Plotinus employed Aristotle's account of the 'maker's mind' (*nous poētikos*) in *De Anima*, Chapter Three, to argue that this special capacity actualizes potential *nous*, and in so doing strives to imitate the cognitive perfection of the supreme *Nous* whose creature and image it is. The embodied soul has the task of bringing order into the corporeal realm, but this is an accident (in the Aristotelian sense), that is, one of the consequences of the world-soul's descent, since its essence is reason: 'The forms of all things have their original home and their truest existence in *Nous*; then *Nous* communicates these forms to the world-soul, and to the souls of human artisans according to their capacities; then these divine and human souls can in turn impose likenesses of the original forms on matter, to the extent that the soul is capable of communicating the form and the matter of receiving it.'[79] Needless to say that in this explanation of the creative power of human artisans, Plotinus follows the Platonic metaphysical scheme linking the timeless original with the imperfect sensible copy, and the fabricated copy of a copy with the sensible object.

Through an inward extension of this analogy Plotinus can lead his pupils (and later readers) from their attachment to bodily things toward an intellectual vision of *Nous*, which must exist as the highest principle, in order to thus actualize the intellectual potential in individual souls. Where the Stoics considered corporeal things and their qualities to be the most real, Plotinus argued that they are merely the result of the soul's transmitting to matter what it has received from *Nous*. Everything real or perfect attributed to sensible things comes from some archetype in *Nous*; the appearance of defects or imperfections in sensible things must be explained by recourse to some other process. In this fashion, Plotinus' problem is the opposite of the Stoics' problem: they have to account for how superior principles emerge as alterations of inferior elements, that is, how the active principles in bodies are organized to order the totality of any bodily thing, including the animal body, into a rational whole. In contrast, Plotinus' problem is 'to explain, given the

---

[78] Menn, 1998, p. 112; on this topic, see also O'Daly, 1973, Chapter 3.
[79] Menn, 1998, p. 113.

existence of Nous and soul apart from bodies, how they come to be *in* bodies, how they come to bestow life and reason, to the extent that they do, on the extended mass which of itself is "the darkness of matter and not-being and what the gods abhor".'[80] When the active principle of soul produces a living body, the soul descends from the intelligible realm and thus becomes present in a material thing. However, in another sense the soul does not itself descend leaving its home behind; rather, the soul cares for its living host without building itself into the work or production. In Plotinus' own words, 'it governs while remaining above; it is ensouled in this way, having a soul not *of* it, but *to* it, [the body] being ruled, not ruling, possessed not possessing' (Enn. 4.3.9).

Although it is most common to say that soul is in the body, Plotinus prefers to say that body is in soul; what is contained in a living body is not the soul as such but the *image* of soul, that is, the irrational psychic powers that operate through the bodily organs and members: 'Soul constructs and animates not only the body of the world but also many smaller bodies, and each one equally receives a "soul" or image of soul: these many souls come to be out of one intelligible soul, and in a sense they still are one soul'.[81] It is in this context that Plotinus rehearses one of his most difficult and perplexing arguments, about which many of his interpreters disagree.[82] The issue concerns the question about whether there is only *one* soul, identical with the world-soul, instanced in many numerically distinct living things, each of which is individuated only by its material properties. Or, on the other hand, whether there are many particular souls, each the partial image of the world-soul, which itself individuates each living thing by imparting to it its material properties. Plotinus' expression of this issue is typically gnomic: 'one and the same soul is present in many bodies, and before this one-in-many there is another not-in-many: the one-in-many [derives] from this, *as if it were* an image coming to many places from the one-in-one, as if many pieces of wax were stamped by one ring and bore the same impression' (Enn. 4.9.4, emphasis added). The use of the phrase 'as if it were' conveys the author's effort to express this ontological derivation by analogy with a material multiple replication. Depending on whether the reader takes the one-in-many or the many-in-one as conceptually prior in the order of derivation, the relation of particular soul to world-soul has two senses (or two directions of fittedness). In one sense, my soul is the same as other souls and the world-soul, and, in another sense, my soul is similar to, but different than, other souls and the world-soul; similar in being one-of-many, each of which is like the world-soul, different in being *only* one-of-many, whereas the world-soul is many-in-one.

After drawing structural comparisons in Homer and Plato between the image and the original, Jean-Pierre Vernant returns to this theme in concluding his synopsis with an analysis of Plotinus' usage.

> For Plotinus, the One, or God, eternally immobile in its complete perfection, produces 'images' by a radiation comparable to the light that emanates from the sun. Insofar as these images express the One, they are inferior to it. Dependent on it, engendered from

---

[80] Menn, 1998, p. 120.
[81] Menn, 1998, p. 121.
[82] See for example, Blumenthal, 1993, III, pp. 56–60.

it, these images draw their existence from the link they must preserve with their source and model ... Like the *eidōlon* of that which has engendered it, the soul is inferior to the *nous*. It revolves around intelligence; it is the light that radiates from *nous*, its trace of the world beyond. On the one hand, the soul remains merged with intelligence, is filled with it, and takes pleasure from it; the *psuchē* takes part in it and itself has the power to think. But on the other hand, it is in contact with what follows, or rather, the *psuchē* also engenders beings that are necessarily inferior to it.[83]

Although the individual soul is not separable *as an entity* from its likeness, that is, its animate host body whose reflection its soul simulates, it is separable *as a likeness* from the world-soul whose (partial) reflection each soul amounts to. Such a capacity for conceptual separation (and eventual reunification) is comprised in the human soul's power to turn inwards in contemplation of its origin:[84]

> A turning of the soul towards Intelligence and the One is always possible ... To be a philosopher would therefore mean to turn oneself away from the body-simulacrum of the soul to return to that of which the soul is also the simulacrum, and from which it remains separated as long as it is content to reflect it instead of being identified with it. The idea is that the soul would lose itself there to find itself again, no longer as an image, a double, similar to the exterior model, but as a single and authentic being in the full coincidence of the self with the self through an assimilation to the god who is the all.[85]

A. H. Armstrong has summarized in an exemplary fashion the special relation Plotinus posits between the individual soul and its animate body; a summary so succinct and accurate it is worth quoting in full:

> Plotinus, when he uses spatial metaphors to describe the relationship of the two [body and soul], prefers to say that body is in soul, rather than soul in body, as in his great image of body floating in soul like a net in the sea. It means that Soul does not work on the universe from outside, making plans to deal with it on the basis of an external knowledge of it. There is no thinking things out or planning, no willing or choosing this or that, in its government of the world. The universal order springs from Soul spontaneously, as a tree grows. The laws of nature are not laid down in advance and then applied, but are the immediate undesigned result of Soul's contemplation of the higher order of Intellect, of which they are a reflection (somewhat distorted by the reflecting medium) rather than a laboriously painted picture. At this point in the system the principle, which applies throughout, that all action is dependent on contemplation becomes particularly important. Soul springs from Intellect as the spontaneous result of Intellect's contemplation of the One, and its own production of an action upon body is the spontaneous result of its return in contemplation to Intellect ... This applies at all levels, even the lowest, of Soul's action as a universal principle in the world of body, space and time.[86]

Plotinus' *Enneads* represents the crowning achievement of Neo-Platonism, the Hellenistic epoch's interpretation of Plato's mystical texts filtered through, and

---

[83] Vernant, 1991, p. 192.
[84] On the idea that separation means living an inner life, see Smith, 1974, p. 21–3.
[85] Vernant, 1991, p. 192.
[86] Armstrong, 1970, p. 253; in more detail, Smith, 1974, pp. 1–19.

adjusted with, Aristotelian, Stoic and anti-Gnostic doctrines. But Neo-Platonism continued for centuries after Plotinus under the Roman Empire; it was the dominant philosophical movement in Rome, North Africa, Athens and the Greek colonies in the Near East. Although its closing dates are mostly ceremonial or commemorative, the last phase of Neo-Platonism in the East occurred in 642 CE with the Arab conquest of Alexandria, and in the West with the closing of the Athens School in 529 CE under the Emperor Justinian.[87] There is general scholarly consensus on some of the core aspects of Late Neo-Platonism from the third to the sixth centuries:[88] first, the refinement and expansion of the Plotinian triad of One, Intellect and Soul; second, an emphasis on personal salvation in the afterlife; and third, the introduction of elements of theurgy, making oneself godlike, or working oneself into god.[89] 'With one notable exception (Themistius), all serious pagan philosophers in late antiquity took a firmly Platonist view of the soul's relation to the body, a view that was, moreover, shared by not a few of their Christian contemporaries', as Blumenthal notes.[90] Andrew Smith claims that the legacy of their attempt to popularize Platonism, in the context of the 'despondent society' of that epoch, resulted in the weakening of the philosophical statement of human stature.[91]

Later Neo-Platonists tended to complicate Plotinus' account of soul by postulating all sorts of intermediate entities at every point in the transition from realm to realm. Such significant teacher-scholars as Iamblichus and Proclus were highly motivated to offer an account of the soul's ascent which promised personal salvation. In pursuit of this ambition, Proclus and others were not averse to using magical spells and charms, reading omens and summoning oracles. Porphyry, Proclus and Julian the Apostate, amongst others, were united in their vigorous opposition to Christianity and attempts to resuscitate pagan theology and worship. The Later Neo-Platonists also shared an ever-growing concern to maintain the soul's freedom from the effects of its union with the body, and an obsession with the 'mechanics' and techniques of psychic life apart from the body, both before birth and after death. It is not feasible here to trace the complex, often baffling pros and cons of late pagan arguments regarding the nature of the Platonic-inspired immortal soul, but it is important to bring out one of the more unusual ingredients of Later Neo-Platonic *psychē-logos* – the doctrine of the *okhema*, or 'soul-vehicle'.[92]

The central Platonic text for this notion is in the *Timaeus* (41d, 44e, 69c) where, it seems, each created soul is accorded its own vehicle. In the *Elements of Theology*, Proclus introduced the notion of two vehicles: one for the upper, and one for the lower soul. On this view, it was easier for the soul to operate with its body in the material world via an intermediate entity, something halfway between the fully

---

[87] Alan Cameron argued that it continued until the destruction of the city of Rome in 580 CE, but Blumenthal convincingly rebuts this, 1993, XVIII, pp. 369–85.

[88] See Merlan, 1967, pp. 473–6.

[89] On this immensely complex topic, see Blumenthal, 1993, XI, pp. 1–7; John Anton, in Wallis, 1992, pp. 9–32; Birger Pearson, in Wallis, 1992, pp. 253–76; Smith, 1974, pp. 81–141; and Dodds, 1951, App. II, pp. 283–311.

[90] Blumenthal, 1993, VIII, p. 75.

[91] A. Smith, 1974, p. 54.

[92] On soul-vehicles, see Verbeke, 1945, pp. 351–85; Smith, 1974, App. 2, pp. 152–8.

material and the fully immaterial. However, Proclus often spoke as if there were *three,* not just two vehicles (*okhemata*): 'the vehicle which is natural to it puts it inside the cosmos, the second makes it [the soul] a citizen of the world of becoming, the one that is like a shell makes it an inhabitant of the earth.' Blumenthal further interprets this passage in terms of the soul-vehicles' functions: 'there is one vehicle for the soul outside the cycles of existence ... one for the soul when it is involved in a series of incarnations, and a third ... which is only needed when a soul is not merely in a condition for embodiment, but is actually embodied.'[93] Proclus claimed that (at least) the first and second vehicles are 'light-like', they are a tunic or garment made of simple components.[94] Simplicius distinguished between two types of ensouled body: the earthly body is *ostreōdes*, while the heavenly body is *pneumatikon*. This distinction, of course, is similar to St. Paul's distinction between the psychical body (in this life) and the pneumatic body (in the next life). Simplicius speculated on the material components of the soul-vehicle which would allow it to mediate between the body (*sōma*) and the soul (*psychē*). Blumenthal examined Simplicius' vehicular terms very carefully and classified them into four groups: (1) *augoeides* = light-like, similar to the light in the intelligible realm; (2) *aitherōdes* = aether-like, that is, celestial or stellar material; (3) *arkhoeides* = archē-like, similar to the originative principle; (4) *pneumatikon* = pneumatic or spiritual, that is, composed of *pneuma*, in the late Aristotelian, Stoic-modified sense.

Perhaps less perplexing in his account of soul-vehicles is an earlier work by Iamblichus where he described the prophetic power illuminating the aethereal and light-like vehicle attached to the soul. On his view, human beings have one soul-vehicle made of a single substance that can be described by three key terms: aether-like, light-like, and pneumatic. On balance, Blumenthal concludes that, 'the vehicle is seen as a necessary bridge entity between immaterial soul and material body ... Secondly, that it is involved with those activities which require the cooperation, in the strict sense, of body and soul, and most particularly those where the contribution of each might be regarded as more or less equivalent, that is, those which are performed by the sensitive faculties of the soul through the organs of the body.'[95] Although Proclus and Simplicius seemed to have held that the lower vehicle vanished upon the body's death, the upper vehicle accounted for the human soul's immortality and its return (ascent) to god's dominion.

In his recent thorough review of the best scholarly studies of Plotinus' account of soul, Emilsson draws the following important lesson about Plotinus' unique place in the Ancient and Hellenistic debates:

> Plotinus' view on the soul-body relation represents a great advance in sophistication from anything we know in his Middle-Platonic predecessors, even if some aspects of [his] doctrine of the soul are and presumably will remain unclear. In particular, his emphasis on the distinction between the intelligible – including all types of soul – and the corporeal, a distinction in terms of the nonextension of the latter, was to prove important in the history of western philosophy. Secondly, through his doctrine of the

---

[93] Blumenthal, 1993, XVII, pp. 174–5.
[94] The imagery of tents, skins and tunics is found in Philo, see Wolfson, 1962, pp. 366–9.
[95] Blumenthal, 1993, XVII, p. 186; see also Emilsson, 1994, pp. 5339–40.

pervasive presence, his notion of an organism and his distinction between the soul proper and the reflection of soul, Plotinus provides at least the sketch of a solution of the question [about] how an unextended soul can ensoul an extended body and nevertheless remain one and transcendent.[96]

In these and other ways, thinkers over the next two centuries, inspired by both the mystical Platonic dialogues and Christian teachings, attempted to reconcile disparate and heterogeneous philosophical elements into a coherent whole, that is, a coherent holistic account of an integrated whole soul.

(3) The Greek and Latin Church Fathers

The centuries from Plotinus to Proclus (c.200–500 CE) witnessed the gradual ascendancy and dissemination of Neo-Platonism in urban centers such as Rome, Syria, Athens, Alexandria and the cities of Graeca Minora, such as Pergamum. During the same period Christian martyrs, apologists and theologians established some of the basic tenets of the Christian doctrine of the soul. The Neo-Platonists had attempted various forms of synthesis of mainly mystical Platonic texts, with admixtures of Stoic, Aristotelian and anti-Gnostic arguments. The Greek and Latin Church Fathers, on the other hand, adopted an orientation that was equally anti-Gnostic and (often, but not always) favorable to pagan philosophy, especially toward the ethically high-minded pagans, such as Plato and the Stoics. Many of the early Church Fathers consciously intended their attitude toward pagan philosophy to follow the lead of Philo Judaeus. Philo, it will be remembered from a previous section, had attempted to render Greek philosophical speculation compatible with Judaic Scripture, though on his view philosophy would always be subordinate to God's word. Philo had been particularly inspired by the Greek notion of rational persuasion and explanation, such that his interpretation of Scriptural passages had to accord with inferential, demonstrative reasoning. The Church Fathers' attitude toward pagan philosophy, and hence their attitude toward the nature and functions of soul, was tied to their understanding of the subordinate relation of philosophy to Scripture. For some of them, the search for rational proofs of what one already believed on the basis of Christian faith diminished the value of such beliefs – faith alone was sufficient to hold such beliefs. But for others, faith in Scriptural teachings supported by rational demonstrations had even greater merit; to still others, simple faith and rational faith had equal merit.[97]

The period of patristic literature, the epoch of the Church Fathers, is usually defined as beginning with the end of the first century when the NT had been completed, and ending with the death of Gregory the Great (604 CE), or Isidore of Seville (636 CE); in the Eastern Church, this period extends to the death of John Damascene (749 CE). The Christian epithet of 'father' was applied to someone who instructed another in the true doctrine, as St. Paul himself said (1Cor. 4:15). The Gelasian Decree of the sixth century established four essential credentials to qualify

---

[96] Emilsson, 1994, pp. 5356–7.
[97] Wolfson, 1970, pp. 97–101.

for the title Father of the Church: doctrinal orthodoxy, holiness in life, ecclesiastical approval, and antiquity. Other significant Christian theologians who lack the credential of antiquity, but exhibit immense erudition, are called Doctor of the Church. In the Latin West, there are four Great Church Fathers: Ambrose, Jerome, Augustine and Gregory the Great; in the Greek East, the four Great Church Fathers are Basil the Great, Gregory Nazianzus, John Chrysostom and Athanasius.[98] The enormous variety and complexity of both internal and external debates, that is, heresies outside and schisms inside the Church, preclude our investigation from following every twist and turn in the patristic efforts to explain the nature and functions of the soul. Instead, our efforts will focus on some of the principal exponents of Christian-inspired philosophical speculation about *psychē* and *anima*.

Justin Martyr in the second century records his conversion from various Greek philosophical schools to Christianity which he regarded as the *true philosophy*.[99] Although he vigorously rejected pagan myth and cult as superstition infected by evil tendencies, he gave the most positive welcome possible to the classical philosophical tradition. He thought that it was remarkable how much Plato got right: his concept of god beyond human comprehension, Socrates' indictment of corrupt religion and impiety, Socrates' execution by the Athenian tribunal because of this indictment, the notion of the soul's close connaturality with the divine – these were all things Justin thought should be admired. He argued that Plato was able to achieve many of his profound insights because he knew about the Hebrew prophets. Although Plato had made some mistakes in his interpretation of these ideas, they still provided him with 'obscure hints of the truth'. Justin also admired Plato's notion, which he considered to be very close to St. Paul's, that humans have access to a universal moral conscience, without any need for a special, privileged revelation. Justin used the concept of the divine Logos or Reason to explain how the Father in heaven deals with the inferior created order of things. He stressed that the creation is the work of the supreme God, acting through the Logos as its mediator, and that in Christ's incarnation the Logos assumed full human status. Christ truly suffered in his passion in order to redeem humankind, and thus the destiny of the human soul is not merely the escape or passage beyond of an immortal soul, but its bodily resurrection at Christ's second coming. Justin's thinking had a decisive influence on early Christian attitudes toward Greek philosophy, especially through the impact of his thought on Irenaeus, Bishop of Lyon.

With Irenaeus the shape of Christian theology became stable and coherent, as Henry Chadwick says.[100] Irenaeus argued that there is a manifest unity in the OT and the NT through the apparent fulfillment of Hebrew prophecies, especially the ones that draw a parallel between Adam and Christ, and the foretelling of the advent of the messiah. He took the trouble to become fully conversant with Gnostic doctrines in order to better refute them, and understood that the main issue was one of Scriptural authority. Where the Gnostics had based their positions on several dubious tractates, apocrypha and testimonies, Irenaeus was the first to attempt to establish the NT canon of genuine gospels. He also had a positive attitude toward

---

[98] Quasten, 1975, vol. I, pp. 1–12.
[99] Quasten, 1975, vol. I, pp. 196–219.
[100] Chadwick (1967), 1993, pp. 80–83.

the best features of pagan Greek thought, accepting Xenophanes' description of God as 'seeing entirely, knowing entirely, and hearing entirely', and quoted with approval Plato's apothegm that 'God is the source of all good things.'

Irenaeus worked out his doctrine of human nature in conscious opposition to Gnostic dualism; where they distinguish between the Demiurge's creation of the natural (or hylic) human, and the Invisible Father's creation of the spiritual or pneumatic human, Irenaeus proposed to show that these two beings are one being. He argued that human being is at one and the same time bodily and spiritual, fashioned by the hands of God in the beginning, and to whom the Holy Spirit has been given through Christ's incarnation. Irenaeus replied to Gnostic teachings about the threefold 'nature' of human being by saying that flesh, soul and spirit are 'parts' of each single individual: 'That which was made by the Father's hands was not one part of human, but human himself in the likeness of God. Soul (*psychē*) or spirit (*pneuma*) may be one part of human, but human cannot exist as such. The complete (*perfectus*) human is the mixture and union of the soul, receiving the Spirit from the Father, and mingled with the flesh which was formed in the image of God' (Adv. Haer. 5.6.1). Here he draws an important conceptual distinction between 'image' and 'likeness', just as Plato and Plotinus had done: the body is the image, which the Father's hands fashioned and into which he breathed its soul; the likeness is the gift of the Holy Spirit. The original endowment of human being with spirit is an integral part of human being, without which an individual is incomplete.

Irenaeus devotes some time and effort to explaining his scheme for the integration of these component parts, an explanation which is of prime importance for understanding his theology of human being as the image of God: 'If we take away the reality of the flesh (*caro*), that is to say, the material form (*plasma*), and consider the spirit (*spiritus*) in isolation, what we have left is not the spiritual human, but the spirit of human or the Spirit of God.' In these terms, *spiritus* does not denote a kind or type (*genos*) of human being, to which another type might be conjoined, but a part or aspect (*meros* or *eidē*) of human being:

> When this spirit, mingled with the soul (*anima*), is united to the material form, then, because of the outpouring of the Spirit, the human becomes spiritual and perfect; and it is such a human who is made in the image and likeness of God. If, on the other hand, the Spirit is missing from the Soul, then what we have is certainly an animate being, but one who remains carnal and imperfect; he indeed possesses the image in the material form, but he does not acquire the likeness by means of the Spirit. In the same way, therefore, as this being is imperfect, so also if we take away the image and despise the material form, we can no longer speak of a human, but only of a part of a human, or of something other than human. [Adv. Haer. 5.6.1]

It is clear here (if not in other contexts) that he equates the 'likeness' (*homoiōsis*) to God, denoting perfection in human nature, as the Holy Spirit's gift, and uses 'image' (*eikōn*) to refer to the human body. It is humans' material form (*plasma*) which will be brought to life again at the resurrection; in this he agrees with the Pauline notion that the spiritual (*pneumatikos*) body, not the psychical (*psychikos*) body, will be brought back to life. In these contexts, Irenaeus speaks of the flesh (*caro, carnis*, from whence 'carnal') in line with the NT Greek term *sarx, sarkikos*, the soft tissues in which humans' tendency to moral evil is manifest.

According to Jean Danielou,[101] it seems that Irenaeus developed his ideas about human nature in the following fashion: God in the beginning created human in his own image and likeness, composed of body, soul and spirit; at the end of time he will come to restore this lost likeness in his creature. But Irenaeus proposes an unexpected line of thought:

> Just as, from the beginning of our formation in Adam, the breath (*aspiratio*) of life which was from God, united to the material form (*plasma*), gave humans life, and revealed him as a rational animal, so in the end the word of the father and the Spirit of God, united to the ancient substance from which Adam was formed, made a living and perfect human who received the perfection of the Father; so that, as in the ensouled human we all died, so in the spiritual human we shall all be made alive. For Adam never escaped from the hands of God, to which the Father addressed these words: Let us make human in our image and likeness. And that is why, at the end, not by the will of the flesh, nor by the human will, but by the Father's decision, his hands perfected human, so that Adam should be in the image and likeness of God. [Adv. Haer. 5.1.3]

In this passage, the lower immaterial form is the soul (*psychē*, or *anima*) which he equates with humans' animal nature, 'united to the ancient substance' (*ousia* or essence) of the kind of living being which can receive the gift of spirit.

The giving of life to the animal body by God's breath at the beginning, as Genesis records, is matched by the gift of true life through God's Spirit at the end, that is, in the final event of the Incarnation and its consequences for all redeemed human beings:

> For the breath (*afflatus*) of life, which makes human an animal, is one thing; and the life-giving Spirit, which perfects him as spiritual, is another thing ... Now Isaiah says: For the Spirit shall go forth from me, and I have made every breath of life, allotting the spirit uniquely to God, who pours it out in the last days upon the human race by the adoption of sons; but the breath of life he links with the creation, declaring it a thing made. Therefore the breath of life is temporal, but the Spirit is eternal ... 'But', says the Apostle [Paul], 'it is not the spiritual which is first, but first that which is animal, and then that which is spiritual.' For it was necessary first that human should be formed, and that having been formed he should receive a soul; and only then that he should in this way share in the Spirit. That is why 'the first Adam was made' by the Lord 'a living soul, and the second Adam a life-giving spirit'. [Adv. Haer. 5.12.2]

In these and other passages, Irenaeus asserts that the body was not created incorruptible, but rather capable of incorruption, that is, it could achieve a state in which it did not suffer from corruption. In making this claim he struck a decisive blow against the Gnostics, who used the text of St. Paul, that 'flesh and blood cannot inherit the kingdom of heaven' (1Cor. 15:20), to declare that it was flesh that inclined humans to destruction. Irenaeus went so far as to claim that certain persons (the prophets) had been granted immunity from fleshy decay even before their own deaths: 'By the very hands by which in the beginning they were formed they were assumed and translated. For the hands of God had in Adam accustomed

---

[101] Danielou, 1973, vol. II, p. 400; see Quasten, 1975, vol. I, pp. 308–10.

themselves to handle, to grasp, and to hold the thing they had formed, and to bear it and set it down where they wished' (Adv. Haer. 5.5.1). The image of God's hands marks an important motif in Patristic thought, one which ties it closely to the Greek notion of the supreme *nous* as demiurge or craftsman.[102] According to this view, humans were incorruptible in their original nature, and thus made potentially in the likeness of God. The second Adam is the perfect likeness of God (Jesus Christ) who will return in the last days: 'In him alone is God's design perfectly realized, he alone is God's total success. Hence all that went before him, though part of the same plan, were no more than rough drafts, inchoate and tentative. It is in the Risen Christ that the Spirit lays hold once for all upon the flesh in order to bestow upon it incorruptibility, and so to realize the perfect man.'[103] Irenaeus expressed this sentiment in clear language: 'When the word of God was made flesh, he established both the one and the other. He manifested the true image by becoming that which was his image; and he restored the likeness by consolidating it, making human like the Father by means of the visible word' (Adv. Haer. 5.16.1–2).

The OT offers many outstanding instances of the creative life force invested in God's hands: Joshua was full of the spirit of wisdom, for Moses had laid his hands upon him (Deut. 34:9); it was through the hands that the dying father transmits his gift (Gen. 48:13; 49:26); for the Jews the hands, as well as the knees, were the seat of strength (Job 4:3; Isa. 35:3), or of the lifeforce itself (Isa. 57:10). (The use of the word 'seat' (*sedes*), as in 'seat of reason' or 'seat of emotions', rarely remarked but often employed, conveys the same sort of metonymical shift.) In ancient Jewish custom, a hand-shaped statue was erected over the grave (2Sam. 18:18; 1Sam. 15:12), or the hand is a protective, apotropaic object (Isa. 56:4), or the God Sabazios, represented by a hand or a human carrying a hand-shaped scepter. In Jewish thought it was the hand that anointed a priest or elder son, transmitting spirit or vital power, for example, 'the spirit of Yahweh came upon him' in many instances (Judg. 3:10; 6:34; 1Sam. 10:6; 16:13, and so on) is parallel with 'the hand of Yahweh came upon him' (2Kings 3:15; Ezek. 1:3; 3:22; 8:1; 37:1). This imagery continues in the NT, where the best-known instance is Jesus' laying on of hands with his disciples (Acts 8:17; 9:17; 19:6, and so on), and the Apostles themselves anointed others in the same manner (Mark 5:23; 6:5; 16:18). In some early Christian artworks, especially tomb paintings, God the father, or perhaps the Holy Spirit, is pictured as a single hand.[104] There is a very good chance that the thought conveyed in these manifold figures of speech is of the divine being, or a divinely inspired being, for example, a priest or a prophet, as a maker or builder, one who works with his hands; as such, this root sense may underlie the technical Neo-Platonic concept of *theo-eurgos*, 'god-worker', or 'one who works on god'. This derivation shows even more clearly the parallel with the early Greek notion of *dēmi-ourgos*, for example, in Homer (Od. 17:383–85), who mentions carpenters, doctors, poets and others; and most famously in the *Timaeus*, though there is some disagreement over what kind of 'work' these makers had in common.[105]

---

[102] On patristic use of *nous* in this sense, see Lampe PGL, 1976, pp. 925–6, sec. F.
[103] Danielou, 1973, vol. II, p. 402.
[104] These details are drawn from Onians, 1951, pp. 494–8.
[105] For H. J. Blumenthal's ingenious derivation from the Mycenean Greek, see his 1993, XI, pp. 1–7.

Irenaeus' perspective on humans' incorruptible nature in the likeness of God signifies an important and unusual feature in his position. Although God granted a certain sort of perfection by bestowing his spirit on humans at the beginning, the earliest humans were only children who must progress stage by stage to another sort of perfection. His imagery in the pertinent section is strikingly literal: 'He who is the perfect bread of the Father offered himself to us in the form of milk, as if to babies; and his coming was rationed to the measure of humans, so that when we had been nourished at the breast of his flesh, and become used by such milk-feeding to chew and drink the word of God, we would be able to hold down within ourselves the bread of immortality, that is, the Spirit of the Father' (Adv. Haer. 4.38.1). Thus the more usual and traditional image of the soul as breath has been replaced by that of bread and milk, partly due to the notion that it is through a special individual event (the Holy Spirit's gift)[106] that humans are granted immortal life. Jean Danielou comments that these passages are quite extraordinary:

> They seem to go utterly against the whole mentality of the world in which Irenaeus lived. In the thought of the ancient world perfection lies in the past, at the beginning of things, and time brings nothing but degradation. This point of view was to exert great pressure on the course of early Christian theology ... The thought of Irenaeus unquestionably forms an exception to the general rule. Nevertheless, such teaching was not wholly original with him, any more than it was strictly biblical. Its affinities are with the concept of *paideia*, training, which was a prominent feature of ancient culture; but it does seem that Irenaeus was the first to apply this concept to the history of mankind as a whole.[107]

And further: 'this means that the philosophical element must be accorded a much greater influence on the development of Irenaeus' theology than it has sometimes been allowed.'[108]

The inheritance of the Platonic division of the soul into three parts or forms becomes more obvious in Patristic writers after the fading away of apologetic concerns in writers such as Justin Martyr and Irenaeus. Clement, Origen and Tertullian repeatedly employed the *Republic* tripartite formulation, although they sometimes had to abandon this scheme when it conflicted with Christian teaching. David Bell nicely summarizes the main features of the Platonic scheme as it appears in the Church Fathers. (A) The three-part scheme tends to be restricted to ethical rather than metaphysical contexts. (B) More important than this scheme is the duality of rational and non-rational; in order to accommodate the latter, they simplify Plato's original doctrine by grouping *thumos* and *epithumia* into the non-rational, leaving *logismos* as the rational element. (C) In order for the soul to be harmonious and balanced, the rational 'part' must govern the non-rational 'part'; if this were not the case then ethical-spiritual progress would be ethical-spiritual regress. (D) In many but not all cases the spatial location of the soul's parts

---

[106] On the Holy Spirit's work in creation, see Lampe PGL, 1976, p. 1100, sec. F.
[107] Danielou, 1973, vol. II, p. 404.
[108] Danielou, 1973, vol. II, p. 408.

according to the *Timaeus* account is given, though sometimes the analogy with the city-plan is used instead. (E) Plato's main scheme is syncretized with Stoic and Aristotelian features, especially the division into three forms of soul, that is, nutritive, sensitive and rational. On the whole, there is general consensus amongst the early Christian writers on these five main points; in other words, dissension and divergence is more rare than explicit (or even tacit) acceptance.[109]

Clement's analysis of the main 'parts' of human nature is somewhat eclectic, drawing from different systems in different contexts. When he comes to his discussion of the symbolic meaning of the number 'three' he analyzes human first into the standard triad of *thumos, epithumia* and *logismos*, and then into the threefold form, according to the NT, of *sarx, psychē* and *pneuma*. In another passage, he makes good use of the Stoic twofold division into *hēgemonikon*, the ruling 'part', and *hypokeimenon*, the subordinate 'part': 'There is, therefore, a kind of decad in a human: the five senses, the voice, the sexual drive, and in the eighth place, the spiritual element [introduced] at the formation of human; the ninth is the ruling "part" of the soul; and the tenth is the distinctive character of the Holy Spirit, which is added by faith' (Strom. 6.16.135). Clement here attempted to gerrymander these diverse partitions by equating (a) the five senses and the active faculty with the body, (b) the soul as life-force with the subordinate element, and (c) the rational faculty (*nous* or intellect) with the Holy Spirit.

According to either the Platonic or the NT scheme, for Clement it is always the case that it is the intellect or mind that gives humans their real dignity. He protested against the view that it is in virtue of his body that a human was fashioned in the image of God (Strom. 6.14.112). For Clement, it is due to their possession of *nous* that humans are made in the image of God, since mind is an endowment unique to the human species.[110] In arguing in this manner he set himself against the view of Irenaeus, who regarded the body as the image, and against other teachers who claimed that the Holy Spirit was the image of God. As Jean Danielou says, 'it is one of the distinguishing marks of Clement that exalts man the intelligent being as the most valuable of all the good things in God's creation.'[111] Since it is intellect that truly makes this animal a human it is in virtue of intellect that a human is a spiritual being. In this he disagreed with Plato and Neo-Platonic trends: 'It is far from correct to say that a human has no share in the divine thought (*ennoia*), since it is written that at this creation he took part in the breath (*emphusōma*), receiving a substance (*ousia*) more pure than any given to other living creatures' (Strom. 5.12.87). His argument in this passage reflects both the OT notion of God's breath (*nepesh*) and the NT notion of God's directive word at creation: 'Whereas Plato makes the intellect (*nous*) dwell in the soul (*psychē*) as an emanation from the divine gift, and the soul in the body, we say that in addition the Holy Spirit has been breathed into the believer' (Strom. 5.13.88).

---

[109] Bell, 1980, pp. 17–18; see Chadwick, in CHLGEMP, p. 171; and Lampe PGL, 1976, pp. 1543–4, sec. B

[110] On the affinity of God and the soul made in his image, see Lampe PGL, 1976, p. 1548, sec. IIA.

[111] Danielou, 1973, vol. II, p. 411.

Clement went on to argue that the human body was formed by God from dust or soil, and that this body is the 'form' or matrix (*plasis*):[112] 'Moses says that the body was formed from the ground, which is what Plato calls the "earthly dwelling", but that the rational soul (*logikē*) which comes from above, was breathed in by God at the face. For there the "ruling part" (*hēgemonikon*) is said to be located' (Strom. 5.14.94). This latter assertion converges with both the Stoic and Galenic thesis that the principal seat of the mind is in the head, and that respiration is an indication of the soul's presence. The Holy Spirit's special endowment is linked with Christ's coming, and as such it is bestowed only on those who believe in Christ as savior, through the action of baptism. On this topic, Clement argued against various Gnostics who thought that every human is both ensouled (*psychikos*) and spiritual (*pneumatikos*) by nature. Clement wanted to demonstrate just the opposite point of view, that a human is not a divine being by nature, one who has fallen from his original perfection, but rather a living being who though entirely human at the creation, can achieve perfection through salvation. He considered it entirely plausible that God could have created humans without the Holy Spirit's gift; as a product of a supremely good creator, each individual would have been good in his own nature. But humans would not be good through their own efforts, that is, by the exercise of their freedom to choose salvation. It was through *knowledge* of good and evil that Adam fell from his perfect state, Clement insisted; if Adam had remained in obedience to the Lord, his perfection would have followed without effort.

One consequence of this first fault was that disorder was introduced into human nature, as Danielou explains:

> As soon as the first man had sinned and disobeyed God, he became like the beasts, lacking reason. It is natural that one should regard him from then on as irrational and liken him to an animal. (Paed. I.13.101) ... Clement is saying that by the fall man lost his logos, and became like the animals – an idea which comes from Plato and Philo – but not that he lost all capacity for rational thought and was reduced to animality. On the contrary, Clement lays great stress on the fact that fallen man preserves his natural faculties intact, and that he is capable of moral effort. The present passage has to be understood in the light of the Platonist conception of the hierarchy of powers of the soul. The soul comprises both the higher part, the *hēgemonikon*, that is the mind (*nous*), and the passions, namely anger and desire, which derive from man's animal nature. If the passions are subjected to the *nous*, then the man is *logikos*, that is to say, the mind is the dominant factor; if the *nous* is subordinated to the passions, however, he becomes like the animals, because it is the animal nature which has gained supremacy.[113]

Henry Chadwick summarizes Clement's reliance on Greek philosophical doctrines while at the same time attempting to strike out on an emphatically Christian account of soul. Clement

---

[112] On *psychē* in relation to *sōma* in these texts, see Lampe PGL, 1976, pp. 1545–6, sec. D.

[113] Danielou, 1973, vol. II, p. 414; on *nous* obscured and numbed by sin, see Lampe PGL, 1976, p. 924.

... accepts the soul's independence of the body as proved by the souls' wandering in dreams and says that death breaks the chain binding the soul to the body. Nevertheless, he has many hesitations about the idea that the soul has fallen from heaven to become imprisoned in earthly matter. Although it is possible to find this idea in Clement, it seemed to him so dangerously like Gnosticism that he formally denied that the soul is sent down to this world as a punishment. He is able to show that the Gnostic interpretation of Plato is one-sided to the point of distortion, but he has to admit that there is much in Plato with marked affinities to the Gnostic world-view. Therefore, it tends to react against both, affirming that immortality is not an inherent and natural possession of the soul but a gift of salvation in Christ. The soul is not a portion of God but is created by God's goodness; as such it is the proper object of divine love. But this love is not automatic, as the heretics assume. It is one of the fundamental grounds for complaint against the Gnostics that their doctrine of the divine spark in the elect obliterates the gulf between creator and creature.[114]

Origen was a younger contemporary of Clement, and both came from Alexandria, an enclave where Origen's father had been a Christian martyr. Origen always wrote with a passionate sense of belonging to a church called to fearless resistance against compromise and oppression. Along with this attitude he maintained a strong world-denying strain of personal detachment and ascetic self-discipline. According to a story told by Eusebius, in his youth he castrated himself, and lived on the minimum of food and sleep, taking seriously the Gospel counsel of poverty.[115] He was a student of the mysterious Ammonius Saccas, with whom Plotinus was later to study, and became renowned in his own day for an exhaustive knowledge of Greek philosophy, heretical sects and an unusual familiarity with Hebrew. Origen's work resembles Philo's and Clement's in many respects, and he employed a complex and sophisticated template for allegorical interpretation of the OT. He was permanently concerned to seek a spiritual meaning that indicates Christ's redemption and a mystical sense that pertains to the individual soul's ascent and union with God. In Origen's hands, the influence of pagan philosophy had a seriously distorting effect on Christian teaching. One aspect of this is his avowal that humans comprise part of a spiritual world, a part that has fallen into the material world and is now called to restore itself to its original state.

Origen devised a picture of humans' relation to the divine and incorporeal world in which souls pre-exist the material world's creation.[116] He thought that this was the only way to save both God's justice and humans' freedom. All of the many differences in particular souls' conditions are due to their merits and demerits in their prior existence: 'When God in the beginning created what he willed to create, that is, rational beings (*logika*), he had no other reason for creating than himself, that is, his own goodness. Since it is he himself who is the cause of everything which has been created, and since in him there is no variation, nor change, nor inability, he created all those whom he did create equal and alike' (De Princ. 2.9.6). Although all creatures were made equal insofar as they had life-force, only rational

---

114 Chadwick, 1970, p. 172.
115 Chadwick, 1970, p. 182.
116 On the pre-existence of souls, see Quasten, 1975, vol. II, pp. 91–2; Lampe PGL, 1976, p. 1544, sec. C.

creatures have freewill, and freedom implies a certain degree of instability: 'The rational natures which were made in the beginning were created, not having existed before. Since, therefore, they once were not, but had a beginning in their existence, they are necessarily changeable and mobile, because whatever may be the virtue transferred into their substance, it does not belong to it by nature, but was given by God' (De Princ. 2.9.3). The created spirit continually receives its own being as God's gift, and its existence is a perpetual progress, namely the progress of becoming godlike. Having free will, those spiritual natures are necessarily moveable, both in the bodily sense and in the spiritual sense, that is, in terms of the diversity of choices available to them: 'In accord with the motions of its own freedom each spirit, neglecting the good to a greater or lesser degree, was drawn toward the opposite of the good, namely evil. It is thence that the creator seems to have derived the springs and causes of variety and diversity, in such a way that he created a diverse and varied world in accordance with the diversity of spirits, that is, of rational creatures' (De Princ. 2.9.2). Origen follows both the Platonic and Pauline division of kinds of humans into three classes. The first consist of those who fell the least (angels), the second comprises those who fell a middle distance (humans), and finally those who fell the furthest and reached the complete opposite (demons).

Origen addressed the question of the relation between the fall from the good and the corporeal world in these terms, as summarized by Jean Danielou:

> The body does not form part of the nature of any being. In the beginning all spirits were entirely incorporeal, but through their fall all became clothed with the bodies of one kind or another. The Fall, however, does not consist, as it does in Plato or Plotinus, in a descent to the realm of sensible realities. Corporeity is not evil; there is in Origen's writings no condemnation of the body – indeed it is a point of primary importance for him that there should not be, since this is an essential part of his reply to the main objection of the Platonists against the Incarnation. His thought is diametrically opposed to those who denounce corporeity, and see in it the principle of evil. Evil is in the will alone; and corporeity is connected not with evil but with diversity: 'The diversity of the world cannot exist without bodies.' Furthermore, these bodies are each appropriate to the degree of the creature's fall. They are therefore a punishment, but for Origen every punishment is a means of restoration.[117]

Thus, he managed to reconcile one facet of Platonic thought, that the body is a tent or garment, made of earthly fabric which binds humans to earth, with the positive aspect of the Pauline notion of flesh, as that which tends towards evil things, but which can be redeemed through the spirit: 'All rational, incorporeal and invisible creatures, if they become neglectful, fall little by little to lower planes, and take bodies appropriate to the places in which they settle; first, for example, ethereal bodies, than aerial, then when they enter the vicinity of the earth, they are clothed with coarser bodies, and finally they are tied to human flesh' (De Princ. 1.4.1)

Origen had an ambivalent attitude toward the Platonic account of soul since in another work, the *Homilies on Ezekiel*, he is prepared to employ the tripartite scheme in a positive manner. He ascribed the powers of the soul to the creatures in

---

[117] Danielou, 1973, vol. II, p. 420; see Chadwick, 1970, p. 190.

Ezekiel's vision: to the human the rational 'part', to anger the lion, to concupiscence the calf, and to the presiding spirit the eagle. According to David Bell, this picture clearly belongs to the same order of speculation as Plutarch's elevation of the mind (*nous*) over the soul (*psychē*) and the later Plotinian thesis of an unfallen part of the soul which remains forever 'above' and which forms a continuum with the divine thoughts (*noēta*).[118] Origen adopted an interpretation of Aristotle's notion of 'maker's mind', which he called *theia aisthesis*, for this purpose. In doing so he attempted to harmonize the Platonic and Aristotelian accounts of the 'nature' of the divine mind in its relation to finite, mortal minds. On this issue Origen offered his own version of the ascent of the soul through the various levels of reality, the sensible, the intelligible and the divine. Origen's notion of the body is not easy to isolate and shows many ambiguities; he asserted three times over that the Trinity alone is absolutely incorporeal, so the body (*corpus*) is a feature of the creature alone. But in the latter instance, 'body' seems to mean something else, as Henri Crouzel explains:

> In fact, Origen applies the word 'body' both to the terrestrial body and to the more subtle bodies which he distinguishes in his speculations on the history of rational beings: 'ethereal' bodies or 'dazzling' bodies, belonging to the pre-existent intelligences; the angels; those raised from the dead to eternal blessedness; the 'dark' bodies of the demons and those raised from the dead for damnation. But the word 'incorporeality', which can express either the absence of any body, however subtle, or simply the absence of the earthly body, has yet a third sense, that of a way of life without regard to the unlawful desires of the body, a meaning that is thus of a moral order: applied to the blessed in eternity, it is also applied fairly often, though obviously in a relative degree, to the righteous living on earth.[119]

It is due to humans' desire to serve the needs of the self at the expense of more spiritual aspirations that their bodies become, like all other sensible things, a constant temptation to remain at the sensible level and thus thwart the soul's ascent to contemplation of the divine mystery. Nevertheless, the earthly body is good in itself since it was created by God, and 'God saw that it was good.' The human body is an image of the divine reality, but the hinge upon which the image pivots is the soul and not the body; in this sense, the human body is the 'shrine' or 'temple' that contains the image. The ethereal body of the pre-existent soul survives in the earthly body after the fall in the form of 'seminal reason'. From these seeds grows the glorious or dazzling body of the resurrection; in other words, the substance (*ousia*) of the body remains the same, but its properties change – from heavenly to earthly and then to heavenly again. For righteous humans now in their earthly life, the body made from clay or dust has also entered the radiance of the spirit that makes itself known through the Holy Spirit, as Henri Crouzel says. An essential difference between those raised into glory and those raised into damnation is that the latter no longer have any spirit (*pneuma*), for God has taken back the gift bestowed upon them at the beginning. With respect to the same passage analyzed

---

[118] Bell, 1980, pp. 25–6.
[119] Crouzel, 1989, p. 90; on soul in relation to body, see esp. Watson, 1989.

earlier in the section on the NT idea of conceptual division between the spirit and the flesh, Origen declares that when God has taken back the spirit, both the soul and the body will go to hell, even though the soul retains its indelible image of God its maker – though now this image is the source of its torment:

> The dominant context of this trichotomic anthropology is more moral and ascetic than mystical: it is the spiritual battle. The soul is torn between the spirit and the attraction of the earthly body, the flesh: of this struggle the soul is both the scene and the stake, and it is the soul, with its free will, that has to decide for one or the other. In itself, by reason of the two elements or tendencies that divide it, the soul is in league with both sides.[120]

This is the crux of the conceptual distinction between soul and spirit in the Christian tradition, and hence the origin of the primary sense of spirit as a divinely bestowed capacity for *another life*; in contrast to the medico-physical sense of spirits (always in the plural) as the material carriers of our ordinary life-force.

There is some resemblance between Origen's view of the cosmos as a whole and Plotinus' picture of the world-soul (though he refused to countenance an identification with the Stoic world-soul[121]), but with the reservation that the Church itself is thought of as the corporate body of Christ: 'Just as our own body is composed of many members, and is held together by one soul, so the whole universe should be regarded as a kind or immense, gigantic living creature, which is, as it were, held together by one soul, namely the power and reason of God' (De Princ. 2.1.2). One single principle guides the order of the world whole, manifest both in the hierarchy of spirits and in the arrangement of material elements – and that is that God has brought about a world in which rational creatures desire to return to him from their own free will.[122] The potential restoration extends to all spiritual creatures, and even the demons in Hell have an opportunity to reverse their descent by climbing back up to God. This doctrine is one of many which sets Origen in stark contrast with contemporary Gnostic beliefs. According to one of their main tenets, each created being has its place by nature, or in its essence, and thus cannot attain any greater degree of release than what has already been granted to it. Origen also rejected some of the implications of extreme dualism, since on his view *all* things (except God alone) are intermediate between spirit and matter. In this respect he was closer to Plotinus than any other philosopher, since Plotinus emphasized free will as the most decisive factor in establishing a created being's place in the cosmic order. But, as Danielou observes, there are profound differences as well:

> For Plotinus, evil is essentially an illusion of the spirit which cleaves to matter instead of turning toward the One. It therefore depends on the spirit in question whether it comes to itself and thus rediscovers its own true nature and returns to the home which it has abandoned. For Origen the fallen souls are utterly impotent to save themselves by their own efforts; salvation can only come by an act of God's love. This act is the sending of the Son, begun in the OT, reaching its climax in the Incarnation, and pursuing an

---

[120] Crouzel, 1989, p. 92.
[121] See Berchman, 1984, p. 133.
[122] On mystical union, see Quasten, 1975, vol. II, pp. 97–100.

unending course through the ages until Christ has once more subjected all things to the Father and restored the spirits to their original integrity.[123]

In the Latin tradition, Minucius Felix's *Octavius* is the earliest work in Latin Christian literature which testified to the encounter between the Christian revelation and the philosophical culture of the classical heritage. This dialogue between Octavius the Christian and Caecilius the pagan survives only in Book VIII of Arnobius' *Adversus Nationes* (c.303–310) Writing about the same time as the more famous Tertullian, Minucius went to some lengths to employ standard Latin prose and avoid Christian lexical inventions. In doing so, he often appealed to Cicero and Seneca in his presentation of some of the main tenets of the Christian faith. Many of his careful Latin turns of phrase were adopted by later Latin Christian writers and helped to establish a stable lexicon for key theological concepts. His theology is derived to a great extent from the early Christian apologists and also from the Platonists and Neo-Platonists.[124] The Late Latin philosophical preoccupation with the 'inner' human being emerges for the first time in Christian literature in Minucius' work, becomes more explicit and systematic in Tertullian, and reaches its fulfillment in Augustine. Minucius' views about human nature took their start from his general picture of humans' nearness to God. These views are expressed in response to the opinions of his main opponent, Caecilius, who voices some standard Stoic arguments. Caecilius accepts some of the main planks of Stoic physics while rejecting much of the theological speculation associated with it. He asks, 'if in the beginning the seeds (*semina*) of all things come together and solidify by nature, why is God the author?' The seeds are the elements whose combination, in a variety of complex mixtures, produces all things by the action of their root-nature. This reflected the Stoic view that, amongst all other things, living beings are no more than specific combinations of elements: 'Human and each living thing is born, lives and grows up and consists of a spontaneous combination of elements into which once again human and every living thing is separated, dissolved and dispersed. So all things flow back to their source and return to themselves without an artificer, a judge or an author of their being.' The constant flux and reflux observable in apparent growth and change was Minucius' way of expressing, in the pagan voice, the Stoic picture of endless cosmic cycles unwinding without direction or providence.

Minucius countered these Stoic claims with a vigorous statement of the evidence for divine providence: 'There exists some sacred power (*numen*) ... by which all nature is inspired, moved, nourished, and directed'. Although *numen* is a distinctly pagan term, usually avoided by early Christian writers, Minucius used it in this context to indicate something like *potestas*; the term *inspiretur* also shows some reliance on the Stoic notion of *pneuma* – breath as the principle of movement. However, in contrast with his pagan opponent Minucius does not draw on the Stoic doctrine that the cosmos is an elemental compound, preferring instead to speak of the world made by God. With regard to human nature, he says that 'the beauty of our form declares that God was its author', and specifically cites 'the upright

---

[123] Danielou, 1973, vol. II, p. 425.
[124] On his life, see Bayliss, 1928, Chap. 1; quotes are from Danielou, 1977, vol. III, pp. 203–10.

stature, the erect head, eyes placed at the top as in a watch-tower and the other senses brought together as in a citadel'. In contrast with other animals, humans possess speech and reason by which they are able to imitate God, that is, to exist in his image. It is the contemplative vision of heaven, the result of their erect posture, which leads humans to knowledge of God, an idea which first appeared in Cicero. Four other special features of human beings are also derived from Cicero's writings: the human body's wonderful contrivance, individuals possessing different outward features, the manner of generation and childbirth, and their adaptation to diverse climates. Minucius also adhered to the Stoic notion of a general conflagration in which the world is bound to come to an end: 'All things which have come into being die, all created things perish ... and thus all the things that are contained in heaven cease as they began.' With regard to the exact fashion in which this *incendium mundi* will take place, Minucius is less than clear. He said that, 'either an earthly fire will fall unexpectedly down onto the world or else heaven itself will begin to melt' – an opinion as ambivalent as current debates about global warming versus an impending ice age. Although he knows that this idea can be found in the Stoic philosophers, he insists that its main import is derived from the OT.

Minucius considered the concept of human destiny, as realized in the final resurrection, had not been entirely foreign to pagan philosophers; both Plato and Pythagoras preserved the traditional belief that although human bodies dissolve their souls are eternal. According to his version, since God was able to fabricate humans at the beginning, he will be able to make them again: 'just as he could be born out of nothing, so he can be renewed out of nothing.' Whereas it is true that the body may dissolve into its original elements, the elements themselves are in God's keeping. According to Jean Danielou, this theme is not found in Tertullian, but it is taken up by Gregory of Nyssa: 'It is quite obviously in accordance with Stoicism, and Minucius is the first Latin Christian author to make use of it, whereas the other associated ideas had already been used by the second century apologists. On the other hand, Minucius does not deal at all with the argument put forward by Celsus, that bodies are devoured by other bodies.'[125] He argued astutely that the idea of bodily resurrection is prefigured in nature itself: 'The sun dips down and is born again; the stars sink and return; the flowers fall and renew their life; shrubs age and then break into leaf; seeds must decay in order to renew their life. The body in the grave is like trees in winter, they conceal their greenness under a show of dryness ... We too must wait for the springtime of the body.' In these terms Minucius did his best to make constructive use of pagan philosophical concepts of human nature and destiny while preserving a strict line on Christian doctrine:

> His teaching is based on Scripture, but he points out that it is prefigured in pagan mythology. The river of fire and the heat which comes from the Styx and from the dark chasm mentioned by Virgil are examples of this. Like the fires of Etna and Vesuvius, which set fire to the land without consuming it, the punishing fire similarly destroys and replenishes its fuel at the same time. Hence the doom of sinners thrown into the *incendium* will be eternal. Minucius, then, uses these themes taken from the Latin tradition to illustrate the Gospel message.[126]

---

[125] Danielou, 1977, vol. III, p. 207.
[126] Danielou, 1977, vol. III, p. 208.

Latin Christian theology and psychology reaches its first great summit in the prolific and brilliant work of Tertullian (*c*.160–225 CE), North African lawyer, jurist and teacher.[127] Tertullian followed Irenaeus' line of thought on several themes, especially in his concern with the triune nature of God: 'He was a well-educated orator rather than a meticulous philosopher', Chadwick says. 'He had been influenced by Stoicism with its doctrine that the immaterial is simply the non-existent, and was prepared to explain that God in all three "Persons" is "Spirit", which he seems to have interpreted as an invisible and intangible, but not ultimately immaterial vital force'[128] – an express formulation not far from the fundamental Greek idea of *psychē* itself. Tertullian's Latin vocabulary decisively shaped medieval theological discussions on many subjects, much as Cicero's Latin had transformed Greek philosophical ideas. As an individual thinker, he was 'brilliant, exasperating, sarcastic, and intolerant, yet intensely vigorous and incisive in argument, delighting in logical tricks, and with an advocate's love of a clever sophistry if it will make the adversary look foolish, but a powerful writer of splendid, torrential prose'.[129]

In his general orientation, Tertullian had a rather negative view of pagan philosophy, but he admitted that it contained grains of truth. What the philosophers 'have discovered has been lost in uncertainty, and from one or another kind of truth has emerged a flood of quibbles' (Ad Nat. 2.2.5–6). He endorsed Justin's opinion that the Biblical texts are the earliest works of philosophy, and that the Greek philosophers, in their desire to know everything, may have borrowed some truths from the Scriptures. In his attempt to define his position with regard to paganism, he took Varro's treatise *De rebus divinis* as his benchmark. Varro's ambition had been to compile a compendium of Roman religion in the first century BCE, grouped under three headings: philosophical, mythical and civil. Tertullian analyzed the interpretation of mythology according to which myths are symbols of the realities contained in the cosmos. The question that concerned him, with regard to natural theology, centered around the deification of the cosmos, the way in which the world had been made like God's work.[130] He referred to Varro's view only to utterly reject the physicalistic implications of such an understanding: 'Varro insists that fire is the soul of the world (*anima mundi*), to such an extent that fire governs everything in the world, just as the soul governs everything in human beings' (Ad Nat. 2.14). Tertullian did not simply criticize the Stoic picture of soul-fire, since he accepted their concept of providence, but not their explanation of its appearance. Against the thesis that the elements are divine principles that condition the world for human good, he argued that God transcends the world and the elements are merely tools for shaping his creation.

Tertullian's knowledge of pagan philosophy was enormous and he was especially indebted to the Stoic Seneca, more so than to the eclectic Cicero. J. H. Waszink has shown that he adopted several Stoic arguments, for example, on the basic unity of the soul.[131] In putting forth his Stoic-inspired points he was not reliant, as was

---

[127] ODCC, pp. 1352–3; Quasten, 1975, vol. II, pp. 246–9.
[128] Chadwick, 1993, p. 89.
[129] Chadwick, 1993, p. 91.
[130] Danielou, 1977, vol. III, p. 211; Varro's work, see OCD 3rd edn, p. 1582.
[131] Waszink, 1955, pp. 129–47.

Minucius, on Cicero's *De natura deorum* and the *Letters to Lucilius*. 'We may therefore say without hesitation', Danielou comments, 'that the Stoic influence in his case was less a matter of detail and more of the spirit. He kept certain basic aspects of Stoic teaching, and these were to provide both the background of his own thought and one of the ways in which he was to leave his mark on Latin Christianity.'[132] One of his modifications of Stoic teaching pertains to his use of the term *corpus*, in the ordinary sense of 'body'; he often uses this term as a synonym for *caro, carnis*, 'flesh', to refer to the material aspect of human nature. T. D. Barnes has documented[133] the fact that he also uses it in a more technical sense to indicate matter or the material constituents of natural things. From his perspective matter is corporeal because all substances are corporeal, and this applies to his discussion of the soul: 'The soul is a body of its own peculiar quality', as he said in his commentary on the *De Anima*.[134] Against Plato and the Platonists, he insisted that the very notion of an incorporeal substance was nonsense; even the angels had bodies, though they were spiritual bodies. One of his most unusual beliefs was that God himself is a body, 'for spirit is a body of a special kind.'

Tertullian's general picture of universal corporeity or body-ness was as follows: 'Everything that exists is a body of a special kind. There is nothing incorporeal except what does not exist. If a being has something by which it exists, it is a body.' He admitted that there are different *kinds of kinds*, that is, different ways in which each kind of body can be special: 'Over against spirit and soul I am not aware in human of any other substance except flesh to which the term "body" can be applied' (Adv. Marc. 5.15.8). Given his identification of existent thing with body what could count as something non-bodily? 'From whence does the force come to an incorporeal soul? How could an empty thing move solid things?' (De Anima 6.3). The essential opposition that his analysis is meant to bring out is between that which has concrete reality, firmness, solidity, resistance and activity with that which does not have concrete reality and efficacy. This does not mean that there is not something the opposite of body, but that this something does not derive from the very substance of reality; rather, it derives from those abstractions by which reality is analyzed in the mind: 'Tertullian's profound vision then is that the name of "body" has to be given to what is real, and what is real is not that which is dependent on the mind, but that which imposes itself on the mind, comes into conflict with it and resists it.'[135]

The most basic features of his position on body are taken from the Stoic system, but with some important provisos. First, he rejected the notion that all bodies are homogeneous (literally, 'of the same kind or class'); there are certain irreducible levels of corporeity. On one hand, there are three degrees of bodily being (spirit, soul and matter), and on the other, there are three levels of souls (angelic, human and animal). He also rejected the Stoic doctrine of change, namely that only created things can change or be changed, since God is immutable and immovable. This proviso also attaches to his concept of the soul, since what is natural in the soul

---

[132] Danielou, 1977, vol. III, p. 215.
[133] Barnes, 1971, pp. 304–6.
[134] On the *De Anima*, see Quasten 1975, vol. II, pp. 287–9.
[135] Danielou, 1977, vol. III, p. 217.

cannot change. Thus against the Gnostics he held that the soul cannot become enmattered by just any means, not even by free will, which, he claims is *not* an essential feature of ensouled beings. For the same reasons he also condemned the doctrine of soul-migration, from living to living being. He asked 'if the soul is in any way capable of being transferred (*translationis*) into animals, will it be changed according to the qualities of the species and their lives, which are contrary to human life...?' – and concluded that this is contrary to the very nature of the cosmos itself. Concrete things can only be subject to accidental changes and can, in that sense of internal change, grow and develop. Such an inner transformation takes place in the soul, a unique substance which develops, according to Tertullian, in the intellect (*mens* or *animus*). With regard to an analysis of the component parts and functions of the soul he went along with his non-Christian contemporaries. He did not use the term 'part' (*pars, partis*, Greek *meros*) but preferred instead Aristotle's terms 'powers' (*vires*), or 'operations' (*operae*). He reconciled the twofold division into rational and non-rational with Plato's threefold analysis in these terms: 'indignation, which is called *thumikon*, and concupiscence, which is called *epithumētikon*, and that which is common to us and lions, the same thing indeed with flies, by reason moreover with God' (De Anima 16.3).[136] He employed the same scheme in his analysis of the human 'nature' of Christ, arguing that Christ felt anger and desire, though he admitted that in Christ's case these emotions were not irrational but perfectly rational.[137]

In his discussion of the problem of metempsychosis he described the movement as *animarum reciproce discursu* or, in other words, 'the movement by which souls pass unceasingly from the dead into the living and conversely', *animarum recidivatu revolubili semper ex alterna mortuorum atque viventium suffectione* (De Anima 38.1). He identified this as a Pythagorean doctrine, though according to his Middle Platonist source, it came from a divine oracle. He objected to this opinion since, in light of Stoic logic, it was possible for death to follow life, but not for life to follow death, for example, blindness can follow sight, but not the reverse. He also objected that, on this view, 'there would always have been the same number of souls, that is, the number of those who first entered life.' But since it is clearly the case that the human species has increased in number the quantity of souls could not have increased. Further, he thought it absurd that human souls could pass into animal or plant hosts, since each animal has a special affinity with one of the elements, whereas the human soul cannot be reduced to any one of these elements.[138] In other animals, the soul's seat is not the same as that in humans:

> The problem of Tertullian's sources in this whole discussion is raised both by his account of Platonist theory and by his refutation of it on the basis of Stoicism. For what

---

[136] David Bell remarks on the strange, unexplained use of flies in this set of images; he conjectures that Tertullian (or his source) may have confused the very similar passage in Origen's *Homilies on Ezekiel* where the calf is compared to the *moskhos,* easily confused with the Latin word *muscis*, 'flies'.

[137] David Bell, 1980, pp. 23.

[138] On patristic writers' rejection of metempsychosis, see Lampe PGL, 1976, pp. 1546–7, sec. F3.

we have is a highly characteristic block of ideas: criticism of the theory of the fall of souls; coming and going between heaven and earth; criticism of the theory of metempsychosis; and the simultaneous origin of the body and the soul. This group occurs, so far as the present writer is aware, only in one other patristic author, namely Gregory of Nyssa.[139]

Tertullian's philosophical approach to certain Christian doctrines was not confined to his appropriation of Stoic opinions about matter and bodies. His work also testified to the then current force of Platonist and Middle Platonist teaching; as such, he was one of the great witnesses to the vitality and influence of Platonism under the Roman Empire in the second century. In the *De Anima* he was especially concerned to refute the Platonist concept of pre-existent souls:

> I am sorry that Plato should, in good faith, have been responsible for spreading all kinds of heresies. In the *Phaedo*, for example, he says that [1] souls come from various places at various times, and [2] in the *Timaeus* that the descendants of God, having been given the task of begetting mortals, received the immortal principle of the soul and made a mortal body freeze around it; [3] he also teaches that this world is simply the image of another world. [De Anima 23.5]

As J. H. Waszink correctly pointed out,[140] the reason he mentioned these three points is that they were developed by the Gnostics into doctrines that Tertullian had just severely censured.

Let us follow Jean Danielou in his comparison of the similarities between Tertullian and Gregory before going on to consider the details of Gregory's account of soul. In the first place, Gregory distinguished between soul-migration from human to human, and from human into animal or plant. He accused the former theory of confusing two different natures and argued that it is absurd to think of the human soul as flying with birds, swimming with fishes, or feeding like animals. He discussed the issue of the fall of souls and argued that the soul has a cyclical movement that leads to a coming and going between the heaven and earth. In the same context he also considered the thesis that the body and soul appear at the same time in the mother's womb, and then argued that, according to the Stoic principles of *hexis* and *sterēsis*, life cannot come from death. He closed this discussion with a question about the number of souls and decided that this is something that can occur only at the end of a growth process:

> It goes without saying that Tertullian could not have influenced Gregory of Nyssa here, but it is at the same time difficult not to conclude that each author made use, in his own special way, of already existing material. If this is so, then the treatise in question undoubtedly came from a Middle Platonist source ... Tertullian would be the earliest witness to a lost treatise ... which was used by Porphyry and also indirectly by Gregory of Nyssa.[141]

---

[139] Danielou, 1977, vol. III, p. 227.
[140] Waszink, 1955, p. 140.
[141] Danielou, 1977, vol. III, p. 228; see Quasten 1975, vol. III, pp. 283–5.

In summary, Tertullian borrows his arguments about the nature and function of the soul from the Platonists and his concept and scheme of the body from the Stoics and Aristotelians. He drew on Cicero, Seneca and Varro with great skill and creative ingenuity, blending Stoic theorems with some of the most basic Christian principles. It has been justly remarked that, because of his profound erudition, ingenious syncretism of diverse elements and superb prose style, Tertullian was the greatest intellect of his age.

In his dialogue *On the Soul and Resurrection*, Gregory of Nyssa[142] addressed the issue of whether opposite feelings such as desire and anger should in fact be thought of as supplementary souls: 'Either anger and desire are both second souls in us, and a plurality of souls may take the place of a single soul, or the thinking faculty in us cannot be regarded as soul either (if they are not).' His correspondent Macrina's answer was that such emotions are faculties of the animal soul, not of the distinctly human soul; they cannot belong to the mind, since the mind is the seat of God's image and God does not have such feelings. Macrina's questions and opinions reflected the then current Hellenistic attitude about the faculties (*dynameis*), whether it is one thing or three parts, whether such conceptual divisions imply real divisions amongst essences (*ousiai*), and whether indeed there may not be multiple souls for each living thing. The overall purport of this dialogue was that irrational feelings cannot exist in the rational faculty since such feelings are not found in God, who is the paradigm for human minds, but not souls. Gregory described the relation between the intellectual faculty and the passions as one of control and transformation; by governing the passions in their basic state something wonderful is brought forth from them.

In the treatise *On the Making of Humans*,[143] he argued that just as the mind is one thing despite its multiple faculties and operations, so also God himself is one. In arguing this line, he used Aristotelian arguments against Plato on the unity of the soul, and then reapplied them to an account of the mind. In other words, he wanted to argue that the mind is one thing despite its obvious multiple powers and operations. His thesis then moved from a general exposition of the resemblance of human nature with divine nature to the unity of action in human and divine operations. He said that God does not have many powers for many operations, but only one power, just as humans have only one power of mind for its many operations. The several senses are animated (literally 'ensouled', or 'soul-driven') by one power, which does not vary with the organ used, but whose perceptions are separable due to physical constraints. He described the soul as consisting of three powers: the nutritive, the perceptive and the rational. In terms of the living thing itself, there are three powers: the moist, the hot and the mixed; he associated these with the liver (and blood), the heart (and breath), and the nervous system. But he cautioned his reader that the three psychical powers are not attached to or seated in one organ.[144]

---

[142] This sub-section draws heavily on Michel Barnes' superb study, 1994, pp. 8–20; see also Sheldon-Williams, in CHLGEMP, 1970, pp. 447–56; Quasten, 1975, vol. III, p. 261–3.

[143] See Quasten, 1975, vol. III, p. 263; on his Platonism, see esp. Cherniss, 1930.

[144] On the twofold and threefold division of the soul, see Lampe PGL, 1976, p. 1543, sec. B4.

His overall argument for the soul's unity was drawn from the Genesis account of creation, according to which the first living things created were those that grew from the earth. Those next created were the non-rational animals, and then finally rational humans. In the Genesis account Gregory discovered an Aristotelian threefold division of the soul, that is, the capacity for growth and nutrition (*threptikon*), the capacity for managing the senses (*aisthestikon*), and the power that orders all else (*dianoetikon*). He also concurred with Aristotle that the higher faculty or power subsumes or contains all the lower powers. Gregory followed the Biblical version in his interpretation of this threefold division: 'Of the bodily things, some have no part in life, while some participate in living powers (*zōtikēs energeias*). Of bodily things again, some have sensation, while some have no part in sensation. Finally what has sensation is again divided into rational and non-rational.' Where the Neo-Aristotelians were concerned to preserve the unity of the soul as a whole, Gregory is concerned to preserve the unity of the mind over against the multiplicity of the mind's faculties and operations.

It is not just the OT account of human nature that Gregory worked through in his treatise on *Human Making*, but the NT version as well. When St. Paul prayed for complete grace to descend 'on body and soul and spirit' (1Thess. 5:23), and again where Christ exhorted his followers to love God with 'their whole heart and soul and mind' (Mark 12:30), Gregory interpreted this threefold division in light of his psychical theory. In this vein he said that 'body' means the nutritive, 'soul' the sensitive, and 'mind' the rational power. The Pauline formula had been Origen's preferred model for an account of soul in *On First Principles*, where it was used in contrast with the Platonic threefold analysis. Origen had been worried that, against the Gnostics and other heretics, he needed a firm basis for the dichotomy between flesh and spirit. In contrast, Gregory interpreted the same scriptural passages in order to diminish the radical separation between the body, the soul, and the spirit:

> While for Origen the trichotomy describes the entire human organism, for Gregory it describes only the human soul: the scriptural term 'body' refers to the nutritive power and not to the corporeal body *per se*. The existence and nature of the body is accounted for by the Aristotelian presupposition that all soul exists in body. Gregory's identification of the scriptural trichotomy with the Aristotelian trichotomy removes the tri*partite* content of the former, for the distinctions no longer name separate natures.[145]

In addition, he spoke of the natural human disposition to recognize Christ's wonders and the moral injunction for humans to respond with love and honor. In the passage cited from Mark's gospel he altered its import slightly in order to affirm that the rational power is the locus of honor and the heart is the locus of love. In the context as a whole, Gregory wanted to move beyond the description of the human soul and instead characterized the whole of human existence, in one dimension as desire and intellect, and in another dimension as corporeal and incorporeal.

Robert Grant has nicely summarized the Patristic contribution to philosophy in the following words:

---

[145] Barnes, 1994, p. 22.

Christian theologians generally shared their doctrine of God with Platonists. Their doctrine of the Logos resembled that of the Stoics, although Christian theologians believed in one Logos (as in Philo) rather than many. They used skeptical arguments against the pagan gods ... Like non-Christians of various schools, they tended to believe that there had once been unified religious philosophy, Oriental in origin, from which later philosophers had deviated. This first philosophy, it was thought, had been based on the inspiration of the divine Logos or borrowing from Moses, or both. The views of the Christian theologians were thus close to the kind of Hellenistic Judaism represented by Philo. Few writers took up the philosophical problems presented by the Incarnation; several of them do not even mention Jesus.[146]

The current investigation into the patristic account of soul considered the ramifications of these themes in third-century Greek thinkers, such as Clement, Origen and Gregory of Nyssa, as well as the Latin thinkers Minucius Felix and Tertullian. It is now our task to consider the complex multi-faceted ways in which Augustine attempted to reconcile all of these points of view in the greatest theological–philosophical synthesis of the early Middle Ages.

(4) Augustine's Christian–Platonist synthesis

An overview of Augustine's various accounts of the soul and soul–body union – for there is no *one* account – has to 'take account' of some exceptional factors in understanding his entire work. These factors include, first, the development of Augustine's understanding of human nature, from his earliest Manichean phase, through his Platonist and Neo-Platonist studies, to his conversion to Christian doctrine, especially through St. Paul's Letters. In the last phase, Augustine's extraordinary genius is turned toward repeated efforts to accommodate (or perhaps reconcile) Platonic concepts with both NT accounts of soul *and* Genesis' two accounts of the creation of Adam. Second, hand in hand with this maturation in his thinking is his willingness to revise and correct his previous exegesis and explanation. Third, the degree of influence accorded to the mystical Platonic dialogues and Plotinus' *Enneads* is open to dispute; various scholars disagree widely on how much Augustine had read and how much his readings shaped his views. Fourth, in his later work there are three accounts, not just one, of the relation of soul to body: (a) in the human being as originally created by God in the Garden of Eden; (b) in our present earthly life after the fall from the previous perfect state, and (c) in our future heavenly life after the resurrection.

In the sections that follow we will consider some of the standard topics in the then current discussion of the nature, function and origin of the human soul. Augustine's distinctive Latin terminology was derived from contemporary translations of Greek texts and the Scriptures; through his subtle handling of these texts his discussions decisively transformed the psychical vocabulary of philosophical speculation. One also needs to take account of his conversion to both Platonist and Neo-Platonist philosophy and to Christian theology. He thought

---

[146] Grant, 1967, p. 58.

that Plato's mystical ideas provided him with the vision of God and the soul, and that Christ's message provided him with the path to that vision. He also follows Plato in allowing that the basic concept of *anima* as principle of self-movement and life-force is closely tied to its immaterial and immortal character. Philosophical arguments for the soul's immortal and immaterial status also concern possible scenarios for the soul's origin and the notion that each individual soul is created by God from nothing. Other long-standing philosophical concerns include: the ways in which he employed the various Stoic recipes for mixture (*krasis*), that is, the total blending of soul and body; his partial rejection and puzzlement about the Neo-Platonist notion of soul-vehicle (*okhema*), and his unusual interpretation of St. Paul's teaching about the soul's taking upon itself a glorious, spiritual body after the Final Resurrection. The doctrine of human double life and double death means that, in the first life, he is born as an ensouled animal, whose first death is the soul's separation from its body, and that the second life is given through the in-breathing of the Holy Spirit, a new life which can only be lost through sin and wickedness.

Augustine's psychical terms reflect his mastery of Latin translations of Greek philosophical works and the Vulgate Latin Bible. The term *anima* (f.) can refer to the souls of humans and animals; it is often used as a synonym or hendiadys (one-for-two) with *animus* (m.), though *animus* is never used with reference to non-rational beings. The mind (*mens*) is a part of the soul (*pars animi*), specifically the best or highest part, that is, that which is pre-eminent in the soul (*quod excellit in anima*). He distinguished three types of soul: (1) the rational soul, seat of mind and will, (2) the irrational soul, seat of appetite, perception, and memory, and (3) the vegetative or living soul, sometimes referred to as 'the merely living soul'. He also employed Latin versions of Greek Neo-Platonic terms; for example, *anima intellectualis* for *noera psychē*, *anima spiritalis* for *pneumatikē psychē*, *spiritus* for the LXX *pneuma*; *spiritus* often means the same as *anima*, when it has the specific sense of *mens*. Gerard O'Daly summarizes Augustine's Latin philosophical vocabulary:

> There is no obvious specific precedent for Augustine's usage; he appears to reflect different aspects of the Latin philosophical tradition. The equation of *anima* with the soul in general, and the description of *mens* as 'part of the soul', are first found in Apulieus, but become thereafter general, so that direct dependence of Augustine upon Apulieus need not be posited. Cicero ... translates both *psychē* and *nous* by *animus*, but *anima* which is frequently equivalent to *psychē* in Augustine, is so only exceptionally in Cicero. Calcidius and Macrobius introduce a new stringency into their usage of *animus* ... and *anima* that reflects the distinctions between the Neoplatonic *hypostases*, and a similar restricted use of *anima* = *psukhē* is observable in Marius Victorinus [Latin translator of Platonic texts]. If the books of the Platonists ... exercised this sort of care in their distinction between the two terms (something which we cannot verify), then such care is not reflected in Augustine's usage, despite his occasional employment of Neoplatonic terminology.[147]

---

[147] O'Daly, 1987, pp. 7–8; Verbeke argues against the identification of Porphyry's *pneuma* and Augustine's *spiritus*, Verbeke, 1945, p. 504.

Augustine had not been satisfied with the Stoics' concept of the soul (via Cicero's redaction of their arguments) nor with the Manichean doctrine of two principles; much of his distaste for their teachings was directed at their corporeal interpretation of the basis for soul. Augustine was resolved to come to an understanding of the Christian God, and hence to God's greatest creation, the living soul, as immaterial and immortal. He found the right approach to this question in 'certain books of the Platonists translated from the Greek language into Latin' (Conf. 7.9.13). Augustine did indeed come to understand God as an incorporeal being, an understanding that allowed him 'to solve to his satisfaction the problems about the relation between God and the soul and about the origin of evil.' In Stephen Menn's words:

> But it did not succeed in giving him the wisdom he was seeking. As Augustine puts it, he could 'see the country of peace from a hill in the forest' (Conf. 7.21.27), but he could not find a path through the dangerous territory between his present position and his goal, and he could not sustain the vision amid the cares of the world. In Augustine's mature judgment, then, Platonism gives a true vision of the goal of wisdom, and specifically of God, while only Christianity gives a rule of life that allows us to attain the goal. For a Catholic bishop ... this is giving remarkable credit to pagan philosophy.[148]

Augustine's double conversion, first to Platonist philosophy and then to Christian theology, was the culmination of an arduous intellectual journey in pursuit of wisdom, a journey that he had embarked upon twelve years before writing the *Confessions*. As a student rhetorician in Carthage (373) he read (the now lost) Cicero's *Hortensius* (itself modeled on Aristotle's *Protrepticus*) and his heart was inflamed with the desire for truth and the true God: 'This book indeed changed all my way of feeling ... Suddenly, all empty hope for my career lost its appeal, and I was left with an unbelievable fire in my heart, desiring the immortal qualities of wisdom, and I made a start to rise up and return to you, my God' (Conf. 3.4.7). Cicero's extensive though eclectic knowledge of Greek philosophy, especially his Stoic ethics and skeptical attitude toward knowledge had a profound and unsettling impact on the young student. He later quoted with approval Cicero's remark that 'if the souls which we have are eternal and divine, we must conclude that the more we let them have their way in their natural activity, that is, in reasoning and in the quest for knowledge, and the less they are caught up in the vices and errors of mankind, the easier it will be for them to ascend and return to heaven' (De Trin. 14.19.26). Fired by this vision of philosophy's privileged access to wisdom (*sophia*) and mind (*nous*), Augustine turned to the teaching of Mani, whose lectures and seminars he followed for many years before leaving their company deeply dissatisfied with internal doctrinal problems and their inability to answer his questions.[149]

Augustine returned to his home town to teach rhetoric, but within two years he was back in Carthage looking for a better-informed Manichean teacher, whom he thought he had found in Faustus of Milevis. At that time, Manicheanism was considered an eccentric and repugnant heresy; Augustine's devoutly religious mother Monica was horrified, but her son had to work through its challenges on his own.

---
[148] Menn, 1998, p. 76; on his use of Cicero, see Cary, 2000, pp. 80–85.
[149] See Brown, 1967, pp. 40–45.

He was disillusioned by the static religious character of Manichean teachings and its overly optimistic view of human nature; the complexities of doubt, ignorance, and deep-rooted tensions within the concept of the will were, in his opinion, deliberately avoided by the Manichees. In 382 he moved from North Africa to Rome, a city that he found sadly disappointed his excited expectations. But he did make several good contacts, one of whom advanced him for the post of professor of rhetoric in Milan where, in the autumn of 384, Augustine met Bishop Ambrose. The Bishop's erudite and wide-ranging knowledge of philosophy, coupled with a profound and other-worldly intimacy with the Christian message, was to change the young teacher's understanding forever.

For Ambrose, a human being *is* his soul; the human body is merely 'a tattered garment'. In going against his soul, a human ceased to exist, and in returning to God, the soul cast off its impediments, 'like washing the mud off gold'. The enemy is right inside you, he said; the cause of your error is there, shut up in you alone. 'One thought runs through Ambrose's preaching: beneath the opaque and rebarbative "letter" of the OT, this "spirit", the hidden meaning calls to our spirit to rise and fly away into another world', in Peter Brown's words. 'This other-worldliness must have appeared as quite revealing to Augustine. With the exception of the Platonists, most thinkers in the ancient world, the most religious included, were "materialists" in the strict sense. For them, the divine was also an "element", though infinitely more "fine", more "noble", and less "mutable",' than earthly things. In the contemporary philosophical context, a human being was thought to be 'a living force that seemed to permeate the universe: and so it was his position in a physical world, infused with divine energy, that concerned most thinkers, not the intangible depths of his soul.'[150] Augustine's second-hand information about Platonic theory, via Cicero's *Hortensius* and doxographical sources, was insufficient to deal with Ambrose's searching questions and complex arguments. The dramatic story of his second conversion in Book VIII of the *Confessions* recounts his almost super-human efforts to integrate both sides of his philosophical understanding of faith and reason in an incorporeal God and his greatest creation, the human soul. Stephen Menn says that 'Augustine and his teacher Ambrose are the first Latin Christian writers to maintain that the human soul is incorporeal; by the 13th century, the scholastics simply assume that this is in the Bible (because they assume that "spirit" means "incorporeal substance").'[151] The astonishing hypothesis that the Christian soul is both immortal *and* immaterial was to reappear more than a thousand years later, after the holding-sway of Neo-Aristotelian and Thomistic metaphysics and psychology, in the seventeenth-century thinkers inspired by Augustine's account – Descartes, Arnauld, Malebranche and Pascal.

Due to his close association with Ambrose and other well-educated and cultured persons of rank in Milan, Augustine took a renewed interest in the Platonic texts, now available in Latin translations by his contemporary African colleague Marius Victorinus. But one important question has been asked over and over again: which books of the Platonists was Augustine talking about? Answers vary from one

---

[150] Brown, 1967, pp. 84–5.
[151] Menn, 1998, p. 23.

scholar to another; the question has inspired heated (and perhaps irresolvable) debate, but it is simply not feasible to enter this debate here.[152] In one of his earliest works, written shortly after his conversion, he said that 'the voice of Plato ... has shone out from the parted clouds of error most of all in Plotinus, who has been judged to be a Platonic philosopher so like to him that one would think that they had lived together, or rather, since there is so much time between them, that he [Plato] had lived again in him [Plotinus]' (Contra Acad. 3.18.41).

In *The City of God* he specifies some of the descendants of these Platonists, 'the most noble recent philosophers': Plotinus, Iamblichus, Porphyry and Apulieus (Civ. Dei 8.12). It is one scholarly task to tease out the traces of these Platonic books in Augustine's works, it is another peculiarly philosophical task to demonstrate what important lessons he learned from them and adopted in his syncretistic program. Stephen Menn draws the following lessons from this issue: first, at a minimum it served a crucial negative function in making Christianity possible by helping to remove intellectual obstacles to finding wisdom in the Church. Second, it made a positive contribution toward the wisdom desired by opening out an intellectual vision of God's true nature: 'Platonism gave him only the vision of God, while Christianity gave him the path; but the vision was what inspired him to seek the path.' Third, it provided him with the idea of a cognitive discipline that could lead a purified soul toward God; his narrative of the ascent of the soul parallels Plotinus' narrative.[153] After his conversion Augustine retired to Cassiciacum, a peaceful and serene retreat, for an *otium liberale*, where he composed several of his most important early treatises: *Contra Academicos, De Beata Vita, De Ordine* and the *Soliloquies*. He returned to Milan the next year, and then to Rome and Ostia (where his mother died), and finally came home to Carthage five years after his departure. He wrote the *Confessions* (397) and *The City of God* (413–25), numerous tracts against heretical sects, hundreds of sermons and letters, as well as lengthy Biblical commentaries. In addition to his prodigious scholarly labors, he found time to establish a monastery and carry out onerous duties as the Bishop of Hippo in North Africa, a title he retained, during years of great upheaval, until his death in 430.

For Augustine, the basic sense of soul pertains to the appearance of life in certain things; in this he follows the most long-lasting concept of *psychē* in Greek thought, as well as the OT notion of life-force. It answers the question of what makes living things breath, move and change states. The kinds of beings that have life are ensouled, and those that do not have life are soul-less. But there are various grades of life and these correspond with levels or grades of the soul. With regard to soul-grades, Augustine's views draw on the Latin writer Varro, who distinguished three levels: the vegetative soul in trees, bones, nails, hair, and so forth;[154] the sensitive or perceptive soul in animals, and the highest level (mind) in humans alone. In *On the Trinity*, he said that, although a human cannot perceive an incorporeal soul, the fact that a human is conscious of itself as a perceiving being shows that it has (or is)

---

[152] See, amongst others, Brown, 1967, pp. 88–100; O'Daly, 1987, pp. 9–11; Menn, 1998, pp. 75–82; and especially O'Connell, 1968, pp. 1–28; Cary, 2000, pp. 33–8; Menn responds to O'Connell's elaborate thesis in a long footnote, Menn, 1998, pp. 79–80, note 7.

[153] Menn, 1998, pp. 130–32, 145.

[154] On nails and hair, Latin *unguis*, see Onians, pp. 246, 494.

a soul (De Trin. 8.9). At this stage, his argument for the soul's immortality drew on the premise that it is not just the presence of soul that keeps humans alive, but rather that its essence as life-force does not admit its opposite, death: 'Those who have held its substance to be some kind of life that is not corporeal, since they have found that it is a life which animates and gives life to every living body, have in consequence tried, each as best he could, to prove it immortal, since life cannot lack life' (De Trin. 10.9). Soul as life and death as not-life are exclusive contraries, just as light and dark are; the soul's death is no more than a metaphor for loss of wisdom, lack of happiness, or removal from God's presence. He has little more than contempt for Epicurus' and Lucretius' belief that the soul decomposes after bodily death; he says that the claim that 'the soul is dissolved like smoke scattered by the wind is ... the view of Epicurean pigs, rather than humans.' O'Daly comments on Augustine's strong words, that 'even if life is indeed the essential characteristic of soul, this does not in itself imply that soul is necessarily immortal, but merely that soul, in so far as it exists, is necessarily alive, unlike bodies, which can be either dead or alive.'[155]

Although he does not mention Plato's *Republic* by name, Augustine is clearly familiar with this dialogue's threefold division (Civ. Dei 14.19): anger (*ira*) and desire (*libido*) correspond with the desire-form (*thumoeides*) and appetite (*epithumētikon*), and the mind (*mens*) corresponds to the rational (*logistikon*) or controlling power (*imperans*):

> Augustine will, however, prefer the rational-irrational bipolarity to the Platonic tripartite division, and will ... elsewhere regard *ira* and *libido* as affections, as it were, on the same level, rather than graduated powers of a differentiated soul-structure. Thus he often emphasized the traditional view that it is the function of the rational soul to control the irrational powers ... and that this controlling power defines soul's proper relation to body.[156]

In his *Literal Interpretation of Genesis*, he discussed several different accounts of the origin of the soul, accounts that vary partly due to discrepant versions of the soul's origin in the *Genesis* texts. At the most primeval level, all souls are created as seminal principles that develop or mature at their own proper times. In his early efforts to deal with the two *Genesis* versions he thought of them as complementary accounts:

> They are allegories of every soul's (and not merely Adam's) resemblance to God through reason, and of soul's formative and cohesive functions in its symbiosis with body. Augustine observes that the divine 'inbreathing' (*insufflatio*) of life referred to in *Genesis* 2:7, if it symbolizes the ensoulment of an already existing body, would be consistent both with soul's pre-existence and with its creation at the moment of the inbreathing. He is not here concerned to choose between these options: more important to him is the scriptural testimony of the *Genesis* account that the human soul is created and not, as the Manichees maintain, a part of divine nature.[157]

---

[155] O'Daly, 1987, p. 12.
[156] O'Daly, 1987, p.13.
[157] O'Daly, 1987, p. 16; see O'Connell, 1968, pp. 148–52.

J. M. Rist observes that from the time of Augustine's conversion 'he wanted to maintain *both* that it is man's soul which is created in the image of God, *and* that man himself is some kind of composite of two substances, a soul and a body. In the end ... he fails to provide a full account of the "mystery" of their coming together to form each of us, though he determines that the "person" formed from the mixture of soul and body has some analogies to the "person" formed by the presence of God as man.'[158]

In his *Treatise on Freedom of the Will*, Augustine catalogues four (or five) then current accounts of the origin of the human soul:[159]

1 The traducian view that all particular souls are derived from one original soul.
2 The creationist view that each particular soul is made at an individual's birth.
3 Divine embodiment, according to which God installs or imparts each particular soul from an inventory of pre-existent souls.
4 Voluntary embodiment, according to which each particular soul, from its pre-existent state, chooses to install or impart itself at an individual's birth.
5 Embodiment as punishment (which may be another version of 3 or 4), derived from Cicero's *Hortensius* and Origen's *De Principiis*, according to which each individual's embodiment is punishment for its pre-existent soul's sins.

In his most complete examination of the soul's origin, he argued against the notion that either the matter or the form of the soul could exist prior to its creation (Gen. Litt. 6.1.1). The soul is created out of nothing at the primeval creation of the world, at the same time as the causal principles of the body: 'The soul indeed was created already, just like the first day was brought into being, and that once created it lay hidden in God's works, until he sowed it at the proper time in the body that is formed out of clay, breathing it in, that is, animating it' (Gen. Litt. 7.24.35). Having dismissed the various other options for the soul's pre-existent divine or voluntary embodiment, he turns to the traducian option; having found no scriptural support for this his discussion remains inconclusive. With regard to the general question of the soul's origin, O'Daly synopsizes Augustine's final verdict thus: 'he is resigned to uncertainty ... on an "inessential question" whose solution is not necessary to man's salvation.'[160]

Aspects of Augustine's Platonist account of soul are already apparent in some of the texts from this period, both with respect to the format of argument and to the metaphorical imagery employed. The grand image from the *Phaedrus* of the charioteer and two horses appears in his meditation on the whole figure or unity of human-rider and horse in this wonderful passage:

> Since it is almost universally agreed that we are made up of soul and body, and since for the purpose of our present discussion such an agreement can be taken for granted, what we must ask now is what man really is: is he both these constituents, or is he

---
[158] J. M. Rist, 1994, p. 94.
[159] For Patristic passages stating some of these views, see Lampe PGL, 1976, pp. 1544–5, sec. C.
[160] O'Daly, 1987, p. 19.

body only, or soul only? For although soul and body are two things, and neither of them alone is called 'man' in the absence of the other (for a body is no man unless it is animated by a soul, nor is a soul a man without a body which it animates), it nevertheless happens that one or the other of these is alone taken for and referred to as man. What, then, shall we say man is? Is he soul and body together, as a pair of horses or a composite beast like a centaur is one thing? Or shall we say that he is a body only, albeit a body used by a soul which rules it? ... Or, finally, shall we call the soul alone man, and so on account of the body which it rules? Just as we call a man a knight, not the man and his horse together, but we do so on account of the horse he rides. The solution of this problem is difficult – or, if it be easy to see, it nonetheless requires a lengthy explanation, and it is not necessary here and now to undertake the labor and delay. [de Mor. Eccl. 1.4.6]

The Stoic attempts to resolve the problem of the presence of soul and body in one substance by recourse to various kinds of mixture appeared in Augustine's imagery of the human body made from earth or clay. No doubt this reflected an effort on his part to build in one of the features of the *Genesis* story about Adam's creation from clay. In the same passage from *On Church Customs* quoted above (where the elision occurs), he draws an analogy with the human as horse-rider and half-centaur with a clay lamp and its flame: 'Shall we say that [a human] is a body only, although a body used by a soul? Just as we call a clay lamp a light. We do not say that the clay vessel and the flame together make up a light; we call the lamp a light, but we do so on account of the flame.' In other words, if the organic body is like a clay vessel and the soul is like a flame, then we should (and do) say that this thing is a human, that is, in virtue of having a soul. In another early work, he is more explicit in his treatment of the Stoic concept of mixture when he draws another analogy for the soul in union with the body from the way in which water and soil are mixed together to form mud, holding its parts together and compacting them (de Gen. Contra Man. 2.7.9). According to R. A. Markus, Augustine 'never seems to have doubted its [mixture's] adequacy for formulating the mode of union of soul and body in man ... [He] stressed the unity of soul and body in man as strongly as his inherited conceptual equipment allowed it to be stressed, certainly far more strongly than Plato himself had done.'[161]

In Letter 137, Augustine defended the doctrine of Christ's incarnation against its pagan critics by arguing that the union of two 'natures' in the single person of Christ is no more or less mysterious than the union in one person of body and soul. He rescued the Stoic notion of mixture by contrasting the way in which two liquids combine with the way in which light mixes with air. In the former mixture, he said, each component loses its purity (*integritas*) whereas in the latter, purity is retained even though light is incorporeal and air is corporeal, as Plotinus himself asserted (Enn. 4.5.7). But Augustine did not follow the Stoics' (and Porphyry's) further distinction between irrecoverable and recoverable mixtures, for example, egg and flour in contrast with oil and water. With regard to the mixture of soul and body, he did not state, along the lines of light and air, that the consequent parts cannot be recovered from the new combination. Indeed,

---

[161] Markus, 1970, p. 358.

... in the case of body and soul mixture of subsequently separable substances would seem to be the one possibly acceptable alternative to the theory adopted by Porphyry and Augustine ... Moreover, in adopting the uncompounded unity (*unio inconfusa*) concept Augustine follows Porphyry in being aware of its paradoxical nature, but, whereas in Porphyry this kind of union seems to contravene all natural laws, in Augustine it even has an analogy in nature with the mixture of light and air.[162]

Augustine used other Latin words to describe the 'blending' of soul and body, as J. M. Rist points out.[163] It is *contemperatio* (Quan. An. 30.59), *mixtura* (Ep. 137.3.11), an ineffable mixture (Gen. Litt. 3.16.25) and conjunction (Civ. Dei 13.24). Rist argues against an overt Plotinian influence on his view and suggests instead that Augustine's ideas about blending were taken from Varro, Celsus and Cicero: 'The body subsists as a body by and through the soul [the soul vivifies the body; a corpse is an empty house]: that seems to be a version of Plotinus' view that the body is "in", that is, caused by the soul. It is the soul that enables the body to be a body. In addition, the soul and body form a unity; the philosophical problem is whether that unity is merely "accidental".' In Letter 137, he introduced the term *persona* to nominate the union of soul and body, a union expressly modeled on the form of union in Christ of God and human. As Rist explains:

It seems that Augustine's growing theological confidence ... about the appropriate language to be used for the incarnation encouraged him to think that he need not worry about the queerness or uniqueness of the relationship between the substances soul and body. If so, it is another example of his view that *only theological* explanations will enable certain basic philosophical problems to be solved, or at least admit of a rational solution (to be fully understood by God, if not by us). [original emphasis][164]

Augustine was also familiar with the *Phaedrus* thesis that the soul is a self-moving principle; the overt indication of its animal (second-level) soul is its ability to move.[165] He argued that the soul's awareness of its self-driven movement is an awareness of its power to will. The power of self-willed movement is given to each creature by God, but he took this to mean that it is exercised voluntarily in specific actions. Although the soul itself is not extended in space, it causes local bodily motions that take place in space. He drew an elaborate parallel with an organic machine (the animal body) whose limbs move around an unmoving pivot or joint: 'an explanation of bodily motion in terms of a series of necessarily moved and necessarily unmoved elements, of which the first unmoved element is the soul'.[166]

This self-moving unextended cause of bodily motions is not itself a body; the soul is not corporeal and not composed of matter. Since the soul is not limited or bounded by space, it cannot be a body that occupies space. If the soul were material, one could not account for the unity of perceptions, that is, the whole

---

[162] O'Daly, 1987, p. 43.
[163] Rist, 1994, pp. 99–101.
[164] Rist, 1994, p. 95.
[165] An interpretation derived from Cicero's Latin synopsis, Tusc. Disp. 1.53; de Re Pub. 6.27.
[166] O'Daly, 1987, pp. 20, 21.

person feels pain when part of the body is injured. The intellect can grasp non-sensible objects like numbers and geometrical figures, the imagination and memory can be directed at non-existent (and hence immaterial) things. With these and other arguments the young Augustine convinced his auditor Evodius in *De Quantitate Animae*. As J. M. Rist explains:

> For Augustine, then, soul and body are two separate substances. Unlike soul, body requires a place and makes contact with other bodily objects which also require a place. Soul, though present in our bodies, need not be so, and can 'live' among non-bodily objects. The [Platonic] Forms and the truths available to the soul are in no way tied to their spatial instantiations. It is the soul, not the body, which 'remembers', understands, and loves. Still less, in Augustine's view, is it my body which loves, understands, or acts justly.[167]

Questions about the source of this self-moving power and the space occupied, not by the soul, but by the soul's effects on bodily members forced Augustine, on some occasions, to deal with the Neo-Platonic concept of soul-vehicle (*okhema*). In an early letter, the well-informed Nebridius said, 'you must remember what was often discussed by us in conversation and disturbed us, keen and agitated as we were, namely the question about some kind of permanent body (so to speak) or quasi-body of the soul, which as you recall is also called a vehicle (*vehiculum*) by some' (Ep. 13.2). Augustine's responses, here and elsewhere, were somewhat less than direct; he mentioned that souls once departed from their earthly body 'are contained bodily in visible places' (Gen. Litt. 8.5), and later said that it is a deep problem that needs much discussion about which no certain conclusion can be reached: 'It is better to remain in doubt concerning arcane matters than to quarrel over what is uncertain.' He was inclined to think that the soul does not have any kind of body between earthly death and heavenly rebirth. The only two features of the soul-vehicle discussed by his correspondent, its fiery nature and its extra-corporeal motions, are perhaps derived from an unknown Neo-Platonic source:

> Given this perspective, the vehicle, far from being what it was for the Neo-Platonists, a psychical envelope to be shed when the heavenly sphere was transcended and the irrational soul dissolved, might rather have become for Augustine the foreshadowing of the resurrected body, the necessary and even desirable substrate of soul between physical death and the final resurrection. But Augustine cannot be sure about the vehicle, and he maintains that it is not necessary to posit a bodily substrate in order that psychical functions may occur.[168]

In addition to the principle of self-movement, the soul also partakes of another kind of inner motion, namely change and growth. Augustine said that 'soul can be said to be changed in accord with the body's affections, or in accord with its own' (Im. An. 7). Instances of the former class are aging, sickness, pain, fatigue, distress and pleasure; in the latter class instances are the emotions of desire, fear, joy and anger: 'What happens to the soul in the case of emotions happens to the body with regard

---

[167] Rist, 1994, p. 97; see O'Daly, 1987, p. 26.
[168] O'Daly, 1987, p. 78; Verbeke, 1945, p. 504

to place, for the former is moved by the will, but the body is moved in space' (Vera. Rel. 28). It is due to its 'extension' (so to speak) in time that the soul can change, both with regard to its particular feelings and knowings, and with regard to its moral state of good or evil. God is truly and perfectly immutable without change or alteration, and outside the temporal order, since God is eternal. Although the human soul shares some of its attributes with God's substance, the soul itself is not eternal, but rather immortal in a special sense: 'The human soul is immortal in some manner peculiar to itself ... but since it dies through estrangement (or alienation) from the life of God, without however entirely ceasing to live its own natural life, it is found with good reason to be mortal and at the same time said to be immortal' (Ep. 166.3). In one of his sermons, he said that the soul is immortal 'after some manner of its own (but it can die) ... How does it die? Not by ceasing to be life, but by losing its life [in God]' (Serm. 65.4). Augustine's unusual doctrine of two lives and two deaths will be further considered below.

The kind of change that the soul undergoes is not substantive, but quantitative and qualitative; the soul's affections or passions alter, the intellect is modified according to its changeable perceptions, and the intellect can modify the soul by means of learning, especially through moral education. The soul *qua* substance provides both life and form (*species*) to its body and the form of the soul itself is God's gift. The informed soul transmits specific forms via perception, sensation and so forth, but does not lose its own intrinsic form: 'If the soul transmits form to body, that the body may exist to the extent that it does, it by no means deprives itself of form in the process' (Im. An. 24): 'Just as the soul's immortality is not that of God, so also its form is not that of the highest good: the soul is rather "like God". It is in this sense that Augustine understands the words of *Genesis* 1:26, that man is made in God's image and likeness. Man, like God, has power over subordinate creation in virtue of his possession of reason ... and indeed he has limited creative powers of his own, as when, for example, the human soul forms and enlivens the body.'[169]

Before turning to Augustine's specific claims about the nature of the human soul it is instructive to consider the importance that he attached to the ideas of image and likeness.[170] Some commentators unthinkingly treat these two terms as one feature with two names, rather than two distinct features. Augustine commented on the dictate that human being was created in the image and likeness of God that these two terms are *not* synonymous; after the fall, human became an impartial image and thus a kind of damaged likeness (De Trin. 9.2.2; 10.12.29). He also criticized the early Patristic view, for example, in Origen, that an image does not have to be any kind of likeness. An image is ontologically dependent on an original in a way in which two things similar to each other, via a higher third term, are not thus dependent. In a careful and detailed article,[171] R. A. Markus shows that the early Augustine spoke of human being as made *in* the image of God, only Christ *is* an image, and thus humans are images *in him*. But in later works Augustine held that each *person* is an image of the whole Trinity.

---
[169] O'Daly, 1987, p. 37; Cary, 2000, pp. 95–104.
[170] Rist, 1994, p. 72, note 47.
[171] Rist cites Markus, 1964, pp. 125–43.

The soul thus has a middle state, a state between the immutable, eternal Creator and the mutable and entirely death-bound state of created things: 'The rational soul ... has been placed in some kind of middle state, in that it has the bodily creation beneath it, but its own and the body's creator above it' (Ep. 140.3). It seems likely that he derived this idea from Plotinus, or perhaps indirectly from Porphyry. In *Ennead* Book Four, Plotinus described the soul's ideal station as *mesē taksis* (Enn. 4.8.7), intermediate between the pure intelligible realm and the impure sensible realm. O'Connell devotes much attention to Augustine's employment of the Plotinian concept of middle state in *De Genesi Contra Manichaeos*, where he says that 'Augustine's "spiritual exegesis" permits him to take extraordinary liberties with what is often the most obvious meaning of the Scriptural text, something of which he seems at times uncomfortably aware.'[172] However, considering Augustine's threefold task in accounting for the nature of soul, this middle state in the order of things (*in meditullio quodam rerum*) is the result of its fallen condition, having declined from the perfection of its original state.

The central chapters of Book XIII of *The City of God* succinctly present his complex view of the interrelations of soul, body, mind and spirit. All three of Augustine's major lines of explanation find their expression in this passage: the primeval state, the current state and the future state:

> Bodies which have a living soul, but not yet a life-giving spirit, are called animal bodies, that is, bodies with soul (*anima*), and yet they are not souls but bodies. In the same way, those other bodies are called spiritual. Yet we must not allow ourselves to believe that they will be spirits; we must think of them as bodies having the substance of flesh, though never having to experience corruption or lethargy, being preserved from such a state by the life-giving spirit. Then a human will no longer be earthly, but heavenly, not because his body made of earth will not be the same, but because the heavenly gift will fit it for living in heaven itself, not by any loss of its natural substance, but by a change in its quality. [Civ. Dei 13.23]

The first human, Adam, was made from earth, made a living soul, but not a life-giving spirit, a condition dependent on his voluntary obedience to God. His body was animal in that it needed food and drink for life, but in the garden Adam was not vulnerable to death due to his having eaten from the fruit of the tree of life. This accords well with the statement by St. Paul that the human body is sown in corruption and humiliation and weakness, though it will rise again after the Resurrection in incorruption and glory. In the former state, it is an animal body, in the latter a spiritual body: 'The first man was made into a living soul' (1Cor 15:42) and 'the last man is made into a life-giving spirit' (1Cor. 15:45). Augustine countered some interpreters who claimed that the first human had spirit, based on their reading of the Genesis verse, 'God breathed into his face the breath (*spiritus*) of life, and man was made into a living soul' (Gen. 2:7). They took this to mean, he said, that soul was already in him and is brought to life by the Holy Spirit: 'If indeed this had been said, we should have taken it to mean that the Spirit of God is in a sense the life of souls, and without that Spirit rational souls are to be considered

---

[172] O'Connell, 1968, pp. 155–72.

dead, although their presence gives to bodies the semblance of life. But this was *not what happened when the human was created*' (Civ. Dei 13.24). He rejected the exegetical assertion that Adam's soul was fashioned from water and earth, though it is true that his animal body was made of those parts;[173] the soul is not the whole human, it is his better part. Perhaps, he said, one should rather declare with St. Paul that the soul is the inner human,[174] and the body the outer human (2Cor. 4:16).

Augustine here made a crucial distinction between the spirit (*spiritus*), to translate the Greek *pneuma*, and the breath (sometimes *flatus* or *afflatus*) to translate *pnoē* which, he astutely pointed out, appears more often in relation to the created world then in relation to the Creator. When God breathed into Adam's face, the breath of life is *pnoē*, but the spirit (*spiritus*) can refer to humans or animals or even physical phenomena (though this last is rare, Ps. 148:8). Another crucial distinction is made again within the same Greek-Latin paired terms *pneuma-spiritus* to refer to the third 'person' of the Trinity, the Holy Spirit. He rejected the interpreters' claim that the Genesis text meant the Holy Spirit when it referred to the living spirit or spirit of life, as if it were (or had been) the case that the Holy Spirit brought to life the creature's soul. But Augustine responded that in those cases where Scripture speaks of spirits of life or living spirits 'it intends us to take the meaning as animals, in the sense of animate bodies, obviously possessed of the bodily sense perception *that comes through the possession of a soul*.' He thus reserved the special connotation of the Holy Spirit's gift to humans alone in virtue of their having *rational* souls: 'Scripture here kept strictly to its usual language to make the point that human did indeed receive a rational soul, which was not produced from water or earth, like the soul of other physical [*sc.* animate] creatures, and created by the breath of God; but that human was nevertheless created to live in an animal body, which comes into life when a soul begins to live in it' (Civ. Dei 13.24). The rational soul comes to live in a human in a second sense of life; it is not the sense of life conveyed by the identification of soul with the principles of self-movement and alteration.

In order to make this interpretation more clear, Augustine relied on yet another distinction in the meaning of breath. (This conceptual scission is perhaps comparable to the Hebrew terms *nepesh* for breath *qua* life-force and *neshama* for ordinary breath.) In the ordinary sense of breath (*anhelitus*), humans and other animals breathe in and out without adding to or subtracting from the creature's natural substance, that is, no more so than through food or drink; to inhale and exhale are functions of an animal body as a living (*sc.* animate) being. This organic notion of breath is not what the Genesis text meant when he said that God 'breathed' into Adam's face:

> Almighty God equally has the ability to produce a breath that was taken neither from his own natural substance, nor from anything in his subject creation; *he could produce it*

---

[173] He followed Cicero and the Latin translator Victorinus in rendering Plato's threefold schema with the terms *pars, partes*, for the Greek *meros*, even when Plato does not speak of 'parts'; he also renders the enigmatic passage from 1Cor 15:42–45 where Paul speaks of the *psychikos sōma* by 'animal body', instead of animate (*anima*) body, thus equating animal-organic with *anima*-soul; on his use of Latin terms, see also Brown, 1967, pp. 101–10.

[174] See esp. Cary 2000, pp. 115–22, 140–46.

from nothing. And to say that he 'inspired' or 'breathed' this breath when he implanted it into a human body is the suitable way of expressing God's action; for he is immaterial, as was the breath, but the breath was mutable, and he is immutable, the uncreated producing a created breath. [ibid.]

Augustine then returned (as we do here) to the enigmatic passage in St. Paul (1Cor. 15) where Paul speaks about the first Adam made into a living soul, that is, an animate (*psychikos*) being, and the last Adam made into a life-giving spirit, that is, a spiritual (*pneumatikos*) being, However, Augustine's double-life thesis permits the understanding that it is a *second life*, granted by the Holy Spirit via God's breath, that makes possible humans' final post-resurrection status. Conversely there are two senses of death and mortality in Augustine' ingenious interpretation of this central Pauline text. The *first death* is the separation of soul from body in its earthly demise, to which all created animate things are subject; the *second death* is the separation of inbreathed spirit from the person in spiritual death, an event to which only the wicked and sinful are subject. As Augustine said in *The City of God*,:

> thus the animal body ... was not made so as to be incapable of dying, but so as not to die, if the human had not sinned. For the body which will be incapable of death is that which will be spiritual and immortal in virtue of the presence of a life-giving spirit. In this it will be like the soul which was created immortal. The soul, it is true, may be spoken of as dead because of sin, in that it loses one kind of life, namely the Spirit of God, which would have enabled it to live in wisdom and felicity. Still, it does not cease to live *with a kind of life of its own*, however wretched, since it is created immortal. [Civ. Dei 13.24, original emphasis]

According to Augustine, if humans had not sinned in the Garden of Eden and turned away from God's grace and beneficence, they too like the angels would have been immortal in the sense of not being vulnerable to the first (soulful) death. It was not part of God's original creation of human nature to make it subject to death, rather this 'sentence' was imposed, along with toil and suffering, as punishment for their disobedience. The corruptible animal body weighs down the soul (Wis. 9:15), but this subjection to decay is the consequence, not of having a body as such, but of having an earthly, sinful body (Civ. Dei 13.15). It is on this point that Augustine rejected Platonist teaching according to the *Phaedrus*, that even good and wise souls regain their animal, corruptible bodies. And he rejected Porphyry's adjustment of Neo-Platonic teaching that the good and wise souls, in order to remain in purity and felicity, must forever avoid attachment to their bodies (Civ. Dei 10.30; 13.19).

Another subtle statement in this context advanced Augustine's brilliant thesis, namely, that in humans alone the ensouled and inspirited 'parts' cohere in one nature. In virtue of its having (or being) a rational soul, God breathes in a spirit which the human can either accept or reject – in accepting, he becomes a new being, and in rejecting he becomes like a beast: 'The second death is so called because it follows the first, in which there is a separation of natures which cohere together, either God and the soul, or the soul and the body. It can thus be said of the first death that it is good for the good, bad for the bad; but the second death does not happen to any of the good, and without doubt it is not good for anyone' (Civ.

Dei 13.2). Therefore, in Augustine's view, human beings have a double nature[175] – a double life and a double death – such that every human exists in some sense as the first Adam, that is, our common humanity is our death-bound earthly existence. But every human also has his or her own individual life that began at conception, the ensoulment of this particular animal being. J. M. Rist adroitly connects this notion to Plotinus' view:

> The relationship between Adam and each of us looks in some respects like that of the Plotinian hypostasis of Soul – though in Plotinus Soul cannot fall – to the individuals which are 'parts' of it ... [F]or Augustine, Adam is in us and beyond us, and yet we share in him, and his guilt; that latter part is unplotinian. Even Eve partakes in Adam, as is shown by the account of her being physically formed from him. There can be no 'man' (*homo* is of course both male and female) who does not share in Adam, and who is not Adam. It is no more surprising that Adam can also exist 'separately' from his 'parts' than that the Plotinian hypostasis can exist 'apart' from individual souls; as 'a one and many'. The difference is that while Plotinus makes the individual souls metaphysically distinct from the hypostasis, Augustine makes them 'historically' distinct. But that is what we should expect a Christianized Plotinus to do.[176]

One of Augustine's favorite expressions when he spoke about human nature is that 'we are all one in Adam'; although he thought this notion best articulated our common life and common death in the spiritual sense, there is no exact Scriptural source for this phrase. (He would never assert that a human was merely the mixture of a particular soul and a particular body, for such a combination would be incomplete.) It is most likely that Augustine developed this double-nature account for theological reasons, but it also does justice to metaphysical claims from Plato and Plotinus about the identity of human beings with one another, as well as the special Christian teaching about the individuality and commonality of human beings.

Augustine followed St. Paul, and not the Platonists, in marking out flesh for special consideration;[177] although having a body (*corpus*) may be a necessary condition for humans to fall away and sin, it is through the flesh (*caro, carnis*) that they do so. In *The City of God*, he actually refers to soul and flesh as 'parts' of human being by means of a part-for-whole figure of speech. Since God the Creator made animal flesh it is good in itself, in its own kind, and on its own level:

> But it is not good to forsake the good creator and live by the standard of a created good, whether a human chooses the standard of the flesh, or of the soul, or of the entire human, who consists of soul and flesh, and hence can be denoted by either term [soul or flesh] by itself. For anyone who exalts the soul as the supreme good, and censures the nature of flesh as something evil, is in fact carnal alike in his cult of the soul and in his revulsion from the flesh, since this attitude is prompted by human folly, not by divine truth. [Civ. Dei 14.5]

---

[175] The Sixth Book of Gen. Litt. contains a reference to the double-life thesis; see also Serm. 10.11; Conf. 10.20; Contra Julian; En Ps. 85; Pecc. Mer. 3.7; DNC 2.5; Op. Imp. 2.177.
[176] Rist, 1994, p. 126.
[177] Stroumsa, 1990, pp. 25–30.

On this issue Augustine found both the Manicheans and the Platonists deficient and misguided: the former execrated earthly bodies as the natural *substance* of evil, and the latter trusted little in our animal bodies from whence desires and fears raise their ugly heads.

Augustine did not always have such a well-balanced view of flesh and body; his earlier strongly accented dualism contained numerous derogatory tropes about the body, where the body is said to be a dark prison (Contra Acad. 1.3.9) or a cave (Sol. 1.14.24). He later modified this Platonic metaphor: if the flesh is a prison, it was not designed to be so; your prison is not a body as a body, but the *corruption* of your body (en Ps. 142.18). According to another early text, he thought that Adam was originally created with a spiritual body made of a special kind of matter that ceased to be spiritual after the fall from grace (Gen. Comm. Contra Man.). It was not made out of flesh, but instead was like an envelope or soul-vehicle (the Greek *okhema*). Adam and Eve before the fall could not procreate because they had no flesh, and after the resurrection the reborn humans will have no flesh. But he abandoned this view and replaced it (about the time of his text *Against Faustus*) by one of his most unusual doctrines: the spiritual post-resurrection body will indeed be made of flesh. The Edenic soul naturally ruled its body and the relation of soul and body was one of mutual love. Even after the fall some trace of this original love remains: for the desire to escape from the body would be an error; the desertion of love for one's body that God intended in his creation of a unified whole being. The mind has a natural appetite for ruling the body and its love of life is the same as its love for its body; but this will only be satisfied at the resurrection when the earthly body will no longer be a burden. When St. Paul says that, 'death is the last enemy to be destroyed' (1Cor. 15:26), Augustine commented, 'my flesh shall be my friend throughout eternity' (Serm. 155.14). The pain associated with bodily death arises when the soul is torn against nature from its embrace with the flesh (Civ. Dei 13.6). In the *Confessions*, he held that the soul *falls into* the body, rather than that it *falls with* the body into the corruptible realm.[178] His later, revised view is that the *person* is ultimately responsible for his free choice in turning toward God. In their fallen state humans are not free from sin, but they are free to choose the truth, free to escape from the bodily claims that incline them toward unfree choice.

Augustine, of course, is concerned not only with a proper account of the human soul and its union with the body in the whole person, but also with the proper discipline that can lead him, and anyone so inclined, to an understanding of God and the relation of God to his best creation, the human soul. The description of the soul's ascent in the *Confessions* (Civ. Dei 7.10) is compressed and puzzling;[179] for those readers familiar with Plotinus' system of levels of being, it might have been comprehensible, but for others it would be a mystery. In the *Freedom of the Will*, he offered clearer and easier-to-follow guidelines that began with knowledge proper to the rational soul, the starting-point for knowledge of God; the relation of one's own soul to God makes possible both our fall and our salvation. For Augustine and Plotinus, all forms of beauty and order have their source in Nous; one ascends to

---

[178] Rist, 1994, pp. 98–101, 111–12; see Cary, 2000, pp. 45–7.
[179] This short section closely follows Menn's superb summary, 1998, pp. 163–7.

God by tracing back to their source the perfections we admire in bodies and souls, along the lines of the intellectual ascent in Plato's *Symposium*. Augustine brought his reader to the recognition of truth as the source of wisdom (the perfection of soul) and number (the perfection of body). God, however, is the source of all the beauties we encounter amongst bodies and souls. All good things come from God and do so by reflecting God's existence, something that Augustine felt he had adequately proved. He then reflected on how it is that wisdom and number come to appear in souls and bodies, because it is a useful discipline to know, not only that there is divine wisdom, but how it can lead a person to a good and happy life. We are often tempted to admire the more accessible beauties of lower things and need a spiritual exercise to call us back from earthly things by reminding us of divine truth and beauty. In Stephen Menn's words, 'both bodies and souls are mutable things which have their being only as they receive form and number; they cannot supply these to themselves, but can only receive them from an immutable form and number, which must exist in the divine truth.'

Although Augustine's version of the soul's ascent in the *Symposium* had obvious similarities with Plotinus' story, it helped to uncover some non-Plotinian aspects of Augustine's distinctive manner of conceiving Nous and its relation to lower things. The cognitive faculty that merely perceives beauty is not the source of that beauty; he refused to attribute to all bodies a soul that molded it and put in it such a shape:

> Augustine's metaphors of fire, light, and heat help to illustrate his transformation of the Plotinian picture of the relations between Nous, soul, and body. Nous is like a fire; it communicates the heat of wisdom to the rational souls that are adjacent to it, and spreads the light of number even to the bodies that are far from it. Augustine certainly thinks that the action of Nous on souls indicates a closer relation, but he does not suggest that the action of Nous on bodies is *mediated* through soul; rather, the transmission of light and the transmission of heat are two distinct actions that both spring immediately from the same source.[180]

He thought that the *Timaeus* and Plotinian doctrine of world-soul is on the right track in positing an intermediate level or stage in the order of beings, but not in the ordered sequence of creation. Instead he assigned the highest level of order to the angels who have not sinned or declined from their celestial natures, but who have free will to sin if they choose. God has the power and foresight to know what is the best for each thing to fulfill its proper function. However, Augustine did indeed draw his initial concepts of God and the soul from Platonist or Neo-Platonist teachings.

Augustine's relations to his revered philosophical mentor Plato are as complex as anything one could ever find in any of the Hellenistic and Patristic writers. He found the concept of the one, true God in Christian teaching and the method of reaching this God, through an internal, psychical discipline, in Plotinus' account of the ascent of the soul. He employed this method of ascent, in Stephen Menn's words, 'to clarify and justify Christian concepts of God as creator and redeemer, and the human soul as his creature fallen or redeemed'. His astonishing philosophical

---

[180] Menn, 1998, p. 165.

and exegetical skills did not constrain him to an awkward compromise between the best of one and the best of the other, with the ill-fitting pieces left out; if anything, he did not shirk from acknowledging these problems:

> He certainly accepts much of the Platonist cosmology, but he is selective, and increasingly so with time. Neither his concept of God nor his concept of soul forces him to believe that the physical universe derives its order from God by means of soul, rather than directly. Augustine experiments with such a picture; but fundamentally he conceives the God-soul relationship and the God-body relationship as two different and irreducible things. This non-Platonic element of Augustine's thought determines the particular way he describes God's relation to lower things, and the particular path he takes to ascend to God.[181]

Phillip Cary said that the greatest problem Augustine set for himself was how to locate God within the human soul, without affirming the divinity of the soul. Careful exposition of Augustine's arguments 'offer[s] strong evidence in favor of the claim that no one before Augustine conceived of the self as a private inner space, by demonstrating that this concept arose as the solution to a quite specific problem that no one before Augustine is likely to have had.'[182] Despite Augustine's remarkable achievements in reconciling Platonic and Neo-Platonic accounts of human nature with Christian doctrines, the towering figure of Plato fades from view after the fall of the Roman Empire in the West and does not fully emerge again for nearly one thousand years. Speculation about soul, mind and spirit passes into the Near East and the Arabic sphere with the migration of Aristotle's works.

---

[181] Menn, 1998, p. 167.
[182] Cary, 2000, p. 140.

Chapter 4

Medieval Islamic and Christian Ideas

(1) Islamic concepts: Alfārābī, Avicenna and Averroes

The first great Islamic philosopher (as defined by Henry Corbin[1]) among those whom the Christian writers of the Middle Ages came to know was Alkindī (*c*.800–73), who lived first in Basra and then in Baghdad. Alkindī was an encyclopedic writer and doctrine-collector, whose work covered almost the whole field of Greek learning: arithmetic, geometry, astronomy, music, optics, medicine, logic and politics. One of his biographers prepared a calendar of his writings, totaling almost 250 separate treatises, of which only about twenty-five survive. Alkindī devoted fifty treatises to philosophical subjects, nearly one hundred to the various branches of mathematics, and thirty-five to medicine and the natural sciences. As someone concerned with philosophical issues he mentions almost no one by name aside from Plato and Aristotle. He appears to have known all of Aristotle's works aside from the *Politics*, which was conspicuously absent from the Islamic corpus of Greek texts, two apocryphal works, *On Plants* and *On Minerals*, but not the highly popular *Theology of Aristotle*, probably written by Porphyry, itself derived from Plotinus' *Enneads*, Books IV–VI. Another alleged Aristotelian work, the so-called *Liber de causis*, was largely excerpted from Proclus' *Elements of Theology*. One consequence of this assimilation of genuine and apocryphal Aristotelian works with Neo-Platonism is that the Islamic philosophers circulated an amalgam of Aristotle, Plato and Plotinus under Aristotle's name, from whence, through its Latin translations, it passed into the hands of twelfth-century Christian philosophers.[2]

One of Alkindī's works, *De Intellectu*, belongs in the family of commentaries on Aristotle's *De Anima*, by way of the later Aristotelian expositor Alexander of Aphrodisias. The purpose of this work was to clarify the meaning of the Aristotelian distinction between the passive intellect which receives intelligible 'species', and the agent intellect which produces intelligible objects. Of special interest to the Latin translators, with their standing obsession about epistemic issues, was the light which Alkindī's discussion of intellectual (or cognitive) operations threw on the function of abstraction, the 'power' which produces universals. Alkindī considered the agent intellect an intelligent or spiritual being distinct and superior to the soul, acting upon the soul in order to actualize its potency for thought. From its earliest phase Islamic philosophy admitted that there is only one agent intellect for all human beings; each individual possessed its own receptive power which the action of the agent intellect 'changes' from potency to actuality. In other words, all

---

[1] Corbin 1993, pp. xiii-xiv.
[2] Marenbon, 1998, pp. 31–2, Corbin, 1993, pp. 154–7.

human concepts flow into our individual souls from a purely spiritual being, one and the same for all humans.³ Davidson attempts to make good sense of these ideas:

> Al-Kindī, in sum, offered two theories of the source of actual human thought. According to one, the human intellect is led to actual thought by the transcendental *first intellect*, by which he probably intended the Neo-Platonic Cosmic Intellect. According to the other, the human intellect is rendered actual by the 'universals of things' with no further clarification ... Kindī [also] describes the heavenly bodies as the 'agent of [human] reason'. There, however, he probably meant that the heavens generate the human rational soul with its potential for thought, not that the heavens lead the human rational soul to actual thought.⁴

The next important stage in Islamic philosophical-theological investigation of the nature and function of the soul is taken up in the work of Alfārābī (*c*.870–950). Born about the time of Alkindī's death, Alfārābī was from a noble family, lived for some time at the Sāmānid court in Baghdad, then under the protection of the Hamdānid dynasty in Aleppo; he made many other long journeys before his death at an advanced age in Damascus. He was known in his own lifetime as *magister secundus*, the second master after Aristotle, especially for his outstanding work on the *Organon*, or logical instrument. He also wrote comments on Porphyry's *Isagogē*, much of the Aristotelian corpus, including the *Physics,* the *Metaphysics,* the *Nichomachean Ethics,* the *Rhetoric,* though not the *Poetics,* and others, all now lost. Amongst his extant works important for our purposes are the *Harmony between the two sages Plato and Aristotle*, the *Little Book of Reasoning*, the *Book of Terms used in Logic, On the Intellect and the Intellectual, On Unity and the One*, and the strange treatise known as the *Book of Letters* (*Kitāb al-hurūf*).⁵ By letters, Alfārābī meant both the Greek letters under which Aristotle's *Metaphysics* had been divided into chapters, and letters in the sense of tool-words by means of which logical operations could be encoded or equipped to express precise concepts. These include the particles and names of the categories and the interrogative particles modeled on the 'what-is', 'how-much', and so forth, of *Metaphysics*, Book Theta.⁶

In his *Letter on the Intellect*, Alfārābī says that the word 'intellect' has diverse senses, in much the same way that his master, Aristotle, refers to the way in which 'being' can be said of many things. He lists six main ways in which 'intellect' is used, although the greatest weight is attached to only one sense; the fifth definition receives the most detailed treatment. The *first* sense of 'intellect' is that by virtue of which an ordinary person characterizes human being as rational; the key Arabic word here is *ta'aqqul*, 'prudence', 'discernment', which connects this sense with the Greek concept of *phronēsis*. The *second* sense is that which scholastic theologians state has a prescriptive function, that is, either in negative and dismissive or in

---

³ Gilson, 1955, p. 184; Davidson, 1992, pp. 27–8, 33–4.
⁴ Davidson, 1992, p. 17.
⁵ Corbin, 1993, pp. 158–65; Marenbon, 1998, pp. 35–8.
⁶ See esp. Corbin, 1993, pp. 75–6, 144–6; Netton, 1992, pp. 44–6; on his life and work, see the entry in EI2, vol. II, pp. 778–81.

positive and affirmative judgments. The *third* sense has the ordinary meaning of natural sensory perception; it is the faculty of the soul that enables humans to grasp the truth of universal, necessary judgments. It is that part of the soul (*juz' mā min al-nafs*)[7] described as 'the faculty of perceiving the primary principles of demonstration, instinctively and intuitively'. The *fourth* sense marks out the mature conscience, the capacity to know good from evil; it has some overlap with prudence in the first sense. The *fifth* sense is by far the most important and complex in his sixfold scheme, and is explicitly fashioned to expand and systematize Aristotle's discussion in *De Anima*, Book III. The *sixth* sense of intellect refers to the First Principle of Divine Reason, in other words, God himself, who is the source of all intellect and intellectual operation in the cosmos.

His analysis of the fifth sense of intellect itself comprises four distinct subdivisions or aspects: (1) the potential intellect (*'aql bi'l-quwwa*) with respect to the knowledge that it can acquire; (2) the actual intellect (*'aql bi'l-fi'l*) – not to be confused with the *agent* intellect – with respect to that same knowledge while acquiring it; (3) the acquired intellect (*'aql mustafād*), that is, the intellect considered as already possessed of that knowledge; and (4) the agent intellect (*al-'aql al-fa'āl*), by means of which the soul ascends to the principle of all intelligible things. It is also identical to the Tenth Intellect (in the second register), an existent spiritual being, who presides over the world beneath the moon and confers both forms on its matter and actual knowledge on all its intellects. According to Gilson's analysis,[8] the agent intellect is immutable in its action and in its being. It eternally radiates all the intelligible forms and does not care in what pieces of matter nor in what intellects it happens to be received. When a certain piece of matter has been conveniently prepared by prior forms to receive the form of human-ness, an individual human is born. When an intellect has been conveniently prepared and trained to receive the intelligible form of human mind, it conceives the essence of human being. The wide variety of effects produced by an eternally uniform action of the agent intellect, namely the innumerable different particular humans, is simply due to the fact that the matters and intellects which come under it are not all, nor always, similarly disposed to receive it. However, one should not identify this agent intellect with the Uncaused Cause or the Prime Mover, in Aristotle's sense, for other intellects ascend above it in rank upon rank. All other higher-order intellects are subordinated to the First Intellect, who resides in an inaccessible solitude. The ultimate end or final 'cause' of all humans is to be united to the separate agent intellect, who is the *immediate* immovable mover and the source of all intellectual knowledge of the world-whole in which humans live. According to Islamic religious beliefs, which are inextricably merged with this account of soul, the prophets and imams are the only privileged humans to realize this union with the godhead. In addition, Alfārābī also claimed that there were two cities inhabited by humans, much as Augustine had also argued: one present here on earth, and another future city in heaven. When the souls of the living leave this world and join the dead in their other world, they are united with

---

[7] The Arabic word *nafs* is from the same lexical root as Hebrew *nepesh*, see TDOT, vol. IX, p. 498; summary from Netton, 1992, pp. 40–48.

[8] Gilson, 1955, pp. 183–5.

them on the level of intelligible being. Each one unites with another whom he most resembles, and through this ceaseless renewal of soul with soul, the joys of the dead are fostered, increased and indefinitely enriched.[9]

Ian Netton has summarized the basic purport of Alfārābī's fifth sense of intellect within the sixfold scheme as follows. He

> posits a fifth major species of intellection which has four different, but related and developing meanings, aspects or qualities. The relation between each of these intellects is expressed in terms of matter and form, potentiality and actuality. This fifth type of intellection has two opposite poles, passive and active, receptor and cause, which are respectively the Potential Intellect and the Active Intellect. Between the two operate the Actual Intellect and the Acquired Intellect. We may thus define [it], even if somewhat simplistically, as follows: Potential Intellect is that which has the *capacity* mentally to abstract and know the essence of things. It is a passive or latent quality. Actual Intellect is that capacity *in action*. Acquired Intellect is the latter in an externally *developing and developed* mode, the external factor being the *agency* of the Active Intellect. The Active Intellect is the motor for this, the 'efficient cause' of thought, and also a cosmic link between the sublunary and transcendent worlds.[10] [original emphasis]

Richard Walzer has made an eminently clear statement showing the intimate connection between Alfārābī's understanding of the active intellect and Aristotle's difficult discussion of this concept in the *De Anima* passage: 'The active intellect (*nous poiētikos*) is no longer identical with the divine mind ... but is described ... as a transcendent immaterial entity placed next to the sphere of the moon and acting as intermediary between the divine mind and the human intellect in transmitting the divine emanation to the human soul once it has reached the stage of the acquired intellect.'[11] If one thinks through this progression, from cause or motor to primary receptor, there is an archetype of intellect caused by the agency of the Active Intellect to *develop* as it *activates* its passive *capacity*. The linchpin of this double register or dimension is the Active Intellect as the chart opposite shows.

According to Netton's excellent overview, there are two distinct registers in Alfārābī's account of the intellect in this complex text. There is the Aristotelian register, carefully underpinned throughout the main sections with references to the relevant *De Anima* passages, with four main entries. Then there is the second, parallel register with ten key terms, clearly indebted to Neo-Platonic sources, such as Plotinus' scheme of cosmic hypostases. In what follows, the reader of Islamic medieval texts should note that Greek and Arabic did not have separate words for *intellect* and *intelligence*. A technical convention that originated in Latin medieval translators distinguished the two concepts with two terms, reserving the word 'intelligence' to designate the incorporeal, purely noetic beings that govern the celestial spheres.[12] From God, the first intellect, emanates ten lesser intellects, culminating in the Tenth Intellect, which is the Agent or Active Intellect. This last power acts as a bridge between the heavenly world and the world below the moon,

---

[9] Gilson, 1955, p. 187; Davidson, 1992, pp. 44–8.
[10] Netton, 1992, p. 50; Davidson, 1992, pp. 48–52.
[11] Walzer, 1962, pp. 209–10; also in EI2, vol. 2, pp. 778–81.
[12] Davidson, 1992, p. 6.

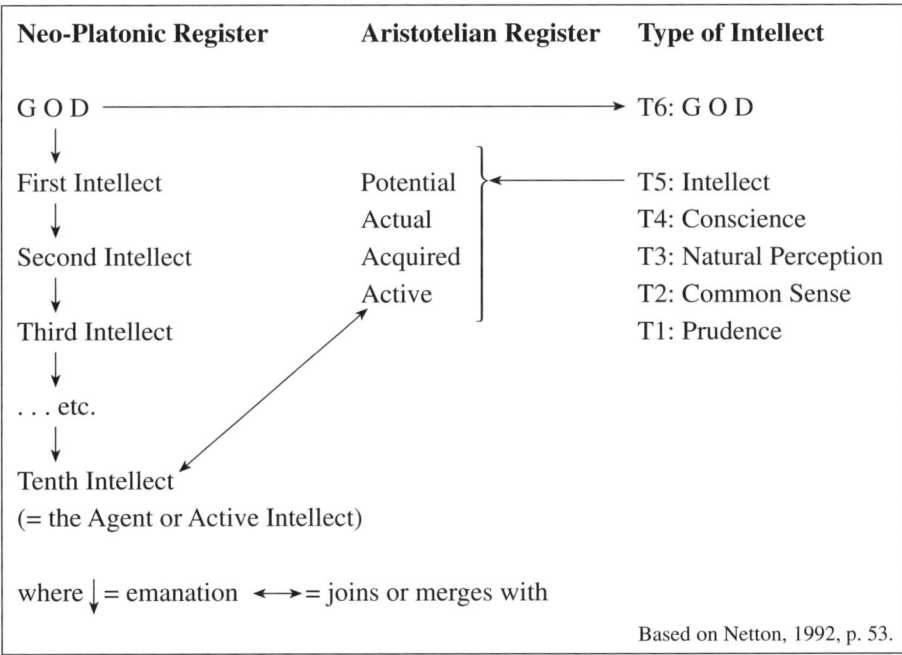

The Active Intellect

and connects with the former register at the point where human intellect takes part in the divine agent intellect. Alfārābī's account of the soul and his theory of knowledge are blunt-edged mixtures of Aristotelian and Neo-Platonic doctrines, organized around two registers: one to account for the ordered appearance of the world-whole, and the other, to account for humans' situation in this order. His perfect epistemic paradigm is 'that in which the Being who knows (al-'āqil), the intellect (al-'aql), and the intelligible or that which is known or comprehended (al-ma'qūl) are merged indissolubly and ineluctably in the One who is, of course, God himself'.[13]

With the work of Avicenna (Ibn Sīnā) (980–1037) the Islamic philosophical vocabulary and conceptual apparatus achieves an outstanding degree of exactitude and rigorous exposition. Like his predecessors, Avicenna had polymathic ambitions and was an insatiable collector of Greek doctrines, commentator on ancient texts, and exegete of Koranic scripture. He was born in Persian Bukhara, the capital of the Samānid dynasty; his father was a member of the heterodox Ismā'ili sect whose theological doctrines drew heavily on Neo-Platonic sources. A precocious student, he was said to have mastered all the current disciplines by the age of eighteen, a report which brought him to the attention of the royal court. Within two years the

---

[13] Netton, 1992, pp. 45–6.

Samānid dynasty succumbed to the onslaught of the Turkish forces and Avicenna fled, roaming for years in Transoxiana and the Iranian country. For seven years he acted as counselor and physician to Sham Al-Dawlah (Sol Regni in Latin), the ruler of Hamdān, but after his protector's death he was thrown in prison. When the city was attacked by 'Alā Al-Dawlah, the ruler of Isfahan, Avicenna was released from prison, and escaped disguised as a dervish. He moved to Isfahan to serve its prince, but the relative peace and calm of this period was rudely interrupted in 1030 when the Turkish forces attacked the caravan he was traveling with. Avicenna's great encyclopedic work *Kitāb al-Insāf*, 28,000 questions in twenty large folio volumes, was destroyed by the soldiers. But most of his other work has survived: *The Direction (al-Hidāya), The Cure (al-Shiftā'), The Deliverance (al-Najāt)* – all in Arabic – and the large Persian encyclopedia, *The Book of Knowledge (Dānish-nāmeh)*. In addition, he wrote many commentaries on Aristotle's texts, including the *Metaphysics, On the Soul*, the apocryphal *Theology of Aristotle,* and others, most of which belonged to *The Book of Right Judgment*. Avicenna constructed a comprehensive philosophical system that owed much to Aristotle, but modified and corrected (in his view) by Neo-Platonic arguments on the basic features of intellect and knowledge.[14] Other influences that have been identified include Plato on his political theory, Galen on medicine and the account of soul, and the Stoics on logic and forms of reasoning. But what makes Avicenna's work distinctive is the complex integration of Islamic theological and cosmological doctrine with Greek philosophical thought, especially through Alfārābī's concepts of divine essence and the dyadic emanation scheme.[15]

According to Avicenna's *Liber de Anima*, the soul considered in itself is a substance endowed with many powers from which flow many diverse operations. The distinct powers of the soul are (1) the nutritive and generative power common to plants and animals; (2) the sensitive power which embraces perception, imagination and memory, and the motile power responsible for self-movement, and (3) the capacity to know intelligible objects, to invent artifacts, to speculate about natural things, and to distinguish between moral good and evil. In agreement with Aristotle, Avicenna holds that there are three kinds of soul: (1) the vegetative soul, the prime perfection of a natural living body with regard to its vital functions; (2) the sensitive soul, the prime perfection with regard to its sensations and perceptions, and (3) the rational soul, the prime perfection enabling it to carry out deliberate actions and to acquire knowledge through meditation since its soul can grasp universals. The rational soul is possessed by humans alone and has two main faculties: the practical and the theoretical (which Gilson calls the 'active' and the 'contemplative') – they are both called intelligence with equivocation: 'Our soul has two faces, one which looks downward to the body, and another which looks upward to the intelligible beings from which it receives its principles.' The practical faculty is the principle of movement driving its host's body into action; as such, it corresponds with the strictly animal faculties of appetite, imagination and estimation. The practical intelligence has to control the irrational

---

[14] On his life and work, see the entry in EI2, vol. III, pp. 941–7.
[15] Marenbon, 1998, pp. 40–44; Corbin, 1993, pp. 167–70; Marmura, 1967, pp. 226–9.

tendencies and, by not allowing them to gain the upper hand, it disposes a human to consider theoretical knowledge.[16]

The special service of the theoretical faculty is to receive the impressions of universal forms abstracted from material things. The functions of the theoretical intelligence occur in temporal stages; Avicenna sometimes says that potency or potentiality is itself equivocal. The first is absolute potency in an infant, the second that of relative potency in an adult, only when the instrument for reception of actual forms has been achieved, and the third is complete potency realized only by those who meditate. This power of the human soul is given different names according to its disposition with respect to intelligible objects. At the lowest level, it is called 'material intellect', not in the sense that it is corporeal or made from matter, but because it is in the same relation of pure potency to actuality as that of prime matter with regard to all its forms. At the next level, the 'habitual intellect' (*al-'aql bil-malaka*) already possesses those thoughts that it can use, but does not actually use them; it can think of those forms whenever it wills without recourse to further perception. For example, someone who knows a certain principle can be said to know its valid consequences even when he has not yet thought about them. The habitual intellect remains in potency whereas the active or effective intellect actually knows and knows *that* it knows. Because intellectual cognition is granted to the intellect by a spiritual being above human nature, it can be called an accommodated intellect, that is, an intellect given to it from outside. At the last stage its relation to the intelligible forms may become completely actualized – when they are present to the intellect and the 'objects' of its contemplation. In this sense then, it is an 'acquired intellect' (*al-'aql al-mustafād*) in that it has acquired these forms from the higher spiritual being.[17]

The plurality of beings in the cosmos proceeds in the wake of the First Intellect from a series of contemplative acts which transform the cosmological scheme into an account of angelic consciousness. The First Intellect contemplates its own internal principle, one that makes its being necessary, as well as the pure possibility of its own being, considered as outside its own principle. From the first act proceeds the Second Intellect, and from the second act proceeds the motive soul of the first heaven (the sphere of spheres); from the third act proceeds the ethereal, supra-elemental body of the first heaven. This heaven's body then derives from an inferior dimension, the dimension of shadow or non-being of the First Intellect. This threefold contemplative activity is repeated from Intellect to Intellect, until the double hierarchy is complete, that is, the scale of the ten cherubic (or angelic) Intellects (*karūbīyūn* or *angeli*) and the scale of celestial souls. These celestial souls (angels) have no sensory faculty, but they do have imagination and intellection; their desire for the Intellect from which they proceeded communicates to each heaven its own motion. The cosmic revolutions which initiate all observable motion are the result of the angelic beings' aspiration to attain the status of the next higher intellect.[18]

---

[16] Gilson, 1955, p. 199; Afnan, 1958, p. 136.
[17] Gilson, 1955, p. 200; Afnan, 1958, p. 139; Davidson, 1992, pp. 84–8.
[18] Corbin, 1993, pp. 170–71.

The Tenth Intellect no longer has the strength to generate another unique Intellect and another unique soul, so the chain of emanation 'explodes', as it were, into the multitude of human beings, while from its material dimension proceeds all matter below the moon. The Tenth Intellect is called the active intellect, since from it our souls emanate, and its illumination projects the ideas of forms of knowledge into those souls. But as the consequence of this 'descent', the human intellect has neither the role nor the power to abstract the intelligible from the sensible. Every particular item of knowledge and memory are, strictly speaking, moments of emanation combined with illumination which derive from the angelic intellects. In addition, the human intellect itself possesses the nature of an angelic potential intellect, as Corbin explains, 'herein lies the secret of the soul's destiny. Of the four states of the contemplative intellect, the one which corresponds to intimacy with the Angel who is the active or acting Intelligence is called the "holy intellect" (*al-'aql al-qudsī*). At its height, it attains the privileged status of the spirit of prophecy.'[19] In this fashion Avicenna adopted the concept of a higher-order intellect that is separate from and extrinsic to the human intellect, and yet at the same time he did not identify this with the concept of God, as had Alexander and Augustine. Alfārābī and Avicenna regarded this supreme intellect as an actual being in the pleroma, through which humans were linked to the pleroma itself. But they were not satisfied with the Aristotelian notion that the soul is the form of an organic body; the informing of bodily matter by its soul is only one of the soul's functions, and in this they agreed with the Neo-Platonists.

It is clear that humans have the power to grasp intelligible objects by receiving them from without; for Avicenna it is also clear that such a power cannot reside in or exist in virtue of anything bodily. If it were extended in space, the immaterial forms could not be received in it without becoming extended, divisible and decomposable. Avicenna wants to draw the conclusion that the subject of the rational power that can grasp intelligible forms must be immaterial. One of his arguments for this is by way of an ingenious thought experiment, one whose later versions resonate in early modern western philosophy. Let us suppose, he said, that

> someone was suddenly created complete, but with his vision veiled so that he could not see anything, and then placed in a vacuum, where there would be no pressure for him to feel, and with paralyzed limbs so that he could not touch himself, nor do anything with them. Then he would see that he could be sure of his own existence. Indeed he would not doubt that he existed, even though he could not detect the exterior of his limbs, and his internal parts, his mind, and his brain would also be hidden, so that he could not feel their length, width or density. If at that time he was able to imagine a hand or some other limb, he would not imagine it to be a part of him or necessary to his existence ... [Hence] he does not need the body to know and perceive the soul. [*Liber de Anima*, vol. I, pp. 100–1][20]

Several commentators on Avicenna's account of soul mention the supposed similarity of this thought experiment with Descartes' hypothesis about the real distinction

---

[19] This account from Corbin, 1993, pp. 171–2.
[20] See comments by Davidson, 1992, p. 83, note 38.

between soul and body in the Second Meditation. But there are important differences, not the least of which is that Avicenna's sense-deprived test subject begins the cognitive process as a whole person, that is, an ensouled body, instead of as a methodically reduced mind. He returns to this thought experiment later to make the further point that:

> Our bodies are really only like that which if we had them for as long we would consider to be parts of ourselves. Indeed, when we imagine our souls, we do not imagine them to be bare, but clothed in bodies, because of the length of time we have had them. We are used to taking off our clothes, which we have not done with our limbs. Hence the belief that our limbs are parts of our nature is stronger than the belief that our clothes are parts of us. [*Liber de Anima*, vol. V, p. 162]

Avicenna offers another proof for the immaterial soul by arguing that the soul cannot know itself by means of a bodily sense due to the fact that it knows itself *and* knows that it knows. The soul even knows that it does not need a bodily sense in order to know itself; it understands by and through itself. It always understands itself as an immaterial essence, that it is not attached perforce to a body of any kind, nor dependent on body in any way for its own being.[21] Since all human souls have the same definition they all belong in the same species (or kind) and are, in the strict sense, one soul. There is no essential difference amongst souls, and their unitary form makes them all one thing. Their apparent multiplicity is due to the diversity of material bodies that they occupy. Since human (and animal) souls are individual and distinct only in virtue of the bodies they inhabit, they begin to exist at the very moment when the matter suitable to be animated by them comes into being. The body-host of each soul is both its domain and the instrument through which it takes care of the whole creature. Due to this natural affection between soul and its body, the soul renounces all other bodies but finds in its own body the origin of its future perfection.

After the death of its body, the rational soul remains numerically distinct, because it then receives from its creator a principle of individuation other than corporeal matter. What this principle is, we know not, but we know for sure that the soul sometimes perceives its own singular essence, when it become aware of affections that are proper to itself. Perhaps these affections, which the soul acquires in its capacity of 'intellect in act', are enough to render it numerically different from other souls. Whatever the reason for it, the intrinsic individuality of each separate soul is certain. As to its survival, it is equally certain.[22] The soul is an autonomous self-subsistent substance in the same sense as the body, and its union with the body is an accidental one. Since the substance *qua* essence of the soul is simple, it cannot 'contain' the cause of its own destruction, as the subject 'contains' all its true predicates in Aristotle's scheme. For Avicenna then, the soul's existence depends on immutable and indestructible causes, that is, its own essence and the divine power by which it is maintained in being. Afnan says that, 'The psychology of Avicenna aims to identify the human soul with the human intellect. It describes the

---

[21] Gilson, 1955, p. 202; an argument taken up by Thomas Aquinas (see below).
[22] Gilson, 1955, p. 204.

soul as a self-sufficient intellectual substance, which needs a body in order to actualize itself, but not in order to subsist after it has achieved its self-actualization. No wonder then that the *Liber sextus naturalium* ends by describing the progressive acquisition of intelligible knowledge by the rational soul.'[23]

Davidson elaborates on the discursive importance of the concept of conjunction or union of human with agent intellect in Avicenna's demonstration of the soul's immortality:

> Conjunction with the active intellect and the resultant state of acquired intellect are integral to all actual human thought. But acquired intellect, besides designating actual human thought at any level of intellectual development, is also the term for human thought at the stage where the soul has a full repertoire of thoughts and can dispense with its body. After the death of the body, a soul possessing acquired intellect in the narrower sense enters permanent conjunction with the active intellect and has 'the intelligible order of all existence' inscribed in it ... Whether the soul with a fully perfected intellect can enter into permanent conjunction with the active intellect during the life of the body or only after the body's demise is not stated by Avicenna.[24]

In order to understand itself the soul does not need to detach itself from the material world, for indeed souls are intelligible in their own right. The soul *qua* rational intellect does not become like the object it understands; the soul is like a mirror[25] in that it conserves in memory the images of particular things, but not the intelligible forms that it has received from the spiritual intellect. When one says that the soul understands some thing this means that the form grasped by the intellect is in the soul. The form has no distinct existence of its own beyond the spiritual intellect that gives it and the human intellect that receives it. Insofar as humans are concerned, as soon as the form ceases to be known, it ceases to exist in the soul. For humans then, to learn is to acquire the perfect aptitude to conjoin the human intellect with the divine intellect in actuality, in order to receive from it the simple power of intellectual abstraction from which other forms will follow. Since Avicenna thought of the soul as one unitary and unified substance, he posited the one organic agency in the body through which it governed – not the brain, but the heart. It is through the heart functions that the soul is dependent on the body. The heart is the source of all the animal spirits and forces that flow into the limbs and other vital organs. The brain's function is to prepare these animal spirits to enable the body to feel and move.[26] In these terms, Avicenna takes up one of the main Stoic psycho-physical hypotheses about the reciprocal relation of animal body with its hegemonic soul, and bequeaths that medical-psychical model to Albert the Great.

The work of Averroes (Ibn Rushd) (1126–98) marks the high point of Islamic medieval philosophy in the century just before the introduction of Aristotle's work

---

[23] For summaries of Avicenna's arguments for the soul's immortality, see Afnan, 1958, pp. 152–5.

[24] Davidson, 1992, p. 115; see the whole section, pp. 103–16.

[25] The soul as a mirror is a potent and long-lasting metaphor, probably derived from Plotinus *Enneads*, 1.4.10; see Davidson, 1992, p. 25.

[26] Gilson, 1955, p. 205.

to the European world. His pre-eminent status is due to his exceptional philosophical acuity, his meticulous scholarly analysis of Greek texts, and the influence which his systematic investigations exerted on European thinkers until the early 1600s.[27] He was born in a family of learned jurists in Cordoba, Spain, and eventually became chief judge of Cordoba. His exhaustive education covered every aspect of Greek *paideia*, including mathematics, astronomy, philosophy and medicine. His scholarly reputation gained him an invitation to work at the court of the caliph Abū Ya'qūb Yūsuf who commissioned Averroes to summarize, with commentary, the extant Aristotelian corpus. At the end of his labors, he had written thirty-eight commentaries, sometimes two or three on one text. These expositions differ in length and are usually referred to as either short (or epitome), middle and long. There are five long commentaries, on the *Posterior Analytics*, the *Physics*, the *Metaphysics*, *On the Heavens* and *On the Soul*. It is generally thought that the variation in length is connected with different stages in the teaching curricula. He also wrote many other topical treatises, including a counter-attack against Al-Ghazālā's attack on philosophical pretensions to understanding, *The Incoherence of the Incoherence* (*Tahāfut al-tahāfut*). Averroes' death

> coincided with the virtual disappearance of the dynamic speculative tradition evidenced in Arabic thinking for the several centuries after 700. Interestingly, it also coincided with the bursting forth of a similarly active tradition in the Latin West, which was greatly stimulated by the translations of Aristotle and Greek science from Arabic and Hebrew manuscripts. All these events – the death of Averroes, the abrupt decline of Arab intellectual dynamism, the translation into Latin of Aristotle ... and the exponential acceleration of Western philosophizing – occurred virtually within two decades. These are perhaps neither radically causative nor dependent events, but their close association is historically remarkable.[28]

In the *Epitome* or *Short Commentary* Averroes reiterates the familiar Islamic division of the human intellect which had been carefully interpolated into Aristotle's *De Anima*, Book III, chapters four and five. This division comprises the 'material' intellect, the First stage of the potential intellect; the 'habitual' intellect (*al-'aql bi'l-malaka*), the perfection of the material stage; the 'active' or 'efficient' intellect (*al-'aql al-fa'āl*) which brings the material and habitual intellects from potency to actuality (in other texts he calls this stage *in actu* (*al-'aql bi'l-fi'l*)); the last stage is the Agent Intellect (*al-'aql al-fā'il*), the eternally active separate substance.[29] It is through the agency of the Agent Intellect that the human intellect, in all its divisions and functions, is perfected and actualized, reaching the ultimate stage of 'acquired' intellect (*al-'aql mustafād*), at which stage it is said to be conjoined with the Agent Intellect, that is, it is the final form of the human intellect.[30] Averroes had some difficulty with the concept of the material intellect, the nature and location of which bothered him during his study

---

[27] On his life and work, see the entry in EI2, vol. III, pp. 909–20.
[28] MacClintock, 1967, p. 220.
[29] For details on the *Epitome*, see Davidson, 1992, pp. 266–72.
[30] Ivry, 1996, p. 203; Gilson, 1955, pp. 224–5.

of Greek texts, and for which he offered various, sometimes incompatible assessments.[31] He considered the material intellect to have two faces, or aspects, the active and the passive, each of which was present in the human soul. Given the basic Islamic perspective that *all* Greek philosophical doctrines belonged to one overarching system, it is not surprising that Averroes favored one later Aristotelian exegesis at one time and another at another.[32]

He definitely followed Alexander of Aphrodisias in thinking that the Agent Intellect is a divine celestial substance, which functions as kind of guarantor for the intelligible nature of all earthly forms, especially the form of reason in the human soul, that is, the rational faculty. It is wrong to think that this faculty is innate in human beings, rather, he said, it is on loan from the Agent Intellect. The material intellect in its potential for rational thought is only connected by accident with the human soul, but belongs by essence to the Agent Intellect itself. The material intellect is thus a temporary instance of the universal intellect, eternal and always actual; the material intellect is the first perfection whereas the Agent Intellect is the final perfection. Averroes thought that,

> the material or potential intellect is best understood as a disposition or ability of the human soul to represent imaginative forms intellectually. The material intellect accordingly relates to the intelligible or ideal dimension of imaginative forms, a dimension which these forms always possess, but only potentially at first. They await an intelligent mind to bring them to actuality by thinking them, even as the potentially intelligent mind requires some active stimulation to become receptive.[33]

The material intellect receives the intelligible aspect (*intention*) of the imaginative form, not the form itself, and thus the intellect keeps its distance from the material and particular character of worldly, sensible things. The objectivity of our thought, its ability to reach an intelligible 'object' and represent it in the mind, is assured by the essential separation of the rational faculty from the other psychical faculties. The nutritive, the sensitive and the imaginative faculties are connected with and affected by material things, both those which are external and those which are internal to the human organism. The human material intellect is the principle of potential thought, a principle that is given form and reality by the Agent Intellect, and by any other faculties with material connections to the soul. The material intellect, and the rational faculty in general, is thus *in* the human soul and person, and not *of* them. This line of argument leads Averroes to the conclusion that the human intellect must be fully immaterial and separate from anything physical in order to remain unaffected by particular, corporeal forms. Its passive nature is entirely that of universal receptivity, that is, it remains impassive to that which it receives, always able to receive new thoughts without bias or distortion from previous thoughts: 'As such, the activity of the intellect, particularly in its initial phase of representing or thinking the intelligible, is inerrant; the thoughts (of a

---

[31] 'Averroes was haunted by the issue, and successive works find him struggling with it and moving restlessly from one position to another', Davidson, 1992, p. 258.

[32] See Davidson, 1992, p. 276.

[33] Ivry, 1996, p. 205.

healthy person) are always accurate, or "true".'³⁴ The material intellect is no more than the potency to think, and its actual thinking requires an active agent. This is supplied by the one Agent Intellect who activates the potential, and thus allows the human being to realize the lifelong process of acquiring knowledge. The material intellect stands to the Agent Intellect as matter stands to form, as Ivry says; it supplies the basis or substrate upon which the Agent Intellect builds. But it does not accomplish this by emanating the forms directly upon the material intellect, rather it *illuminates* the 'objects' of understanding, it casts light upon them so that they can be received by an immaterial thing.

Averroes attempts to answer an important question which he feels has not been adequately addressed by Aristotle in the *De Anima* text. What is the origin of the form received by the matter prepared to receive it? The converse of this question would be: what accounts for this particular piece of matter having the disposition to receive the form appropriate to it? Averroes also feels obligated to accommodate any hypothesis about informed matter with the Almohad theological picture linking the Creator's efforts with its worldly effects. In his view it is not an issue about the transmission of something from outside, but of bringing some thing from potency to actuality: 'All forms and the relations between them exist in potential in the prime matter and to an extent in actuality in the Prime Mover which moves the Celestial bodies so that they free precisely those forms that are potential in matter. No immaterial being can act on matter, nor give it form, without using as instruments immutable immaterial beings, i.e. the Heavenly Bodies.'³⁵ Urvoy comments that Averroes exaggerates the similarity between the Almohad creationist theory and the philosophers' non-creationist theory: 'If divine wisdom produces an ordered world, by bringing into actuality potential forms which group concrete individuals into genera and species, so, inversely, through the act of abstraction the human spirit can make these forms exist separately. This is both the most characteristic act of [human] and that which brings him closest to divinity.' This sounds very much like Neo-Platonist doctrine (at least what they understood through the sometimes faulty texts), but Urvoy argues that the pertinent issues arise within Averroes' own metaphysical problematic: 'If Ibn Rushd's solution has been seen as neoplatonic in tone, it is because he wishes to take into account all the interpretations and do justice to each one, not through syncretism, but by integrating the particular aspect that justified its formulation.'³⁶

The Agent Intellect is the last principle in the celestial hierarchy of beings; each sphere has its own regnant principle responsible for the formal nature of that domain. Strictly speaking, the human material intellect does not think 'under its own power'; it is only the disposition or capacity to think, since the Agent Intellect establishes the potential form of human being as a rational animal in each individual. To represent a form in the intellect is thus an active as well as a passive force, which consists first in abstracting the essential and universal aspect of an imaginative form and then receiving it as an intelligible form. For the human soul to grasp such

---

34 Ivry, 1996, p. 206.
35 C. Touati, quoted in Urvoy, 1991, p. 105.
36 Urvoy, 1991, pp. 106, 108.

forms brings the individual closer to the Agent Intellect, affording it the chance to conjoin with the universal eternal Agent: 'Unlike Avicenna', Ivry says, 'Averroes does not believe the acquired intellect establishes an identity which can transcend the death of the individual, at most for Averroes one is granted a glimpse of eternity, of eternal truths, while alive.'[37] The imaginative faculty serves as the material substrate for the material intellect, just as the sensory organs are the substrate of the imaginative faculty, providing it with the intentions contained in sensory forms. In this context, Averroes is less naturalistic than Aristotle, who in each field of study drew inferences from observations about specific psychical functions. According to Jolivet, Averroes' grand synthesis attempts to state a unified theory under which accounts of intellectual knowledge, cause and effect, and astronomy are subsumed:

> Situated, by virtue of his imagination (which is corporeal) and his contact with the Intellect, between the material world and that of the Intelligences, human's function is to take back forms to their origin by thinking them. This vision is characteristic of neoplatonism, in which the dispersal of the intelligible in the sensible must be compensated for by a reunification and a return to [its] source, of which the agent is none other than the soul.[38]

Averroes' proposed location of the material intellect is one of the most unique features of his approach, and distinguishes his theory from that of his predecessors. Both the active and passive powers of the Agent Intellect, according to the *Long Commentary*, are located in the heavens, and the material intellect is called 'the last of the separate intellects in the celestial hierarchy', located immediately under or after the Agent Intellect. In positing the Agent Intellect as an entirely separate and eternal substance, he guaranteed the incorruptible nature of the material intellect, but retained its character as the psychical disposition to integrate the rational faculty with the whole process of cognition along Aristotelian lines. In the *Middle Commentary*, he located the imaginative faculty in the human soul as such; but unlike the Neo-Aristotelians he does not consider this disposition to be an extant substance in its own right, neither in the soul nor in the body. In the *Middle Commentary*, the material intellect's 'place' is not clearly defined, and functions *as though* it belongs to the human soul, since this makes the best sense of its immaterial, intelligible functions.[39] In the *Long Commentary*, the material intellect is posited in the celestial realm, as a fourth kind of being, in order to preserve its substantial autonomy. It is clearly the case that humans have the capacity to think in abstract and intelligible concepts, and Averroes must now account for its power to do so.[40]

He attempts to resolve some of these problems by positing various surrogates for the material intellect by means of which the power of thinking can be regarded as corporeal and hence located in the brain. At the same time he thinks that it has the

---

[37] Ivry, 1996, p. 208.

[38] Jolivet, quoted in Urvoy, 1991, p. 103.

[39] On the place of the *Middle Commentary* in the development of his treatment of the soul, see also Davidson, 1992, pp. 276–82.

[40] See Davidson, 1992, pp. 290–93.

capacity to perceive intelligible intentions within particular forms, thereby engaging the process of abstraction that the material and agent intellect combine to complete. The Agent Intellect is not present in its essence in the human soul, for its activity is entirely bound up with that of the material intellect, such that they appear to be two in one way, and one in another way. Thus, according to the *Long Commentary*, the rational faculty and the passible intellect suffer the same mortal fate as the imaginative faculty. As Ivry observes:

> It could hardly have escaped his notice that this very corporeality and corruptibility of the cogitative faculty and passible intellect render them unreliable as objective, unaffected transmitters of intelligible forms, however preliminary and restricted their role in abstracting universal intelligibles was conceived. The material intellect is not any more protected from material particularity by relating to the cogitative faculty or to the passible intellect than it is in relating to the imaginative forms themselves.

So this new attempt to resolve an old problem throws up an unexpected new problem: 'The passible intellect and/or cogitative faculty face the same dilemma Averroes first encountered with the material intellect, that of bridging corporeal and incorporeal reality. Averroes has created a second bridge to do so, with these quasi-immaterial powers, but it is no more sturdy than the first bridge, now relocated in the heavens.'[41]

He argues for the soul's immortality by turning to Aristotle's notion that the active intellect (*nous poētikos*, more properly the 'maker mind') alone is spiritual and hence immortal, but modifies it such that the soul has an impersonal immortality, since the 'maker mind' is alien to everything that makes an individual an individual.[42] With regard to the other aspects of the soul, that is, the other psychical functions considered as specific subjacent forms, insofar as each is linked to one or more sensory organs, they can grow weak and lose their effective function. This question is beyond the limit of scientific inquiry; Averroes declares only those with special gifts of insight can discern an answer. But the Koran does provide an image that can be used to draw an analogy: in sleep the soul has no activity because it does not use its sensory organs, and yet the soul subsists. Averroes reviews the various proposals put forward by the Greek and Islamic philosophers and concludes that each offers only hints or indications that ultimately can be reconciled with Koranic images from revelation.[43] With regard to the question of resurrection, he says that, 'our existence there is another creation, superior to this existence'; in agreement with Christian doctrine he claims that in this superior life each human regains its body, but not the spiritual body, rather the original, earthly body.

Averroes' greatest influence, however, was not on Islamic thought but on European Latin philosophy after its transmission through the Spanish schools, especially in Toledo, after 1200. In MacClintock's limpid words, 'the dynamic speculative activity vital for five centuries in the Arabic tradition, which was founded in large part on Greek writings in philosophy and science ... disappears after 1200, reappearing

---

[41] Ivry, 1996, p. 215.
[42] On these arguments, see Davidson, 1992, pp. 335–8.
[43] Urvoy, 1991, p. 88.

almost immediately in Western Latin thought.' In the centuries after Averroes' death, a large number of translations were made from Arabic and Hebrew into Latin, from Greek originals that had already been translated into Syriac and Arabic. These efforts caught the attention of powerful rulers who wanted to establish centers of excellence in research and recruited talented polyglot scholars to assist their endeavors: 'The impact of this solid and integrated corpus of natural science on the Western intellectual world was enormous, coming as it did into a climate where for centuries scholars eager for knowledge had had to content themselves with third-hand encyclopedic compilations of inadequately developed science and scientific methodology.'[44]

Latin translations of Aristotle's texts were usually accompanied with their attendant later commentaries; those by Alexander and Simplicius were common, but Averroes' had the most influence.[45] Much of Averroes' work was eagerly taken up by young scholars hungry for new ideas, but it also met some strong opposition. His writings were banned by the University of Paris in 1210 and again in 1215, deemed usable only with corrections in 1231, and not officially sanctioned until 1255. Several significant thirteenth-century theologian-philosophers studied Averroes with great attention, including Albert the Great, William of Auvergne, Alexander of Hales and Robert Grosseteste. Albert the Great felt strongly enough about the Second Master that he published one tract, *Against Averroes*, and his student Thomas Aquinas also devoted enough attention to this opponent to merit a special title, *Treatise on the Unity of Intellect against Averroes*. In sum, the Islamic commentator's principles were thought to run counter to some basic Christian doctrines: the world was eternal, and not created in time; individual immortality was not possible; the very existence of the world was deeply contingent, and faith and reason each accorded with a separate standard of truth.[46] In the 1270s the Paris Council again condemned Averroes' position and university masters, such as Siger of Brabant, Boethius of Dacia and Bernard of Nivelles, were indicted. The last self-proclaimed Averroist was Cesare of Cremona (sadly famous perhaps for his refusal to use the 'stupid' telescope), whose name as late as 1631 could be linked with Galileo himself as an enemy of orthodox Christian teaching.

Urvoy argues that in addition to the Latin Christian writers there were at least two other continuators of Islamic philosophy in the thirteenth century: Raymond Marti (*c*.1230–*c*.1285) and Raymond Lull (1232–1316). Marti, like Albert and Aquinas and Bacon, was a Dominican monk, an expert in Arabic, Hebrew and even Aramaic. He studied with Albert the Great and must have known Thomas Aquinas in Paris; his major work *The Fight for Faith* employs many Islamic works, including Averroes' *The Incoherence of the Incoherence*, otherwise little-known to his contemporaries. Raymond Lull was more of a maverick, unaffiliated with any university; he issued various demands for the creation of colleges of oriental languages to train missionaries, the unification of military religious orders, and the allocation of budgets for the Crusades to the Holy Land. It is unfortunate that Lull

---

[44] MacClintock, 1967, pp. 223–4.
[45] For details on this huge topic, see Davidson, 1992, pp. 298–314.
[46] On this double standard of truth see, amongst others, Urvoy, 1991, p. 101.

relied quite heavily on faulty summaries of Islamic philosophical opinions and hence condemned Avicenna and Averroes for mistakes they never made: 'Thus, on one hand, Ramon Marti makes use of Ibn Rushd in a scrupulous but impersonal way ... Ramon Lull, on the other hand, is guilty of grave factual errors – even dishonesty – but sets out a completely new path which was to have considerable repercussions, although it was marginalized by the "philosophically non-professional" character which permeates it.'[47]

In H. A. Wolfson's famous phrase,[48] Averroes was 'twice revealed' to European philosophy – first in the thirteenth century and again in the sixteenth century. With regard to the second event, his commentaries on Aristotle's texts were widely read and studied and copied, despite the Church's repeated condemnations of his doctrinal position. Many of the Arabic originals had been lost, but through Hebrew translations virtually all of his writings became available to Latin translators. Most of Averroes' commentaries were included in sixteenth-century collected editions of Aristotle's works; twenty-six out of thirty-four translations were made from Hebrew, six of which replaced older translations from the thirteenth century made directly from the Arabic. But the Islamic thinker's reception the second time was much different than the first time: it was not the Christian scholastics who declaimed his heretical stance, but the classical scholars who decried his ignorance of Greek antiquity and lack of access to properly edited texts. Wolfson's own painstaking studies led him to a contrary view: in his 1929 book on *Crescas' Critique*, he said that the Arabic and Hebrew translators preserved clear-cut analyses, exact terminology, and forms of expression. The successive translators maintained a literal and faithful attitude, and the various versions 'suffered comparatively little corruption'. More than thirty years later, Wolfson had not changed his opinion, but added that he was now convinced that there had been a continuous oral tradition which accompanied every translation, explaining all the new shades of meaning. It is in large measure due to Wolfson's own efforts that there has been a *third* revelation, with the grand plan for publishing three series of texts, each with critical apparatuses and glossaries, devoted to Averroes' monumental encounter with Aristotle's philosophy.

(2) Theological summation: Albert the Great and Thomas Aquinas

The course of Albert's life (*c*.1200–80) follows the course and fortunes of the entire thirteenth century; he was without doubt the dominant figure of his epoch, the most prolific writer, the most influential teacher; an experienced traveler, studious observer of nature, and the one person so consummately learned that he was called *Magnus*, 'the Great', even in his lifetime.[49] In 1223 he entered the Dominican Order, studied at Padua and Bologna, then lectured at various convents in Germany; he was master of theology in Paris from 1240–48, when Thomas Aquinas studied under him. He

---

[47] Urvoy, 1991, p. 131; Lull's place in the development of occult thinking deserves a section of its own, perhaps in a second volume.
[48] Wolfson, 1973, vol. I, pp. 383–97.
[49] Catania, in EEP, vol. 1, p. 64.

was sent by his superiors to organize the plan of studies at Cologne in 1248, and in 1260 was consecrated Bishop of Ratisbon (Regensburg), which he resigned after two years, to devote all his mighty efforts to teaching and writing. His principal works include the *Summa de Creaturis,* several long commentaries, on the *Metaphysics, On the Soul,* the *Ethics,* on *The Causes and Procession of the Universe* (based on the pseudo-Aristotelian *Book of Causes*), on *The Books of Pseudo-Dionysius,* and *The Fourth Book of the Sentences,* as well as his final great summation, the *Summa Theologiae.* Although scholars have agreed in assigning him the central role in making Aristotle the supreme pagan authority for university studies, Albert's grand Aristotelian system is actually mixed with many Neo-Platonic elements, sometimes muddled and confused. It is more clear now, however, that Albert did attempt to advance a bold view, not so much about specific problems in philosophy, but about the very nature and scope of philosophy as an intellectual activity.[50]

The arrival of Graeco-Arabic scholarship in the form of Islamic treatises and commentaries posed some difficult problems for Christian thinkers, namely, how to reconcile conflicting statements about crucial Christian beliefs.[51] In an overly simplified way, one could say that the books of the mystical Plato (for example, the *Timaeus*) and the Neo-Platonists, especially Plotinus, but also Porphyry and Proclus, had been accommodated into the Christian doctrinal framework through the syncretistic labors of the Church Fathers, reaching its brilliant culmination in Augustine. But Aristotle was another matter; reconciliation of his metaphysical principles with Christian teaching was one of the pre-eminent tasks for western theologians after the recovery and reception of Aristotle's work via the Islamic route. The proliferation of Christian commentaries on Aristotle's *De Anima* in the twelfth and thirteenth centuries testifies to their authors' efforts to reinterpret the First Master's understanding of the nature and functions of soul and mind. Their task was to make it accord with some of the basic tenets of the OT, especially the *Genesis* accounts, and the all-important NT statements about human soul and divine spirit.

In his early work, the *Summa de Creaturis,* Albert juggles several different approaches to account for the nature and functions of soul. In addition to the mainline Aristotelian account, he also tries to make good use of Neo-Platonic arguments, especially through the filter of St. Augustine and Pseudo-Denis, as well as Avicenna's technical improvements on Aristotle's hylomorphic scheme. One of his most ingenious efforts involves Avicenna's distinction between partial form (*forma partis*) and total form (*forma totius*), applied to the composite of soul and body in the animate being. The partial form is the source of all the perfections that are present in the material and the composite, giving them their essence and 'reason'. The form provides the essence by producing and diffusing itself in the whole; it is the main feature of the essence and reason of any animate thing. It is also the reason of the common nature, that is, the nature common to the composite of both soul and body; it is also the act of matter and the first act of the whole. According to Ducharme's summary:

---

[50] Marenbon, in Marenbon, 1998, p. 230
[51] For details, see Davidson, 1992, pp. 209–17.

Within an individual being, form is the principle of unity and cohesion and identity, and it gives the being to be what it is, sealing in perfection, so to speak, a separation which, of itself, it would not have produced. The division (*divisio*) is a result of matter, but the diversity (*diversitas*) of distinct identities is attributed to form. Earthly individual beings are true beings, and their diversity is not a screen which would hide a more basic identity. Their diversity and their unity have a substantial source, their form, which is part of them and gives them unity, just as it gives them *esse* [essence] and *ratio* [reason] ... Even if that form is submitted to the laws of matter, it assumes them and elevates them to perfection. Nothing is, but the individual, and it truly is, thanks to its form.[52]

In his *Commentary on the Sentences*, Albert compares the composition of human nature, in terms of soul and body, with the composition of the divine natures in Christ, carefully segregating the two concepts of composition according to partial form and total form:

The first composition, properly called, is that of soul and body; soul which is said to be the act of an organic physical body, having life in potency. And to that composition follows the total form, which is 'human' or 'humanity', if one may speak about it in abstraction; and that form is the species in this particular individual. Indeed form is twofold (*duplex*), namely the form of the matter, or partial form, or potential; that form is the end of generation in nature, and it is a part of the thing, and such a form, the soul, is in a human. There is another form, which is the reason of the thing, and its whole essence according to its reason; that form follows the composition of the natural form and of natural potency, which is matter. [III Sent., d.2, art. 5, sol.]

The first composition of natural matter and natural form gives an existent being its definite nature; that which gives this nature is the substantial form which radiates through the composite. The total form follows (in the logical sense) the partial form, and makes present the species in the individual, for example, 'humanity' in Socrates; it is the reason in Aristotle's sense of *logos* as the *archē* of natural things' nature.[53]

Albert employs both the distinction between partial and total form, and the manner in which each gives 'reason' to the essence of both the species and the individual, in his intricate account of the identity of the concrete earthly human before and after his bodily death. He says one must counter the argument that either the substantial forms of an individual before and after death are different, or that the substantial form of humanity *in* the individual perishes with his death and hence can no longer be present. If (a) one agrees with Avicenna that the total form is other than the partial form, and if (b) the essence of the species 'humanity' can subsist without any individual instantiating it, and if (c) it is only the material elements that individuate particular humans, then (d) there is nothing *in* the individual human that subsists (survives) after the death of his material body. But, in contrast with this argument, if one agrees with Aristotle, as interpreted by Averroes, that (a) the total form is the substantial form of the whole composite, and (b) the whole

---

[52] Ducharme, 1979, p. 138; see also Bonin, 2000, pp. 47–50.
[53] See Ducharme, 1979, pp. 141–2 on details of the relation of partial form to total form; Baldner, 1996, pp. 103–8.

composite is distinct from the matter component according to reason, and (c) the form only is destroyed with respect to its predication of the composite, then (d) the individual after death is identical with the one before death. Since Albert is primarily concerned with the Christian doctrine of resurrection and the soul's immortality, the substantial form he has in mind is the spiritual nature of human being.[54] Albert himself explains:

> The soul is completely subject to suffering in the body ... But one must understand that two points are to be considered about the soul, namely that it is the nature of human, and the principle of human activities. From this point of view it can be considered in three ways: some features belong to it as substantial form, some as soul, some as human nature precisely as human. According to its being a substantial form, it is itself the perfection of the human body. The balance of temperaments that it produces in the human body amongst the various elements is superior to the balance obtained in other bodies due to their forms; in this respect the human body resembles celestial bodies. Therefore the reason of form and act in it is the most noble of all.

This superior balance is closely tied to the goodness (nobility) intrinsic to the perfect state it aspires to attain:

> As the soul, it is the act of a body, which is not only the result of such a balanced composition, but also as having life; it is found in all organic things, and thus it belongs to the soul to radiate various powers in various parts of the body; the human soul possesses this in the most noble way. Since the soul is the nature of human as human, nature gives human being the essence and reason of human. And thus, the rational soul, considered as the nature of human, must have something more than a mere form, and more than a mere soul.

The essence and reason of the noble or ruling 'part' partakes of both a nature dependent on a living body and a nature independent of any living body:

> It must have, flowing from it, some powers that are linked to organs, because it is a form giving essence as a nature docs, and other powers that are not linked to organs; these are related to powers that are linked, inasmuch as they receive their [sensible] species from them, and they are related to separate substances, inasmuch as they participate in their light. And that is what the philosopher [Aristotle] says: the noble soul has three operations, viz. divine, animal, and intellectual; thus considered, the whole of a soul united to a body shares in the sufferings [of its body]. Soul is also to be considered as being the principle of human activities, and seen as such, it is not necessary that it shares in its totality the body's sufferings, because some of its powers may be taken up with the contemplation of eternal things, and some others submitted to passivities proper to bodies. [III Sent., d. 15, art. 3, sol.]

Albert sums up his whole philosophy of the human soul in these terms: soul is a true substantial form; it is even superior to all other forms; it is also an authentic soul, the act of a body; again, it is superior to all other souls. But it is also the 'nature' of human as human; it gives a human the *esse* and the *ratio* of human

---

[54] Ducharme, 1979, pp. 143–5.

[being]; and, so considered, it appears as human's very 'substance'. Now, since it is rational, it is more than a mere form, and more than a mere soul. Albert, quoting an unnamed philosopher, goes on to say that, while some of that soul's resources of activity are linked to an organic support, others are not. The latter are indeed related to the former, since they receive their 'species' from them, but they are also akin to separate substances and share some of the light which is proper to them. And so, the human soul, in most of its activities, is entirely involved with its body, but its 'divine' activity, the contemplation of eternals, is not impeded because of that involvement: its species may come from functions that are bound to a bodily organ, but its 'light' is of a different order.[55]

For Albert, the existence of the soul (*anima*) is evident from the obvious fact that some creatures have an internal principle of motion and others do not; with some kinds of creatures this is clearly due to the presence of the will. Albert devotes one whole chapter to a review of the Church Fathers' various definitions of soul, then another chapter to unpacking the definitions and subject-status of the soul in Aristotle. Irrespective of its eventual definition, it is clear, he says, that the soul is an immaterial substance united with a material body. Its first act is to give its own body being, and its second act is to give its body its own powers and operations. Albert says that Plato was right to define the soul as 'an incorporeal substance that moves a body', and Aristotle was right to define the soul as 'the form of an organized body that is capable of life'. He uses Avicenna's interpretation to reconcile these two seemingly incongruent statements: considered in itself, from the point of view of its essence, the soul is an incorporeal substance; but considered with respect to its body, the soul is its first act and its mover. In other words, there is a certain incorporeal substance which, insofar as it is the first act and mover of its body, is called the soul.[56] He now has to account for this substance's union with its body, on which point he says that Avicenna was right and Averroes was wrong. The soul, considered in itself, is a substance from which emanate operations and powers closely allied with its body; as an incorporeal substance it brings about secondary acts in which no bodily organ has any role.[57]

He follows Aristotle to the letter when he says that there are three powers in the human soul: the vegetative, the sensitive and the rational. However, against Platonist opinions, these three powers comprise a single substance, a single soul and a single act. It is the one human soul that unites all three powers in one being.[58] The five external senses are dealt with in some detail before he turns his attention to the nature and scope of sensory knowledge and its relation to intelligence. Although he argues that the sensitive power as such is both a material and a passive power, he admits that after it has been actualized by the sensible form of external objects it can make judgments; it does this through the communal sense. He accepts the argument that there is an agent intellect in the soul that abstracts and thus actualizes intelligible species, but rejects the parallel argument that there is an active sensory

---

[55] Ducharme, 1979, pp. 146–7; Bonin, 2000, pp. 50–52.
[56] Gilson, 1955, p. 283; Baldner, 1996, pp. 108–12.
[57] Baldner, 1996, pp. 113–16.
[58] Michaud-Quantin, 1955, pp. 60–65; on the soul's roots in the elements, Ruegenberg, 1979, pp. 54–5.

power that abstracts and thus actualizes the sensible species. Instead he claims that it is something in the nature of intellect that renders the potentially intelligible actually intelligible, whereas it is something in the nature of the external world that renders material things actually sensible. That which is present in the sensory faculty is definitely not the form united with the material properties of an externally existing thing, but rather an 'intention' or species of material thing that enables the soul to have knowledge of that thing.[59] The concept of intention here follows the early medieval, patristic term for entity in receipt of sensory 'species', for example, in its earliest version as introduced by Augustine; its source is external to the defining essence of an ensouled being.

Albert expands on Aristotle's views about the agent intellect insofar as it is given from without: 'The intellectual soul is not educed from matter; instead, it enters from without; ... the light of the agent intellect is its root, in such a way that [the soul] is sometimes called by philosophers the result of the divine intellect in the physical body that has life.' The standard Aristotelian position is that the lower soul and the passive intellect are capable of destruction, whereas the active principle of the intellect alone, considered to be separate from the passive intellect and its phantasms, is not open to destruction. Albert thus adduces four groups of basic faculties in the human soul: first, the powers of knowing, perceiving and forming opinions; second, the generic power of appetite; third, the power of locomotion, and fourth, the power of growth (*De Anima* I, tract 2, cap. 15). This differs in significant respects from the general Islamic category of internal sense, and also from Aquinas' later position.[60]

The overriding philosophical questions and disputations in these twelfth-century writers were directed not at the nature and functions of *soul*, but at the powers and operations of the intellect. Gilson's astute comment here is that

> Albert's approach to the problem of the intellect is typical of his general attitude. Naturally, he has first exhausted all the literature available on the subject ... But he also realized, with great acumen, that they did not all apply to the same problem. For instance, he clearly saw that the division of Avicenna and that of Aristotle did not add up, because Aristotle intended to divide the human intellect into its essential parts (the agent intellect and the possible intellect), whereas Avicenna intended to distinguish the various stages which attend the acquisition of learning ... The same remark applies to the division of Averroes, which is taken from the degrees of perfection of the intellect. These penetrating remarks justify the extensive use which he himself occasionally makes of several different divisions and classifications of the human modes of intellection.[61]

Albert makes his own position quite clear: the agent intellect and the possible intellect are *in* the soul. The agent intellect is not a habit, that is, the permanent possession of certain intelligible thoughts, nor is it a separate intelligence which confers intelligible forms onto the possible intellect. The human intellect, he says,

---

[59] Mahoney, in Kretzmann, CHLMP, 1982, p. 602.
[60] For a summary classification of the internal senses in Albert the Great, Thomas Aquinas and Roger Bacon, see Wolfson, 1973, vol. I, pp. 295–310; see also Harvey, 1975, pp. 45–62.
[61] Gilson, 1955, pp. 284–5; Ruegenberg, 1979, pp. 58–62.

is 'conjoined to the human soul; it is simple, it has no intelligible features, but it produces them in the possible intellect from the phantasms, as Averroes expressly says in his commentary on the *De Anima*.' This is a peculiar assertion since Albert knows quite well that for Averroes the two intellects are separate substances; he thought that once this doctrine had been corrected it was more satisfactory than any other attempt to make sense of Aristotle's remarks.[62]

The agent intellect flows from the human soul insofar as the soul is an actuation of its substance; the possible intellect flows from the soul insofar as it is the soul's potency. The proper action of the agent intellect is that of an efficient and formal cause whose effect is to draw the possible intellect from potency to actualization. Thus the agent intellect transmutes something in the possible intellect from potency to actuality, and Avicenna and Averroes are both correct when they claim that there are degrees in this transmutation. With regard to knowledge as such (*scientia*), the possible intellect has three degrees, not powers or faculties: first, since it is the potentiator for all intelligible things, the possible intellect is material (*hylealis*), that is, it resembles prime matter to the extent that its possibility is completely indeterminate. Second, the same intellect can be said to already possess the knowledge of principles which are necessary for the acquisition of secure knowledge (*intellectus in habitu*). Third, the same intellect can be said to already possess that scientific knowledge, with the ability to make use of it at will (*intellectus in effectu*). In Albert's redaction of Avicenna's scheme, he has omitted the latter's highest degree of intellectual cognition, the accommodated or acquired intellect, since from Albert's point of view it implies some sort of communication or alliance with an autonomous agent intellect. Since each human being has its own agent intellect, there is no reason to believe, with Avicenna, that humans must employ the power of a separate intellect every time it thinks an intelligible entity. On the other hand, Avicenna was correct to claim that the rational soul has no genuine memory, in which it could store its already acquired knowledge of intelligible things. The possible intellect already has that power; in this proper function it receives intelligible beings, retains them, and then reconsiders them through the soul's own agent intellect.[63]

Given his definition of soul as an immaterial substance, Albert offers various arguments to demonstrate its immortal status, some based on Avicenna's view. The soul is not some sort of corporeal energy, the human intellect is not the act of any kind of body, the soul is not there in view of the body – rather, in each case, the reverse is true. In short, the rational soul is a substance that exists in itself, and since it has subsistence apart from its body, it can exist after its bodily host's death. Albert quotes Avicenna with approval: 'this name *anima* does not designate the essence of the thing that it names, nor is it taken from the category in which it is contained [substance]; it is taken from an accident that happens to it; and this is the reason why the name of the soul (*anima*) is derived from the verb, to animate.' The same definition implies that soul *qua* substance is the mover of its body (*movens corpus*), in addition to being the first act of its body. One dimension of the intellect

---

[62] Gorman, 1940, pp. 223–30.
[63] Gilson, 1955, pp. 285–6; Ruegenberg, 1979, pp. 58–62.

is called practical because through cognition and rational inquiry it directs the human will and actions. The practical and the theoretical intellect are one substance, they are the same intellect, at some times directed toward the good, at other times directed toward the truth. In Gilson's words: 'The practical intellect first turns toward the good in general, which is the prime mover in the order of actions and operations; then it turns toward good things which can be done or made, in which case it deals with singulars; thirdly, it moves desire toward these particular goods apprehended as desirable ends. Goodness is, in the practical order, what truth is in the speculative order.'[64]

In the proper sense of the concept of will, it is the natural appetite of the rational soul and its objects are of three kinds: first, within the soul it holds sway over all other powers; second, outside the soul, the will applies to that which can maintain and protect nature; third, it concerns that which outside the soul is not required to maintain nature, such that it can tend towards impossible things (and thus become irrational) or towards possible but not actual things (and thus become inventive). Free choice then belongs to human beings alone; *liberum arbitrium* is the liberty to arbitrate (not 'arbitrary liberty'), to decide by means of arbitration between what is good and what is evil. The liberty of desire consists in the rational power either to yield to the judgment of reason, or else to turn away from it. As an arbitrating power, it belongs to reason, and as free, it belongs to the will; but to be an act of arbitration is the very substance of the will, to be free is incidental to this main power. Free choice is the power to do what one pleases, without being under the sway of some higher power, whereas liberty must be defined with respect to some goal, and is the power to preserve the rectitude of the will, desired for the sake of uprightness itself.

With St. Thomas Aquinas (1224–74), our story reaches the apogee of medieval scholastic summation of then current philosophical and theological doctrines of the soul. Thomas was born into a noble family in the Kingdom of Naples; his parents initially opposed his decision to enter study with the Benedictines, but he spent several years at the monastery in Monte Cassino, before moving to the University of Naples. At the age of twenty he entered the Dominican Order and studied theology, first at Paris and then under Albert the Great in Cologne. After seven years' teaching in Paris as master of theology, he moved to Rome and its environs continuing his prodigious teaching schedule amongst the monks at several locations. His enormous written output was achieved during his twenty years' teaching (1252–73), as well as sermons, notations, letters and other works.[65] He held public disputations, the standard medieval component of university education, usually once every two weeks; the transcripts of two of these, *Disputed Questions on the Soul* and *Questions on Spiritual Creatures*, are of special concern here, as well as his meticulous commentary on Aristotle's *De Anima*, and relevant passages in two of his great works, the *Summa Contra Gentiles* (Book II) and the *Summa Theologiae* (Book I). One should bear in mind that Thomas always considered himself to be master of *theology*, or sacred doctrine, and not philosophy, but such a proviso

---

[64] Gilson, 1955, p. 288; on liberty, p. 290.
[65] Brian Davies, in Marenbon, 1998, pp. 241–2; V. J. Bourke, in EEP, vol. 7, p. 105; Jan Aersten, in Kretzmann & Stump, 1993, pp. 12–14.

should not diminish the respect that Thomas had for philosophy's capacity to bring the student to correct insight. In Bertrand Russell's evergreen *History of Western Philosophy,* Thomas is peremptorily dismissed from inclusion in the proper subject matter of the history of philosophical doctrines, but Anthony Kenny has argued forcibly for a more balanced assessment.[66]

Thomas does not often use the word 'mind' (*mens, mentis*), preferring instead to talk about the rational soul (*anima rationalis*) or the rational part of the soul. Kretzmann opens his recent discussion of this issue with the remark that 'Aquinas's philosophy of mind can be understood only in the context of his more general theory of soul, which naturally make use of many features of his metaphysics.'[67] Thomas' formulaic definition of soul is 'the first principle of life', and much of his preliminary efforts are focused on the meaning of the concept of life in the basis of actual living things. There are, he says, vital activities that normally have bodies and bodily parts among their principles; *some* principles of life clearly are in bodies, and hence have material 'natures', but those are not souls. There are some bodies that are not only not principles of life but even by nature without life; thus no body considered solely as a body has life as its essence:

> But a *first intrinsic principle* of life (which imbues everything else in an animate body with life) must have life essentially. If it did not, its having life would be explained on the basis of something else intrinsic to that living body, and it would not be that body's *first* principle of life. Therefore, *no* soul, *no* first principle of life, is a body. If a soul is in any respect corporeal ... it will not be in virtue of its corporeality that it animates the thing whose soul it is. [original emphases]

He accounts for the fact that only some specifically organized bodies have the principle of life by employing the Aristotelian concept of substantial form: 'The *first* principle of life in a living body, its soul, is not a bodily part of that body, but rather its form, one of the two metaphysical parts of the composite of matter and form that absolutely every body is.'[68]

The soul as the form of living organized mater is immaterial and incorporeal; as such it is the most humble of forms. However, all souls are graded according to their level in the hierarchy of ensouled beings, and the human soul is the highest of all souls connected to animate bodies (the angels do not have corporeal bodies, and hence are the highest of all). The human soul is capable of knowing many things, and since in order to know something it is necessary that the knower not be the same species as the thing known, the knower (or the knowing agent) cannot be a bodily thing. The power that humans have to know things is the operation of a substantial form that is alien to, that is, essentially different than, anything of a corporeal nature. To operate by itself it must subsist by itself, because being is the cause of its operations, and everything acts according to its essence. The only being that can subsist by itself is a substance, not an accident of something more basic, and hence the human soul must be both substantial and immaterial. For Thomas, to

---

[66] Kenny, 1993, pp. 1–13.
[67] Kretzmann, 1993, p. 128.
[68] Kretzmann, 1993, p. 130; see Bourke, 1967, p. 108.

see that the human soul is an immaterial substance is, at one and the same time, to see that it is immortal.[69] Since the human soul *qua* basic substance exists in itself, it cannot lose its nature by accident. Since the human soul is immaterial and only tied to its host's body by an act of God, the death of the human body does not entail the death of its soul. In the strict sense, the *rational* soul *qua* immaterial form is not affected by the corruption or diminution of the animate body. The human body, that is, the corporeal component of the soul–body composite, exists *in virtue of* the soul, whereas it is not true to say that the soul exists *in virtue of* the body it is joined with.[70]

Bernard Bazan has presented several attempts to reconcile two divergent views about Thomistic metaphysical principles, used in support of his account of soul: that the soul is the form of a body, and that a human is a soul that uses a body. One arbitrative interpretation distinguishes two types of metaphysical subordination: in the case of essential subordination, there is a direct relation between two forms; in the case of dispositional subordination, the forms are independent between them, but they maintain an indirect relation founded on their attachment to one and the same matter. Insofar as it concerns essential substance, it also makes a subdivision according to which the concept is considered either as a plurality of forms or a plurality of degrees of the same form. Bazan responds to this suggestion that the central point is the notion of an incomplete substance, susceptible to receiving successive perfect acts; it is never a question of admitting a relation between two substances. Rather, he argues, the intellectual soul is not only the last formal perfection, but a true substance, complete in itself; this accords with the ordered arrangement amongst the partisans of dualism as they have defined the concept. The thirteenth century thinkers considered the soul as a reality independent of the body, within the order of being, but also complete within the order of essence and the order of acts. The soul does not need a body as an extrinsic instrument to its nature as a spiritual substance. Since the universal matter-form scheme does not posit a plurality of forms, it prejudges nothing about the number of forms of composition, but only affirms the immateriality of separate substances. In terms of the infrastructure of constitutive principles, the rational soul plays the role of a competing form *vis-à-vis* a composite already actualized for inferior forms; pluralism supposes, then, the conception of the soul as a corporeal form.[71]

The thesis of the soul's autonomous subsistence has both an advantage and disadvantage to Thomas' general theory about the human soul. The advantage is that it establishes one of the necessary conditions for the soul's immortality, but the disadvantage is the implicit threat to the unity of the human being. Since the distinctively human character of human being is its having a subsistent, separable rational intellect or mind, it looks as though the human being is *identified* with its rational part. The fact that a human is united with its body appears to be an accident, though an accident of a special kind, namely through God's grace. Thomas attempts to dispel the serious difficulties involved in this twofold picture by

---

[69] On immortal discussions in this context, see esp. Pegis, 1934, pp. 95–120.
[70] Gilson, 1957, pp. 187–8; see also Kenny, 1993, pp. 129–43.
[71] Bazan, 1969, pp. 33, 36, 69; synopsis of main points in my literal trans.

introducing a further distinction between a real particular, 'this something' (*hoc aliquid*) and the substance as such or in itself.[72] Strictly speaking *hoc aliquid* applies to an individual in the category of primary substance, that is, if and only if it is not *in* something else as its subject, and it is something that occupies a place of its own in the natural order of things. In Kretzmann's concise words:

> The human soul is *in* the human being, not as heat is in coal, but as a part is in a whole, such that it is capable of subsisting on its own. Moreover, the human soul as the form of its own body has the role of fulfilling or completing the human species, that is, the soul is not only the *rationality* but indeed, the full *rational animality* of the human body, specifying that corporeal thing as a human being. Without the soul that body is a corpse, which can be called a human body only equivocally. Although the soul itself has no place of its own among individuals sorted out in the species and genera of substances, it is what gives the human being its unique place in that system, what enables that human being to satisfy [the criterion], and so it is more nearly a *hoc aliquid* than any bodily part could be.[73]

Kenneth Schmitz has argued[74] that Thomas formulated one of the strongest arguments ever presented for the immortality of the human soul. This proof proceeds through three moments: first, it establishes the immaterial nature of the intellectual operations performed by the human soul (its incorporeity). Second, it establishes the soul's capacity to exist in and through itself (its subsistence), and third, it establishes the actual survival of the soul after death (its incorruptibility). One of the keys to understanding the distinctively rational appeal of Thomas' argument is that worldly things, including human beings, are not merely limited substances of certain kinds of creatures, beings created by God, who possess a positive principle of existence received from another being. An additional key pertains to Thomas' doctrine of self-knowledge; according to the principle of epistemic purity or transparence, only humans can know themselves and in doing so realize that the soul which knows, as both knower and known, is an immaterial being.

However, in satisfying his discursive requirement for a demonstrative proof, Thomas confronts an embarrassing aspect of the post-mortem soul's separation from its body which only the Christian doctrine of resurrection can cope with. Thomas considers the hope for such a later state as 'the vision of the way things really are, the glory towards which reason gropes, into which faith peers darkly, and in which the blessed take joy'. Thomas grasps this dilemma by the horns, not shrinking from the inevitable consequences of an attempt to reconcile two contrastive points of view. Schmitz says that:

> The farthest he can go as a philosopher in parting the mysterious veil that lies at the boundary of our present life, however, is expressed in his formula: the human soul, by virtue of its intellectual nature, is both a substance in its own right and yet the spiritual life of the body (*forma et hoc aliquid*). Without the body, it subsists only as a radically incomplete being, since it is by nature meant to inform, structure and vivify its human

---

[72] On this distinction in Albert, see Baldner, 1996, pp. 106–8.
[73] Kretzmann, 1993, p. 135.
[74] Schmitz, 1986, pp. 396–405; Kenny's synopsis of this argument, 1993, pp. 153–9.

body. In the end, then, St. Thomas' proof delivers to us something not unlike a Greek shade.[75]

And with this discursive end to Thomas' incongruous demonstration, one could turn to the opening canto of Dante's *Divine Comedy*, where the Christian pilgrim, in search of the philosophical truth at the heart of the strange Christian doctrine of the soul's immortal status, encounters an entire realm of departed shades.

Thomas rejects any idea that matter as such is evil or deficient or imperfect:

> It would be completely foreign to the Thomistic perspective to regard the material universe as the result of some calamity and the union of soul and body as the consequence of a fall. A radical optimism runs through this doctrine because it presents a universe created out of pure goodness. It interprets all its parts, in the measure in which they subsist, as so many reflections of God's infinite perfection. Origen's teaching that God created bodies in order to imprison sinful souls in them is most repugnant to St. Thomas' thought. The body is not the prison of the soul, but a servant and instrument placed in its service by Almighty God. The union of soul and body is no chastisement of the soul but a salutary bond through which the human soul will reach its full perfection.[76]

Since it is in the concept of the good that sufficient and final 'causes' must reside, one must examine the soul itself to uncover the body's 'reason' for existing. If the soul were an intelligence of the same degree of perfection as an angel, it would be pure form subsisting and operating without the aid of an outer instrument, fully realizing its own definition, and thus concentrating in the individual the total perfection of an essence. But the human soul is lower on the ladder of being than the angels, midway between pure (though finite) immaterial intellect and insensate, inanimate material 'nature'. The perfection to which the human soul can attain is achieved only through the successive generation of humans as the *species*, that is, the creation of an omnipotent and beneficent God. Each human being as an individual is only the incomplete realization of an ideal archetype: 'Insofar as it satisfies its own essential definition, it is an act and has the pleasure of being what it ought to be. But insofar as it only realizes its definition imperfectly, it is in potency; that is, it is not all that it could be. Indeed, it is even in a state of privation, because it feels that it ought to be what it is not.'[77]

Thomas' discussion of the nature of human being examines certain typical activities and then, by means of persuasive reason draws inferences about what kinds of powers would be needed to explain these activities, and then concludes by offering the best candidate for what could be the subject of such powers. He classified human biological activities into three sorts: growth, digestion and reproduction; the next higher level comprised sensation, affections and locomotion; the highest level comprised the cognitive functions of understanding, judgment and reason, as well as the various correspondent appetites toward and away from the

---

[75] Schmitz, 1986, pp. 409, 413.
[76] Gilson, 1957, pp. 189–90.
[77] Gilson, 1957, pp. 190–91.

objects of perception and understanding. To these various functions he assigned generic powers or potencies in accord with the Aristotelian maxim that each potency is ordered towards its proper action, and the nature of each power derives from the action to which it is ordered. Thomas further distinguished five special sensory powers for perception of external particular things, and four special internal senses, or inner-directed powers: the communal sense, imagination, memory and practical reason (or cogitation). The appetitive power was divided into two versions based on the type of good or evil (moral or non-moral) perceived in the objects towards which or away from which desire was directed: either concupiscible or irascible, derived from the Classical Greek psychical concepts of *thumos* and *epithumia*. (Thus, *concupio* had already long stood for the notion of desire, in the sense of sensuous desire for some thing; and *ira* for strong-willed 'anger' or powerful petition to overcome obstacles – the Latin translation itself slants the interpretation of these two key aspects of the 'lower' soul.)

Thomas attributes eleven distinct types of emotion ('passions' in the original sense) to these two sensory appetites: love, desire, delight, hate, aversion and sorrow to the former; and fear, daring, hope, despair and anger to the latter: 'Much of this psychological analysis is quite sophisticated, employing data from Greek, Roman, and early Christian thought and also using the physiological and psychological treatises of Islamic and Jewish scholars. It also forms the basis of the analysis of human conduct in Thomistic ethics.'[78] At the highest level, which pertains to the human soul alone, the general capacity to understand (*intellectus*) comprises simple apprehension, judgment and reason. One version, that is, specific function, of this power involves the abstraction of universal meanings (*intentiones*) from the particular 'objects' of sense experience – this is the agent intellect. The other version or function of the intellect is the overall grasping (*comprehensio*, from *com-* and *prehendo*, 'grasp') of these universal meanings in one unified cognitive act – this is the possible or passive intellect.[79]

Marenbon closes his succinct discussion of Thomas' treatment of the nature and functions of the human mind and soul by knocking back the superficial view that Thomas did little more than express the fullest medieval version of Aristotle's account of *psychē*. He says that, first, this neglects the extent to which the Aristotelian elements in Thomas' discussion belong to a broader and fuller theory that depends on a Christian theologian's concept of the grades of intelligent beings. These grades comprise humans in their earthly life, incorporeal souls (or angels), and the substance of God himself. Second, where Aristotle's arguments for perception, memory and imagination, as well as the autonomous inorganic character of *nous*, have little resonance with modern, 'scientific' concerns about consciousness and its causal support, Thomas' analysis of intellectual operations goes far beyond the 'first master', and poses questions more relevant today: 'How might the ways of human thought – which seem to be intrinsically linked with the functioning of the brain and the senses – be related to the ways in which an incorporeal being would think? St. Thomas' bold solution both underlines the distance and difficulty of the

---

[78] Bourke, in EEP, vol. 7, p. 108; for details, see Gilson, 1957, pp. 201–6.
[79] Kretzmann, 1993, pp. 140–43; Kenny, 1993, pp. 49–57.

relationship, and yet uses it as a means towards understanding the slow, fallible and distinctively human activity of reasoning.'[80]

(3) Dante's soul in the service of love

The great medieval Italian writer Dante (1265–1321) is not usually considered in histories of philosophical speculation, and yet he was more than a Christian poet with an acquaintance and interest in philosophy. Dante's greatest achievements are philosophically inspired journeys of self-discovery. Many of his major works, such as *The Banquet, On Monarchy,* the *Letters*, and select cantos of *The Divine Comedy*, contain overt exposition and analysis of philosophical themes, and are well informed about the teachings of Averroes, Aquinas and Albert the Great. Two hundred years after his death, Marsilio Ficino referred to him as 'by parentage celestial, by habitation Florentine, of a lineage angelic, and in profession a poetic philosopher'. Etienne Gilson and Bruno Nardi, perhaps more than any other contemporary scholars, established the very idea of the intimate connection in his works to then current debates in philosophy, theology and poetic theory. Gilson declared that 'Dante's conception of the nature and role of philosophy was such a personal one precisely because it was required for the solution of the essentially personal problem that he set himself in the *Monarchy*' and elsewhere.[81] Patrick Boyde says at the outset of his outstanding recent study, *Dante: Philomythes and Philosopher*, that, 'Dante is first and foremost a poet of the intellectual life ... most of the distinguishing features of his mature poetry derive from his study of philosophy.'[82] It is one of our tasks to trace Dante's informed philosophical understanding of the human mind and soul.

Dante Alighieri was born in Florence into a family on the fringes of the nobility, and received a rather patchy, nondescript education; he did not attend university and had no formal training in philosophy. His youthful decision to make poetry his vocation was given a personal focus and artistic theme in his rapturous love for the beautiful and unattainable Beatrice. When she died in June 1290, a few days after Dante's twenty-fifth birthday, he felt that his 'first age' had closed; he chose thirty-one inter-linked poems to document all the main stages and events in the maturation of his vision of perfect love, and he called this work *Vita Nuova*. In an effort to overcome his all-consuming grief at Beatrice's death, Dante turned to philosophy, especially Cicero's *On Friendship* and Boethius' *Consolation of Philosophy*. Boethius' dialogue with the allegorical woman Philosophia was an ideal introduction, since long passages of dense argument are regularly interrupted with meditations in verse form. Dante later spoke of his conversion to philosophy, his genuine love of wisdom (*amatore di sapienza*); the goal of philosophy, he said, is 'that perfect

---

[80] Marenbon, 1987, p. 131; Zupko, 1997 underlines Aquinas' relevance as an empirical investigator of the human mind.

[81] Gilson, 1963, p. 224 (first published in French in 1939); Bruno Nardi's seminal work, *Note critiche di filosofia dantesca,* was published in Florence, 1938.

[82] Boyde, 1981, p. 5; on his rapport with classical philosophical texts, see Curtius, 1979, pp. 348–79.

loving which admits no interruption or shortcoming, that is, true happiness won through contemplation of the truth'.

For two or three years he attended the Franciscan and Dominican schools nearby, listening to the philosophers' disputations, and began his long study of Aristotle's works. But he could not equally well serve two mistresses, as Boyde puts it:

> so Dante had to choose between his love for Beatrice in glory and his new love for philosophy. He had to say in effect that he loved Beatrice – *amica quidem Beatrix* – but he loved wisdom more – *sed magis amica sapientia*. In short, philosophy demanded that he should entirely forsake his early love, his early culture, and his early poetry ... The second age brought a second love. It was only in his *third* age ... and only in the *Comedy* itself, that he felt able to heal the breach and to reconcile the second Dante with the first.[83]

In his lifelong study of philosophy Dante never committed himself to any one major figure or school. He was more like Cicero than any other classical exemplar, eclectic in his tastes and distant from any particular approach. Although he was especially devoted to Aristotle in his later thought, he turned more and more to Christian teachings and came to distrust the reach of unaided reason straining to understand through the intellect alone.

Florentine political intrigues embroiled Dante in some serious difficulties for several years, at the end of which he may have traveled to Bologna and Paris for further studies. Between 1304 and 1308, he embarked on two ambitious projects: the *Convivio* (or *Banquet*), prose commentaries on various philosophical topics (only four of fifteen projected books were completed), and *De Vulgari Eloquentia* (or *The Eloquence of the Vulgar Tongue*). These two original and audacious works are generally regarded as ground-breaking attempts to establish the Italian vernacular as a worthy language to rival Latin. With the election of Henry VII as Holy Roman Emperor, Dante had high hopes that a just and wise ruler would bring some peace to the troubled Italian North, hopes soon crushed with Henry's premature death three years later (August 1313). In response to the promise of competent, temporal governance Dante wrote *On Monarchy*, but it was in his 'third age' that his most cherished dreams of a universal harmony of loving order were expressed. *The Divine Comedy* is an astonishing literary achievement that succeeds in extolling several messages on different levels. In what follows our attention will be focused on the explicit, acknowledged philosophical aspects of this (and earlier works). In *Paradise* the Beatrice-figure delivers five major treatises and Statius offers a sophisticated scholastic disputation worthy of any twelfth- or thirteenth-century master of arts:

> There is no escaping the fact that the author of the *Comedy* is a repentant sinner, but an unrepentant intellectual. The *Comedy* is the story of a journey on which he traveled from ignorance and bondage to a state of freedom in the final apprehension of the whole truth, the full and simultaneous perception of all things seen in their unchanging essence in the mind of God. The protagonist is a philosopher *in fieri*. The philosopher who narrated

---

[83] Boyde, 1981, p. 27; on the three ages, see references in Foster & Boyde, 1967, pp. 225–7.

that personal journey to the Truth was a philosopher *in actu*. To revert to the language of the *Convivio*, he was one who 'by diligence and study had won the love of wisdom and received the gift of understanding'.[84]

Dante blended Christian, philosophical and medical ideas in his various discourses on the human soul, its functions and its aspirations. One physical model standard at that time, ultimately derived from Galen's medical works, posits three kinds of spirit as the means by which the soul irradiates its host body, equips its organs and causes them to discharge their functions. In several early works Dante clearly holds to the medical scheme enunciated most fully by Statius in the *Purgatory*: the natural spirit is generated from imperfect blood in the liver, the vital spirit is produced in the heart through the mixture of imperfect blood and air from the lungs, and the animal (that is, soulful) spirit is produced from the vital spirit in the *rete mirabile* at the base of the brain. The third highest spirit flows through the brain, filling the cerebral nerves and then flows down through the spinal cord into the motor nerves that activate and control all the diverse sorts of bodily movement (Purg. 25). This scheme appears as early as the *Vita Nuova*, when the adult Dante describes his reaction to his first sight of the beautiful Beatrice; in his internal dialogue, each spirit is given a voice in his recollection.[85]

The vital spirit, which dwells in the innermost chamber of his heart, began to tremble violently, making his pulse flutter. This spirit calls the amorous thinker's attention to the next higher spirit, who is like a god and rules over him. The animal spirit, whose seat is in 'the high chamber where all the spirits of sensation bring their perceptions', began to feel wonder, knowing that the lover's true joy had appeared. The natural spirit, who resides in the nutritive parts, began to weep, knowing that it would often be obstructed, that is, overridden by the soul's desire for the wondrous Beatrice. It is clear from this inner counsel that the god who comes to rule is love; forever after that initial encounter, love governed Dante's soul. His natural spirit's forecast, that his physical desire to see her again would be impeded, was correct – it was another nine years before he saw her again. After the young woman's death, the poet's spirit would have to wait even longer to see the glorious Beatrice in Paradise, and thus be reunited with his joy again in heaven. The young Dante calls his desire 'the spirit of love', and it was so strong that it 'crushed all the other sensory spirits, and made possible a vivid vision of his beloved even when she was no longer present'[86] – perhaps one of the poet's greatest gifts.

Five or six years later, after his education in Aristotle and the scholastic commentators, Dante's appreciation for philosophical definitions and arguments was much more sophisticated. In the *Banquet* he endorses the Aristotelian scheme[87] of three kinds of soul, finding them equally present in human nature, with vertically arranged powers, each subsuming its next lower power. He abridges one of the main

---

[84] Boyde, 1981, p. 40.
[85] On this medical-spiritual imagery, see Gilson, 1963, pp. 50–72.
[86] Boyde, 1981, pp. 147–9; Foster & Boyde, 1967, pp. 338–40.
[87] E. R. Curtius argues that Dante's thought here is close to Albert Magnus and Alexander of Hales, Curtius, 1979, pp. 221–5

arguments of *De Anima* Book Two, that there are three capacities of the *psychē*: life, sensation and thought: 'It is perfectly obvious that the powers are arranged in such a way that each one acts as the basis for the next. The first can exist independently, but the second must rest on the first. Thus the vegetative power, which is the principle of life, is the basis for sight, hearing, taste, smell, and touch; but it can also exist as a soul in its own right, as we see in all the plants.' Presumably Dante means that a substance with the vital principle can exist as such without 'realizing' either the second or third principles. Moreover, the form (*forma* or *eidos*) of some things, such as plants, comprises life-conferring properties, but without making that thing a soul. He continues this line of thought in comparing the three powers: 'The sensitive power is the basis for the intellectual power, that is to say, reason. In mortal animate beings, the rational power is never found disjoined from the sensitive power; but the power of sensation does exist without reason, as we see in beasts, birds, fish, and indeed all brute animals. And the psyche which includes all these powers, being the most perfect of them all, is the human soul' (Conv. 3.2.11–14).[88]

Although in his later work he will insist on the unified and single 'nature' of the human soul, in the *Banquet* he considers the soul's three 'natures' to be united through Divine Wisdom by means of a miracle. The discrepancy between Dante's two versions perhaps reflects some confusion about whether each form has its own nature (*natura* or *ousia*). In addition to the admirable harmony amongst the three forms of soul, he praises the harmony of soul and body, and the harmony that obtains among the various bodily organs. The soul is the form of its living body, the ground of its existence, the actualizer of its various potencies, the efficient cause of its organic functions, and the self-moving agent that employs these organs to carry out its operations.[89] In addition to (or perhaps in parallel with) the perfection to which the soul can aspire through its most noble part (the mind) via its return to the divine source of its being, the soul-body composite has its own 'idea' of perfection, an outward beauty that radiates in the human face. Dante the poet surpasses Dante the thinker in superbly expressing the soulful beauty a human being can attain in these memorable images (it is conceivable that here his vocabulary was influenced by Biblical Wisdom texts, that is, by Hebrew verses filtered through Greek and then Latin concepts):

> The soul dedicates its greatest care and solicitude to those parts of the body where it carries out its proper task most fully. That is why it lavishes such care on the human face, where the highest potentiality of its matter is actualized, such that no two faces are alike. Within the face there are two areas, the eyes and the mouth, to which the soul devotes its greatest efforts, since it could be said that all three powers of the soul have jurisdiction there. [Conv. 3. 8. 6]

He employs an elaborate simile comparing the human body to a domestic building, a set of images to which the section on medieval mentality returns at the close of this section:

---

[88] On his use of *mente* and *intelletto* in his early poetry, see Foster & Boyde, 1967, pp. 174–5, 223–4.
[89] Boyde, 1993, p. 160.

> To adopt a beautiful simile, these two places might be called the balconies belonging to the mistress of the body's mansion, because it is there that she often makes her appearance, even though she is, so to speak, under a veil. She shows herself so openly in the eyes that any attentive observer can know her current state of feeling. And since there are six human passions ... none of them can affect the soul without its likeness appearing in the window of the eyes, unless it is concealed by a great effort ... She stands revealed in the mouth like a color seen through glass. For what is laughter but the coruscation of the soul's delight, that is, a light whose brightness corresponds to its inner state? [Conv. 3. 8. 9–10]

Patrick Boyde provides a useful précis of Dante's psychical vocabulary in the second and third chapters of the *Banquet* Book Three.[90] Dante refers to the distinctly human power as *mente* ('mind', for Latin *mens* and Greek *nous*); it is only one part of the human soul, but with regard to the other powers, it is 'the most excellent', the most precious, the most perfect, the noblest, ultimate and sovereign. It is through the mind that humans are linked, in the great chain of being, to higher incorporeal beings: 'Mind takes part in the divine nature like the sempiternal intellects [angels]; it is divine, and in this sense it is so ennobled and denuded of matter that the divine light shines into it as it does into an angel.' Dante points out that due to the human mind's interlinkage and participation in the divine intellect, some philosophers have called a human a god-like animal (Conv. 3.2.14–19). The significance that Dante accords to the human soul's light-like character, to its infusion with the body of light, will become more explicit in his treatment of the resurrected good souls in the *Paradise*.[91]

He adduces several powers (or virtues) specific to the human mind, that is, the human *psychē* 'in virtue of' its having a rational part. He makes a fairly standard distinction, also found in Averroes, between the speculative intellect (in the *Banquet* it is called the 'scientific virtue') and the practical intellect,[92] though he draws very different consequences from this than does Averroes. The speculative intellect finds its raw material in the sensible species, the images and visible forms, received from the communal sense, and then directs its attention to some of these species, stored in the 'treasure house' of memory. It then compares and contrasts images derived from various things, or the same thing at different times, and thus grasps the intelligible species, that is, concepts that pertain to the thing's inner nature or essence. In Boyde's summary statement: 'The goal of the speculative intellect is *scientia*, and that consists of a coherent set of acquired concepts and propositions which are "true" (*verum*). In this context, however, "truth" (*veritas*) entails a condition which is not necessarily required in ordinary usage: the concepts and propositions must be all-embracing, because "knowledge bears on universals".' In saying this, Dante, of course, agrees with the epistemic focus of the scholastics' insistence on the close connection between perception via species and conception via invariant form: '"Truth" is the text "written within" the natural world. "Truth"

---

[90] Boyde, 1993, p. 175.

[91] 'Dante sometimes treats light metaphorically as if it were a body. Thus it is that even light itself, in order to be somehow representable, has to double itself as an image.' Shapiro, 1998, p. 165.

[92] See Gilson, 1963, pp. 136–8.

is what the mind "reads" in the act of intellection (*intus legere*) and what it subsequently "gazes on" in the act of speculation (*speculari*).'[93] Boyde, however, is incorrect in thinking that 'intellect' is from *intus-legere*; rather, it is almost certainly derived from *inter-lectus* (past participle of *ligo*), 'gather from among', thus closely allying it with 'collect' and 'recollect'.[94]

The other principal aspect of the human mind is the practical intellect; in the animal domain this corresponds with the estimative power carried out by instinct. In the human domain it is the power to make things and carry out projected courses of action; in both cases the exercise of these powers is based on rational decisions. Dante typifies the practical intellect with four main qualifiers; it is, in his words, either *ragionativo, inventivo, consigliativo* or *giudicativo*. The first term merely indicates its rational force and directedness; the second literally means to discover or uncover; that is, the mind finds out solutions to problems and answers to questions. The third means to weigh up in the balance, to deliberate (from *libera*, 'scales'); the term *consiglio* (from *consilium*) refers to an internal counsel. And the fourth clearly indicates the notion of judgment in favor of the best option, the best way to achieve some goal:

> The practical intellect is 'discursive'. But instead of moving ever further away from the scattered phenomena of the material world towards an ordered set of abstractions and archetypes, it takes these 'universal forms' as its *principia* – its 'points of departure' – and it returns step by step towards the concrete world with the intention of working on particular bodies in a particular place and time, either by 'making' or by 'doing' (*faciendo vel agendo*).[95]

The rational part, Dante avers, consists of the intellect and the will (*voluntas*), the power that grasps and the power that brings the body into freely chosen motion. The will comes into play when deliberation has resulted in a judgment about the best means to achieve a good discerned by the mind. When he refers to the 'operations that are proper to the rational soul', he clearly indicates that it is the manifest performance of speech and other forms of meaningful exchange. Rational operations are those in which 'the divine light shines most clearly, that is, in speech and in the actions which are usually described as manners or conduct. For it must be made clear that, among animate beings, a human alone is able to speak, and a human alone is said to have actions or conduct called rational, because he alone has reason' (Conv. 3.7.8).

Dante agrees with Averroes and Aquinas when he identifies the form proper to human being with the faculty or power of reason; and further he defines the life lived by humans, in the sense of the fullness of its potential, as the exercise of the reasoning power:

> Things should be defined and named in accordance with the highest perfection of their form, as human is defined by his reason and not by his senses or any less perfect power.

---

[93] Boyde, 1993, p. 180.
[94] This derivation is confirmed by the OLD, 1968–72, pp. 935 (col. c) – 936 (col. a).
[95] Boyde, 1993, p. 183.

Hence, when we say that a human 'lives', we ought to understand that he is using reason, which is the life proper to his species and the actualization of his most noble part. And so the human who abandons reason and uses only the sensitive part of his soul does not live as a human but as a beast. As Boethius puts it so well, 'he lives the life of a donkey'. [Conv. 2.7.3]

Dante ties his understanding of this essential definition with his reading of Aristotle in *De Anima*:

Living is the mode of being proper to living things ... It is clear that, for animals, living consists in sensation, whereas for humans living is using reason. Using reason, therefore, is the human mode of being, and so to renounce that use is to renounce being, and therefore to be dead. And is it not renouncing the use of reason if one fails to take thought about the end of our life? And is it not renouncing the use of reason if one does not take thought about the route? [Conv. 4.7.12]

In his middle period work *On Monarchy*, Dante develops a more complex picture from the same premises as those in the *Banquet*.[96] Each individual human endeavors to acquire a certain amount of knowledge through the exercise of his reason, but what he can acquire in this fashion is only a small portion of the total knowledge accessible to all of humankind. Only the human species as a whole can lay claim to this total knowledge, 'but it may aspire to such an achievement only on condition that it exists as a universal community, endowed with a kind of existence of its own, and having this as its special function.' The specific goal of this collective function cannot be realized by any portion less than the entire species, 'for it is a question of organizing things in such a way that at every moment of its existence the human race, thanks to the great number of the individual intellects of which it is made up, is continually realizing the total power of the possible intellect.' But in arguing in this manner Dante knew that he ran counter to Averroes' controversial assertion that the possible intellect is a single entity and that an individual human's knowledge is no more than a share in this permanent intelligible intellect. As Gilson says, 'The possible intellect of Averroes presented Dante with a kind of individual human race whose unity would always be realized in a concrete way, while at every moment of its duration it would actualize the whole of the knowledge accessible to humans.'[97]

If the inbuilt goal of the human species is to know all that it is possible to know, and the essence of human nature is defined in accord with its highest function, then the total possible knowledge would already exist eternally and permanently within humans' intellectual grasp: 'In short, to him what is involved is a multitude, that very multitude of individuals which the universal human community will render capable of attaining its goal by imposing on it the unity which is essential to the independent possible intellect of Averroes, though humanity as conceived by Dante does not yet possess it and will, moreover, enjoy it only if it accepts the unifying hegemony of the Emperor.' If there is no peace in the universal human community, then there can be no chance for humans to develop to the highest degree their

---

[96] See Gilson, 1963, pp. 167–70.
[97] Gilson, 1963, p. 169.

aptitude for discovering the truth or the attainment of their divinely designed end-state.[98]

Human in its kind occupies the middle point between corruptible and incorruptible beings; he is at the horizon of two hemispheres, corruptible in terms of his corporeal nature and incorruptible in terms of his ensouled nature. Dante thus argues that humans alone have two final goals, as well as two natures, each dimension of which corresponds to the perfection of that nature:

> Ineffable providence has therefore set human to attain two goals: the first is happiness in this life, which consists in the exercise of his own powers and is typified by the earthly paradise. The second is the happiness of eternal life, which consists in the enjoyment of the divine countenance, which human cannot attain on his own power but only by the aid of divine illumination, and which is typified by the heavenly paradise. [Mon. 3.15]

Dante's teaching about the twofold ultimate goal (*hominis duplex finis*) of human nature is skillfully married with the idea that the pursuit of wisdom and the acceptance of Christian faith can coexist in harmony: 'These two sorts of happiness are attained by diverse means ... We attain to the first by means of philosophical teaching, being faithful to it by exercising our moral and intellectual virtues. We arrive at the second by means of spiritual teaching, which transcends human reason, insofar as we exercise the theological virtues of faith, hope, and charity'[99] (Mon. 3.16).

Although Dante has gone to some pains to carefully separate and analyze the three types of material spirits and the three powers of the human soul, he emphasizes that human being as such has only *one* soul, not three souls, one aspect for each level of activity. It is 'one soul that lives and feels and reflects inwardly upon its own nature' (Purg. 25.75). The unitary soul is the form of its human body, and the soul's highest part (the mind) gives direction and purpose to that whole; however, the mind is neither composed of nor attached to any bodily organ. Dante thus agrees with his scholastic teachers that, since the intellect abstracts concepts from the species of material things, it cannot itself be material. Nor can the will be material since it is able to make decisions and bring about projected actions that are themselves denuded of matter, that is, they are merely phantasms 'acted upon' by the active intellect. There is no part of the mind (though not, of course, no part of the soul) that can be imprinted, impressed, stamped, sealed, influenced or impeded by images from any earthly or heavenly body (see Purg. 16.67–84; Para. 7.67–72).

In his masterpiece, *The Divine Comedy*, Dante presents a more complex twofold picture of human nature, a picture articulated through several principal figures' voices. It is complex also because it attempts the difficult task of interweaving both an Aristotelian matter-form account of psychical stages, and an essentially Christian account, filtered through his reading of Neo-Platonism, whose core doctrine is the

---

[98] This issue is analyzed in some detail by Prue Shaw, Introduction to Dante, 1995, pp. xxiii–xli.

[99] See Gilson's interpretation of this argument, Gilson, 1963, pp. 191–6.

post-mortem attainment of a glorious new body.[100] The pilgrim's initial entry into the underworld, in the opening canto of the *Inferno*, presents him and the reader with a profound conceptual problem. Patrick Boyde says that it is a ghost story in reverse: 'Instead of the ghost returning to his earthly haunts to terrify the living, it is Dante, a creature of flesh and blood, who penetrates the realms of the afterlife and alarms the souls of the newly dead who populate the shores and lower slopes of Mount Purgatory.' Where the dead souls marvel at the miracle that has brought a living soul amongst them, Dante does not express wonder that these souls have survived as individual beings. He does not marvel *until* he seeks to embrace his old friend Casella, and finds that three times his arms return empty to his own breast. This startling moment of insight, when the living soul confronts the 'double' of the dead soul, is modeled on similar incidents in the *Aeneid* and the *Odyssey*:[101]

> The episode is a little unsettling to the reader[s] ... They suspend disbelief, and they do not ask how the shadow bodies may be visible and yet transparent, or intangible and yet subject to torments by the tangible qualities of heat and cold. Least of all do they ask what a good Aristotelian ought to ask: if the soul is simply the structure by virtue of which a living *compositum* exists, and is 'what it is', how can it take on an independent existence at the moment when that *compositum* ceases to be and its structure is destroyed?

Shapiro points out that, right from the start, the writer associates his guide Virgilio's faintness with his form as a shade (*ombra*); he is a member of the 'court of the silent'. She also argues, quite plausibly, that Dante was familiar enough with Virgil's own philosophical thinking to reproduce the Virgilian (and hence Stoic) notion of the soul as a tenuous, indistinct body-double. Good evidence for this view is found in the ancient commentary on the *Aeneid* by Servius, who complained that poets have routinely confused the ideas of simulacrum and shade. According to Servius, 'the souls of the dead are simply supposed to form simulacra. And later Charon [the ferryman in Hades] refuses to take living bodies across the Styx, stressing that only the bodily species, the simulacrum can go (Aen. 6.391). Here is the text that would most forcefully stimulate a reaction by the Christian poet seeking to reconcile imagery with doctrine.'[102]

In his early work on Dante's philosophical attitude to these issues, Etienne Gilson pointed out that there is no precedent in Christian literature before the *Divine Comedy* that presents any details about the corporeal semblance of the human soul after death – modern readers just assume that such iconic imagery was always there. Shapiro gives full credit to the thirteenth-century Italian poet for this precedent: 'It is ultimately a poetic invention pure and simple, whose success is due to its distant but enduring provenance in human imagination, and in Dante's case, to the astounding variety of significance Dante can attach to a few principal terms.'[103]

---

[100] The following sub-section on Dante's treatment of soul in the *Divine Comedy* draws heavily on two recent studies, Boyde, 1981, pp. 270–95 and Shapiro, 1998, pp. 161–97, from which the following quotes are extracted.

[101] The double or shade was discussed in detail at the end of Chapter 1, sec. 1.

[102] Shapiro, 1998, p. 162.

[103] Shapiro, 1998, p. 163; see Dante, 1970–75: Singleton, 1970, *Inf. Comm.*, pp. 9, 14, 53.

The poet quite obviously felt the need to explain his assumptions about the condition of human souls after their earthly death, but he does not feel that these early infernal encounters exhaust the subject. 'Instead', as Boyde states, 'a delicate trail of reminders and anticipations leads from the encounter with Casella in the second canto to the twenty-fifth canto where Statius makes a detailed and authoritative statement on the subject'[104] – one that a pagan thinker could simply not lay claim to.

In the *Purgatory,* Canto XXV, Statius is given a treatise-length speech that agrees closely in most details with then current scholastic descriptions of the development of the human soul, analyzed into three successive forms which are recapitulated in the maturation of a single living being: 'The active power becomes a soul, like that of a plant, except that it has not yet reached its journey's end, while that of a plant has already come to the shore. It goes on working until it can feel and move like a sea-sponge.' (The sea-sponge was a standard, textbook example of something with a minimal power of sensation and movement.) The third stage is partly incepted with the formation of distinctly human organs and members, but the rational soul can only be informed through the active intervention of God. Statius concurs with Aristotle's claim that the intellect cannot be transmitted by any material species, such as sperm, nor even by an ethereal, highly tenuous *pneuma*. Where Aristotle had said that such an intellect alone must enter from outside, Averroes had claimed that it was an entirely separate substance, one for all humankind.[105] For Averroes, each individual human participates in the cosmic pool of intellect, but it was not an essential element of the human soul, and hence not related to the individuality of each human. However, Dante knew that Averroes' denial of personal immortality was vehemently rejected by Aquinas, and he has Statius obliquely refer to Averroes when he says, 'this is a point that led a wiser man [Averroes] than you into error, so that in his teaching he made the possible intellect distinct from the soul, because he could not see any bodily organ assigned to the intellect' (Purg. 25.63–6).

At this juncture, Statius deftly weaves the Genesis story of human creation into his discourse. God, he says, 'rejoices over such a masterpiece of nature's handiwork, and he breathes into it a breath, a spirit, which is newly created and filled with power. The spirit draws up into its own substance all that it finds active in the foetus, and becomes a single soul that lives, feels, and considers itself within itself' (Purg. 25.70–5). In making this synoptic statement, Dante has adroitly interlinked the Biblical, Pauline and Aristotelian strands of his multiplex account into one definition. In Statius' discourse, Dante attempts to hold together, in careful balance, two otherwise opposite views about the human soul. One, that God alone created each individual human as an individual; and the other, that each human is produced by a natural physical process of generation. Boyde says that 'this nine-line sentence contains perhaps the single most important doctrinal statement in the *Comedy*, and the vehicle is worthy of the content. It holds fast to the principle that the exact word

---

[104] Boyde, 1981, p. 271.
[105] See the background texts provided by Dante, 1970–75: Singleton, 1973, *Purg. Comm.*, pp. 595–616.

is always best ... But the language of Aristotle and his philosophy is enriched with Christian elements.' The poet plays on the deeply buried, but always immanent ambiguity in the notion of spirit (*pneuma*) as breath of life and the Holy Spirit as God's actual breath, giving life.[106] In this way, 'using the simplest prepositions, conjunctions, and verbs, he reproduces Aristotle's characterization of the nutritive, sensitive, and intellectual powers in the human psyche; and yet the phrasing and rhythm of the line, coupled with the insistence that our psyche is formally *one*, recalls the language of Christian marvel and paradox in the presence of the mystery of the Three Persons in One God.'[107]

Statius' main ideas can be reduced to this three-pieced argument, according to Boyde. (1) Major premise: *agens agit sibi simile*; that is, every agent causes an effect by reducing something to its likeness, and therefore every effect must resemble its cause. (2) Minor premise: human alone has two efficient causes, since he is both generated and created. (3) Conclusion: human alone has a dual nature and a double goal. Statius claims that humans have three likenesses to the Creator God, or perhaps, they have a likeness to God in three dimensions. The first likeness is the capacity for self-awareness, that is, the actualization of the human potential for God-given intellect. The second likeness is through their intrinsic freedom; since human actions are as free as the original acts of the Creator; in claiming this, he rejects deterministic explanations of humans as merely animal beings. The third likeness is through the intellect and will whose source and goal is God; the highest perfection, or 'final cause', consists in becoming like God in truth and goodness. In the *Banquet* Dante had said that 'God is the principle of our souls and he creates them in his likeness, as the Bible testifies ... Therefore, the human soul desires above all other things to return to its beginning in him' (Conv. 4.12.14).

The natural place toward which our desire should lead does not lie anywhere on earth, not even in the long-lost Garden of Eden, but rather in heaven with God. In the *Divine Comedy*, 'Dante represents the "concreated and everlasting thirst for the kingdom that is like God" as the sole and sufficient cause of his *ascent* through and beyond the physical heavens to the Empyrean. When man is made whole, and the whole man chooses and loves God, there is no longer any impediment to restrain his natural movement.'[108] This reference to the soul's ascent indicates Dante's intelligent appropriation of one of the main tenets of Plotinus and Porphyry, which Dante would have known through Augustine's *City of God*. The soul at birth clothes itself in successive, cumulative bodies; these cloud-like envelopes descend through the atmosphere, become heavier with thicker layers of vapor, until they are captured by the earth's surface or dragged yet deeper into the abysses. In addition to the idea of the soul's return to its source through spiritual discipline, Dante's use of the concept of *person* accords with Augustine's new name for this special

---

[106] 'Dante preserves the double meaning for "spirito" by his use of the word to mean "breath" as well as soul; in the reunion scene with Beatrice, the compassion for the sinning pilgrim, which the angels convey by means of sighs, causes the ice around his heart to melt into "spirito e acqua" (Purg. 30. 98) in weeping', Shapiro, 1998, p. 173.

[107] Boyde, 1981, p. 279.

[108] Boyde, 1981, p. 287; see Para. 1.121–6, 139–41; 2.19–21.

creation, one that captures the very essence of a being with a double life and a double death.[109]

Dante's doctrine of dual creation and generation gives prominence to the uniqueness of each individual human being. The substantial form of each person differs so greatly that it cannot be explained in terms of material-organic properties: 'Each one of us originates in a distinct "idea" in the Divine Mind. And this is tantamount to saying that each one of us constitutes a distinct *species*, distinguished by our form, rather than by the composition and dimensions of the matter in which the common form of the species is individuated.'[110] In *The Eloquence of the Vulgar Tongue* he says that, 'human actions proceed not from natural instinct, but from reason. And reason is so diversified in individuals in respect of differences, judgment, and choice that it almost seems as if each human rejoices in his own distinct species.' Boyde links this line of thought with Dante's thesis about humans' creation and generation:

> Dante gives great prominence to the fact that man is generated before he is created, and to the fact that the qualities and powers in his generated nature are drawn up into the *spirito novo* to make the single human soul. He reminds us that we have no less than *four* natures lying below the fifth and last, the truly human or angelic, that is, the rational nature, and that the complexion of the elements, the formative power of the father's seed and the influences from the heavens all help to determine our temperament and aptitudes.[111]

Perhaps the most beautiful and stunning image that Dante employs to capture the dual nature of human being is through posing this rhetorical question: 'Don't you realize that you are worms born to form the angelic butterfly that soars without defenses to the seat of judgment?' (Purg. 10.124–6). As the Psalms said, in the sight of God the supplicant is a worm (*vermis*) not a human (Ps. 21:7); Augustine, in his commentary on St. John's Gospel had said that all humans born in the flesh are worms, and from worms God makes angels (in John 1.13). On one rare occasion, Aristotle referred to the *psychē* as a butterfly (HA 551a14) and Christian funerary imagery in the early centuries sometimes depicted the soul released as a butterfly soaring toward heaven.[112] The worm crawls about, it is bound to the ground, it lives in the earth, it is an immature, rudimentary being, and so forth,[113] whereas the butterfly (*papilia*) lives in the air, it can both ascend and descend, it displays the perfection and beauty of its form, it is the most mature realization of its created being. In the great scale of being, humans can exercise both their will and their

---

[109] On Dante's relation to Augustine, see Mazzotta, 1979, pp. 147–91; Shapiro, 1998, pp. 169–70, 173.

[110] Boyde, 1981, p. 289.

[111] Boyde, 1981, p. 290.

[112] Leclercq, 1924, cols. 1490–1500.

[113] The current zoological term for the initial stage is larva, and *larva* in Classical Latin, for example, Plautus' comedies, meant 'ghost', and by tropic extension it came to mean 'mask'; thus it became synonymous with the Latin usage of *persona*; in addition, *larvatus* also means 'masked', as in the theatre, and in the Sicilian dialect *masca* means both 'mask' and 'ghost'; see also Shapiro, 1998, p. 171.

intellect in attempting to achieve their souls' greatest perfection, but our life here on earth is preparation for what can only be truly achieved in a better world yet to come. In Boyde's dynamic words:

> Our role is to join the two halves of the Scale of Being in our persons ... Our task here on earth is to live out a life-span which will resemble that of all generated beings, except in the crucial respect that it will be guided by the dictates of reason. We are to live *secundum rationem*. We are to exist as conscious 'agents', and not as unconscious 'patients' of external forces or instincts. We are to live neither as caterpillars, nor as butterflies, but as 'winged caterpillars'.[114]

Dante expresses through his evocative and stunning imagery some of the central features of the late medieval attitude that individuals had toward their own human nature. Detailed examination of peripheral social, religious and material achievements of human activities, including sculpted and painted portraits, the syllabus of secular studies, personal records, the care of one's body, and so forth, provide indirect evidence about the centre in which mediaeval mentality must reside.[115] What one can reconstruct from this evidence shows that individuals' attitudes toward their own bodies and the bodies of others were governed by the dualist conception upon which every representation of the world was built. No one doubted that each individual was composed of both body and soul, or flesh and spirit. The body was perishable and ephemeral, subject to disease and decay and would return into the dust. Yet, it is called upon to reform its ways in this life with a view towards eventual resurrection, and thus must be considered the immortal component. The person is weighed down by the burden of the 'flesh', by the heavy, inferior properties of carnal pleasures; but at the same time, the person aspires to heavenly perfection. In accord with this twofold picture, the body was deemed to be dangerous, susceptible to temptation; from the body's parts, especially those below the waist, emanated animal impulses. Since it was the person's body which was susceptible to disease and infection, it was toward the body that punishments were applied to wipe away sin and blame. The soul showed through its envelope of flesh, the body being merely its dwelling place, or rather, in an architectonic image, its court or enclosure. The human body was the outer zone of a protected core, restricted in a manner similar to the domestic space around the person.[116]

One of the clearest and most illuminating accounts of the human body as the soul's dwelling place comes from a medical treatise by Henri de Mondeville, written in Paris in the early fourteenth century.[117] Mondeville's terms and analogies provide the key to the symbolic system of which the body was a part, a system understood not only by learned scholars, but also by the ordinary person; in fact, the author claims to have included the layman's thoughts and language into his treatise. It is immediately apparent that the human body was seen as some kind of

---

[114] Boyde, 1981, p. 293.
[115] On characteristics of this general mentality, see Morris, 1973, pp. 150–73.
[116] Duby, 1988, pp. 520–52.
[117] This synopsis relies on the archival research of Marie-Christine Pouchelle, in Duby, 1988, pp. 522–4.

residence – its interior is called 'domestic' and its exterior 'sylvan', terms which resonate with allusions from romantic literature, the court and the forest. The body's interior is like a court, for the whole body is like a large and complex building which consists of a hierarchy of spaces or rooms. There is a noble portion, a service portion, and between them a wall (the diaphragm), similar to the wall which separated the workers from other tenants. Below this wall lie the body's 'lower' parts which must be subjugated and dominated by the 'higher' parts. The most dangerous rebellions smolder in the lower or crude parts, the place where everything superfluous and noxious is eliminated. As in a noble residence, the lower section performs a nutritive function, furnishing food to the organs located in the noble space above, the delicate organs associated with the higher functions of morality and wisdom. In each of the two sections, there is an 'oven': the lower oven cooks the nutritive humors and, like a great kitchen fire, it is designed for slow burning; whereas the upper oven contains a blazing fire which lights the heart with joy. Here, as in a castle's or monastery's chapel, the humors are distilled in the upper reaches of the flame where tongues of fire lick the air and matter is made into spirit.[118]

The bodily house is surrounded by an enclosure as secure as the wall around any private dwelling. The body's envelope is the ultimate enclosure, the most secret and intimate place of all, and violating it is prohibited by the strictest taboos. The human body is a fortress or hermitage, but one constantly under threat, encircled with dangerous and wicked temptations. Hence it is important that the body is kept under surveillance, especially the apertures through which devilish forces might infiltrate the boundary walls. Moral dictates urged that a guard monitor the posterns and windows of the eyes, the mouth, the ears and the nostrils, portals through which worldly delights might enter. But, of course, the soul showed through this fleshly envelope, the eyes and mouth are the windows or balconies of the soul, in Dante's beautiful image cited above. This complex of metaphors and analogies encapsulates an important cognitive and affective transformation in the understanding that humans had of their own 'natures', that each person's *human* nature was similar to but different than Nature in general. One especially important shape this difference took was the production or generation of the very idea of an inner private sphere.

It is at about this time that one reads about private, inner rooms in the better houses; these studies were the equivalent of monastic retreats and permitted solitary meditation. According to the *Vita Nuova*, Dante closeted himself in his private room so that he could weep over his lost love without being seen by others. Petrarch became so absorbed in reading Augustine's account of the inner torment leading to his conversion that he cried aloud, struck his forehead and wrung his hands. In such a personal retreat, an individual could eliminate every distraction in order to be fully prepared to receive Christ within. The great German mystic Meister Eckhart said that, 'so high above the world and so mighty, this little castle is impregnable to all but the gaze of the Almighty. And because he is one and

---

[118] This is the same domestic imagery used by Spenser in the *Faerie Queene*, Book II, Canto ix; see below, pp. 262–4.

simple, he enters in his oneness what is called the fortress of the soul.' The ideal retreat, of course, was not an actual room in a building, but the deeply inward, private sphere of one's own soul. But the leisure for contemplation and meditation was not available to everyone, only those with both the education and inclination for such an intense endeavor. Many writers in this period testify to this turning inward: 'they looked to the future with sincere and fervent anxiety. Indications of this can be seen in the revival of ascetic orders, the success of devotional confraternities, in some of the more spectacular aspects of the Mendicants' preaching, and above all in innumerable manifestations of personal piety.'[119] The epoch-making setting in which these private retreats and interior studies find their home is the Renaissance of the fourteenth and fifteenth centuries.

---

[119] Braunstein, in Duby, 1988, pp. 616–24; quote from Eckhart, p. 618.

Chapter 5

Renaissance Platonism, Hermeticism and Other Heterodoxies

(1) The centrality and dignity of human being

The Renaissance is the name given to the great European epoch of the rebirth of classical learning, but it is an epoch whose birth and death have been assigned to different times and figures, according to different scholarly interpretations. The central characteristics of this rebirth have not been in as much dispute as the names of those who best represented these characteristic features. There is a nuclear cluster of factors, like the set of symptoms for a specific condition, perhaps only some of which are exhibited by any major figure, but whose abiding presence can be traced from the late 1300s to the late 1500s. Charles Trinkhaus, in the Foreword to his massive study of the idea of image and likeness in Italian humanist writings states this with admirable simplicity:

> The central conclusion of this book is that the Italian Renaissance ... was accompanied by a powerful assertion of a philosophy of will by leading representatives of Italian humanism and among philosophical circles influenced by them. Humanist moralism, rather than stressing rationalistic restraint and inhibition of human action, emphasized the dominance of irrational or arational elements in man's psychic make-up. In so doing this movement was consistent with its rhetorical nature and with its conception of its educational role as one of psychagogy [soul-education]. Moreover, some of its leading proponents found inspiration in the pre-scholastic Christian theological tradition, drawing the full eudemonist and voluntarist implications from the theology of St. Augustine for the first time.[1]

In turning to the texts of classical antiquity the humanists discerned an abiding concern with the essential nature of human being. Though their initial interest had been sparked by Greek and Latin writers' excellence in rhetoric and style, most of the original texts dealt with moral edification. To a greater or lesser degree the writers in this period found scholastic moral theory and accounts of the soul to be irrelevant to the topical problem of how an average Christian should lead a good life. In many writings of the 1300s one finds the persistent plea for a renewal of the religious doctrine of grace, according to which divine force alone is capable of remaking the naturally selfish character of humankind towards higher ethical and spiritual goals. One finds also the basic idea that humans' capacity and drive to command and shape their world was regarded as an emulation of God's divine

---

[1] Trinkhaus, 1970, vol. I, pp. xx–xxi.

nature. The humanists reacted against the prevalent Aristotelian and Scholastic doctrines about human conditions and motivations, and began to accord more respect to the realistic, even pessimistic views of human nature in the recently rediscovered texts of the Stoics and Epicureans, especially in doxographical material preserved in Augustine's voluminous writings.

With this more realistic attitude about what one could reasonably expect of actual human behavior, and not just what one could hope for from an ideal human in an ideal world, the humanists brought out a challenging paradox. As Trinkhaus says, an individual human's life was seen as the triumph of his energy, irrational desires and selfish achievements, but now understood as the fulfillment of a high status in the hierarchy of beings granted to him by divine creation. This new picture of human nature took for granted humans' capacity for both good and evil works on a grand scale. In its mature expression in the works of Ficino and Pico, 'it saw mankind not as meekly awaiting the ministrations of a quasi-angelic clergy, not as lying in a torpor of decay like rotting vegetables waiting for the few sound fruits to be plucked from the refuse, but as alive, actively assertive, cunningly designing, storming the gates of heaven.'[2] This heroic vision of humans' essence and action was more inclined to admire and elevate the exemplum of the great person, whether his words and deeds brought him closer to, or drove him further from, an emulation of the image and likeness of God.

There were several dimensions to the Renaissance writers' interest in human nature and action; the rebirth of classical studies on the physical, natural and moral elements of human being drew on many ancient sources. The long-standing texts of Aristotle on these subjects, especially the *de Anima*, were translated into the best possible Latin editions and formed the principal reading of the university syllabus.[3] But parallel with these new Latin texts was an increasing interest in the original Greek language; the Aldine edition of Aristotle's *Opera Omnia* (1495–98) established an unprecedented standard for exact and careful reproduction of his works. For the first time on an institutional scale, scholars of Aristotelian topics had to be concerned with more than philosophical argumentation, they also had to take account of philological and historical issues. In connection with these monumental efforts to recover the exact text of the 'First Master', scholars began to carefully separate, analyze and publish the many long-attested commentaries on Aristotle's works. These included the commentaries on the *de Anima* by ancient authors, such as Themistius, Simplicius and Alexander, as well as medieval Islamic-Arabic authors such as Averroes.[4]

But the most far-reaching and profound influence on the novel speculations of the Renaissance thinkers was the rediscovery, translation and dissemination of Platonic and Neo-Platonic works.[5] Where the major works of Aristotle had reached the Christian West and been assimilated by the great scholars of the late twelfth and thirteenth centuries, Plato's dialogues had been mostly unknown, filtered and

---

[2] Trinkhaus, 1970, vol. I, p. xxii.
[3] Copenhaver, in CHRP, 1988, pp. 77–92.
[4] For details, see Grafton, in CHRP, 1988, pp. 767–91.
[5] Popkin, in CHRP, 1988, pp. 673–6.

excerpted through other ancient writers. It was largely through the extraordinary efforts of one person, Marsilio Ficino, under the patronage of the wealthy and powerful de Medicis, that the complete Greek texts of Plato's works were recovered and translated into Latin. Following his Latin edition of Plato's *Opera Omnia* in the 1490s, Ficino turned his attention to the Neo-Platonists and in the next decade produced editions of Plotinus' *Enneads*, Iamblichus' *De Mysteriis*, Synesius' *De Insomniis* and Proclus' *Theologia Platonica*.[6] One of the unexpected consequences of the now readily available texts of the *Timaeus*, the *Enneads*, and Proclus and Iamblichus' theurgical texts was an explosion of interest in the more ancient and esoteric doctrines of magic and divination. The greatest impetus behind this 'secret' movement in heterodox (and often heretical) theoretical and practical magic was the discovery and translation, by the indefatigable Ficino, of the 'lost works' of the Hermetic Corpus. In addition to the astonishing rediscovery of the vast tradition of Platonic and Neo-Platonic philosophy, one should not ignore the equally important, though less immediately influential, publication of the works of other ancient schools, such as the Stoic Epictetus' *Enchiridion*, and the Skeptic epitome by Sextus Empiricus, *Outlines of Pyrrhonism*.[7]

Eckard Kessler also draws our attention to the noticeable change in fortunes of the great medieval summations, such as those by Thomas Aquinas, Albert the Great, Duns Scotus and William of Ockham, after the 1520s.[8] Although these theologians continued to enjoy outstanding prestige in universities in the 1400s, their accounts of the nature and function of the human soul became less and less popular in contrast with the humanist and vernacular writings. Kessler claims that the reasons for this rupture are quite clear: the 'barbarous Latin prose' of the earlier commentators 'grated on the ears' of readers in the 1500s, readers who were more accustomed to the superb Latin style of Ficino, Pomponazzi, and others. They were also sophisticated enough to know that these earlier writers had been ignorant of the original Greek material, and that factor usually rendered their analyses obsolete:

> It is the abrupt confluence of classical and medieval currents that lends Renaissance psychology its drama and uniqueness. From 1490 on, writers on the soul struggled to accommodate the new materials of the classical revival and the new religious imperatives of the Protestant and Catholic reformations. The period was a complicated and confused one, and the diversity of the philosophical materials, collected from different schools and traditions, makes it burdensome to exhume the position of a given author.

Kessler also observes some of the consequences of this endemic confusion and diversity: 'This may have been the reason why psychological discussion declined in manuals and textbooks ... It is certainly the reason why philosophers after Descartes attempted to circumvent the whole problem and why modern attempts to reconstruct Renaissance debates remain so tentative, fragmentary and incomplete.'[9]

---

[6] Though Proclus' work was not printed until 1618, Ficino provided excerpts in his commentaries on the *Phaedrus* in 1496.
[7] Popkin, in CHRP, 1988, pp. 678–84.
[8] Kessler, in CHRP, 1988, pp. 459–61.
[9] Kessler, in CHRP, 1988, p. 463.

Kristeller was one of the first scholars to call attention to the continuity between the Middle Ages and Renaissance, that is, to the similarities in some of the central issues which underlay the more remarked upon ruptures and points of divergence. But Renaissance thinkers did make some important changes, both in terms of original elements introduced in this period and in terms of the latent elements they transformed. The changes Kristeller feels deserve attention are:

> the strengthening of classical influences which had been less effective during the Middle Ages; new approaches to familiar sources, for example, to the works of St. Augustine; a new emphasis given to certain elements of the medieval tradition that had been present but less prominent during the Middle Ages; and finally, a recombination and rearrangement of the very same older elements as they appear in a new and different looking whole.[10]

In this regard the Humanists formulated an entirely new educational and cultural ideal that directly or indirectly furthered their prestige and influence. The ideal they sought fell more properly under the aegis of literary culture, rather than philosophy or theology, the most prevalent versions of which they identified as scholasticism. The Humanists were engaged to one degree or another in transforming the entire system of secondary education and imposing their scholarly and stylistic standards upon the other academic disciplines. In Kristeller's words, 'The main contribution of Renaissance humanism seems to lie in the tremendous expansion of secular culture and learning which it brought about in the areas of literature, historiography, and moral thought. This development was not entirely new and to some extent may be traced back to the later Middle Ages; but it did reach its climax during the Renaissance.'[11]

Petrarch (1304–74) is generally considered to mark the first steps in the beginning of Renaissance attitudes towards classical studies, humanist rhetoric, and disapproval of scholastic philosophy. His father was exiled from his native city of Florence a few months after Dante's expulsion in 1302. From his father the young Petrarch was to learn the fluent mastery of rhetoric and style that later elevated him to the highest rank, and from his reading of Cicero and Virgil he acquired his lifelong passion for Latin prose and poetry. He spent the first half of his life near Avignon, the French seat of the alternate papacy, and thus had access to powerful patrons and an exceptional collection of books. In the 1330s he succeeded in assembling a complete text of Livy's *History of Rome* by collating and amending various manuscripts; in so doing he set down some of the earliest rules for textual analysis. About the same time he also discovered an important collection of Cicero's Letters, *Pro Archia*, and manuscripts of Propertius and Pomponius Mela. He carefully constructed for himself an ideal of the classical poet and then worked assiduously to attain this ideal. He was crowned with laurels by King Robert of Sicily for his outstanding poetic acheivements, which include most famously the *Canzoniere*, celebrating his youthful love for the fictitious Laura, the *Bucolicum carmen*, modeled on Virgil's *Eclogues*, and an epic about Scipio Africanus.

---

[10] Kristeller, 1972, p. 115; see also Copenhaver, in CHRP, 1988, pp. 92–6.
[11] Kristeller, 1972, p. 127; Kristeller, in CHRP, 1988, pp. 133–7.

In addition to his many other occasional pieces, Petrarch's distinctive themes appear in *Rerum familiarium libri*, letters he collected and rewrote until the late 1350s and revised until 1366, and *De remediis utriusque fortune*. In 1352 he moved to Milan, living under Visconti patronage for eight years, and then Venice until 1368, and in Padua until his death in 1374. Near the end of his life, Petrarch had achieved one other ambition, an ambition that had profound overtones in the centuries that followed: he initiated the first-hand study of Greek texts and brought into Northern Italy the first Greek teachers. Nicholas Mann emphasizes the significant step forward in the scholarly understanding of our classical heritage when the Byzantine diplomat Manuel Chrysoloras instituted in Florence a regular series of lectures on the Greek language: 'It is thus 1397 which has to be seen as a key date in the history of humanism and even of European culture. Chrysoloras numbered among his pupils some of the most outstanding scholars of the new generation ... With them, and the advent of the fifteenth century, Greek regained its status as part of the *studia humanitatis*, and humanism may be said to have entered a new phase.'[12]

Petrarch's works illustrate, to a greater or lesser degree, some of the main themes of Italian humanism: his works include many Latin poems, a few speeches, historical studies, invectives, dialogues and private letters. The invective documented 'affirmative praise of the humanities against the sciences'; as such they 'represent an interesting episode in that continuing battle of the arts and of various "cultures" that is still with us'.[13] The treatises *On Religious Leisure* and *On the Solitary Life* offer defenses of the contemplative approach, the latter work also illustrates the secularization of this scholarly ideal. The *Secret Dialogue* recounts a discussion between Franciscus (Petrarch) and Augustinus (St. Augustine), one of Petrarch's favorite authors, and offers a highly personal and moving account of the author's moral conflicts and his reflections on the value of fame and honor. Petrarch's self-conscious fabulation of his own life is revealed in his *Letters on Familiar Things*, as Nicholas Mann has recently argued. It was perhaps his discovery of Cicero's *Letters to Atticus* that inspired the idea of editing and reshaping his own letters. It seems to be axiomatic in Petrarch's use of such literary models that imitation is almost always accompanied by an awareness and assertion of his own individuality: 'One might indeed say that as Petrarch spends much of his life writing letters, so he spends much of his letters writing his life.'[14] Mann also argues persuasively, but more contentiously, that Petrarch may even have invented the incident that he (and his friend Boccacio) made famous, the royal crowning with laurels, and the name and character of his great youthful beloved, Laura.[15] In one way or another, these works exemplify the essential characteristics of the early humanist sentiments that Kristeller succinctly lays out prior to his treatment of Petrarch's position. The humanists' literary production, he said, 'was characterized throughout by a desire to imitate ancient authors and to emulate them in the elegance of their style, vocabulary and literary composition'. But they also added something largely new:

---

12 Mann, in Kraye, 1996, pp. 7–17, this quote p. 17.
13 Kristeller, in CHRP, 1988, p. 128–9.
14 Mann, 2000, pp. 18, 23, 24.
15 Mann, 2000, pp. 28–32, 33–42.

'the tendency to take seriously their own personal feelings and experiences, opinions and preferences. An air of subjectivity pervades all humanist literature. It accounts for the often uninhibited gossip, flattery and polemics present in much humanist literature, and it also helps to explain the Renaissance preference for such literary genres as the invective, the dialogue, the speech, the letter and the essay.'[16]

According to Trinkhaus, Petrarch lacked the natural philosopher's interest in the workings of the cosmos except insofar as these workings affected human beings. The physical world in its operations was the manifestation of the cycles of an impersonal fortune. The world in its manifold aspects was entirely God's creation, but in most respects this divinely inspired, fortune-governed domain was remote and irrelevant. The blows and gifts that fortune meted out to each and every individual were emotional, social and political ones: 'To Petrarch the irrelevance of both physics and metaphysics was almost absolute; he couldn't have cared less.' Petrarch repeatedly disparages scholastic speculation as vain and empty posturing, fatuous efforts to comprehend in an elaborate jargon those things that will forever remain mysterious. The focus of many of his letters and polemics was the moral and physical well-being of humankind, as Trinkhaus says:

> the only things that concerned him were man's metabolism and mortality. Men were born, matured, grew old and died. Or they died unexpectedly before their life cycle was completed. And what mattered here was not the physiological processes but the psychological and spiritual attitudes that a man should have towards his physical being, his body. His physical needs and his physical appetites might distract and distort his psychic existence and cause conflicts and anguish spiritually; a wrong attitude towards one's body might jeopardize the eternal destiny of one's soul, might involve it in worse than spiritual death along with the physical death of the body.

But against all this Petrarch reiterates the essential dignity of the ordinary human being.[17]

Petrarch rarely addresses topics of distinctly philosophical concern, and when he does touch upon them, he certainly does not treat them in a philosophical manner. But, of course, that accords with his general attitude toward philosophical disquisition: that it is remote from the everyday features of human life on this earth. However, on several occasions in the *Remedies* the voice of reason takes up claims made by joy or sorrow regarding these very issues. Conrad Rawski summarizes the main points in the *Remedies*:

> [They] address the life of man on this earth. Of all living creatures, man alone is endowed with the powers of reason – memory, intellect, and foresight – hence [he is] capable of thinking in terms of the past, the present, and the future. This unique gift allows man to consider, to weigh, and to judge before he wills and acts; yet he remains subject to his natural emotions and impulses which, more often than not, deceive the

---

[16] Kristeller, in CHRP, 1988, p. 126; on Petrarch's invective against medical doctors, see Streuver, 1993, who unfortunately insists on interpreting this treatise in terms of C. S. Pierce's semiotic theory.

[17] Trinkhaus discusses Petrarch's views on human dignity in the *Remedies*, Trinkhaus, 1970, pp. 179–99.

mind and interfere with its findings. Man has to negotiate the inner conflicts between reason and the senses as he tries to cope with the *conflicts of this world*, the exigencies of life. [Rem. I. xxiii, original emphasis]

Rawski's notes to this passage cite Augustine's discussion of his own bondage to the flesh (Conf. 8.5.10–12) as the key medieval text on this topic, one that Petrarch knew well and admired (Rem. II. xlviii):

This action is represented as man's everlasting war with Fortune, the ancient goddess Fortune, fickle and inexorable, who smiles and frowns on all men, granting prosperity today, inflicting abject adversity tomorrow – the hidden cause behind the ups and downs of man. The battle involves each man's reactions to the 'two Fortunes', fair and foul, as they beset him. Victory or defeat is implicit in his state of mind at the end of each encounter, which in turn decides how he will fare during the next one. Fortune herself is beyond these earthly circumstances. Whether she reigns supreme as willed by God, or is invoked as a popular figure responsible for the inexplicable, she remains forever man's existential dilemma. [Rem. I. xxiii]

Petrarch repeatedly refers to the course of a person's life as a road or path and the traversal of this path as a journey.[18] In one of his most famous letters, recounting his ascent of Mount Ventoux with his brother, Petrarch vividly describes one path as steep and narrow, difficult at first and then rewarding further on, and another path as gentle and broad, easy at first and then arduous further on (Fam. iv.4). The Wheel of Fortune, with its personified cardinal points, appears in many manuscripts from this period.[19] The allegorical battle

within every individual takes place in the concrete, ordinary world familiar to contemporary readers. Against a background of universal instability and cosmic strife, Reasons contends with the Four Passions, offspring of Fortune's emissaries, Prosperity and Adversity. These two sisters gave birth to two sets of twins: Prosperity's passional offspring are Joy (*Gaudium*) and Hope or Desire (*Spes sive Cupiditas*); and Adversity's offspring are Sorrow (*Dolor*) and Fear (*Metus*). Where Joy and Sorrow are concerned with the past and the present, Hope or Desire and Fear are concerned with the future; both sets of passions afflict the mind as diseases of the body. [Rem. I. xxiii]

In Petrarch's somewhat awkward rendition of this contest (where Reason has all the good lines), the ordinary, unreflective human has an innate tendency to give vent to these four passions, and thus become dominated by them. Reason can contend against these tendencies or natural impulses by recourse to moral virtue, the intellectual power of contemplation, and the desire to act according to God's will. Reason urges the exercise of moderation in the face of prosperity and patience in the face of adversity:

Within this sparse allegorical framework, Reason argues the propositions posed by the four Passions ... by juxtaposing contraries to each statement that is made ... As the

---

[18] The same imagery that Descartes uses again and again; see MacDonald, 2000, pp. 66–73.
[19] For some good examples and analyses, see Rem. vol. II, pp. 24–37.

double face of Fortune is explored, paradoxical situations emerge, since Reason, countering with opposites, is often reduced to binary choices, as it were, and consequently forced to adopt and to advocate in one argument what was condemned in another. This ambiguity points to a paramount objective akin to Abelard's ... doubt [which] naturally leads to inquiry, and through inquiry we obtain the truth. To follow the argument, to weigh the alternatives presented, and to arrive at an enlightened choice ... with noble courage and a mind undaunted by theatrical make-believe – this is the desired result of Petrarch's therapy, attempting to provide awareness of the *vera bona* – the true goods – and thus a ground for wiser action, for living this life – the *vita activa* of the troubled Trecento – more peacefully, more happily. [Rem. I. xxiv]

In *Remedies*, Book Two, Section 93, Reason responds to Sorrow's dejection when it dwells on the misery of the human condition in these words:

You have a body, admittedly mortal and frail, but commanding in appearance, beautiful and erect, able to view the sky. You have an immortal soul, a road to heaven, and inestimable goods bought at a paltry price ... they are so great that I myself could not comprehend them without the teachings of the faith: the hope of resurrection of the body after burial, whole and shining, without guilt, cleansed to resume in great glory the erstwhile place, which surpasses all human dignity on earth and also that of the angels. ... Does not this alone seem to ennoble somewhat the human condition and to relieve a little of its misery? [Rem. II. 93; vol. 3, p. 225]

Trinkhaus synopsizes Petrarch's enumeration of God's divine gifts to humankind, endowments that future humanists would reiterate as the essential qualities of human dignity. They are 'a soul created in the image of God with marvelous inborn qualities of mind, memory, eloquence, inventive capacity, and artistic capacity; the utilities and beauties of the external world; the erectness and beauty of the body; the immortality of the soul; the heavenly reward promised it; the resurrection of the body; the reflected glory of the Incarnation; the exaltation of man through the Incarnation and consequent salvation above the angels'.[20]

In his lengthy invective *On His Own and Others Ignorance*,[21] Petrarch argued vigorously against his critics, who had said that he was 'a good man but a poor scholar'. He argued that their professed learning depended heavily on Latin translations of Averroes' commentary on Aristotle, that they had not made an impartial inquiry into the truth of their philosophical claims. True ignorance, Petrarch said, was knowing what you did not know and attempting to remedy the deficit, whereas their ignorance was thinking they knew more than they did and not attempting to learn more than their original assumptions had led them to believe.

Between the time of Petrarch's death and Ficino's foundation of the Florentine Academy, one outstanding thinker was to make ignorance his theme, but for Nicholas Cusanus learned ignorance was extolled as a cognitive condition worthy of our ambition. Copenhaver quite rightly says that Cusanus' place in Renaissance and early modern philosophy 'strains the usual categories', but then admits that he 'fits the broad context of European intellectual history better than the immediate situation

---

[20] Trinkhaus, 1970, vol. I, p. 191.
[21] Petrarch in CKR, 1968, pp. 47–133.

of his own time, where it has been easier to locate analogies with his ideas than to identify precise influences'.[22] Ernst Cassirer once said that Cusanus' thought 'reflects the entire manifold of the age', but D. J. Hawkins accepts Cusanus' historical importance with some reservations. His philosophy, Hawkins says, 'is not only astonishing in itself, but it is astonishing that such a system should have been put forward not by some obscure eccentric but by one of the leading European figures of the age.'[23] Charles Lohr says that his metaphysics is 'an achievement of great originality', and that his synthesis represents 'a high-water mark in the evolution of the new understanding of reality' in Western Europe since the twelfth century.[24] Perhaps Andrew Weeks' nice image is the best place to start: his work 'seems to project the inwardness of the medieval monk's cell outward by envisaging the boundlessness of divine being and the universe'. Cusanus turned away from the mystical themes of the inner human's union with the divine, the birth of the Son of God in the soul, and instead articulated a new form of speculation involving number and measure.[25]

Nicholas of Cusa (1401–64) studied at the universities of Heidelberg, Padua and Cologne, an excellent preparation for his rapid rise in the church hierarchy, and received his doctorate in canon law. He came to prominence at the Great Council of Basle in 1432, and wrote an important tract defending the conciliar position, a compromise among the competing factions. In 1437 he was sent to Byzantium with an ecclesial delegation whose mission was to invite the Greek Orthodox to the Council of Ferrara and Florence; in the next year he was sent on a papal mission to Germany. One of his most important works, *On Learned Ignorance*, was printed in 1440, one of more than forty works that this busy church administrator found time to compose. He was elevated to the rank of Bishop and then Cardinal in time for the Jubilee Year 1450, working tirelessly for the cause of church reform. After the fall of Constantinople in 1453 he published *On the Peace of Faith*, an appeal for unity amongst the many far-flung Christian churches. His defection from the conciliarist camp to more partisan support for the papacy angered some of his former colleagues, and his immense efforts to achieve ecumenical reform were ultimately frustrated. Cassirer summed up the relation between Cusanus' thought and life in these words: 'The opposing forces that Cusanus tried to reconcile intellectually diverge in his life. What he had tried intellectually to bring together into a systematic unity and harmony fell apart in the immediate reality in which he stood.'[26] Cusanus died one year after Pico's birth, one year after Ficino's commission to translate Plato's complete dialogues, thus living long enough to witness the secular revelation of the Greek texts whose mystical teachings he had presaged.

Cusanus was a peculiar figure even in his own time: at once a late medieval apologist for the established church hierarchy and the dismantler of those very structures of order and authority he had worked so hard to uphold. Cassirer argues forcefully that Cusanus was 'the first modern thinker because his first step consists

---

[22] Copenhaver & Schmitt, 1992, pp. 177–8.
[23] Hawkins, quoted in Levao, 1985, pp. 39–40.
[24] Lohr, in CHRP, 1988, p. 556.
[25] Weeks, 1993, p. 99.
[26] Cassirer, 1963, p. 60.

in asking not about God, but about the possibility of knowing God.'[27] At the most basic level Levao sees this two-faced character in Cusanus' attitude toward the various philosophical and theological traditions in his own background: 'At times Cusanus takes classical and medieval traditions to be a series of symbolic approximations to the truth, even playing the *bricoleur* who builds a world out of the materials at hand. Yet the mental operations that are meant to figure forth images of union also impress him with their astounding diversity and fecundity.'[28] Cusanus said, 'I think there is not, nor ever was, any perfect human that did not frame some conception of the mind [for] the mind is the bond and measure of all things.' But Cusanus' own perfectly human conception of the mind took many shapes, employed many frames, such that it is hard to take the measure of *his* measure of things. 'The mind's store seems boundless', Levao says, 'its metaphors and enigmas ostensibly point to a final rest in the highest wisdom, but the very process of their invention significantly alters the map upon which the pilgrimage is imagined to take place.'

One of the themes of *On Learned Ignorance* is the nature of the human soul and its intrinsic dignity. Cusanus brings into play an unusual variety of thinkers whose combined theological visions he thought perfectly expressed the imperfect and approximate picture humans had of their own and God's nature. *On Learned Ignorance* draws on Albert Magnus, Thomas Aquinas and Raymond Lull, as well as the fullest scholastic and humanist interpretations of Aristotle available at that time. But in addition he also draws on the Platonic inspired Pseudo-Dionysius, Augustine, Proclus, Calcidius, Eriugena and St. Anselm, and the mystical works of Meister Eckhart, Hildegard of Bingen, Thierry of Chartres and Hugh of St. Victor.[29] Cusanus said that the inspiration for this work came while on a voyage to Byzantium and much of its imagery relies on the notion of philosophical inquiry as a soulful journey. Here he brilliantly reformulates the Pseudo-Dionysian negative theology devoted to humans' intellectual distance from God, a distance which can be bridged only through the ineffable mystery of Christ's incarnation. Humans, he said, by natural impulse express their need to know by comparing the more known with the less known. But even the more precise, abstract operations like counting and measuring end in some thing that cannot be furthered compared. Just as a polygon whose sides can be multiplied toward a circle as its limit, so also each epistemic claim only approximates one step closer to the truth without ever reaching the truth itself. Finite human attempts to grasp divine and cosmic infinities remain permanently out of alignment with humans' limited concepts. Like Petrarch before him, Cusanus endorsed the notion of Socratic ignorance, the deep and abiding sense of knowing just how little one knew or could ever know.

Cusanus prayed to be released from the chatter of scholastic disputation and rescued by a more profound silence: 'mystical theology leads to respite and silence where we are granted a vision of an invisible god, while the knowledge that trains us for conflict [and] hope for victory in words ... is far from that which hurries us

---

[27] Cassirer, 1963, p. 10.
[28] Levao, 1985, p. 3.
[29] For these influences, see Copenhaver & Schmitt, 1992, pp. 177–8; Lohr in CHRP, 1988, pp. 548–52.

on to God, who is our peace' (Apol. 7–8). Since God cannot be grasped by a finite mind, human beings know about divine things only through symbols, metaphors and enigmas. But even the best of these symbols and images, derived from geometry, for example, are mere likenesses or simulacra that bear no true proportion to their divine model. Cusanus claims that even the most profound metaphor, that of the coincidence of opposites, where the opposite extremes of each positive attribute meet in an abyss that swallows all contradictions, fails to achieve comprehension of the divine paradox.[30]

In Copenhaver and Schmitt's synopsis, humankind is estranged from its creator and also strange to other creatures because objects in the world lack the common proportion that would make them knowable. One of Cusanus' main premises equates knowing with the operation of measuring or comparing and, since human knowledge can only ever come close toward the truth, he could find no real measure between humans and God or between humans and other worldly things. Only the special, unique event of Christ becoming human, an undying God who became a mortal being, proffers the opportunity to resolve the disjunction between human and divine being in his own person. The Incarnation of Christ symbolizes the fact that the human creature is a juncture of a higher and a lower nature, a little world that recapitulates in miniature the extremes of the larger world. But if humankind relies entirely on its human cognitive capacities, the species itself will remain exiled from God and from the cosmos. Genuine understanding, he said, begins with faith, which 'enfolds every intelligible thing in itself'. Since God cannot be comprehended through the study of worldly things, 'reason, opinion, and learning lead from the more known through symbols to the less known, only where arguments stop and faith starts do we grasp him. Faith carries us in simplicity beyond all reason and intelligence up to the third heaven of simplest intellectual reality' (Doct. Ign. 3.11). Even in our bodily being we may contemplate God in his incorporeal nature. Through this contemplation we come to see that God cannot be comprehended due to the immensity of his excellence. *This* knowledge, Cusanus said, is learned ignorance, learned when intelligent persons confess their lack of comprehension, an implication of which is that mystical faith has to displace rational discourse as the right path for the soul to return to God.[31]

Cusanus expressed one of the richest versions of the notion that the human creature is a microcosm or little-world of the entire cosmos. But he took this antique image and radically modified it; human being is a microcosm not because he comprises in himself all the many degrees of reality and is subject to conflictual forces, but rather because he unites in himself the lowest level of intellectual reality and the highest level of sensible reality. With regard to the creator's generative power, the human is 'a second god', invested with a creative power that imitates in germ that divine power: 'Human is God then, but not in an absolute sense, for he is human; thus, he is a human God. Human is also a world, but he is not all things through contraction, for he is human; thus, human is a microcosm – a human world at any rate. Human can be a human god then, and as God in a human manner he can

---
[30] On the coincidence of opposites from a modern perspective, see Weeks, 1993, pp. 103–14.
[31] Copenhaver & Schmitt, 1992, pp. 178–80; Levao, 1985, pp. 21–33.

be a human angel, a human beast, or whatever else. Within human potency all things exist in their way' (De Conj. 2.14). These are very strong words indeed; they predate by fifty years Pico's declaration of the enormous reach of human potential, and invest humans with a mastery of their own nature that is only hinted at in Descartes' shocking departure from traditional views of human capacity almost two hundred years later.

The creative power of the human mind resides in its ability to produce tools and art-works; these products are distinct not because of the natural material they are made from, but because of the non-natural forms they are given. The human creative power thus approaches that of God's power, but whereas God brings forth what he understands, humans are only able to understand what God has brought forth. Unlike God, human does not produce real beings, but instead can only represent and appropriate them:

> Even the things which the mind itself produces – a geometrical theorem or the form of a spoon – are objects appropriated by the mind to itself. The proper object of the mind must be an interior reality ... The proper object of the mind can only be the mind itself as knowable. To discover its true self, the mind must withdraw from the otherness which is involved in sense-perception and rational knowledge and turn inward. [Idiota, sec. 2]

Cusanus clearly has Augustine's interior discipline in plain view here, encouraging the notion that through cognitive self-mastery the soul can achieve its true nature. The mind must turn away from its exterior activities, as Charles Lohr says, and

> ascend to its own necessary, intrinsic dynamism. The condition of the mind's return to itself is a deliberate, prior choice. Man's ultimate autonomy is grounded not only in his faculties of knowledge, but also in his ability freely to choose. Through his faculties of knowledge man can comprehend all things; through his freedom he can become all things, a human god, angel or beast. He has the ability to choose to belong to himself, to free himself from the world and realize all the interior potentialities of his nature.[32]

In the short tract *On Conjectures* four years later, Cusanus tempers his skeptical view that all human claims to knowledge are approximations of the truth; instead he adopts a more optimistic view about humans' intellectual abilities. He now thinks that humans stand in the same relation to the rational products of their minds as God stands in relation to the real objects of the natural world. Where God created real things, humans create conjectures about things; and more than that, they can devise an art or technique of conjectures that can bring their understanding closer to the actual structure of divinely created realities. The conjectural technique 'exemplifies human creativity, weakened by its divorce from infinity yet wielding great power within a finite domain. The fact that a person can keep thinking anything at all shows that the thinker is immortal; thought, a function of soul, replicates itself perpetually and requires a perpetual faculty.'[33] Cusanus proposed several metaphors to capture the essential connection between the divine immortal

---

[32] Lohr, in CHRP, 1988, pp. 553–4.
[33] Copenhaver & Schmitt, 1992, p. 181.

nature and humans' soulful imitation of that nature. In one striking instance he compared the movement of a spinning top (or ball) with the soul's animation of the body, and the soul's capacity for invention to the game of ball playing.

In a recent paper, Emily Michael has argued that from ancient times to the early modern period the human soul or *psychē* played a double role in relation to the body:

> First it was believed to be integrally linked to the human body as the locus or cause of its vital and cognitive activities; and second, it was believed to be the vehicle, as separable from the human body, of personal immortality. Different aspects of this double role were emphasized at different times and by different thinkers. The story of the human soul's career during the Renaissance is that of the progress from general agreement on the harmony of these two roles to a common preoccupation with their reputed conflict.[34]

She goes on to claim that the prevalent account of the human soul in this period was the Thomistic interpretation of Aristotle's account, but that after an early stage in which it held almost complete authority, the Neo-Aristotelian view began to fall away in the 1500s under the impact of competing non-Thomistic views.[35] Where Petrarch had deliberately and vehemently argued that philosophical descriptions of the human soul's nature and functions were beside the point in dealing with everyday concerns, later humanists, employing the recently rediscovered Platonic accounts of the soul's capture by the body and descent to the mundane world, elevated the soul's self-education through wisdom to something that any thoughtful person could achieve.

(2) The rediscovery of Plato, Plotinus and the Hermetica

Marsilio Ficino (1433–99) is the source and the symbol of the greatest achievements in Renaissance philosophy and the revival of an entire tradition that had been almost completely obscured by the dominance of the Aristotelian system, harmonized and integrated with Christian doctrine under Albert the Great and Thomas Aquinas, and promulgated in the early university settings as orthodoxy. Ficino's earliest surviving works show an unremarkable, pedestrian treatment of standard curricular topics, but this was to change under the patronage of the de Medicis. In the mid-1450s Ficino began to study Greek and devoted his attention to the works of Epicurus, as well as his Latin proponent Lucretius. By the early 1460s he felt that he was ready to start work on the enormous task assigned him by his patron, a complete Latin translation of the entire Platonic corpus in 1462. He received from Cosimo de Medici the Villa Careggi, a grand house near Florence, and the foundation

---

[34] Michael, in Wright & Potter, 2000, p. 147.

[35] Between 1967 and 1982, C. H. Lohr published sixteen lengthy bio-bibliographical studies of the principal medieval and Renaissance Aristotelian commentaries in various issues of *Traditio* and *Renaissance Quarterly*; these now comprise the most complete scholarly repository of information on these figures; for a brief overview, see also Mercer, in Sorell, 1997, pp. 33–67.

charter of the Florentine Academy. One of his first commissions was to render into intelligible Latin the fourteen discourses known as the *Corpus Hermeticum*. Cosimo had obtained an exceptionally rare manuscript of these tractates which his scholars agreed should be dated 'around the time of Moses', thus making their protagonist, Hermes Trismegistus, an Egyptian priest-magician, the predecessor of Socrates and Plato by several centuries. Before Ficino's superb (second) printing of this text, which he called *The Book on the Power and Wisdom of God, whose Title is Pimander* (hence known under its short-title as *The Pimander*), only one Latin text of the *Asclepius* had been known in the Christian West.[36] Ficino's *Pimander* was to become the single most important and most influential presentation of *prisca sapientia* until the end of the eighteenth century. Ficino's diligent work on the Hermetica may now seem like an unaccountable digression, given his impending work on the Platonic corpus, but he clearly thought that the figure of Hermes stood on an equal footing with the other great god-speakers of the most archaic epoch, and inaugurated the idea of a personal quest to achieve an immortal soul.

It took him almost six years to finish his Latin edition of Plato (until 1469), but it was not published until fifteen years later (1484). This monumental edition was accompanied by short commentaries and/or argument summaries for each dialogue; six fuller commentaries on individual Platonic dialogues were printed separately in 1496. While working sporadically on some of these texts (not all of which are complete), Ficino took up another enormous task, the translation with running commentary of Plotinus' *Enneads* (begun in 1484 and printed in 1492). His translations of Porphyry, Iamblichus, Proclus and other related Neo-Platonic works appeared in 1497, shortly after the publication of some of his letters, which he had begun to collect twenty years earlier. His first collection of 120 letters written between 1457–76 was circulated amongst his friends, a common practice at the time; he may have been prompted to start this collection due to the fact that letters falsely purported to be his were also in circulation.[37] Somehow, in the midst of these prodigious scholarly endeavors he found time to write his massive summation of ancient theology, *The Platonic Theology* (printed in 1482), his apologetic treatise, *On the Christian Religion* (1474) and the strange digest of medical, magical and hermetic thought, *Three Books on Life* (1489). After the expulsion of the de Medicis from Florence in 1494, Ficino retired to the country where he carried on guiding and instructing his far-flung pupils through letters.[38]

It is not feasible in this short section to rehearse the many occasions when Ficino addressed his newly acquired understanding of the Platonic teachings on the soul before his great syncretistic study in *The Platonic Theology*. But it is worth looking at one paradigmatic Ficinian kind of interpretation, one which appeared in scattered texts devoted to the *Phaedrus* dialogue. Socrates' mythical story of the chariot-driver and his two horses is one of the most dazzling and memorable pictures of the soul in philosophical literature. Michael Allen, the editor of the variorum edition of

---

[36] On the reception of the Latin *Asclepius*, see Yates, 1964, pp. 44–61, 169–89.

[37] Translators' Note in Letters, vol. I, 1975, p. 27.

[38] For brief accounts of his life, see Copenhaver & Schmitt, 1992, pp. 143–9; Kristeller, 1943, pp. 11–29; Letters, vol. I, 1975, pp. 19–24.

all Ficino's Phaedran-associated texts, says that it is 'also the most self-consciously poetic in terms of its diction, gorgeous rhythms and figures, dramatic juxtapositions, elaborate allegory, and symphonic structure'. Instead of the usual cautious dialectical exchange on a given topic, Plato presents another Socrates: 'the ecstatic seer, the poet-prophet, singing in Corybantian measures of man's agonistic ascent to heaven, of the fall, of true knowledge, of immortality'.[39] With his immense erudition, and recently acquired knowledge of Socrates' forerunners, Ficino would have been familiar with Parmenides' poem, where the narrator describes an ecstatic chariot ride through the gates of Night and Day to an audience with an unnamed goddess. He would also have known about the Biblical prophet Elijah taken up to heaven in a whirlwind, the four-wheeled chariot of the Cherubim witnessed by Ezekiel, and St. Paul's reference to extra-somatic travel to the third heaven. Coupled with this, Ficino drew inspiration from the accounts of Plotinus and Iamblichus about the human soul's ascent to its rightful divine home. But unlike most of the other Platonic dialogues, the *Phaedrus* had made an impact before Ficino's translation, although not before Ficino had begun to unpack its secrets.

Allen conjectures that there may have been three reasons that influenced Ficino's decision to single out this dialogue from others concerned with soul-related topics. The first related to the high status accorded to the *Phaedrus* after Plotinus elevated its argument beyond its previous lesser stature. Following Plotinus' lead, Iamblichus insisted, perhaps for the first time, 'on interpreting the Phaedran Zeus, not as a cosmic deity, as the celestial world-soul, but as the supramundane, supracelestial demiurgic leader from the intelligible realm'. This view was bolstered by Ficino's unique grasp of Proclus' theurgical reworking of this central Socratic vision. Second, Ficino considered the *Phaedrus* to be the fourth member of the third tetralogy, composed of the *Parmenides, Philebus* and *Symposium.* The third reason could have been the outcome of an unwitting scholarly error that assigned the composition of the *Phaedrus* to Plato's youth, along with the *Meno* and the *Phaedo* (this accorded with the then current understanding of the dialogues' chronology offered by Diogenes Laertius) and thus thought of it as the product of poetic inspiration. Ficino even declared this view in these words: 'our Plato was pregnant with the madness of the poetic muse, whom he followed from a tender age or rather from his Apollonian generation. In his first youth, Plato gave birth to his first child, and it was itself almost entirely poetical and radiant.' On Ficino's interpretation, the speaker in the dialogue is the Phaedrus of the *Symposium,* 'the archetypal youth at the foot of the Diotimian ladder of ascent to ideal Beauty, waiting to become the godlike charioteer. By the same token, he is the archetypal pupil inspiring the teacher to his heuristic task. Hence, Ficino observes, though devoted to beauty in all its forms, the dialogue is especially concerned with beauty as we perceive it via our three cognitive powers: intelligence, sight, and hearing.'[40]

Ficino's commentary on the *Phaedrus* must be reconstructed from his running notes, the argument synopses, various appended chapters, and the fifty-three summae. Allen has gone to great lengths to reorder these heterogeneous texts and provide

---

[39] Introduction to Allen, 1981, p. 1.
[40] Introduction to Allen, 1981, p. 11.

them with an overall scheme. The eight additional chapters are basically concerned with the soul's ascent:

> first, with the individual soul's ascent through the four divine inspirations, then with the ascent to immortality of Soul, generically conceived, and finally with the ascent of Soul, and all souls, as a company of gods led by Jove, the world-soul, beyond the arch of the intellectual heaven to gaze upon the supracelestial place, the portals of the transcendent One. This drama of cosmic ascent is inadvertently heightened by Ficino's failure to deal with the crippling of the wings, the rebellion of the dark steed, and the soul's ... descent again to earthly beauty and desire.

Ficino may have found some of the textual passages uncongenial, and no doubt his considerable energies and enthusiasm were redirected elsewhere; hence, in this commentary there are flashes of genius, but also many loose ends. Allen says that Ficino 'carved out an epic fragment to the glory of his passion-mastering intelligence, concentrating, as it were, on the shape of the head rather than the musculature of the torso'.[41]

In an early letter to Agli (December 1457), long before his official version of the *Phaedrus* text, Ficino already espoused distinctively Platonic ideas about the soul. Plato had learned from Hermes Trismegistus, he said, that God is the supreme source and light within whom shine the models of all things; that the soul in contemplating the eternal mind of God also beholds with greater clarity the natures of all things; and thus that the soul saw justice, wisdom, harmony and the beauty of the divine nature itself. In this heavenly state, human minds were nourished with perfect knowledge; but then human souls were depressed into bodies through thoughts about and desire for earthly things. In their descent to earth they forgot their original state and will remain like this unless they turn their thoughts to the divine light again. The human soul can fly back to heaven on two wings, the virtues of wisdom and justice, virtues which exemplify contemplation and moral conduct. The philosopher's mind can regain these wings, and through their recovery the soul is separated from the body. Filled with divine light, the soul strives with all its might to reach heaven and is drawn towards it; Ficino says that Plato calls this drawing-away 'divine frenzy'. The embodied soul perceives only shadows and images of things, but these are clues to a fuller knowledge: 'We remember what we knew before when we existed outside the prison of the body. The mind (*animus*) is fired by this memory and, shaking its wings, by degrees purges itself from contact with the body and its filth and becomes wholly possessed by divine frenzy.'[42] In this letter and other texts, Ficino shows commendable sensitivity to nuances in Latin terms for rendering Plato's Greek; thus, for example, he almost always carefully discriminates between *anima* (f.) for 'soul' and *animus* (m.) for 'mind' or 'rational soul'.[43]

Ficino adopted an explicitly Platonic orientation in the initial setting-forth of the *Platonic Theology*, not only with respect to the central issue of the nature of the

---

[41] Introduction to Allen, 1981, pp. 22–3.
[42] Letters, vol. I, pp. 43–4.
[43] See, for example, the clever dialogue between God and the Soul in Letters, vol. I, pp. 35–9.

human soul, but also with respect to the character of philosophy itself as the disciplined pursuit of truth and wisdom. He agreed with Plato that the soul is related to God as the power of vision is to the sun's light. Just as poor finite humans cannot see things without the sun casting light on them, so also humans cannot know anything without the illumination of the divine light. No matter what the domain of knowing inquiry, human beings, in seeking the truth, are directed toward the contemplation and reverence of God. Insofar as the human soul is God's greatest creation, in attempting to understand the natural truths that God has instituted in this world, every one attempts to understand their own soul. The human soul bears within it the image of God's work and this manifests an eternal destiny, namely its final end in its original source. Thus, the central theme of Ficino's entire work can be accurately characterized under the rubric of the subtitle of his book, 'arguments for the immortality of the soul'. However, as Kristeller pointed out long ago, 'the thesis of immortality in the *Theologia Platonica* is really no more than a guiding principle that is lost sight of over long sections. [But] beneath the formal plan of division we can recognize a rational distribution of material.'[44]

The general thrust of Ficino's argument for the human soul's immortality is that the object of human longing for fulfillment of one's inmost nature, beyond the transient dissatisfactions of earthly life, points toward another, more perfect life, and justifies humans' belief that there is such a new life. In the synoptic version of his first proof, he concludes:

> with the assurance that when the soul loses its body, it passes into a life of excellence in which the contemplation of the light is unimpeded by the darkness and uncertainty of the earthly prison. This description of the afterlife implies that the source of our unhappiness is our imperfect relationship to the light. The assurance of our immortality shows that we are destined for a more perfect contemplation than this world can afford, and in this vision we shall be made whole.[45]

In his understanding of Plato's mature position on the essential nature of human being, Ficino asserted that the definition of the human species also comprises human aspirations. Given humans' congenital, innate inability to achieve a perfect vision of the light while tied to his wretched bodily prison, it surely must be conceded that the proper end of human being must be the form to which he aspires, and not the form to which he is confined. Ficino takes up one of the central Renaissance concerns with human dignity by pointing out that the proper activities connected with knowledge, desire and practical action are directed at 'objects' beyond the self. The overarching strategy of the *Platonic Theology* is oriented towards three tasks as Collins explains. The first task is to mount a concerted attack against the secular version of Aristotle by proving that philosophical speculation cannot be separated from religious devotion. The second task concerns the fundamental requirement to establish the immortality of the human soul; but in the author's view, arguments for this thesis directly serve the first task. The intimate connection between philosophical and religious inquiry reveals that the ineluctable

---

44 Kristeller, 1943, p. 34.
45 Collins, 1974, p. 4.

desire for God goes beyond the limits of mortal existence and cannot be an empty, vain endeavor. This second task introduces the third task, one that 'transforms the whole enterprise', in attempting to teach the attentive reader an entirely new point of view: 'It tries to lay open to him the divine dimension of his world; its arguments and conclusions are meant to show that man himself and the world around him are flooded with the divine presence. The purpose of all this is to make human life on this earth continuous with the life hereafter by drawing man even now to his proper place with God.'[46]

In the opening book of the *Platonic Theology*, Ficino distinguished five levels of unity and efficacy in the world whose structure offers a stepwise access from the inner soul of each human to the divine power at the highest level.[47] The lowest level in the great chain of being is that of corporeal matter; extended in space and time, pieces of matter lack unity and the power of action. For some thing to be an agent means that it has the power to act within itself, it is disposed toward motion, and it can be united with what it acts upon. Ficino thus directly links power with unity, and the root of power is being. Further, since form is the principle of being, it is also the principle of unity, that which unites all the component parts of the corporeal thing. In the vertical order of the world, this unifying function is attributed to form; without form to unify it any piece of matter would be undetermined in its species or kind, it would flow from one state into another. He assigns to the concept of quality the explanatory role of determining any body to be a certain kind of body. In basic agreement with Aristotle on this point, Ficino argues that by making a thing to be of a certain kind the form makes it active only if it is directly connected or manifest in the extension and hence composition of the bodily thing. In order to avoid an infinite series of conditions that must be met for some thing to have a specific form for its matter, the incorporeal form must have unity of its own, and not as the result of being in-*formed* by some other principle. In both its spatial and temporal extent, the human body, for example, is one thing, united by its incorporeal form, one thing that unifies its subordinate parts. Ficino calls the principle that unifies the formed matter of a human its soul. Since death occurs through the division of its bodily parts and the dissolution of its unity, life is an indissoluble power (PT I.3.1).

In addition to the intrinsic feature of material unification, the soul *qua* form must also account for its power to move itself. The soul gives to its body the internal power of self-motion; without soul any body can only be moved by an externally acting agent (PT III.1.1). Ficino does not deal at any length with what role the lower forms of life have to play in this grand scheme. On one occasion he does mention the relation between the irrational and rational soul, like that between an object and its shadow, but does not explain whether this irrational soul is one that animals possess. In any case, it is clear that animals are in less control of their actions than humans, since the action of humans' rational souls are directed towards the universal form (idea) of the good. In its power of self-motion and organization the rational soul compensates for its body's corporeal inadequacies; its outward actions are drawn out in time and divided into moments. Just as its animal nature

---

[46] Collins, 1974, p. 7; the following summary is derived from pp. 12–15.
[47] See Kristeller, 1943, pp. 92–120.

nourishes itself little by little, so also the soul acquires knowledge little by little. The human soul moves between potency and action, between the capacity for something and the possession of it. That which is in motion under its own power is not satisfied with itself; in other words, it is moved through the desire to attain that which will render it more perfect than its present state permits. It is in the very nature of a finite imperfect soul, therefore, to seek for something more perfect than itself and better endowed with qualities that are self-sufficing (PT I.4.1).

Ficino's demonstration cleverly suggests that understanding is what the soul seeks as the form of its host's body and what it does not already possess in terms of its incomplete nature. Above the human soul in the vertical order there is something that does not move itself, because it has no need, and does not seek to know, since it is always in the act of knowing (PT I.5.1). Taking his lead from Plotinus and Proclus,[48] more than from the mystical Platonic texts, Ficino theorizes that above the level of soul is the level of mind, the exemplar of which is an angel. According to his estimate, the soul is an imperfect mind, the angel is a perfect mind, and God alone is the truth above the level of minds. Although the human rational soul is justly called mind (*animus*) in terms of its capacity for intellectual cognition, it is not mind in its proper essence. Animals have soul (*anima*) as the principle of life and self-motion and humans, insofar as they are in fact animal beings, have organic powers and functions through the principle of life. For humans to possess a rational soul means that this is the highest 'part' or power of mind capable of being realized in them; it does not mean that their use of reason exhausts the essence of mind. Although it is fitting, that is, fits within the ordered whole, that mind *per se* can exist separate from any body, the rational soul in humans is intimately linked with the whole soul, itself the inseparable form of its animal body.

However, even an angel's perfect mind does not mean that it does not need something greater than itself. In what it does know, the angelic mind is perfect and complete; but it is finite and limited, it does not know everything and is not simple in its completeness. Ficino claims that an angel is not mobile, because it does not need to move toward what it lacks, but it is multiple since it is not unified in its being. The angelic mind is dependent on God, the most powerful of all beings, whose intrinsic power is self-unity and other-unifying (PT I.6.1). Above the angel there must also be goodness itself; since all things strive for the good, but all do not strive for mind. Some things that have mind are not satisfied with this possession but seek beyond it for the good; moreover, understanding is itself thought to be a good worth striving for. At the summit of Ficino's cosmos stand unity, truth and goodness: 'the truth of a thing consists in its simplicity or lack of composition; a thing is true because it is one; it is good for the same reason. It has well-being when it is united with itself and its principle; for a thing to be good is for it to be itself, pure and unadulterated. Thus, unity, truth, and goodness are the same in things.'[49]

God is not only the final end or 'object' of all lesser beings' striving, he is also the creative source of all beings' existence. Ficino offers an ingenious hypothesis

---

48 Plotinus, *Enneads*, 5.1.3; and Proclus, *Elements of Theology*, 20, 175, 190.
49 Collins, 1974, p. 16; see the Letter to Cavalcanti, Letters, vol. I, pp. 85–8.

about the dual concept of god in Plato's texts: in the *Parmenides* god is called the infinite because he does not receive a limit from outside himself; and in the *Philebus* he is called the term or limit because he determines all things by means of the infusion or imparting of forms. In Collins' evocative words: 'Suspended from God like a shadow is a potency, in a sense a material potency, which by its very nature is unformed and undetermined. This potency reflects God's character as unlimited or infinite. But to the extent that God as the term or limit looks at its shadow as in a mirror, he is reflected in the shadow as an image, and thus infinity itself, i.e. common matter, is determined by forms.'[50] But this twofold character of god, one being that is both finite and infinite, boundless and bounded, causes deep problems for Ficino's account of the overall scheme, and especially for his account of the difference between the being and the essence of the human soul. He devotes considerable effort to finding his way out of this explanatory impasse in his discussion of the immortality of the human soul. He is compelled to distinguish the actuality–potency relation between form and matter from the actuality–potency relation between being and essence.

The essence of some thing is the what-it-is expressed in its definition, whereas its being is the actuality of its essence and its presence in the contingent nature of things. The essence of human is true for all times and all places; immortality belongs to the nature of the form of human, but not to its matter. Some forms, such as angels, are not determined to exist in bodies, but other forms, such as humans and animals, are determined to exist in bodies; they cannot exist *as the forms they are* without being manifest in matter. If the determinate essence in itself is immortal, then it receives its being in an immortal mode; thus forms that do not have their being in matter are immortal according to their essence *and* their being (PT V.7.1). The definition of human expresses something that it can become, unaffected by the state of the actually existing things that correspond to it. That thing's intrinsic content can remain eternally true even though the things in which this content exists are changed by generation and corruption. It is clearly the case that humans in their animal nature are composite beings, and if the composite ceases to exist through loss of life, so also do those parts that exist in virtue of the being of the composite. The human essence is neither like geometrical objects, timeless and perfect (though bounded in their definition), nor like material things which can lose their being through decomposition. The human rational soul resists this kind of decomposition, for it is different in its essence from the forms of material things with no capacity for intelligence. Strictly speaking, it is the human who exists, it is the human who thinks, and not just the mind. Any given mind exists only because it belongs to an actual human (or angelic) being. Ficino's argument reaches its inescapable conclusion. In Collins' terse summary statement:

> Hence, the mode of thinking is a human one as is the mode of being. But the rational soul has an action in which matter cannot be involved; it knows things in separation from matter and material conditions. Whereas a material thing is composite, changing, impenetrable even by those things which are its like in essence, the soul has knowledge which is immutable, reduces things to their simple parts in knowing them, and unifies

---

[50] Collins, 1974, p. 44; the next summary is from pp. 45–50.

under one universal idea. But if the soul acts in separation from matter, it must *be* separate from it. Thus, it exists in itself and is independent of the body.[51]

Ficino turned his attention again and again to rational demonstrations of the soul's immortality, often in self-contained short treatises, for example, the Letter to Cavalcanti on the soul's perceptions after death, the Letter to Lorenzo de Medici on eternal happiness, and especially the lengthy Letter, 'Five Questions Concerning the Mind'. This latter piece was written in 1476, two years after the completion of the *Platonic Theology*, incorporated into the collection entitled *Five Keys of Platonic Wisdom* in 1477, and also in the second book of his *Letters*, first printed in 1495.[52]

Ficino firmly believed that there was a unitary theological tradition that stretched back to Orpheus, Hermes Trismegistus and Zoroaster, and that this same tradition culminated in Jesus' teachings, the works of Dionysus the Areopagite and Augustine's Christian–Platonist synthesis. In Michael Allen's Introduction to the excellent new five-volume Latin-English edition of the *Platonic Theology*, he says that Ficino's great work was 'a bold, albeit problematic, attempt to appropriate ancient philosophy, and particularly late ancient philosophy, for the *ingeniosi*, the intellectuals, the forward wits of the republic and its governing elites'. The many-faceted character of Ficino's complex work may account for its peculiar style which set out to emulate in the Latin language what Plotinus had achieved in the Greek. In other words, 'to approach sublimity in an unadorned and apparently artless way that is nonetheless syntactically and rhetorically challenging, with its frequent asyndeton (making the reader work it out), its unbalanced periods (drawing the reader into the mazes of the argument), its occasional direct address, and its intermittent flights of poetic imagery contributing to a sense of allocutionary trance.'[53] Allen insists on viewing Ficino as more of an original, even radical thinker than the derivative and expository place usually allotted to him in standard accounts of fifteenth-century history of ideas. An attentive reading of the work reveals many unorthodox, sometimes heretical views just below the surface: these include Pelagianism, Origenism, Docetism, Arianism and even Gnosticism, with its emphasis on the 'light-filled nature' of human beings and their 'stellar origins and ends'.

Ficino had the good sense, or innate political canniness, to not make the sort of outrageous proclamations later associated with Giordano Bruno or Tommaso Campanella, ones that precipitated their disastrous ends. But he did subscribe to two ancient ideals, submerged during the scholastic Middle Ages, and resurrected, largely due to his own indefatigable efforts, through the recovery of late Greek texts. In Allen's concise words:

> the first was that of the magus with his power over a nature dominated by sympathies and hidden ciphers and signs, and in pursuit of the secrets of macrocosmic transformation. The second was the ideal of the daimonic soul in search of poetic, amatory, prophetic, even priestly ascent into the realm of pure Mind and Will, of Knowledge and Love – the soul, that is, in search of interior transformation and illumination both in the traditional

---
51 Collins, 1974, p. 51; see PT VIII.14.
52 Letters, vol. I, pp. 79–82; 171–8; CKR, 1968, pp. 193–212.
53 Allen, in Ficino, 2001, p. ix.

terms of faith and belief, and in the necessarily more elite terms of understanding, of intellectual consciousness.[54]

Allen has also identified the intellectual debts Ficino owed to his great predecessors in treating these themes: in addition to the obvious and overt allegiance to Plato's more 'mystical' dialogues, he also drew upon Aquinas' *Summa Contra Gentiles*, Book II;[55] the eccentric Neo-Platonist Proclus' almost forgotten work, *The Platonic Theology*; Plotinus' treatment of the soul's immortality in *Enneads*, Book Four, chapter 7, and Augustine's early interpretations of the Neo-Platonic doctrines espoused by Porphyry and Iamblichus.

The bulk of Ficino's *Platonic Theology* consists of many interconnected arguments concerned to show the immortal status of the human soul. Until the researches of Kristeller, Eugenio Garin and others about fifty years ago, it was commonly thought that the Renaissance theological and academic obsession with immortality was the consequence of Ficino's Florentine Academy. Although it is true that Ficino, in full possession of the great Platonic and Neo-Platonic texts, gave the fullest and most articulate expression to these ideas, there were many other specialized treatises on this subject written in the mid to late 1400s. These works vary a great deal in length, acuity and access to earlier sources; there is no unified approach, nor is there any doctrinal agreement. But unlike his predecessors and contemporaries, Ficino is not content to merely restate and expand Aquinas and Augustine, but also develops novel arguments of his own. His summation of immortality arguments also has a polemical purpose; he was implacably opposed to the Averroist doctrine of the unicity of intellect – that there is only one all-embracing cosmic mind – since he thought that this undermined the Christian doctrine of the individual soul's immortality. Kristeller claims that Book XV of the *Platonic Theology* is the most detailed refutation of Averroism after Aquinas' monumental rebuttal two centuries before.[56] In addition to this polemical objective, Ficino also had a more profoundly philosophical motive, and that was to revive the view that the true goal of humankind was a return to the divine source of its soul-nature by means of an ascent through contemplation. Like Plotinus, Proclus and other *priscae theologiae*, Ficino even hints that he himself was able to attain a direct vision of God during his earth-bound life. However, Ficino quickly points out that this only shows a more privileged vantage on what is, after all, an intrinsic human characteristic, that is, the soul's capacity to transcend its material conditions. Indeed, there are other hints in this massive, over-stuffed work that show Ficino's collateral, and partly hidden, interest in magical and theurgic practices (to which we shall turn shortly.)

It is difficult to gain an overall view on the complex network of paths traced out in theological-philosophical accounts of the soul between the early 1400s and the late 1500s. There are many motives for holding a specific line of thought, not all of

---

[54] Allen, in Ficino, 2001, p. x.

[55] In an appendix Collins provides one hundred pages of side-by-side extracts from Ficino and Aquinas to show either paraphrase or near-verbatim quotation, 1974, pp. 114–215.

[56] Kristeller, 1972, p. 33.

them philosophical; there are several frameworks in which such lines of thought converge, and there are also wide discrepancies in the degree of scholarly erudition brought to these debates, degrees of expertise that increased as the original Greek texts became available in better Latin translations. Alessandro Achillini (1463–1512) can be taken as an exemplary academic in this period; his works were fairly popular, eleven titles going through twenty-four editions from 1494.[57] Achillini distinguished two human souls: an organic soul with powers similar to those catalogued by Aquinas; but went against the Neo-Aristotelian scheme in claiming that the intellect is not a power of the organic soul. He insisted that Averroes' assertion that the human intellect is a separate substance, one for all humans, is a correct interpretation of Aristotle's claims in *On the Soul*:

> The single human soul, separated from matter and common to all human beings, acts in conjunction with the cogitative power of individual human souls to produce, for each individual, intellective cognition. But the Averroist view that body and mind are two really distinct substances – that is, the Averroist distinction between a *single* eternal human mind and each human body with its mortal organic soul – entails a denial of personal immortality.

However, Achillini's line of thought on this was caught up in contradictions, as Kessler explains: 'he maintained that this single intellect was both the assisting form, using man as instrument for its operations as a captain uses a boat, and also the *forma informans* of man, which gave him a specific essence and provided the subject of intellection for the individual being.'[58] His espousal of Averroes' position was not greeted warmly, since it was generally agreed that it would lead very shortly to a direct collision with basic Christian tenets.

Concerted opposition to Averroes' interpretation had consolidated not long after his Islamic commentaries on Aristotle's texts made their way into the Latin West in the mid-1200s. Albert the Great's attack in 1256, and then Aquinas' attack in 1270 were shortly followed by the Bishop of Paris' condemnation of Averroist teachings in 1277.[59] But Achillini's work brought the simmering discontent to the boil again, prompting another wave of virulent counter-attacks. Making the situation even worse, in 1495 the Venetian humanist Jerome Donato published his Latin translation of the *De Anima* of Alexander of Aphrodisias,[60] an ancient commentator who held the heretical view that the human soul is mortal. This newly discovered support for the Averroist position acquired a certain amount of risqué popularity in the University of Padua and the University of Bologna,[61] raising the hackles of the Church authorities. The furor generated by these scandalous views culminated in one of the decrees of the Lateran Council in 1513 which issued a dogmatic declaration asserting the immortality of the human soul. The Lateran Council also issued the unprecedented injunction that philosophers attack these pernicious errors and prove

---

[57] Michael, in Wright & Potter, 2000, pp. 149–50; see CHRP, 1988, pp. 271–2, 495–6.
[58] Kessler, in CHRP, 1988, p. 495.
[59] See Grant, in CHLMP, 1982, pp. 537–9.
[60] See Cranz, in CTC, 1960, vol. I, pp. 77–135, vol. II, pp. 411–22.
[61] See Kristeller, 1965, vol. 2, pp. 111–18.

the soul's personal immortality by natural reason, and not merely as an article of faith alone.

But the full force of the Church's repudiation of Averroist teaching was brought against the short text *On the Immortality of the Soul* by Pietro Pomponazzi, first printed in 1516. Pomponazzi (1462–1525) had been the student of Thomist instructors at the University of Padua, where he also took up the cause of Averroes' interpretation of Aristotle on the nature of soul. Although he did not know Greek, like Ficino and Pico, he was open to philosophical arguments from the Neo-Platonists, the humanists, and recently printed Greek commentators such as Alexander of Aphrodisias. Pomponazzi's famous (or infamous) treatise was, in Kessler's words, 'the culmination of his life-long endeavour to solve a problem regarding which he had repeatedly affirmed that he would prefer to be taught than to teach'.[62] In his lectures on the soul in 1500 his main concern seems to have been a careful exposition of Aristotle's *On the Soul*, according to Averroes' commentary. But within a few years he had begun to question the central Averroist doctrine of the unicity of the intellect. He thought that whether one argued that the intellect is merely the assisting form of human, like a captain in a boat, or that the single intellect is the informing form of human being, there is no way of maintaining the individual unity of human as a rational animal. Against Averroes' version of Aristotle, he began to argue with Thomas Aquinas that such a position reduced human to an entirely animal status. But Pomponazzi was caught between two equally untenable positions, since Aquinas' view that the human soul is immortal, although in accord with Christian faith and revelation, could not be held as the consequence of rational argument. Aquinas' position was based on the assumption that the human soul was the product of divine creation, and this was opposed to the principles of nature. Since Aquinas and Averroes supposed the soul to be an immaterial form acting in a material subject, a whole composed of parts, 'they had to come to terms with the problem of how the different parts of the body, moved by one and the same soul, act differently; and neither could do so without admitting different material dispositions as additional causes of these actions.'[63]

Pomponazzi devised a schedule of questions that revolved around two groups of arguments that seemed to require the soul to be both immortal and immaterial. The first group of arguments concerned the operation of intellectual cognition, that is, with regard to the immateriality of intellective objects, while the second group concerned the operation of the will, that is, with regard to the final end of moral virtue, one that seemed to lie beyond this earthly life. With respect to the latter argument he argued that moral virtue did not depend on the assumption of a better life in heaven, but agreed with the Stoics that moral goodness was valued most highly when sought as an end in itself. The sticking point concerned the first argument and Pomponazzi's response to this drew on a clever use of the Neo-Platonic view of the soul's intermediate status between the material and immaterial realms. If one claimed that the soul's proper place was in the immaterial realm, and thus elevated humans to a higher ontological status, then all the problems connected

---

[62] Kessler, in CHRP, 1988, p. 501–5.
[63] Kessler, in CHRP, 1988, p. 502.

with the material conditions of humans' animal nature came into play. He agreed that the intellectual soul could not operate without the faculty of imagination, and insofar as sensible images are dependent in their 'object' on material things, the intellective power was an integral and inseparable part of the human soul.[64]

Pomponazzi made a valiant effort to deal with these and related problems in his short treatise *On the Immortality of the Soul*, a complex and dense work that begins with the salutary proviso that the human soul is indeed immortal, but that such a belief can only be held as an article of faith, and not shown by means of reason. Pomponazzi has been called the last scholastic and the first Enlightenment thinker, as J. H. Randall said: 'He did indeed partake of the natures of both: of the latter in his fiery zeal against the theologians, his scorn for all comfortable and compromising modernism in religion, and his sober vision of the natural destiny of man; of the former in his refusal to leave the bounds of the Aristotelian tradition, in his meticulous use of the medieval method of refutation, and in his painstaking attention to the reasons by which a position was defended.' In this respect he was not unlike other illustrious figures in the Renaissance period, philosophers, polemicists, painters and others, who shared a median between two extremes, or at least, between two well-defined and often incompatible views. This shared spirit was manifest in 'its concentration on man and his destiny, its view of human nature as the link between heaven and earth, its reverence for the authority of the ancients – for him, Aristotle – and, despite all theory, its Stoic temper of mind'.[65] But Pomponazzi did not agree with the Stoics that the human soul is some kind of body, even a special body composed of very subtle matter. Rather, his initial premise was that there are two sorts of substantial form: first, there are separate immaterial forms wholly independent of matter and hence indestructible; second, there are material forms which inhere in prime matter and thus constitute and activate the body. A material form is integral to its body and has no activity apart from its body; it is thus wholly dependent on that body and inseparable from it.

He claimed that the rational soul, like all other forms that inhere in prime matter, is inseparable, material and mortal. He rejected the Thomistic claim that the rational soul is a third type of substantial form, that is, one that can inhere in prime matter and activate a body, but is separable from that body. He maintained against this view that the human soul is an intermediate entity in the sense that it has activities that are proper to both separate and material forms.[66] The human soul has both intellectual and organic powers; in this manner he affirmed that the soul is essentially and properly mortal, but relatively and improperly immortal. He based his position on an analysis of the soul's operations in the function of knowing; all types of knowing are functions of one and same soul, and all types of knowing abstract from matter. However, there are three types of separation from matter corresponding to the three types of cognitive abstraction. First, there is the total separation from matter by which angelic intelligences know; second, there is the lowest type of

---

[64] Kessler, in CHRP, 1988, p. 503.
[65] Randall, in CKR, 1968, p. 268; Randall claims here that Pomponazzi had 'a better understanding of Plato than Ficino or Pico', a highly dubious and implausible assertion.
[66] Michael, in Wright & Potter, 2000, p. 154.

separation by which the sensitive powers know, since they need bodies both in the subject and the object condition. The third type of separation from matter is one that needs bodies as objects of knowing operations, but not in the subject condition – this is the mean between the two, namely human intellect. Therefore, on one hand, the soul is a material form, an organic being generated by human parents, and not created by divine fiat; it is the supreme and most perfect of material forms, though incapable of existing or acting apart from its body. On the other hand, the soul's essential operation of knowing shows that it partakes of the divine immortal nature. In Randall's words, 'while knowing requires material conditions, and is thus the activity of a human body, it does not function materially but rises above the limitations of those conditions to grasp universals and truth. Knowing needs a body, but it does not take place in any localized part of the body ... Knowing takes place in the body as a whole ... since intellect includes all the powers of the body.'[67]

Pomponazzi concluded his essay with the formal contention that the immortal status of the human soul is 'a neutral problem', like that of the eternity of the world, and that neither its affirmation nor its denial can be shown by natural reason. The Venetian clergy found this conclusion highly offensive and persuaded the Patriarch and the Doge to burn the book and declare him a heretic. Cardinal Bembo at the Vatican did not find anything heretical in his treatise, and Pope Leo X encouraged both parties to fight it out. Pomponazzi responded with an *Apology* in 1518 and the next year followed this with the *Defense*. In the *Apology* he said that the soul's immortality was *not* a neutral problem, but actually went squarely against natural principles. He said that he was prepared to die for the truth of the doctrine of immortality, but solely on the basis of its standing as an article of faith. Little by little, he began to retract his more outrageous assertions, defending an orthodox position that placed presumptive credence in the Christian concepts of spiritual resurrection, supernatural grace and redemption, and the blessing of a second, better life in the world to come. On his deathbed Pomponazzi left an ambiguous testament that will never settle the argument about his final philosophical position, beyond an allegiance to his personal conviction that he would now go gladly 'to where all mortals go'. Copenhaver and Schmitt posed an insightful query that perhaps marks an ending to the story of where his investigation took him, but without finalizing a definitive statement: 'May it not be that in contending honestly with difficult and dangerous questions, questions that he could not resolve, he simply located the boundary between faith and reason differently from the way most of his contemporaries dared or, indeed, otherwise than church officials would have liked?'[68]

---

[67] Randall, in CKR, 1968, pp. 272–3; see the argument summary in Michael, 2000, pp. 154–5.

[68] Copenhaver & Schmitt, 1992, p. 110.

(3) Magic and occultism in the service of science

Ficino's scholarly studies into Platonic, Neo-Platonic, and Hermetic sources were not solely concerned with standard philosophical issues about the nature and functions of the human soul.[69] His wide-ranging and erudite commentaries also inspired an entire company of thinkers whose interests either had been, or were now, stimulated by an intense curiosity about ancient magic, astrology and alchemy. In 1489, Ficino published the single most influential statement of magical theory since the waning of Neo-Platonic Greek magic and theurgy in the Fourth Century. In the *De Vita Libri Tres* (sometimes referred to as the *De Vita Triplici*) Ficino took natural magic to be as much the province of philosophy as cosmology, astronomy, or matter-theory. In the final chapter he says that nature itself is a magician, having devised a complete scheme of correspondences between foods, minerals, stars, humors, and so forth, which the investigator can uncover and make use of: 'The philosopher, who is learned in natural science and astronomy, and whom we are wont to call a magician, likewise implants heavenly things in earthly objects by means of certain alluring charms used at the right moment.' One could distinguish between the wisdom of the magus and the learning of the philosopher, but they are actually interdependent aspects of the same enterprise: 'The *magus* is a scientist, as he investigates the hidden laws of the cosmos, learns of the correspondences between all things, and seeks to understand the world from the perspective of the Creator himself. But he is also a diviner, as he does this through action, perfecting the techniques and rituals which may lead him to the deeper level of insight required to reap divine gifts.'[70] Ficino had already clearly voiced this impartial view in his commentary on the *Symposium*, where he said that the power of magic consists in love, an erotic attraction of one thing for another in accord with a natural affinity. Natural objects, such as plants and minerals, are organs in an enormous living being; they borrow and loan each other their 'natures'. The magician is simply a person learned in such occult matters and skillful at manipulating them.

The First Book of *The Threefold Life* is concerned with the health of scholars, the Second with prolonging their life, and the Third with astral influences on their bodies and souls. The Third Book, entitled *De Vita Coelitus Comparanda*, became Ficino's *Summa Magica* and took on an unplanned life of its own. Near the opening of the First Book, Ficino draws an elaborate analogy about the proper instruments of the physician and the magician: 'Only the priests of the muses, only the hunters after the supreme good and truth are so negligent (alas) and so unlucky that they seem to utterly neglect that instrument by which they can in some way measure and

---

[69] The editors of CHRP have created an artificial segregation in their treatment of two groups of philosophers: twenty sober, serious Neo-Aristotelians, affiliated with established universities, are dealt with in two chapters, 'The Organic Soul' and 'The Intellective Soul', chapters that do not even mention Ficino and company; whereas those thinkers inspired by Plato, Plotinus and the Hermetica are dealt with only in the chapter on 'Astrology and Magic'. This unhappy editorial policy obscures the basic fact that most (if not all) of these thinkers shared the same concerns about the nature, function and origin of the soul.

[70] Voss, 2001, p. 5.

grasp the whole world. An instrument of this sort is the spirit (*spiritus*), which is defined by the physicians as a certain vapor of the blood, pure, subtle, hot and lucid.' In making this claim, Ficino clearly aligns himself with an understanding of *spiritus* as *pneuma* in Stoic and Galenic terms, an understanding supported by his reading of Plotinus and Porphyry. He continues in this vein (*sic*): the spirit is 'formed from the more subtle blood by the heat of the heart, flies to the brain, and there the soul carefully employs it for the exercise of both the interior and exterior senses. Thus the blood serves the spirit, the spirit the senses, and finally the senses serve reason.'[71]

The spirits of the studious investigator of nature's secrets need special care, he says, due to their constantly drawing on its resources in thinking and imagining. It has to be replaced from the more subtle parts of blood, and this renders the remaining parts of blood dense, dry and black. This is one reason why scholars often appear melancholic,[72] filled with black bile; since spirits that comprise black bile are very fine, hot, agile and combustible, they are likely to ignite and produce a state of mania. This temporary exalted state is followed by extreme depression and lethargy, caused by the smoke left over after the heart's fire. But it can be tempered with phlegm and more blood, when the spirits will glow again and not burn; this makes possible continuous study of the highest caliber. Thus, Ficino argues, it is quite easy to see why the studious philosopher is prone to both madness and stupidity.[73]

In the Third Book the concept of spirit is widened beyond its technical medical meaning. Ficino accepts the Stoic-inspired theory of astral influences that posits a world-spirit, flowing through the entire sensible cosmos, which provides a channel between the stars and the earth. Since the world is one animate being, its soul, like our own human souls, must have an instrument that transmits its power to its own body. The medium of the world-soul and the world-body is not made out of the four humors or the four elements, but is an element or essence unto itself, the fifth essence. Here Ficino agrees with Aristotle, that the fifth essence is an incorruptible ether, which contains the powers of the lower four elements. This world-spirit is 'a very subtle body, as if it were not body and almost soul. Or again, as if it were not soul and almost body. Its power contains very little earthly nature, but more watery, still more aerial, and the maximum of fiery and astral nature ... It brings to life everything, everywhere, and is the immediate cause of all generation and motion.' The world-spirit is similar enough to human spirits that it can nourish and purify our souls by attracting and absorbing them: 'Without doubt, the world lives and breathes, and we may absorb its breath through our spirits.' This can be done by making it yet more similar to the fifth essence, by making it as celestial as possible. There are many ways to accomplish this work

---

[71] See also Yates, 1964, pp. 62–83

[72] On the humoral doctrine and melancholy in Ficino, see Klibansky et al., 1964, pp. 254–72.

[73] See Walker, 1958, pp. 3–4; the medical model of spirits as very fine particles mediating between the bodily organs and the soul is similar to the model employed by Descartes, as we shall see below.

in addition to the mental contemplation of divine things; these ways involve the magical use of music, plants and charms.[74]

The Third Book forms an excursus to Ficino's commentary on Plotinus' *Enneads*, whose central text is a passage (Enn. 4.3.11) where Plotinus briefly mentions the magical animation of cult statues. For Plotinus, this specific example of magical craft is an instance of the soul's ability to affect bodies, and it exerted an extraordinary influence on Proclus, Porphyry and Iamblichus, whose works Ficino knew well. Plotinus claimed that the seminal reasons (*logoi spermatikoi*), associated with Soul as the intermediary between Mind and Body, linked species or forms in matter with ideas in Mind. 'The soul of the world', Ficino said, 'possesses at least as many seminal reasons of things as there are ideas in the divine mind, and with these reasons [Soul] makes the same number of species in matter. Thus, each and every species corresponds through its own seminal reason to an idea, and often through this reason it can easily receive something of value from on high.' In Copenhaver's words, 'seminal reasons were the dynamic terms in a system of causation and communication joining material objects to immaterial ideas through the medium of Soul. ... Equipped with this metaphysical information, the philosopher-magician had reason to manipulate species of material objects to attract the higher immaterial powers with which they are joined through Soul and its *logoi*.'[75] Ficino agreed with the Thomistic doctrine that the substantial form of any material object is educed from its material potency by the power of the heavenly bodies, in virtue of every body's participation in the divine scheme of things, whose perfect expression is the starry heavens.

In this chapter Plotinus argued that the efficacy of prayer and magic does not show that the gods intend the specific effects of these human acts; they are not the effective consequences of prayers as direct causes. Rather, the response to the magical charm or invocation springs spontaneously from the organic sympathies that bind the living cosmos together. Plotinus did not make any distinction between two kinds of magic, natural and demonic, rather it became an important distinction brought into play by his theurgical interpreters, and one that proved crucial in Renaissance efforts to maintain the probity and propriety of magical doctrines against Christian dogma. Copenhaver has examined Ficino's use of Neo-Platonic texts, the Corpus Hermetica, and the Arabic treatise *Pimander* in great detail and draws an admonitory conclusion. The great reviver of Plato and Plotinus ends his Third Book with studied ambiguity; the idea of religious magic, aimed at contemplation and union with the divine nature, would have been seductive to his Platonist leanings, 'but the Christian in him must have trembled to approach heaven on paths not blessed by the church.' Contrary to scholarly opinion, Ficino's theory of natural magic 'cannot reasonably be called Hermetic any more than it can be called Galenic or Thomist'; although he had already translated the fourteen tractates in the Corpus Hermetica, he cites them nowhere in *Three Books on Life*. Copenhaver's

---

[74] Walker, 1958, pp. 12–13; in Plato's dialogue, Charmides wanted to make a charm or amulet to ward off headaches; Socrates referred to charms as 'noble words or discourses' (Charm. 157a); ordinary Greeks commonly employed magical amulets or charms (*epōdē*), most of which contained written incantations.

[75] Copenhaver, in CHRP, 1988, p. 276.

choice of words is quite robust in this respect: he says that the Hermetica contain little of any philosophical value, they are 'banal expressions of spirituality', they have 'little to offer anyone who requires a consistent conceptual and terminological framework for analysis of the problems it presents'.[76]

However, this does not mean that Ficino did not accord astral and talismanic magic efficacy as operations carried out on the natural affinities between material objects.[77] If these charms or talismans were cleared of any demonic influence, then they could be used with safety, as Thomas Aquinas himself had admitted (SCG 3.104–5). As long as the marks were not words, which could only be addressed to another intelligence, but if they were images or pictures then they could 'capture' the essential character of the composite object. The graphic figure is something like a substance since it locates the artificial composite in a species. 'The engraving of the figure put the talisman in the species (the *taxis* of Proclus) of its heavenly analogue, thus assuring their taxonomic kinship', Copenhaver continues. 'And the truly expert *magus*, who had read his Aquinas, would also stimulate an ontological connection by matching a material quality of the talisman, such as its colour, taste or texture, to the series of forms, earthly and heavenly, with which the talisman was meant to communicate.' Ficino also endorsed the Thomistic notion of hidden or occult qualities associated with the substantial forms educed in matter by stellar and planetary powers.

Angela Voss is more positive than Copenhaver in her assessment of Ficino's appropriation of Neo-Platonic natural magic. Iamblichus thought that for the soul to succeed in its attempts at ascent, it first had to strip off its habitual ways of thought to come into contact with 'an innate knowledge of the gods co-existent with our very essence'. Ficino reserved the term 'notion' to translate this idea of divinely instilled innate knowledge,[78] and expanded upon this at some length. He considered it to be 'a preeminent, intuitive, experiential contact with the profoundest level of being, quite distinct from any conceptual mental activity'. Following logical rules of right reasoning will never lead to the realization of one's own divinity, he cautioned. Instead, Ficino declared, 'the perfect efficacy of ineffable works, which are divinely performed in a way surpassing all intelligence, and the power of inexplicable symbols, which are known only to the gods, impart theurgic union.' Voss draws a salutary lesson from this attitude:

> Thus images, prayers, invocations, talismans – in whatever ritual use appropriate for the particular condition of the individual – may all contribute to the process of realigning his or her soul. It is important to understand that divination does not originate from the energies used in everyday life, or from human fabrications or ingenuity. Rather, the devotion, intent and desire of the operator will allow a superior power to 'perfect' the ritual and impart its authority to it. In other words, human beings may partake of Divine Revelation through their own efforts.[79]

---

[76] Copenhaver, in CHRP, 1988, pp. 280–81.

[77] On Ficino's advocacy of natural magic, see Walker, 1958, pp. 36–55.

[78] As George Berkeley did in his last major work, *Siris* (1744), for which see Chapter 8, sec. 2.

[79] Voss, 2000, p. 4.

In the year 1484, under the astrological conjunction of Saturn and Jupiter, Ficino decided to publish his translation of Plato's dialogues. But this date was highly significant for another reason, since on the very day it appeared Pico arrived in Florence and persuaded Ficino to translate Plotinus. The great Florentine Platonist himself thought the coincidence was symbolic: 'It would seem to be divinely brought about that while Plato was, so to speak, being reborn, Pico was born under Saturn in Aquarius. In fact I too was born thirty years earlier under the same sign. And so, arriving in Florence on the day that our Plato was produced, the old wish of the hero Cosimo de Medici [to translate Plotinus] which had previously been hidden from me, was divinely inspired in Pico, and through Pico in me.'[80] Pico's arrival was to inaugurate a new stage in the appropriation of Platonic metaphysics and Neo-Platonic magic into Renaissance debates on the compatibility of philosophical rationality and theological faith. But where Pico began his precocious work in expanding the mystical-hermetic ancestry of the revitalized Platonism, he was to finish his very short life's work by back-pedaling on many principles that Ficino had held dear.

Giovanni Pico della Mirandola (1463–94) studied canon law at Bologna, and then scholastic philosophy in Ferrara, Padua and Paris. Through his interest in Averroes, he began to study Hebrew and Arabic, an unusual linguistic accomplishment at that time, and one that was to prove decisive in his grand scheme to unify the various ancient strands of *prisca sapientia*. In the autumn of 1486, Pico wrote the *Oration on Human Dignity* to introduce his most audacious project, the *Conclusions*, nine hundred theses he intended to publicly defend in Rome early the next year. Pope Innocent VIII was seriously concerned about various heterodox opinions in these *Conclusions* and attempted to forestall the public disputation by appointing an official commission to investigate them, but Pico pre-empted this move by having them printed. The Papal Commission found three theses heretical and ten suspect, so Pico then printed an *Apology* which was so weak that the Pope felt obliged to condemn the entire work. Although Pico originally intended that the *Oration* should only introduce the main arguments in the *Conclusions*, the text took on a life of its own after his death. It is a powerful and disturbing tract, though open to many divergent interpretations and attempts to situate its exact context. Copenhaver and Schmitt said:

> Pico's theological adventures may have been imprudent and provocative, but there was no insincerity in his wanting to die in a friar's habit nor any inconsistency in the friendship with Savonarola that guided his final years ... The meaning of Pico's *Oration* still evades the learned consensus which has settled these other points; it may be that the form, content, and history of this best-known of all Renaissance philosophical texts have doomed it to ambiguity.[81]

Where Ficino had added a metaphysical dimension to humans' central place in the divine scheme of things as the master of earthly creation, Pico claimed that God had endowed humans with the power to transcend their earthly condition. He

---

[80] Quoted by Voss, 2001, p. 4.
[81] Copenhaver & Schmitt, 1992, p. 165.

confabulated his own version of the Genesis account of humans' creation and pictured God telling Adam before the Fall from Grace that, unlike all other creatures, humans had no fixed place. Through the exercise of his own free will, Adam could choose either a lower animal status or a higher nearly divine status. Pico advised human beings, through Adam's example, to emulate the Cherubim, the second angelic rank below the Seraphim. The Seraphim have their being in an intense love of God, the Cherubim in contemplation, and the third rank, the Thrones, in judgment. Pico claimed that the pursuit of wisdom in philosophy teaches humans how to live like these angelic intellects, who can rise to divine peace or descend to the world and engage in an active life. He viewed this epistemic pursuit as a gradual ascent, but not a discipline or ascesis as Augustine had advocated; instead the soul's journey ended in an earthly death and a spiritual union with other souls conjoined in the highest mind. He described this stepwise inner movement in terms taken from the ancient Stoics: moral teachings tames the passions, dialectic calms the storms of discursive reason, and natural philosophy deals with diversity of opinions about the natural world and humans' place in it. The final stage of this *progressus* leads to theological peace which Pico phrased in words taken from mystical initiation (*epopteia*).[82]

Pico declared that he had roamed through all the great philosophers looking for 'scraps of true belief' and came to think of these pieces as fragments of a greater whole. In this regard he planned a vast syncretistic project that would reconcile the main principles of Plato and Aristotle *and* those who had taken their inspiration from one or both of these thinkers, such as Aquinas, Duns Scotus, Averroes and Avicenna. Pico's grand project was indeed more ambitious than any before him had attempted, since the concord he discerned behind the philosophical masters would be further strengthened by other ancient 'wisdom teachings'. Those teachings he intended to build into his system included Pythagoras' number cosmology, Orphic and Chaldean mysticism, the Hermetic Corpus, natural and demonic magic, and the Jewish Cabala. After citing these venerable soul-guides, Pico concluded with a metaphor that connects his uncovery of such teachings with the veiled presence of a hidden god in the ancient mysteries:[83]

> As was the practice of the ancient theologians, even so did Orpheus protect the mysteries of his dogmas with the coverings of fables, and conceal them with a poetic veil, so that whoever should read his hymns would suppose there was nothing beneath them beyond idle tales and perfectly pure trifles ... What a task it was for me, how difficult it was to draw out the hidden meanings of the secrets of philosophy from the deliberate tangle of riddles and from the obscurity of fables, especially since I have been aided, in a matter so serious, so abstruse, and so little known, by no toil, no application on the part of other interpreters.

He had little respect or patience for his detractors who 'barked like dogs' at his labors, who had wanted to do no more than tear down everything he had done. Thus he has been compelled to speak and 'join battle to the sound of a trumpet'; or, in his

---

[82] Pico, in CKR, 1968, pp. 223–32; see Trinkhaus, 1970, vol. II, pp. 505–29.
[83] On Pico's use of ancient Greek initiatory imagery, see Wind, 1967, pp. 8–11.

own ringing words, 'I have wished to give assurance by this contest of mine, not so much that I know many things, as that I know things of which many are ignorant.'[84] In saying this he carries forward the theme of learned ignorance found in Petrarch and Cusanus.

The main body of the *Conclusions* comprises nine hundred statements, divided into six groups; the last two groups, Pico said, represented his own position. A large proportion of the first four groups are synoptic statements drawn from ancient, patristic and scholastic philosophers, but also includes Orpheus, the Hermetica and Neo-Platonism; his favorites were Proclus, from whom he took fifty-five theses, and the Cabbala, with forty-seven theses. The thirteen theses that troubled the church authorities covered a wide variety of topics: whether the controversial patristic writer Origen had been saved, how the cross has been venerated, how the sacrament of the Eucharist works, whether God can assume an irrational nature, and others. He also proposed answers to three questions considered heretical by the commission: in descending to hell Christ was not really present, raising the problem of an incorporeal being's location; in claiming that mortal sins were punished forever in hell he argued that there was an insupportable disproportion between finite causes and infinite effects. But his most troubling claim was that the sciences of magic and Cabbala provided certainty about Christ's divine nature. Perhaps Pico meant to contrast the great miracles performed by Christ with the lesser wonders of natural magic and Cabbala, but the judges interpreted this outrageous declaration as a threat to the divine science of theology. Pico tried to defend his position by distinguishing between practical Cabbala as magical technique for manipulating names and symbols, and theoretical Cabbala as the right path for contemplation of the divine attributes.[85]

But Pico's various half-hearted attempts at apology were not enough and he fled from Florence, roaming from university to university in search of greater knowledge about the 'pristine theology'. His primary focus at this time was on the Jewish mystical teachings, first introduced to him by Elia del Medigo in Padua; but his real Hebrew teacher was Samuel Abulfaraj (also known as Guglielmo Moncado and Flavius Mithridates) whom he had met in Florence. Abulfaraj translated thousands of pages of Hebrew text for Pico, including the twelfth-century *Book of Splendor*, commentaries on Maimonides, and Recanati's fourteenth-century interpretation of the Torah. Pico's employment of Hebrew material in the *Conclusions* and the short treatise *Heptaplus* was unprecedented and was to have an immense influence on Christian Cabbalists for centuries. Charles Lohr provides an admirable summary of Pico's use of the Cabbala:

> Cabbala ... was essentially a method of contemplation on God's attributes. Man can know nothing of God's hidden, inner nature. Only through his attributes can man know something of the divine life. The attributes describe God's inner life and are not – like the Neoplatonic emanations – outside of him. They name the stages in which the divine life pulsates. Cabala used ... the image of the tree to describe the way in which creation reflects this divine life. God's inner nature is the hidden root of the tree, while the

---

[84] Pico, in CKR, 1968, pp. 253–4.
[85] Copenhaver & Schmitt, 1992, pp. 168–9.

attributes are represented by its branches. The tree forms the skeleton of the universe, spreading its branches throughout the whole of creation to form the primordial man, Adam ... Cabala used techniques for manipulating letters of the Hebrew alphabet in order to discover such hidden meanings behind the text of the Bible. It was believed that when God gave the law to Moses, he also revealed to the chosen its secret meaning. This cabalistic tradition was said to have been passed down orally through the ages.[86]

Pico's prodigious, if somewhat eccentric, reading led him to infer that Cabbalistic teachings were similar to the core ideas of Pythagorean doctrine and the mystical Platonic doctrines expounded by Ficino:

> In the *Oration* Pico tells us that when he had procured the books of the science of cabala, he found in them a religion which was not so much Mosaic as it was Christian: the mystery of the Trinity, the Incarnation of the word, the divinity of the Messiah, the same things about original sin, its expiation by Christ and the end of the world that we read in Paul and Dionysius the Areopagite, in Jerome and Augustine. Similarly, in the *Heptaplus* Pico maintained that Moses hid, behind the account of creation, not only all the secrets of philosophy, but also fore-shadowings of the coming of Christ. The mutual correspondences found in creation between the angelic, celestial and elemental worlds lead by way of the microcosm – which is man – to Christ, through whom alone creation can return to the creator.[87]

The brief but intricate text of the *Heptaplus* employed an intersecting Cabbalistic and Neo-Platonic scheme of four worlds: the supracelestial, the celestial, the sublunary and the human realms. By means of this cosmic division Pico attempted to justify a sevenfold system of cosmic order that corresponded to the six days of active creation and the seventh day of rest. Pico made ingenious use of the threefold design of the tabernacle, the triune nature of God, the seven-branched menorah candle, and related gematric devices to connect the hidden meanings of the Hebrew Genesis account. But he also discussed the human condition in a manner that has led some scholars to think that the author had been chastened by the church's punitive measures. Here Pico claims that the human body and soul correspond to heaven and earth, joined together by a third spiritual substance. The intellectual and sensory faculties of human beings had analogies with the biblical waters above and below heaven: 'Humankind is not so much a fourth world, like some new creature, as the bond and union of the three already described.' Where before he had said that humans lacked a proper nature, but had the power to attain the natural properties they aspired to, he now said that 'humankind contains all things in itself as their centre.' Even if Pico had toned down his more extreme views, he still strongly held to an optimistic vision of human excellence and dignity.[88]

In the short work that appeared two years after the *Heptaplus*, the treatise *De ente et uno*, Pico no longer propounded these various proofs for the threefold division of worlds and humankind, but instead argued around the central notion

---

[86] Lohr in CHRP, 1988, p. 580; see esp. G. G. Scholem, *On the Kabbalah and its Symbolism*, Ralph Manheim, trans. New York: Schocken Books, 1996.
[87] Lohr in CHRP, 1988, p. 581.
[88] Copenhaver & Schmitt, 1992, pp. 173–4.

that God dwells in darkness. In order to ascend into the dark cloud where God dwells, humans must enter into the light of ignorance; by this he meant that all affirmations and negations about God's nature are equally impossible. At this stage in his rapidly changing exploration of pristine theology, all references to Orpheus, Hermes, the Neo-Platonists, the Cabbala, and so forth have been excised. Pico attempted a full frontal assault on Ficino's account of Platonic metaphysics and adopted the Christianized Aristotelian position of Thomas Aquinas. As Charles Lohr says: 'The rejection of the idea of a higher type of intellectual knowledge, through which the dynamic implications of the Christian doctrines of the Trinity and Incarnation could be harnessed for a new metaphysics, involved a radical change in the Renaissance view of man. Although Pico makes an appeal for the unity of mankind based on oneness, truth and goodness, his idea of man ... had become an abstract idea.' In this section of the treatise Pico's words reflect St. Paul's words in his Letter to the Colossians, but without mentioning the resurrection of humans' spiritual body. In doing so, however, he follows Aquinas' interpretation of this basic Christian message, and not Augustine's Platonized interpretation. One consequence of this discursive move is the repudiation of Ficino's attempt 'to introduce a dynamic moment into the divine unity by transferring a number of the attributes of the Plotinian mind to the One. To establish the agreement of Plato and Aristotle on Thomistic terms he was compelled to abandon the active conception of reality which had, up to his time, been the foremost characteristic of Renaissance philosophy.'[89]

Pico's critique of astrology and magic, *Disputationes adversus astrologiam divinatricem*, was published only after his death in 1496. In its Third Book he endorsed some of the main tenets of Ficino's theory of astral influence, namely, that the heavens are the cause of all motion and life in the world below the moon. The source of motion and life is a cosmic heat that contains in perfection and virtue all the elemental qualities. This cosmic heat is conveyed by celestial spirit which penetrates everywhere and in doing so nourishes, tempers, informs and vivifies all things. The cosmic spirit is akin to the spirit which unites soul and body in humans and animals; it is 'a very fine, invisible body, most closely akin to the light and heat of the stars'. The spirits in animals 'are not capable of generating or preserving bodies, or performing the functions of sense perceptions, unless they have the help of celestial spirit, which since it is more mobile, efficacious, and thus closer to life, strengthens the infirmity of the inferior [that is, animal] spirit and, by its commerce with it, makes it more akin to the soul.'[90] Pico stressed that matter was the single cause of disorder, irregularity and imperfection in the earthly realm and stated that to regard the stars as the cause of individual phenomena was to deny their essential nature and intrinsic dignity: 'Having restricted the influence of the stars to the Aristotelian principles of motion, heat and light, Pico divorced philosophy, understood as the correct attitude towards nature, from astrology, magic and any other superstitious practice.'[91] This attempt to divorce what had been seen for

---

[89] Lohr in CHRP, 1988, p. 583.
[90] Quote from Walker, 1958, pp. 55–6.
[91] Ingegno, in CHRP, 1988, p. 240; on Pico's magic, see Thorndike, vol. IV, pp. 485–8, 493–8, 508–11, 529–43; Walker, 1958, pp. 54–9, 146–51.

centuries by some thinkers as an intimate linkage between the contemplative metaphysics of the natural world and the active magical operations based on that metaphysics encountered resistance from many quarters. But Pico's position was defended by many other thinkers, and the major scientific discoveries in the next two centuries were to reinforce the skeptical derogation of occult and hermetic interpretations of natural philosophy. To some degree, the cumulative effects of the skeptical challenge, ecclesiastical condemnations and natural scientific progress were to drive the heterodox currents of occult philosophy underground.

In November 1494, Pico della Mirandola died in mysterious circumstances (some suspected he had been poisoned); he died on the very day that an invading army occupied Florence, now deserted by the de Medicis. Ficino survived Pico by five years, but he had noted the extraordinary coincidences of Pico's short, meteoric career: born when Ficino received the commission to translate Plato's dialogues, arrived in Florence on the day Ficino's edition of Plotinus was printed, and died at the close of the golden age of Medician Platonism. Charles Lohr makes a very strong claim about this terminal date:

> the continuity of the [Platonic] tradition which understood reality dynamically ... was broken or became at least irrelevant for metaphysics as the science of God. After Pico, the history of metaphysics shifted from the problem of God to the problem of being ... [But] the tradition of a dynamic understanding of reality which had been represented by Lull, Nicholas of Cusa and Ficino became associated with Renaissance magic and occultism. The idea of man's creativity was paralleled by the notion of a magical control over nature and by the vision of a new technology. These ideas led, in turn, to the demand for a new system of the sciences.[92]

But these ideas also formed the basis for the great magical *summae* that populate the other, more hidden stream of speculative thought about human nature.

The occult and magical stream of thought had existed for several centuries before the apogee of the Florentine Academy under Ficino, but Ficino deserves the utmost credit for setting forth this philosophy's venerable ancestry, especially through the texts of the Thrice-Greatest Hermes, the first and most pure of the pristine theologians. Within the compass of this present work[93] it is simply not feasible to discuss the manifold shapes taken on by the magical, occult metaphysics of a dynamic, spiritual reality in the centuries before the triumph of a natural philosophy grounded in an empirical physics. The most that can be done here is to headline those figures who bodied forth those many shapes.[94] The pre-eminent figures include Cornelius Agrippa (1486–1535) who, in Copenhaver's scathing words, 'overwhelmed his blatantly derivative theory with a tonnage of recipes and anecdotes that leave the impression of chaotic wonder-mongering'. Paracelsus

---

[92] Lohr in CHRP, 1988, p. 584,

[93] Detailed examination of these writers' concepts of soul, mind and spirit might comprise a major chapter in the second volume of the *History of the Concept of Mind*.

[94] For an impartial but brief assessment, see Copenhaver & Schmitt, 1992, pp. 303–28; see also the expert but more polemical analyses by Copenhaver, in CHRP, 1988, pp. 285–96; Yates, 1964, pp. 130–56.

(1493–1541), in Copenhaver's words again, 'transferred to the plane of natural philosophy or natural magic the mystic's direct, inward vision of God's word. Likewise, faith more than learning became the basis of the Paracelsian magician's operations, as of the Christian mystic's union with God.' Girolamo Cardano (1501–76) wrote over two hundred works on medicine, mathematics, physics, theology, music, and whatever else struck his fancy. Della Porta (1535–1615) wrote on astrology, the art of memory, natural magic, various forms of divination, and several stageplays. He thought that natural magic should be the complement of scientific investigation; and stressed that the interrelation between soul and body could be understood through the concept of inner correspondence. Bernardino Telesio (1509–88) taught that empirical observation and sense perception are the only true foundations of natural philosophy, that spirit was the most potent combination of heat and matter, and that this material soul performed all the psychic functions necessary for human life. Tommaso Campanella (1568–1639), member of the Dominican Order, was twice censured for his Telesian opinions, but disregarded his superiors; arrested and imprisoned many times over nearly thirty years, he maintained that the world was a sentient animal whose parts partake in one and the same kind of life.

Giordano Bruno (1548–1600) deserves a special place in this brief review of later Renaissance occult philosophy. Bruno was one of the first serious proponents of Copernicus' heliocentric hypothesis, argued for an infinite universe, unbound by celestial 'orbs', considered the stars to be other suns around which earth-like planets revolved, and rejected the church as an authority on issues of natural reason.[95] His second Italian dialogue, *Cause, Principle and Unity* follows immediately after his first, *La Cena de le Ceneri* (*The Ash Wednesday Supper*), which, with four other Italian titles, were first published in London after his visit to England in 1584–85. Bruno's Copernican arguments had an unfriendly, even contemptuous reception at Oxford University, and the *Supper* is to some extent an account of that confrontation, filtered through the Nolan's savage and clever parodies of English Scholastics and Neo-Aristotelians.[96] He continued this line of argument through his spokesman Filoteo in the five dialogues of *Cause, Principle and Unity*, of which the first is an apology and synopsis of the *Supper*. In the brief, highly incisive Introduction, the Italian scholar Alfonso Ingegno comments that Bruno had attempted to reunify terrestrial with celestial physics on the basis of a principle of universal becoming. From this metaphysical basis, he moves on to derive a new concept of the divinity which was to assume a radically anti-Christian character. This doctrine led in some measure to his condemnation and eventual execution at the hands of the Inquisition in 1600, when he had been found to be 'an impenitent, stubborn and obstinate heretic'. In limpid terms, Copenhaver and Schmitt express their dismay at this gruesome sentence: 'Bruno burned for philosophy; he was killed for moral, physical, and metaphysical views that terrified and angered the authorities. While pondering our irritations with his changes on such questions, it will be well to recall the price he paid to the hobgoblin of little minds and the demon of clear convictions.'[97]

---

[95] Ingegno, in CHRP, 1988, pp. 254–6, 293–4.
[96] On his visit to England, see Yates, 1982, pp. 210–21, and esp. Bossy, 1992.
[97] Copenhaver & Schmitt, 1992, p. 315.

Two of Bruno's other works, *On Magic* and *General Account of Bonding (De Vinculis in Genera)* were composed during Bruno's visits to Prague and Helmstedt in 1588–90 and copied by an admirer named Besler. In these two short works, Bruno focused his attention on the notion of cognitive or spiritual 'contraction' through which the magus can realize certain powers. But, he said, this can have an opposite effect if the magical power is directed towards a higher level or if it is carried out so as to render the agent no longer master but servant of his imagination. Bruno's concept of bonding refers to a spiritual linkage which the magus establishes between himself and another soul. Ingegno remarks that 'the magus is acquainted with the dynamics not only of magic but also of demonic action, and knows how demons can take possession of us through unguarded avenues, and this opens up to him a new field of action, permitting him to link other men to himself and, in fact, to establish a whole series of magical bonds between himself and others.'[98]

Hilary Gatti concisely blocks out the two principal orientations which Bruno studies have taken in the past half-century and carefully situates her own reaction to the Yates-inspired reading of Bruno as an Hermetic and Magical thinker:[99]

> It appeared to me that [Bruno's] attention was more often directed elsewhere, to subjects such as the new cosmology and the revival of ancient atomism, to number theory and the possibility of investigating, measuring, and mapping out anew the shape of the natural world. To stress these aspects of his thought could well seem a simple return to earlier readings of Bruno, which tended to treat with distaste his references to magic, astrology and the art of memory ... But was it really necessary to denigrate those aspects of Bruno's thought? I became convinced that Bruno's concern with such subjects ... could be seen as surrounding and complementing his concern with the new science.[100]

Gatti attempts to explain what it means for Hermetic and magical thought to 'surround' and 'complement' his concerns with natural-scientific hypotheses about terrestrial and celestial physics. The Copernican elements in several Bruno texts, especially the *Supper* and *De Immenso*, show that Bruno was able to appreciate some of the grander implications of the heliocentric theory, including most importantly the insight that the physics of matter most closely associated with pre-Copernican cosmology would have to be abandoned. Despite the fact that Bruno himself never made any astronomical observations, and seemed to genuinely disparage experimental investiagtion, he was able to make some improvements (as well as some mistakes) in the celestial model. His main achievements center

---

[98] Ingegno, in Bruno, 1998, Introduction, p. xxvii.

[99] Where Frances Yates insisted on seeing Bruno (almost) entirely as the last great exponent of the Hermetic or Occult tradition and relegated his natural-scientific, metaphysical and ethical theses to the status of eclectic rhetorical devices and digressions, recent Bruno scholars, such as Ramon Mendoza, G. Aquilecchia, Rita Sturlese (whose excellent research remains mostly untranslated) and others, have reversed this interpretation, stressing the importance of his forward-looking picture of the cosmos and bracketing his magical and occult remarks as literary allusions.

[100] Gatti, 1999, p. 7; echoed by Copenhave & Schmitt, 1992, pp. 316–17.

around five hypotheses: an infinite universe, an order of infinite worlds, the concept of a minimal unit, an idiosyncratic understanding of mathematics, and a visual or pictorial logic:

> Bruno uses both neo-Platonic and Hermetic sources and vocabulary to express his sense of the divinity of his infinite universe [and] questions such as the nature of death, the problem of time, and the immortality of the soul. It is a mistake, however, to separate the consideration of such aspects of his thought from his natural philosophy. Precisely because Bruno sees the infinite material substance as rationally ordered by the divine intelligence, its infinite extension must necessarily assume a coherent physical ontology which he expresses as an infinite number of worlds.[101]

Bruno himself was a great soul, and in his many works he staunchly held that the human soul is great indeed due to its place in the cosmic order. Although Bruno often drew on Aristotle's matter-form account of the human soul, he made severe modifications such that matter and form no longer comprise independent principles of explanation. Copenhaver and Schmitt claim that Bruno did not care about individual human beings, but thought that particular things of any kind were no more distinct than ripples in the calm sea of being:

> Nature thrives and breeds transitory forms out of living matter through her own internal force of soul. The single universal form is the world-soul that drives things from within as their principle. Causes that act externally are superficial; a deeper dynamism belongs to principles that move inside. Matter and form unite in the infinite substance that comprehends all ... Individual souls in Bruno's system cannot be discrete specific forms because soul is really one; what enlivens a human and a fly are fragments of the same world-soul, which is like a light reflected in a shattered mirror whose splinters are the souls of particular beings.[102]

Bruno's dreadful death at the hands of the Roman Inquisition in 1600 symbolically marks the end of the figure of the two-faced philosopher-magician, one who could reasonably and confidently maintain both the Magical-Hermetic view of occult powers hidden in the natural world *and* the empirical-scientific view that intelligible laws governing these powers were disclosable to rational inquiry. Within a few decades of Bruno's death, the Cartesian-Galilean understanding of the mathematical order of the natural world and the mechanical laws that govern change and motion would definitively overthrow the fundamental principles of the late medieval and Renaissance picture of a dynamic, spiritual nature. The model of a world-machine would supplant the model of a world-spirit, imbued with celestial and terrestrial intelligences that could be intuited and handled by wisdom-seekers. Wisdom would no longer be the special endowment or privilege of a few initiates, but a collective achievement that can be realized through cooperative endeavors, pieces of which can become available to anyone with the right scientific education. The occult philosophy and its many heterodox variants are not so much driven underground as channeled into side-roads, away from the

---

[101] Gatti, 1999, p. 122; see also in agreement Copenhaver & Schmitt, 1992, pp. 298–9.
[102] Copenhaver & Schmitt, 1992, p. 315.

main highway; dusty roads traveled by amateur alchemists, juridical astrologers, counterfeiters, and the other conjurers and tricksters commonly satirized by the Elizabethan and Jacobean playwrights.

Chapter 6
Mind and Soul in English from Chaucer to Shakespeare

(1) The various senses of 'soul' from 1200 to 1500

The key psychical term 'mind' in English derives its root-sense from Latin *mens, mentis*, which itself perhaps has its root source in Greek *menos*, but clearly comprises meanings associated with *nous*, especially after Aristotle's definitive statement in *De Anima*, chapter three. But 'mind' also subsumes connotations associated with Latin *animus* (m.), in contrast with *anima* (f.), a linguistic subtlety first articulated in Cicero's *Tusculan Disputations* and Lucretius' *On the nature of things*. The key term 'spirit' has a collateral source in Latin *spiritus*, used by the early Church Fathers, especially Jerome in the Vulgate, to translate the Hellenistic and LXX term *pneuma*, although *pneuma* was also used as a technical Stoic term for the special material stuff which accounted for the lifelike properties of beings with *psychē* or *anima*. English language use of 'psyche' and all its cognates, as well as 'animal', 'animistic', 'animate', and so forth exhibit solid, well-attested lines of development. *Anima* (f.) is the Latin term used by Cicero, Lucretius and the early Church Fathers to render the Greek *psychē* in the cluster of meanings stabilized around it in the Middle and Late Platonic dialogues and in Aristotle. But the source and trajectory of the English word 'soul' is very different from any of the above; it does not have Latin or Greek ancestors, but springs from Anglo-Saxon, Old English and Middle English usage. It is the task of this chapter to show how the English word 'soul' was best suited to render the same or similar concepts for which Greek had used *psychē* and Latin had used *anima*.

The exhaustive philological analyses undertaken by the editors of the *Middle English Dictionary* provide a very detailed, comprehensive catalogue of thousands of instances in the usage of soul-words during the period *c.* 1150 to 1500. The compilers of the entry for 'soul' divide the principal meanings into fourteen categories, of which the first eight are relevant to our inquiry:[1]

1. The spiritual and rational element in humans: (a) to animate and control the body; (b) to have an eternal destiny as a moral agent; (c) to be engaged in a moral struggle with the body; (d) in contrast or in combination with the body.
2. The disembodied spirit of a dead person, or the soul of a transported person in an ecstasy.

---

[1] MED, Part S.11, 1989, pp. 295–308; very helpful short summaries of most of the principal figures and anonymous works of this period can be found in Bennett, 1965, pp. 264–318.

246   *History of the Concept of Mind*

3   (a) One of three species or types of soul; (b) the animating principle of beast or human; (c) the principle of bodily life in humans; (d) a living creature.
4   (a) In Biblical passages, a person or an individual; (b) pronominal for myself or himself; (c) a human in light of his spiritual condition; (d) the whole being of a person.
5   The soul's faculty of understanding divine truths, mysteries or visions.
6   The mind or intellect; also occasionally, the imagination.
7   The seat of emotions and feelings; to set one's heart on some thing.
8   The will or purpose or desire, as intentional direction.

Nearly half of all instances in the entire entry fall under the first heading, whose most basic concept seems to be the principle of life or life-force in animal beings, which in humans is manifest as the rational governance of the bodily nature, itself referred to in a broader sense of 'soul'.

An outstanding expression of this core meaning comes from John Trevisa[2] (one of the Wycliffite translators) in his translation of Bartholomew's *De Proprietatibus Rerum* (*c.*1400), which in several closely connected passages gives clear expression to the notion of life-force, the place of the heart and mind in this scheme, its overt equation with the Latin *anima*, and, perhaps most noticeably, an emphatically philosophical attitude to these issues and others:

> [a] Remigius diffineth a soule in this manere: a soule is a bodiles substaunce rulinge a body. [b] The soule is noght istreight nothir isprad in lengthe nothir in brede in the body ... but abidinge in the middel of the herte withoute spredinge of hitself geveth lif to alle the body. [c] The soule is [in] a maner spiritual and resonable substaunce that god made of noght for to geve lif and perfectioun to mannes body. [d] And thatte anima while he is in the body and geveth it life, mens while he hath mynde, animus while he hath wille, racio while demeth rightfulliche, spiritus dum spirat breeth, sensus dum senteth felith.

The author is reporting on Remigius of Auxerre,[3] a ninth-century monastic writer, often associated with the Scottish philosopher Eriugena; the author explicitly identifies Remigius' definition of *anima* with 'soul' in the following respects: [a] it is a bodiless or incorporeal substance that rules the body; [b] it is unextended, neither in spread or length or breadth of the body; [c] it is in some way spiritual and rational insofar as God gave the body life, and in so doing made it perfect; [d] while the *anima* (f.) is in the body it supplies life to the body, *mens* while it has mind, *animus* (m.) while he has will, *ratio* (reason) while he exercises right-thinking or acting, *spiritus* while he has breath, and *sensus* while he senses and feels.

The repeated use of 'while' in this passage can be understood in two ways: to mean both *during* bodily life, and *insofar as* the body has life. The fact that the soul is not extended and the further claim that it is simple appears again in the Lambeth ms. of *Secret of Secrets* (*c.*1425): 'man ys maad of body thyke, togedyr mesuryd, and of saule simple, and substance spirituell.' The threefold division of the soul with respect to its various functions or powers had been stated by Chaucer in the

---

[2] Hargreaves, in CHB, vol. 2, 1969, pp. 390, 404.
[3] Marenbon, 1988, pp. 78–9.

Parson's Tale: the 'goodes of nature of the soule be good wit, sharp understondynge, subtil engyn, vertu naturel, [and] good memorie.' In John Trevisa's translation of Higden's *Polychronicon* he says, 'manis soule ... holdeth the lowest degre of spiritis and of gostes that haveth knowleche and understondinge.' The *Cursor Mundi*[4] says: 'An saul has proper thinges three, minning, understand[ing] ... schilwisnes of will.' Somewhat later (*c*.1450) this is expressed in the following terms by Osbern Bokenham: 'Man thou formydyst to thi lykenesse, indewyng hym wyth ... Mynd, Resoun, Wyll & yet essencyally But one soule their ben al three.' And again, 'Richard of Saint Victor settes in a buke, that he makes of contemplacioun, three wyrkyngs of cristen mans saiule ... Thoght, Thynkyng, and Contemplacioun.' In *The Mirror of the Blessed*: 'The sowle hath three strengthes ... racionabilite, concupiscibilite, and irascibilite.' In the historical movement of these statements one can discern an earlier stage in which the three faculties or powers[5] of soul (*anima*) are identified with reason, understanding and the will, and a later stage in which the three powers have taken on decidedly Thomistic and Avicennan connotations, with literal English renderings of Latin terms for rationality, concupiscence and irascibility.

But the most primitive meaning underlying this later, more complex threefold division is the notion of principle of life or life-force.[6] This occurs as early as *c*.1150 in the *Vespasian Homilies*: 'maen he gescop mid gaste & mid lichame; nytene & deor, fisces & fugeles he gescop on flaesce buten sawle.' Some short time later in the *Bodleian Homilies*: 'The sawle sodlice is thaes lichames lif ... Gif deo sawle forlete thone lichame, thone swelt the lichame' (where 'lichame' means 'bodily'). The direct gloss with Latin *anima* appears in another nearby passage: 'hyre nomae is anima, thaet is, sawul & the nomae bilimpaed to hyre lyfe' (where 'bilimpaed' means 'belongs to'). The root-sense of life-force occurs in all the previous citations concerned with the triplex division, and reappears *c*.1425 in *Orch. Syon.*: 'the body in hymsilf is deedly and hath no liif but that it hath of the soule, and as longe as the soule is in the body, so longe it resceveth liif and no lengir.' This statement clearly indicates the mortal stature of human as an ensouled being, or perhaps one might say, insofar as human is considered *merely* in terms of his ensouled character, a human is bound to death. The life-force of soul is sometimes located in the heart or blood, as in *The Memorial of Faith* (*c*.1450): 'wyne gladith the hert in the which is the princepal stede of the soule'; or even earlier, in Shoreham's poems (*c*.1330): 'the bible seythe that mannys blod is hys ryght ther saule giste.'

That the soul alone cannot account for humans' capacity to enter another post-mortem life through redemption in Jesus Christ, is captured in the numerous early uses of soul-words indicating some thing *more* about humans' moral status. For example, *Vices and Virtues* (*c*.1200): 'Durh dessere senne ic, ungesali [troubled] saule, fell in to an oder senne, de is icleped propria voluntas, that is, augen-wille.' Thus, the soul's tendency to fall into other sins, or from one sin to another, is properly called the will. The *Ancrene Wisse* (*c*.1200) also said that, 'the sowle is

---

[4] See CHB, vol. 2, 1969. p. 383.
[5] See Doubleday, 1969, for these three faculties in *The Wanderer*.
[6] See Orton, 1980 on Old English concepts of soul in contrast with body.

widewe the haved forloren hire spus [spouse], thet is iesu crist, wid eni heaved sunne.' An *Apocalypse* from *c.*1350 asserts that, 'by the swerd that kerveth bothe half bitokneth goddes word, that one half departeth the soule fro his desire & that othere half departeth the flesshe fro his delices.' This sentiment is echoed in Chaucer's *Parson's Tale* (*c.*1390): 'naked shul they ben of [or in] soule of alle manere vertues which that is the clothyng of soule'; and further, 'By fastynge ben saved the vices of the flessh and by preyere the vices of the soule.' Here the reference to clothing (and in other instances to garments) takes up the ancient theme of the body in its fleshly dimension as the skin, tent or covering of the soul. In addition, it also shows the intimate relation between the English sense of 'flesh' and the Greek sense conveyed by *sarx*, as well as the Latin *caro*, each equally well indicating the characteristic of human tendency toward sin and falling away from God.

One can also clearly discern the Pauline notion that the so-called 'goods' of the body incline one away from God, and the true 'goods' of the soul incline one toward God. Aelred's *Institutes* (*c.*1400) speak on behalf of all sinners when he says, 'we dredeth so muche syknesse of body that we dredeth to comyngge, that siknesse of soule that we feeleth present we take noon hede of.' *Desert Religion* (*c.*1450) states: 'for when a man for-sakens his flesch and all thyng that delycius es and lyfes in saule be hardnes, than enters he in to wildernes.' The English version of Higden's *History* (*c.*1425) contains two glosses which connect this notion with the Latin version: 'Hit myghte be that spirittes gate gigantes, in whom hugenesse of sawle [or 'gretnesse of herte', Latin *immanitas animorum*] was correspondente to the hugenesse of theire body.' Evident in many passages is the psychical tension between opposing inclinations. On one side, the flesh's delight in earthly pleasures; on the other, the soul's delight in future bliss. Canon Orm's strange attempt (*c.*1200) to harmonize the gospels[7] resulted in some peculiar expressions, but he caught the tone of this internal moral struggle in these lines: 'uss birrth clippenn all awegh the flaeshess fule wille, that allre werrst & allre mast werdeth the wrecche sawle.' At about the same time, the *Ancrene Wisse* says, 'Laurd, thu havest imaket foder to federin wid the sawlen, thet is thet hevie flesch thet drahed hire duneward.' In Gower's *Confessio Amantis* (*c.*1393) he says: 'The bodi and the Soule also among them ben divided so that what thing that the body hateth the soule loveth and debateth.' An anonymous tract (*c.*1450) states that reason holds sway over the moral struggle between body and soul: 'therfore shuld be the soules mocion the flesche to holde under be reason.' In the *Battle Text* (*c.*1500) an unusual identification is made, one that perhaps shows the influence of the author's reading of Plato's *Phaedrus*: 'Take hede of thy horse, whyche ys thy body, that he be made buxome and mylde unto the soule whyche ys hys master.' This is clearly an echo of the *Phaedrus'* image of the driver (reason) ruling two horses, one wild and dark, the other docile and light (though there is no mention of the dark horse).

However, despite the compilers' declaration that the passages which deal with the moral strife between flesh and soul[8] show that soul can be construed as an

---

[7] See CHB, vol. 2, p. 381.
[8] For details, see Canuteson, 1977.

immortal 'part' of human being, there appears to be only privative evidence, that is, deprived of soul humans are indeed death-bound. One has to look elsewhere in the Middle English sources for more positive assertions about the immortal soul. The many references that draw on the root-sense of life-force would seem to preclude this connotation. But perhaps one needs to expand the meaning of life itself to include the kind of life that only the gift of God's spirit can imbue in human being. One paraphrase of *Genesis and Exodus* (*c*.1250) leans in this direction: 'Bi-seke we nu godes might, that he make ure sowles bright ... and lede us to blisse and in to light.' One fourteenth-century catechism says, 'Dede has sondred our bodies and oure saules for a certeyne tyme'; and somewhat later, the prayer *Jesu who art in heaven*, 'for sunne that hath my soule [or herte] bounde thi blisful blod mot be my bote.' And the *Cursor Mundi* draws the link between Christ's life and humans' life in these words: 'That king of all that ai has bene his sete made in hir saul scene, to gesten in hir leif licam.' The *Life of Soul* (*c*.1400) calls the soul's clothing provided by God's teachings the virtues: 'Telle me opunly the virtues that Crist techith to clothe with my soule, that I be not naked in the comyng of my Lord.' The *Dialogue of Reason and Soul* (*c*.1425) says: 'Thoow thi bodi fele bondache, thi soul may perse hevene & have contemplacion of hevene delices.' The soul's power to see into heaven is underlined in another important lexical division, as we shall see.

The root sense of life-force is stressed in numerous passages from the thirteenth to the fifteenth century, but often with some indication that *another* life is vouchsafed through personal acceptance of God's grace. One of the so-called St. Katherine texts[9] (*c*.1225) has its speaker declaim: 'The thet ded me to death ... neome thet he neome mei, thet lif of mi licome; mi sawle ich sende to the [God], healent in heovene.' An equivalent sentiment expressed by the *Ancrene Wisse* about the same date: 'Milci hare sawle the us god idon habbed, hare sawle & alle cristene sawles.' The *Vespasian Homilies* provide a salient clue in this regard, making a clear reference to Augustine, which one could rightfully interpret concerns the Bishop's doctrine of the double life and the double death: 'Augustinus the wise us maned, to ure sawle thearfe, mid thysen worden.' The notion of psychical or soulful healing, in addition to bodily healing, as witnessed by the St. Katherine text above, is taken up in many passages like the following, in the *Bodleian Homily*: 'The sceolden ilome gan to tham halge husle eowre sawle to haele.' *Vices and Virtues* (*c*.1200): 'Hi laened here emcristen ... the fared thar mide be londe and be watere on michele hahte on live and on saule.' The *Gaytrian Catechism*: 'Mikill folke ne serve him [God] als thai shuld do ... In grete peril of thaime to lyve and to sawle.' In the *Parsons Tale*, Chaucer says, in imitation of the NT instruction, 'Love thy neighebore as thy self, that is to seyn, to savacion bothe of lyf and of soule.' Another text about the same date accords the distinction between one and the other life to the soul's goods in contrast, one would think, to the body's goods: 'Hyt ys an ydulnes yn here lyfe, alle that outher man or wyfe travayleth for the lyves fode and lytyl for the soules gode.'

Yet another slight but significant modification of meaning concerns the double or shade of the departed. It seems most likely that the origin of the English word

---

[9] See CHB, vol. 2, 1969, p. 378.

'ghost' in the early and middle period is derived from the Germanic (not Latin) word *geist* which much of the time also rendered the Latin *spiritus*.[10] However, unlike *spiritus* and the Greek NT *pneuma*, the Germanic *geist* and the English 'ghost', 'ghoul', 'ghastly', etc. exclusively refer to the spirit of the dead person, and not to some component or aspect of the living person. According to St. Paul's First Letter to the Corinthians and St. Augustine in Book XIII of *The City of God*, the ensouled body comes to an end with an individual's death and the soul does not gain its spiritual body until the Final Resurrection. Whatever the exact meaning of another life in heaven, the intermediate status of the individual soul, after one and before the other, definitely does *not* comprise some sort of corporeal existence; hence, references to a ghost can only be construed along the lines of a simulacrum or *eidolon*. Amongst other passages, these texts are good examples to establish this psychical nuance of double or shade: *Vices and Virtues* (c.1200) states that, 'swa scule tha gastliche stieres-menn [steersman, that is, guide] steren tha arche of the hali cherche, that hie tharof ne for-liesen ne lichame ne saule'; Lychefelde (c.1450) says that: 'With thi right, lord, mercy mynge, and to my soule goosteli salve thou sende'; and Hoccleve (c.1415) says that: 'The preest, hir soules norice, hem goostly fedde & gaf hem the notice of Crystes lore.'

Lydgate in his *Troy Book* (c.1420) preserves a rare nuance of the soul's second life in connection with reincarnation, but explicitly with regard to Pythagoras: 'A knyght up rose that son was to Euforbius ... in to whom ther was whilom the sowle of Pyctagoras holy transmewed, so as writ Ovide.' As we have seen in our investigation of the non-Greek sources of Presocratic speculation about the immortal soul, characters like Pythagoras, Empedocles and Pherecydes, amongst others, often claimed the power of extra-somatic projection. Through an ecstatic technique of self-induced trance their souls 'traveled' to remote regions of the earth, even into the celestial heavens, or into some future time. In addition to pagan citations of such journeys, the English Bible translations preserve the Biblical notion of prophetic ecstasy in several passages, where the basic idea is usually rendered with the English word 'ravish'. Thus, for example, the Wycliffe Bible (c.1384) identifies this idea with the Latin *mentis excessus* (an interlinear gloss) but translates it with the phrase 'an excess of soul', to some degree obscuring its source in the mind or intellect: 'An axcess of soule, or ravysching of spirit [Latin *mentis excessus*], fel on hym, and he sygh [saw] hevene opnyd.' Then again, making the same unwarranted equation with mind: 'It is don to me, turnynge agen into Jerusalem and preinge in the temple, me for to be maad in ravyssching of soule [Latin *in stupore mentis*] and to see him.' One of the St. Katharine texts (c.1450) predicates this special power of vision to the soul: 'These too persones were lyfte up in soule wiche sightis for to see; Seynt Poule hym-selve was one of thoo that was thus iravyshed.' Tundale about the same date says much the same thing: 'Tundale yn a transynge lay, hys sowle was in a dredefull way ... hit sawe mony a hydwysse payne ere hit come to the body agayne; in purgatorye and in helle all that he saw he cowthe well telle.'

The *Mirror of the Blessed* (c.1500) states, 'the angel of God come to hym and with a ravyschynge toke his sowle and bare it up into hevene, and there it sawe the

---

10 OED s.v. 'ghost', vol. VI, pp. 492–4.

kynge of kyngis sitte in an hye precious sete.' This usage is intimately related to the fifth principal division under the entry 'soul', that is, the soul's faculty of understanding divine truths, mysteries, visions and the future. For example, in an *Apocalypse* from the mid-fourteenth century: 'The third manere of sight is cleped intellectuel, that is, whan the gost alighteth the understondyng of the soules & doth hem seen ... the privetes of god als mychel as his wille is to shewen hem.' The mystic Walter Hilton[11] (*c*.1390) says that, 'ure lord openeth the sight of thi soule in to biholdyng of him ... schewyng to the in gret reverence the sight of his privetes.' And again, relating this idea of divinely granted insight to the ghost's special privilege, 'The lovere of god, that hath the eighe of his soule clansed from al synnes, hath his biholdyng with swetnes of love in gostly gode.' The *Book of Margery Kemp* (*c*.1400) repeatedly refers to the nun's soul's sight of Christ in his living presence, as does the somewhat later *Book of Tree and Fruits*: 'contemplacioun is no thing ells to mene but a sight be the wiche a soule seith into heven.'

More pertinent to the philosophical usage of soul in connection with the Biblical and secular usage of *anima* is the perennially popular discussion of the three species or types of soul, the third main division of meaning. Numerous passages from *S. Leg. Mich.* (*c*.1300) make this threefold division, which whatever its original sources, would have been well known from the English monastic appropriation of Thomas Aquinas and Averroes, for example, through Roger Bacon[12] and John Blund: 'In eche manne thre soulene beoth, ake nought alle iliche guode ... In the nethemeste bolle [nethermost level] thare comez manere soule ase it were amanere liif that sent norischinge to the limes al aboute and biginnez in is wexinge ... thulke manere soule is in eche nought ells springue.' There are three souls, though not alike equally good; the lowest level is the nourishing soul, the source of the other levels of soul. The author continues: 'Thanne comez hare in the heorte a soule that bringuz that liif ... of thulke soule hath ech man that he mai wawi an gon [have gone away] ... thulke soule hath ech thing, best and foul and fisch' – one of the subordinate senses of animal soul. The author further declares that, 'soule of witte and of live comez fram the kuynde of aungles and in this fourme alight And miengez [mingles] with this wreche flesch' – an unusual association with angelic nature by way of its form, not its matter. John Trevisa (*c*.1400) makes the connection with Aristotle and Scholastic thought eminently clear: 'In divers bodies beth thre maner [of] soules ... vegetabilis that gif lif & no felinge as in plauntis ... sensibilis that geveth lif & felinge & noght resoun in unskilful bestes, racionalis that geveth lif, felinge & resoun in men.' In another passage, Trevisa mentions the three names associated with more technical features of Averroes' doctrines and their Latin translations: 'The cercle tokeneth the soule racional ... The soule of felyng hath thre vertues of the soule of lif and thereover the vertu of conceyvynge and concupiscibili and irascibili; for the soule of feelyng is soule of lyf and nought ageinward.' The Cleanness text, Lydgate's poems and Chaucer's *Boece*, all in the early fifteenth century, make similar divisions with similar criteria of differentiation. But it is Reginald Pecock's *Rule* (*c*.1443) which articulates this threefold division in the most detail:

---

[11] On Walter Hilton, see esp. Clark, 1979, 1982, and Baldwin, 1984.
[12] On Roger Bacon's theory of mind and soul, see Sharp, 1930, pp. 155–67.

The thing that makith liif in a body is a soule which is called the growyng soule or the norisching soule, which is in herbis, in plauntis, and in trees ... Every body which may knowe bodily thingis othere than hym silf ... and if he may move hym fro place to place hath a worthier liif and soule than plauntis ... The now seid soule muste be called a knowing soule or a sensitive soule, [in] whiche maner liif and soule han al maner of beestis ... That he hath a soule which is a growyng soule and that he hath a soule feelyng and that he hath a soule resouning may no man avoide for the open experience of her affectis and werkyngis.

It is the presence of soul that accounts for life in plants, animals and humans, though the level (or manner) of soul differs in the three stages; for the animal soul this involves the power of self-movement and sensory knowledge, and for the human soul this involves the rational power.[13] The Wycliffe Bible, especially in its translation of Genesis Chapter One, explicitly identifies the living soul with the Latin *anima vivens* in marginal and interlinear glosses. But gradually over the next century the word 'soul' (*anima*) is deleted from references to plants (except in alchemical texts) and becomes reserved for the life of beasts and humans. It remains true that plants have life, in the sense of the internal power of nourishment and growth, but beasts have life, in the sense of the powers of self-movement, feeling and reproduction, in virtue of the presence of soul – hence the English word 'animal' becomes reserved for them alone. This fairly new idea is clearly expressed in John Trevisa: 'Al that is comprehended of fleissh and of spiryte of lif and so of body and of soule is ycleped animal, a beast, whether it be ayry as fowil, or wattry as fissh ... other erthy as men and bestes.' An animal has its ensouled life through the soft tissues of flesh and the breath of spirit (in the broad sense), an opinion about animal nature that entails its mortal status.

This latter opinion is expressed about the same time by Chaucer's *Boece*: 'Whanne the body and the soule ben conjoyned in one ... it is cleped a beeste, and whanne her unyte is destroyed it is a deed thing.' The *Memorial of Faith* (*c*.1450) employs imagery from Plato and other classical sources to convey by metaphor the basic idea of the life-giving soul in humans: 'Nyce maydons fareth as whete ere with outen corn, a lampe with owten oyle, a purs with oute silver, and eye with outen syght, a body with oute soule.' About the same time Reginald Pecock associates this animal soul with its material composition: 'ech beestis soul is causid, gendrid, and brought forth into his beyng bi the mater and the bodi in whom he dwellith.' Guy de Chauliac's medical text (*c*.1425) offers this conjecture about the most likely seat or locus of the animal soul: 'The potte off the heed, other the brayn panne ... is cleped the partie that is hered in the whiche membra animata, that is to seien members that have soule, ben conteined.' The contemporary source known as the *Secret of Secrets*, an over-edited textual stew, falsely attributed to Aristotle, further differentiates animal from human souls by invoking the criterion of intelligible speech: 'The sensibilitez of the eres ar harkenyng of souns, and therof ar two maners, of sawle and noght of sawle [Latin *animalis et non animalis*]; soun of sawle ys double, one resonable, fallyng to man spekyng, another unresonable, as

---

[13] For full details on the Old English soul's power of cognition and reason, see Matto, 1998.

hyneyinge of hors, chaterynge of byrddes, and swylk lyk souns.' This point is reinforced later: 'Soun noght of sawle ys a rappyngge togedre of stones, hewynge of wode, and swylk lyk, that haven no lyf, as of the thoner, of tympans, and other instrumentz.' The eclectic alchemist George Ripley in his *Compendium of Alchemy* (or *The Twelve Gates*)[14] preserves the use of soul in connection with plants and even non-living things in numerous passages; its most likely meaning there is the hidden essence of some thing. For example, in *The Book of Quintessence* (*c*.1475): 'oure quinta essencia hath iii names by the philosophores, that is to seie, bernnynge watir, the soule in the spirit of wyn, & watir of liif.'

Glosses on the Wycliffe Bible, in conjunction with comparisons to the Vulgate text of these passages repeatedly show that the fourteenth-century translators deliberately rendered *anima* with 'soul', especially in those cases where the human soul is discussed. In addition, in concord with both the Hebrew use of *nepesh* and the LXX use of *psychē*, 'soul' can be used both as a count-noun, for example, in Genesis, Deuteronomy, Jeremiah, Ezekiel, and so forth; and as a pronominal or periphrastic construction to refer to one's self. Other contemporary texts with an emphatic mystical and/or salvational orientation, such as the *Ancrene Wisse*, *Piers Plowman, Pearl, Cloud of Unknowing* and others, follow this same pattern.[15] One of the most interesting English-Biblical patterns of development concerns the replacement of 'soul' for some instances of the Latin words for mind, or, in other cases, instances of Hebrew and LXX references to organs that serve or support cognitive functions. For example, in Wycliffe's version of Daniel there occurs this pivotal verse: 'Ther is not in this tyme prince and prophete, nether brent sacrifice, nether offring ... that we mown fynde thi mercye; bot in contrite soule, or ynwitt [Latin *animo*], and in spirit of mekenesse be we resceyvyd.' Here the Germanic and OE word 'wit' (moreover, inward wit, 'inwit') is identified with this sense of soul, and identified with the Latin *animus* (m.), usually distinguished from *anima* in its special sense (or power) of cognition. In this respect, there are many instances of the formulaic saying, 'with heart and mind and soul'; perhaps some semantic leakage occurred, through which features properly belonging to soul (*anima*) became partially appended to mind (*animus*).[16]

However, there are sufficient instances of unequivocal identification of soul with some Latin word that indicates mind, or mental power, or cognitive function, that one cannot rest too much weight on any accidental slippage. From the same book of Daniel in Wycliffe's version one finds this statement: 'This sacrament, or hid[den] trewthe, is shewid ... that thou shuldist wite the thoughtis of thi soule [Latin *mentis*].' John Trevisa draws attention to the 'objects' and medium of the soul's perception in these words, though one may question the dubious medical claim about causal impact on the fetus: 'Wommen conceyveth children iliche to thinges that they seeth ipeynt and ischape, for the worchynge of the soule while the body is in getynge of a childe sendeth inward likness and schappes that they

---

[14] Ripley's works were printed with other related manuscript sources in Elias Ashmole's great *Theatrum Chemicum,* London, 1652.

[15] See Baldwin, 1984, for analyses of all three texts on this topic.

[16] For full details on the intimate connections between Old English heart, soul and mind, see Phillips, 1986.

seeth with oute.' His translation of Bartholomew makes further medical claims, situating the three powers of the soul in specific portions of the brain. Note well also that the soul's power(s) (Latin *vis, viris* Greek *dunamis*) is rendered 'might' and the soul's function(s) (Latin *functio* or *opus*, Greek *ergon*) is rendered 'working':[17] 'The brayne hath thre holowgh places ... In the formest celle is ymaginacioun conformed and imaad; in the middel, resoun ... the celle in the middel hath moche of spirit [that is, breath] to have myche mevynge & meche of marough to tempre the meving of the soule that he may the bettir deme and knowe what he conseyveth.'

Chaucer in *Troilus and Criseyde* refers to the heart as the seat of the soul's thought about an absent loved one, in concord with the NT and later Greek sense of *kardia*: 'Although the body sat among hem there, hire advertence is alwey ellswhere; for Troilus ful faste hire soul (or herte) soughte; withouten word, on hym alwey she thoughte.' And again in *Boece* his character muses, 'Yif the thryvynge soule [Latin *mens vigens*] ne upliteth nothing by his propre movynges, but suffrith and lith subgit to the figures of bodies ... and yeldith ymages ydel in the manere of a mirour ... whennes comith thilke knowynge in our soule, that discernith alle thinges?' The *Foundation of St. Bartholomew* several times seems to take the Latin *animus* to be synonymous with *anima*, thus altering its basic meaning of 'life-force' in favor of more properly mental characteristics: 'He to his flittyng soule [Latin *fluctuanti animo*] was mevyd to have a dowtable sentence whethir it shulde be take for a fantastyke illusyoun or for an hevynly warnyng.' This passage marks an early use of rational soul (that is, mind, *animus*) as the capacity to 'see through' perceptual illusions to the real truth. The same text in another passage makes evident the proper reference to mind: 'The man awakid that he saw besyly revoluyd yn his mynde ... And by hym-self no thyng certeyn myght comprehende ... he gave way to a flittyng and a tempestuous varyaunte soule and began to aske a preste.' The capacity for inner sight, the 'agenbite of inwit' (in James Joyce's words), is the power proper to the human mind alone, as the great English mystic Hilton states: 'Though thou see me nought with thi bodili eighe, thou maight see me with thi sowle bi ymaginacion, and so maight thou don of alle other bodili thinges.' John Trevisa, as ever one of our best sources for such insights, renders Higden's Latin as follows: 'Short lyfe, a slawe sawle (dul witte and slowe understondynge) [Latin *sensus hebes, animus torpens*] and a slipper memory lete us to knowe mony thynges.'

The next-to-last main division of the meaning of 'soul' groups instances under the heading of soul as the seat of emotions, feelings and desires. It is certainly curious to note that several significant instances of this usage involve the mind or rational soul, and not the soul as such. For example, the Wycliffe Bible's version of Second Maccabees states: 'He that seeth the chier of the heighist prest was woundid in sowle [Latin *mente*]; forsothe the face and colour inchaungid, declaride the ynward sorrewe of soule, or ynwitt [Latin *animi*]' – two clear target words for mind, rendered in English by 'soul'. Other instances of soul as the seat of emotions,

---

[17] For example, *non animi solum vigore sed etiam corporis viribus excellens*, Livy 9.16, 12; *omnibus viribus atque opibus repugnare*, Cicero, Tusc. Disp. 3.11, 25.

such as dread, merry[ness], joy, gladness, loving, and so forth, can be found well sprinkled in texts from Mannyng, Piers Plowman, *Troilus and Criseyde*, the Paston Letters, Lydgate, etc. An exemplary instance is from the *Foundation of St. Bartholomew* (c.1425): 'By the which iiii wyndys be signified iiii passions of the soule, that ys to seye, drede and hevynesse, love and gladnesse.' Another outstanding example is from *The Court of Sapience* (c.1450–70): 'Thanne lawheth the herte, the sowle gladeth, the conscience is clerede & alle inwarde mightes & affecciones, togeder rejocynge, loovene & wirchepene godde' – inward might or power indicating the function of reflection clearing or voiding the mind in order that the soul can experience these positive feelings.

The final sense of 'soul' to be considered here shows the close connection English writers of this period made between the Latin *anima* (f.) and *animus* (m.) and the will (*voluntas*). Chauliac's medical text declares that 'signez when it is for thing divine or evyl soule or will [Latin *animum*] ar when al thingz stondeth wele and netherlez it may not gone out in to dewe acte of deling with, namely with his wife, both al he myght with other.' The *Secret of Secrets* is less well informed than Chauliac about the organic bodily causes of such desires (let alone advice for how to overcome problem cases), but concurs well in its assessment of the soul's responsibility for having such desires and appetites: 'It seems bettir that the eres of the folk be thirsty to the wordes of the kynge thanne thay be fillyd of his tales, forr whanne the eres and the sawles [gloss: the affeccion or dysyre of the spyryt] ar so fillyd, they here nought bleghtly the kyng.' The *Foundation of St. Bartholomew* says something comparable: 'Than to-gidyr with one soule, and inwarde affeccioun of hert, with grete clamoure of voice, we callid yn the holy Apostle to geve his helpe.' Even when one discounts the occasional slippage in use of English 'soul' for Latin terms for mind or intellect (*mens* or *animus*) the preponderance of textual evidence clearly and unequivocally identifies the basic meaning of soul with *anima* as the life-force or vital principle. It is the *principium* that explains the human capacity for knowledge via the senses, moral conscience, the higher (more noble) emotions, and reflection through the right use of reason.

(2) The various senses of 'mind' from 1200 to 1500

The Editors of the *Middle English Dictionary* compiled a detailed comprehensive catalog[18] of thousands of instances in the usage of mind-words during the period c. 1150 to 1500. The compilers of the entry for 'mind' divided the principal meanings into nine categories, the bulk of which are devoted to instances where 'mind' clearly conveys a meaning associated with memory. These categories are:

1   (a) The human mind as the seat or instrument of memory, thought, reason, will, imagination, emotion, etc. (b) frame of mind or mental disposition.
2   The faculty of memory, that is, one of the three constituents or powers of the soul and the Trinity.

---

[18] MED, Part M.4, 1977, pp. 484–92.

3 (a) Individual remembering or remembrance; (b) the thinking process, mental attention, thought, consideration, contemplation, etc.; (c) a particular memory or thought; (d) in verb phrases with 'haven', to remember or consider, to take thought or meditate; (e) in miscellaneous verb phrases, for example, 'beren', 'bringen', drauen', and 'taken'.
4 (a) Preserved memory, people's collective remembrance; (b) in temporal phrases, for example, 'before', 'out of', 'from', etc.; (c) something to be remembered, a memorial or reminder; (d) a commemorative service for a deceased soul.
5 Mention, record; also, something recorded.
6 Reason, understanding; also used in reference to God.
7 Will, desire, purpose; in the sense of inclination or intention.
8 Control of consciousness or reason; sound mind or sanity.
9 In compound phrases, for example, 'mind-day', 'mind-bread', 'mind-place', etc.

Our analysis has little need to consider verb and noun-phrases, such as those in 3(d), 3(e), 4(b) and 9, and half the remainder consist of multifarious uses connected directly or indirectly with memory, either as a cognitive power, an object of such a power, or the externalized storage of such 'objects'. Approximately half of the categorized instances fall under one or another rubric connected with the core ideas of intellect, reason, and reflection. One of the peculiarities of this lexical taxonomy is that one sub-category (3b) would have belonged better with either the first or the sixth categories. Specific citations listed under 3b show clear parallels with characteristics of either the faculty or the properties of intellectual operations.

The basic frame for the preponderant notion of mind as the seat of the higher cognitive functions appears as early as Shoreham's *Poems* (c.1330): 'Sonderliche his man astoned in his owene mende, wanne he note never wannes he cometh ne wider he schel wende.' In the *Parson's Tale*, Chaucer tells us that, unlike the human soul, the mind ceases function during sleep: regarding the effects of sin, 'somtyme of vileyns thoghtes that ben enclosed in mannes mynde, whan he goeth to slepe, which may not been withoute synne.' Gower's *Confessio Amantis* (c.1393) tells us also that thinking takes place only in the active exercise of the mind's power: 'Noght half the minut of an houre ne mihte I lete out of my mende bot if I thoghte upon that hende'; as also does Lydgate (1420): 'up & doun thei casten in her mynde, out of resoun if thei koude fynde rote & gronde of this wondir wirke.' The sinless individual sleeps well, according to an anonymous ms about the same time: 'if that the pacient be of good cheer & is in good mynde & slepith kyndely.' Chaucer again, in *Troilus and Criseyde*, provides another, very important image in connection with the mind, the Arabic-inspired idea of the mind as a mirror: 'thus gan he make a mirour of his mynde, in which he saugh al holly hire figure.' This metaphor nicely conveys the notion of intuition beyond the reach of sensory vision.

An important English language terminal setting is established by the use of 'might' to render the Latin concept of *virtus*, 'power', that is, the essential operation of a mindful being. There are numerous texts in which the psychical division of labor is accomplished by according various operations the status of 'might', for example, *The Cloud of Unknowing* (c.1400): 'Reson & wille, ymaginacion & sensualite alle thees foure mightes & theire werkes mynde conteneth &

comprehendeth in it-self.' Another related passage makes an identification of mind's might with the 'ghost' (that is, spiritual-double) of each of its various physical powers: 'Minde is clepid [called] a principal myghte, for it conteneth in it goostly not only alle the other mightes, bot therto alle tho thinges in the whiche their worchen.' The *Orch. Syon* text of slightly later date asserts that the mind alone is (or can be) divorced from the senses and feelings: 'The gate also of mynde is schutt, that it hath no mynde of the world ne of his owne sensible feelynge.' But in another passage, the same writer seems to equate the mind with memory: 'Thou gaf to man a mynde or a memorye, with which he schuld kepe and remembre thi benfetis'; and again, 'Graunte to me that my mynde mowe be able for to kepe thi benefetis retentifly & that my will mowe brenne in the fier of thi charite.'

Walter Hilton clearly endorsed the view that the human mind is one might or power of the soul, 'the sowle of a man is a life made of thre mightes: mende, reson, and will', though it should be remarked that in making this division, Hilton seemed to separate mind and reason as *two* separate powers. The identification of mind *qua* reason with understanding (along the late Latin lines of the equation *mens qua ratio est intellectus* or *ingenium*) is made in other texts one century later, such as the late fifteenth-century version of *Wisdom*: 'Thre myghtys every Chresten sowll has, wyche bethe applyede to the Trinyte ... Mynde, Wyll, Undyrstondynge'. Other passages from this edition associate these three powers with the mind of God, thus following the Augustinian scheme which correlated the three persons of God with the three faculties of the human soul. The *Chartier Treatise on Hope* (1500) provides a further important philosophical specification when it locates these three powers in the *substance* of the human soul: 'Oh thou undirstondinge, figure or patron of the Trinite, which by the three powers, that is to say, knowinge, will and mynde, owned in the substaunce of a sowle.' But the *Cambridge Precepts* of the same date classify five 'wits', more along the lines of an Avicennan medical scheme, and describe them as 'ghostly', that is, powers of the inner vital spirits: 'The v goostly wytts [are] Mynde, Undirstandyng, Wylle, Reson, Ymaginacion. Mynde of the kyndnes of God, Undirstandyng of his benefetis and his lore. Wylle to wyrshyp hym in thoght ... Reson to rewle thi dedys ... Ymaginacion to medfull warkes.' The function of the preposition 'of' in the first two clauses is somewhat ambiguous, since, on one hand, it can mean 'about', for example, the mind's operations are *about* God's kindness; or, on the other hand, it can mean 'from', for example, the mind's power is granted *from* God's beneficence; the same can be said for understanding. But it seems that in the latter three clauses the function of the preposition 'to' means 'for the purpose of'. Thus, the purpose of God's gift of will is to worship him in one's inner being, reason is for ruling one's actions (the dominant 'part'), imagination is for planning suitable works. The *Orch. Syon* text makes this connection between God's benefits and the human mind's operation in these words: 'thy mynde shulde be full ocupied with the benefetis of me [God], whiche thou hast resceyved.'

One is more likely to find an association of mind with heart in some of the mystical works; for example, Margery Kempe (1438) says, 'than was hir mende all [w]holy takyn owt of al erdly thyngs & set al in gostly thyngs', thus indicating the cognitive move from contemplation of sensible things to contemplation of spiritual things. Her reference to 'ravishing' follows the lexical setting of *exstasis* as 'standing out of' into contemporary English terms when she says that such spiritual contemplation can be directed at the divine nature.[19] An anonymous English translation of Bonaventure's *Meditations* (c.1440) renders this thought: 'who so wolde besy hyme [self] with all his herte and all his mynde it shulde bryng hym ... in to a new state of lyfyng ... sett thy-selfe, that is thi mynde, therto all holly.' One can clearly read in this text both the hendiadys of heart-and-mind for mind and the notion that, according to Christian doctrine, there is another better life, attainable through salvation; moreover, the author wants to convey the idea that this new life is one's real self. One of the most peculiar locutions in the framework of mind as the higher or dominant power of human soul is Hilton's statement that counterposes the flesh's desires for earthly things with the soul's desire to turn toward divine things: 'For to agein stonde the venemouse dartis of alle fleschli loves, and for to put out her malice fro the mynde of her soule.' An equally convoluted locution occurs in the *Gesta Romanorum* (c.1450) 'the seke man herde what they seydyn, and keste up the mynde of his herte to god.' Both of these strange phrases may be straining to express the conceptual intersection of an older idea of the heart as the organic seat of cognition, and the newer idea of the mind as the name of an abstract power.

Lanfranc and Chauliac (both c.1400) propose the brain as internal site of this power or faculty, thus Lanfranc says, 'the substaunce of the ventriclis of the brayn, of the which mynde is maade', and Chauliac: 'a little of the substaunce of the brayne went oute, the whiche was knowen by hurtunge of the mynde.' Chauliac can be precise in his situation of the various cognitive powers in the brain: 'In the myddel ventricle is sitede the vertu cogitatif and resonable; in the hyndermore forsoth the vertu servatyf and memoratif [that is] having in mynde.' Mondeville's medical ms. (c.1475) is more specific in locating this internal function, without doubt following the Arabic version of neural study,[20] when it says, 'the thirdde partie of his brayn that is bihinde in the brayne panne, there that virtus memorativa dwelllith, that is to seie, vertu of mynde.' These medical texts employ the Latin *virtus* (not *vis, viris*), an animate being's internal potency.

Less common, but not unknown, are instances where the mind is the seat or source of various emotions, for example, in Chaucer's *Legend of Good Women*: 'moche sorwe hadde he in his mynde, or that he coude his felaweship fynde.' An influential English translation (c.1450) of the fifth-century Roman military administrator Vegetius says, 'youre softe pesible studie of an hygher counseil than erthliche manis mynde may conseyve desireth olde thinges of dedes of armes.' The overwhelming number of instances where the mind is said to experience an affective state concern negative or privative emotions, such as this text (c.1400): 'whatswa of this wil take hede may be stird ... til drede, thrugh mynde of the hydusnes of payne and sorow that in helle es.' Margery Kempe's glorious and ecstatic experiences could be matched with equally wretched and disgusting thoughts: 'so had sche now as many owrys of fowle thowtys & fowle mendys of letchery & alle unclennes as thwo sche shulde be comown to al maner of pepyl.' Notice the very distinctive use

---

[19] Kempe, 1996, Chapter 3.
[20] For de Mondeville's work, see Duby, 1988, pp. 522–4.

of 'mendys' to signify particular thoughts or mental events. Another similar text also indicates that these gloomy, depressing and harrowing feelings are connected with humans' sinful nature: 'gif it be the mynde of thi wrechidnes, the passyon of Criste, or eny soche that longeth to be comoun entre of Cristen men.' Casting one's mind on the pains of future hellish torment was a favorite trope, as *Jacob's Well* shows: 'Ye shuldyn wyth a spade, that is, mynde of cristes deth, of the doom & of helle-peyne, delvyn out of the gravel of hevy & ydell thoughts.' But *The Cloud of Unknowing* offers more positive guidance: 'a mynde of any special seinte or of any clene goostly thing wil hindre thee so muche.' So also does *Ludus* (c.1475), emphasizing that mental cleanness is without sin, and that without sin one can become closer to Christ: 'For as ye [Mary] were clene in erthe of alle synnys greyn, so shul ye reyne in hefne clennest in mend.' Of course, one has to grant the special proviso that only the Virgin Mary could have been completely clean of sin even during her earthly life.

It is not unknown for writers of this period to predicate mind or mental powers of animals, for example, John Trevisa, in his translation of Bartholomew, says, 'Some [beasts] beeth swithe wratheful and angry & with stronge mynde, as the hound, the camel, and the asse, and some haveth but feeble mynde, as the strucio, the ostrugge, and culvere.' Or the same author (always one of our best sources) in another context: 'the oxe is slowe and stable ... the hounde with mynde of frinedschipe.' Vegetius says the same of the camel, but qualifies his remark by lauding the animal's memory (much as one now says something like 'the memory of an elephant'): 'Also he [the camel] hath a greet mynde of that he hath be taught bifore.' But it is far more common to read that it is precisely through the absence of mind that animals are deprived of spiritual comfort and the second life; for example, the Wycliffe text (c.1375) declaims, 'God sendeth thus his son to socour us atte nede, so wonder a wilde beste, that weldes no mynde.' One could speculate that in these cases the writer has drawn attention to the ways in which some animal species exhibit behavior similar to the more pronounced cognitive achievements of humans.

In addition to the use of 'mind' to nominate the specific power of intellect or understanding, mind can also nominate the (usually) separately named power of will. Gower in the *Confessio Amantis* says, 'and who that happeth hir to finde, for charite tak in his mynde, and do so that sche be begrave with this tresor.' One of the Wycliffe tracts issues this injunction: 'As a childe turnith hym awey fro alle thinghis that his mayster hath forbedun hym and forgetith hem for the greet mynde that he hath to done his maystirs wille.' And *Orch. Syon* makes an ambiguous claim about God's will when humans have it in their power to follow his instructions; the ambiguity rests with the 'onedness' of the body and soul united with God's nature: 'The body and soule oonyd with my dyvyne nature, as I tolde thee, if thou have mynde, in the begynnyng of thi conversyoun.' In this passage, 'if you have mind' could mean 'if you remember' what occurred when you turned toward me, or 'in virtue of having mind' the body and soul are made one with God's nature. John Trevisa underscores the mind as the power of memory in more than one instance, for example, 'Forgetful and unkonnynge, he hath no mynde that he schal geve to his lord accountes of his outrage.' Trevisa's adroit English prose connects not-knowing (un-konnen) with the notion that having-in-mind in this sense means an intention. So does an English version of the romance *Castle Perseverance* (c.1450): 'whanne all othyr synnys man hath forsoke, evere the more that he hath, the more is in hys mynde togadyr to gete good wyth woo and wyth wrake.'

The normal possession of sound mind, as the governance of thought, intention and memory, sometimes is brought to the fore in passages that dramatically highlight the *loss* of sanity. In this fashion, 'mind' is often used, not merely to indicate the specific higher-order faculty or power of reflection and right judgment, but the continuous smooth exercise of that power. As early as the Wycliffe *Book of Judith* this usage stands out: 'whan al the host hadde herd Holofernes of-heveded [raised over] fleigh mynde & counseil fro them.' In *Troilus and Criseyde*, Chaucer has his character voice this plaint: 'I am, till God me bettre mynde sende, right at my wittes end'; though he feels much better on the next occasion, 'at the last, he gan his breth to drawe, and of his swough sone after that adawe [soon after his swoon dawn came], and gan bet mynde and reson hym take.' It is not only the medical texts that speak of loss of mind through serious injury or disease, but ordinary expressions about bodily fatigue, grief and infirmity, as John Trevisa does when he complains about 'sore hedache, wakinge, changing of mynde, [such as in] griseliche sightes in slepe'; or some of the signs of apoplexy, 'an evil that bynemeth a mannes mynde, mevynge, & feelinge'.

One of the most commonly cited culprits for loss of conscious control was overindulgence in alcohol, as the *Cursor Mundi* (c.1425) bluntly states: 'dronkin hede makes a man oft fole-hardy so es his minde mased and mad.' Or, even better, the inveterate boozer John Lydgate, in his paean to the delights of beer declares: 'your bewte causeth men ful ofte to wandryn in mynde, and make men full unsage to walke alone.' Chaucer has the Summoner say that 'wyn maketh man to lesen wrechedly his mynde', a sentiment echoed by the Pardoner in his story, 'he seith he kan no difference fynde bitwix a man that is out of his mynde and a man which is dronkelewe.' Where too much drink can cause the loss of mindful control, too little food can have the same effect, as *Firumbras* (c.1380) says: 'nad sche ther noght of hure bone fulich ymade an ende, or he for hunger had forgone hir wit & ek hur mende.' The *Castle Perseverance* issues this caution: 'meatys and drynkys whanne thei are out of mesure toke, thei makyn men mad and out of mende.' The late fourteenth-century *St. Erkenwald* text makes this more general statement: 'bot quen matyd is monnes myght, and his mynde passynd, and al his resons are torent', parallel with the late fifteenth-century *Mankind* text: 'my mynde is dispersyde [and] my body trymmeleth as the aspen leaffe.' Margery Kempe describes another devout meditator in terms that suggest that deprivation of spiritual goods can have as injurious an effect on one's sanity as deprivation of bodily nourishment: 'This creatur went owt of hir mende & was wondyrly vexid & laboryd wyth spiritys.'

However, by far the greatest preponderance of English language usage of 'mind' between 1200 and 1500 denotes some dimension of human memory: either the cognitive power itself, or an internal episode, or an external testament. Several short passages from Trevisa's various translations in the mid-1300s indicate the general sense of individual or collective remembrance: 'Hit is to be hade in memory that alle the province of Westsaxon hadde alwey oon bishop from the begynnyng'; and 'For kynde wole that the yghen & the kneen haven mynde [Latin gloss *rememorari*] where they were [be]fere in the modir wombe.' Trevisa relies on the commonly accepted medical idea that the fetus can receive impressions in the womb, impressions stored in memory traces; though it surely seems anomalous to claim that this memorial power of mind is invested in the eyes and knees. An anonymous tract of the same date says that 'ever hath mind in thi hert of thos thinges thre: whan thou commist, whan thou art, and what shal come of the.' An even earlier text, the *Trinity Homilies*, records a close connection between heart and mind: 'Listed nu and under-nimed hit on heorte, and habbed hit on minde yiu is ned michel wi the devel is nemd sinful and hunte.' There are scores of passages that employ verbal phrases, such as 'haven in mind', 'bringen to mind', 'keepen in mind', and so forth. Some of these phrases, such as 'keepen in' and 'haven in', connote the passive, receptive character of memory, where others, such as 'bringen to' and 'draven to', connote the active character. It may be the case that someone retains in the 'store-house' or 'treasury' of memory certain events or words or images, but just as well someone may make an effort to actively retrieve or recollect an item from memory storage.

There seems to be little point in illustrating the prodigious frequency with which 'mind' is used in connection with both collective and individual memory. It is so ubiquitous in temporal phrases, such as 'time out of mind' or 'before time of mind', that it loses any real association with a distinct cognitive power and simply refers to an earlier period in one's own life. This particular usage of 'mind' to convey some sense of storage permits an unusual lexical deposit, when 'mind' is externalized in an actual memorial or reminder. Trevisa's *Dialogue Between Master and Clerk* (*c.*1400) offers several excellent examples of this usage: 'Seye nought freres this is another reule, for it is mynde and warnyng & chargyng & my testament'; and again, 'his testament is nought another reule, but mencioun & mynde of the rather rule that was hem y-geve.' Not more than twenty years later, Lydgate's poems employ similar turns of phrase; for instance, 'Nynus an ymage dide make ... and sette it up for consolacioun, and for a mynde and a memorial'; and again, 'he bilt a roial toun, which stant ther yit for a manier mynde for his arryvaile into this regioun.' Closely connected with this derivative sense is the use of 'mind' in reference to a special church service for the dead, for example, this will from 1418, 'to do, make & holde my mynde every yere duryng vii yere next folowyng after my desese', or this *Primer* (1450): 'for a soul in mynde dai, Lord ... graunte thou to the soule of thi servaunt, whose yeris mynde we maken to dai, a seete of refresching blisse.'

Perhaps the single most noticeable feature of the voluminous number of citations under the various sub-headings for mind in its capacity of memory is that such instances are the only occurrences of mind before the mid-1300s. There are no entries for the other principal headings 1, 3b, 6, 7, and 8, that is, those that connote the distinctively rational faculty and its operations, reflection, intention, contemplation, and so forth, before the early and mid-1300s. It is not feasible for us to speculate here on this striking feature of recorded usage of the English word 'mind', except to remark on the possible connection with English translations of Islamic and Neo-Aristotelian medical canons in that period.

The conclusions that we can infer with some justification from the textual evidence brought forth with regard to the English usage of mind and soul between 1200 and 1500 are as follows. First, the human soul, and not the mind, contains or comprises the life-force or principle of life for the human species in their animal nature. Second, it is the human soul, and not the mind that is accorded an immortal status, that is, one not bound to death by its animal being. Third, the tension between these two pictures of the human soul can only be resolved by an appeal to the Pauline notion (amplified by Augustine's superb synthesis) that humans alone have a double life and a double death: the first is an earthly, corporeal life, the second is a heavenly, spiritual life. Fourth, the mind retains some association, through older connections with late Latin terminology, with the emotions and passions, but 'mind' is more and more displaced by 'heart' where deeply private feelings and desires are concerned. Fifth, only mental (not soulful) achievements, in the derivative sense of 'mind' as memory's repository, can be externalized in monuments and memorials. Sixth, where the human soul is accorded higher-order attributes of reflection, deliberation and self-scrutiny, it is normally an abbreviation or contraction for *rational* soul. And finally, with regard to the relation of spirit to soul and mind, one notices the same conceptual separation that began to emerge in late Hellenistic and Patristic writings. The use of the word 'spirit' shows two separate and unconnected meanings: on one hand, in virtue of the gift of spirit from the Holy Spirit, each human possesses a double life, and this accords with the Genesis story that God's breath (*spiritus*) brought Adam to life. On the other hand, 'spirits' are the vehicles of organic life in humans as animal beings, and this accords with the medieval medical concept of *pneuma* in the material frame of the body. As John Trevisa says, 'we shall not beleve that this spyryte is mannis resonable soule, but more sothli the chair therof & cariage & propre instrument, for by suche a spryte the soule is pyned to the body & withoute the servyce of suche a spyryte the soule usyth no perfighte werkynge in the body.'[21]

(3) The natural shape of 'soul' and 'mind' in Shakespeare

At the end of the section on the late medieval concept of the domestic relations between the human soul and body, we emphasized the extensive use of the analogy of the soul as principal tenant of the bodily house. The interior of the human body is like a court, for the whole body is like a large and complex building which consists of an arrangement of rooms, organized according to the more noble or less noble services performed there. The bodily house is surrounded by an enclosure as secure as the wall around any private dwelling. The body's envelope is the ultimate enclosure, containing the most secret and intimate place of all, and violating it is prohibited by the strictest taboos. The human body is a fortress or citadel, but one constantly under threat, encircled with dangerous and wicked temptations. Hence it is important that the body is kept under surveillance, especially around the apertures through which forces might infiltrate the boundary walls. One of the most extensive uses of this analogy occurs in Spenser's *Faerie Queene* (1589), Book II, Canto IX, when the travelers stop to visit Alma's castle of temperance:

> Of all Gods workes, which do this worlde adorne,
> There is no one more faire and excellent,

---

[21] Quoted in Harvey, 1975, p. 70, note 118.

Then is mans body both for powre and forme,
Whiles it is kept in sober government;
But none then it, more fowle and indecent,
Distempred through misrule and passions base:
It growes a monster and incontinent
Doth loose his dignitie and native grace. (FQ II.ix.1)

The next forty-five stanzas describe, in rather heavy-handed metaphors, a tour around Alma's bodily house, a superbly made castle, 'that was so high, as foe might not clime | And all so faire, and fensible withall | Not built of bricke, ne yet of stone and lime'. Even though it is constructed according to a wondrous plan it will not endure forever, 'soon it must turne to earth; [for] no earthly thing is sure' (FQ II.ix.21). The next stanza offers what, on first glance, is a baffling geometrical-numerical picture of the whole plan. Kenelm Digby's first written work was an ingenious Neo-Platonic interpretation of this stanza (as we shall discover in a later section). The visitors are conducted into the castle porch (her lips), a stately hall (her mouth), whose steward is called Diet and whose marshal is called Appetite, and thence into the great kitchen (her stomach) whose chief cook is Concoction and whose clerk is Digestion. Some other less salubrious passages are mentioned before the tour wends its way into 'a goodly parlor' (the heart) where laughter, love and other diverse delights appear; sadness, anger and boredom are banished to another room.

But our studied interest is focused on those lines that describe the 'stately turret' which stands at the highest level of the castle. The uppermost citadel within the castle is, of course, the human head (Latin *caput*) which oversees everything beneath it by means of 'two goodly beacons' (the eyes). Spenser explicitly equates the construction of the human head, and its internal functions, to the intellectual dimensions of the divine nature: 'This part [shows] great workmanship, and wondrous power, | That all this other worlds worke doth excell, | And likest is unto that heavenly towre, | that God hath built for his owne blessed bowre' (FQ II.ix.47). There are many rooms in the human head, but in the three most important rooms there are three sages who provide advice. In these stanzas Spenser personifies the 'inward wits', the three principal faculties of the human rational soul: 'The first of them could things to come foresee: | The next could of things present best advize; | The third things past could keep in memoree' (FQ II.ix.49). The first counselor is named Phantastes, his room is brightly painted with many colors and shifting shapes, images of imaginary things fly about: 'devices, dreames, opinions unsound | Shewes, visions, sooth-sayes, and prophesies; | And all that fained is, as leasings, tales, and lies.' This sage represents the power of fantasy and although he appears young and fresh, he is full of melancholy, and might be thought by some to be close to madness. In the second room sits an unnamed personage, clearly symbolizing the power of perception; his room is decorated with images of magistrates, courts, tribunals and policy; here sensible judgments are made. This counselor has 'meditate[d] all his life long, | that through continual practice and usage, | He now has growne right wise, and wondrous sage.' The noble visitors are much impressed at 'his goodly reason', such that his disciples desire to become like him.

The third chamber is the most removed from the others and here sits an old man, 'halfe blind, | And all decrepit in his feeble corse, | Yet lively vigour rested in his mind, | And recompenst them with a better scorse: | Weake body well is chang'd for minds redoubled forse' (FQ II.ix.55). He is called Eumnestes (his servant is Anamnestes) and his function is to lay things up 'in his immortal scrine | Where they for ever incorrupted dwell.' His room is filled with ancient rolls and records, 'that were all worm-eaten, and full of canker holes'. The visitors ask to hear one of the stories contained in the library; the recitation of the mythical Kings of Briton occupies Canto X. In the opening of Canto XI the visitors are ready to depart from Alma's castle-body but not before reflecting that no warlike siege of a fortress exerts such deleterious effects as the strength of affections: 'Against the fort of reason evermore | To bringe the soule into captivitie: | Their force is fiercer through infirmitie | Of the fraile flesh' (FQ II.xi.1). In the ordinary course of events, sinfulness, disease and accident exercise 'most bitter tyranny' upon the bodily parts. But the author tells the reader to not despair; if one follows the counsel of reason to control the passions, to resist temptation, and become moderate in appetite, then good health will attend one's life. Thus, in contrast, 'in a body, which doth freely yield | His partes to reasons rule obedient, | And letteth her that ought the scepter wield, | All happy peace and goodly government | Is settled there in sure establishment' (FQ II.xi.2). The second grand analogy makes an appearance here: in addition to considering the human body like a house within which the soul dwells, the component parts of the living body are like the members of a nation-state, subject to proper governance by a dominant power. This political-corporeal metaphor will be taken up and extended in profound ways by Thomas Hobbes.

Edmund Spenser (1552–99) and William Shakespeare (1564–1616) lived and worked in the same capital city during the same period. But an enormous gulf separates Spenser's antiquated, cliché-ridden picture of mind and soul from Shakespeare's radical, perhaps unprecedented, reconceptualization of human nature. Shakespeare's plays deploy a sophisticated battery of psychical concepts in what Harold Bloom calls his 'invention of the human'. In his latest book, Bloom makes us aware of the distinctive features of Shakespeare's most fully realized characters: Falstaff's vitalism, Hamlet's intellect, Macbeth's imagination, Lear's capacity for love, Cleopatra's sense of theatre, and so forth. In this fashion, one comes to an understanding of some of the playwright's own obsessions, as well as the one great English writer who created our modern conception of ourselves, and that includes our modern concept of 'mind':

> More even than all the other Shakespearean prodigies ... Falstaff and Hamlet are the invention of the human, the inauguration of personality as we have come to recognize it. The idea of Western character, of the self as a moral agent, has many sources ... [but] personality, in our sense, is a Shakespearean invention ... Insofar as we ourselves value, and deplore, our own personalities, we are the heirs of Falstaff and Hamlet, and of all the other persons who throng Shakespeare's theater of what might be called the colors of the spirit.[22]

---

[22] Bloom, 1998, p. 4.

In contrast to the next generation of English writers, for example, Hobbes and Locke, who focus almost exclusively on the concept of mind, Shakespeare manages to sustain and even deepen our understanding of both concepts: 'soul' as the creative, immortal and spiritual dimension of human being, and 'mind' as the intellectual, cognitive and rational power.

There has been a prodigious amount of scholarly study on Shakespeare in the two centuries since Samuel Johnson, an encyclopedic critic whom many contemporary scholars regard as the first great writer to take the measure of Shakespeare. This section approaches the topic of mind and soul in his plays and sonnets with the utmost caution, acknowledging that almost every perspective on almost every issue has been adopted and defended with a degree of conviction that intimidates all but the most well equipped or the most reckless. It is somewhat surprising, then, to discover that the philosophical question about Shakespeare's picture of human nature and functions of the human psyche has been rarely addressed in the scholarly literature. One of the few exceptions is Paul Cefalu's recent study of the anti-dualist and radical behavioral elements in *Hamlet*. This section makes an overview and assessment of Cefalu's arguments, and offers some comment on guiding clues in Shakespeare's texts that may assist in identifying some of the psychical characters in his *dramatis personae*.

Paul Cefalu persuasively argues that those scholars who have addressed the issues involved in Shakespeare's theory of mind have either overtly or tacitly assumed that one can expect to find some sort of early modern version of substance dualism: 'Part of the reason that *Hamlet's* critics have assumed that Hamlet is preoccupied with inspecting the contents of his private self is that they have mistaken the obsession shown by Hamlet's peers in the play to "pluck out" Hamlet's "mystery" for what is usually described as Hamlet's own inner gaze.' Although Cefalu does not spell this out, it is correct to say that some scholars (notably Hilary Putnam and Daniel Dennett) have incorrectly claimed that Cartesian-style dualism unavoidably commits one to notions of privileged access, inner privacy and irreducible mental content: 'Critics have conflated the third-person statements about Hamlet's mental states with Hamlet's first-person reports, reports which aim to understand the role of behavior, habit and custom in knowing and acting, rather than explore any Cartesian theater of the mind.' One could perhaps support Cefalu's negative assessment of these scholars' efforts to impute some form of proto-Cartesian dualism to Shakespeare by noting how some of them (again notably Daniel Dennett) have invented the very idea of an inner, private theatre, upon which mental contents are projected. This idea is then retrojected onto the early modern period and becomes an important part of an entirely specious Cartesian picture of the mind. Against this unwarranted imputation about early modern psychical theory, Cefalu proposes his own unusual reading: 'For most of the play Hamlet is a radical Rylean behaviorist, inasmuch as he believes mental phenomena and predicates gain meaning only when they are identified in a one-to-one relationship with behavioral predicates, while at least some of the other characters in the play are functionalists, inasmuch as they associate mental events with innumerable subserving physical states and behavioral events.'[23] There is some irony

---

[23] Cefalu, 2000, p. 400.

in this identification of radical behaviorism with Gilbert Ryle's version of functionalism, since Ryle himself was responsible for the gross caricature of Descartes' model of the mind–body relation as 'the ghost in the machine', a cartoon caption for which there is not a shred of textual evidence.

Cefalu offers his own best guess about the sources of Shakespeare's early modern version of such a behaviorist understanding of *at least one dimension* of Hamlet's presentation of himself in the play. What shaped Hamlet's version was an Augustinian-Protestant theory about the ineradicable nature of vicious habits, which in its more extreme strains mutated into a holistic theory of sin, 'according to which an inveterate evil habit was considered a sin unto itself, superadded to the individual sins which comprised the offending habit.' To suppose that this is what Hamlet understands the character of habitual sin to be helps 'to explain both his irresolution ... and his sense that personal identity or subjective states are identical with customary behavioral dispositions. Because he reifies and objectifies habits, Hamlet imagines persons to be constituted by behavior, custom, and dispositional states all the way down.' Hamlet could not think that other persons are endowed with any further psychical facts, such as their having separable minds.[24]

An exemplary instance of Hamlet's supposed inwardness and deep privacy occurs in the opening ceremony of Act I, scene 2, where the Queen discusses the King's death with her son. She informs him that 'Thou know'st tis common, all that lives must die, | Passing through nature to eternity', to which Hamlet replies, 'Aye madam, it is common.' The Queen then asks him, 'Why seems it so particular with thee?', to which he answers, 'Seems, madam? Nay, it is, I know not "seems"' (H 1.2.72–76). In other words, the Queen remarks that it is common for most persons to respond to death in a certain manner, but Hamlet's behavior seems unusual or eccentric. Hamlet follows the last phrase, that he does not know the meaning of semblance, with these strange words: 'Tis not alone my inky cloak, good Mother, | Nor customary suits of solemn black', nor other ordinary outward signs, 'that can denote me truly. These indeed seem | For they are actions that a man might play. | But I have that within which passes show | These but the trappings and the suits of woe.' This exchange is taken by numerous commentators (whom Cefalu quotes at some length) as clear textual support for the innate dualist view cited above. But Cefalu offers an unusual reading: what Hamlet says first in his response does not imply 'a necessary chasm between *is* and *seems* ... but rather suggest[s] that how he *is* is equivalent to how others think he *seems*, and that his particular behavior, which has been duly witnessed by the observing court, should not be construed as false seeming.' What he says in closing about what it is that does not truly denote him shows that there are two states of being that complement each other: 'He does not say that being is more true or valid than seeming; he says only that a person can be a certain way in addition to seeming a certain way ... Hamlet suggests that his behavior is a partial record of his turmoil; he does not suggest that it is misleading, unsubstantial, or falsifiable.'[25]

---

[24] Cefalu, 2000, pp. 400–401.
[25] Cefalu, 2000, p. 404.

Further examples of Shakespeare's use of psychical terms are not meant to cover all the nuances of the playwright's enormous range of expression.[26] Nor can it take account of the fact that simply because one (or more) characters express anti-dualist, behavioral opinions about the human mind that that is sufficient ground to attribute such a view to the author himself. Moreover, it is not impossible that Shakespeare's expert knowledge about many things may extend to an informed understanding of *several* different views of human nature current at the time, different views expressed or exhibited by different characters. In one of its primary connotations, the soul is often referred to as the seat of emotion. When North says, 'Had he been slaughter-man to all my kin, | I should not for my life but weep with him. |To see how inly sorrow gripes his soul' (3H6 1.4.170–2). He avers that he too feels dreadfully sad when he sees the outward signs of the Duke of York's sorrow, even though this sorrow is felt by the Duke in an inward fashion. Or when King Henry says, 'Oh, how this discord doth afflict my soul! | Can you, my Lord of Winchester, behold | My sighs and tears and will not once relent?' (1H6 3.1.106–8). Mowbray reflects on his disgrace before King Richard: 'but my fair name, | Despite of death that lives upon my grave, | To dark dishonor's use thou shalt not have. | I am disgraced, impeach'd and baffled here, | Pierced to the soul with slander's venom'd spear' (R2 1.1.168–71). In *Henry VIII*, Cardinal Wolsey says, 'The hearts of princes kiss obedience, | So much they love it; but to stubborn spirits | They swell, and grow as terrible as storms. | I know you have a gentle, noble temper, | A soul as even as a calm ... ' (H8 3.1.162–6). The soul's emotional condition is often conveyed with fluid-like, fluctuating words and images from tempest and storm. In *The Comedy of Errors*, Egeon tells the Duke of Ephesus about his wife's death in a sea storm: 'Her part, poor soul! seeming as burdened | With lesser weight but not with lesser woe, | Was carried with more speed before the wind' (CE 1.1.107–9). And the devious Iago, reflecting on how to sow dissension between Othello and Desdemona, speaks to himself: 'All seals and symbols of redeemed sin, | His soul is so enfetter'd to her love, | That she may make, unmake, do what she list, | Even as her appetite shall play the god | With his weak function' (Oth. 2.3.345–8).

The rational soul is sometimes responsible for reflection or consideration about some course of action, weighing and measuring evidence. King Henry: 'Oh, Thou that judgest all things, stay my thoughts, | My thoughts, that labour to persuade my soul | Some violent hands were laid on Humphrey's life!' (2H6 3.2.136–8). Lorenzo reflects on Jessica's outstanding attributes: 'Beshrew me but I love her heartily; | For she is wise, if I can judge of her, | And fair she is, if that mine eyes be true, | And true she is, as she hath proved herself, | And therefore, like herself, wise, fair and true, | Shall she be placed in my constant soul' (MV 2.6.52–7). Lorenzo overtly states that his love for her is based on various judgments about her character, and that these judgments follow from his conscientious observation of her words and actions. On rare occasions references to the rational soul can be construed as indicating an intention or purpose in one's words or actions. For example, King Edward IV says, 'Sweet widow, by my state I swear

---

[26] The textual clues extracted below follow the main lexical divisions of the OED and MED schemes for 'soul', 'mind' and 'spirit'.

to thee | I speak no more than what my soul intends; | And that is, to enjoy thee for my love' (3H6 3.2.93–5).

In addition to those passages that instance the reflective exercise of the soul's ability to form judgments and take inward counsel, the rational soul is also the faculty or seat of reason. Holofernes: 'If knowledge be the mark, to know thee shall suffice; | Well learned is that tongue that well can thee commend, | All ignorant that soul that sees thee without wonder' (LLL 4.2.112–14). Leonato: 'There thou speak'st reason: nay, I will do so. | My soul doth tell me Hero is belied; | And that shall Claudio know; so shall the prince | And all of them that thus dishonour her' (Ado 5.1.41–4). Sebastian reflects on falling in love with the disguised Viola, voicing skeptical doubts about appearances in relation to her real character:

> For though my soul disputes well with my sense,
> That this may be some error, but no madness,
> Yet doth this accident and flood of fortune
> So far exceed all instance, all discourse,
> That I am ready to distrust mine eyes
> And wrangle with my reason that persuades me
> To any other trust but that I am mad
> Or else the lady's mad ... [12N 4.3.9–14]

Luciana, on the other hand, may be merely expressing a common opinion about human nature when she says, 'Men, more divine, the masters of all these, | Lords of the wide world and wild watery seas, | Indued with intellectual sense and souls, | Of more preeminence than fish and fowls' (CE 2.1.20–23). But by far the most extensive statement about the rational faculty of the soul is uttered by King Richard:

> I have been studying how I may compare
> This prison where I live unto the world:
> And for because the world is populous
> And here is not a creature but myself,
> I cannot do it; yet I'll hammer it out.
> My brain I'll prove the female to my soul,
> My soul the father; and these two beget
> A generation of still-breeding thoughts,
> And these same thoughts people this little world,
> In humours like the people of this world,
> For no thought is contented. The better sort,
> As thoughts of things divine, are intermix'd
> With scruples and do set the word itself
> Against the word ... [R2 5.5.1–14]

There are several philosophical ideas that underpin this soliloquy: comparing the world as a prison for his person to his body as a prison for his soul; his thoughts are products of this inner microcosm; some of his thoughts are morally better than others, as such they are like thoughts about divine things: and the strangest image, that which marries the female brain to the male soul. It may be that in this latter identification, Richard expresses the idea that underlies the distinction between *anima* (f.) the principle of bodily life, and *animus* (m.) the rational soul or mind.

Holofernes mocks this sort of scholastic jargon when he says, 'if their sons be ingenuous, they shall I want no instruction; if their daughters be capable, I I will put it to them: but vir sapit qui pauca I loquitur; a soul feminine saluteth us' (LLL 4.2.77–80). There is only one instance of a character who mentions the three soul-parts or threefold division, a comic character in *Twelfth Night* whose opinions are often little more than mockery. Sir Toby Belch: 'To hear by the nose, it is dulcet in contagion. I But shall we make the welkin dance indeed? shall we I rouse the night-owl in a catch that will draw three I souls out of one weaver? shall we do that?' (12N 2.3.55–8).

There are numerous occasions when 'soul' is used to refer to either the faculty of memory or to an instance of remembrance, in line with the Middle English use of 'rational' soul. Henry: 'I count myself in nothing else so happy I As in a soul remembering my good friends' (R2 2.3.46–7). Sebastian: 'Oh, that record is lively in my soul! I He finished indeed his mortal act I That day that made my sister thirteen years' (12N 5.1.246–8). Gloucester, on having known the now dead Hastings: '[I] made him my book where in my soul recorded I The history of all her secret thoughts. I So smooth he daubed his vice with show of virtue I that his apparent open guilt omitted' (R3 3.5.27–30). Gloucester's words indicate the behavioral picture stressed by Cefalu; Hastings was so skilled at disguising his evil thoughts with an outer display of good qualities that even his worst guilt was hidden from view. Iago is highly skilled at personal dissemblance, using outward artifices to conceal his inward deceit and baleful plans: 'When my outward action does demonstrate I The native act, and figure of my heart, I In complement extern, 'tis not long after I But I will wear my heart upon my sleeve, I For doves to peck at: I am not what I am' (Oth. 1.1.61–5). As part of his secret plot, Iago (falsely) attributes this same duplicitous skill to the loyal Cassio, who is 'no farther conscionable than in putting on the mere form of civil and humane seeming, for the better compassing of his salt and hidden affections ... that [he] has an eye can stamp and counterfeit the true advantages never present themselves' (Oth. 2.1.237–41).

In addition to these first-person reflections, descriptions of others' views of human nature in behavioral terms also appear in many places. Portia reflects on the sorry state of affairs that has left Antonio in debt to Shylock: 'I never did repent for doing good, I Nor shall not now: for in companions I That do converse and waste the time together, I Whose souls do bear an equal yoke of love, I There must be needs a like proportion I Of lineaments, of manners and of spirit' (MV 3.4.10–15). In other words, those persons bound together as friends share not only the outward displays of their mutual affection, but also the inner 'spirit' that animates their friendly behavior. However, Portia continues: 'If it be so, I How little is the cost I have bestow'd I In purchasing the semblance of my soul I From out the state of hellish misery!' (MV 3.4.18–21). Buckingham employs 'mind' in the same sense when he greets Richard, Duke of Gloucester: 'Withal I did infer your lineaments, I Being the right idea of your father, I Both in your form and nobleness of mind' (R3 3.7.12–14).

In many different circumstances Shakespeare's characters speak of the soul as an inner, private 'place'; there are many ways in which this inwardness is or can be manifest. In *Richard II* the Queen says, 'yet again, methinks, I Some unborn sorrow, ripe in fortune's womb, | Is coming towards me, and my inward soul | With nothing trembles' (R2 2.2.9–11). And then again, shortly after: 'It may be so; but yet my inward soul | Persuades me it is otherwise: howe'er it be, | I cannot but be sad; so heavy sad | As, though on thinking on no thought I think, | Makes me with heavy nothing faint and shrink' (R2 2.2. 28–32); that is, a conscious intention can be empty, the soul within can become hollow. King Richard himself says, '''Tis very true, my grief lies all within; | And these external manners of laments | Are merely shadows to the unseen grief | That swells with silence in the tortured soul; | There lies the substance ... ' (R2 4.1.285–9). Richard's outward show of grief is slight compared to the inward torment he feels, but which others cannot hear. Duke Orsino says, 'Stand you a while aloof, Cesario, | Thou know'st no less but all; I have unclasp'd | To thee the book even of my secret soul' (12N 1.4.12–14). This behavioral sense of inner and outer is equally well conveyed by 'mind' when Talbot says, 'Be not dismay'd, fair lady; nor misconstrue | The mind of Talbot, as you did mistake | The outward composition of his body' (1H6 2.3.73–4).

However, perhaps the fullest expression of the author's view comes across in the poems:

> The deep vexation of his inward soul
> Hath served a dumb arrest upon his tongue;
> Who, mad that sorrow should his use control,
> Or keep him from heart-easing words so long,
> Begins to talk; but through his lips do throng
> Weak words, so thick come in his poor heart's aid,
> That no man could distinguish what he said. [RL 255]

The poet's inward soul as the seat of strong emotions is here identified with the heart; the heart is so overcome with the internal conflict of sadness and anger that it renders him temporarily incapable of verbally expressing that very trouble. And again, the poet reflects on the divide between outward semblance and inward reality:

> Those parts of thee that the world's eye doth view
> Want nothing that the thought of hearts can mend;
> All tongues, the voice of souls, give thee that due,
> Uttering bare truth, even so as foes commend.
> Thy outward thus with outward praise is crown'd. [Son. 69]

The soul is often spoken of in direct contrast with the body, in many cases such phrases indicate the soul as life-force or vital principle. Anne: 'Though it be temporal, | Yet, if that quarrel, fortune, do divorce | It from the bearer, 'tis a sufferance panging | As soul and body's severing' (H8 2.3.13–16). Antonio: 'I once did lend my body for his wealth; | Which, but for him that had your husband's ring, | Had quite miscarried: I dare be bound again, | My soul upon the forfeit, that your lord | Will never more break faith advisedly' (MV 5.1.249–53). Benedick: 'And though you know my inwardness and love | Is very much unto the prince and Claudio, | Yet, by mine honour, I will deal in this | As secretly and justly as your soul | Should with your body' (Ado 4.1.244–9). To aver that one's words and actions are 'as secret and as just' as the soul's compact with the body does not, of course, imply that personal intentions cannot be discerned by others. Rather, it conveys the idea that the secrecy with which they are hidden is as strong as an individual's skill in covering them over. Morton says to Northumerlnad: 'My lord your son had only but the corpse, | But shadows and the shows of men, to fight; | For that same word, rebellion, did divide | The action of their bodies from their souls' (2H4 1.1.191–4). The love-struck poet reflects that if his soul betrays him then, 'My nobler part to my gross body's treason; | My soul doth tell my body that he may | Triumph in love; flesh stays no father reason; | But, rising at thy name, doth point out thee | As his triumphant prize' (Son. 151).

The human soul as principle of life or life-force clearly comes across in many passages where the soul is carried or borne by blood or breath. Henry says about the death of the traitorous Mowbray, 'like a traitor coward, | Sluiced out his innocent soul through streams of blood: | Which blood, like sacrificing Abel's, cries' (R2 1.1.102–4). Benedick remarks this about humans' animal bodies: 'Now, divine air! now is his soul ravished! Is it | not strange that sheeps' guts should hale souls out | of men's bodies?' (Ado 2.3.58–60). Graziano exclaims on Shylock's execrable behavior that it makes him want to 'hold the opinion with Pythagoras, | That souls of animals infuse themselves | Into the trunks of men thy currish spirit | Govern'd a wolf, who, hang'd for human slaughter, | Even from the gallows did his fell soul fleet, | And, whilst thou lay'st in thy unhallow'd dam, | Infused itself in thee; for thy desires | Are wolvish, bloody, starved and ravenous' (MV 4.1.130–7). Other characters express one or another view about the ancient doctrine of soul-migration, such as Malvolio: 'That the soul of our grandam might haply inhabit a bird ... I think nobly of the soul, and no way approve his opinion.' To which the Clown responds: 'Fare thee well. Remain thou still in darkness: | thou shalt hold the opinion of Pythagoras ere I will | allow of thy wits, and fear to kill a woodcock, lest | thou dispossess the soul of thy grandam' (12N 4.2.48–53).

Pythagoras was not the only pre-Socratic the poet knew about, since he also is aware of another archaic doctrine, that the soul is a seed whose body is a bark-like skin: 'My body or my soul, which was the dearer, | When the one pure, the other made divine? | ... the bark peel'd from the lofty pine, | His leaves will wither and his sap decay; | So must my soul, her bark being peel'd away' (RL 167). There are other instances of Platonic soul-imagery, such as those that play on the soul's wings and its ascent to upper regions. Queen Elizabeth says about her young children: 'My unblown flowers, new-appearing sweets! | If yet your gentle souls fly in the air | And be not fix'd in doom perpetual, | Hover about me with your airy wings | And hear your mother's lamentation!' (R3 4.4.9–14). Lorenzo rhapsodizes on the same imagery, compounded with the Christian notion of angelic beings, the human body's corruptible condition, and an astrological strophe about souls as stars: 'There's not the smallest orb which thou behold'st | But in his motion like an angel sings, | Still quiring to the young-eyed cherubins; | Such harmony is in immortal souls; | But whilst this muddy vesture of decay | Doth grossly close it in, we cannot hear it' (MV 5.1.60–5). Viola uses the same stellar imagery: 'And all those sayings will I overswear; |And those swearings keep as true in soul | As doth that orbed continent the fire | That severs day from night' (12N 5.1.269–72). And Bedford says of the dead King Henry V that 'A far more glorious star thy soul will make |

Than Julius Caesar or bright ... ' (1H6 1.1.55–6). The poet is also well aware of the idea of a world-soul (*anima mundi*), though this may be no more than a rhetorical trope: 'Not mine own fears, nor the prophetic soul | Of the wide world dreaming on things to come, | Can yet the lease of my true love control, | Supposed as forfeit to a confined doom' (Son. 107). The poet sometimes uses rather negative terms to describe the body, from whose prison death releases the soul:

> Even here she sheathed in her harmless breast
> A harmful knife, that thence her soul unsheathed:
> That blow did that it from the deep unrest
> Of that polluted prison where it breathed:
> Her contrite sighs unto the clouds bequeath'd
> Her winged sprite, and through her wounds doth fly
> Life's lasting date from cancell'd destiny. [RL 247]

Despite the many passages that support a behavioral view of the soul in relation to its outward manifestation, Shakespeare allows his characters to express a common Christian belief in the soul's basic immortal status. Warwick: 'And after all this fearful homage done, | Give thee thy hire and send thy soul to hell, | Pernicious blood-sucker of sleeping men!' (2H6 3.2.224–6). Suffolk: 'If I depart from thee, I cannot live; | And in thy sight to die, what were it else | But like a pleasant slumber in thy lap? | Here could I breathe my soul into the air. | ... So shouldst thou either turn my flying soul, | Or I should breathe it so into thy body, | And then it lived in sweet Elysium' (2H6 3.2.388–98). Plantagenet says about the dead Mortimer: 'And peace, no war, befall thy parting soul! | In prison hast thou spent a pilgrimage | And like a hermit overpass'd thy days' (1H6 2.5.115–17). Joan of Arc, visited by fiends in her prison cell, implores their help in these words: 'Cannot my body nor blood-sacrifice | Entreat you to your wonted furtherance? | Then take my soul, my body, soul and all, | Before that England give the French the foil' (1H6 5.3.20–3). King Henry himself says, 'For what I speak | My body shall make good upon this earth, | Or my divine soul answer it in heaven' (R2 1.1.36–8). The Bishop says of Norfolk's death in Venice, that 'he gave his body to that pleasant country's earth, | And his pure soul unto his captain Christ, | Under whose colours he had fought so long' (R2 4.1.97–100). Richard takes up the same theme in a later scene: 'Join not with grief, fair woman, do not so, | To make my end too sudden: learn, good soul, | To think our former state a happy dream; | From which awaked, the truth of what we are | Shows us but this: I am sworn brother, sweet, | To grim Necessity, and he and I | Will keep a league till death' (R2 5.1.16–22).

Shakespeare's use of 'mind' is compatible with both the behavioral interpretation of inwardness and its outward manifestation, and with the common view of mind as the noble or rational part of the human soul. One of its principal meanings is to mark out the rational faculty or power of reflection, as in these remarks by Queen Margaret: 'The mutual conference that my mind hath had, | By day, by night, waking and in my dreams ... | Makes me the bolder to salute my king | With ruder terms, such as my wit affords | And over-joy of heart doth minister' (2H6 1.1.25–30). And again shortly after, following the same theme: 'I thought King Henry had resembled thee | In courage, courtship and proportion: | But all his mind is bent to holiness, | To number Ave-Maries on his beads' (2H6 1.3.53–6). The Queen in another play comments in the same vein on another person's 'change of mind', after observing perplexing changes in his behavior: 'What, is my Richard both in shape and mind | Transform'd and weaken'd? hath Bolingbroke deposed | Thine intellect? hath he been in thy heart?' (R2 5.1.50–2). Various references to mind can also be used to distinguish intellect from the will or emotion. King Henry remarks that the mind can be stimulated by present discomfort to refuse further indecision and thus rouse the body to action: ''Tis good for men to love their present pains | Upon example; so the spirit is eased: | And when the mind is quicken'd, out of doubt, | The organs, though defunct and dead before, | Break up their drowsy grave and newly move, | With casted slough and fresh legerity' (H5 4.1.18–23). Nathaniel paints a delightful picture of the proper food for the mind, its education is a kind of eating conducted by the noble part of the human soul. He likens the human sensitive soul, whose functions are maintained by ordinary food and drink, to an animal's soul:

> Sir, he hath never fed of the dainties that are bred
> in a book;
> He hath not eat paper, as it were; he
> hath not drunk ink:
> His intellect is not
> replenished; he is only an animal, only sensible in the duller parts:
> And such barren plants are set before us, that we thankful should be,
> Which we of taste and feeling are, for those parts that
> do fructify in us more than he.
> For as it would ill become me to be vain, indiscreet, or a fool,
> So were there a patch set on learning, to see him in a school. [LLL 4.2.23–31]

The contemplative lover dwells on the power of the mind's eye to recreate his beloved's form. His rational 'part' is so distracted by memories of her beauty that it is partly disconnected from the sensory-motor 'parts'. The ordinary sensible features of delightful things cannot displace her image from his love-struck mind, which renders all he sees only seeming or semblance:

> Since I left you, mine eye is in my mind;
> And that which governs me to go about
> Doth part his function and is partly blind,
> Seems seeing, but effectually is out;
> For it no form delivers to the heart ...
> Of his quick objects hath the mind no part,
> Nor his own vision holds what it doth catch:
> For if it see the rudest or gentlest sight ...
> ... it shapes them to your feature:
> Incapable of more, replete with you,
> My most true mind thus makes mine eye untrue. [Son. 113]

It is in virtue of the intellectual powers of the mind that reason is able to make sound judgments and deliver opinions that can lead to genuine knowledge. Suffolk says, 'But, in my mind, that were no policy: | The king will labour still to save his life, | The commons haply rise, to save his life' (2H6 3.1.238–40). Helena reflects on Demetrius' obvious qualities: 'Things base and vile, folding no quantity, | Love can transpose to form and dignity: | Love looks not with the eyes, but with the mind; | And therefore is wing'd Cupid painted blind: | Nor hath Love's mind of any judgement taste' (MND 1.1.232–36). Love is not the only emotional state that can cloud one's mind and lead to hasty and ill-formed judgments; the mind is also the seat of other emotions and passions. Salarino: 'Your mind is tossing on the ocean; | There, where your argosies with portly sail, | Like signiors and rich burghers on the flood' (MV 1.1.8–10). Achilles: 'My mind is troubled, like a fountain stirr'd; | And I myself see not the bottom of it.' To which Thersites replies, 'Would the fountain of your mind were clear again, | that I might water an ass at it! I had rather be a | tick in a sheep than such a valiant ignorance' (Tro. 3.3.8–12). Cressida is bereft when her lover leaves, uttering the same sentiments about eye and mind as Sonnet 113: 'Troilus, farewell! one eye yet looks on thee | But with my heart the other eye doth see. | Ah, poor our sex! this fault in us I find, | The error of our eye directs our mind: | What error leads must err; O, then conclude | Minds sway'd by eyes are full of turpitude' (Tro. 5.2.107–12). Prospero confronts the dreadful consequences of his schemes: 'I am vex'd; | Bear with my weakness; my, brain is troubled: | Be not disturb'd with my infirmity: | If you be pleased, retire into my cell | And there repose: a turn or two I'll walk, | To still my beating mind' (Temp. 4.1.158–63). King Lear's sanity nears the limits set by his tormented thoughts: 'The body's delicate: the tempest in my mind | Doth from my senses take all feeling else | Save what beats there' (Lear 3.4.12–14). Edgar later reflects on Lear's mental degeneration: 'When we our betters see bearing our woes, | We scarcely think our miseries our foes. | Who alone suffers suffers most in the mind, | Leaving free things and happy shows behind: | but then the mind much sufferance doth o'er skip, | When grief hath mates, and bearing fellowship' (Lear 3.6.95–100). Macbeth says that he would 'better be with the dead, | Whom we, to gain our peace, have sent to peace, | Than on the torture of the mind to lie | In restless ecstasy' (Mac. 3.2.21–24). Insofar as the human mind can contain or bear the load of sin or guilt it can alter the inner equilibrium that comprises a normal, sane condition.

On many occasions those stricken with remorse or shame or those who infer that others should have these feelings in virtue of their actions pause to reflect on how it is that they bear their sin or guilt. Gloucester says, 'Suspicion always haunts the guilty mind; | The thief doth fear each bush an officer' (3H6 5.6.11–12). Lady Anne laments over the corpse of King Henry V and curses his foul, devilish murderer, Richard, of whom she says, 'Thou hast made the happy earth thy hell, | Filled it with cursing cries and deep exclaims. | If thou delight to view thy heinous deeds, | Behold this pattern of thy butcheries.' She knows exactly where to lay the blame: 'Thou wast provoked by thy bloody mind. | Which never dreamt on aught but butcheries: | Didst thou not kill this king?' (R3 1.2.100–2). Henry Bolingbroke (later Henry IV) says to Mowbray, Duke of Norfolk, that if Richard had allowed him then 'One of our souls had wandered in the air, | Banished this frail sepulchre of our flesh | As now our flesh is banished from this land.' But he also gives Norfolk fair warning: 'Confess thy treasons ere thou fly the realm | Since thou hast far to go, bear not along | The clogging burden of a guilty soul' (R2 1.3.188–93). Antonio mocks Shylock's thrifty parable about ewes and rams: 'The devil can cite Scripture for his purpose. | An evil soul producing holy witness | Is like a villain with a smiling cheek' (MV 1.3.97–9).

The sonnet poet even feels the sinful burden of *amour propre*, for he considers that 'Sin of self-love possesseth all mine eye | And all my soul and all my every part; | And for this sin there is no remedy, | It is so grounded inward in my heart' (Son. 62). The sentiment or passion of love is properly found in the heart, but it affects the whole soul and not just one soul-part. In *The Rape of Lucrece*, sin is often compared to a stain or blemish, which, depending on one's basic inner virtue, can either be absorbed or repelled: 'Though my gross blood be stain'd with this abuse, | Immaculate and spotless is my mind' (RL 237); 'What is the quality of mine offence, | Being constrain'd with dreadful circumstance? | May my pure mind with the foul act dispense, | My low-declined honour to advance?' (RL 244); 'With this, they all at once began to say, | Her body's stain her mind untainted clears' (RL 245). But these statements about sin staining the soul or mind do not imply that the soul or mind is a separate substance which assumes these properties. When Cefalu discusses Hamlet's preoccupation with customary sin and habitual conduct he says that Hamlet's beliefs 'perhaps contribute to his miscalculated decision to unburden himself of all memories and dispositional attitudes ... But if on the one hand he believes habits are pernicious for the reasons he adduces ... he seems on the other hand as convinced as his peers that inveterate behavioral patterns are infallible clues to one's private attitudes and intentions.'[27]

Shakespeare's expert knowledge of medical models for the diagnosis and explanation of physical and mental diseases has been studied in some detail.[28] On one or another occasion he seems to rely on either Galenic or Paracelsan terms to describe characters' insane or deranged words and actions. These passages clearly show that he thought of normal and abnormal conditions in psycho-physical terms, that is, as a balance or imbalance that affected the whole person. Queen Margaret: 'Oft have I heard that grief softens the mind, | And makes it fearful and degenerate; | Think therefore on revenge and cease to weep' (2H6 4.4.1–3). Clarence bewails King Henry's reaction to shocking news: 'No, no, he cannot long hold out these pangs | The incessant care and labour of his mind | Hath wrought the mure that should confine it in | So thin that life looks through and will break out' (2H4 4.3.117–20). Salerio reports to Bassanio about Antonio's state of health: 'Not sick, my lord, unless it be in mind; | Nor well, unless in mind: his letter there | Will show you his estate' (MV 3.2.232–4). Macbeth faces ruin near the final scene, but has utter resolve: 'The mind I sway by and the heart I bear | Shall never sag with doubt nor shake with fear.' But he does not hesitate to ask the Doctor if he cannot assist his wife: 'Canst thou not minister to a mind diseased, | Pluck from the memory a rooted sorrow, | Raze out the written troubles of the brain | And with some sweet oblivious antidote | Cleanse the stuff'd bosom of that perilous stuff | Which weighs upon the heart?' (Mac. 5.3.42–6). No more intense depiction of madness could be expressed than King Lear's wretched final state, presaged in several subtle lines before his total collapse.[29] King Lear: 'Infirmity doth still neglect all office |

---

[27] Cefalu, 2000, pp. 417–18.
[28] Hoeniger, 1985, pp. 113–27.
[29] Hoeniger, 1985, pp. 307–38.

Whereto our health is bound; we are not ourselves | When nature, being oppress'd, commands the mind | To suffer with the body' (Lear 2.2.278–81). In one scene with the Fool and Edgar he says, 'When the mind's free | The body's delicate. This tempest in my mind | Doth from my senses take all feeling else | Save what beats there' (Lear 3.4.11–14). Ophelia is distraught at Hamlet's bizarre words, his sarcastic jibes at her affection, and his inexplicable actions: 'Oh, what a noble mind is here o'erthrown! | The courtier's, soldier's, scholar's eye, tongue, sword; | The expectancy and rose of the fair state, | The glass of fashion and the mould of form, | The observed of all observers, quite, quite down!' (Ham. 3.1.153–7). It is Hamlet's outward demeanor that is observed by all observers, but from this one can indeed infer an inward collapse.

One of the principal meanings of 'mind' is inclination or disposition, for example, when King Edward rebukes his courtiers for not telling him of Clarence's death: 'All this from my remembrance brutish wrath | Sinfully pluck'd, and not a man of you | Had so much grace to put it in my mind' (R3 2.1.119–21). Buckingham: 'Who knows the lord protector's mind herein? | Who is most inward with the royal duke?' To which the Bishop of Ely replies, 'Your grace, we think, should soonest know his mind' (R3 3.4.7–9). This usage is very close to the sense of 'mind' conveyed in passages which indicate someone's intention. Clarence gives his opinion on King Edward's choice of wife and his offer to provide one for Clarence: 'In choosing for yourself, you show'd your judgment, | Which being shallow, you give me leave | To play the broker in mine own behalf; | And to that end I shortly mind to leave you' (3H6 4.1.60–2). King Edward asks Montague and Hastings to resolve his doubt about their loyalty to Warwick: 'if you mind to hold your true obedience, | Give me assurance with some friendly vow, | That I may never have you in suspect' (3H6 4.1.137–9). In *Taming of the Shrew*, Kate insists on speaking her mind, that is, disclosing her wishes and desires, which here she attributes to her heart: 'Your betters have endured me say my mind, | And if you cannot, best you stop your ears. | My tongue will tell the anger of my heart, | Or else my heart concealing it will break, | And rather than it shall, I will be free | Even to the uttermost, as I please, in words' (TS 4.3.73–80).

By far the most significant Shakespearean passages about the mind and mental functions in terms of the proposed behavioral and functional framework are those that refer to the inner person. It is surely one of Shakespeare's most distinctive descriptive principles that the nobility or baseness of an individual's true nature shines through by way of its outward forms. Petruchio says it very neatly: 'Our purses shall be proud, our garments poor | For 'tis the mind that makes the body rich; | And as the sun breaks through the darkest clouds, | So honour peereth in the meanest habit' (TS 4.3.169–72). Kate expounds on women's special virtues in these words: 'Why are our bodies soft and weak and smooth, | Unapt to toil and trouble in the world, | But that our soft conditions and our hearts | Should well agree with our external parts? | Come, come, you froward and unable worms! | My mind hath been as big as one of yours, | My heart as great, my reason haply more, | To bandy word for word and frown for frown' (TS 5.2.170–7). Viola says to the Captain just now arrived in Illyria: 'There is a fair behavior in thee, captain; | And though that nature with a beauteous wall | Doth oft close in pollution, yet of thee | I will believe thou hast a mind that suits | With this thy fair and outward character'

(12N 1.2.43–7). Sebastian echoes this same theme in the next act when he describes his sister: 'she much resembled me, [though she] was yet of many accounted beautiful: but, though I could not with such estimable wonder overfar believe that, yet thus far I will boldly publish her; she bore a mind that envy could not but call fair' (12N 2.1.21–7). Antonio reproaches Sebastian: 'But O how vile an idol proves this god | Thou hast, Sebastian, done good feature shame. | In nature there's no blemish but the mind; | None can be call'd deform'd but the unkind: | Virtue is beauty, but the beauteous evil | Are empty trunks o'er-flourish'd by the devil' (12N 3.4.357–62).

Shakespeare sometimes uses 'mind' in adverbial and prepositional clauses to refer to the memory alone, that is, to the collective or individual memory, either in an instance or through an observance. It is uncommon, however, for 'mind' to be used in periphrasis for the whole person. On the other hand, soul is often used in phrases that are periphrastic for the self, such as 'poor soul', phrases that are usually couched in the third person, in an address to others, either present or absent. It is also used in oaths, for example, 'upon my soul' or 'by my soul', to convey the sense of something spoken sincerely or with the truth. Shakespeare also employs 'spirit' or 'spirits' in numerous passages; such usage seems to fall under one of two main headings. 'Spirit' is often used in a standard medical sense denoting vital or animal spirits; these were understood to be rapidly moving, small corpuscles, carried either through the blood or breath or both. But he also used 'spirit' to refer to disembodied entities, composed of non-earthly material, such as fairies or demons. This accorded fairly well with Renaissance ideas about non-human spiritual intelligences, such as one finds in Giordano Bruno and other magical writers.

In his thorough analysis of the behavioral concept of mind in *Hamlet*, Paul Cefalu concludes that 'there is no sufficient evidence that *Hamlet* anticipates Cartesian dualism or any of the varying innatist or idealist philosophies critics have traditionally attributed to it … Hamlet inherits a widely-held Augustinian-Protestant preoccupation with the tortured relationship among habit, sin, and action.' This is not so distant from some of the other trends that began to emerge in the century before Shakespeare's exploration of the intricacies of human nature: 'Early modern theories of the mind and subjective states were often conceived not solely in terms of their privacy, secretness, or inaccessibility, nor in terms of their distinction from bodies, behavior, or the outer world, but simply in terms of their use and contingent relationship with various physical states.'[30] There is lots of textual evidence to support the functional interpretation; there are numerous references to an inner or inward aspect of human nature, but this aspect is not hidden or private. It is (almost) always manifest in an individual's countenance or speech or actions, though sometimes such outer signs can be mistaken or pass unnoticed. It takes skill and insight to discern the 'inner' meaning of these signs and to dissemble in ways that lead the observer astray. The functionalist interpretation is supported by numerous passages where characters attribute their mental state to a specific disposition of their organic parts, a disturbance in their humoral balance, or even the physical effects of severe emotional stress, such as grief, anger or lust. There

---

[30] Cefalu, 2000, pp. 427–8.

are no references to an incorporeal or immaterial mind or rational soul; only if one reifies relevant noun-phrases can one turn subject statements into substantial referents. This does not overlook the fact that Shakespeare often employs standard Christian imagery about the human soul's immortality and its second life in heaven or hell; but then, this elaborate imagery is part of his extraordinary theatre of the world.

Chapter 7

The Triumph of Rationalist Concepts of Mind and Intellect

(1) Descartes: mind as simple, immaterial thinking thing

In the history of the concepts of mind and soul, the philosophical speculations of René Descartes (1596–1650) occupy a crucial position. His thinking marks a decisive turning-point in the good fortune of mind's career, at the expense of soul's place in the scheme of things. Descartes offers two accounts of the basic nature of human being: a physical theory about soul, couched in medical–organic terms, and a metaphysical theory about the mind and its relation to ensouled living bodies. His theory of soul is solidly situated in the prevailing medical model of organic functions and deploys concepts from a fairly standard arsenal, whereas his metaphysical theory comprises a radical overthrow of the standard Neo-Aristotelian account. He had contemplated a revolutionary physical theory, the first part on light, the second on human nature, which he called *The World*, but withheld the texts from publication when he heard of Galileo's condemnation in 1633. Four years later, in *The Discourse on the Method*, he took up the theme of a new rational 'science' of the human soul (perhaps originally planned as the third part of *The World*), explained entirely in mechanistic terms. But his most concise, sophisticated attempt to articulate this new position appeared in the *Meditations* in 1641. There are two highly condensed passages in the Second Meditation that encapsulate the most significant watershed in the history of modern speculation about the significance of soul and mind in theories of human nature.

At this point in the chain of reasons, the meditator synopsizes his backward-looking rejection of false beliefs about the soul and his new forward-looking concept of the mind. His response to the evil demon hypothesis has left him in possession of one valuable and certain thing, the 'I' that has these thoughts, including the thought that he might be deceived. But he wants now to know in what this 'I' consists: 'What then did I formerly think I was? ... I propose to concentrate on what came into my thoughts spontaneously and quite naturally whenever I used to consider what I was ... As to the nature of this soul (*anima*), either I did not think about this or else I imagined it to be something tenuous, like a wind or fire or ether, which permeated my more solid parts.' But, he reflects, these ideas are imagistic thoughts, derived from sensory perceptions of sensible things like fire and breath, and, at that moment, he has no good reason to trust what sense perceptions tell him about the world. The one certain achievement of the inward process of methodical doubt, that he thinks these thoughts, does license an inference to the next stage: 'I am then in the strict sense only a thing that thinks; that is, I am a mind or intelligence or intellect or reason – words whose meaning I have been ignorant of until now' (CSM II.17–18).

The first statement is one of the most overlooked passages in the Second Meditation; here the meditator repudiates his previous belief that the soul (*anima*) is a tenuous thing, like a wind or a fire or ether. His reference to 'what he used to think' recalls one of the most prevalent ideas in popular thought, that the soul is some sort of 'breath' or 'fire' or 'inner heat'. One of Descartes' greatest tasks will be to introduce an entirely new account of the nature and function of the mind (*mens*) in a coherent explanation of human nature. The principal attribute of mind, not soul, is thinking and its modes are willing, doubting, affirming, and so forth. But this new concept is not one that the meditator can begin with, for there is no justification for presuming that *anima* is anything more than another prejudice or false belief. One of the well-remarked puzzles about the *Meditations* is the discrepancy between a promise he made in the Letter to the Reader and the Synopsis about the soul, and his alleged failure to fulfill this promise in the text itself. Before his meditations began, the author stated that he would offer a proof of the soul's immortal status; but by the end of the Sixth Meditation no such proof has been offered. Perhaps this is because in the course of the Second Meditation he had to abandon the very concept of soul and all of its preconceived attributes in favor of its replacement, the mind, for which he cannot elicit the attribute of immortality.[1]

Descartes had a long-standing interest in the organic properties and functions of animal beings, especially those features that conferred life on animate things. With regard to his physical theory about the presence of soul in some beings, perhaps one should pay more attention to his hypothesis about an artificial human, or perhaps more accurately, a human-beast conceived as the artifice of a great craftsman. In the *Treatise on Man* he says, 'I suppose the body to be nothing but *a statue or machine made of earth*, which God forms with the explicit intention of making it as much as possible like us. [He also] places inside it all the parts required to make it walk, eat, breathe, and indeed to imitate all those of our functions which can be imagined to proceed from matter and to depend solely on the disposition of our organs.' Shortly after this he defines the animal spirits as 'a certain very fine wind, or rather a very lively and pure flame' (CSM I.99, 100). This definition is clearly connected with the notion of soul dismissed in the Second Meditation, when he says that he used to think of the soul as 'something tenuous, like a wind or fire or ether'; on the next page, it is 'a wind, fire, air or breath' (CSM II.17, 18). He often refers to the animal heart as a source of fire: again in the *Treatise on Man* (CSM I.108), in the *Description of the Human Body* (CSM I.316), and in the letter to Vorstius, June 1643 (CSM III.225). Richard Carter has examined these organic-mechanical images in some detail, underlining the novelty and peculiarity of Descartes' hypothesis, explicitly with regard to the template of an automaton made of earth or clay.[2]

In Part Five of the *Discourse*, Descartes recapitulates some of the principal theses of the *Treatise on Man*, which he had withheld from publication when he learned about Galileo's condemnation.

---

[1] This issue is dealt with in detail by Fowler, 1999, pp. 18–53.
[2] Carter, 1983, pp. 175–9; see also Carter, 1985, pp. 223–49.

I supposed too that in the beginning God did not place in this body any rational soul or any other thing to serve as a vegetative or sensitive soul, but rather that he kindled in its heart *one of those fires without light* [like] that of the fire which heats hay when it is stored before it is dry, or which causes new wine to seethe when it is left to ferment from the crushed grapes. And when I looked to see what functions would occur in such a body, I found precisely those which may occur in us *without our thinking of them*, and hence without any contribution from our soul ... Those functions are just the ones in which animals without reason may be said to resemble us. [CSM I.134; and again CSM I.138]

An important part of Descartes' physical account of the animate nature of living beings pertains to the concepts of vital spirit and mixture. In the Sixth Meditation, he twice asserts that the mind is intermingled (*permixtio*) with the body, and this is not a chance use of the term 'mixture', since 'permixture' has a special meaning. Descartes was obsessed with ways of explaining various types of mixture and returns to this issue again and again;[3] this topic is rarely (if ever) addressed in scholarly studies. In the *Principles*, he spells out some of the salient mechanisms involved in the mixture of spirits: empty space is actually full of imperceptible, self-subsistent matter (CSM I.230); this is similar to the spatial permixture of the soul in an animate body (CSM I.286); there is no real difference between artifacts and natural bodies except in degree of the fineness of its 'parts' (CSM I.288). The simple–complex formal ontology that he lays down in Rule XII of the *Rules* is an early modern version of part–whole theory[4] that allows him to describe the material ontology of particles as the smallest 'parts' of elements, not of whole bodies. All these features come together in his explanation of the life-force manifest in ensouled beings in terms of the motion of animal 'spirits', and hence in terms of the even more basic internal motions of particle-mixtures (CSM I.104, 107–8).

It is not uncommon to hear Cartesian scholars assert that Descartes did not distinguish between mind and soul, that one term can be interchanged with the other without loss of truth. Indeed there are many passages where Descartes does seem to use the two terms as synonyms, but then there are other passages where he goes out of his way to carefully segregate their meanings. In the Second Replies, for example, he says that, 'the substance in which thought immediately resides is called mind. I use the term "mind" rather than soul since the word "soul" is ambiguous and is often applied to something corporeal' (CSM II.114). He is even more explicit in his response to Gassendi in the Fifth Replies, where he clearly underlines an ambiguity in the meaning of 'soul'. He says that one of the proper tasks of the philosopher is 'not to change the names after they have been adopted into ordinary usage', in this case *anima* (soul); rather, 'we may merely amend their meanings when we notice that they are misunderstood by others.' He then goes on to speculate about the origin of the concept of 'soul': 'primitive humans probably did not distinguish between, on the one hand, the principle by which we are nourished and grow and

---

[3] Attempts to explain mixture: in *The World*, CSM I.88–90; in the *Principles*, CSM I.258, 272, 322; in the *Letters*, CSM III.33, 52, 101.

[4] For details on his simple–complex ontological schema, see MacDonald, 2000, pp. 95–110.

accomplish without any thought all the other operations which we have in common with the brutes, and on the other hand, the principle in virtue of which we think. He therefore used the single term "soul" to apply to both.' If the author had been reflecting on ancient Greek or Hebrew usage of soul-terms then this conjecture is a very good estimate indeed. In contrast with this customary usage the author emphasizes that the term 'soul' is ambiguous, and hence should be avoided. 'If we are to take "soul" in its special sense, as meaning the "first actuality" or "principal form of human", then the term must be understood to apply only to the *principle* in virtue of which we [humans] think. For I consider the mind not as a part of the soul, but as the thinking soul in its entirety' (CSM II.246). He makes the same response to the obdurate Father Bourdin in the Seventh Replies, where he reiterates that it was only habit that inclined him to imagine that thinking was an attribute of the soul, as opposed to the principal power of the mind (CSM II.332).

K. V. Wilkes draws attention to Descartes' disambiguation of soul and mind in her article on 'Psuchē versus the mind' in Aristotle's works. She says that Descartes needed a certain foundation in order to combat skeptical arguments and found it in the concept of consciousness, the essence of which is thinking: 'How he reached this conclusion is independently absorbing, of course, but just as intriguing is the sheer speed with which he moved from Aristotle's *Psuchē* to the conscious *mens*.'[5] Wilkes argues that the present range of senses of the term 'conscious' date from the mid-1600s, appearing in the wake of neo-skeptical assaults on claims to certain knowledge: 'It took the challenge of skepticism to hoist consciousness – as we now have it – to the pedestal it still occupies today. (And then, alas, such pseudo-entities as impressions and ideas; qualia, sense-date, raw feels, [and others] came in to put their feet up on the pedestal).' Since that time, she says, philosophers have been stuck with a concept of mind that purports to accommodate both the Cartesian notion of conscious being as the seat of thought and Brentano's notion of intentionality (modified by Empirical–Analytic thinkers) – and these two dimensions are not compatible:

> Phenomena that fit the 'Cartesian criteria' of consciousness, such as feeling pain, are not easily regarded as being intentional; whereas the battery of pre-, sub-, un-, or simply non-conscious phenomena, which the 'intentionality criterion' can easily absorb, fail the Cartesian criteria. The latter criteria (of immediacy, incorrigibility, privileged access) are epistemological; what makes a proposition intentional is a logical matter. In short, the mental, and with it the mind, are a mess.[6]

Michael Frede makes a similar claim about Descartes' rejection of the concept of soul in his account of human nature: 'If we look at Descartes we see that he uses both the term "mind" and the term "soul" to talk about the same thing.' This is a peculiar statement, since it could mean either that Descartes uses both terms in his discussion of human being, who has both mind *and* soul, or that mind and

---

[5] Wilkes, in Nussbaum & Rorty, 1992, p. 114.
[6] Wilkes, In Nussbaum & Rorty, 1992, p. 116; on Descartes' introduction of the crucial notion of *conscientia*, see Baker & Morris, 1996, pp. 100–24.

soul *mean* the same thing, but this is patently false (*pace* John Cottingham[7]). Thus, Frede immediately qualifies his previous assertion: 'If there is a preference for the term "mind", it is because Descartes is rejecting a certain conception of the soul, that of the scholastic Aristotelians, which he wants to replace by another conception. And so he finds it convenient and appropriate to use the term "mind", rather than the term "soul", when he wants to talk about *the soul* as he himself conceives it.'[8] This is an astute insight, for it expresses very succinctly the notion that Descartes' analysis of the functions and powers of mind is not meant to capture or carry forward the earlier notion of *nous, intellectus* or *ingenium*. Rather, it is designed to replace or cover completely the earlier notion of *psychē* or *anima*, in terms of which 'mind' was a separate 'part' or power. Frede is correct in arguing that Descartes rejected both the 'primitive' and scholastic versions of soul as that which explains a living thing's life, including nourishment, self-motion and reproduction. Instead, Descartes has a new scientifically informed concept of the physical world as a whole, in terms of which everything, whether living or non-living, can be explained by means of matter and its properties, expressed through mechanical laws.[9] The concept of the soul that Descartes adopted is the same one that Aristotle rejected, the Platonic concept of the soul as the autonomous thinking being:

> On this Platonist conception it is, properly speaking, the soul which is thinking or feeling anger, and the living organism only derivatively can be said to do these things, namely insofar as its soul is doing them. Now later Platonists, under the influence of Stoicism, give up the assumption that our soul makes us alive. They, too, came to think that bodies, whether alive or not, are part of nature and can be explained in terms of it. But they retain the notion of the soul as the thinking self, distinct from the body, and the proper subject of the mental functions. It is in this way that the notion of the soul attacked by Aristotle is the historical ancestor of Descartes' notion of the mind; a Platonist notion of the soul freed of the role to have to animate a body.[10]

However, beyond the basic Platonist concept of the soul, Descartes also follows, via Augustine's interpretation, the template of the soul's ascent to higher states through mental discipline.

My own conjecture on the contentious issue about whether 'mind' and 'soul' mean the same thing in Descartes' works has several component theses.[11] First, after a certain date (perhaps as early as the *Discourse*), whenever Descartes uses the word 'soul' (*anima*, French *âme*) without any modifier, he is talking about the *rational* soul (or mind); on other occasions he modifies the term 'soul' with the prefix 'animal' or 'sensitive', an endowment that humans as animal beings also have.[12] Second, he routinely describes the material constituent 'parts' of the animal

---

[7] Cottingham, in Cottingham, 1992, p. 236.
[8] Frede, in Nussbaum & Rorty, 1992, pp. 93–5.
[9] See Baker & Morris, 1996, pp. 69–87, 118–24, 127 note 187.
[10] Frede, in Nussbaum & Rorty, 1992, pp. 93–5.
[11] For an alternate but compatible exegesis of these terms, see Fowler, 1999, pp. 161–75.
[12] This claim is supported by Baker & Morris' findings, 1996, p. 70.

soul in terms of particles in motion; the 'animal spirits' are a very subtle material stuff. The supporting medical–physical scheme makes use of the organic processes of decoction of food, the circulation of blood, the rarefaction of air in the lungs and heart, seepage through pores, and so forth.[13] Third, the immaterial simple mind is joined with its host's body *by means of* the animal soul; the mind is not joined immediately or directly with an inert, non-living body, but with an animated, living body.

With this cautious separation of soul and mind observed by Descartes in his physical account of ensouled beings that have mind, one can now turn to his metaphysical account of the true nature of mind in the *Meditations*. The concept of mind, he argues, not the concept of soul, can be made the content of a clear and distinct intuition only through the chain of reasons, and this means securing it firmly as a link in the progressive stages of the Meditations. The initial arguments of the First Meditation were devoted to discrediting sensory evidence; their conclusion is that only the science of 'the simplest and most general things, which do not care whether or not these things exist in nature, contain something certain and undoubted' (CSM II.14). In the Second Meditation, he advanced the rule that a clear and distinct idea was purged of minimal doubt, that the idea of the mind could be made the content of a clear and distinct intuition, but that the idea of the soul could not.[14] Moreover, the self-evident character of the idea that the thought that he thinks entails the existence of a thinking thing confirms the intuition that this thing is a mind, and that the essence of mind is a simple, immaterial substance. In the Third Meditation, he turns his attention to ideas other than the idea of mind, whose existence is uniquely guaranteed by the apodictic certainty of the previous insight. He will only endorse the science of pure essences once he has acquired knowledge of God, because without such knowledge he does not have a criterion for deciding *which* of his perceptions are clear and distinct. The Fifth Meditation proceeds from the idea of God as the source of eternal truths and offers a direct affirmation of the science of pure essences. The Sixth Meditation argues from God as the source of the order of beings and can only partially restore the evidence of the senses; it concedes that at least some of the doubts raised in the First Meditation are permanently valid.

At the final stage in the Sixth Meditation, the meditator has an intuitive knowledge of himself as a thinking thing and God as the guarantee of the perfect linkage amongst beings. God is the pre-eminent agent intellect and human beings are all potential intellects, since they are made in God's image (like the mark of a craftsman, stamped on his work).[15] Since he distinctly conceives of himself as a thing that thinks, he knows that the content of this concept is a real essence which he himself is actually an instance of. This is sufficient to establish that the thinker's essence consists in being only a mind and that he is really distinct from all other things. But he finds that he possesses, beyond this thinking essence, various passions, sensations

---

[13] For details on his medical scheme, see Hatfield, in Cottingham, 1992, pp. 335–70.

[14] On the specific features of mind in the Second Meditation, see Carriero, in Rorty, 1986, pp. 199–221.

[15] This particular argument outline follows Menn, 1998, pp. 366–70.

and emotions which he seems to derive from some body with which he is very closely conjoined, and from its alleged interactions with other bodies. He does not immediately assume that these passions (in the sense of passive affections) really do arise from the union of mind with body. His next task is to argue for this claim and then explain how these non-intuitive thoughts arise and how they are directed toward the perfection of the mind–body composite. If Descartes can accomplish this, then he will be in a better position to evaluate the argument from the teachings of nature. 'There is no doubt that everything which I am taught by nature has some truth', since these composite ideas, like the ideas seen in the natural light, proceed ultimately from God.

The problem now revolves around an answer to the question about which things genuinely belong to our nature as we receive it from God and which things are the result of our own actions. By coming to understand himself as an essentially intellectual soul which appears in the world united to its own body, the thinker can discover what his true nature is and can thereby discern what *this* nature is teaching him. Descartes thus distinguishes between two senses of 'nature': in the broad sense, nature is nothing other than God himself and his creation, the order of beings; in the strict sense, it is *my human* nature, the complex of all those things which have been bestowed on me by God. When he speaks of being taught something by *his* nature, he is concerned with what he understands through his own essence. And what does his nature teach him? 'This nature does indeed teach [us] to flee those things which produce a sense of pain and pursue those things which produce a sense of pleasure, and the like.' In other words, the proper function of human nature, in contrast with the intellect alone, is to give practical guidance for action, and *not* to perceive the truth of things. The operations of the intellect tend toward the perfection of the mind which is knowledge of reality; but the operations of human nature tend toward the perfection of the mind–body composite, its continued survival. It is obvious that the proper usage of the passions is practical rather than theoretical, but we mistakenly think that the *senses* also have a theoretical value, that is, that they give us knowledge of the truth of things outside our subjective domain.[16] But Descartes clearly does provide a justification for the teachings of nature, a justification which applies primarily to the passions and only secondarily to the sensory faculties.

An interpretation of the manner in which his account of the teachings of human nature is closely tied to his causal-interactive account of mind–body union is summarized by Baker and Morris:

> Our Nature consists in a strict correlation between thoughts and movements of the pineal gland. But additionally, given the way the body-machine works, our Nature induces a *normal* correlation between sense-based thoughts and local movements in the sense-organs or between rational and animal voluntary actions; and less immediately, between thoughts and the perceptible properties of perceived things. Finally, mechanical connections between welfare-related conditions of the body get mirrored back into 'Naturally confused thoughts' ... Since to have a Nature is to be a substantial union of mind and body, it follows that only a soul united to a body can possess the faculty of

---

[16] An argument supported by A. O. Rorty, in Rorty, 1986, pp. 516–18.

sensory perception, and only a body substantially united to a soul can possess the power of the body to act on the soul.[17]

However, the thinker of the Sixth Meditation is not seeking practical advice, rather he is seeking knowledge about the world of bodies, as Menn explains. He gains this knowledge only by drawing theoretical inferences from the fact that such teachings are generally reliable; if he did not follow these, he would cease to exist. This conclusion is true even for the most basic assumptions, such as 'there really is a world, that men have bodies, and the like, which no one of sound mind has ever seriously doubted.' The thinker knows that his confused sensory impressions of bodies proceed from some *active* power, in *some* substance; he also knows that his own essence involves only the powers of intellect and volition, and so he infers that he himself does not contain the power that generates these impressions. Although this is as far as his intuition of essences can take him, he still has a great inclination to believe that his sense impressions proceed from bodies and not from God. He thinks we can be sure that, although we interpret our sensations in different ways, our basic inclination to predicate them of bodies is not a human artifact, but is given through our human nature, and therefore from God alone. Since God is not a deceiver and has not given us an inclination towards non-existent things, we can conclude that bodies really do exist. Now, this is different from the structure of the assent compelling judgment that the angles of a triangle equal two right angles. We were inclined to believe these geometrical judgments simply because our attention was then directed at a clear and distinct idea. Here, however, we have two distinct inclinations to believe that bodies exist: first, a natural and scientifically worthless impulsion, without any clear and distinct perception; and then an intuitive perception which deduces that bodies exist, from the very fact of the former natural impulse. Only this intellectual perception allows us to make the *scientific* judgment that bodies really exist in the world.[18] One should carefully attend to what Descartes means when he says that he has re-established the world, for this is *not* the world with which the doubter began, not the world which one takes for granted, filled with sensible things. Instead, it is 'an entirely *new* world brought into being in imaginary spaces', as he says in the opening of *The World or Treatise on Light* (CSM I.90).

Descartes' discussion of the way in which mind and body are united occurs after he has defined the essence of mind as thinking and the essence of body as extension. He states that one might consider the human body as 'a kind of machine', like a clock, whose actions could be explained in an entirely mechanistic manner.[19] But the human being is a composite, this mind united with this body; a human being whose mind is indivisible (not composed of parts) and whose body is divisible (composed of parts):

> Although the whole mind seems to be united to the whole body, I recognize that if [a part] of the body is cut off, nothing has thereby been taken away from the mind. As for

---

[17] See the whole section on human nature in Baker & Morris, 1996, pp. 168–77; this quote pp. 172–4.

[18] This summary statement from Menn, 1998, p. 369.

[19] For details on the beast-machine, clockwork and automata, see Baker & Morris, 1996, pp. 88–100.

the faculties of willing, of understanding, of sensory perception and so on, these cannot be termed *parts* of the mind, since it is *one and the same* mind that wills and understands and has sensory perceptions ... The mind is not immediately affected by all *parts* of the body, but only by the brain, or perhaps just one small part of the brain, namely the part which is said to contain the common sense. [CSM II.59, original emphasis]

It is the common sense that integrates the apprehensions of material simples and composites through the external senses and makes them available to the mind, which can then formulate common natures, that is, common to the material and intellectual domains. The composite formed from an immaterial simple (the mind) and an entirely material composite (the body) can itself be made a theme of an analysis of a clear and distinct idea. An ontological analysis of the mind–body whole is called for and this is signalled by the word 'seems'; the whole mind *seems* to be united with the whole body. That the meditator *seems* to see, to hear and to be warmed provoked him into thinking about what that seeming-ness (or semblance) consists in, and so too here. One can indeed have an intellective simple *idea* of the mind, but the mind itself is not a simple idea, it is an immaterial simple *thing*. And what one can rightfully say about ideas and about things partly depends on where, in the process of reasoning, one comes to have knowledge of one or the other. Descartes has already warned the reader not to confuse or misplace the two formats, order of reasons and order of essences, and it is in ignorance of this that readers will have problems with the interaction of mind and body.[20]

Every time the brain, or just the pineal gland, is in a given state, the meditator continues, it presents the same signals to the mind, even though other parts of the body may be in different conditions at the time. But what these signals present are not isolated, unconnected sensory simples; they usually present *organized* or patterned sense impressions to which the mind can apply abbreviated or synoptic figures, for example, in terms of the science of most simple things. One of the most important 'figures' of such patterned sense impressions in our ordinary experience is the complex of ideas presented by a living, moving human being. The complex appearance of a human being comprises not just the observable properties of an inert object, but the patterns exhibited by their actions, words and gestures. What Descartes tells us is that only the soul can 'breathe life into' these patterns of behaviour; a human's bodily disposition, actions and speech are *animated* by a *sense-giving* being, one 'whole self' which is a mind united with its body.[21]

Descartes' account of human nature is not completely constrained by the causal-interactive explanation that centres on the pineal gland, neural spirits and branching networks of pneumatic tubules. One way in which he can respond to the charge that *only* an interactive account will perform the right work is to point out that he has stressed the need to differentiate the simple–composite scheme when applied to real things and when applied to our *ideas* about things. The different uses of this ontological scheme correspond to the way in which we come to understand the connections between things, on one hand, and the way in which such connections exist in themselves, on the other. With respect to how such things as

---

[20] On mistaken interpretations of this account, see Baker & Morris, 1996, pp. 55–8.
[21] This summarizes my earlier argument, MacDonald, 2000, pp. 108–12.

mind and body are in themselves: the mind is simple, single and immaterial; the body is an extended composite of material simples and composites; and the human being is a composite of both an immaterial simple and an extended composite. But this is *not* how we come to understand a real being as a human being. If Descartes is not as explicit about this issue as one might wish in the Sixth Meditation, his position is quite clear in the Fifth Replies: 'In fact I have never seen or perceived that human bodies think; all I have seen is that there are *human beings*, who possess both thought and a body' (CSM II.299). He attempts to straighten out this crucial problem in a late letter to Arnauld: 'That the mind, which is incorporeal, can set the body in motion is something which is shown to us not by any reasoning or comparison with other matters, but by the surest and plainest everyday experience. It is one of those self-evident things that we only make obscure when we try to explain them in terms of other things' (CSM III.358).

This alternate explanation of the union of mind and body as revealed by our ordinary experience is one of the main points that Descartes stressed in his correspondence with Princess Elizabeth. David Yandell has argued that Descartes 'came to realise that it was a mistake to try to offer a mechanistic or "scientific" explanation of the action of the mind on the body. Given [his] view that the principles of physics do not apply to the activities of the mind ... interpreting the interaction of mind and body as analogous to the operations of either could not possibly produce any understanding of their interaction.' Instead, Yandell suggests, Descartes fell back on one of his fundamental epistemic principles, that there are primitive notions, the most general and simplest ideas, not reducible to yet more simple ideas that explain them. With this doctrine in mind, Descartes can claim that there are three equally primitive notions at work in his metaphysical theory – mind, body, and mind–body union – and that these correspond with three aspects of the natural world – the mental, the physical, and their interrelation. Descartes responded to Elizabeth's entreaties to explain how it is that mind and body are united with some clarifications about the sources of our knowledge about mind and body interaction as we observe it in things in our experience. Descartes argued that 'the various types of primitive notions come to us in different ways. The soul is known purely through the intellect, the clearest knowledge of body is achieved by the intellect aided by the imagination ... and knowledge of the union of mind and body is acquired by means of the senses.'[22]

Yandell draws an important lesson from his ingenious reconstruction of this line of thought:

> Descartes came to the conclusion that the ability of the mind to cause certain physical movements was known through normal experience and sensation ... Any attempt to explain mind-body interaction by applying notions of physical interaction is as much an error as an explanation in terms of purely mental concepts would be. Its concept is 'primitive' or basic, and cannot be understood in terms of (nor by analogy to) mechanistic relations among bodies.

---

[22] Yandell, 1997, pp. 250–53.

Perhaps indeed our failure as limited, finite intellects to understand *how* mind and body could actually be united in human beings, despite the obvious fact that our ordinary experience shows them to be so united, is not itself an internal problem that Descartes' theory has to contend with. Baker and Morris remark on the hidden irony of the common criticism that it is impossible on his substance dualist thesis to rationally explain mind–body interaction:

> that is precisely his *doctrine*, not a *problem* for it. It is part of what he meant to be understood, not something that he would have preferred to pass unnoticed. He expressed it in the claim that the interaction of body and soul is a *primitive* notion. In his view, this is consistent with treating it as something 'ordained by Nature', since this description, by invoking the action of God, expressly puts the matter beyond the reach of metaphysical or scientific explanation.[23]

Serious conceptual confusions arise in an appreciation of Descartes' formulation of mind–body union if one mistakes the essence of mind and the essence of body as exclusively determining the essence of their union in the human being as a mindful body. This mistake begins with a misreading of the famous statement: 'I have a clear and distinct idea of myself, insofar as I am simply a thinking, non-extended thing; and ... I have a distinct idea of body, insofar as this is simply an extended, non-thinking thing. And accordingly, it is certain that I am really distinct from my body and can exist without it' (CSM II.54). It is easy and natural to read this 'I' as this person, the meditator, instead of from the somewhat unnatural (that is, methodically reduced) standpoint, as this mind which has uncovered these essential features through an elaborate process of abstraction.

This discursive abstraction is reiterated in the further statement that 'I am not merely present in my body as a pilot is present in a ship,[24] but that I am very closely joined and, as it were, intermingled [*permixtio*] with it, so that I and the body form a unit' (CSM II.56). It should be very clear from the last clause that 'I' refers to the mind alone, which with the body forms a unit. Reading the mind alone for 'I' in the above two passages gives a much different picture than reading person or human being for that same 'I'. It is rare in the Sixth Meditation for Descartes to talk about this 'unit', the human being. Virtually the entire discussion is taken up with the essential natures of the two things that make up this unit. One hint, that is only fulfilled much later, is that it is, 'quite certain that my body, or rather my *whole self*, insofar as I am a combination of body and mind, can be affected by the various beneficial or harmful bodies which surround it' (CSM II.56).

This last phrase points the reader to a much later work, *The Passions of the Soul*, which explicitly discusses the 'whole self'. As a natural scientist, Descartes made great efforts to explain the interaction of psychical and physical events at a hypothetical brain site, the pineal gland. But irrespective of the success or failure of this mechanistic account, he provides a profound, if sometimes cryptic, explanation of how mind and body can coexist in one whole self. It is a distorted and unjustified

---

[23] Baker & Morris, 1996, p. 154.
[24] It is really quite baffling how many times this statement is misquoted to read that Descartes claimed that the mind is present in the body as a pilot is present in his ship.

caricature of so-called Cartesian dualism to reduce the latter explanation to the former hypothesis. For commentators to observe that there are serious deficiencies in the *causal account* of actual psycho-physical interactions, especially in the domain of sensory perception, is one thing; to insist that an adequate *description* of the mindful body is liable to the same sort of problems, is another thing. Recent studies by a number of scholars have done much to correct this pervasive misconstrual and to point the reader of the Sixth Meditation straight to Part One, section 30, of *The Passions of the Soul*. The point of this comment is that, *in the order of reasons* the essence of mind is a thinking immaterial thing and the essence of body is an extended material thing. But *in the order of beings*, the human is a composite of two dependent wholes, mind and body; further, one is not licensed to conclude that things are connected together in the way that our thoughts about those things are linked together.[25]

In *The Passions of the Soul*, Descartes first wants to carefully delimit the actions of the mind from the passions in the most general sense. Mental actions are, properly speaking, predicated only of volitions which the mind undertakes with respect to its thoughts. The passions, on the other hand, are of three sorts: sense perceptions, bodily sensations, and the emotions. Sense perceptions refer to things outside the body which produce certain movements in the external sense organs and hence correspondent movements in the brain. Bodily sensations, such as hunger, thirst, pain, and so forth, are not predicated of things outside the body. Their essential characteristics are not to be found in objects, although, of course, sensations may be caused by the presence or absence of those objects. The passions in the proper sense are the emotions, such as anger, sadness, joy, and so forth, whose essential characteristics are predicated entirely of the soul. There is an *auto-affectivity* to the emotions, comparable to the self-evident status of the cogito, which is indicative not of the mental nor of the physical domains alone, but of the person as a *mindful body* – a primitive notion: 'We cannot be misled ... regarding the passions [emotions] in that they are so close and so internal to our soul that it cannot possibly feel them unless they are truly as it feels them to be' (CSM I.388).

If sense perceptions, which are unreliable and excluded by the first stage of methodical doubt, were the only kind of passion, then it would be valid to conclude that the mind is conjoined with only one part of the extended body, whether the pineal gland or any other site. But that gland is in fact a functional *part* of a *whole* extended body whose boundaries and conditions are discovered through bodily sensations and emotional affects. In terms of the whole person, the mind is intermingled with (*permixtio*) the whole body as its (the person's) own extension. According to the order of reasons, as developed through the *Meditations*, clear and distinct knowledge of the essence of mind and the essence of body reveal a *real* distinction between the two, such that they can be conceived as existing independently of each other. But according to the order of essences, clear and distinct knowledge of the whole person reveals that the whole mind and the whole body are related as

---

[25] On the crucial importance of distinguishing the order of beings and the order of reasons, see Gueroult, 1984, vol. I, pp. 200–210; and in more detail, see MacDonald, 2000, pp. 63–85.

interdependent parts that contribute to a functionally greater whole (CSM I.339). In Amélie Rorty's words:

> The passions proper [the emotions] reveal that the entity formed by the mind's pervading its own body can form a single whole, a unity whose distinctive benefits and harms are not reducible to those of its contributing constitutive substances. The passions show that the mind is not only permixed with the body but that, taken together, mind and body form a whole with interlocked functions, directed to the well-being of that whole. The we who is served by the passions is not only the machine organism, but the combined mind-and-body, taken as a composite whole.[26]

The issue here, with regard to simple–complex natures, is to understand how the mind-body union of a person is experienced through apprehensions of various 'common natures' which partake of both the material and immaterial domains. In other words, to experience a human being *qua* person is to understand that he or she is corporeal, living and conscious. Serious problems arise when a univocal and unilateral conceptual schema, that is, physical versus psychical, is brought to bear on the concept of a unified mindful body. Entirely physicalistic and reductionist accounts of mind–body union can never adequately 'build in' consciousness and hence are prone to dismiss it as an epi-phenomenon, a product of an imperfect explanatory hypothesis which further empirical research (such as cognitive neuroscience) can remedy. On the other hand, entirely immaterialist or anti-physicalist accounts, though less common, are inevitably faced with the enigma of the soul's insertion in an intersubjective world, a world in which our pre-theoretical understanding of human beings shows them to be sense-*giving* creatures, animated by a lively intelligence which shines forth through all their movements, speech and gestures.

(2) Spinoza: mind as the idea the body has of itself

In contrast with Descartes' substance dualism, Spinoza (1632–77) professes a metaphysical picture whose basis is substance monism.[27] Spinoza does not merely assert this as a ground assumption, but offers a dense and cryptic argument for this on the opening page of the *Ethics*, Part One. Jonathan Bennett has argued that in addition to his 'official' argument, Spinoza also has an alternate, unofficial argument that supports his primary contention. In other words, what Spinoza must agree with is that, first, there is only *one* extended substance, and second, that any thinking that occurs in this world must be done by extended substances. Spinoza has a solid and cogent reason for saying that this one thing, insofar as it is extended and hence co-extensive with the world, must have all possible attributes. If there were an attribute, that is, a basic way of being, that was not instantiated, nothing could

---

[26] A. O. Rorty, in Rorty, 1986, p. 518; see also A. O. Rorty, in Cottingham, 1992, pp. 371–92; James, 1997, pp. 94–108.

[27] On the general philosophical setting in which Spinoza's thesis about the soul has its place, see Garber & Ayers, 1998, CH17CP, pp. 778–80, 815–18, 842–5.

explain this fact, and that conflicts with his core thesis of explanatory rationalism. Spinoza names this one infinite and eternal substance God or Nature, where Nature is the perfectly suitable name for everything in its totality (not just the sum of its material parts). Bennett says that his 'use of the term God as one name for the natural world is evidently based on his believing that descriptions of God in the Judeo-Christian tradition come closer to fitting the natural world than to fitting anything else.'[28] There is, therefore, only one infinite and eternal substance, and it has two principal attributes, thought and extension. There are an infinite number of individuals, each of which can be considered a dependent part of that one substance. Spinoza's position attacks the dualist opposition of God and created world and the dualist opposition of mind and body. For various reasons, Spinoza was not satisfied with answers proposed to problems produced within the Cartesian framework.

God or Nature is the one substance, Spinoza insisted; it has two infinite attributes, thought and extension, each of which has an infinite and eternal mode; for extension, this mode is motion-or-rest; for thought, this mode is intellect. The two attributes under which we conceive the infinite substance should be thought of as different ways of 'seeing' one and the same reality. The entire world can be thought of either as a series of extended things, that is, physical bodies ordered in causal linkages; or as a series of ideas ordered in intelligible sequences. The two series correspond exactly, not because of any external contingent connection between them, but because they are the same ordered sequence viewed in two different ways. The way in which we think of extended things is due to our modes of thought, or strictly speaking, due to our power of imagination which presents our consciousness with images of those things, rather than to the nature of extension as it is *per se*. We think of extended substance as divided into separate bodies which occupy a limited area in space and time, but extension *itself* cannot be thought of as other than limitless in time and space: 'It is mere folly or insanity to suppose that extended substance is made up of parts or bodies really distinct from each other' (Letter 29). And the way in which we think of the other attribute, thought, will depend upon the level of knowledge which our particular finite mind has reached.

The infinite and eternal mode of extension is motion-and-rest; the finite mode, which constitutes individual bodies, that is, the medium-scale things that surround everyone, are *configurations* of simplest particles. In this context, one might think of Descartes' discussion of the simplest 'natures' that provide the basic building blocks of his universal science of extension and motion. Spinoza considered motion as the ultimate basis or most natural state (*hexis*), and rest as a special case of motion. The system of moving bodies is one in which each state of the system can be accurately described in terms of prior states. Explanation of change in state is in terms of a differential distribution of motion and rest among the ultimate particles, which are similar to energy-points or quanta, in contrast to the classical notion that the ultimate units are atoms. The basic configurations that compose individual physical objects in the manner in which humans experience them, are elements in a *hierarchy* of such organized systems. In such a system there is an ascent from the

---

[28] Bennett, in Garrett, 1996, p. 65; for more details, see Bennett, 1984, pp. 70–79, 81–96; for other interpretations of this argument, see Curley, 1969, pp. 20–47; Delahunty, 1985, pp. 89–104.

simplest particles at one end to the whole world at the other end. The latter extreme is one complete individual substance in which all other entities are dependent parts; Spinoza calls this the *facies totius universi* – 'the face of the whole universe'.

All individual things are configurations of particles in a charged energy state which possess a drive (*conatus*) to maintain themselves in being. The hierarchy of beings then is a plenary order of *power* – the higher an individual is on the scale, the less it is acted on by external forces and the more its changes come from within itself. In this hierarchy, the more an individual is acted upon by others without its *drive* being diminished, the higher it is on the scale. There is an equation, therefore, between being more or less active as a causal agent upon others and being more or less real. The hierarchy which emerges from Spinoza's new picture of the world is a modified version of an Aristotelian hierarchy: in ascending order, the 'principles' are the inorganic, the organic, the animal and the human. The human body is more real than merely animal bodies because it maintains itself in being more effectively than other bodies, it does so more under its own control, and it interacts more foresightfully with its environment.[29]

In parallel with the infinite mode of extension, motion-and-rest, is the infinite mode of thought, that is, intellect or mind. In addition to the hierarchy of beings, there is also a hierarchy of ideas, which are the finite modes of thought, and there is a highest order idea, correlative with 'the face of the whole universe' – and that is the infinite idea of god. Neither ideas or bodies belong to the one infinite substance, conceived as the cause of all things (or the Prime Mover). Rather particular ideas and particular bodies belong to the finite modes of the infinite attributes which come into being through the mediation of the infinite modes, motion-and-rest and intellect. The relations between ideas and bodies can be understood from the point of view of either framework. Every body has an idea that corresponds to it and this idea is its soul (*anima*). The human body's idea alone is worthy of being called a mind (*mens*). Or, from the point of view of intellect, every idea has that of which *it is an idea* – the human mind is the idea its own body has of itself.[30] This might sound like a peculiar doctrine; it is surely more common to say that your mind *contains* the ideas of many things, including your own body and lots of other bodies. But Spinoza would say that if you have an *adequate* idea of some thing other than your own body, then this is not a mental entity *in* your mind, towards which you have some sort of mental relation, such as intentional directedness. Rather, your mind, as a finite mode of the infinite intellect, at the moment in which it mentally 'grasps' the thing in the form of an idea, is correlated with the precise finite mode of infinite extension which is this particular body as the 'object' of its idea.[31]

Spinoza's exposition of the schematic correspondence between ideas and bodies is supported by his doctrine about the hierarchy of ideas. For Spinoza there are

---

[29] As Hampshire phrases these claims, 1987, pp. 45–8.

[30] On this exceptionally fruitful doctrine, see *inter alia*, Harris, 1973, pp. 77–87; Daniels, 1976, pp. 542–58; Mark, 1979, pp. 401–16; Bennett, 1981, pp. 573–83; Bennett, 1984, pp. 125–51; Lucash, 1984, pp. 619–34.

[31] On Spinoza's theory of ideas, see esp. Bennett, 1984, pp. 153–67; Donagan, 1988, pp. 38–47; Wilson, in Garrett, 1996, pp. 111–16.

three levels of knowledge laid out in the following fashion (EIIP40Schol2). First, there are confused and vague ideas of experience, which are the result of whatever causal association our bodies enter into with other bodies. There is a purely mechanistic explanation for the formation of such ideas; they are essentially sensible images rather than thoughts and are essentially passive rather than active. The connection between such confused and obscure ideas is one of *association* rather than logical sequence. The repetition of similar experiences when similar interactions with other bodies occur results in the abstraction of composite images which he calls *general ideas*. The recurrent association of one image with other images results in one image being taken as a *sign* for the other and the system of such signs is a language. Thus, the degree to which humans share general ideas and understand each other's meanings depends upon how far they share experiences, that is, how far their minds have undergone similar modifications.[32]

Second, at the next higher level there are adequate ideas which are the result of constructing universal notions based on similarities amongst the inadequate ideas at the previous level. Common notions are general ideas of features that every individual thing which participates in that specific mode of extension must necessarily possess. The most elementary spatial and temporal properties of bodies are the subject matter of common notions and upon them is built the whole scheme of scientific knowledge. For an idea to be adequate means that an idea stands in a logical relation with other ideas such that one can see the necessity of its being thus and not otherwise. One cannot have an adequate idea without being aware that one has knowledge by means of these ideas. The task of correcting the understanding depends upon the original possession of at least one adequate idea to provide a criterion of clarity and distinctness. But how would one know, beyond a reasonable doubt, that this original idea is adequate? Spinoza's answer is that 'truth is the criterion of itself and of the false, as light manifests both itself and the dark.' Phrases in Spinoza's texts, such as 'it is manifest by the natural light' or 'it is self-evident', are indications of the adequate status of ideative content. A true idea is always self-evident because it exhibits the *logical necessity* of the genuine relations between the characteristics of that of which *it is an idea*.

Third, at the next higher level, is the scientific idea; it is an element in a theory that allows one to explain how the 'object' of an adequate idea can appear as a sensible image at the inadequate level. With a full understanding of the actual size and position of the sun, for example, one can explain why the sun appears to be a disc-shaped object at the outer boundary of the atmosphere. Beyond the achievement of scientific ideas is the highest level, *intuitive knowledge*, itself based on the previous stage of comprehensive knowledge, but which in its furthest extent approaches the 'infinite idea of God'. Only God possesses an adequate idea of himself, but insofar as the human mind approaches the comprehension of such an idea then one approaches to the condition of god-hood oneself.

The ordered arrangement of beings corresponds with the hierarchy of levels of knowledge. The first level comprises confused and vague ideas of experience, the

---

[32] Floistad speculates that there is a straight correlation between levels of knowledge and the character of egoistic interests, Floistad, 1978, pp. 1–14.

second comprises adequate ideas, and the third and highest level comprises intuitive knowledge that approaches the 'infinite idea of God'. About this highest level, Spinoza says that, 'the more each of us is able to achieve in this kind of knowledge, the more he is conscious of himself and god, that is, the more perfect and blessed he is' (EVP31Schol). Since God is the same as Nature as a whole, and since Nature is defined as perfect, every being is oriented towards its own perfection or completeness of essence. From this vantage point arises the individual's desire or striving to unite with the source of that which causes the experience of joy or bliss: 'There necessarily arises an intellectual love of god; [and] joy which is accompanied by the idea of god as its cause, i.e. love of god, not insofar as we imagine him as present, but insofar as we understand god to be eternal' (EVP32); 'Although this love of god has had no beginning, it still has all the perfections of love, just as if it had come to be. The mind has had eternally the same perfections which now come to it and that is accompanied by the idea of god as an eternal cause. If joy then consists in the passage to greater perfection, blessedness must surely consist in the fact that the mind is endowed with perfection itself' (EVP33). One can readily appreciate how the German Romantic poet Novalis later referred to Spinoza as 'the god-intoxicated man' and Goethe dubbed him 'the most Christian one'.

In Spinoza there is no simple equation of thought with the mental and extension with the physical, since extended things and ideas correlative to them must both belong to the unique self-caused substance, God or Nature. There can be no ideas which are not as such ideata of external things, nor can there be extended things of which there are no ideas. In correspondence with each level of knowledge or class of idea, there is an ideatum of that same idea; degrees of rationality and degrees of reality must be linked at every stage. Thus, insofar as we purify our understanding in order to consider ideas of the highest level of rationality, we come close to or approximate the condition of godhood; in this way we cease to be merely dependent parts of nature. Our status as natural beings, that is, as entities under the aspect of extension and its infinite mode, motion-and-rest, wholly depends on the class of idea (confused, adequate or intuitive) which constitutes our minds, and vice versa. Spinoza has an unusual and seemingly paradoxical claim about the union of mind and body in the human – namely that, in the special case of humans, the complex idea which the human body has of itself *is* its mind. This union under two aspects which constitutes a person is only a special case of a general, uniform principle.

There is thus an equal novelty in his notion of psycho-physical causation; in contrast with Descartes' position, there is no natural basis for the supposition of causal interaction between immaterial mental things and material non-mental things.[33] Spinoza does not claim that changes in one *produce* or generate changes in the other; rather, every bodily change *is* a mental change and vice versa. Spinoza can insist on this identity since there is only one Nature and one order of natural events that expresses itself, or is conceived by our minds, *under two different attributes*. In his view, there is a virtual identification of mental and physical changes; but this also seems paradoxical on a classical view of substances and

---

[33] On Spinoza's denial of mind–body interaction, see Jarrett, 1991, pp. 465–85; Koistinen, 1996, pp. 23–38.

changes. Spinoza was well aware of the paradoxical character of his thesis and knew that it involved a drastic revision of ordinary language, let alone the terminology of metaphysics.

The particular finite mode of extension which is my body exchanges energy with its own proximate environment; and every such 'interaction' (as one supposes it to be) is reflected in an idea. Since Spinoza construed the moral dimension as coterminous with the perfectibility of things as parts, exchanges which diminish living beings' energy states are poisons, and hence evil, while exchanges which augment their energy states are healthy, and hence good. Changes of state which are the effects of external bodies impinging on particular finite modes in my body (via the sense organs) are *ideas in imagination*, that is, they fall under the lowest level of knowledge. In perceiving an object, a modification of my body occurs which is necessarily reflected or expressed in an idea; this idea, which constitutes part of my mind at that moment (the occurrent mental event), has as *its* object (*ideatum*) a modification of which both the state of my body and the state of the object are causes.[34]

To describe an idea as true for Spinoza is never merely to state that it corresponds with or is a 'picture' of some external object or event; *all* adequate ideas are true and *all* true ideas are adequate. This adequation or ideal of self-evidence is both the necessary and the sufficient condition of truth. Thus, as we ascend the scale of knowledge from mere daydreams and vague experience through clear and distinct perceptions to scientific insight, our ideas of modifications of bodies becomes more and more concatenated or logically coherent. It is the mark of an adequate idea that as soon as it is given to the mind's eye (intuition), it conveys certainty; that is, it provides a standard of certainty and self-evidence by comparison with which other ideas can be assessed. This is another way to understand the significance of the common Spinozistic phrase, 'this proposition is manifest (or evident) through itself.'

Human beings maintain their identity for a limited period of time by preserving a constant adjustment of their parts, as Hampshire explains. This self-maintenance is not the result of some choice or decision by the person, but occurs as a natural process for all things as parts of Nature. Other things are susceptible to fewer modifications because their structures are less complex and thus have less 'reality' than human beings. They can manage only a lesser field in their environment and hence the cohesion of their components is liable to disruption by a more narrow range of external causes. Let us remind ourselves at this point that, for Spinoza, all things and their modifications can be conceived as 'parts' of the cosmic whole either under the aspect of thought or under the aspect of extension. Human beings have a high degree of complexity which, under the attribute of thought, is captured by saying that they have *mind* and that they are *self-conscious*.[35] Thus, a human mind consists of ideas which reflect the effects of external causes insofar as they modify the balance of motion-and-rest (the infinite mode of extension) which

---

[34] This sub-section follows the analysis in Hampshire, 1987, pp. 50–60.

[35] On the often neglected topic of self-consciousness in Spinoza, see Rice, 1990, pp. 201–11.

constitutes the human body. Such a modification arises out of the body's so-called interaction with other things and may be either an increase or a decrease in energy, its 'life-force'.

There is thus a wide range of internal energy states within which a human cohesion of parts may remain united, without the individual being destroyed. These changes in state can be described both in physical terms as an increase or decrease in the organism's vitality, and they can be described in mental terms as pleasure and pain. Thus, every increase in vitality is a pleasure and every decrease in vitality is a pain. Now Spinoza is not making a crude hedonistic observation about the real purposes which underlay our desire for pleasure and our avoidance of pain. Rather, by pleasure he means 'the passion by which the mind passes to a higher state of perfection, and by pain the passion by which it passes to a lower state of perfection' (EIIIProp11N). Any increase in the power or perfection of the human body must be an increase in the power or perfection of the mind and vice versa; in other words, an increase or decrease in vitality or life-force can be construed in neutral terms with respect to the mental or physical domain.[36]

For Spinoza, pleasure and pain, desire and aversion are the primary passions; all the other passions are defined in terms of these. These are passions in the seventeenth-century sense of affects,[37] passions which arise from the passive association of ideas; but in this sense they are confused and obscure states because the mind is not aware of the causes of its ideas. In experiencing these emotions, we are merely reacting to external causes; our conscious life is conducted, not at the level of logical thought, but at the level of sense perception and bodily sensation. So when we experience love or hate, joy or sorrow, the ideas which constitute our mind are inadequate and the judgments we make about the 'object' of love or hate are unscientific. These judgments express ideas about the interaction between our bodies and other parts of nature, but they do not show the true causes of the modifications of our mindful body (our self). These ideas indicate the actual constitution of our own body rather than that of the external bodies, which we *assume* to be the actual cause of our feeling just this way rather than some other way.

Thus Spinoza makes an important distinction between active and passive emotion which derives from the distinction between the inadequate ideas of imagination and the adequate ideas of the intellect. Since every modification of the body involves at the same time its correlative idea, every type and phase of consciousness involves its correlative complex of ideas, including the experience of an emotion. An emotion (*affectus*) represents a whole modification of the person, under both the mental and the physical aspect; it is a *passion* insofar as the cause of the modification does not lie within oneself. A person is passive insofar as his thoughts are a sequence of ideas which can be explained only in terms of causes whose sources are not in his mind. It is an *action* if the cause of the modification does indeed lie within one's mind. A person is active insofar as he is thinking logically, that is, insofar as the

---

[36] Hampshire, 1987, pp. 61–70.

[37] See James, in Garber & Ayers, 1998, CH17CP, pp. 913–49; in contrast with Descartes and Malebranche, see esp. Hoffman, 1991, pp. 153–200.

succession of ideas constituting his mind is a self-contained and self-generated series.[38]

The degree of power or perfection of any finite thing depends on the degree to which it is causally active, and not passive, in relation to things other than itself. The one infinitely powerful and perfect being is God or Nature who is, in every respect, active and not passive. A human being conceived as a finite mode of thought has greater power and perfection insofar as the succession of ideas which constitutes its mind are linked together as cause and effect. A human is active and not passive insofar as the succession of ideas in his mind is a logical one. Remember that, for Spinoza, to explain anything in a legitimate manner is to *prove* the chain of cause and effect that links idea with ideata. Since the order of thoughts and the order of things are the same, the chain of cause and effect can be expressed in a valid logical sequence. A human being has less power or perfection as a thinking being insofar as his present ideas are not explicable as the logical consequences of previous ideas in his mind. In God, there would be an infinite sequence of ideas, each one of which would be logically entailed by its predecessors. But human minds, for the most part, consist of more or less random sequences of ideas. However, they are not random in the sense that they are not the effects of causes of some kind, but in the sense that the causes are external to the sequence. In other words, for the human mind the sequence of ideas is not self-contained and hence cannot be completely intelligible – there are always gaps. The power and perfection of an individual mind is increased in proportion as it becomes less passive and more active in the production of its ideas. The equivalent for the individual human body of this increased cognitive activity is the internal stability of the organism, which enables it to carry on living without any violent perturbations produced by external causes. Thus, the mind is relatively free and active in its thinking when the body is in a relatively constant state *vis-à-vis* its own proximate environment.[39]

Human beings, unlike animals, can be aware of the tendency toward self-maintenance and the increase of their own power and activity which constitutes their real 'nature' as a human being. The reflection in a conscious idea of this *conatus,* the drive to maintain oneself in being, is called desire. Spinoza defines desire as appetite together with conscious awareness of its occurrence and the 'object' towards which it is directed. Now pleasure and pain are not to be found in the 'objects' which desire and aversion afford, nor can they be discovered by any form of abstract reasoning. They represent a change in the psycho-physical state of the whole individual, that is, they are the mental reflection of a rise or fall in an organism's life-force. Such a change may be produced by any number of external causes, for example, being too hot or too cold, being hungry or thirsty. Which specific things will promote or depress the life-force of any particular thing depends on the constantly changing 'nature' of the individual organism, that is, on the particular configuration of its ultimate elements at the moment of its interaction with the external cause.

---

[38] On the notion that there are two kinds of ideas, active and passive, that correspond to two kinds of motion in the body, see Lucash, 1992, pp. 11–23.

[39] Hampshire, 1987, pp. 97–101.

It may be difficult to understand how *conatus* pertains to inanimate things – how could a stone, for example, be said to have a drive to maintain itself in being? The problem for the common-sense view is that we think of a stone as an individual thing or substance; but of course, for Spinoza, this is incorrect. A stone, a plant, an animal are all no more than temporary configurations of finite modifications of the infinite attributes of one thing, God or Nature. They are all parts of the self-aware cosmos that work together toward the maintenance of the whole. Thus, for example, plants consume soil and water, animals consume plants and animals ... and so forth, each thereby participating through an exchange of energy in the greater whole, from whence all derive their life. Thus pleasure and pain, desire and aversion and the consequent doctrine of the passions is built on Spinoza's insight that human judgment and willing are entirely explicable in terms of the natural and necessary tendency of the human organism to maintain and increase its own power and perfection.

Spinoza's ethical theory adopts certain key ideas from the Stoics, especially with regard to acceptance of what is not within our power to change: 'We do not have an absolute power to adapt things outside us to our use ... If we are conscious that we have done our duty, that the power we have could not have extended itself to the point where we could have avoided those things, and that we are a part of the whole of nature, whose order we follow.' He makes an important connection between the realization of our limited power and the attainment of inner clarity: 'If we understand this clearly and distinctly, that part of us which is defined by understanding, i.e. the better part of us, will be entirely satisfied with this, and will strive to persevere in that satisfaction. For insofar as we understand, we can want nothing except what is necessary, nor absolutely be satisfied with anything except what is true' (EIVApp2). As Nadler says, what in the end replaces the passionate love for worldly goods is an intellectual love for an eternal, immutable good that human beings can indeed possess – God.[40] Spinoza argues that the mind's natural love of God is the same as our understanding of the universe, our virtue, our happiness, our well-being and our salvation.

Nadler goes on to say that this virtue 'is also our freedom and autonomy, as we approach the condition wherein what happens to us follows from our nature ... alone and not as a result of the ways in which external things effect us. Spinoza's "free person" is one who bears the gifts and losses of fortune with equanimity, does only those things which he believes to be "the most important in life", takes care for the well-being of others ... and is not anxious about death.' Spinoza's ethical picture of thankful acceptance and humility is directly tied in with his view about the relative permanence of the human soul:

> The free person neither hopes for any eternal, otherworldly rewards nor fears any eternal punishments. He knows that the soul is not immortal in any personal sense, but is endowed only with a certain kind of eternity. The more the mind consists of true and adequate ideas (which are eternal), the more it remains – within God's attribute of thought – after the death of the body and the disappearance of that part of the mind that

---

[40] Nadler, 1999, p. 240.

corresponds to the body's duration. This understanding of his place in the natural scheme of things brings to the free individual true peace of mind.[41]

(3) Leibniz: soul as an infinitely small incorporeal automaton

Here we move from one extreme on the metaphysical spectrum, Spinoza's single infinite substance, to the other extreme, Leibniz's infinite plurality of simple substances, which he called 'monads'. Leibniz (1646–1716) can be considered either a substance monist (one kind of thing) or a substance pluralist (many kinds of thing), since each monad is a species unto itself; hence, there are an infinite number of kinds of things. Our history of the concept of mind proceeds in a direction opposite to Spinoza's orientation: from an infinite whole (the cosmos) to the infinitely small, the monadic elements of the universe, but where in each case the extreme is itself thought to be a living thing. The word 'monad' is from the Greek for 'unit', a term that indicates Leibniz's attempt to avoid the term 'simple substance'. Like Descartes and Spinoza, he agrees with the Aristotelian definition of substance as ontologically independent: something whose existence does not depend on the existence of any other thing. But for Leibniz this means that substance can have no parts, for if it did then the whole would depend on its parts. Thus Leibniz's monad has no material or physical parts at all; it is quantitatively simple and indivisible, like a mathematical point through which many angles can be drawn, or a center whose circumference is nowhere. However, it must have features of some kind or else one thing could not be distinguished from another thing. Thus a monad does have properties such that a description of its composition is complex.

No one can experience basic monads in any way according to Leibniz, they are not parts of the observable world. What humans experience are the results of the organized conjunction of basic monads. They are 'metaphysical points', along the lines of geometrical points, but with no spatial dimension. The medium-sized things we experience in our surrounding world are actually composites or aggregates, considered to be substances 'by courtesy only'. They are no more than the assemblages of totally separate units integrated and coordinated by the dominance of a linking substance (an entelechy), itself just a very complex monad. Monads are not accessible to empirical experience, which could either confirm or disconfirm their existence as a matter of fact, but only to theoretical projection: 'Every extended body, as it is really found in the world, is in fact like an army of creatures, or a herd, or a place of confluence, like a cheese filled with worms' (M 67, MES, p. 228). Although there is only one type of substance, the basic monad, there are an infinite number of instances of this type – every monad is a complete instance of its own kind – every individual thing is a species *sui generis*.

Leibniz thought of nature as having two levels: the micro-level of monads and their linkages, and the macro-level of organized composites, that is, collectives of monads that are the fundamental fabric of observable nature. The key concept here

---

[41] Nadler, 1999, pp. 242–3; see Lucash, 1990, pp. 103–13; on the immortality of the human soul in his earlier *Short Treatise*, see Curley, 1977, pp. 327–36; on ambiguities in the key ideas of eternity and duration, see Parchment, 2000, pp. 370–82.

is that of entelechy: that which unifies the aggregate is synopsized (or present in germ) in a single substance. It serves as the unifier of the whole by representing all its parts through linkages. The idea of the two levels and the idea of an entelechy do not comprise just the trivial point that composites require units because composites are pluralities, but the profound idea that composites which are themselves unified require true units to serve as unifiers (Rescher, in MES, p. 51). Leibniz said that to discover (that is, invent) these real unities, he was forced to have recourse to the notion of a *formal atom*, to rehabilitate the Aristotelian notion of substantial form. Aristotle did not consider the form (*eidos*) to be actually or really separate from the matter whose form it was. Hence, according to his doctrine the soul is totally dependent on its host's body.

The number of monads never increases or diminishes; for Leibniz, there is no real birth or death. All simple substances have their beginning and ending only by a miracle, that is, by God's setting that monad in the actual world or making it nothing. Monads cannot be altered or changed in their internal make-up; 'monads have no windows through which something can enter into or depart from them' (M7, MES, p. 58), and thus our experience of causal connections is also by courtesy only. Leibniz also rejected any interactive theory of perception: there is no causal interaction between a sensible thing and its being sensed. Nothing can affect monads from without, and their supposed changes are strictly the result of an unfolding of their inner programs. In Benson Mates' acutely simple formulation, 'all monadic changes are generated internally through the chronological exfoliation of the exigencies of their own inner natures'.[42]

Despite their quantitative simplicity, monads are qualitatively complex; each one has many properties (MES, pp. 72–4). Substances require qualities to endow them with a character that allows for a distinction of each from the rest. These qualities represent the inner reflections of outer conditions unfolding over time. The universe as a whole is an integrally connected system of monads (a plenum). The qualitative complexity of monads lies in the fact that each provides a representation of the entire universe, each from its own point of view. No two individual things can be perfectly alike, they must differ more than just numerically. With this thesis Leibniz confutes Locke's idea that the soul is an empty tablet, 'a soul without thought, a substance without action'. Experience does not inform the mind, rather, contingent events are merely the occasions through which internal movements emerge into conscious awareness.

According to Leibniz's principle of pre-established harmony there is a strict parallelism that operates in two dimensions (MES, pp. 253–60). Like two clocks that are perfectly synchronous, monadic inner changes exactly correspond to observable interactions between particular things. There is also an exact correspondence between such monadic inner changes and sentient beings' ideas about those changes. According to his super-essentialist position, there are no accidental properties and no contingent events; everything that can truly be predicated of a particular thing belongs to the essence of that thing. Of the infinite number of possible worlds, God brought about this actual world. God always works to bring

---

[42] Mates, 1986, p. 59.

about the best, and the best world is the one that optimizes the best state for all covariant particular things.

The action of the internal principle of change Leibniz called appetition (MES, pp. 79–81); it provides each substance with an internal program that specifies how the entire history of that thing unfolds in a predetermined fashion. He conceived the radical idea that information could be encoded in the internal make-up of an individual substance in such a way as to pre-program the entire course of its subsequent development. He considered the internal principle as an analogue to the algebraic rule (or algorithm) for generating a numerical series or the equation for a continuous curve. All monads have a complex inner structure, an internal complexity of differential detail that runs into endless variations, something like the infinite decimal expansion of pi, according to Rescher's metaphor. In this framework, substantial changes for composite things organized around monadic forms consist in an alteration of specifiable detail.

All monads have perceptions, which are the determinate relations each monad holds with all other monads in its immediate vicinity. Apperception, however, pertains to conscious beings alone, such as animals and humans (MES, pp. 75–8). Leibniz strongly opposed the Cartesian view that animals are organic automata, as well as the idea that all mental processes must be conscious. Leibniz thought that unconscious perceptions lie beneath the threshold of conscious awareness; perception is not a cognitive operation or capacity exercised by some kinds of things, but pervades nature entirely. Even when unconscious, humans are aware of sound, although the component sensory simples are below the level of discriminable perception. Where perception was construed as a monad's determinate relations, appetition is the drive or tendency from one perception to another. Spinoza had conceived of *conatus* as the drive for self-preservation that maintains the existing conditions of things, whereas for Leibniz, it is the drive for self-development striving to bring emergent features into actualization.

The capacity for abstract thinking, through which self-knowledge becomes possible, endows higher-level creatures with the ability to perform inductive and deductive reasoning and make valuations. Thus while soul-endowed animals have sensation, memory, association, anticipation and affection, only self-conscious spirits achieve theoretical knowledge and rational evaluation (MES, pp. 273–4). Rational spirits are also capable of attaining metaphysical insight, including comprehension of one of Leibniz's most basic metaphysical requirements, that there are two levels of reality, the monadic and the phenomenal. The apparent world comprises well-founded phenomena, the coherent and total expression of more fundamental monadic properties. In order to grasp the point of this notion of expression one might think of the way that the sound of a trumpet expresses the specific shape of the grooves in a vinyl record. It would be wrong to think that the trumpet sound and the record grooves have some 'nature' or property in common; rather the pattern of sound is isomorphic to the pattern of grooves. According to the same analogy, one might think of the musical score as the algorithm that encodes the program for how the substantial form of that piece of music unfolds. Leibniz also thought of the relation between impressions and thoughts (or rather, idea and ideata) in the same way that he thought of the relation between the sound and the grooves. The pattern in the 'grooves' of the animal corporeal automaton is 'contained' in the individual thing's inner program, itself governed by the dominant monad of the animal soul or human mind. The interface between corporeal and incorporeal nature is occasioned *by* the precisely determined state of both mind and world.

Leibniz's unusual concept of mind and soul is the consequence of several large-scale metaphysical assumptions: (1) the only genuine substance is an immaterial, simple unity; (2) the complete concept of the subject logically contains all of the predicates that can be ascribed to it; (3) the actual essence of the subject contains all of the properties that can be attached to it; (4) monadic internal changes can only be explained in terms of final causes; (5) observable behavior at the phenomenal level can be explained in terms of efficient causes; (6) the phenomenon of life in living things is not reducible to matter in motion; and (7) individual middle-sized things are preformed and postformed at the monadic level, that is, monadic constituents pre-exist an individual's birth and exist after an individual's death:

> The soul is a spiritual automaton still more admirable and ... it is through divine preformation that it produces these beautiful ideas, wherein our will has no part and to which our art cannot attain. The operation of spiritual automata, that is, of souls, is not mechanical, but it contains in the highest degree all that is beautiful in mechanism. The movements which are developed in bodies are concentrated in the soul by representation as in an ideal world which is in God, that most of the perceptions in the other substances are only confused. [Theo. 40, MES, p. 84]

Leibniz borrows from and transforms several Aristotelian metaphysical notions. A true unity is one that is indivisible and self-subsistent; a simple substance exists independently of the existence of any other thing. The universe is a continuum of infinitely graded spatial–temporal regions, and hence matter is infinitely divisible. If a simple substance was material it could be divided into its uniform constituent atoms and hence would depend for its existence on the collective existence of its parts. Hence, a true unity is an immaterial substance whose paragon instance is a soul. He sometimes refers to monads as units of force; thus, a monad's fundamental characteristic, in addition to its complex properties, is self-activated force (MES, pp. 264–71). At the middle-level, this is manifest in each individual's tendency to move from state to state along pre-programmed lines.

Leibniz wanted to avoid what he saw as some of the pitfalls of Aristotelian physics, but he employs the concept of soul in the Aristotelian sense of intrinsic form: 'By means of the soul or form there is a true unity corresponding to what is called "I" in us. Such a unity could not occur in artificial machines, or in a simple mass of matter, however organized it may be' (NS sec. 11, MES, p. 47). With the final clause he rejects the Aristotelian notion that an individual's form is the consequence or concomitance of the entire assemblage organized in that specifically complex manner. An individual's tendency and source of motion could only be manifest in the phenomenal realm if the formal unity were already there in the monadic realm. Thus, the concept of soul in the strict sense refers to the simple, most basic monad. But in the taxonomic scheme of things, soul in the broad sense refers to an animate, sentient being. Moreover, his concept of machine also embraces two senses: in the strict sense every monad is a machine or automaton – 'in all corporeal nature there exist only machines some of which are alive' (Letter to

Arnauld, MES, p. 48). In the broad sense, a machine is manifest in the phenomenal realm as an artifact with design features.[43]

Given his advocacy of the principle of pre-established harmony, not only are all monads perfectly aligned in terms of their overall internal changes, our ideas about such changes are perfectly congruent with their phenomenal manifestations. This is clearly the case with the cognitive operations of the animal and human soul: 'I have compared the soul with a clock only with regard to the regulated precision of its changes ... And one can say that the soul is a most exact immaterial automaton' (PPL, p. 495, MES, p. 86). This statement reverses the Cartesian imagery of an animal *body* being like a machine. Leibniz says that he is 'in agreement with the Cartesians, except that [he] includes the beasts and believes that they too have sense and souls which are properly described as immaterial and as imperishable as atoms are, according to Democritus and Gassendi' (NE. 66, MES, p. 84). He clearly conceptualized the notion of a machine or automaton in organic, plant-like terms, not in terms of inert, material parts with push–pull functions.[44] With respect to a compound substance such as an animal, the body is organic when it forms a kind of automaton or natural machine; it is properly described as a machine not only in the whole, but also in its smallest observable parts (PNG sec. 3, MES, p. 88). He revived and corrected the Aristotelian notion of substantial form in a way that makes this notion intelligible. On his view, the original notion lacked coherence because it failed to explain such forms' natures in terms of force: 'Just as the soul ought not to be used to explain the details of the economy of the animal's body, so I concluded that one ought not to use these forms to explain the particular problems of nature, though they are necessary to establish its true general principles. Aristotle calls them first entelechies; I call them, more intelligibly perhaps, primitive forces' (NS sec. 3, MES, p. 52).

Daniel Garber has recently attempted to unpack Leibniz's insight about primitive force:

> Leibniz characterized the ultimate individuals in terms of what he calls primitive active and primitive passive force. Primitive active force, which he associated with soul or substantial form, is the ground of derivative active force, which includes both the living force found in bodies actually moving, and the dead force found in stretched strings and taut bows. Primitive passive force, associated with matter, is the ground of derivative passive force, which includes impenetrability and resistance. These two primitive forces come together to make up corporeal substances, the individuals that ground the reality of the world.[45]

L. J. Russell offers a similar assessment of this issue in Leibniz's physics, but cannot make sense of his doctrine in detail: 'Derived active force (*vis viva*) belongs to *materia secunda*. Since primary active forces in the monads display themselves as derived active forces to the degree made possible by the interlinking of matter in space, a body can get the amount and kind of movement allowed it only through the

---

[43] On these broad issues, see Duchesneau, 2000, pp. 225–36.
[44] For which, see Russell, 1967, p. 428.
[45] Garber, in CH17CP, 1988, p. 783.

moving bodies that environ it ... It does not seem that there is any way of making out Leibniz's view in detail.'[46]

Although a monad may be simple in nature, its description may be complex; so also, a composite substance mirrors a complex of determinate relations. Leibniz's definition of perception is the set of determinate relations a monad has with other monads in its proximate environs, and thus a complex thing's perceptions mirror a complex array of relations with other complex things. He defines appetite as the tendency of a thing to move from perception to perception, and thus a sentient, animate being (soul) has the self-directed capacity to move from state to state. All ensouled beings, he said, are 'always images of the universe. They are, after their manner, worlds in abridged form, fruitful simplicities, substantial unities, but virtually infinite by the multitude of their modifications, centers which express an infinite circumference' (Letter to Bayle 1712, MES, p. 74).

On Leibniz's view the history of each composite thing is the unfolding of its constituent monads' own inner natures. Each monad has an internal program, designed to run through a very precise sequence of stages, and since a composite thing's particular profile or aggregate shape is the 'result' of a dominant monad's organization of its subordinate monads, its entire history is contained in its concept. Thus, a composite thing's perceptions and sensations at any given time and place are, strictly speaking, the consequences of its ordering principal monad's internal phase of development. Hence, the soul's perceptions and appetites have their source entirely within the organism: 'Everything in [the soul] must arise from its own nature by a perfect spontaneity with regard to itself, yet by a perfect conformity to things without.' The stipulative condition of conformity is due to both the principle of efficient causation at the phenomenal level, and the principle of pre-established harmony. This train of thought continues: 'and thus, since our internal sensations, that is, those that are in the soul itself and not in the brain or in the subtle parts of the body, are merely phenomena which follow upon external events ... These perceptions internal to the soul itself come to it through its own original constitution, that is to say, through its representative nature, which is capable of expressing entities outside itself in agreement with its organs' (NS. 14, MES, p. 95).

Given his unusual definition of perception, Leibniz is able to assert that every true unity, in virtue of being a simple substance, always has perceptions, even on those occasions when a sentient or conscious being is not aware of them. He refers to these as petite or minute perceptions,[47] and likens them to the innumerable wavelets, each inaudible on its own, which together compose the roaring noise of the surf (NE. 54–5, MES, p. 95): 'In short, insensible perceptions are as important to pneumatology [account of spirit] as insensible corpuscles are to natural science, and it is just as reasonable to reject the one as the other on the pretext that they are beyond the reach of our senses' (NE. 57, MES, p. 100). Against the Cartesians who held that thoughts must be transparent to reflection, that is, that one must be capable of thinking *that* one has thoughts, Leibniz separated conscious from unconscious perceptions. On several

---

[46] Russell, 1967, p. 430.

[47] On petite perceptions, see Mates, 1986, pp. 201–2; Rutherford, 1995, pp. 80, 164; Jolley, 1984, pp. 106–12.

occasions he implied that the existence of unconscious perceptions could be adduced in the same way as the existence of minute particles in physics. Nicholas Rescher once commented that the 'doctrine of unconscious perceptions ... may be seen as a bold stroke of innovative genius in the history of psychology, but it may also be seen in the less dazzling light of an inescapable necessity of Leibniz's system.'[48] According to Leibniz's Law of Continuity, 'nature never makes leaps' (NE. 56, MES, p. 73); there are always further gradations between one state and another, such that it is only the degree of distinctness that certifies a given level of perception. Thus, every simple monad has perceptions, a sentient being such as an animal has more distinct sensations, including consciousness and memory, and a self-conscious being such as a human has apperception (reflective awareness) and reason. With regard to the sentient character of a living being, its perceptions are 'accompanied by memory, a perception of which there remains a kind of echo for a long time, which makes itself heard on occasion. Such a living being is called an animal, as its monad is called a soul' (PNG sec. 4, MES, p. 91).

Although simple monads are immutable, imperishable and eternal, individual things seem to come into being and pass away. But it is only the aggregate of monads that is composed and decomposed; transience and mortality are features of the phenomenal world. The appearance of an individual's death is nothing more than a kind of sleep or quiescence, during which perceptions become less distinct and vivid. An animal or human in ordinary sleep approaches the perceptual status of a bare monad: 'It is true that animals are sometimes in the condition of simple living beings, and their souls in the condition of simple monads, namely, when their perceptions are not distinct enough so that they can be remembered. This happens in a deep sleep without dreams or in a swoon' (PNG sec. 4, MES, p. 95). Leibniz's view here is at the other extreme from the archaic notion that the psyche or soul actually leaves the human body during sleep or fainting. But then in this 'primitive' view the psyche is the life-force superadded to an organic body and separable from it. In contrast, Leibniz locates the life-force in the very elements that compose the individual and identifies it with their essential nature. During dreamless sleep, he says, 'an infinity of small, confused sensations occur in us. Death itself cannot affect the souls of animals in any way but that; they must certainly regain their distinct perceptions sooner or later, for in nature every thing is orderly' (NE. 113, MES, p. 95). God has brought about an optimal world, filled at every point with the greatest compossible life, a world in which all things collectively flourish and thrive: 'Thus nothing is fallow or sterile or dead in the universe' (M sec. 69, MES, p. 231); 'There is never either complete birth or complete death, in the strict sense of a separation of the soul from the body. What we call births are unfoldings and growths; even as what we call deaths are enfoldings and diminutions' (M sec. 73, MES, p. 240).

In Leibniz's rambling and disorganized response to Locke's *Essay* his main concern, he said, was to establish the immortality of the soul. Leibniz seems to have studiously ignored the hypothetical character of Locke's materialist thesis. If God is all-powerful could he not have brought it about that certain systems of

---

[48] Rescher, 1967, p. 133.

matter were designed for thinking? Nicholas Jolley astutely argues that Leibniz systematically treated Locke's outrageous query as an assertion that the soul is indeed material and hence mortal. Jolley reconstructed Leibniz's argument as follows:

> The soul is a simple, and hence immaterial, substance.
> If the soul is a simple, immaterial substance then it is naturally immortal.
> Therefore, the soul is naturally immortal.
> If the soul is naturally immortal, then it always perceives.
> Therefore, the soul always perceives.
> If the soul always perceives, then it has innate ideas.
> Therefore, the soul has innate ideas.[49]

Leibniz also thought that Descartes had denied souls to animals and thus could have thought that Locke, in attempting to refute the scandal of soulless beasts, wanted to replace a separate and separable immaterial substance (the mind) – which Descartes did *not* deny to animals – with a specific arrangement of complex matter. Thus, in a strange double twist around a misattributed doctrine, Leibniz rejected Locke's alleged thesis in order to revive the notion that animals have immortal souls because souls are immaterial. As Jolley puts it, 'Leibniz must admit that the souls of animals, being monads, are naturally indestructible, but that does not mean that they are immortal; true immortality implies self-consciousness which animals, unlike men, do not possess.' Immortality as such and immortality by nature may seem to mark out a strange and tortured distinction, but Leibniz seems to hold the view that only those beings with mind have a sufficiently complex dominant entelechy that the 'echo' of their past perceptions and appetites can be recalled as resonant with the individual identifiable as one's ego: 'The intelligent soul, knowing that it is and having the ability to say the word "I", so full of meaning, not only continues and exists ... but it remains the same from the moral standpoint, and constitutes the same personality' (DM sec. 34, MES, p. 109).

Leibniz also incorrectly ascribed a materialist position to Newton whom he thought Locke had appealed to in formulating his derivative argument. Newton's astute associate Samuel Clarke responded (with Newton's approval) to Leibniz arguing that the soul was immaterial and immortal, extended through its host's body, and united with its body via composition based on close-fitting mutuality. Leibniz retorted that if the soul was extended then it had parts, and if something had parts then it was liable to decomposition and hence mortal. And further, he said that causal interaction between material and immaterial entities could not be explained in mechanical language and could only be supported by continuous divine action (miracle).[50] Oddly enough, Newton thought that Leibniz was committed to a thorough materialism in which human being was nothing more than a clockwork machine and the mind an unnecessary appendage. Ezio Vailati says that, 'Newton saw Leibniz's denial of universal gravitation as a consequence of incipient materialist leanings much in the same way in which Leibniz had viewed Locke's acceptance of universal gravitation as a prelude for materialism.'

---

[49] Jolley, 1984, p. 119; next quote ibid.
[50] Vailati, 1997, pp. 66–77; see also Yolton, 1983, pp. 132–7.

With regard to his view about self-conscious beings, only at the highest level of monadic organization does one have cognitive access to the order of substances in normal experience; the understanding of this order is called reason: 'In the true sense [reason] depends on necessary or eternal truths ... which make the connection of ideas indubitable and their conclusions infallible. Animals in which such consequences cannot be observed are called beasts, but those who know these necessary truths are the ones properly called rational animals, and their souls are called spirits' (PNG sec. 5, MES, p. 107). In this passage and others he makes use of a technical, stipulative definition of spirit, one that is divorced from both religious and medical overtones: 'Intelligences or higher souls, which are also called spirits, are ruled by God, not only as machines, but also as subjects, and [these] intelligences are not subject to those radical changes to which other living things are subject' (Against Descartes 1702, MES, p. 224). Nicholas Rescher comments on this further adjustment of Leibniz's hierarchical picture:

> Leibniz takes rational spirits of humans to differ from the more primitive souls characteristic of lower animals through the possession of a capacity for conceptual thinking with its concomitant access to knowledge of universal generalizations and truths of reason ... The capacity for abstract thinking (through which self-knowledge becomes possible) endows these higher-level creatures with an ability to perform inductive and deductive reasoning, and also enables them to make evaluative assessments ... It transpires that only the apperceptively self-conscious spirits can attain to the theoretical knowledge and rational evaluation which involve conceptualization and universal judgment. They alone are capable of *science* and *morality*. [Rescher, in MES, p. 110]

There is a subtle and far-reaching connection regarding the aggregate of infinitely small entities across several Leibnizian themes: (a) messo-scopic things as aggregates of monads; (b) noticeable perceptions compounded out of unnoticeable perceptual quanta; and (c) self-directed life-forms composed of tiny animacula. One of Leibniz's favorite images is that the individual thing is like 'a pond full of fish' or 'a cheese full of worms'. But for him this is more than a metaphor, since on a very real level, Leibniz meant these statements to be taken literally. He was fascinated with microscopic discoveries reported from about 1650 onward by Robert Hooke, Schwamerdam and van Leeuwenhoek, amongst others, as some of these comments demonstrate: 'In addition to the soul which constitutes the real unit of the animal, the body of the sheep is actually subdivided, that is to say, it is also an aggregate of invisible animals or plants (which are likewise compound) besides that which constitutes also their real unity' (MES, p. 50); 'There is no portion of matter in which there are not numberless organic and animated bodies ... but for all this, it must not be said that each portion of matter is animated, just as we do not say that a pond full of fish is an animated body, although a fish is so' (MES, p. 232).

Nor are his references to seeds entirely metaphorical either since he clearly thought of seeds as containing the embryonic form of the composite whose inner program instructed progressive differentiated unfolding. Hence, Leibniz would have endorsed the Stoics' claim that life resides in *sperma*, but would have disagreed that these were a special class of elements. One can imagine that Leibniz would have welcomed Jacob von Uexkull's description of the *umwelt* of the tiny tick, here synopsized by Gilles Deleuze:

The tiniest of all animals has glimmers that cause it to recognize its food, its enemies and sometimes its partner. If life implies a soul, it is because proteins already attest to an activity of perception, discrimination, and distinction – in short, a primary force that physical impulsions and chemical affinities cannot explain ... In most cases, the soul gets along quite well with a very few clear or distinct perceptions ... Everything else in the great expanse of Nature, which the tick nevertheless conveys, is only a numbness, a dust of tiny dark and scattered perceptions. But if an animal scale exists, or an 'evolution' in the animal series, it is insofar as increasingly numerous differential relations or a deepening order are determining a zone of clear expression that is both more extensive and increasingly hermetic. Each of the conscious perceptions that comprise the zone is associated with others in the infinite process of reciprocal determination.[51]

In a recent well-documented study, Catherine Wilson has convincingly argued that Leibniz's repeated attentions to infinitely small animals or organisms were positive attempts to incorporate new microscopic discoveries into his metaphysics.[52] These efforts had two principal dimensions: the evidence about the infinite distribution of living creatures of an extremely small size, and the doctrines of preformation and postformation of the forms of living things. There are many references in his works and letters, especially after 1686, to the microscopic investigations of Swammerdam, Malphigi and van Leeuwenhoek, with whom he corresponded in the last two years of his life. Where his predecessors had examined the parts and layers of small insects and other tiny, but observable specimens, marveling at the superb skill of the divine fabricator, van Leeuwenhoek made an enormous leap forward. He studied the structural details of protozoa, spermatozoa and bacteria, the very existence of which had not been observed before. Leibniz was fascinated with these results and quickly became convinced that everything, everywhere, was inhabited by these animaculae – every thing was living all the way down.[53]

The more orthodox position at that time was that the appearance of life was the functional consequence, according to some as yet unspecified process, of the mutual interrelations of inanimate, inorganic parts with one another; thus, sentience and consciousness were emergent phenomena. Leibniz vigorously rejected this view and held that life could be explained in entirely mechanistic terms, but with the proviso that the concept of mechanism was itself organic. This view blends well with his other doctrines of the subject being contained in the predicate, the present being pregnant with the future, and the divine installation of pre-established harmony. Wilson says that:

> this leads to the question whether the theory of monads is, in the last analysis, a theory of animals and animacules which recede into the regions of indefinite smallness, or a theory of non-spatial, immaterial, perceivers. On the former view, every substance has an organic body and so a place relative to other organic bodies ... On the latter, phenomenalistic theory, the objects encountered 'in' space are the representations of

---

[51] Deleuze, 1993, pp. 92–3.

[52] Robert Latta, more than one hundred years ago, had proposed just such an account of Leibniz's appropriation of microscopical studies; see the extract from Latta in Rescher, in MES, p. 247.

[53] Wilson, 1996, pp. 166–71.

perceivers, each of whom experiences its own 'world' as a more or less adequate version of the world perceived by God.[54]

Given his views about individual birth and death, and the underlying stability at the monadic level, one can readily understand (if not agree with) his belief that the nascent form of an organism was contained in the seed which then unfolded into a mature individual, and that, even after death, in the ashes of consumed matter, the living thing was recapsulated in the hidden *opusculum*. Wilson speculates that the notions of pre- and post-formation in Leibniz's metaphysics may have been influenced by chemical experiments with crystals in solution, especially through their interpretation in occult literature.

However, Leibniz still has to account for the aggregative character of aggregates of monads, that is, what it is about certain aggregates that *results* in their being stones or sheep or humans. He realized that it was not a wise policy to attempt to interpret bodies as merely spatial collections of monads; to do so, he said, was 'to enter the labyrinth of the continuum'. In terms of the whole individual, monads are not the basic parts of matter but its 'immediate requisites'; one thing is the requisite of another if the former's nature is conceptually presupposed by the latter. Leibniz's constant recourse to analogies with a flock of sheep or a pond of fish are not entirely helpful here, since a flock is a collection of things by accident; its constituent members are enflocked by the shepherd's actions. Of course, Leibniz would respond that God is the universal shepherd for all substantial aggregates, but perhaps it would have been more germane for him to distinguish different *kinds* of aggregate, as the Stoics had done – mixture, blending and fusion, for example. Aggregates of monads result in different kinds of things according to three basic factors: the contribution of component monadic natures, the connections established amongst the aggregated monads, and the dominant entelechy which imparts to the whole its distinctive profile. In Leibniz's ontology, aggregate beings occupy a curious middle ground between what is genuinely real, a true unity or simple substance, and what is merely ideal. He refers to them, on one occasion, as *semirealia* or *semimentalia*; although their existence is dependent on minds that perceive them, they are not mental entities, such as thoughts or images: 'They are pluralities of individuals, which together determine a single complex being insofar as they are apprehended as having a certain sameness or connection with respect to one another.'[55]

Aggregate beings comprise monads connected in such a way as to determine the complex idea of a collective being. When Leibniz moves his discussion to treatment of issues about soul and mind, he is then faced with the task of accounting for the intimate connection between an organic living body and its soul, specifically its soul-like dominant monad. It seems to make the best sense of Leibniz's doctrine to impute to him two senses of 'body': first, the mere appearance, that is, what the monadic structure represents its body as looking like; and second, the body as it is in itself, the aggregate of constituent monads. Thus Leibniz needs to show how these two concepts of body are correlated: 'under what conditions a plurality of

---

[54] Wilson, 1996, p. 174.
[55] Rutherford, 1995, p. 222.

monads can be said to result in the organic body of their dominant monad or soul'. Rutherford poses this very question and then offers an ingenious solution: it is a safe assumption, he says, that 'a monad characteristically represents an organic body as *its* body to the extent that it represents that body as where it is and as the instrument through which it acts. An organic body is thus in this sense subordinate to its soul: it only persists as the body of that soul, or as that organic body, insofar as it is represented as such by the soul.' This representation defines the body's dimensions in space and time and its capacity for action. The monads that provide a ground for the body's relation to the soul must be such that they express themselves as subordinate to that soul. Since monads are only able to express their relatedness through what they represent as the relations of their organic bodies, these grounding monads must represent their own organic bodies as subordinate to the soul's body. Therefore, 'for a plurality of monads to result in an aggregate that is identifiable with the organic body of a dominant monad is for there to be a specific correlation among their perceptions, such that a mind with access to each monad's expression of the relation of its body to the universe would judge that the organic bodies of the lesser monads indeed exhausted the organic components of the body of the dominant monad.'[56]

The unity of corporeal substance depends on the fact that the substantial form is a unity in itself, one that endures by its own nature. In addition, this form provides its body with a principle of unity by virtue of representing it *as* a single enduring thing. No matter how its parts may change, the body remains the thing it is insofar as it continues to be perceived as such by the soul. Further, it is only through the animate body that the soul is located with respect to other middle-sized things, such that it is able to act on and be acted on by other things. Although the soul is a genuine unity in itself it does not *confer* the true unity of an individual substance on the multiplicity of its bodily parts. Rather, this substantial unity is the consequence strictly entailed by the perfect harmony between the two realms. According to the *New System*, the union of soul and body consists of nothing more than the fact that the soul's perceptions are in harmony with its bodily states. However, from this consequence one should infer that the soul–body whole comprises an accidental or contingent unity, not an essential one: 'If Leibniz accepts the theory of monads, he is committed to the rejection of organic creatures as animated bodies that possess the property of being an *unum per se*. At the deepest level, the unity of the organism resides in the soul alone, which persists as an embodied creature insofar as it always represents some plurality of lesser monads as its organic body.'[57]

Whether or not Leibniz was fully aware of the unresolved tension in the implications of his twofold account of soul and body, one of his Jesuit critics brought it sharply to his attention. In an article in 1703, Father Tournemine commented that no simple harmony or parallelism between the soul and its body could make it the case that the two conjoined together formed *one* thing, the individual human being. Although there could be a permanent and total synchrony between bodily and spiritual operations, such that no empirical evidence could ever

---

[56] Rutherford, 1995, pp. 224–5.
[57] Rutherford, 1995, p. 273.

refute this thesis, why should Leibniz want to claim that the individual substance was a unity in itself? In his reply, Leibniz played the diplomat, claiming somewhat disingenuously that he had never offered an account of soul–body union, and then backing down still further when he said that an explanation of this kind of unity is one of the theological mysteries. This tactical move was similar to the one that Descartes made when asked to explain *why* mind and body were conjoined in the manner he described in the Sixth Meditation.

Despite his efforts to mollify his critics, Leibniz must have been troubled by his apparent failure to establish the metaphysical grounds for the essential unity of an ensouled being. He returned to the dilemma with a modified version when pressed even harder on the same question by Des Bosses, to whom he said that he could now communicate those teachings 'intended for the wise', but not for 'the popular audience'. Here for the first time he proposes the notion of a continuous or substantial linkage (*vinculum*) between the soul and body, in virtue of which they compose *one* thing. Over several years he discussed this issue with Des Bosses, concerned to provide a coherent account of the Christian doctrine of transubstantiation in the Eucharist. Rutherford summarizes Leibniz's conclusions about this radically modified version.

1. A plurality of monads comprising an organism counts as a unity in itself if and only if its members are united by a substantial linkage.
2. A substantial linkage is itself a substantial thing, not a mode or accident; it realizes the bodily phenomenon.
3. A given set of monads is naturally required by the linkage that unifies them, but not essentially required; monads can continue to exist without that linkage, and the linkage can be united with another set of monads through a miracle.
4. The phenomenal accidents of bodies are grounded in their monads, but these accidents are also modifications of the linkage.
5. In the miracle of the Eucharist, God destroys the substantial linkages in the bread and substitutes the linkage that defines Christ's body; the bread monads remain, but their phenomenal properties are now modifications of the linkage with Christ.

In conclusion, Rutherford says that this account is 'a theory of baroque complexity', and even Leibniz himself considered it little more than an academic exercise. Although the notion of substantial linkages was an embarrassment to Leibniz's metaphysical picture, 'the most reliable texts come down firmly on the side of monads alone, with real union and composite substance rejected. And this is exactly what we should expect given his deep and abiding commitment to the ideality of relations.'[58] Leibniz's attempted overthrow of the most primitive ontological categories of substance and property, cause and effect, soul and body, was of staggering proportions – it is little wonder that he did not have time to sort out all the loose ends. Nicholas Rescher puts Leibniz's astonishing achievement in perspective:

---

[58] Rutherford, 1995, pp. 279–81.

Leibniz was the first metaphysician in the western tradition who sought to construct reality out of units which possess a property structure wholly beyond the reach of our everyday experiences. Anticipating 20th century physics in this respect, Leibniz dared for the first time to envision a reality that *emerged* from the operation of a reality that lies totally beyond the reach of human observation. His theory of substance is a leap into an order of reality which, for the sake of being intelligible, leaves the sensible domain almost totally behind.[59]

---

[59] Rescher, Introduction to MES, p. 12.

Chapter 8

The Empiricists' Advocacy of Matter Designed for Thought

(1) Early attempts at a mechanical account of matter in motion

Descartes' radical overthrow of traditional philosophy terminated some of the Neo-Scholastic arguments as well as answering some of the principal challenges thrown out by the Neo-Skeptics, though some were not aware of these endings, and continued for some time in happy ignorance. His overthrow also inaugurated many new lines of thought, or, in the case of the revival of Epicurean materialism, made an antiquated doctrine seem attractive again. In contrast to his substance dualism and the thesis that the mind is simple, immaterial and immortal, by the time of his death in 1650, substance monism (materialism) and the mind as a system of matter suitable for thought had gained credence through the efforts of such thinkers as Thomas Hobbes and Pierre Gassendi. Other thinkers, most notably Kenelm Digby, agreed with Descartes' principal theses about the immaterial nature of mind, but thought that such a view could be better fitted into a naturalistic atomism whose laws were explicitly compatible with mechanism.

The materialist thesis about the nature and composition of mind has its origins in the work of Thomas Hobbes (1588–1679), whose contribution to the debate about soul and life is unprecedented in the early modern period.[1] According to Hobbes, since sensation and imagination are nothing but 'diverse motions, (for motion produceth nothing but motion)', there is no need to posit an incorporeal soul over and above the material body. Responding to the distinction between imagination and intellection, he suggested that reasoning is simply manipulation of names, from which he drew the conclusion that 'reasoning will depend upon the motion of corporeal organs, and thus mind will be nothing but motion in certain parts of an organic body.' But Hobbes went beyond this; since he believed that all of our notions come to us through the senses, 'a man can have no thought, representing any thing, not subject to sense. No man therefore can conceive any thing, but he must conceive it in some place; and indued with some determinate magnitude; and which may be divided into parts.'[2] At the very least, this means that the sorts of incorporeal souls posited by both Descartes and his scholastic critics are not possible

---

[1] It is a curious fact about Bernard Gert's recent chapter on Hobbes' psychology that he nowhere discusses the materialist thesis about the nature of the human mind; see Gert, in Sorell, 1996, pp. 157–74.

[2] On Hobbes' account of perception and sensation, see R. S. Peters, in EEP, 1967, vol. 4, pp. 37–9.

315

objects of knowledge. In a more radical vein, Hobbes held the view that the very notion of an incorporeal substance is incoherent and self-contradictory. The immaterial soul that Descartes and others attempted to introduce along with the mechanical model of the world is incomprehensible. The pretended notion of an incorporeal substance, along with popular beliefs about ghosts and the scholastic notion of substantial form or separate essence derive, Hobbes thought, from a misuse of language, from treating terms such as thought, the names of faculties, or acts of a living body, as if they named things, viz. a soul or a mind. In this way, Hobbes linked Descartes' position with his scholastic forebears and criticized them for the same improper arguments.[3]

There has been much scholarly debate on how early in his career Hobbes' philosophical views were formed;[4] it seems most likely that the major portion of his distinctive theories about matter, motion and mind were formed as the result of Descartes' response to his criticisms of the *Discourse on the Method* (1637) and Descartes' response to his Third Replies to the *Meditations* (1641). In response to Descartes' claim that the one thing that resists the hypothesis of an evil demon is a thinking thing disengaged from its body, Hobbes said that, 'it seems to follow from this that a thinking thing is something corporeal. For it seems that the subject of any act can be understood only in terms of something corporeal, or in terms of matter.' Hobbes insisted that by analogy with his analysis of the piece of wax in the Second Meditation, the meditator should have concluded that the subject of all these changes remains the same, and the only secure instance of an invariant essence has been established for matter alone. Hence, Hobbes continued, 'knowledge of the proposition ["I am thinking"] depends on our inability to separate thought from the matter that is thinking. So it seems that the correct inference is that the thinking thing is material rather than immaterial' (CSM II.122–3). In response to Descartes' assertion that it is the mind alone (intellect) that conceives the true nature of the piece of wax, Hobbes' nominalistic view of universals comes through: 'inferences in our reasoning tell us nothing at all about the nature of things, but merely tell us about the labels applied to them.' All we can validly infer from our observations about the properties of things to which we have given names, is that 'we are combining the names of things in accordance with the arbitrary conventions which we have laid down in respect of their meaning.' Hobbes then tied his account of our use of names to the function of imagination, which operates over sensible images unlike the intellect, and tied the imaginative process to motions in our bodily organs (CSM II.125–6).

Hobbes flirted with the outrageous notion that there is no acceptable evidence that we have an innate idea of God, and, in contrast to Descartes' claim that each one has an idea of his inner self, Hobbes insisted that any such idea must 'arise from sight, if we are thinking of "myself" as my body'. This comment marks an important point in their debate, since with this figure of speech Hobbes laid great stress on the notion of 'inner' observation, intro-*spection*, a notion that will be taken up with much force by Locke and Hume. If it is not the whole self (or person)

---

[3] Garber, in CH17CP, 1998, pp. 774–5.
[4] For summary details, see Tuck, in Rogers & Ryan, 1988, pp. 11–41; Malcolm, in Sorell, 1996, pp. 21–8.

that Descartes here refers to, then it must be something like what we normally call our soul: but 'if we are thinking of my soul, then the soul is something of which we have no idea at all. We rationally infer that there is something within the human body which gives it the animal motion by means of which it has sensations and moves; and we call this "something" a soul, without having an idea of it' (CSM II.129). It is ironic that Hobbes did not seem to observe the Cartesian distinction between mind and soul, and then goes on to predicate characteristics of animal soul that Descartes would have endorsed. Hobbes denied the cogency of the very idea of substance itself (as will Locke and Hume), that is, that its definition has an empty extension; 'substance, insofar as it is the matter which is the subject of accidental properties and changes, is something that is established solely by reasoning [according to names]; it is not something that is conceived, or that presents any idea to us' (CSM II.130). Since the mind is claimed to be an immaterial, thinking *substance*, it has that ontological status only according to our linguistic conventions, and only to the extent that its 'subject' remains the same across *material* changes of its bodily properties. Hobbes further criticized the notion of innate ideas, including the ideas of God and the soul, by insisting that innate ideas would have to be always present to the mind, thus ignoring Descartes' important distinction between cognitive disposition and cognitive performance. In sum, Hobbes did raise some intriguing questions, but in this context failed to follow through on them, and Descartes, though definitely arguing from a better worked out position, was far too brusque in dealing with Hobbes' points.

On and off for the next twenty years Hobbes worked on a massive systematic presentation of his ideas, a system that he envisioned in several sections. Each of these sections had longer or shorter gestation periods; they were copied and recopied, transposed into larger or shorter tracts, and were in enough demand to be pirated more than once. The earliest printed version of *De Cive* (*On the Citizen*) appeared in 1642, and was reissued with additional scientific studies in 1647; at Marin Mersenne's request, Hobbes wrote a detailed, but haphazard rebuttal of Thomas White's *De Mundo* (lost for centuries, it was not published until 1973); the first draft of *De Corpore* (*On Matter*) written in the mid-1640s, but not published until 1658; various drafts of *De Homine* (*On Human Nature*) written in the late 1640s, but not published until 1658; and his most famous work, *Leviathan*, first published in 1651.

Hobbes vigorously declared his advocacy of the materialist thesis about human nature in the opening paragraph of the Introduction of *Leviathan*:

> Nature (the Art whereby God hath made and governes the World) is by the Art of man, as in many other things, so in this also imitated, that it can make an Artificial Animal. For seeing life is but a motion of Limbs, the beginning whereof is in some principall part within; why may we not say, that all Automata (Engines that move themselves by springs and wheeles, as doth a watch) have an artificiall life? For what is the Heart, but a Spring; and the Nerves, but so many Strings; and the Joynts, but so many Wheeles, giving motion to the whole Body, such as was intended by the Artificer? Art goes yet further, imitating that Rationall and most excellent worke of Nature, Man.

In the first chapter Hobbes dealt with sense perception, in the second with imagination, in the third with mental discourse (that is, the train of images), before turning his attention to speech and the passions. In sum, he argued that when a sentient organism encounters objects the sense organs react to them; the sense organs' motion endeavors outwards, while external objects' motion endeavors inwards. These conjoint motions travel to the brain and then to the heart where the internalized motions either weaken or strengthen the vital spirits, resulting in blood circulation. On Hobbes' view, the nature of animal and human being is a sort of engine governed by the mainspring of the heart from which the mechanical effects of particle impacts branch out through the other main organs. In those cases where the incoming motion is great enough to influence the vital motion, the impact tends to either reinforce or retard the subserving motions. In the former instance, the organism responds with a minute incipient motion (endeavor), to retain contact with the assisting motion or its actual source. In the latter instance, the incoming motion hinders or dampens the vital motion, such that it endeavors away from the assisting motion or its actual source. This ties in directly with his account of the passions: the cumulative effect of incoming motion impinging on the heart consists in appetite toward or aversion away from the motile object.[5]

The explanation of the human passions in terms of endeavor in *Leviathan* is derived from an earlier version in his *Elements of Law*, where he said that the two principal parts of human being are allocated according to two kinds of powers or faculties – one in the body, the other in the mind. The natural powers of the animal body are nutritive, motive and generative, and the natural powers of the human mind are cognitive, imaginative and conceptive; each bodily and mental power is manifest through *conatus* ('endeavor' in *Leviathan*). These powers are diversified according to their proper function, but they all consist in strength and motion. Through their elemental interactions, human beings take their place in the universal mechanism, and their natural behavior is explicable in an exclusively deterministic scheme: 'All vital motions and animal motions marking natural life are sufficient to explain the kind of life accorded him only if, as a pure working hypothesis, this existence were to be led solely in accordance to natural conditions apart from the acquisitions of civilization. Such [an] existence would be nothing more than animal life, the resultant of a balance of forces.'[6]

Hobbes abandoned his description of the mechanical forces behind animal sentience and passion for more pressing moral and political concerns, and only returns to his opening theme thirty chapters later in the third part on the Christian Common-wealth. In Chapter XXXIV, his analysis of human nature is explicitly situated in terms of the use of the words 'body' and 'spirit' in Holy Scripture:

> The word body, in the most generall acceptation, signifieth that which filleth, or occupyeth some certain room, or imagined place, and dependeth not on the imagination, but is a reall part of that we call the Universe. For the Universe, being the Aggregate of all Bodies, there is no reall part therof that is not also Body ... The same also, because Bodies are subject to change, that is to say, to a variety of appearance to the sense of living creatures, is called Substance, that is to say, Subject to various accidents

---

[5] On Hobbes' concept of motion in relation to his materialism, see Garber, in CH17CP, 1998, pp. 581–4; R. S. Peters, in EEP, 1967, vol. 4, pp. 36–7.
[6] Goyard-Fabré, in van der Bend, 1982, p. 20.

such as sensible qualities; 'And according to this acceptation of the word, Substance and Body, signifie the same thing; and therefore Substance Incorporeall are words, which when they are joined together, destroy one another, as if a man should say an Incorporeal Body' (Lev. pp. 269–70). In making this curious argument, Hobbes elides one of the crucial distinctions Aristotle invoked when treating this issue in the *Categories* and *Metaphysics*, Book Zeta between the grammatical concept of subject and the ontological category of substance. Hobbes, ever vigilant about natural language usage,[7] is aware of another common meaning for 'body', one that refers to seemingly non-material entities. These, he said, are commonly spoken of in terms of 'aire and aeriall substances', and are called 'wind or breath or spirits'. But he said that such things are 'idols in the brain, which represent Bodies to us, where they are not, as in a Looking-glass, [or] in a Dream, or to a distempered brain waking, they are ... nothing.' He debunked words in contemporary speech associated with the notion of an incorporeal being, laying the blame squarely on both learned and unlearned ignorance. Such persons may be easily persuaded 'to call them Bodies, and think them made of aire compacted by a power supernaturall, because the sight judges them corporeall; and some to call them Spirits, because the sense of Touch discerneth nothing in the place where they appear, to resist their fingers. So that the proper signification of Spirit in common speech, is either a subtile, fluid, and invisible Body, or a Ghost, or other Idol or Phantasme of the Imagination' (Lev. p. 271).

Hobbes devoted a great deal of attention to dealing with passages in Holy Scripture alleged by many interpreters to support the Christian doctrine[8] of the human soul's immaterial and immortal status. One by one he passes in review often-cited Old Testament passages, for example, Genesis 2:7, Ezekiel 2:30, Deut. 34:9, as well as New Testament dictates, such as Romans 8:9, John 4:2, Luke 4:1, and others. His typical exegesis of these texts makes two interconnected claims: that there is no concept of nor reference to an independent substance, separable from humans' bodily nature, such as one finds in Plato's dialogues; and that the real problem emerged from a faulty translation of the central terms, imposing later connotations without warrant. For example, he said that he will not examine 'how we came to translate Spirits by the word Ghosts, which signifieth nothing, neither in heaven nor earth, but the Imaginary inhabitants of mans brain', but cannot resist the conjecture that 'the word Spirit in the text signifieth no such thing, but either properly a reall substance, or metaphorically, some extraordinary ability or affection of the mind, or of the body' (Lev. p. 273). When he turned to those texts that mention good or bad angels, he does *not* argue that such entities are no more than imaginary figments, since God has the power to shape things as he wills, according to an *extra*-ordinary and *super*-natural manner. However, 'when he hath so formed them they are Substances, endued with dimensions, and take up roome, and can be moved from place to place, which is peculiar to Bodies; and therefore are not Ghosts incorporeall, that is to say, Ghosts that are in no place.' Given his commitment

---

[7] On Hobbes' doctrine of names and language conventions, see R. S. Peters, in EEP, 1967, vol. 4, p. 33.
[8] On Hobbes' attitude toward religion, see R. S. Peters, in EEP, 1967, vol. 4, pp. 44–5.

to a thoroughgoing materialism about *natural* things and their causal connections, Hobbes' method of avoiding the stigma of atheistic tendencies (incurred by Epicurus and Lucretius) is to allow that an all-powerful God could produce immortal beings by means *outside* of the natural order, but they would still be corporeal. On this view then, this 'substance incorporeal [is] a thing not imaginary, but reall, namely a thin Substance Invisible, but that hath the same dimensions that are in grosser Bodies' (Lev. p. 274).

Having solidly debunked the notion of the soul as an incorporeal substance, in Part Four, Chapter XLIV, 'Of Spirituall Darknesse from Misinterpretation of Scripture', he turned his scathing attention to the collateral belief in the human soul's natural immortality.[9] Substantial forms and abstract essences are empty pieces of spurious jargon, he says here, which are 'built on the vain philosophy of Aristotle, [who] would fright them from obeying the laws of their Countrey, with empty names' (Lev. p. 465). Only by thinking that these words stand for real things could one give any credence to reports of apparitions, the dead walking in graveyards, pursuing the shadowy goals of their former lives. Having fallen into the error of granting existence to separated essences the credulous are led into other absurd beliefs, amongst which he has special contempt for the Catholic doctrine of Purgatory, Heaven and Hell (Lev. p. 432). There is no natural attribute of human beings such that they can live beyond their earthly lives; only at the Final Judgment and Resurrection, by God's divine grace, are good persons granted another *bodily* existence, thus reconciling his view with the unequivocal declaration in St. Paul (1Cor. 15). In the second edition (1680) of his *Considerations Upon his Reputation* (first published 1662), Hobbes responded to criticisms of his analysis of the Christian concept of human nature in these forceful words (quoted at some length since this text is rarely brought into discussions of Hobbes' theory of mind):

> What kind of attribute I pray you is immaterial, or incorporeal substance? Where do you find it in Scripture? Whence came it hither, but from Plato and Aristotle, heathens, who mistook those thin Inhabitants of the Brain they see in sleep for so many incorporeal men; and yet they allow them motion, which is proper only to things corporeal ... But seeing there is no such word in Scripture, how will you warrant it from natural reason? Neither Plato nor Aristotle did ever write of or mention an incorporeal Spirit; for they could not conceive how a Spirit, which in their language was *pneuma* (in ours a wind) could be incorporeal ... Substance is something you'll say, that being without Body, stands under — ! Stands under what? Will you say, under accidents? Almost all the Fathers of the Church will be against you; and then you are an Atheist. Is not Mr. Hobbes his way of attributing to God, that only which Scripture attribute to him, or what is never anywhere taken but for honor, much better than this bold Undertaking of yours, to consider and decypher God's nature to us?[10]

Another of Descartes' inquisitive contemporaries argued in a direction almost opposite to that of Hobbes, insisting on a literal interpretation of the relevant Scriptural passages and their congruence with an incorporeal concept of human spirit. Henry More (1614–87) arrived at Cambridge University in 1631 where he

---

[9] See Springborg, in Sorell, 1996, pp. 360–69.
[10] Quoted in Mintz, 1970, p. 42.

began his academic studies at Christ's College. But after much study of ancient and scholastic philosophy, he found that most of what they said 'seemed to me either so false and uncertain, or else so obvious and trivial' that it was not worth further scrutiny. More began to wonder whether knowledge of things would yield supreme happiness or whether there was some greater and more divine route to a good life. His study of Platonic, Neo-Platonic and Hermetic writers showed him that purgation or mental cleansing has to precede illumination from God. More read Descartes' works with great avidity, but then rejected his philosophical project for a universal science. According to More in his *Collection* of early works in 1662, Descartes took the low road toward materialism while More himself took the high road of Platonism, though they met at the entrance to Holy Scripture. At this juncture, More tried to expound the most approvable interpretation of the first three chapters of *Genesis*, since the ancient Jewish Cabbala had been lost. Using Cartesian and Platonic insights, More found the hidden key to unlock the secrets of Genesis: 'those two dazzling paradoxes of the motion of the earth and the pre-existence of the soul', for More this was the basis for a new science of the spirit.

In the early 1640s, More composed two Platonic-mystical poems about the soul's immortality,[11] inspired by his reading of 'the Platonic writers, Marsilius Ficinus, Plotinus himself, Mercurius Trismegistus, and the Mystical Divines, among whom there was frequent mention made of the purification of the soul, and of the purgative course that is previous to the illuminative.' In the first poem, *Psychozoia*, he constructed an elaborate, if somewhat incoherent, Christian-Platonic hierarchy starting with the trinity of Ahad or Atove, the first principle of all beings (Father), Aeon, the universal intellect (Christ), and Psyche, the principle of love (the Holy Ghost). In the second poem *Psychathanasia*, he claimed that everything that exists depends on God for his ideal and central presence, completely included in every 'atom-ball'. Just as light rays infuse every part of the 'overspreading latitude' of the physical universe, so God penetrates all things to varying degrees of 'differential profunditie'. Individual souls are 'free effluxes' from the divine source and may be taken back when God wills. While free will can explain the fall of souls, the immortal status of good souls is assured by their intimate bond with God's Love.[12]

More employed astronomical imagery to describe the way in which the mind expands beyond the limits of the earthly realm into the sun itself and then its ideal archetype, God. The soul's outward movement is aided by its immaterial nature and the attractive force of the pure flame of Love. The human soul has three parts[13] – the vegetative, the sensitive and the rational – each of which has its own distinctive operations but whose common character is self-motion. He attempts to account for the soul's spiritual extension by defining its proper region as a set of points that cannot be measured. Where Ficino had emphasized the soul's incorporeality by drawing out the differences between the inert body and its life-giving form, More explained the basic power of the soul as derived from a universal vitality that moves both the great and small worlds. In other words, the lower plastic part of the

---

[11] For a survey and analysis of seventeenth-century poems on the soul's immortality, see Allen, 1964, pp. 150–85.
[12] Jacob, 1985, pp. 505–10.
[13] For details, see esp. Henry, 1986, pp. 175–80

soul is continuous with the spirit of nature that molds all things in their proper form. Jacob argues that More's most original contribution to the immortality debate was the notion of total self-reduplication: 'Though Ficino, too, attempts to explain this Platonic mystery by quoting Augustine, [his] notion of "vital intensity" is not as carefully worked out as More's unique conception of spirit as a substance capable of self-reduplication on account of what he was later ... to call its "essential spissitude".'[14] The concept of spiritual inspissation or spissitude is more or less the opposite of material thinning or rarefaction. It probably originated with Lady Anne Conway (1631–79) in an effort to counter the revived Epicurean thesis that some kinds of matter could be very subtle; Conway and More claimed that spirit thickened into solid bodies.[15]

Conway disagreed with both Descartes and More about the essential difference between spirits and bodies – for her there was no difference. Bodies, she said, were condensed or congealed spirit, and spirits were subtle, volatile bodies. Body and spirit were not contrary entities; matter was not dead, stupid and lifeless; rather, there was an intimate bond between them, and an organic unity that existed all the way down. There was one basic kind of substance, with one essential nature, of which spirit was the superior partner; spirit was more excellent in such respects as swiftness, penetrability and life-force. If More was right, she said, that spirit was the principle of motion in dead unorganized matter, then spirit would have no need of body at all, nor of corporeal sense organs. She vigorously disagreed with Cartesian dualism, arguing that body and spirit were inter-convertible because they only differed as *modes* of one and the same underlying substance. Both the materialists like Hobbes and the dualists like More went wrong at the very start, on her view, since in neither case could the inert, lifeless building blocks of material substance, including animal bodies, ever give rise to an animate organism. Leibniz thought very highly of Conway's monistic vitalism which he considered to be superior to any other contemporary explanation of the sources of self-motion and sentience in animal beings.[16]

Given his rejection of Cartesian physics, More worried that a materialistic or mechanistic explanation of the world might lead to atheism. In 1655 he published *An Antidote against Atheism, or an Appeal to the Natural Faculties of the Mind of Man whether there be or not a God*, dedicated to Lady Anne Conway. More felt that he had to base his argument on the free use of the human mind's natural faculties; the very idea of free will would overcome the atheist's skepticism. If the atheists 'will with us but admit one postulate or hypothesis, that our faculties are true' then he will profess that there is a God. But when regarding the evidence for this hypothesis, More admitted that his arguments are not such that 'a man's understanding shall be forced to confess that it is impossible to be otherwise than I have concluded.' In fact, More went on to say that nothing of this sort can be shown by rational persuasion, 'for it is possible that mathematical evidence itself may be

---

[14] Jacob, 1985, p. 511.

[15] For an overview and analysis of Conway on spirits and bodies, see Frankel, 1991, pp. 41–58.

[16] On Conway's monistic vitalism and her influence on Leibniz, see Merchant, 1979, pp. 255–69.

but a constant undiscoverable delusion, which our nature is necessarily and perpetually obnoxious unto, and that either fatally or fortuitously there has been in this world time out of mind such a being as we call man, whose essential property it is to be most of all mistaken, when he conceives a thing most evidently true.'

But even if there were no God, why could not this deluded, mistaken human being exist? More did not attempt to prove that God could not be a deceiver; he would not produce arguments, 'that the reader shall acknowledge so strong as he shall be forced to confess that it is utterly impossible that it should be otherwise.' Nonetheless, More felt that his arguments deserved approval and would win full assent from an unprejudiced mind. He clearly felt that he had established an incurable skepticism in order to eliminate the possibility of necessarily true arguments. Since the value of an argument depends on the valuative function of our rational faculties, and since our senses can be deluded and our reason misled, the result of a process of reasoning could be 'otherwise'. But instead of abandoning rational discourse, More went on to offer his own specially devised antidote to atheism. This antidote consists in pointing out that a person who does not assent to certain evidence is 'next door to madness or dotage', and does great violence to the free use of his faculties. This does not answer or remove incurable skepticism, for the atheist can say over and over again that, in spite of any evidence, it could still be otherwise. More's rejoinder to this was that if a person can accept mathematical truths which rely upon the rational faculty alone, then he could accept a proof for the existence of God. Only the mad, senile, or obtuse would refuse to accept certain evidence, though it may turn out to be false due to our fallible faculties.

More also had to counter the prevalent doctrine that truth was manifest through 'inner persuasion', an internal criterion advanced by Protestant reformers. He distinguished between a false enthusiasm, which he claimed indicated a form of insanity, and genuine inspiration, which would lead only to an expression of what was 'holy, just and true'. In his 1659 work *The Immortality of the Soul*, More seemed to realize that his version of incurable skepticism with regard to human faculties might be carried too far and render knowledge impossible or unreachable. Thus, he said, 'to stop all creep-holes and leave no place for the subterfuges and evasions of confused and cavilling spirits', he would offer some axioms which are so plain and evident, 'that no man in his wits but will be ashamed to deny them, if he will admit anything at all to be true.' To doubt these axioms would comprise 'perfect skepticism ... a disease incurable and a thing rather to be pitied and laughed at, than seriously opposed. For when a man is so fugitive and unsettled that he will not stand to the verdict of his own faculties, one can no more fasten any thing upon him, than he can write on the water, or tie knots in the wind.' One of his axioms is that, 'whatever is clear to anyone of these three faculties is to be held to be undoubtedly true, the other having nothing in evidence to the contrary.'

When he came to lay out the grounds for certainty in faith and religious matters, More managed to present a basis for a faith which was true in spite of this incurable skepticism. This would be endorsed by all those who were 'impartial and unprejudiced examiners', whose judgments had not been perverted by education, passion or special interest. Reason is needed to persuade us that reported testimony is infallible and proper use of the senses is needed to guarantee the right use of our testimony. The senses are 'properly circumstanced' when the sense organs are sound, the medium 'fitly qualified', and the distance of the object duly proportioned. Reason functions properly in a mind that has been freed from prejudices and preconceptions and is turned toward the truth irrespective of whether it accords with what had been expected. From this, More concluded that there are ordinary truths in logic, physics and math, so patently true that they 'appear so as well to the wicked as to the good, if they be *compos mentis* and do not manifest violence to their faculties.' One aspect of this conclusion that More did not address was that these truths *appear* or *are assented* to as certain, provided that our faculties can be trusted. In any event, he went on to build his case that Christian doctrine could be supported and strengthened by applying these criteria to the testimony of the prophets and gospels.[17]

More's initial enthusiasm for Descartes' mechanical philosophy was short-lived and he slowly came to think that it was invalid in many respects, especially in the intelligible world where matter was the slave of spirit. 'For my owne part', More said, 'I think the nature of a spirit is as conceivable and easy to be defined as the nature of anything else.' Indeed he offered his own definition: spirit is a substance 'possessing Self-penetration, Self-motion, Self-contraction and dilatation and Invisibility ... Penetrating, Moving and altering the Matter'. By the 1650s he was inclined to see evidence for spirits in various paranormal phenomena (as they are now called) reported to him by numerous informants. More edited and enlarged upon his colleague Joseph Glanvill's eclectic work exposing agnosticism, *Saducismus Triumphatus,* in 1681 and 1688. Although More was rather cautious about imputing to Plato his own beliefs in ghosts, demons and witches, Glanvill showed little scholarly restraint when he argued that every conceivable combination of matter and spirit must actually exist. Glanvill said that he:

> had made use of the Platonick Hypothesis, that Spirits are embodied ... Since then the greatest part of the World consists of the finer portions of matter, and our own Souls are immediately united unto these, 'tis infinitely probable to conjecture, that the nearer Orders of Spirits are vitally joined to such Bodies; and so Nature by degrees ascending still by the more refined and subtile matter, gets at last to the pure *Noes*, or immaterial minds, which the Platonists made the highest Order of created Beings.[18]

More shared Glanvill's belief in the existence of such disembodied beings and used this belief to justify his Spirit of Nature, a universal agent acting as an omnipresent vehicle for the Divine Will of God. In the Second Edition, More wrote in the Preface, that he was 'very industrious and zealous to support the belief of Spirits and Apparitions and of whatever is true that contributes thereto'. Taking account of the rampant agnosticism and even atheism of the present age, it would be negligent of him 'not to have a great zeal and inclination against the stupour and besottedness of the men of these times, that are so sunk into the dull sense of their Bodies, that they have lost all belief or conceit that there are any such things as Spirits in the World.' In the Third Edition he went further and declared that the Bible itself provides evidence enough to assure anyone that there are angels and spirits, deriding

---

[17] This summary follows Garber's rendition, in CH17CP, 1998, pp. 776–8.
[18] Glanvill, quoted in Hall, 1990, p. 133.

those who follow Hobbes or Spinoza in slighting the approved interpretation of Holy Scripture. He said that he thought it was 'a special piece of Providence that there are ever and anon such fresh examples of Apparitions and Witchcrafts as may rub up and awaken their benumbed and lethargic minds into a suspicion, at least, if not assurance, that there are other intelligent Beings besides those that are clad in heavy Earth or Clay.'[19]

In his later works, More worked very hard to define precisely what he meant by spirit; in Rupert Hall's summary, spirit is a genuine substance because it occupies space and is capable of affecting matter by shaping and moving it. In most respects, spirit is the antithesis of matter: since matter is not self-moving, something must exist that is self-moving; since matter is 'discerpible' (divisible) and impenetrable, spirit must be 'indiscerpible' and penetrable; material particles have fixed dimensions, but spiritual substance can expand and contract. The human soul is formed of spirit and the source of intellect and reason, which can be the product neither of the whole body nor of any single organ within it. The soul is essential to the living body, but not the body to the soul, which exists both before and after the body's existence. He affirmed the notion of extra-somatic projection, that is, that the human soul can leave its body and travel through material objects. This kind of spiritual motion is as natural to the soul as 'the fire will ascend upwards, or a stone fall downward, for neither are the motions of these meerly mechanicall, but vital or magicall, that cannot be resolved into meer matter.'[20] The claim that human and animal souls pre-exist their bodily vehicles struck More as highly plausible; they lived in the interim as ghostly beings inhabiting the airy realms. In one of his late letters to Descartes (July 1649), More said that he could not understand Descartes' claim about how one moving particle could impart or transmit its motion to another particle. In contrast with this mechanistic explanation, More said that, 'all we call body has a dull and sottish life, though destitute of sensation and perception, as being the last and lowest shadow or image of that divine essence which I take to be the most perfect life.' The mechanical transfer of motion from body to body, 'represents very well the nature of my extended spirits, which can contract and expand again, easily penetrate matter without filling it, impell it and move it any way you please' (AT V, p. 383).

The single overarching theme that More's considerable intellectual energies revolved around was the mysterious world of spirits. In More's eccentric scheme there were three principal constituents: the Spirit of God which ruled the universe in all respects; the Spirit of Nature, similar to the Hellenistic *anima mundi*, Nature personified; and the Spirit of Humankind, immortal and everlasting, capable of good or evil actions, and manifest on an earthly plane in ghosts or apparitions. He explicitly equated these three realms with the Platonic Ideal Forms: the Christian spirit world was the equivalent of Plato's ideal realm, the Spirit of Nature is the Idea of all that exists in the universe, and the Spirit of Humankind is the Ideal of humans in their species. The material world and the human body are no more than contingent realizations of the perfect ideas of Nature and Humankind that result

---

[19] More, quoted in Hall, 1990, pp. 138–9.
[20] More, quoted in Hall, 1990, p. 134.

from God's choosing to create this actual world and letting it run its course. Although he chose to dispute with the great natural scientists of his time, More was not their intellectual equal, and failed to understand the genuine import of mathematical and experimental advances. His postulation of a dynamic nature imbued with spirit was not compatible with the well-grounded theories of Descartes, Boyle, Hooke and others. In Rupert Hall's words, More was 'a poetically religious metaphysician whose ideas of God and Nature were glowing, romantic, mystical, and often barely intelligible.' Although More began his amateur scientific studies by praising Descartes as the 'sublime mechanic', twenty years later he had succumbed to some very strange beliefs. The major parts of More's vast output were: 'his positive proclamations of the existence of God and the immortality of human souls, his lengthy expositions of the role of Spirits in the universe, both beneficent and devilish, [and] his exaltations of the long and divinely inspired idealist stream in the evolution of human wisdom of which true Christianity was the supreme expression'.[21]

Another contemporary philosopher who was also strongly motivated by the skeptic's practical approach to an ethical life was Pierre Gassendi (1592–1655). In his earliest work, the *Exercises against the Academics* (1624), Gassendi praised Charron, Montaigne, Lipsius, Seneca and Cicero, and stated that, but for lack of worldly experience, he would have considered himself a disciple of Sextus Empiricus. The *Exercises* is a very curious and precocious work, since it embraces quite a wide variety of scientific, theological and philosophical positions. Gassendi is in many respects one of the earliest empiricist philosophers and elaborated a detailed if confusing theory of knowledge based on sensible experience and a posteriori reasoning. He accepted the Copernican revolution in astronomy and the anti-Aristotelian conception of atoms and the void, and developed some of the most virulent, if not most persuasive, arguments against standard logic, universal statements and the primacy of mathematical principles. And yet he would have adhered to a complete relativism and solipsism if not rescued from total darkness and ignorance by the surety of divine illumination. On a number of points he prefigured Descartes' *Discourse* by reworking skeptical doubt and the technique of suspension from judgment. But he was sufficiently biased by the standard interpretation of Sextus' *Outlines* that he failed to see that his own doubts about sense experience did not go as far as Sextus' original doubts. It is certainly an anomaly of the *Exercises* that many of the conceptual confusions which he highlighted reach their clearest formulation in even more obscure terms, that is, the confusions become more pronounced and incommensurable epistemic claims are stretched to the breaking point.

In his rebuttals to Descartes' Fifth Replies,[22] Gassendi argued that one of the reasons which would prevent subjective appearance from being construed as a candidate for genuine knowledge is the explicit identification of intellectual ideas with the mental images of corporeal things. Since indubitable knowledge of things can only be founded on ideative cognition of a thing's essence and, since the

---

[21] Hall, 1990, pp. 4, 7, 9.

[22] On their exchanges over the *Discourse* and *Meditations*, see Lennon, 1993, pp. 106–17.

images the mind receives are only of accidents and not of substance, therefore there can be no certain knowledge of any thing whatsoever. If his early work in the *Exercises* of 1624 was entirely critical in its vigorous championing of a thorough skepticism, his more mature work in the *Compendium* of the 1640s shows a concerted effort to find a middle way between the skeptics and the dogmatists. Despite his propensity for pedantry and his almost complete evasion of the questions and arguments brought forward by Descartes, Gassendi was a dedicated and assiduous scientist. Twenty years of his own experiments, coupled with close scrutiny of those of Copernicus and Galileo, led him to a notable advance in dealing with skeptical problems and the establishment of a more reliable scientific method.[23]

In several recent papers, Margaret Osler has presented a very convincing case that Gassendi's entire *oeuvre* can best be understood as an attempt to restore and Christianize Epicurean Atomism.[24] One of his challenges was to expunge atheistic elements in Epicurus' pagan views, especially his doctrine that the soul was death-bound. In the final chapter of his posthumous work, *Syntagma Philosophicum*, Gassendi turned his attention to Epicurus' and Lucretius' original arguments designed to demonstrate that the soul is not immortal. The nature of soul, according to Gassendi, is what distinguishes living from non-living things. In claiming this, he agreed with and adopted Lucretius' important distinction between *anima*, that by which animals are sentient and nourished, and *animus*, that by which some animals (humans) reason. He agreed that the *anima* is present throughout the body, but disagreed that the *animus* was located in the chest, rather its seat was in the head (*caput*). Because humans differ from animals by uniquely possessing rational souls, the souls of animals correspond to the irrational parts of the human soul. Animal souls live in their bodies and leave at their death, and hence animal souls are a very fine matter dispersed throughout their bodies. Thus, 'the soul seems to be a very tenuous substance, just like the flower of matter (*florem materiae*) with a special disposition, condition, and symmetry holding among the crasser mass of the parts of the body.'[25] The soul is composed of extremely mobile and active corpuscles, not unlike those that compose fire or heat, made of a most subtle texture: 'The soul seems to be like a little flame or a most attenuated kind of fire, which thrives or remains kindled while the animal lives, since if it no longer thrives or is put out, the animal dies.'

But Gassendi's further claim that the rational soul (*animus*) in humans is incorporeal marked the boundaries of his mechanical view of the world. In this respect, despite the acrimony shown in his earlier controversy with Descartes in the Fifth Replies, he was in much closer agreement with Descartes than with Hobbes.[26] After reviewing the various ancient and medieval theories of human nature, Gassendi declared that 'the human soul is composed of two parts: the irrational, embracing

---

[23] On Gassendi's early espousal of skepticism, see Popkin, 1979, pp. 99–109.
[24] Osler, 1985; on Gassendi's new version of atomism, see Lennon, 1993, pp. 133–40; Garber, in CH17CP, 1998, pp. 569–73.
[25] Gassendi, 1972, p. 421; Epicurus had likened the soul to its body as a scent to a flower.
[26] On his view of the mind's incorporeal nature *vis-à-vis* Descartes, Hobbes and Digby, see Garber, in CH17CP, 1998, pp. 769–75

the vegetative and sensitive, is corporeal, [it] originates with the parents, and is like a medium or fastening (*nexus*) joining reason to the body; ... and reason, or the mind, which is incorporeal, was created by God, and is infused and unified as the true form of the body.' Gassendi made it eminently clear that this picture of the human rational soul accords with Holy Scripture: 'In agreement with the holy faith, we say that the mind, or that superior part of the soul, which is appropriately rational and unique to human, is an incorporeal substance, created by God, and infused into the body; ... it is like an informing form.' His close adherence to Christian doctrine allowed him to assert that the nature of the human soul does not make it something beyond the ordinary; it is not outside the natural order. Wherever and whenever a human being is born, God creates a rational soul for that individual; the rational soul of each person is specifically and directly created by God. If the sensitive soul can thus be regarded as the form of the animal body, then the rational soul, even though it is an independent substance, can also be regarded as the form of the individual person.[27] Although the sensitive soul, as a very subtle, fiery matter, is dispersed throughout the body, the rational soul has its seat in the brain.

In closing that chapter, Gassendi turned his attention to the rational soul's immortal status. He considered this an issue of Christian faith, not of an assent-compelling argument: 'truly after death it survives or remains immortal; as it bore itself in the body, either it will be admitted to future happiness in heaven, or it will be thrust down unhappy in hell, and it will regain its own body in the general resurrection, just as it was in itself, and will receive its good or evil.' He then attempted to offer an account of the rational soul's immortality on physical grounds, the main premise of which was that the mind's immaterial character guaranteed its immortal stature. On this issue, he was again in accord with the sort of argument that Descartes had put forward: since the mind lacks matter, it also lacks mass and parts into which it could be divided and analyzed. And since what cannot be divided cannot be dissolved into its parts, it remains one simple thing forever. Osler says that Gassendi's discussion of the mind's immaterial and immortal nature illuminates certain general features of his thought, as well tying his work into the broader contexts of earlier attempts to formulate a theologically acceptable version of the mechanical philosophy. His above-mentioned discussion 'reveals the eclectic and transitional nature of his position', as Osler says. 'On the one hand, he was clearly and quite self-consciously trying to articulate a philosophy of nature to replace the Aristotelianism he despised and to provide metaphysical foundations for the new science which he promoted so actively. On the other hand, his thought is deeply marked by the Humanist adulation of the classics.'

Unlike Descartes, who made an intellectual virtue out of not relying on earlier authorities, 'Gassendi felt obliged to base his views on the work of an ancient model', Epicurean atomism, which he tried to reconcile with Christian doctrine. 'Neither ancient nor modern, Gassendi contributed to the new worldview by relying on traditional methods of argument', thus making a modified atomism safe for the Christian faith: 'Once the mechanical philosophy was widely accepted

---

[27] Osler points out that this view has a well-respected pedigree in Thomistic doctrine, Osler, 1985, p. 176.

in the following generations, its wider implications for the traditional debate about human nature were more thoroughly explored.'[28]

In contrast to Gassendi's reactionary approach to some aspects of the exciting new mechanical philosophy, Kenelm Digby (1603–65) has been justly regarded by some modern scholars as the first English thinker to comprehend and advocate the Cartesian–Galilean system.[29] Digby's interests in philosophy, mechanism, alchemy and hermeticism may have been instigated by his tutor at Oxford University, the brilliant mathematician Thomas Allen who, in his spare time, dabbled in numerology, cabalism and other occult arts. On an early visit to Europe in 1623 as part of his 'grand tour', Digby went to visit Galileo in Padua, and had several long interviews with a mysterious 'Brahmin' who introduced him to Indian wisdom doctrines. For two years he operated as a naval commander charged with harassing French ships, but had time on board to write his *Memoirs* and *Private Journal*, as well as a brief, very clever exegesis of mystical Pythagorean elements in one stanza of Spenser's *Faerie Queene* (Book II, Canto IX, stanza 22). After his naval adventures he returned to England with fond thoughts about a quiet rural life, but was drawn into some serious religious debates which led to his conversion to Anglicanism and a long-lasting association with the Catholic priest and scientist Thomas White. In London, his close friendship with the Dutch painter Van Dyck, then resident as official court painter, opened the way to his lifelong fascination with alchemical experiments.[30] However, after the death of his beloved wife, and shortly before his move to Paris, he reconverted to Roman Catholicism, and upon his arrival in the French capital, became involved with another English ex-patriot, Thomas Hobbes, in the circle around Marin Mersenne.

Through his entrée into Mersenne's circle Digby quickly came to learn about Descartes' work; he sent Hobbes in London a copy of Descartes' *Discourse* hot off the press in 1637, and commented in his letter to Hobbes that, 'I doubt not but you will say that if he [Descartes] were as accurate in his metaphysical part as he is in his experience [that is, experiments], he had carryed the palme from all men living' (HW VI. Ltr 27). Sometime early in 1641, Digby went to great lengths to obtain a private interview with Descartes at his retreat in Egmont, Holland, according to the memoir of des Maizeaux (AT XI.670; AT III.90). Digby wanted to persuade Descartes to visit England, and questioned him about the construction of the human body, its application for the prolongation of life, and other 'useful and agreeable knowledge'. Digby also made numerous secret trips across the English Channel in futile efforts to raise money from English Catholics in France to support the English Monarch. He was captured and imprisoned in August 1642; finally compelled to take some time off, he had sufficient leisure to compose his annotations on Thomas Browne's *Religio Medici*. His Catholic mentor Thomas White had published his major work *De Mundo* in Paris that year (the same work that Hobbes devoted so much attention to refuting), and Digby's nascent ideas

---

[28] Osler, 1985, pp. 182–3; for a more positive estimate of Gassendi's success, see Lennon, 1993, pp. 26–34; for more about his association with Descartes, see MacDonald, 2002.
[29] B. J. Dobbs, 1971, p. 6; John Henry, 1982, p. 213; Garber, in CH17CP, 1998, p. 566.
[30] On his relation with Van Dyck, see Dobbs, 1975, pp. 75–83.

about mechanism began to take shape.[31] Three years after first meeting Descartes, Digby published his own lengthy Hermetic–Cartesian work, *Two Treatises: of Bodies and of Man's Soul* (1644), and again returned to France where he met Descartes in Paris. Digby regained his adventurous spirit, making trips back and forth across Europe, wrote three books of culinary recipes and chemical secrets, and was active in the early circle around the formation of the Royal Society, chartered in 1663. This strange, multi-faceted character, who had pursued pirate treasure, alchemist's gold, the mechanical philosophy, and the interests of persecuted Catholics, died after the outbreak of plague in 1665.

In the first part of his major work, Digby developed an impeccable heuristic of the mechanical philosophy, dubbed by John Henry, 'an Aristotelian atomism'.[32] He did not think of this as some strange sort of hybrid theory, but an authentic extension of Aristotle himself: 'Let any man read his books of Generation and Corruption, and say whether he doth not expressly teach, that mixtion (which he delivereth to be the generation or making of a mixt body) is done *per minima*, that is, in our language and in one word, by atomes' (2T p. 343). The natural qualities that emerged from combination of elements were brought about by 'the mingling of the least partes or atomes of the said elements, which is in effect to say that all the nature of bodies, their qualities and their operations, are compassed by the mingling of atomes.' Unfortunately, Digby's choice of an Aristotelian framework in which to develop an emergent atomism has cast him in the role of a rear-guard thinker, but this rather simplistic view obscures his genuine significance. John Henry argues that Digby's theory of bodies is the culmination of the *minima naturalia* tradition, which held that there were smallest particles operant in physical and chemical processes. But his *Treatise on Body* is so different from other works that it is almost in a class of its own: 'Digby did not merely tack on bits of atomist doctrine in order to shore up the crumbling structure of Aristotelianism, rather he re-built the whole edifice using atomism or mechanism as his mortar.'[33]

However, Digby himself thought that the really important part of his work was the second treatise where he intended to articulate a comprehensive physiology of the human soul through the study of corporeal agents. In his *Observations on Religio Medici*, he had confuted Browne's claim that the immortality of the soul could be known on the basis of faith alone. Digby replied that the soul's immortal status was natural, and that only those who were not well versed in rational proof would think that such a belief was an article of faith. He said that he would endeavor 'to shew by a continued progresse, and not by leapes, all the motions of nature; and unto them to fit intelligibly the termes used by her best secretaries; whereby all wilde fantasticke qualities and moods (introduced for refuges of ignorance) are banished from my commerce' (Obs. p. 4). He repudiated Browne's credulous superstition that spirits and devils haunt the earth for moral reasons, for 'all causes are so immediately chayned to their effects, as if a perfect knowing nature get hold but of one linke, it will drive the entire series or pedegree of the

---

[31] On the significance of White's work in the mid-1600s, see Southgate, in Sorell, 1993, pp. 107–27.
[32] John Henry, 1982, p. 214; for details, see Dobbs, 1971, *passim*.
[33] John Henry, 1982, p. 215.

whole to each utmost end' (Obs. p. 7). But he did affirm the basic Christian doctrine of post-mortem existence, citing Plotinus' theory with approval:

> Soules that goe out of their bodies with affections to those objects they leave behind them doe retaine still even in their separation, a byas, and a languishing towards them ... For life which is union with the body, being that which carnal soules have straightest affections to, and that they are loathest to be separated from, their unquiet spirit, which can never naturally loose the impressions it had wrought in it at the time of its driving out, lingereth perpetually after that deare comfort of his. [Obs. p. 12]

In Daniel Garber's summary, Digby's straightforward strategy is to catalog the main operations of the human soul: simple apprehension, knowledge as judgment, discourse as method, and bodily actions. For each of these operations, the soul comprises features that preclude it from being performed by body alone. From these inferences, he concluded that there must be some thing in human nature other than our bodies. He admitted that the real nature of the soul in its union with an animate body is ultimately unknowable, but his concept of the human soul is quite close to Descartes' concept. It is unextended and without place, even outside time; it is a thinking thing from which all vital functions have been removed and situated in bare matter. He concurred with the Cartesian new way of ideas, that ideas are internal representations of external things, and abstracted from particular things, shows that the mind is an incorporeal substance. But Descartes and Digby also differed on some important issues: for Descartes, the distinction between soul and body 'follows from the very ideas we have of the soul and body, and God's power to create separately what we conceive as separate. Digby, on the other hand, depends mainly on arguments from the limits on the behavior of mechanical systems.' In this fashion, his metaphysical position is indeed closer to Aristotle's view that the human intellect has an operation in itself that it does not share with its body:

> Although the conceptions of body are radically different [between Descartes and Digby] ... in both cases the argument proceeds from a claim about faculties humans have that cannot be performed by a body to a claim that it must be something non-bodily that is the seat of the faculty. In a sense, Digby's main arguments for the existence of an incorporeal soul in man can be regarded as simply the older arguments, adapted to the new mechanist context.[34]

(2) Locke, Berkeley and Hume for and against the materialist thesis

Many of the philosophical controversies in the seventeenth century, although they may have been overtly devoted to highly abstract metaphysical issues, were also concerned with threats to orthodox religion. A wide variety of views about the structure of the natural world, human nature, the origin of knowledge, and so forth were thought to threaten traditional religious doctrines and authority. Hobbes' view of mind as matter in motion was considered by many critics to lead either directly

---

[34] Garber, in CH17CP, 1988, pp. 770–71.

to atheism and religious apathy or indirectly to undermine moral and spiritual values. Even those philosophers with an avowedly strong religious attitude, such as Descartes and Spinoza, were accused of the worst atheistic tendencies. Their critics focused on the fundamental scientific thesis which asserted that an explanation of human actions could be given entirely in terms of bodily mechanisms, thus derogating the importance of mind and spirit, if not rendering them altogether redundant. There were thought to be two ways in which the human mind (or spirit) might be neglected in the mechanistic framework. On one hand, if matter is inert and passive all the way down then there seems to be no room for an active, productive, and hence free power of mind. On the other hand, if matter is considered to have inherent active principles, or if it is receptive to having such principles imposed upon it, there is also no need for mental or spiritual causality in the natural world. In brief, for those who maintained an orthodox religious attitude in all things, the human soul's immaterial status was an essential requirement for its immortal character. Hobbes' ingenious (and premature) proposal in the mid-1600s faced hugely difficult internal problems, when he attempted to reconcile his utterly materialist account of all corporeal beings with the Christian teaching of resurrection and heavenly life.

Ralph Cudworth, in his gargantuan 1678 work, *The True Intellectual System of the Universe*, argued vigorously (if not always cogently) that any kind of materialism leads to atheism, and identified four kinds of atheism in these highly charged words:

> First, the Hylopathian or Anaximandrian, that derives all things from Dead and Stupid Matter in the way of Qualities and Forms, Generable and Corruptible; Secondly, the Atomical or Democritical, which doth the same thing in the way of Atoms and Figures; Thirdly, the Cosmoplastick or Stoical Atheism, which supposes one Plastick and Methodical but Senseless Nature, to preside over the whole Corporeal Universe; and Lastly, the Hylozoick or Stratonical, that attributes to all Matter, as such, a certain Living and Energetick Nature, but devoid of all Animality, Sense, and Consciousness.[35]

John Locke (1632–1704) tried to steer his way around (or through) these quaintly named atheistic dangers. Several prominent elements came together in Locke's grand scheme: an account of things as matter in motion, the mechanistic laws that governed their motion,[36] an experience-based theory of ideas, and nominalism about the meaning of universal ideas, including the ideas of mind and soul. In the *Essay on Human Understanding* (1690), his empirically motivated project was to catalog and describe the general ideas which humans actually have, as opposed to deriving them from a priori principles which would be based on innate ideas. Later thinkers in the eighteenth century were to commend Locke's project to provide a 'natural history' of human faculties, instead of an imaginary 'romance of the mind'. His model of human knowledge is both atomistic and constructive: it is *atomistic* in that general ideas are reducible to simple ideas for each of which there corresponds

---

[35] Cudworth, 1678, pp. 134–5, quoted in Yolton, 1983, p. 5.

[36] On the importance of this topic in then current discussions, see Gabbey, in Garber & Ayers, CH17CP, 1998, pp. 649–79.

a simple percept; it is *constructive* in that general principles are built up entirely out of those simple ideas. But one should be alert to an ambiguity in his use of the term 'idea'; it can mean either the occurrent perceptual act or the perceptual content – his usage is not always as clear as one might wish.

According to Locke's theory, ideas are the immediate objects of thinking or perceiving; and for Locke thinking and perceiving mean the same thing. All our ideas are *about* some thing; moreover, every idea is specific to its cognitive mode, that is, remembering, imagining and perceiving, in virtue of the object towards which it is directed. Thus, sensory ideas are about something in virtue of having a really existent object; imaginative ideas are about something in virtue of having an 'inner' object, where there is no really existent outer object, and so forth. Some modern interpreters have argued that Locke held the view that thought is essentially characterized by its intentional structure. One basis for the charge that Locke's use of the term 'idea' is ambiguous is that he applies it to entities of different kinds. He makes a number of divisions within the domain of ideas; ideas are simple or complex, particular or general, concrete or abstract, adequate or inadequate, and so forth. Locke said, 'I have used [the word idea] to express whatever is meant by *phantasm, notion, species*, or whatever it is, which the mind can be employed about in thinking' (E I.1.8). Locke's peers and some modern scholars severely criticized Locke for this rather vague statement, but if one bears in mind the core insight that he is marking off ideas' distinctively intentional character, making all ideas the immediate *objects* of thought, then perhaps his further reflections will not seem as open-ended and will be less likely to lead to unwarranted difficulties.

Over and above the fact that Locke's simple ideas correspond to Descartes' sensory simples, rather than to compound sensory ideas, the main difference between Lockean and Cartesian ideas is that Locke rejected ideas of pure intellect or intuition. When Locke writes about the resemblance between primary qualities and our ideas of them, and says that 'a circle or square are the same, whether in idea or experience', it seems that the comparison is between the intentional 'object' and the real object, the thing as one perceives it and the thing as it is in itself. In addition, his assumption is that the first use of names of sensible qualities is for ideas rather than things: in secondary qualities, there is 'nothing like our ideas existing in the bodies themselves. They are in the bodies, we denominate from them, only a power to produce those sensations in us; what is sweet, blue or warm in an idea is but the certain bulk, figure and motion of the insensible parts in the bodies themselves, which we call so' (E.II.8.15).

Although Locke followed Descartes in his dualism of properties, thought and extension, he did not confidently accept a dualism of substances. He held instead that there is a radical separation between properties which have to do with mentality or mental actions, and properties which have to do with materiality or material actions. But unlike Descartes, Locke thought that a single thing could in principle have properties of both kinds.[37] As for whether any individual thing does indeed

---

[37] Bermudez claims that the only position consistent with his skepticism about knowledge of real essences is property dualism, and not substance dualism, Bermudez, 1996, pp. 223–30.

have both kinds of properties, Locke remarked that the question, 'Do any material things think?' is a prime example of an inquiry to which we probably can never know the answer. In a long, intricate chapter in Book II (E II.23.15–18, 22–32), Locke defended the notion of an *immaterial* thinking substance, but this did not seriously conflict with his later defence of the possibility of material thinking substances. Locke did not take it for granted that there are thinking things, and then ask whether they are extended or not. Rather, he confronted the radical materialist's argument which questioned the entire category of thought, and argued in opposition that there are indeed thinking things. He did not and need not argue that thinking things are immaterial. He did often say that that they are immaterial, using that term fourteen times, but as Michael Ayers has pointed out, these uses of the term 'immaterial' may have been a reaction to Bishop Stillingfleet's accusation that Locke was a materialist.[38]

In a famous later passage, Locke took for granted that there are thinking things and confronted the question of whether or not they are extended. The notion of matter that thinks is difficult to accept, he admitted, but the notion of a real thing that has no extension is equally difficult to accept; thus the most reasonable stance to adopt is that of the agnostic: 'He that considers how hardly sensation is, in our thoughts, reconcilable to extended Matter; or Existence to any thing that hath no Extension at all, will confess, that he is very far from certainly knowing what his soul is ... He who will ... look into the dark and intricate parts of each hypothesis, will scarce find his Reason able to determine him fixedly for, or against the Soul's materiality' (E IV.3.6). Locke framed the hypothesis about the genuine nature of mind as an example of a question beyond the limits of human knowledge:

> We have the ideas of matter and thinking, but possibly shall never be able to know whether any mere material being thinks or not: it being impossible for us, by the contemplation of our own ideas, without revelation, to discover whether Omnipotency has not given to some system of matter, fitly disposed, a power to perceive and think, or else joined and fixed to matter, so disposed, a thinking immaterial substance: it being, in respect of our notions, not much more remote from our comprehension to conceive that God can, if he pleases, superadd to matter a faculty of thinking, than that he should superadd to it another substance with a faculty of thinking. [E IV.3.6]

In other words, there is no logical contradiction in supposing that God could equally well endow 'certain systems of senseless matter' with the power of thought as he could produce an immaterial thinking thing joined to some bodily matter. Locke commented that the second alternative is beyond our ability to comprehend because bodies are only able to strike or affect bodies by impulse and motion. Hence, it is just as mysterious how motion could produce sensation and ideas as it is how ideas could be properties of matter. Having voiced the absence of intrinsic contradiction in either of these alternatives, Locke hastened to add that none of what he has said lessens the ordinary belief in the soul's immaterial status.

---

[38] This summary of Locke's theory of ideas follows Ayers' detailed exposition, Ayers, 1991, vol. I, pp. 55–70; for a more concise version of his interpretation, see Ayers, in CH17CP, 1998, pp. 1090–94.

Locke then went on to raise a series of objections to the materialist thesis that he has just proposed.[39] First, regarding the supposition that every particle of matter can think, he said that the notion that there are as many eternal thinking beings as there are particles of matter is unavoidable. Since, 'if they will not allow matter as matter, that is, every particle of matter, to be as well cogitative as extended, they will have as hard a task to make out to their own reasons a cogitative being out of incogitative particles, as an extended being out of unextended parts.' Second, the supposition that only one atom of matter thinks 'has as many absurdities as the other, for then this atom of matter must be alone eternal or not.' If this one atom alone is eternal then by its own power it made all the rest of matter.[40] The consequence of this is that the creation of matter was accomplished by a single powerful thought, an idea that the materialist would want to *reject*. Third, Locke pointed out that there is an important difference between pieces of matter (corpuscles) and those same pieces organized into a system of interrelated parts, for example, an animal or plant. But this supposition ascribes all the wisdom and knowledge of an eternal being to the mere juxtaposition of its parts, an absurd consequence also: 'For unthinking particles of matter, however put together, can have nothing thereby added to them but a new relation of position, which it is impossible should give thought and knowledge to them.' Fourth, on the materialist view that thinking can only be a function of the motion of the constituent parts, the property of thought would be accidental, 'since all the particles that by motion cause thought, being each of them in itself without any thought, cannot regulate its own motion, much less be regulated by the thought of the whole.' This results in an unwanted diminishment of the concept of human freedom, since if thought is not the cause of motion, but the result of motion, then 'freedom, power, choice, and all rational and wise thinking or acting will be quite taken away; so that such a thinking being will be no better nor wiser then pure blind chance' (E IV.10.17). Taking account of all these objections, Locke was firmly convinced that thought cannot be a property of matter in motion, but he also insisted that it would be possible for God to endow a system of matter with the power of thought.

Locke also confronted the question whether animals were mere machines in distinguishing precisely between masses-of-matter and the life-force of plant and animal beings. The identity of masses-of-matter rests only in 'the cohesion of particles of matter any how united', while the identity of living organisms consists in the requisite disposition of the constitutive particles that makes them suitable to receive and distribute nourishment. It is the specific organization of the material particles that constitutes the life of an organism and distinguishes it from other individual organisms. The same account is true of more complex organisms, which Locke explicitly compared to a mechanical artifact. He remarked that a watch is 'nothing but a fit organization, or construction of parts, to a certain end, which when a sufficient force is added to it, it is capable to attain.' An individual unified thing like a watch is 'very much like the body of an animal, with this difference.

---

[39] This summary follows the outline in Yolton, 1983, pp. 16–17.
[40] For more details on the eternal being argument, see Ayers, 1991, vol. II, pp. 169–83, and the masses-of-matter argument, vol. II, pp. 207–15.

That in an animal, the fitness of the organization, and the motion wherein life consists, begin together, the motion coming from within; but in machines the force, coming sensibly from without, is often away, when the organ is in order, and well fitted to receive it' (E II.27.5). Yolton comments on this passage that, 'few in Britain objected to Locke's strong endorsement of this Cartesian understanding of animals, but it may have influenced some to take the next step in predicating human consciousness and reason of organized matter in motion.'[41]

In the next section Locke turned his attention to the identity of human beings, which, he said, consists in 'nothing but a participation of the same continued life, by constantly fleeting particles of matter, in succession vitally united to the same organized body' (E II.27.6). Locke did *not* claim that there is some special force that constitutes the unity of a living thing, including human being. The sense in which life is the unifying principle presupposes that the concept of unity can be understood in terms supplied by the recognition of material coherence and discreteness. The concept of life deserves to be called the principle of material unity because unity is open to explanation in each case in more primitive terms, as Michael Ayers says: 'The point that the causal principle of an animal's or plant's unity has this kind of relevance to its continuing identity presupposes that animals and plants are, at least normally, coherent and discrete, i.e. that they are characteristically physically or materially unitary objects.'[42]

In the case of human beings, the principle of unity is found in consciousness, which unites such items as sensations, perceptions, thoughts and actions, that is, modes or operations of the human mind. But Locke went on to argue that this involves the uniting of substantial parts of the whole human in two ways. In Ayers' words, 'First, the unknown, material or immaterial, simple or complex substance which underlies and sustains a single consciousness is united "into one person" by that consciousness. Second, the intimate consciousness we have of the outlying parts of the body incorporates them too into "our thinking conscious self".' It might seem that an unnoticed conceptual slippage takes place here from the *subject* of conscious awareness to the *object* that consciousness is aware of. But Locke can answer this potential objection by marshalling some of the main features of his theory of identity of *persons*. He identified the consciousness of one's past with interconnected recollections, offered an explanation of consciousness in terms of the necessary self-conscious feature of mental operations, and made a crucial analogy between consciousness and life as a natural unifying principle that overlays the flux of substance.[43]

In a highly significant move, Locke distinguished the concepts of human and person, and made the identity of the human consist in the organization of bodily matter over time, whereas the concept of person was 'forensic', that is, tied in with the assignment of praise and blame. Locke's suggestion that matter might think was an integral factor in his rejection of thought as the essence of human being,

---

[41] Yolton, 1983, p. 35; on Locke's account of living things, see Ayers, 1991, vol. II, pp. 216–28; Lennon, 1993, pp. 314–33; Lennon criticizes Yolton's view of Locke's agreement with Descartes on this point, p. 323, note 129.

[42] Ayers, 1991, vol. II, p. 225.

[43] Ayers, 1991, vol. II, pp. 265, 267.

with his allowing consciousness to animals, and with the account of personal identity that he introduced. In contrast with other vitalist doctrines of soul at that time, as Lennon says: 'it is the materialist who can give the richest expression to the great chain of being, for while all is material, the material may be indefinitely graded with respect to these (and all other possible) attributes. Not so for the friend of the [Platonic] Forms, who in this period has seen his friends reduced to at most two, with the result that the chain of being is as great as it can be with two links.' This dispute unbalanced the various positions: 'this division between qualitative monism and dualism, between (let us say) Gassendist atomism and Cartesian dualism, is far too simplistic to categorize the dispute over the bestial soul. On the one hand, there is no reason why the atomist must allow that animals think – animals and man too could be no more than atoms organized into machines. On the other hand, there is no reason why the Cartesian cannot extend thinking souls to animals – this after all was Plato's view.'[44] But the central issue is far more complex than this 'simplistic view' suggests, Lennon continues, since the very concept of soul was an elusive notion at that time, and ambiguities in its meaning were constantly exploited by defenders of religious orthodoxy. Thus, the reason that Locke's suggestion that matter might think came under such virulent attack was that it allowed the claim that some portions of matter (the ones that made up the human brain) might think in a *rational* manner. While Descartes' and Locke's views were equally regarded as dangerous, namely, through the evaporation of the essential difference between humans and masses-of-matter, the danger itself sprang from opposite sources: 'Descartes was seen to denigrate matter, Locke to glorify it. The explanatory success of mechanism created an impulse that had to be deflected in one of these two directions.'[45]

John Yolton argues, on the basis of numerous lesser-known texts of the early 1700s, that it was not the abstract argument about substance, property, extension, and so on, that eventually led to the rejection of Locke's suggestion that certain systems of matter, suitably arranged, could think:

> The force at work in those who reacted against that suggestion was the fear of the automatical man. This image of the man-machine had widespread implications. It accompanied the debates over liberty and necessity, which concerned many writers in the century: mechanism, automatism, and clockwork were consistent with necessitarianism; immateriality, spontaneity, and indivisibility of soul were consistent with libertarianism. Thus the debate over thinking matter, the tensions between materialists and immaterialists, were the focus of many themes in eighteenth-century British philosophy. Immaterialism was on the side of the angels. Materialism was that 'hideous hypothesis' that everyone identified with Spinoza.[46]

Charles Taylor argues that Locke reified the mind to an extraordinary degree and that this was integral to the materialist making the mind into an object of observational study: 'First, he embraces an atomism of the mind; our understanding

---

44 Lennon, 1993, pp. 319.
45 Lennon, 1993, p. 320.
46 Yolton, 1983, p. 45.

of things is constructed out of the building blocks of simple ideas. Metaphors to do with constructing and assembling stuff are very prominent in Locke, and not just in the usual mode, where one speaks of "constructing" a theory or a view.' In Lockespeak, ideas are 'materials', and humans have the constructive power to 'compound and divide' these materials; since humans do not have the productive power to make or destroy these materials, this power properly consists in uniting or separating them (E II.12.1). He talked of the brain as the mind's 'presence-room' (E II.3.1) or as a dark room (E II.11.17), and of ideas in the mind as furniture[47] (fifty years later Hume used a comparable reifying image when he describes the mind as 'a kind of theatre', T. p. 252): 'Second, the atoms themselves come into existence by a quasi-mechanical process, a kind of imprinting on the mind through impact on the senses. ... And third, a good part of the assembly of these atoms is accounted for by a quasi-mechanical process of association.' The consequences of this picture are profound, on Taylor's analysis: 'the aim of this disassembly is to reassemble our picture of the world, this time on a solid foundation, by following reliable rules of concatenation ... In effecting this double movement of suspension and examination, we wrest control of our thinking and outlook away from passion or custom or authority and assume responsibility for it ourselves.'[48]

Immaterialism as an alternative hypothesis remained nascent until its fully fledged expression in the early 1700s. George Berkeley (1685–1753) adopted an unusual, and some would say eccentric, position on the true nature of the human mind. Berkeley's position shares some of the basic features of Descartes' concept of substance, and also shares some of the basic features of Locke's theory of ideas;[49] but otherwise his views put him at odds with every other thinker in this period. Henry More was quite willing to countenance some version of materialism about inanimate things and the mechanical laws that governed their interactions, but held that for animate things the most significant elemental building blocks were immaterial spirits. Berkeley, on the other hand, held that there were *no* material things whatsoever, that all that existed were minds and their ideas. According to his famous ontological maxim, *esse est percipi aut percipere*, 'to be is either to perceive or to be perceived.' Ordinary ideas were 'things' perceivable by our finite human minds, human minds were the 'things' that perceived ideas, and God is the infinite, eternal mind which contains our finite minds the way our minds contain ideas. It is not our purpose to review the premises upon which Berkeley built his argument for immaterialism, nor to examine internal problems in his metaphysical picture.[50] Rather, our attention is focused on the place of soul and mind in this framework and the way in which his doctrine of names is closely linked with the derivation of mind's true nature.

---

[47] Bailey recently made a good case that Locke restricts the soul to inner chambers of the skull using the root metaphor of the 'camera obscura' to model the human mind itself, Bailey, 1989.

[48] Taylor, 1989, pp. 166–7.

[49] McCracken plausibly argues that, in repudiating Locke and Malebranche on the nature of mind, Berkeley's original position was very close to that of Descartes, McCracken, 1988, pp. 596–611.

[50] For detailed reconstruction see Winkler, 1994, pp. 137–203; Tipton, 1974, pp. 57–95.

Berkeley's theory of the nature of mind was closely bound up with his views on the meaning of words, according to which every word stands for (or signifies or denotes) some idea, and this relation of signifying renders words meaningful. In his *Philosophical Commentaries*, Berkeley explored the possibilities of what some scholars have called his 'unofficial view'.[51] Here he said that one must distinguish two kinds of mental element: ideas, images, dreams, sensations, feelings, and so forth; and that which entertains or is conscious of the former elements. In the main part of the PC, he denied the existence of any self-subsistent thing that has or could entertain ideas. The mind, he said, is nothing more than the ideas that occur over its course; it is a 'congeries of perceptions', in much the same language as Hume's bundle of perceptions. His argument is that no one is aware of the alleged thing that has ideas, one is aware only of the ideas themselves. Any word that purports to denote the alleged thing (for example, substance) that has ideas signifies nothing, and hence is without meaning: 'Say you the Mind is not the Perceptions, but that thing which perceives. I answer you are abused by the words that and thing, these are vague empty words without meaning' (PC 581). One might infer from this that one's mind does not exist when one has no ideas, that it simply goes out like a candle flame; at one point he even said that, 'in sleep and trances the mind exists not' (PC 651).

But Berkeley soon recognized difficulties in this extreme point of view and began to show some concern about the basic unity that everyone experiences in their mental lives. A mere congeries of ideas cannot provide its own unity; no one idea could be said to perceive the rest. Later, in the *Three Dialogues*, he said that 'I know that I, one and the same self, perceive both colours and sounds', and took this insight to show that, 'I my self am not my ideas ... [but] one individual principle, distinct from colour and sound, and, for the same reason, from all other sensible things and inert ideas' (3D p. 233). At an earlier stage he was not willing to admit what he would allow later, namely, that this one unifying thing is a substance. In addition, he also seemed to be aware of another difficulty: given the congeries of ideas thesis, that the perceptions which constitute a mind happen to be bundled together, it should be possible for an occurrent perception to be detached from all other perceptions, that is, for it to be perceived by no mind at all.[52] Still another worry concerned the concept of activity or power. Berkeley seems to have been convinced throughout his writings that the only active thing in the world is the human will, and that the will is always active (PC 461).

Thus he abandoned his original congeries view, for the will is clearly not a mere bundle of volitions (PC 463). He adopted a drastic course away from this position, determined to expel any kind of inactivity from the mind, identifying the mind with the will: 'The Spirit [is] the Active thing that which is Soul and God is the Will alone' (PC 712). Given his initial premise that all ideas are basically inactive, none of them can resemble by way of a copy any volition of the will. Pitcher remarks that, 'If Berkeley were to hold on to the Idea Doctrine, he would have to say that it is nonsense to talk about volitions or the will – and this would mean, since the mind

---

[51] On the relation between the PC and later views, see Grayling, 1986, pp. 154–8.
[52] This self-criticism on Berkeley's behalf was made by Pitcher, 1977, p. 184.

has now been identified with the will, that it is nonsense to talk about the mind. In that case, Berkeley would of course have to deny the existence of the mind, just as, earlier, he denied the existence of that (alleged) thing that has perceptions.' By rejecting the nominalist thesis about an idea's relation to word-meaning, he 'creates a problem for himself that he will struggle with throughout the rest of his philosophical career; for if we have no idea of mental acts or of the mind itself, how is it that we are able to talk about them intelligibly?'[53]

Berkeley therefore abandoned the view that the will (= the mind) is a mere congeries of volitions in favour of the view that the will (= the mind) is an immaterial or spiritual substance. In the PC he did not assert this as the conclusion of his self-critical examination, but held it out as an hypothesis (PC 829). Shortly after this remark (virtually the opposite of Locke's hypothesis about thinking matter), he mentioned that, in addition to the faculty or power of will, one must also include the power of understanding. Since it now seems to be clear that it is one and the same thing that performs all one's volitions, it is equally clear that the same thing that performs one's volitions also perceives one's ideas. His final view in the PC was that the mind is an unknowable spiritual substance that both wills and perceives, and that since it is unknowable it is not feasible to distinguish various mental faculties in its composition. By means of this circuitous route Berkeley arrived at his official published theory, that the mind is an unextended spiritual substance.[54] His mature view is expressed in these symptomatic passages: 'Besides all that endless variety of ideas or objects of knowledge, there is likewise some thing which knows or perceives them, and exercises diverse operations, as willing, imagining, remembering about them. This perceiving, active being is what I call *mind, spirit, soul* or *my self*' (PHK I.2, original emphasis). And later, this single thing is identified as spirit: 'One simple, undivided, active being; as it perceives ideas, it is called the understanding' (PHK I. 27). And in the *Three Dialogues*, he says that 'I my self am not my ideas, but somewhat else, a thinking active principle that perceives, knows, wills, and operates about ideas' (3D p. 233).

These passages are mostly privative, expressing what the mind is not, that is, the denial of composite, extended material substance. In order to accommodate his new positive doctrine about the nature of mind, Berkeley also enlarged his initial doctrine of ideas and meanings. He now said that a word has meaning if it denotes an idea, a group of ideas, or any other actually existing thing of whose existence we have an idea: 'If there is no idea signified by the terms *soul, spirit,* and *substance,* they are wholly insignificant, or have no meaning in them. [But] I answer, those words do mean or signify a real thing, which is neither an idea nor like an idea, but that which perceives ideas, and wills, and reasons about them' (PHK I.139). In the *Three Dialogues*, his speakers claimed, in rather oblique phrases,[55] that one can have an immediate, direct knowledge of one's own mind (or soul). Philonous makes an irrefutably obvious assertion when he says that 'my own mind and my

---

[53] Pitcher, 1977, p. 187.
[54] See, for example, Tipton, 1974, pp. 256–96; Winkler, 1994, pp. 276–312.
[55] Interpretation of these indirect statements, Pitcher, 1977, pp. 213–15.

own ideas I have an immediate knowledge of' (3D p. 232). Pitcher dubbed this the Self-evident Existence Doctrine, according to which, it is 'not that one has an immediate awareness of one's own mind and its ideas, but that one has an immediate – i.e. an intuitive, as opposed to discursively reasoned – knowledge *that* one's own mind and its ideas exist.'

When he returned to his later edition of the *Principles of Human Knowledge*, Berkeley introduced a new term of art into his fundamental framework – *notion*. Thus, he says in this context that 'it must be owned at the same time, that we have some *notion* of soul, spirit, and the operations of the mind, such as willing, loving, hating, in as much as we know or understand the meanings of these words' (PHK I.27; see also I.140). In the very opening he said that it was important that one survey the objects of human knowledge either as (a) ideas actually imprinted on the senses, (b) such as they are perceived by attending to the passions and mental operations, or (c) ideas formed by means of memory or imagination in compounding any of the former. In this context, he appealed to a reflective notion whose 'object' was an idea of an actual thing, an existent substance. He thus felt licensed to draw an important conclusion: let anyone attempt 'to reflect and try whether he can by any abstraction of thought, conceive the extension and motion of a body, without all other sensible qualities' (PHK I.10). The essence of the mind is an unextended, immaterial thing wholly different in kind from ideas, one that perceives ideas and performs volitions. Pitcher comments that, on Berkeley's view of what reason demands that one assert about the nature of mind, 'the existence of such an entity is the only possible hypothesis that can explain certain phenomena that we encounter in our so-called "mental life", so we *must* posit the existence of a mental substance.'

This has far-reaching consequences in various domains of Berkeley's philosophy, for 'to call the mind a mental or spiritual substance – and, more specifically to call it a simple mental substance – would tend to foster the belief that it is immortal ... and this belief has the most beneficial moral results.'[56] He would also maintain that the term 'mental substance' has significant intellectual uses, since it figures prominently in what he regards as the correct explanation of both the unity of consciousness and the mental activity that all thinking beings find within by means of reflection. Grayling closes his helpful summary of Berkeley's official view with these words: 'In short then, [his] claim we know ourselves to be *minds* as he defines them is more defensible than is generally allowed, for it could be argued that certain facts justify postulating a determinate self or subject, which in turn is most readily characterisable in terms of its being at least in part a conscious, thinking, and often active thing (an *agent*).'[57]

The official version of Berkeley's immaterialist account of spirit in these works is not the end of the story, however, since in his later life he felt the need to situate this doctrine within a 'chemical' frame, one supported by both ancient authorities and modern scientific studies. His final treatise, *Siris: A Chain of Philosophical Reflexions and Inquiries* (1744) is rarely included by current scholars in their assessment of his theory of mind and spirit; it is not uncommon for them to express

---

[56] Pitcher, 1977, pp. 222–3.
[57] Grayling, 1986, p. 167.

some embarrassment when *Siris* is mentioned.[58] Jessop, the editor of this text in the *Collected Works*, has little doubt about Berkeley's overall consistency: 'in *Siris* I can see a deep alteration of temper and a larger theatre of interest, but no *volte-face*; an excursion from his older doctrines, not a cancellation of them.'[59] He argues that every general doctrine and almost every particular doctrine found in the *Principles of Human Knowledge* can be found in *Siris*, and this includes the fundamental immaterialist thesis about the true nature of mind. In any case, it is not our concern in this historical review and assessment to show that all of Berkeley's works fit into one scheme. Rather, we are looking at the ways in which the concepts of mind, soul and spirit evolved in this period, and *that* brief must embrace his later, more eccentric views.

The most pronounced philosophical influence at work in *Siris* is Neo-Platonic, an eclectic mixture of Plato's *Timaeus*, Plotinus' *Enneads* and the Hermetic Corpus. The most pronounced matter-theory influence is an elemental chemistry and corpuscular physics, whose prime constituents are fire and air. At the mid-point of *Siris*, Berkeley declared that, 'This aether or pure invisible fire, the most subtle and elastic of bodies, seems to pervade and expand itself throughout the whole universe. If air be the immediate agent or instrument in natural things, it is the pure invisible fire that is the first natural mover or spring from whence the air derives its power' (Siris 151). It is always restless and in motion, in rising and falling it actuates and enlivens the whole world mass 'pregnant with forms which it constantly sends forth and resorbs. So quick in its motions, so subtle and penetrating in its nature, so extensive in its effects, it seemeth no other than the vegetative soul or vital spirit of the world' (Siris 152). The natural order of things shows that there must be a highest order mind that governs and actuates the entire world system; as such, it is the proper agent and cause of every thing, whereas pure aether, fire and light are the instruments of the infinite mind. Thus, Berkeley said, when one speaks of corporeal agents or causes, these words should be understood 'in a different, subordinate, and improper sense' (Siris 154). He reiterated his long-standing adherence to the idea-name thesis mentioned earlier: 'in compliance with established language and the use of the word, we must employ the popular current phrase.'

The human mind is an agent whose actions are constrained by necessity, but the infinite mind presides in the world by free actions in the employment of its various instruments (Siris 160): 'In the human body the mind orders and moves the limbs: but the animal spirit is supposed the immediate physical cause of their motion. So likewise in the mundane system, a mind presides, but the immediate, mechanical, or instrumental cause that moves or animates all its parts, is the pure elementary fire or spirit of the world.' His thought here swerved close to the Stoic and Neo-Platonic idea of the *spiritus mundi*, whose essential 'nature' is the element of pure (as opposed to ordinary) fire (see also *Siris* 282–4). Later, he attempted to integrate this idea of world-spirit as principal agent with the chemical composition and

---

[58] For example, Winkler says that 'if we can arrive at an interpretation of *Siris* that is consistent with the best interpretation of Berkeley's earlier works, fine; if not, then it is *Siris*, composed of hints rather than principles, that ought to give way', Winkler, 1994, p. 270.

[59] Jessop, in WGB, 1953, vol. 5, p. 12.

mechanical activities of the vital spirits that all living things possess as parts of the greater whole: 'The principles of motion and vegetation in living bodies seem to be delibations from the invisible fire or spirit of the universe, which, though present to all things, is not nevertheless one way received by all, but variously imbibed, attracted, and secreted by the fine capillaries and exquisite strainers in the bodies of plants and animals' (Siris 214). By this complex process it is evident that the infinite mind, through its restless manifestations in corporeal instruments, is the actual vital power or force behind motions and changes in mundane things, whereas the vital spirits in living things is called force only in a derivative sense: 'Force or power, strictly speaking, is the Agent alone who imparts an equivocal force to the invisible elementary fire or animal spirit of the world, and this to the ignited body or visible flame, which produceth the sense of light and heat.' He hereby endorsed the Neo-Platonic idea of a great chain or scale of being from the purely incorporeal to the crudely corporeal: 'In this chain the first and last links are allowed to be incorporeal: the two intermediate [links] are corporeal, being capable of motion, rarefaction, gravity, and other qualities of bodies' (Siris 220).

He held to the same metaphysical principle expressed in his earlier works, that God alone, as the pre-eminent agent mind can account for the observable phenomena: 'We cannot make even one single step in accounting for the phenomena without admitting the immediate presence and immediate action of an incorporeal Agent, who connects, moves, and disposes all things according to such rules, and for such purposes, as seem good to Him' (Siris 237). But Berkeley admitted that these connections, movements and dispositions may not be amenable to strictly mechanistic explanations, and may instead be comprehensible only in terms of hidden 'idiosyncrasies, sympathies and oppositions' resident within things. These are 'specific virtues' that should be thought to follow 'peculiar motions of the insensible parts, and peculiar properties depending thereon' (Siris 239). Berkeley thus brought about a return to a dynamic concept of reality, one more akin to Marsilio Ficino's interpretation[60] of Platonic and Neo-Platonic theories of the natural world and human beings' place in that world. He was one of the few thinkers in this period to seriously consider the relevance of the Hellenistic concept of soul-vehicle (*okhēma*), a tunicle perhaps made from pure aether or light-particles or animal spirits. He cautions readers that Plato's *Phaedrus* 'not unfitly' called the chariot which the mind or soul drives the *augoeides*, 'a luciform aethereal vehicle', a word that nicely expresses the 'purity, lightness, subtlety, and mobility of that fine celestial nature in which the soul immediately resides and operates' (Siris 171). He even ventured onto paranormal ground when he said that there are 'undoubted instances' of the vital flame 'visible on diverse persons' (Siris 205).

Where Berkeley zealously embraced an immaterialist notion of the natural world in general and the human mind in particular, David Hume (1711–76) took forward Locke's original hypothesis and argued that matter in motion was indeed the most likely explanation. Hume thought that failure to recognize the true extent to which

---

[60] Berkeley approvingly cites Ficino several times: *Siris* 194, 206, 207, 210; on Hermes: 178, 270, 272, 273, 287, esp. 298, 325; references to Neo-Platonism *passim,* but esp. 342–55.

Newtonian laws could be applied to all phenomena played into the hands of the skeptics. Many of Hume's immediate predecessors, especially the Cartesians, had attempted to refute philosophical skepticism, in particular the resurgent version championed by Montaigne, Gassendi and Pierre Bayle. In contrast to these thinkers, Hume described himself as neither an extreme skeptic nor an anti-skeptic; rather, he was a cautious skeptic who worked hard to develop a philosophical position which was both skeptical *and* constructive.[61] His position is skeptical insofar as he showed that knowledge has nothing like the firm reliable foundation the Cartesians and other Rationalists had claimed to provide it with; his position is constructive insofar as he undertook to articulate a new science of human nature that would provide a unique and defensible foundation for all the branches of human knowledge, including morals and politics. Hume much admired Newton's *Principia Mathematica* (1686) and resolved to produce an equivalent experimental science of the human mind.[62]

Hume's extensive reading would have made him well acquainted with the sources and consequences of the revived skepticism. Hume knew those sections of Pierre Bayle's *Dictionary* and Locke's *Essay* which exposed the inadequacy of Descartes' attempts to prove that there is an external world and his doctrine of innate ideas. He also knew about Bishop Berkeley's criticisms of Locke's distinction between primary and secondary qualities, and that, since the mathematical science of nature rested on the validity of the basic notion of primary qualities, the collapse of primary (objective) into secondary (subjective) qualities threatened to destroy this new science. In addition, he considered that every philosophical theory had failed to adequately explain the interaction of mind and body. One of the leading Cartesians, Malebranche, had concluded that there are no natural causes of any kind, and that there can be no human knowledge of cause–effect relations or the existence of objects. What we do know about these things, Malebranche argued, is entirely the result of an act of divine grace. In Norton's words: 'In short, Hume was satisfied that the battle to establish reliable links between thought and reality had been fought *and lost* and hence made his contributions to philosophy from a post-skeptical perspective that incorporates and builds on the skeptical results of his predecessors.'[63]

Hume's new science of the mind turns its attention to the immediate objects of the mind, that is, what is given to the mind before the construction of an elaborate metaphysical picture. Hume argued that the immediate 'objects' of the mind are perceptions, but he did not take these to be representations of really existent objects in the world. His new way of ideas focused on perceptions *as perceptions*, elements or objects of the mind, instead of representations of external existences. In Book One of the *Treatise*, Hume showed how some of these perceptions are interrelated or associated to produce still further perceptions, which are then projected onto a world which is alleged to exist outside the mind. It seems to be the case that

---

[61] See esp. Fogelin, in Norton, 1993, pp. 111–13.

[62] On Hume as a natural scientist of the human mind, see Pears, 1990, pp. 3–15; Stroud, 1977, pp. 1–16.

[63] Norton, in Norton, 1993, p. 7.

somehow the mind is furnished with impressions conveyed from the sense organs. But on further examination, we find that not one of these impressions can by itself be taken as an accurate representation of space or time, cause and effect, an external object, or even our own mind. It is a simple, brute fact that we do *not* have sensory impressions of space and time, cause and effect, external existence, and so forth. But despite this disturbing finding, we do indeed have *ideas* of space and time, cause and effect, external existence, and so forth. Moreover, we are totally committed to the belief that there are real entities which correspond to each of these ideas. Given the success of the revived skeptical assault on the certainty of knowledge, the mystery to be explained is how we come to have these crucial ideas; and in addition, how we come to the belief that these ideas represent, not sensory impressions, but external realities. In Norton's succinct words, 'Hume's greater goal is to show how, despite the success of skepticism, we are rescued from skepticism.'[64]

The first book of the *Treatise* is an effort to show how our perceptions cohere to form ideas about those basic features of the world, such as space and time, cause and effect, and the continued and distinct existence of objects. Another way to put this is, to speak with Hume, that the question is not 'what is the real nature (or structure) of cause and effect, or external existence, or one's own mind?'; but rather, 'How do we acquire the natural belief in cause and effect, or external existence, or one's own mind?' Although we do have ideas of space and time, Hume argued that we have no direct impressions of space or time, but rather of items located *within* space and time. His account of our idea of space appealed to the specific manner of appearance of things in space; by means of two senses, sight and touch, we have impressions that arrange themselves as so many points related to one another in a sensory field. These impressions are transformed by the *imagination* into a complex impression which represents extension or the abstract idea of space itself; the idea of time is accounted for in the same way. The abstract idea of time, like all other abstract ideas, is represented in the imagination by 'a particular individual idea of a determinate quantity and quality joined to the term "time" that has a general reference'. In short, the imagination, one of the mental faculties which plays a lesser role in rationalist metaphysics which favors intellect or intuition, achieves what neither the senses nor reason can achieve.

Hume's general answer to questions about how we come to have the various beliefs that humans actually have was that they are the products of a non-rational faculty, the imagination. This faculty, which often carries through its course according to habit or custom, is defined by a certain propensity to form ideas or beliefs. The raw materials upon which the imagination works, and from which all mental contents are constructed, are impressions and their faint copies, ideas. In John Biro's summary, many of Hume's more skeptical arguments in the *Treatise* were devoted to showing that our stock of these materials is more limited than some philosophers have supposed. He showed again and again that the impressions from which some putative idea posited by rationalist metaphysics would have to derive are just not found in experience. But he did not deny the obvious and remarkable

---

[64] Norton, in Norton, 1993, p. 8.

fact that from the rather limited stock of impressions available to ordinary humans, we are able to construct an edifice of beliefs that goes far beyond those impressions and the ideas which can be traced back to them.[65]

First, my complex ideas are not confined to the complex impressions which one actually has, for one can combine simple impressions in unusual ways, into new complex ideas, which Hume often called *fictions*. Some of these may give rise to natural beliefs, that is, the conviction that they represent real things, but other complex ideas do not do so, in the usual sense of 'fiction'. Second, the course of one's experience, and the various regularities among the perceptions that compose one's experience, are exploited by the mind in forming certain sorts of beliefs. In both these ways the mind must be considered as basically an active power. It is what the mind does with what it receives that really matters and it is this which Hume's new science is an attempt to describe. According to his empirical inquiry, the mind is led from one idea to another idea by three principles of association, namely, resemblance, contiguity, and cause and effect. These associations involve the mind taking notice of certain properties and regularities amongst its perceptions. But this does not mean that such a process has to be conscious, it can be below the level of conscious belief-formation. These properties and regularities are detected by the mind in such a way that it makes a difference to its subsequent operations and contents. If it were not for this active contribution by the mind, the mere presence of such properties and regularities would not be sufficient to explain the combinations and transitions that actually occur among our ideas, nor the acquisition process of the beliefs human beings actually form.[66]

Hume's advice, when confronted with the skeptical challenge, was to replace endless and fruitless cogitating, in an effort to provide a philosophical justification for our beliefs, with an effort to find a scientific explanation of their origin. Thus he said that one must give up metaphysics and become instead an 'anatomist' of human nature. This advice bears a striking resemblance to the fairly new programs in cognitive science and naturalistic theory of knowledge in the late twentieth century.[67] Here too the guiding thought has been to abandon an a priori method of study into consciousness, now perceived as bankrupt, in favor of an empirical investigation which holds the promise of genuine progress. Many theorists in cognitive science have come to feel that the pursuit of conceptual analysis will never tell us anything interesting about the real character of human knowledge.

In the section of the *Treatise* concerned with the immaterial status of the human soul, Hume started by challenging the concepts of substance and inhesion. Hume felt that he had showed that we have no impression of substance as such, and hence can have no legitimate idea of substance. Moreover, even on the approved definition of substance and property, the soul's accidents could just as well turn out to be things as accidents. He contended with various arguments designed to show that composition from extended parts would indicate that the soul would have to have

---

[65] Biro, in Norton, 1993, pp. 39–40.
[66] Biro, in Norton, 1993, pp. 40–41.
[67] The relevance of Hume's position to current cognitive science is discussed by John Biro, in Norton, 1993, pp. 51–6.

some location. But thoughts as the properties of the thinking thing would then also have to have parts and that seems to be nonsense. He then constructed a rather peculiar argument to show what can and cannot be conjoined to a thing with spatial location. He did admit that some perceptions and objects can be localized in a place, but efforts to fit the mind to a place take this category in a too literal sense. Instead, he argued that the coexistence of perceptions at any given time, for any given perceiver, need not be spatial coexistence. He remarked that it is not a good idea to attempt to provide a place for a thing that is utterly incapable of being in a place – such as the mind. Hume thought that both the materialists and immaterialists had fallen foul of this problem, since, for the former, it would entail that all thought would have to be located in the way that bodies are, and for the latter, it would impugn the notion that some thoughts are indeed shaped and figured, and hence located.

Hume then explicitly said that he would show that 'this hideous hypothesis is almost the same with that of the immateriality of the soul, which has become so popular.' An earlier stage in the argument had shown that, since ideas are derived from preceding perceptions, it is impossible that 'our idea of a perception, and that of an object or external existence can ever represent what are specifically different from each other.' In other words, if it is the case that external existences differ from our perceptions of things, one cannot learn this difference by merely inspecting our perceptions. There are only two choices: (1) we can conceive of the external object as a relation without a relative, an empty notion; or (2) we can make it the very same thing with a perception or impression. Yolton comments that 'his conclusion from the above principle is that we cannot with certainty transfer the connection or repugnance of impressions to objects, but we can transfer conclusions about the relation of objects with certainty to impressions. The latter is so because, even though an object is different from an impression, the quality of the object which I think of (and which will be transferred) is thought of or conceived of by the mind.'[68] For the immaterialists, all thoughts and perceptions are modifications of one simple and indivisible substance, and this is an exact parallel, as Hume pointed out, with Spinoza's doctrine of substance and mode. But where Spinoza's account has been treated with detestation and scorn, the second has been treated with applause and veneration. Both accounts, however, are equally unintelligible, Hume said, though for different reasons; but here the metaphysical 'reasons' adduced have extended beyond their proper scope.[69]

He then drew attention to the materialist hypothesis that matter in motion could produce thoughts by way of his previous demolition of the concept of cause-and-effect. He argued that, just as one can never have any sensible impression of the connection between causes and effects, but only of the constant conjunction of the idea of a cause and the idea of an effect, so also for all that we know, 'anything may produce anything', and that is equally plausible for systems of matter *causing* the effect of thoughts. He skillfully turned the tables on the immaterialist by saying that, if they want to prove by reason alone that 'such a position of bodies can never

---

[68] Yolton, 1983, p. 55.
[69] Yolton, 1983, p. 57.

cause thought, because turn which way you will, 'tis nothing but a position of bodies', they might just as well conclude that the position of bodies can never produce motion either. It is still the case that we have a natural belief that bodies do cause motion, since we find constant conjunctions in our experience of bodies followed by changes in the position of those bodies: 'Thus the condition necessary for assigning cause with respect to matter and motion is also met with [respect to] motion and thought.'

This conclusion has positive consequences for the materialist, however, as he declared unequivocally in the passages on the soul's alleged immortality, yet another presumptive doctrine for which we have no evidence:[70] 'Experience, being the only source of our judgements of this nature [cause and effect], we cannot know from any other principle, whether matter, by its structure or arrangement may not be the cause of thought.' Yolton draws the salient lesson that

> Hume is not far from Locke's suggestion that it is not inconsistent, as far as we know the nature of substance, for God to add to matter a power of thinking. Hume says, as far as we know about causal relation, matter and motion can be regarded as the causes of thought. If anything, Hume's conclusion is much closer to the materialists' conclusion, since God has no part in his argument. But just as Locke saw no danger in his supposition for religion or morality (even for immortality), so Hume asserts that what he has said ... 'takes nothing from' the arguments for religion: 'everything remains precisely as before'.[71]

Hume's unswerving allegiance to an empirical-experimental approach to the human mind leaves little options for those who want to avoid excesses of metaphysical fancy. With regard to the question of consciousness, Waxman says:

> we have no alternative but to resist the urge to speculation and accept that the ultimate support and operating principles of the successive perceptions which furnish the 'raw material' to associative imagination are veiled in impenetrable obscurity. In posing questions which ask for unobservable causes, capable neither of furnishing an easy transition of thought nor the vivacity (belief) possible only in the presence of an impression, 'we either contradict ourselves, or talk without a meaning'.

Hume's proposed solution to the problem of personal identity[72] brought his anatomy of the human mind to an abrupt halt, since further insight into the facts were impossible within the bounds of his phenomenological approach. Hume's 'true idea of the human mind' comprises 'a fourfold basis in phenomenological feeling: memory-resemblance; causal relations between distinct perceptions; ... the scarce-felt passage from moment to moment essential to the fiction of perfect identity; and the myriad phenomenological cross-currents that yield the illusion of an imperfect identity'.[73]

Hume understood 'the need to find the right balance between the subjective, phenomenological approach so central to the [Cartesian] tradition, and the objective,

---

[70] On Hume's various arguments against the soul's immortal status, see Gaskin, 1988, pp. 166–82.
[71] Yolton, 1983, pp. 59–60.
[72] On which, see Biro, in Norton, 1993, pp. 47–56.
[73] Waxman, 1994, p. 232.

third-person, experimental methods needed in scientific theory', and in his works this comprehension of the problem is 'more pressing than for anyone before or since', as John Biro says. But Hume has a much more complex task than the now current tasks that face the cognitive scientist, since he had to try to fit into a coherent whole basic elements that would not easily work together: 'innocent scientific theorizing; self-conscious and self-reflective, even self-referring, philosophical analysis; and an ultimate allegiance to common sense as the touchstone for both'. Although perhaps he does not succeed in weaving these disparate strands in his thought, he was well aware of the tensions pulling him in different directions: 'More than any other thinker of the modern period, he feels the pressure to find an accommodation between the scientific spirit of his era and the perennial ambitions of philosophy. This explains the complexity of his thought, as well as the puzzles and perplexities that have plagued interpretations of it.'[74]

(3) Summary overview and general conclusions

In closing these investigations, our thoughts return to the initial setting-forth of the very problem of the human mind and soul. The concept of soul (*psychē* or *anima*) began its career in human thought about human and animal nature as the principle of life itself or as a life-force present in conjunction with other factors, such as breathing, self-willed motion and blood flow. These other factors are observable properties of humans and animals, and when taken to indicate the presence of soul they comprise a cluster of over-determined elements, some of which *must* be present for ensouled life to take place. But in Homeric and Old Testament texts these elements are articulated like the muscles and tissues depicted on Archaic and Geometric vases and bas-reliefs, pieces connected by means of joints, functional components that hinge around a more solid frame.[75] Obvious emotional states, such as anger, sadness and lust, were considered little more than the external manifestations of an inner, invisible, but concrete life-force. There are even textual clues that soul was only thought to be present when these affects were strongly displayed; *psychē* and *nepesh* are absent (or at least dormant) when an animal or human is quiet and immobile, sleeping or unconscious.

In Ancient Hebrew and Homeric Greek, each of the main psychical words has many nuances which subtly alter its meaning, nuances that depend on whether the word is the subject or object of an action, whether it is predicated of an animal or a human or God, and with which verbs of action it is linked. In addition, each word has undergone an evolution, or at least an attenuation, in its total reference field. In an approximate manner the first chapter outlined the evolution or progression of these various meanings according to the following scheme:

(concrete + outward) → (concrete + inward) → (abstract + inward) →
(self-referring or reflexive)

---

[74] Biro, in Norton, 1993, p. 58.
[75] An unusual analogy made by Snell, 1953, pp. 6–7.

This is only one vector of development, however, since it became apparent that various ambiguous meanings of both (concrete + inward) and (abstract + inward) could reciprocally influence each other.

$$(\text{concrete} + \text{inward})_1 \rightarrow (\text{abstract} + \text{inward})_1 \leftrightarrow (\text{concrete} + \text{inward})_2 \rightarrow$$
$$(\text{abstract} + \text{inward})_2$$

And hence each antecedent meaning can become detached from its initial consequent meaning and destabilize the process in several different directions, becoming more closely associated with other lines.

$$(\text{concrete} + \text{inward})_1 \rightarrow (\text{abstract} + \text{inward})_2 \leftrightarrow (\text{concrete} + \text{inward})_2 \rightarrow$$
$$(\text{abstract} + \text{inward})_3$$

It is important to consider the details hidden within the various shadings of the key Hebrew and Greek terms, since the details provided the framework in which much later conceptual precipitates would fit. The transition in meaning from (concrete + internal) to (abstract + internal) for all three central Hebrew psychical terms is paralleled by an equivalent triform transition in archaic pre-Platonic Greek usage. Remnants of this threefold concept formation survive in contemporary English (and cognate Romance) language expression, though the 'seat' or internal location has sometimes shifted. Thus, one says of a deeply held conviction, 'with heart and mind and soul' and this conveys more than just three words standing for one thing. The further part-for-whole conceptual shift is profound since it signifies not just a greater whole of which an organ or power is a lesser whole but the *kind of being* that has (or more properly *is*) the control or investment of this vital power. Thus the shift to the abstract and inward moves the concept of *nepesh* beyond the outwardly observable, into the individual's inner depths, and here the Hebrew word approaches the later meaning of *anima* or soul. Although each of the main Hebrew psychical terms originate in separate and distinct concrete parts of the human body, they all signify, at an intermediate level, the vital desire of humans as living beings. This occurs before each term precipitates further into more abstract meanings which refer, not to concrete independent parts (pieces) of the human body (as flesh and bone do), but to dependent parts (aspects) of the interior, hidden dimension. In Homeric Greek, the best candidate for the meaning of *psychē* is 'life-force'; but the part-for-whole force of the other main soul-words can also work in reverse (whole-for-part) where the individual is said to be 'full of life'. In this framework it is *psychē* that uniquely differentiates human beings from other living, animate beings, by means of vital attributes such as self-moved action, desire for what is absent, and by means of intellectual powers, those attributable to *nous*, that is, imagination, memory and reflection.

One might speculate that in the past half-century the direction of explanation has followed the reverse course. Some extremists have argued that the word 'mind' has no proper reference and is no more than an item in our 'folk account' of human nature. By an unwavering process of elimination they have deleted the sense of 'mind' as periphrastic for the self, banishing it as an archaic vestige of false beliefs about an inner private sphere. The sense of 'mind' as internal and abstract fares no better, since substance dualism is thought to be fatally flawed; mental predicates are no more abstract than physical predicates of neural states, they serve only to pick out the same events and 'objects' under different descriptions. Current versions of emergent materialism and functionalism have stabilized this downward spiral at the internal and concrete stage; mental terms properly refer to concrete neural coordinates. Perhaps it is only a short step to the next stage in devolution where a much-promised unified theory will discover some deeply buried proto-mechanism, pieces of which are manifest in our middle-sized environment as living, conscious beings.

In his illuminating Introduction to Stephen Strasser's *Phenomenology of Feeling*, Robert Wood lays out a graphic model of the historical evolution of the concept of 'heart'[76] that reveals several parallels with the linguistic analyses conducted in the first two sections of Chapter One. In Woods' own words, at the bottom level, (1) heart is the *physiological blood pump*, closely connected with the lived experience of (2) *vitality* as a vigorous feeling rooted in healthy physiological functioning. It is the 'hearty' who are best predisposed by nature toward (3) *courage* as a virtue of the '*coeur*' – though such virtue bears a close connection with the will as well. In (4) *moods* appear closely bound up with physiological functioning, whether as effect or as cause or both; and in (5) *sympathy* appears as a kind of disposition, but one which is clearly directed toward another. Intentional directedness becomes evident in (6) *memory*, which involves keeping something in mind, pondering it in one's heart, and so forth. Where in (7) the *will* can be considered as either the heartless result of calculation, or as the actual giving of one's heart in love. In terms of (8) *thought*, the heart can be either a computer-like calculation or a pondering in the heart that recollects itself. The concept of 'heart' can slide from a close relation to these functions downwards to vitality (that is, life-force), or upwards toward (9) *one's heart of hearts*, the apex of the self where one's deepest desires, most fundamental choices and most profound thoughts are harbored. Finally, in (10) there is the transcendental extension of the concept to *the heart and core* of any given matter.

In any case, the earliest stages in our historical overview were seriously disturbed by some unexpected incursions. Sometime in the late eighth or early seventh century BCE, Greek travelers return from, or pass along tales about, remote lands to the North and East; they import into popular culture 'foreign', shamanistic ideas about an immortal soul, going-under, ecstatic foresight, and so forth. It is difficult for scholars to form a coherent picture of what the Pre-Socratic thinkers understood the soul to be. On some occasions, the soul is referred to as a thing, or a substance, with a nature or essence, whose functions are explained in terms of the predominance of one element, or the outgrowth of a mixture of elements with a predominant 'profile'. At other times, psychical powers seem to be the properties of one specific element which, when combined in a highly determinate manner, produces a living thing manifesting such underlying functions (or properties). The idea that the human soul is immortal was initially deeply interlinked with ecstatic foresight and magical practices. The problem for these transitional thinkers was to map the non-

---

[76] Wood, in Strasser, 1977, pp. 9–11.

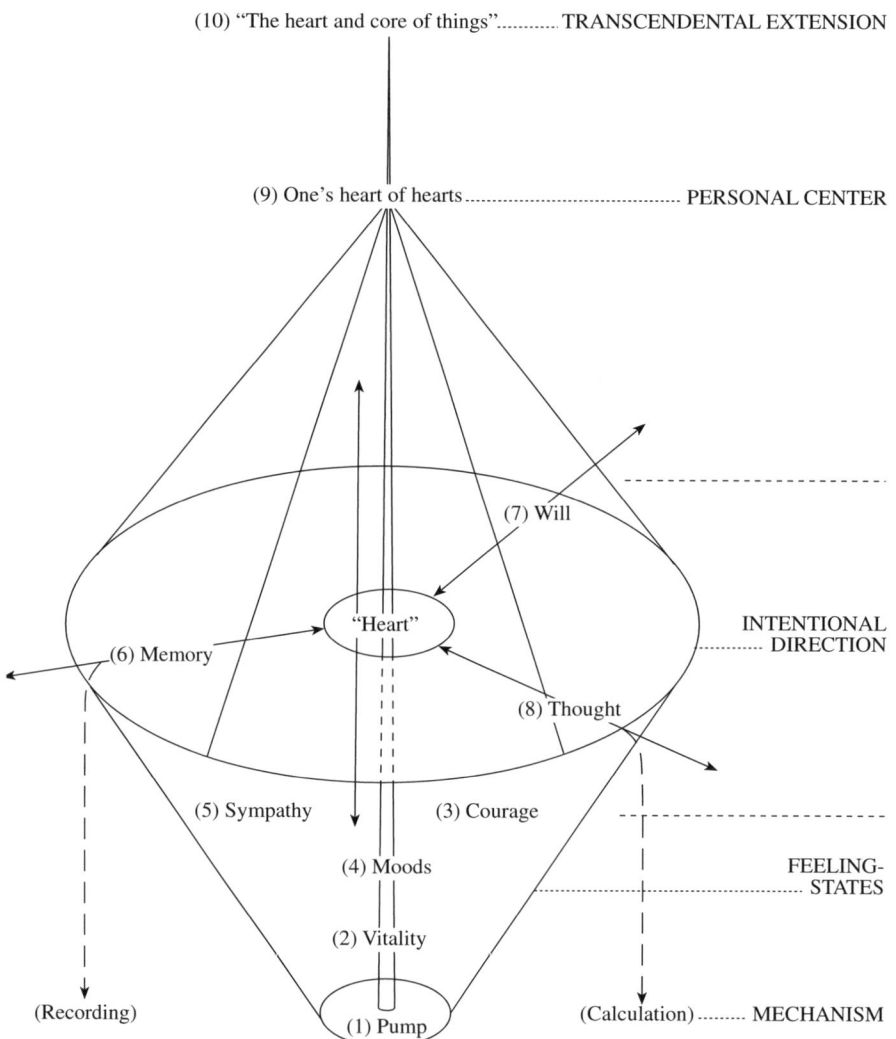

Ordinary language usage of the term 'heart'

Greek concept onto the popular, accepted usage of *psychē*, linguistic usage embedded in the long-standing Homeric framework which understood the soul to be a cluster of life-forces and thus, in its nature, mortal and death-bound.

In some of Plato's dialogues, Socrates seems to be making an effort to reconcile the Homeric-inspired, popular view of *psychē* with this radically new doctrine of the soul as an immortal and immaterial element in human nature. In the middle and late Platonic dialogues the soul becomes a unifying and unitary entity which has various powers (*dunameis*) and can be conceptually divided into forms or kinds (but not 'parts'). On this view, the soul is incorporeal and immortal, like the eternal, immutable Forms. Aristotle did not accept the concept of soul as a separate and separable substance; rather, he said that the soul is the form of an animal being as whole; its special form (*eidos*) imparts or informs life-force to the material body. The very concepts and terms 'informing' and 'imparting' originate in Aristotle's explanatory scheme. For both Plato and Aristotle, spirit (*pneuma*) is an awkward notion, an observable feature of animal beings not fully worked into the whole scheme. The Stoics, however, placed a great explanatory weight on the concept of spirit, and moved it to the front of their analysis of living things, and hence into their account of soul. However, since for the Stoics everything is material, spirit must be some kind of matter, in this case a very fine, subtle matter. This rarefied spiritual matter is not bound to death and can only be destroyed in one of the great cosmic conflagrations which the universe cycled through. Epicurus and Lucretius agreed with the Stoics that spirit confers life and thought on the human soul, but in their view, spirit's material composition means that any animal soul is indeed mortal. At roughly the same time as Lucretius, Cicero translates into Latin many Greek philosophical treatises; his translations decisively influenced later Latin readers' understanding of some principal Greek ideas. He rendered Plato's discussion of the three forms or aspects of the soul into part-terms, Aristotle's central concept of *ousia* by *substantia* (thus severing its connection with the Greek word for 'being'), *phusis* by *natura* (thus fixing its meaning in terms of 'inborn' or 'innate'), *psychē* by *anima* (thus fixing its meaning in life-like terms), and *nous* by *mens*, amongst others.

The most important change in early accounts of soul and mind comes with Christian teaching, through efforts by St. Paul (and to some degree by Philo) to accommodate Greek philosophical concepts with Christian eschatology and soteriology. Although Paul adopts, in somewhat garbled language, the term *pneuma* as breath (translated into Latin as *spiritus*), it does not refer to the same sort of thing as the Hellenistic *pneuma*, but interpolates a radically new concept. In the New Testament's view, not every human has spirit from birth or by nature, it is conferred by baptism, by accepting Christ as Savior. In virtue of having spirit, each individual will achieve redemption in heaven and resurrection at the Second Coming. Those without spirit are damned, both body *and* soul, they are not redeemed and not resurrected. Disagreement then arose over whether only some pre-existent souls had the special capacity to accept the gift of spirit, or whether each soul, now in its earthly body, could earn its spirit through the exercise of its free will.

For Origen the Church Father, righteous humans can expect that their earthly bodies will enter the radiance of the spirit that makes itself known through the Holy Spirit. An essential difference between those raised into glory and those thrown into damnation is that the latter no longer have any spirit (*pneuma*), for God has taken back the gift bestowed upon them at the beginning. With regard to the conceptual division between the spirit and the flesh, Origen declared that when God has taken back the spirit, both the soul and the body will go to hell, even though the soul retains an indelible image of God its maker. Henri Crouzel synopsized this crucial insight when he said that the dominant context of the two-fold and three-fold division of human being is more moral and ascetic than mystical – it is the spiritual battle: 'The soul is torn between the spirit and the attraction of the earthly body, the flesh: of this struggle the soul is both the scene and the stake, and it is the soul, with its free will, that has to decide for one or the other. In itself, by reason of the two elements or tendencies that divide it, the soul is in league with both sides.'[77] This is the crux of the conceptual distinction between soul and spirit in the Christian tradition, and hence the origin of the primary sense of spirit as a divinely bestowed capacity for *another life*; in contrast to the medico-physical sense of spirits (always in the plural) as the material carriers of our ordinary life-force.

Augustine's exceptional achievement was to effect a comprehensive synthesis of the Christian and Platonic understanding of human nature. Plato's mystical thought provided him with the vision of God and the soul, and Christ's message with the path to that vision. Augustine offered an ingenious interpretation of St. Paul's teaching about the soul's taking upon itself a glorious, spiritual body after the Final Resurrection. He proposed that human beings have a double life and double death; this means that, in the first life, he is born as an ensouled animal, whose first death is the soul's separation from its body, and in the second life, it is given through the in-breathing of the Holy Spirit, a new life which can only be lost through sin and wickedness. On Augustine's view, human beings have a double nature, a double life and a double death, such that every human exists in some sense as the first Adam, that is, our common humanity is our death-bound earthly existence. But every human also has his or her own individual life that began at the moment of conception, that is, the ensoulment of the particular animal being.

Aristotle's works passed into the Eastern Roman Empire and, from about 800 CE onward, into the Islamic world, where they were avidly taken up by Arabic and Persian scholars. One consequence of Islamic scholars' assimilation of genuine and apocryphal Aristotelian works with Neo-Platonic texts was that an amalgam of Aristotle, Plato and Plotinus circulated under Aristotle's name, from whence, through its Latin translations, it passed into the hands of twelfth-century Christian philosophers. Alfārābī's account of the animal soul, the rational intellect and his theory of knowledge are rather crude mixtures of Aristotelian and Neo-Platonic doctrines, organized around two registers: one to account for the ordered appearance of the world-whole, and the other, humans beings' situation in that order. Avicenna thought of the soul as one unitary and unified substance, and posited one organic agency in the body through which it governed – not the brain, but the heart. Through this scheme, Avicenna carried forward one of the main Stoic psycho-physical hypotheses about the reciprocal relation of animal body with its hegemonic soul and bequeathed the medical–psychical model to Albert the Great and Thomas Aquinas. Averroes located the human intellect in the vast storehouse of the cosmic Agent Intellect, and thus uniquely distinguished his theory of mind from that of his Islamic predecessors. In positing the Agent Intellect as an entirely separate and eternal substance, he guaranteed the incorruptible nature of the material intellect, but retained its dispositional character integrating the rational faculty with the whole process of cognition along Aristotelian lines.

---

[77] H. Crouzel, 1989, p. 92.

Averroes' greatest influence, however, was not in Islamic thought but in European Christian philosophy, transmitted through Latin translators sometime after 1200. The dynamic speculative activity which characterized the Arabic tradition for five centuries, founded in large part on Hebrew and Arabic translations of Greek texts, disappeared in the Middle East after this period, and reappeared almost immediately in Western Latin speculation. These efforts caught the attention of powerful rulers who wanted to establish centers of excellence in research and recruited talented polyglot scholars to assist their endeavors: 'The impact of this solid and integrated corpus of natural science on the Western intellectual world was enormous, coming as it did into a climate where for centuries scholars eager for knowledge had had to content themselves with third-hand encyclopedic compilations of inadequately developed science and scientific methodology.'[78]

Albert the Great was devoted to establishing just such centers of excellence and had a central role in making Aristotle the supreme pagan authority for university studies. Albert's grand Aristotelian system is actually mixed with many Neo-Platonic elements, sometimes in a muddled and confused manner. The arrival of Graeco-Arabic scholarship in the form of Islamic treatises and commentaries posed some difficult problems for Christian thinkers, such as Albert and his greatest pupil, Thomas Aquinas, especially about how to reconcile 'pagan' statements that conflicted with central Christian beliefs. Although the mystical Platonic dialogues and the main Neo-Platonic works had been accommodated into the Christian doctrinal position through the labors of Augustine and other Church Fathers, Aristotle's works were another matter. The intertextual reconciliation of Aristotle's doctrines with Christian teaching was one of the pre-eminent tasks for Western theologians after the recovery and reception of Aristotle's work via the Islamic route.

Aquinas' formulaic definition of soul is 'the first principle of life', and much of his early efforts are focused on the meaning of the concept of life as the basis of actual living things. There are, he says, vital activities that normally have bodies and bodily parts among their principles; *some* principles of life clearly are in bodies, and hence have material 'natures', but those are not souls. He accounts for the fact that only some specifically organized bodies have the principle of life by employing the Aristotelian concept of substantial form. The soul as the form of living organized matter is immaterial and incorporeal and the human soul is the highest stage of all souls connected to animate bodies. The only being that can subsist by itself is a substance, not an accident of something more basic, and hence the human soul must be both substantial and immaterial. For Aquinas, to grasp the insight that the human soul is an immaterial substance is, at one and the same time, to understand that it is immortal. In the strict sense, the rational soul (mind) as an immaterial form is not affected by the corruption of its host's animate body. The human body, that is, the corporeal component of the soul–body composite, exists *in virtue of* the soul, whereas it is not true to say that the soul exists *in virtue of* the body it is joined with.

Concurrent with the great Christian-Aristotelian summations of the 1300s, Italian humanist writers found scholastic accounts of the soul to be irrelevant to

---

[78] MacClintock, in EEP, vol. 1, pp. 223–4.

the pressing problems about how an average Christian should lead a good life. In many writings of this period, one finds the persistent plea for a renewal of the religious doctrine of grace, the personal acceptance of the idea that divine force alone is capable of remaking the naturally selfish character of humankind towards higher ethical and spiritual goals. The most far-reaching and profound influence on the philosophical speculations of the next generation was the rediscovery, translation and dissemination of Plato's works and the Neo-Platonic commentaries and expansions. Largely through the intense labors of Marsilio Ficino in the late 1400s, the complete Greek texts of Plato's dialogues, Plotinus' *Enneads* and the Hermetic Corpus were recovered and translated into Latin. In his own *magnum opus*, Ficino adopted an explicitly Platonic attitude toward the central issue of the nature of the human soul, and also toward the character of philosophy itself as the disciplined pursuit of truth and wisdom. He agreed with Plato that the soul is related to God as the power of vision is to the sun's light; human beings, in their search for the truth, are directed toward the contemplation and reverence of God, their creator. Insofar as the human soul is God's greatest creation, in attempting to understand the natural truths that God has instituted in this world, every one attempts to understand their own soul. The human soul bears within it the image of God's work and this manifests an eternal destiny, namely its final end in its original source.

But Ficino also subscribed to two other ancient ideals of 'pristine theology', submerged during the scholastic Middle Ages and returned to life through his recovery of Hermetic and Theurgic Greek texts. The first ideal was that of the adept with magical power over the natural world in search of transformation by means of hidden ciphers and occult powers, the second was the ideal of the daimonic soul in search of interior transformation by means of the soul's ascent. Charles Lohr offers an astute insight about the confluence of philosophical and magical strains in Renaissance speculation:

> the continuity of the [Platonic] tradition which understood reality dynamically ... was broken or became at least irrelevant for metaphysics as the science of God. After Pico, the history of metaphysics shifted from the problem of God to the problem of being ... [But] the tradition of a dynamic understanding of reality which had been represented by Lull, Nicholas of Cusa and Ficino became associated with Renaissance magic and occultism.[79]

In the first half of the seventeenth century, the Cartesian–Galilean understanding of the mathematical order of the natural world and the mechanical laws that govern change and motion would definitively overthrow the fundamental principles of a dynamic, spiritual nature. The model of a world-machine would supplant the model of a world-spirit, imbued with celestial angels and demons that could be intuited and handled by wisdom-seekers. The occult philosophy and its many heterodox variants were not so much driven underground as channeled into side-roads, away from the main highway of European philosophical speculation about the nature and functions of the human soul and mind.

---

[79] Lohr, in CHRP, 1988, p. 584.

Descartes' extraordinary achievements in algebraic geometry and the mathematical model of mechanical interactions are closely tied to his metaphysical speculation about the nature of bodies and minds. Descartes' place in the history of the concept of mind is absolutely crucial; his meditations thematize a turning-point in the good fortune of mind's career, but at the expense of soul's place in the scheme of things. In various works he offered two accounts of the basic nature of human being: a physical theory about soul, couched in medical-organic terms, and a metaphysical theory about the mind and its relation to ensouled living bodies. His theory of soul is solidly situated in the prevailing medical model of organic functions and deploys concepts from a fairly standard arsenal, whereas his metaphysical theory comprises a radical overthrow of the standard Neo-Aristotelian account. Two passages near the opening of his Second Meditation mark the most significant watershed in the history of modern speculation about the relevance of soul and mind in theories of human nature. In these two closely conjoined passages the meditator synopsizes his new forward-looking concept of the mind and his backward-looking rejection of previous false beliefs: 'What then did I formerly think I was? ... As to the nature of this soul, either I did not think about this or else I imagined it to be something tenuous, like a wind or fire or ether, which permeated my more solid parts ... [But] I am then in the strict sense only a thing that thinks; that is, I am a mind or intelligence or intellect or reason – words whose meaning I have been ignorant of until now' (CSM II.17–18). The earlier statement is one of the most overlooked passages in the Second Meditation; here the meditator repudiates his previous belief that the soul (*anima*) is a tenuous thing, like a wind or a fire or ether. His reference to 'what he used to think' recalls one of the most prevalent ideas in popular thought, that the soul is some sort of 'breath' or 'fire' or 'inner heat'. One of Descartes' greatest tasks will be to introduce an entirely new term in the discussion of human 'nature', *mens* or mind, whose principal attribute is thinking and whose modes are willing, doubting, affirming, and so forth. But this new concept is not one that the meditator can begin with, for there is no justification for presuming that *anima* is anything more than another prejudice or false belief.

From our contemporary situation, we are indeed the inheritors of a philosophical tradition which was shaped by reactions to the Cartesian project for a universal science, and this includes reactions to and rejections of the Cartesian method of systematic doubt. But his unprecedented approach to issues about the origin and warrant for our beliefs opens a framework in which entirely novel questions are raised. There are at least three principal questions whose answers underpin many of Descartes' detailed assertions. What is easy to lose sight of when one contemplates his radical overthrow of dogmatic and scholastic metaphysics about the nature of the human mind is that these questions reoriented future philosophical arguments. In other words, the answers to these questions, first proposed by Descartes, are now usually taken for granted, as Myles Burnyeat argues.[80] First, how did it come about that philosophers accepted the notion that truth can be obtained without going outside subjective experience? Second, when and why did philosophers first claim knowledge of their own subjective states? Third, given that no skeptic before

---

[80] Burnyeat, 1982, p. 32.

Descartes had ever doubted the existence of his own body, when and why did one's own body become part of the external world?

Scholarly efforts to reconstruct and interpret ancient doctrines of human nature and the criteria of life face many difficulties, not the least of which are attempts to assign each thinker with a specific position in the slippery and shifting arena of dualist schemes. Contemporary scholars have indulged in protracted discussions of the relative merits of various paired opposites such as monism and dualism, dichotomy and trichotomy, bipartition and tripartition, and so forth. On numerous occasions their attempts to adjudicate between various concepts of human nature, as they are supposed to be found in the original authors, ultimately founders on ontological and categorical obfuscations. In most of the torturous debate on soul-doctrines in Plato or Aristotle or St. Paul, for example, there is often complete opacity about *what* is being divided, cut or parted; the status of the resultant parts or items cut; the conditions that some item must satisfy in order for it to be cut, rather than parted; whether the conceptual separability of two or more entities implies anything at all about their real separateness, and so forth. In addition to these questions, assertions about the soul's mortality or immortality often provide a helpful indicator (though not, it must be admitted, a sufficient condition) about the oneness or two-ness of human nature. Thus, on first glance, without other premises to the contrary being advanced, to claim that the soul survives the bodily death of the person whose soul it was would seem to indicate both a conceptual and a real separability between two entities, body and soul, excluding claims about whatever comprises the parts or aspects of the soul itself. However, on the issue of the soul's immortal status, Paul's stated position is very peculiar indeed; it is difficult if not impossible to reconcile his claims about this with *any* of the prior Greek or Judaic doctrines.

In addition to the soul's composition, the soul also has its own duration, which can be either: (a) mortal, that is, subject to, or bound to the death of its host's body; (b) immortal, that is, not subject to, or bound to the death of its host's body; (c) quasi-immortal, that is, not directly bound to death, but vulnerable to cessation due to an accident at some indefinite future time. The third option is often overlooked in historical surveys, but it reflects a position held by the Stoics who believed that airy matter continued to exist after the extirpation of life in an animal body, though it was eventually dispersed, and hence lost its unity. In connection with this view, the souls of Greco-Roman demigods are half-human and half-divine, live in Mt. Olympus, but can die by misfortune. However, mortal and immortal are strange terms when one considers that they define the soul's *life* in terms of the host body's *death*. The notion of an immortal status can be qualified by either pre-natal and/or post-mortem existence; on the Pre-Socratic and Platonic view, all souls have both characteristics. But on the Christian view, souls have only post-mortem existence, since God alone creates the immortal portion (or part) of the human soul by the gift of the Holy Spirit infused at birth. Moreover, on the Platonic view all human souls in their very nature are immortal, whereas on the Christian view only those who accept Christ through baptism are saved and live again.

Whereas material and immaterial are indeed opposite terms, they do not pick out the opposition proper to the soul's composition. It is the concept of matter itself that is salient to the opposition: for matter can either be dynamic, where the life-force 'goes all the way down', or it can be static, where the life-force only emerges at a certain level of complexity. The opposition between mind and body expressed in the phrase 'the mind–body problem' is also misleading since for almost all these theories, body was first contrasted with another term *before* an attempt to account for the presence of the rational soul. In the early sections of this history it has been shown that *sōma* and *sarx*, *corpus* and *caro*, body and flesh (as well as German *körper* and *leib*) are the salient terms in the oppositional contrast. It is in virtue of having *caro* that the animal *corpus* is alive, the soul is em-*bodied* by way of the flesh.

The core factor of the definition of soul as life-force, or as the principle of life, that which provides and explains how some things are living, constantly obstructs argumentative efforts to demonstrate the immortality of the human (rational) *soul*, since it cannot go on *living* after the death of its host's body in virtue of the same properties or functions that provided and explained an earth-bound ordinary *life*. Thus, the concept of life itself is highly unstable; it is ambiguous between the principle of self-motion, sentience and so forth (on one hand), and continuous existence or perduration (on the other). In an obvious, but still baffling sense, the continued post-mortem existence of the human rational soul cannot be any kind of *life* after life, although this continued existence is itself called an *after-life*. Only the mind or intellect alone, the rational soul as an independent part, does not have as a core factor of its definition the feature of an organic life-force, but that feature (sadly) makes it nothing like the original whole individual.

Just as the concept of twoness can be open to many different interpretations, so also can the concept of oneness; monism, from the Greek *monos* in Latin becomes *unum*, and this latter term assumes many guises. Among the diverse applications the concept of oneness takes are unity unicity, union, and unit (that is, unitary particle). (1) Unity means that one individual soul binds together many different faculties or powers, and that, as a conscious power, it binds together all conscious episodes or events as properties of one thing. This underlying sense of binding-together is the basic meaning behind common psychical terms formed from *lecto, lectus*, such as 'intellect' and 'recollect'. (2) Unicity means that the human rational soul as a part of a whole living individual can itself be considered a dependent lesser whole of a greater whole, that is, a cosmic universal mind. (3) Union is often used to convey the notion that the whole rational soul is capable of forming with a whole living body a greater functional whole, which, since Augustine's times, has come to be called the person. (4) In the sense of 'unit', or smallest particle, oneness means that the lowest-level whole is a single simple thing, and in virtue of its 'containing' the principle or force of life, is itself soul-like. Thus, the concept of oneness pertains not only to the number of *kinds* of things of which individuals are composed, in the usual way in which monism is contrasted with dualism, but also to the *order* of oneness to which the soul itself, irrespective of its composition, is said to belong.

In addition to the ambiguities hidden behind oneness and twoness, mortality and immortality, the paired terms material and immaterial do not mark off the same opposition as corporeal and incorporeal; the semantic extensions of the two pairs are not coincident. It is not in virtue of a body (*corpus*) having material 'parts' that life could inhere or emerge from its particular arrangement, but in virtue of matter being the kind of thing its parts are composed of that a body is suited to receive the form that confers life (soul). Even on the view that the soul is not an informing form but an independent thing with causal powers of its own, it is still the case that only certain kinds of bodies are suited to be united to an individual soul. This is not because matter as such is fitted for union, but because the disposition of a certain kind of matter (for example, vital spirits) is suited for the expression of lifelike properties proper to the soul of the whole individual. In terms of at least one metaphysical scheme (Leibniz), in the phenomenal world a body occupies a region of space–time, but its role as a space–time occupier is not filled by its being a material thing. For Leibniz to assert that every simple monad is an 'incorporeal automaton' means that, on its own, lacking integration with other simple monads into a greater whole, a formal atom does not have space–time coordinates properly predicated of its concept. But, of course, simple monads do not exist on their own; rather, fully integrated entities in our middle-sized environment are indeed marked out by space-time coordinates. According to another scheme (Berkeley), a finite mind represents some of its 'objects' as bodies that occupy space and time, but these representations in no way indicate a material substrate those bodies could be instances of. Berkeley could coherently maintain that a physical theory about what kinds of things there are and their mode of existence would comprehend a world of immaterial particulars (spirits).

In historical discussions of the evolution of the concepts of mind and soul, scholars often use the term 'psychology' to refer to an identifiable position on psychical functions; Aristotle's psychology, for example, or Augustine's psychology, and so forth. But the use of this discipline-name with respect to ancient, medieval and early modern accounts is entirely inappropriate, and has been deliberately and consistently avoided in the previous chapters. There are several ways in which 'soul-account' (*psychē-logos*) can be distinguished from what one would now accept by the word 'psychology'. First, Aristotle established the domain of inquiry when he said that it was the task of the philosopher to provide an account (*logos*) of soul (*psychē*), that is, an account of the nature and functions of soul; but soul-nature and soul-functions are not themselves *accounts* of anything. Second, to the same extent that natural philosophers provided competing versions of physical theory (which came to be called 'physics'), so also they proffered versions of psychical theory (which should then be called 'psychics'), and psychics is what the conceptual analysis of soul is about. Consistently following this parallel linguistic structure, physiology is as different from physics as psychology is different from psychics. Third, psychologists in the past century have been concerned, in a very general manner, with the contingent properties and functions of an individual personality, with its lifetime development, internal integration, and cohesion with other individuals; secure results are achieved through empirical investigation. On the other hand, in previous centuries natural philosophers were concerned with the necessary, universal 'nature' (*phusis*) and structures of the soul as such; valid claims are accessible through rational insight. Fourth, with the exception of Epicurus and, much later, Hobbes and Hume, all philosophical accounts of soul connect it closely with an intelligible world, variously described as 'hidden', 'other', or 'beyond'. The many types of dualism or twoness mentioned above presuppose some fundamental distinction between an intelligible and a sensible *world*. This distinction is often built on an explicit cosmic twoness, variously described as 'two-leveled', 'two-tiered' or similar. In contrast, psychologists since the time of Locke and Hume are explicitly concerned only with the sensible world, which itself is not the same, nor reducible to, another world.

Contemporary theorists of mind are almost uniformly dismissive of pre-twentieth-century accounts of mind and soul (except for Hume, perhaps); they often make appeals to 'our ordinary intuitions' about the absurdity of substance dualist claims for an autonomous, usually immortal entity. Aside from the Epicureans, every theorist before the seventeenth century held that the soul outlived the death of its feeble, corrupt host; Thomas Hobbes' unabashed materialist thesis, only feasible from an anti-Catholic perspective, revived this long-despised Hellenistic model and set the course for later explorers. However, moral thinkers take Plato's theory of justice seriously, others draw strength from Aristotle's virtue ethics, semiotic theorists find a treasury of insights in medieval sign-theory, and so forth. Without doubt, ancient accounts of the nature and functions of mind and soul suffered from serious deficiencies in their understanding of biological processes and the physical laws that govern mechanical interactions. But it is also eminently clear that neither Plato nor Aristotle nor Augustine's accounts of the functions of mind are dependent on their models of biological and physical laws. Some apocalyptic thinkers have recently held out the promise of 'a grand theory of everything', one that will unite all known physical and psychical principles in an as yet unknown, undefined theory of something even more basic than the realms of mind and body. But that promise is surely exactly the same sort of cosmic, overarching theory that the pre-Socratics hoped to achieve; it is little wonder, then, that some 'new age' cosmologists wistfully want to rehabilitate Heraclitus.

Bibliography

Chapter 1, Section 1

Childs, Brevard (1992) *Biblical Theology of the Old and New Testaments*. London: SCM Press.
Durr, C. (1925) 'Hebrew Nepesh', in ZAW, pp. 262ff.
Eichrodt, Walter (1967) *Theology of the Old Testament*. London: SCM Press, vol. II, pp. 131–45.
Fabry, H.-J. (1998) '*leb, lebab*', in TDOT, vol. VII, pp. 399–437.
Johnson, A. R. (1964) *The Vitality of the Individual in the Thought of Ancient Israel*, 2nd edn. Cardiff: University of Wales Press.
Lys, Daniel (1959) *Nepesh: Histoire de l'ame dans la révélation d'Israel*. EHPhR, annual issue.
Lys, Daniel (1962) *Ruach: Le souffle dans l'Ancien Testament*. EHPhR, annual issue.
Padel, Ruth (1992) *In and Out of the Mind: Greek Images of the Tragic Self*. Princeton, NJ: Princeton University Press.
Seabass, Horst (1998) '*nepesh*', in TDOT, vol. IX, pp. 498–519.
van Uchelen, Nico (1994) 'Death and the After-life in the Hebrew Bible of Ancient Israel', in Bremmer, *Hidden Futures*, pp. 77–90.
Vriezen, T. C. (1970) *An Outline of Old Testament Theology*, 2nd edn. London: Blackwell, pp. 404–29.
Westermann, Claus (1997a) '*nepesh*, soul', in TLOT, pp. 743–59.
Westermann, Claus (1997b) '*ruach*, spirit', in TLOT, pp. 1202–20.
Wolff, H. W. (1974) *Anthropology of the Old Testament*, London: SCM Press.
Yamauchi, Edwin (1998) 'Life, Death and the Afterlife in the Ancient Near East', in R. N. Longenecker (ed.) *Life in the Face of Death*. Grand Rapids, MI: Eerdmans, pp. 21–50.

Chapter 1, Section 2

Adkins, A. W. H. (1970) *From the Many to the One*. London: Constable.
Bremmer, Jan (1983) *The Early Greek Concept of Soul*. Princeton, NJ: Princeton University Press.
Bremmer, Jan (1994) 'The Soul, Death and the After-life in Early and Classical Greece', in Bremmer, *Hidden Futures*, pp. 91–106.
Burkert, Walter (1985) *Greek Religion*. Trans. by John Raffan. Cambridge, MA: Harvard University Press.

Burnet, John (1916) 'The Socratic Doctrine of the Soul', in *Proc. British Academy*, **10**, pp. 235–59.
Calasso, Roberto (1993) *The Marriage of Cadmus and Harmony*. Trans. by Tim Parks. London: Jonathan Cape.
Caswell, C. P. (1990) *A Study of thumos in Early Greek Epic. Mnemosyne*, special issue.
Claus, David B. (1981) *Toward the Soul: An Inquiry into the Meaning of* ψυχη *before Plato*. New Haven, CT: Yale University Press.
Dodds, E. R. (1951) *The Greeks and the Irrational*. Berkeley: University of California Press.
Furley, D. J. (1956) 'The Early History of the Concept of the Soul', in BICS, **3**, pp.1–18.
Gundert, Beate (2000) 'Soma and Psyche in Hippocratic Medicine', in Wright & Potter, pp. 13–36.
Halbwachs, Maurice (1930) 'La Representation de l'Ame chez les Grecs', in *Rev. Meta et Morale*, **37**, pp. 493–534.
Padel, Ruth (1992) *In and Out of the Mind: Greek Images of the Tragic Self*. Princeton, NJ: Princeton University Press.
Redfield, James (1985) 'Le sentiment homerique du moi', in *Le Genre Humaine*, **12**, pp. 90–105.
Rohde, Erwin (1920) *Psychē: The Cult of Souls and Belief in Immortality among the Greeks*. Trans. by W. B. Hillis. New York: Arno Press (Reprint, 1972).
Russo, J. & Simon, B. (1968) 'Homeric Psychology and the Oral Epic Tradition', in JHI, **29**, pp. 483–98.
Snell, Bruno (1953) 'Homer's View of Man', in *The Discovery of the Mind*. Trans. by T. G. Rosenmeyer. Oxford: Blackwell, pp. 1–22.
Vernant, Jean-Pierre (1991) 'Psuchē: Simulacrum of the Body or Image of the Divine?', in Froma Zeitlin (ed.) *Mortals and Immortals*. Princeton, NJ: Princeton University Press.
West, M. L. (1971) *Early Greek Philosophy and the Orient*. Oxford: Oxford University Press.

Chapter 1, Section 3

Bolton, J. D. P. (1962) *Aristeas of Proconnesus*. Oxford: Clarendon Press.
Claus, David B. (1981) *Toward the Soul: An Inquiry into the Meaning of* ψυχη *before Plato*. New Haven, CT: Yale University Press, pp. 105–40.
Dodds, E. R. (1951) *The Greeks and the Irrational*. Berkeley: University of California Press.
Furley, D. J. (1956) 'The Early History of the Concept of the Soul', in BICS, **3**, pp. 1–18.
Gottschalk, H. P. (1971) 'Soul as Harmonia', in *Phronesis*, **16**, pp. 179–98.
Granger, Herbert (1996) *Aristotle's Idea of the Soul*. Dordrecht: Kluwer Academic.
Kahn, Charles (1973) 'Religion and Natural Philosophy in Empedocles' Doctrine of the Soul', in A. P. D. Mourelatos (ed.) *The Pre-Socratics: A Collection of Critical Essays*, rev. edn. Princeton, NJ: Princeton University Press, pp. 426–56.

Kahn, Charles (1979) *The Art and Thought of Heraclitus.* Cambridge: Cambridge University Press.
Kinglsey, Peter (1995) *Ancient Philosophy, Mystery, and Magic: Empedocles and Pythagorean Tradition.* Oxford: Clarendon Press.
KR: Kirk, G. S. & Raven, J. E. (1960) *The Presocratic Philosophers.* Cambridge: Cambridge University Press.
KRS: Kirk, G. S., Raven, J. E. & Schofield, M. (1980) *The Presocratic Philosophers*, 2nd edn. Cambridge: Cambridge University Press.
Laks, André (1999) 'Soul, Sensation, and Thought', in A. A. Long (ed.) *Cambridge Companion to Early Greek Philosophy.* Cambridge: Cambridge University Press, pp. 250–70.
McKirihan, Richard (1994) *Philosophy Before Socrates.* Indianapolis, IN: Hackett.
Nussbaum, Martha (1972) '*Psuchē* in Heraclitus', in *Phronesis*, **17**, pp. 1–16, 153–70.
Padel, Ruth (1992) *In and Out of the Mind: Greek Images of the Tragic Self.* Princeton, NJ: Princeton University Press.
Schibli, H. S. (1990) *Pherekydes of Syros.* Oxford: Clarendon Press.
Schofield, Malcolm (1991) 'Heraclitus' Theory of Soul and its Antecedents', in Stephen Everson (ed.) *Companions to Ancient Thought 2: Psychology.* Cambridge: Cambridge University Press, pp. 13–34.
von Fritz, Kurt (1964) 'Der *nous* des Anaxagoras', *Archiv für Begriffsgeschichte*, **9**, pp. 87–102.
von Fritz, Kurt (1973) '*Nous, Noein*, and their Derivatives in Pre-Socratic Philosophy', in A. P. D. Mourelatos (ed.) *The Pre-Socratics: A Collection of Critical Essays*, rev. edn. Princeton, NJ: Princeton University Press, pp. 23–85.
West, M. L. (1971) *Early Greek Philosophy and the Orient.* Oxford: Oxford University Press.
West, M. L. (1983) *The Orphic Poems.* Oxford: Clarendon Press.
Wright, M. R. (1989) 'Presocratic Minds', in C. Gill (ed.) *The Person and the Human Mind.* Oxford: Oxford University Press, pp. 207–25.

Chapter 2, Section 1

Annas, Julia (1981) *An Introduction to Plato's Republic.* Oxford: Clarendon Press.
Bell, David, N. (1980) 'The Tripartite Soul and the Image of God in the Latin Tradition', in RTAM, **47**, pp. 16–52.
Burkert, Walter (1972) *Lore and Science of Ancient Pythagoreanism.* Trans. by E. L. Minar. Cambridge, MA: Harvard University Press.
Burkert, Walter (1985) *Greek Religion.* Trans. by John Raffan. Cambridge, MA: Harvard University Press, Chapter VII, 'Philosophical Religion', pp. 305–37.
Burnet, John (1916) 'The Socratic Doctrine of the Soul', in *Proc. British Academy*, **10**, pp. 235–59.
Calasso, Roberto (1993) *The Marriage of Cadmus and Harmony.* Trans. by Tim Parks. London: Jonathan Cape.
Claus, David B. (1981) *Toward the Soul: An Inquiry into the Meaning of* ψυχή *before Plato.* New Haven, CT: Yale University Press, pp. 156–83.

Cornford, F. M. (1930) 'The Division of the Soul', in *Hibbert Journal*, **28**, pp. 206–19.
Cornford, F. M. (1937) *Plato's Cosmology*. London: Routledge & Kegan Paul.
Cornford, F. M. (1965) *Principium Sapientiae: The Origins of Greek Philosophical Thought*. New York: Harper & Row.
Courcelle, P. (1966) 'Le corps tombeau', in *Revue des études anciennes*, **68**, pp. 101–22.
Crombie, I. M. (1962) *An Examination of Plato's Doctrines*. London: Routledge & Kegan Paul, vol. I.
Cross, R. C. & Woozley, A. D. (1964) *Plato's Republic*. London: Macmillan.
Dodds, E. R. (1945) 'Plato and the Irrational', in *J. Hellenic Soc.*, **65**, pp. 16–25.
Dodds, E. R. (1951) *The Greeks and the Irrational*. Berkeley: University of California Press.
Frede, Dorothea (1996) 'The Philosophical Economy of Plato's Psychology… in the Timaeus', in Michael Frede & Gisela Striker (eds) *Rationality in Greek Thought*. Oxford: Clarendon Press, pp. 29–58.
Griswold, Charles (1986) *Self-Knowledge in Plato's Phaedrus*. New Haven, CT: Yale University Press.
Guthrie, W. K. C. (1957) 'Plato's View on the Nature of the Soul', in *Recherches sur la tradition Platonicienne*. Fondation Hardt, Entrietiens III, pp. 3–19.
Guthrie, W. K. C. (1965) *History of Greek Philosophy*. Cambridge: Cambridge University Press, vol. II.
Hackforth, R. (1952) *Plato's Phaedrus*. Cambridge: Cambridge University Press.
Hackforth, R. (1955) *Plato's Phaedo*. Cambridge: Cambridge University Press.
Hall, R. W. (1964) *Plato and the Individual*. The Hague: Nijhoff. Chapter on Psychē.
Kinglsey, Peter (1995) *Ancient Philosophy, Mystery, and Magic: Empedocles and Pythagorean Tradition*. Oxford: Clarendon Press.
Lebeck, Anne (1972) 'The Central Myth of Plato's Phaedrus', in *Greek, Roman & Byzantine Studies*, **13**, pp. 267–90.
Lovibond, Sabina (1991) 'Plato's Theory of Mind', in Stephen Everson (ed.) *Companions to Ancient Thought 2: Psychology*. Cambridge: Cambridge University Press, pp. 35–55.
Ostenfeld, Erik Nils (1982) *Forms, Matter and Mind*. The Hague: Nijhoff, Part Three.
Plato (1997) *Complete Works*. John M. Cooper (ed.). Indianapolis, IN: Hackett.
Rees, D. A. (1957) 'Bipartition of the Soul in the Early Academy', in *J. Hellenic Soc.*, **77**, pp. 112–18.
Rist, J. M. (1964) *Eros and Psyche: Studies in Plato, Plotinus and Origen*. Toronto: University of Toronto Press.
Robinson, T. M. (1970) *Plato's Psychology*. Toronto: University of Toronto Press.
Robinson, T. M. (2000) 'The Defining Features of Mind-Body Dualism in the Writings of Plato', in Wright & Potter, pp. 37–56.
Solmsen, F. (1950) 'Tissues and the Soul', in *Phil. Review*, **59**, pp. 435–68.
Solmsen, F. (1983) 'Plato and the Concept of the Soul', in JHI, **44**, pp. 355–68.
West, M. L. (1983) *The Orphic Poems*. Oxford: Clarendon Press.

Chapter 2, Section 2

Ackrill, J. L. (1973) 'Aristotle's Definition of Psuchē', in *Proc. Aristotle Society*, **73**, pp. 119–33.
Aristotle (1984) *Complete Works*. Jonathan Barnes (ed.) 2 vols. Princeton, NJ: Princeton University Press.
Barnes, Jonathan (1972) 'Aristotle's Concept of Mind', in *Proc. Aristotle Society*, **72**, pp. 101–14.
Barnes, Jonathan (ed.) (1995) *Cambridge Companion to Aristotle*. Cambridge: Cambridge University Press.
Brentano, Franz (1977) *The Psychology of Aristotle*. Trans. by Rolf George. Berkeley: University of California Press.
Eijk, Philip van der (2000) 'Aristotle's Psycho-physiological Account of the Soul-Body Relationship', in Wright & Potter, pp. 57–78.
Everson, Stephen (1995) 'Psychology', in Jonathan Barnes (ed.) *Cambridge Companion to Aristotle*. Cambridge: Cambridge University Press.
Furth, Montgomery (1988) *Substance, Form and Psyche: An Aristotelian Metaphysics*. Cambridge: Cambridge University Press.
Gottschalk, H. B. (1971) 'Soul as Harmonia', in *Phronesis*, **16**, pp. 179–98.
Granger, Herbert (1996) *Aristotle's Idea of the Soul*. Dordrecht: Kluwer Academic.
Hardie, W. F. (1964) 'Aristotle's Treatment of the Relation between the Soul and the Body', in *Phil. Quart*, **14**, pp. 53–72.
Hartman, Edwin (1977) *Substance, Body and Soul: Aristotelian Investigations*. Princeton, NJ: Princeton University Press.
Irwin, T. H. (1988) *Aristotle's First Principles*. Oxford: Oxford University Press.
Irwin, T. H. (1991) 'Aristotle's Philosophy of Mind', in Stephen Everson (ed.) *Companions to Ancient Thought 2: Psychology*. Cambridge: Cambridge University Press, pp. 56–83.
Nussbaum, Martha & Rorty, A. O. (eds.) (1992) *Essays on Aristotle's De Anima*. Oxford: Clarendon Press.
Robinson, Daniel M. (1989) *Aristotle's Psychology*. New York: Columbia University Press.
Shields, C. (1988a) 'Soul and Body in Aristotle', in *Oxford Studies in Ancient Phil.*, **6**, pp. 103–37.
Shields, C. (1988b) 'Soul as Subject in Aristotle's De Anima', in *Classical Quart.*, **38**, pp. 140–49.
Solmsen, F. (1957) 'The Vital Heat, the Inborn Pneuma, and the Aether', in *J. Hellenic Soc.*, **77**, pp. 119–23.
Sorabji, Richard (1974) 'Body and Soul in Aristotle', in *Philosophy*, **49**, pp. 63–89.
Wedin, M. (1988) *Mind and Imagination in Aristotle*. New Haven, CT: Yale University Press.

Chapter 2, Section 3

Annas, Julia (1992) *Hellenistic Philosophy of Mind*. Berkeley: University of California Press.

Arnold, E. V. (1911) 'Kingdom of the Soul', in *Roman Stoicism*. NY: Arno Reprint, 1970, Chapter XI.
Bailey, Cyril (ed. & trans.) (1947) *Lucretius' De Rerum Natura*. vol. I Text & trans; vols. II & III Commentary. Oxford: Clarendon Press.
Clay, D. (1983) *Lucretius and Epicurus*. Ithaca, NY: Cornell University Press.
Clay, D. (1990) 'Diogenes of Oenoanda', in ANRW, vol. 36.4, pp. 2446–559.
Colish, M. L. (1985) *The Stoic Tradition from Antiquity to the Middle Ages*. 2 vols. Leiden: E. J. Brill.
Everson, Stephen (1999) 'Epicurean Psychology', in CHHP, pp. 542–59.
Gould, J. B. (1970) *The Philosophy of Chrysippus*. Albany, NY: SUNY Press.
Hallie, Philip (1967) 'Stoicism', in EEP, vol. 8, pp. 19–22.
Kerferd, G. B. (1971) 'Epicurus' Doctrine of the Soul', in *Phronesis*, **16**, pp. 80–96.
Konstan, D. (1973) *Some Aspects of Epicurean Psychology*. Leiden: E. J. Brill.
Kristeller, P. O. (1993) *Greek Philosophers of the Hellenistic Age*. New York: Columbia University Press.
Long, A. A. & Sedley, David (eds) (1987) *The Hellenistic Philosophers*. Cambridge: Cambridge University Press.
Long, A. A. (1999) 'Stoic Psychology', in CHHP, pp. 560–84.
Padel, Ruth (1992) *In and Out of the Mind: Greek Images of the Tragic Self*. Princeton, NJ: Princeton University Press.
Segal, Charles (1990) *Lucretius on Death and Anxiety*. Princeton, NJ: Princeton University Press.
Staden, Heinrich von (2000) 'Body, Soul, and Nerves: Epicurus, Herophilus, Erasistratus, the Stoics, and Galen', in Wright & Potter, pp. 79–116.
SVF: Arnim, H. von (1905) *Stoicorum Veterum Fragmenta*. Leipzig, 1901–5. Reprint, Darmstadt, 1976.

Chapter 3, Section 1

Berkouwer, G. C. (1962) *Man: The Image of God*. Trans. by D. W. Jellema. Grand Rapids, MI: Eerdmans.
Best, E. (1955) *One Body in Christ*. London: SPCK Press.
Betz, Hans Dieter (2000) 'The Concept of the "Inner Human Being" (ὁ εσω ανθρωπος) in the Anthropology of Paul', in NTS, **46**, pp. 315–41.
Brown, Colin (1978a) 'Soul – *Psychē* ', in NIDNT, vol. 3, pp. 676–89.
Brown, Colin (1978b) 'Spirit, Holy Spirit – *pneuma*', in NIDNT, vol. 3, pp. 689–709.
Bultmann, Rudolf (1952) *Theology of the New Testament*. London: SCM Press.
Burkert, Walter (1998) 'Towards Plato and Paul: The "Inner" Human Being', in A. Y. Collins (ed.) *Ancient and Modern Perspectives on the Bible and Culture*. Atlanta, GA: Scholars Press.
Chamblin, J. K. (1993) 'Psychology', in G. F. Hawthorne & R. P. Martin (eds) *Dictionary of Paul and his Letters*. Intervarsity Press, pp. 765–75.
Childs, Brevard (1992) *Biblical Theology of the Old and New Testaments*. London: SCM Press.
Crossan, John D. (1998) *The Birth of Christianity*. San Francisco: Harper Collins.

Dautzenberg, G. (1966) *Sein Leben bewahren: ψυχή in den Herrenworten der Evangelien*. Munich: Kösel.
Dunn, James (1998) *Theology of Paul the Apostle*. Grand Rapids, MI: Eerdmans, pp. 51–78.
Gundry, Robert H. (1976) *Sōma in Biblical Theology*. Cambridge: Cambridge University Press.
Heckel, Theo K. (2000) 'Body and Soul in Saint Paul', in Wright & Potter, pp. 117–32.
Jewett, R. (1971) *Paul's Anthropological Terms*. Leiden: E. J. Brill.
Kirk, G. S. & Raven, J. E. (1960) *The Presocratic Philosophers*. Cambridge: Cambridge University Press.
Lys, Daniel (1966) 'The Israelite Soul according to the LXX', in *Vetus Test*, **16**, pp. 181–228.
Martin, D. B. (1995) *The Corinthian Body*. New Haven, CT: Yale University Press.
Motyer, J. A. (1978) 'body – sōma', in NIDNT, vol. 1, pp. 232–41.
Moule, C. F. D. (1966) 'St. Paul and Dualism', in *NTS*, **12**, pp. 106–23.
Neusner, Jacob (2000) 'Soul in Judaism', in Jacob Neusner (ed.) *Encyclopedia of Judaism*. Leiden: E. J. Brill, vol. 3, pp. 1342–46.
Reicke, B. (1965) 'Body and Soul in the New Testament', in *St. Th.*, **19**, pp. 200–212.
Reitzenstein, R. (1926) *Hellenistic Mystery Religions*. Trans. by John E. Steely. Pittsburgh, PA: Pickwick Press (Reprint 1978).
Robinson, H. W. (1926) *The Christian Doctrine of Man*. Edinburgh: T & T Clark.
Robinson, J. A. T. (1952) *The Body: A Study in Pauline Theology*. London: SCM Press.
Schmidt, W. H. & others (1984) 'Geist', in TRE, vol. 12, pp. 170–217.
Schmidt, W. H. & others (2000) 'Seele', in TRE, vol. 30, forthcoming.
Schnelle, Udo (1996) *The Human Condition: Anthropology in the Teachings of Jesus, Paul and John*. Edinburgh: T & T Clark.
Schweizer, E. & others (1975a) 'sarx', in TDNT, vol. VII, pp. 98–151.
Schweizer, E. & others (1975b) 'sōma', in TDNT, vol. VII, pp. 1024–94.
Schweizer, E. & others (1975c) 'psychē', in TDNT, vol. IX, pp. 608–60.
Thiselton, A. C. (1978) 'flesh – sarx', in NIDNT, vol. 1, pp. 671–82.
Wolfson, H. A. (1962) *Philo: Faith, Religion and Philosophy in Judaism, Christianity and Islam*, 3rd edn, Rev. Cambridge, MA: Harvard University Press, vol. I, pp. 360–423.
Wolfson, H. A. (1967) 'Philo Judaeus', in EEP, vol. 6, pp. 151–5.

Chapter 3, Section 2

Armstrong, A. H. (1967) *The Architecture of the Intelligible Universe in the Philosophy of Plotinus*. Amsterdam: North Holland (first pub. Cambridge University Press, 1940).
Blumenthal, H. J. (1971) *Plotinus' Psychology*. The Hague: M. Nijhoff.
Blumenthal, H. J. (1993) *Soul and Intellect: Studies in Plotinus and Later Neoplatonism*. London: Ashgate.

Brehier, Emile (1958) *The Philosophy of Plotinus*. Trans. by Joseph Thomas. Chicago: University of Chicago Press.
Chadwick, Henry (1993) *The Early Church*, rev. edn. New York: Penguin Books.
CHLGEMP: Armstrong, A. H. (ed.) (1970) *Cambridge History of Later Greek and Early Medieval Philosophy*. Cambridge: Cambridge University Press.
Culianu, Ioan P. (1983) *Psychanodia I: A Survey of the Evidence*. Leiden: E. J. Brill.
Dillon, J. M. (1977) *The Middle Platonists*. London: Duckworth.
Dodds, E. R. (1951) *The Greeks and the Irrational*. Berkeley: University of California Press.
Dodds, E. R. (ed.) (1960) *Les Sources de Plotin*. Entretiens Hardt, Tome V. Geneva: Vandoeuvres.
Emilsson, Eyjolfur (1991) 'Plotinus and soul-body dualism', in Stephen Everson (ed.) *Companions to Ancient Thought 2: Psychology*. Cambridge: Cambridge University Press.
Emilsson, Eyjolfur (1994) 'Platonic Soul-Body Dualism in the Early Centuries of the Empire to Plotinus', in ANRW, vol. 36.7, pp. 5331–62.
Gersh, Stephen & Kannengiesser, Charles (1992) *Platonism in Late Antiquity*. Notre Dame, IN: University of Notre Dame Press.
Gerson, Lloyd & Wallis, Richard (1995) *Neoplatonism*. Indianapolis, IN: Hackett.
Hadot, Pierre (1993) *Plotinus or The Simplicity of Vision*. Trans. by Michael Chase. Chicago: University of Chicago Press.
Menn, Stephen (1998) *Descartes and Augustine*. Cambridge: Cambridge University Press, Chapter 3.
Merlan, Philip (1967) 'Plotinus', in EEP, vol. 6, pp. 351–9.
O'Daly, G. J. (1973) *Plotinus' Philosophy of the Self*. Shannon: Irish Universities Press.
Rist, J. M. (1967) *Plotinus: The Road to Reality*. Cambridge: Cambridge University Press.
Schwyzer, H. R. (1951) 'Plotinus', in RE, vol. xxi (i), cols. 471–592.
Smith, Andrew (1974) *Porphyry's Place in the Neoplatonic Tradition*. The Hague: M. Nijhoff.
Steel, C. (1978) *The Changing Self: A Study of the Soul in Later Neoplatonism ...* Brussels.
Verbeke, G. (1945) *L'evolution de la doctrine du pneuma du stoicisme à S. Augustin*. Paris & Louvain.
Vernant, Jean-Pierre (1991) 'Psuchē: Simulacrum of the Body or Image of the Divine?', in Froma Zeitlin (ed.) *Mortals and Immortals*. Princeton, NJ: Princeton University Press.
Wallis, Richard (1972) *Neoplatonism*. London: Duckworth.
Wallis, Richard (ed.) (1992) *Neoplatonism and Gnosticism*. Albany, NY: SUNY Press.
Wolfson, H. A. (1962) *Philo: Faith, Religion and Philosophy in Judaism, Christianity and Islam*, 3rd edn, Rev. Cambridge, MA: Harvard University Press, vol. I, pp. 360–423.

Chapter 3, Section 3

Barnes, Michel (1994) 'The Polemical Context and Content of Gregory of Nyssa's Psychology', in *Medieval Phil. and Theology*, vol. 4. Notre Dame, IN: University of Notre Dame Press, pp. 1–24.
Barnes, T. D. (1971) *Tertullian: An Historical and Literary Study*. Oxford: Oxford University Press.
Bayliss, H. J. (1928) *Mincucius Felix and his Place Among the Early Fathers of the Latin Church*. New York: Macmillan.
Bell, David N. (1980) 'The Tripartite Soul and the Image of God in the Latin Tradition', in RTAM, **47**, pp. 16–52.
Berchman, Robert (1984) *From Philo to Origen: Middle Platonism in Transition*. Chico, CA: Scholars Press (Brown Judaic Studies).
Bercot, David (1998) 'Soul' in *Dictionary of Early Christian Beliefs*. Peabody, MA: Hendrickson.
Blumenthal, H. J. (1993) *Soul and Intellect: Studies in Plotinus and Later Neoplatonism*. London: Ashgate.
Chadwick, Henry (1993) *The Early Church*, rev. edn. New York: Penguin Books.
Chadwick, Henry (1970) 'Philo and the Beginnings of Christian Thought', in CHLGEMP, pp. 137–92.
Cherniss, H. F. (1930) *The Platonism of Gregory of Nyssa*. Berkeley: University of California Press.
Crouzel, Henri (1989) *Origen*. Trans. by A. S. Worrall. Edinburgh: T & T Clark.
Danielou, Jean (1973) *A History of Early Christian Doctrine, vol. 2: Gospel Message and Hellenistic Culture*. Trans. by John Austin Parker. London: Darton, Longman & Todd; New York: Westminster.
Danielou, Jean (1977) *A History of Early Christian Doctrine, vol. 3: The Origins of Latin Christianity*. Trans. by John Austin Parker. London: Darton, Longman & Todd; New York: Westminster
Gilson, Etienne (1955) *History of Christian Philosophy in the Middle Ages*. London: Sheed & Ward.
Grant, Robert (1967) 'Patristic Philosophy', in EEP, vol. 6, pp. 57–9.
Kemp, Simon (1996) *Cognitive Psychology in the Middle Ages*. Westport, CT: Greenwood Press.
Leclercq, H. (1924) 'Ame', in *Dictionaire D'Archéologie Chrétiènne*. Paris: Letouzey. Tome I, cols. 1470–554.
Quasten, Johannes (1975) *Patrology*. 4 vols. Trans. anon. Utrecht-Antwerp: Spectrum.
Verbeke, G. (1945) *L'evolution de la doctrine du pneuma du stoicisme à S. Augustin*. Paris & Louvain.
Waszink, J. H. (1955) 'Observations on Tertullian's Treatise against Hermogenes', in *Vigiliae Christianae*, **9**, pp. 129–47.
Watson, Gerard (1989) 'Souls and Bodies in Origen's *Peri Archon*', in *Irish Th. Quart*. **55**, pp. 173–92.
Wolfson, H. A. (1970) *The Philosophy of the Church Fathers*, 3rd edn. Cambridge, MA: Harvard University Press.

Chapter 3, Section 4

Bell, David N. (1980) 'The Tripartite Soul and the Image of God in the Latin Tradition', in RTAM, **47**, pp. 16–52.
Brown, Peter (1967) *Augustine of Hippo: A Biography*. Penguin Books.
Cary, Phillip (2000) *Augustine's Invention of the Inner Self*. Oxford: Oxford University Press.
Champoux, R. (1962) 'L'union du corps et de l'âme selon S. Augustin', in *Dialogue*, **1**, pp. 309–15.
Courcelle, Pierre (1969) *Late Latin Writers and their Greek Sources*. Cambridge, MA: Harvard University Press.
Couturier, C. (1954) 'La structure métaphysique de l'homme d'après S. Augustin', in *Augustinus Magister*. Paris: Aug. Congress, vol. I, pp. 543–50.
De Roy, O. J.-B. (1967) 'St. Augustine', in NCE, vol. I, pp. 1041–58.
Gilson, Etienne (1961) *The Christian Philosophy of Saint Augustine*. Trans by L. E. M. Lynch. London: Sheed & Ward.
Hölscher, Ludger (1986) *The Reality of the Mind: St. Augustine's Philosophical Arguments*. London: Routledge & Kegan Paul.
Markus, R. A. (1967) 'St. Augustine', in EEP, vol. 1, pp. 198–207.
Markus, R. A. (1970) 'Marius Victorinus and Augustine', in CHLGEMP, pp. 331–419.
Matthews, Gareth (2000) 'Internalist Reasoning in Augustine for Mind-Body Dualism', in Wright & Potter pp. 133–46.
Menn, Stephen (1998) *Descartes and Augustine*. Cambridge: Cambridge University Press, Chapter 4.
O'Connell, Robert (1968) *St. Augustine's Early Theory of Man*. Cambridge, MA: Harvard University Press
O'Connell, Robert (1969) *St. Augustine's Confessions: The Odyssey of Soul*. Cambridge, MA: Harvard University Press.
O'Connell, Robert (1987) *The Origin of the Soul in St. Augustine's Later Works*. New York: Fordham University Press.
O'Daly, Gerard (1987) *Augustine's Philosophy of Mind*. London: Duckworth.
Rist, J. M. (1994) *Augustine: Ancient Thought Baptized*. Cambridge: Cambridge University Press.
Schindler, A. (1975) 'Augustine', in TRE, vol. 4, pp. 646–98.
Schwarz, R. (1954) 'Die leibseelische Existenz bei Aurelius Augustinus', in *Phil. Jahr.*, **63**, pp. 323–60.
Stroumsa, G. G. (1990) '*Caro salutis cardo*: Shaping the Person in Early Christianity', in *Hist. Rel.*, **30**, pp. 25–59.
Stump, Eleanor & Kretzmann, Norman (eds) (2001) *Cambridge Companion to Augustine*. Cambridge: Cambridge University Press.
Trapè, Agostino (1996) 'Saint Augustine', in *Patrology*. Joh. Quasten (ed.) Trans. anon. Utrecht-Antwerp: Spectrum. vol. 4, pp. 342–462.
Verbeke, G. (1945) *L'evolution de la doctrine du pneuma du stoicisme à S. Augustin*. Paris & Louvain.

Chapter 4, Section 1

Afnan, S. H. (1958) *Avicenna: His Life and Works*. London: Allen & Uniwn.
Amid, M. (1940) *Essai sur la Psychologie d'Avicenne*. Geneva: Vandrouves.
Bakos, Jan (1956) *Psychologie d'Ibn Sīnā (Avicenne)*. 2 vols. Prague: Académie Czecho des Sciences.
Corbin, Henry (1993) *History of Islamic Philosophy*. London: Routledge.
Davidson, Herbert (1992) *Alfarabi, Avicenna and Averroes on Intellect*. Oxford: Oxford University Press.
Endress, Gerhard & Aersten, Jan (eds) (1999) *Averroes and the Aristotelian Tradition*. Leiden: E. J. Brill.
Gilson, Etienne (1955) *History of Christian Philosophy in the Middle Ages*. London: Sheed & Ward.
Goodman, Lenn (1995) *Ibn Sīna (Avicenna)*. London: Routledge.
Hyman, Arthur (1996) 'Averroes' Theory of the Intellect and the Ancient Commentators', in Endress & Aersten, 1999, pp. 188–98.
Ivry, Alfred L. (1991) 'La Logique de la science de l'âme', in *Penser avec Aristotle*. Paris: Editions Erès, pp. 687–700.
Ivry, Alfred L. (1996) 'Averroes' Three Commentaries on *De Anima*', in Endress & Aersten, 1999, pp. 199–216.
Jolivet, Jean & Roshdi, Rashed (1984) *Etudes sur Avicenne*. Paris: Les Belles Lettres.
Leaman, Oliver (1985) *An Introduction to Medieval Islamic Philosophy*. Cambridge: Cambridge University Press.
Leaman, Oliver (1997) *Averroes and His Philosophy*, 2nd edn. London: Curzon Press.
MacClintock, Stuart (1967) 'Averroes' and 'Averroism', in EEP, vol. 1, pp. 220–26.
Marenbon, John (ed.) (1998) *Medieval Philosophy*. London: Routledge.
Marmura, Michael (1967) 'Avicenna', in EEP, vol. 1, pp. 226–9.
Netton, Ian Richard (1989) *Allah Transcendent: Studies in the Structure and Semiotics of Islamic Philosophy, Theology and Cosmology*. London: Routledge.
Netton, Ian Richard (1992) *Al-Farabi and His School*. London: Routledge.
Rahman, Fazlur (1952) *Avicenna's Psychology*. Oxford: Oxford University Press.
Rosenthal, Franz (1975) *The Classical Heritage in Islam*. London: Routledge & Kegan Paul.
Taylor, Richard C. (1996) 'Remarks on *Cogitatio* in Averroes' *Commentarium Magnum*', in Endress & Aersten, 1999, pp. 217–55.
Urvoy, Dominique (1991) *Ibn Rushd (Averroes)*. London: Routledge.
Walzer, Richard (1962) *Greek into Arabic Essays on Islamic Philosophy*. Oxford: Oxford University Press.
Wolfson, H. A. (1973) 'The Twice-Revealed Averroes', in his *Studies in the History of Philosophy and Religion*. Twersky & Williams (eds) Cambridge, MA: Harvard University Press, vol. I, pp. 371–86.

Chapter 4, Section 2

Aquinas, Thomas (1993) *Selected Writings*. Trans. by Tim McDermott. Oxford: Oxford University Press.
Baldner, Steven (1993) 'Is Albert the Great a Dualist on Human Nature?', in *Proc. of American Catholic Phil. Assoc.*, **67**, pp. 219–29.
Baldner, Steven (1996), 'St. Albert the Great on the Union of the Human Soul and Body', in *American Catholic Phil. Quarterly*, **70**, pp. 103–20.
Bazan, Bernardo (1969) 'Pluralisme de Formes ou Dualisme de Substances?', in *Revue Phil. de Louvain*, **67**, pp. 30–73.
Bazan, Bernardo (1983) 'La Corporalité selon Saint Thomas', in *Revue Phil. de Louvain*, **81**, pp. 369–409.
Bonin, Therese (2000) 'The Emanative Psychology of Albertus Magnus', in *Topoi*, **19**, pp. 45–57.
Bourke, Vernon (1967) 'Thomas Aquinas', in EEP, vol. 8, pp. 105–16.
CHLMP: Kretzmann, Norman & others (eds) (1982) *The Cambridge History of Later Medieval Philosophy*. Cambridge: Cambridge University Press.
Craemer-Ruegenberg, Ingrid (1979) 'The Priority of Soul as Form and its Proximity to the First Mover', in *Southwestern J. Phil.*, **10**, pp. 49–62.
Ducharme, Léonard (1979) 'The Individual Human Being in Saint Albert's Earlier Writings', in *Southwestern J. Phil.*, **10**, pp. 131–60.
Geiger, L. B. (1962) 'La vie, acte essentiel de l'âme', in *Arch. Hist. doctr. litt.*, **17**, pp. 49–116.
Gilson, Etienne (1945) 'L'âme rationelle selon Albert le Grand', in *Arch. Hist. doctr. litt.*, **7**, pp. 5–72.
Gilson, Etienne (1955) *History of Christian Philosophy in the Middle Ages*. London: Sheed & Ward.
Gilson, Etienne (1957) *The Christian Philosophy of St. Thomas Aquinas*. Trans. by L. K. Shook. London: Gollancz.
Gorman, William (1940) 'Albertus Magnus on Aristotle's Second Definition of the Soul', in *Mediaeval Studies*, **2**, pp. 223–30.
Kenny, Anthony (1970) 'Intellect and Imagination in Aquinas', in Anthony Kenny (ed.) *Aquinas: A Collection of Critical Essays*. London: Macmillan.
Kenny, Anthony (1993) *Aquinas on Mind*. London: Routledge.
Kretzmann, Norman (1993) 'Philosophy of Mind', in N. Kretzmann & E. Stump (eds) *Cambridge Companion to Aquinas*. Cambridge: Cambridge University Press, pp. 128–59.
Lehrberger, James (1998) 'The Anthropology of Aquinas' *de Ente et Essentia*', in *Review of Metaphysics*, **51** (4), pp. 829–47.
Marenbon, John (1987) *Late Medieval Philosophy*. London: Routledge.
Marenbon, John (ed.) (1998) *Medieval Philosophy*. London: Routledge.
Michaud-Quantin, Pierre (1955) 'Albert le Grand et les puissances de l'âme', in *Revue du moyen âge latin*, **11**, pp. 59–86.
Michaud-Quantin, Pierre (1966) *La psychologie de l'activité chez Albert le Grand*. Paris: J. Vrin.
Pegis, Anton C. (1934) *St. Thomas and the Problem of the Soul in the 13th Century*. Toronto: Pontifical Institute.

Schmitz, Kennel (1986) 'Purity of Soul and Immortality', in *The Monist*, **69**, pp. 396–415.
Schneider, Arthur (1906) *Die Psychologie Albers des Grossen nach den Quellen dargestellt*, in *Beiträge Zur Gesch der Phil und Theologie des Mittelalters*, Band IV, Heft 5, Munster.
Sharp, D. E. (1930) *Franciscan Philosophy at Oxford in the Thirteenth Century*. New York: Russell & Russell.
Zupko, Jack (1997) 'What is the Science of the Soul?', in *Synthese*, **110** (2), pp. 297–334.

Chapter 4, Section 3

Boyde, Patrick (1981) *Dante: Philomythes and Philosopher*. Cambridge: Cambridge University Press.
Boyde, Patrick (1993) *Perception and Passion in Dante's Comedy*. Cambridge: Cambridge University Press.
Colish, Marcia (1983) 'Dante: Poet of Rectitude', in her *The Mirror of Language: A Study of Medieval Theory of Knowledge*, rev. edn. Lincoln, NB: University of Nebraska Press.
Curtius, E. R. (1979) *European Literature and the Latin Middle Ages*. Trans. by W. R. Trask. London: Routledge & Kegan Paul (first pub. 1953).
Dante (1970–75) *The Divine Comedy*. Trans. with Commentary by Charles S. Singleton. Princeton, NJ: Princeton University Press. *Inferno*, 2 vols (1970); *Purgatorio*, 2 vols (1973); *Paradisio*, 2 vols (1975).
Dante (1990) *The Banquet*. Trans. by R. H. Lansing. New York: Garland. [Conv.]
Dante (1995) *Monarchia*. Trans. and ed. by Prue Shaw. Cambridge: Cambridge University Press. [Mon.]
Duby, George (ed.) (1988) *Revelations of the Medieval World*. Cambridge, MA: Harvard University Press.
Gilson, Etienne (1963) *Dante and Philosophy*. Trans. by David Moore. London: Sheed & Ward, 1949. (Reprinted, New York: Harper & Row.)
Foster, Kenelm (1977) *The Two Dantes and Other Studies*. Berkeley: University of California Press.
Foster, Kenelm & Boyde, Patrick (1967) *Dante's Lyric Poetry*. vol. I Text, vol. II Commentary. Oxford: Clarendon Press.
Mazzotta, Giuseppe (1979) *Dante: Poet of the Desert*. Princeton, NJ: Princeton University Press.
Mazzotta, Giuseppe (1993) *Dante's Vision and the Circle of Knowledge*. Princeton, NJ: Princeton University Press.
Morris, Colin (1973) *The Discovery of the Individual 1050–1200*. New York: Harper & Row.
Shapiro, Marianne (1998) *Dante and the Knot of Body and Soul*. New York: St. Martin's Press.

Chapter 5, Section 1

Cassirer, Ernst (1963) *The Individual and the Cosmos in Renaissance Philosophy*. Trans. by Mario Domadi. New York: Barnes & Noble.
CKR: Cassirer, Kristeller & Randall (eds) (1970) *The Renaissance Philosophy of Man*. Chicago: University of Chicago Press. (First pub. 1948.)
Copenhaver, Brian & Schmitt, Charles (1992) *Renaissance Philosophy*. Oxford: Oxford University Press.
Hopkins, Jasper (1981) *Nicholas of Cusa on Learned Ignorance*. Minneapolis, MN: Banning Press.
Kraye, Jill (ed.) (1996) *Cambridge Companion to Renaissance Humanism*. Cambridge: Cambridge University Press.
Kristeller, P. O. (1956) *Studies in Renaissance Thought and Letters*. New York.
Kristeller, P. O. (1961) *Renaissance Thought: The Classic, Scholastic and Humanist Strains*. New York: Harper & Row.
Kristeller, P. O. (1965) *Renaissance Thought II: Papers on Humanism and the Arts*. New York: Harper & Row.
Kristeller, P. O. (1972) *Renaissance Concepts of Man and Other Essays*. New York: Harper & Row.
Levao, R. L. (1985) *Renaissance Minds and Their Fictions: A Comparative Study of Nicholas of Cusa, Sir Philip Sidney, and Shakespeare*. Berkeley: University of California Press.
MacDonald, Paul S. (2000) *Descartes and Husserl: The Philosophical Project of Radical Beginnings*. Albany, NY: SUNY Press.
Mann, Nicholas (2000) 'From Laurel to Fig: Petrarch and the Structures of the Self' in *Proc. British Acad.*, **105**, pp. 17–42.
Petrarch (1975) *Rerum Familiarum*. Trans. by A. S. Bernardo. 3 vols. Albany, NY: SUNY Press. [Fam.]
Petrarch (1991) *Remedies for Fortune Fair and Foul*. Trans. with Commentary by Conrad H. Rawski. 5 vols. Bloomington, IN: Indiana University Press. [Rem.]
Sorrell, Tom (ed.) (1997) *The Rise of Modern Philosophy*. Oxford: Oxford University Press.
Struever, Nancy (1993) 'Petrarch's *Invectiva contra medicum*: An Early Confrontation of Rhetoric and Medicine', in *Modern Language Notes*, **108** (4), pp. 659–79.
Trinkhaus, Charles (1970) *In Our Image and Likeness: Humanity and Divinity in Italian Humanist Thought*. 2 vols. London: Constable.
Weeks, Andrew (1993) *German Mysticism from Hildegard of Bingen to Ludwig Wittgenstein*. Albany, NY: SUNY Press.

Chapter 5, Sections 2 and 3

Allen, M. J. B. (1981) *Marsilio Ficino and the Phaedran Charioteer*. Berkeley: University of California Press.
Allen, M. J. B. (1984) *The Platonism of Marsilio Ficino*. Berkeley: University of California Press.

Bossy, John (1992) *Giordano Bruno and the Embassy Affair*. New Haven, CT: Yale University Press.
Bruno, Giordano (1998) *Cause, Principle and Unity*. Trans. & ed. by Robert de Lucca; *Essays on Magic*. Trans. & ed. by R. J. Blackwell. Intro. by Alfonso Ingegno. Cambridge: Cambridge University Press.
Collins, Ardis B. (1974) *The Secular is Sacred: Platonism and Thomism in Marsilio Ficino's Platonic Theology*. The Hague: Nijhoff.
Ficino, Marsilio (2000) *Commentary on Plato's Symposium on Love*. Trans. by S. R. Jayne, 2nd edn. New York: Spring Publishers.
Ficino, Marsilio (2001) *Platonic Theology*. Ed. & trans. by M. J. Allen & John Warden. Cambridge, MA: Harvard University Press.
Ficino, Marsilio (1989) *Three Books on Life*. Ed. & trans. by Carol Kaske & John Clark. Renaissance Society of America.
Ficino, Marsilio (1975–80) *Letters*. Trans. by various (LSE). 6 vols. London: Shepheard-Walwyn.
Gatti, Hilary (1999) *Giordano Bruno and Renaissance Science*. Ithaca, NY: Cornell University Press.
Harvey, Ruth (1975) *The Inward Wits: Psychological Theory in the Middle Ages and the Renaissance*. London: The Warburg Institute.
Klibansky, R. & others (1964) *Saturn and Melancholy: Studies in the History of Natural Philosophy, Religion and Art*. London: Nelson.
Kristeller, P. O. (1943) *The Philosophy of Marsilio Ficino*. Trans. by Virginia Conant. New York: Columbia University Press.
Michael, Emily (2000) 'Renaissance Theories of Body, Soul, and Mind', in Wright & Potter, pp. 147–72.
Sorrell, Tom (ed.) (1997) *The Rise of Modern Philosophy*. Oxford: Oxford University Press.
Thorndike, Lynn (1923–58) *History of Magic and Experimental Science*. 8 vols. New York: Columbia University Press.
Voss, Angela (2000) 'The Astrology of Marsilio Ficino', in *Culture and Cosmos*, **4** (2), pp. 1–23.
Walker, D. P. (1958) *Spiritual and Demonic Magic from Ficino to Campanella*. London: Warburg Institute.
Wind, Edgar (1967) *Pagan Mysteries in the Renaissance*. Penguin Books.
Yates, Frances (1964) *Giordano Bruno and the Hermetic Tradition*. London: Routledge & Kegan Paul.
Yates, Frances (1982) Collected Essays vol. I: Lull and Bruno. London: Routledge & Kegan Paul.
Zanier, Giancarlo (1987) 'Platonic Trends in Renaissance Medicine', in JHI, **48**, pp. 509–19.

Chapter 6, Sections 1 and 2

Baldwin, A. P. (1984) 'The Tripartite Reformation of the Soul', in Marion Glasscoe (ed.) *The Medieval Mystical Tradition in England*. Cambridge: D. S. Brewer.
Bennett, H. S. (1965) *Chaucer and the Fifteenth Century*. Oxford: Clarendon Press.

Boitani, Piero & Torti, Anna (eds) (1999) *The Body and the Soul in Medieval Literature*. Cambridge: D. S. Brewer.
Butterworth, C. C. (1971) *The Literary Lineage of the King James Bible 1340–1611*. NY: Octagon Books.
Canuteson, J. A. (1977) 'The Conflict Between the Body and the Soul as a Metaphor of the Moral Struggle in the Middle Ages', Unpub. Ph.D. Dissert.
Clark, J. P. H. (1979) 'Image and Likeness in Walter Hilton', in *Downside Review*, **97**, pp. 207–20.
Clark, J. P. H. (1982) 'Augustine, Anselm and Walter Hilton' in Marion Glasscoe (ed.) *The Medieval Mystical Tradition in England*. Exeter: D. S. Brewer.
Doubleday, James (1969) 'The Three Faculties of the Soul in *The Wanderer*', in *Neophilologus*, **53**, pp. 189–94.
Duby, George (ed.) (1988) *Revelations of the Medieval World*. Cambridge, MA: Harvard University Press.
Harvey, Ruth (1975) *The Inward Wits: Psychological Theory in the Middle Ages and the Renaissance*. London: The Warburg Institute.
Hayes, Stephen (1995) 'Of Three Workings in Man's Soul', in Anne Clark Bartlett (ed.) *Vox Mystica: Essays on Medieval Mysticism*. Cambridge: D. S. Brewer.
Kemp, Simon (1996) *Cognitive Psychology in the Middle Ages*. Westport, CT: Greenwood Press.
Kempe, Margery (2000) *The Book of Margery Kempe*. Lynne Staley (ed.) New York: W. W. Norton.
Marenbon, John (1988) *Early Medieval Philosophy*. London: Routledge.
Matto, M. E. (1998) 'Containing Minds: Mind, Metaphor, and Cognition in Old English Literature'. Unpub. Ph.D. Dissert. New York University.
'mind' (1977) in *Middle English Dictionary*. University of Michigan Press, Part M.4, pp. 484–92.
Orton, P. R. (1980) 'The OE Soul and Body: Further Examination', in *Medium Aevum*, **48**, pp. 173–97.
Phillips, M. J. (1986) 'Heart, Mind, and Soul in Old English: A Semantic Study'. Unpub. Ph.D. Dissert.
Ross, Ann Brown (1993) 'Anglo-Saxon Teaching on the Soul'. Unpub. Ph.D. Disscrt. Univ. North Carolina.
Schaffner, Paul (1999) 'Life of Soul', in Anne Clark Bartlett (ed.) *Cultures of Piety: Medieval English Devotional Literature*. Ithaca, NY: Cornell University Press.
Sharp, D. E. (1930) *Franciscan Philosophy at Oxford in the Thirteenth Century*. New York: Russell & Russell.
'soul' (1989) in *Middle English Dictionary*. University of Michigan Press, Part S.11, pp. 295–308.
Whitehead, Christiania (1998) 'Making a Cloister of the Soul in Medieval Religious Treatises', in *Medium Aevum*, **67** (1), pp. 1–29.

Chapter 6, Section 3

Bloom, Harold (1998) *Shakespeare: The Invention of the Human*. London: Fourth Estate.

Cefalu, Paul (2000) '"Damned Custom... Habit's Devil": Shakespeare's Hamlet, Anti-Dualism, and the Early Modern Philosophy of Mind', in *English Lit. Hist.*, **67** (2), pp. 399–431.
Cody, Richard (1969) *The Landscape of the Mind: Pastoralism and Platonic Theory in Tasso's* Aminta *and Shakespeare's Early Comedies*. Oxford: Clarendon Press.
Greenblatt, Stephen (1994) 'The Eating of the Soul', in *Representations*, **48**, pp. 97–116.
Hoeniger, F. David (1985) *Medicine and Shakespeare in the English Renaissance*. Newark, NJ: University of Delaware Press.
Ide, Richard (1975) 'The Theatre of the Mind: An Essay on Macbeth', in *English Lit. Hist.*, **42**, pp. 338–61.
Johnson, Paul (1997) 'Battle Within Shakespeare's Brain', in *J. Consc. Studies*, **4** (4), pp. 365–73.
Levao, R. L. (1985) *Renaissance Minds and Their Fictions: A Comparative Study of Nicholas of Cusa, Sir Philip Sidney, and Shakespeare*. Berkeley: University of California Press.
Soellner, Rolf (1968) 'Shakespeare, Aristotle, Plato and the Soul', in *Shakes. Jahrbuch*, **4**, pp. 316–33.
Waddington, R. B. (1990) 'All in All: Shakespeare, Milton, Donne and the Soul-in-Body Topos', in *English Lit. Hist.*, **20** (1), pp. 40–68.

Chapter 7, Section 1

Aliqué, Ferdinand (1987) *La Decouverte Metaphysique de L'Homme chez Descartes*, 2me edn. Paris.
ATI–XI: Descartes, René (1996) *Oeuvres de Descartes*, Charles Adam & Paul Tannery (eds) New Edition. 11 vols. Paris: J. Vrin.
Baker, Gordon & Morris, Katherine (1996) *Descartes' Dualism*. London: Routledge.
Beck, L. J. (1965) *The Metaphysics of Descartes*. Oxford: Oxford University Press.
Carter, Richard (1983) *Descartes' Medical Philosophy*, Baltimore, MD: Johns Hopkins University Press.
Carter, Richard (1985) 'Descartes' Bio-Physics', in *Philosophia Naturalis*, **22**, pp. 223–49.
Caton, Hiram (1973) *The Origins of Subjectivity: An Essay on Descartes*. New Haven, CT: Yale University Press.
CH17CP: Garber, Daniel & Ayers, Michael (eds) (1998) *Cambridge History of Seventeenth Century Philosophy*. Cambridge: Cambridge University Press.
Cottingham, John (ed.) (1992) *The Cambridge Companion to Descartes*. Cambridge: Cambridge University Press.
Cottingham, John (ed.) (1994) *Reason, Will and Sensation*. Oxford: Oxford University Press.
CSM I–III: Descartes, René (1985) *The Philosophical Writings*. Trans. by Cottingham, Stoothoff & Murdoch. 2 vols; *The Correspondence* (1991) Trans. by Cottingham, Stoothoff, Murdoch & Kenny. Cambridge: Cambridge University Press.
Curley, Edwin (1978) *Descartes Against the Skeptics*. Oxford: Blackwell.

Fowler, C. F. (1999) *Descartes on the Human Soul*. Dordrecht: Kluwer Academic.
Gaukroger, Stephen (1996) *Descartes: An Intellectual Biography*. Oxford: Oxford University Press.
Gouhier, Henri (1962) *La Pensee Metaphysique de Descartes*. Paris: J. Vrin.
Grene, Marjorie (1985) *Descartes* [Philosophers in Context Series]. London: Harvester.
Gueroult, Martial (1984) *Descartes ... According to the Order of Reasons*. 2 vols. Trans. by Roger Ariew. Minneapolis, MN: University of Minnesota Press.
Hooker, Michael (ed.) (1978) *Descartes: Critical and Interpretive Essays*. Baltimore, MD: Johns Hopkins University Press.
James, Susan (1997) *Passion and Action: The Emotions in 17th Century Philosophy*. Oxford: Oxford University Press.
Judovitz, Dalia (1988) *Subjectivity and Representation in Descartes*. Cambridge: Cambridge University Press.
Loeb, Louis (1981) *From Descartes to Hume*. Ithaca, NY: Cornell University Press.
MacDonald, Paul S. (2000) *Descartes and Husserl: The Philosophical Project of Radical Beginnings*. Albany, NY: SUNY Press.
MacDonald, Paul S. (2002) 'Descartes – The Lost Episodes', in JHP **40**, pp. 437–60.
Marion, Jean-Luc (1981) *Sur L'Ontologie Grise de Descartes*. Paris: J. Vrin.
Marion, Jean-Luc (1986) *Sur Le Prisme Metaphysique de Descartes*. Paris: P.U.F.
Marion, Jean-Luc (1991) *Sur La Theologie Blanche de Descartes*. Paris: P.U.F.
Menn, Stephen (1998) *Descartes and Augustine*. Cambridge: Cambridge University Press.
Miles, Murray (2000) *Descartes' First Principles*. Toronto: University of Toronto Press.
Nussbaum, Martha & Rorty, A. O. (eds) (1992) *Essays on Aristotle's De Anima*. Oxford: Clarendon Press.
Popkin, Richard (1979) *History of Skepticism from Erasmus to Spinoza*. Berkeley: University of California Press.
Rodis-Lewis, G. (1971) *L'Oeuvre de Descartes*. two vols in one. Paris: J. Vrin.
Rodis-Lewis, G. (1991) *L'Anthropologie Cartesienne*. Paris: P.U.F.
Rodis Lewis, G. (1998) *Descartes: His Life and Thought*. Trans. by Jane Marie Todd. Ithaca, NY: Cornell University Press.
Rorty, A. O. (ed.) (1986) *Essays on Descartes' Meditations*. Berkeley: University of California Press.
Rozemond, Marleen (1999) *Descartes' Dualism*. Cambridge, MA: Harvard University Press.
Shea, William (1991) *The Magic of Numbers and Motion*. Washington, DC: Science History.
Voss, Stephen (2000) 'Descartes: Heart and Soul', in Wright & Potter, pp. 173–96.
Wagner, Steven (1984) 'Descartes on the Parts of the Soul', in *Phil. & Phen. Res.*, **45**, pp. 51–70.
Wilson, M. D. (1978) *Descartes* [Arguments of the Philosophers Series]. London: Routledge.
Yandell, David (1997) 'What Descartes Really Told Elizabeth: Mind-Body Union as Primitive Notion', in *Brit. J. Hist. Phil.* **5**, pp. 249–73.

Chapter 7, Section 2

Bennett, Jonathan (1984) *A Study of Spinoza's Ethics*. Indianapolis, IN: Hackett.
Curley, Edwin (1969) *Spinoza's Metaphysics: An Essay in Interpretation*. Cambridge, MA: Harvard University Press.
Curley, Edwin (1977) 'Notes on the Immortality of the Soul in Spinoza's *Short Treatise*', in *Giornale Critico Filosofia Italiana*, **8**, pp. 327–36.
Curley, Edwin (1988) *Behind the Geometrical Method*. Princeton, NJ: Princeton University Press.
Daniels, C. B. (1976) 'Spinoza on the Mind-Body Problem: Two Questions', in *Mind*, **85**, pp. 542–58.
Delahunty, R. J. (1985) *Spinoza* [Arguments of the Philosophers Series]. London: Routledge & Kegan Paul.
Della Rocca, Michael (1996) *Representation and the Mind-Body Problem in Spinoza*. Oxford: Oxford University Press.
Donagan, Alan (1988) *Spinoza* [Philosophers in Context Series]. London: Harvester Wheatsheaf.
Floistad, Guttorm (1978) 'Mind and Body in Spinoza's *Ethics*', in *Synthese*, **37**, pp. 1–14.
Garrett, Don (ed.) (1996) *Cambridge Companion to Spinoza*. Cambridge: Cambridge University Press.
Hampshire, Stuart (1987) *Spinoza: An Introduction to his Philosophical Thought* (rev. edn). London: Penguin Books.
Harris, Errol (1973) *Salvation from Despair: A Reappraisal of Spinoza's Philosophy*. The Hague: Nijhoff.
Hoffman, Paul (1991) 'Three Dualist Theories of the Passions', in *Phil. Topics*, **19**, pp. 153–200.
Jarrett, Charles (1991) 'Spinoza's Denial of Mind-Body Interaction and the Explanation of Human Action', in *Southwest J. Phil.* **29**, pp. 465–85.
Koistinen, Olli (1996) 'Causality, Intensionality and Identity: Mind-Body Interaction in Spinoza', in *Ratio*, **9**, pp. 23–38.
Lermond, Lucia (1988) *The Form of Man: Human Essence in Spinoza's Ethics*. Leiden: E. J. Brill.
Lucash, Frank (1984) 'The Mind's Body: the Body's Self-Awareness', in *Dialogue*, **23**, pp. 619–34.
Lucash, Frank (1990) 'Spinoza on the Eternity of the Human Mind', in *Phil. & Th.*, pp. 103–13.
Lucash, Frank (1992) 'The Activity and Passivity of Mind and Body', in *Phil. Inquiry*, **14**, pp. 11–23.
MacIntyre, Alasdair (1967) 'Benedict Spinoza', in EEP, vol. 7, pp. 531–41.
Mark, Thomas C. (1979) 'Spinoza's Concept of Mind', in JHP, **17**, pp. 401–16.
Matson, Wallace (1977) 'Death and Destruction in Spinoza's *Ethics*', in *Inquiry*, **20**, pp. 403–17.
Mcrae, Robert (1983) 'The Mind, Simple or Composite: Leibniz versus Spinoza', in *Southwest J. Phil.*, **21** (Suppl.), pp. 111–20.
Nadler, Stephen (1999) *Spinoza: A Biography*. Cambridge: Cambridge University Press.

Parchment, Steven (2000) 'The Mind's Eternity in Spinoza's *Ethics*', in JHP, **38**, pp. 349–82.
Parkinson, G. H. R. (1983) 'Spinoza's Philosophy of Mind', in Guttorm Floistad (ed.) *Contemporary Philosophy: A New Survey.* The Hague: Nijhoff, pp. 105–31.
Rice, Lee (1990) 'Reflexive Ideas in Spinoza', in JHP, **28**, pp. 201–11.
Spinoza, Benedict (1985) *The Collected Works.* Ed. & trans. by Edwin Curley. Princeton, NJ: Princeton University Press.
Stock, Barbara (2000) 'Spinoza on the Immortality of the Mind', in *Hist. Phil. Quart.*, **17**, pp. 381–403.

Chapter 7, Section 3

Adams, Robert M. (1994) *Leibniz: Determinist, Theist, Idealist.* Oxford: Oxford University Press.
Deleuze, Gilles (1993) *The Fold: Leibniz and the Baroque.* Trans. by Tom Conley. London: Athlone Press.
Duchesneau, Francois (2000) 'Stahl, Leibniz, and the Territories of Soul and Body', in Wright & Potter, pp. 217–36.
Jolley, Nicholas (1984) *Leibniz and Locke.* Oxford: Clarendon Press.
Jolley, Nicholas (ed.) (1995) *Cambridge Companion to Leibniz.* Cambridge: Cambridge University Press.
Kulstad, Mark (1983) 'Leibniz on Consciousness and Reflection', in *Southwest J. Phil.*, **21** (Suppl.), pp. 39–65.
Mates, Benson (1986) *The Philosophy of Leibniz: Metaphysics and Language.* Oxford: Oxford University Press.
MES: Leibniz, G. W. (1991) *The Monadology: An Edition for Students.* Nicholas Rescher (ed.) London: Routledge.
NE: Leibniz, G. W. (1981) *New Essays on Human Understanding.* Trans. by Peter Remnant & Jonathan Bennett. Cambridge: Cambridge University Press.
PPL: Leibniz, G. W. (1970) *Philosophical Papers and Letters.* Leroy Loemker (ed.) Amsterdam: Reidel.
Rescher, Nicholas (1967) *The Philosophy of Leibniz.* Newark, NJ: Prentice Hall.
Rescher, Nicholas (1981) *Leibniz's Metaphysics of Nature.* Amsterdam: Reidel.
Russell, L. J. (1967) 'G. W. Leibniz', in EEP, vol. 4, pp. 422–33.
Rutherford, Donald (1995) *Leibniz and the Rational Order of Nature.* Cambridge: Cambridge University Press.
Smith, Barry (ed.) (1997) *The Monist,* **80**, Special Issue on Leibniz.
Sleigh, Robert (1990) *Leibniz and Arnauld: A Commentary on their Correspondence.* New Haven, CT: Yale University Press.
Vailati, Ezio (1997) *Leibniz and Clarke: A Study of their Correspondence.* Oxford: Oxford University Press.
Wilson, Catherine (1990) *Leibniz's Metaphysics: A Historical and Comparative Study.* Princeton, NJ: Princeton University Press.
Wilson, Catherine (1997) 'Leibniz and the Animalcula', in Tom Sorrell (ed.) *The Rise of Modern Philosophy.* Oxford: Oxford University Press, pp. 153–75.

Yolton, John (1983) *Thinking Matter: Materialism in Eighteenth-Century Britain*. Minneapolis, MN: University of Minnesota Press.

Chapter 8, Section 1

Allen, Don Cameron (1964) *Doubt's Boundless Sea*. Baltimore, MD: Johns Hopkins University Press.
Bloch, R. O. (1971) *La philosophie de Gassendi: nominalisme, matérialisme, et métaphysique*. The Hague: Nijhoff.
Dobbs, B. J. (1971) 'Studies in the Natural Philosophy of Sir Kenelm Digby Part I', in *Ambix*, **18**, pp. 1–25.
Dobbs, B. J. (1975) *The Foundations of Newton's Alchemy*. Cambridge: Cambridge University Press.
Frankel, Lois (1991) 'Anne Finch, Viscountess Conway', in Mary Ellen Waithe (ed.) *History of Women Philosophers*. Dordrecht: Kluwer Academic, vol. III, pp. 41–58.
Gassendi, Pierre (1972) *The Selected Works*. Ed. & trans. by Craig Brush. NY: Johnson Reprint.
Gert, Bernard (1996) 'Hobbes' Psychology', in Tom Sorrell (ed.) *The Cambridge Companion to Hobbes*. Cambridge: Cambridge University Press, pp. 157–74.
Gert, Bernard (1997), 'Thomas Hobbes', in Tom Sorrell (ed.) *The Rise of Modern Philosophy*. Oxford: Oxford University Press, pp. 157–74.
Hall, A. Rupert (1990) *Henry More: Magic, Religion and Experiment*. Oxford: Blackwell.
Henry, John (1982) 'Atomism and Eschatology', in *Brit. J. Hist. Science*, **15**, pp. 211–39.
Henry, John (1986) 'A Cambridge Platonist's Materialism: Henry More and the Concept of Soul', in *J. Warburg & Courtauld Institute*, **49**, pp. 172–95.
Hobbes, Thomas (1991) *Leviathan*. Richard Tuck (ed.) Cambridge: Cambridge University Press. [Lev.]
Hobbes, Thomas (1991) *On Human Nature*, in Bernard Gert (ed.) *Man and Citizen*. Indianapolis, IN: Hackett, pp. 35–85. [De Hom.]
Hobbes, Thomas (1998) *On the Citizen*. Richard Tuck & M. Silverthorne (eds) Cambridge: Cambridge University Press. [De Cive]
Hutton, Sarah (ed.) (1990) *Henry More 1614–1687: Tercentenary Studies*. Dordrecht: Kluwer Academic.
Jacob, Alexander (1985) 'Henry More's *Psychodia Platonica* and its Relationship to Marsilio Ficino's *Theologia Platonica*', in JHI, **46**, pp. 503–22.
Lennon, Thomas (1993) *The Battle of the Gods and Giants: The Legacies of Descartes and Gassendi 1655–1715*. Princeton, NJ: Princeton University Press.
Merchant, Carolyn (1979) 'The Vitalism of Anne Conway: its Impact on Leibniz's Concept of the Monad', in JHP, **17**, pp. 255–69.
Mijuskovic, Ben Lazaro (1974) *The Achilles of Rationalist Arguments*. The Hague: Nijhoff.
Mintz, Samuel (1970) *The Hunting of Leviathan*. Cambridge: Cambridge University Press.

Osler, M. J. (1985) 'Baptizing Epicurean Atomism: Pierre Gassendi on the Immortality of the Soul', in M. J. Osler & P. L. Farber (eds) *Religion, Science and Worldview*. Cambridge: Cambridge University Press.
Peters, R. S. (1967) 'Hobbes, Thomas', in EEP, vol. 4, pp. 30–45.
Popkin, R. H. (1967) 'Gassendi, Pierre', in EEP, vol. 3, pp. 269–73.
Popkin, Richard (1979) *History of Skepticism from Erasmus to Spinoza*. Berkeley: University of California Press.
Rogers, G. A. J. & Ryan, Alan (eds) (1988) *Perspectives on Thomas Hobbes*. Oxford: Clarendon Press.
Rosenfeld, L. C. (1968) *From Beast-Machine to Man-Machine: Animal Soul in French Letters from Descartes to La Mettrie*. New York: Octagon Books.
Staudenbaur, C. A. (1968) 'Galileo, Ficino, and Henry More's *Psychathanasia*', in JHI, **29**, pp. 565–78.
van der Bend, J. G. (ed.) (1982) *Thomas Hobbes: His View of Man*. Amsterdam: Editions Rodopi.

Chapter 8, Section 2

Aaron, Richard (1971) *John Locke*, 3rd edn. Oxford: Oxford University Press.
Acton, H. B. (1967) 'George Berkeley', in EEP, vol. 1, pp. 295–304.
Ayers, Michael (1991) *John Locke*. 2 vols. London: Routledge.
Bailey, Lee W. (1989) *The Skull's Darkroom*. Dordrecht: Kluwer Academic.
Bennett, Jonathan (1971) *Locke, Berkeley, Hume: Central Themes*. Oxford: Oxford University Press.
Bermudez, José Luis (1996) 'Locke, Metaphysical Dualism, and Property Dualism', in *Brit. J. Hist. Phil.*, **4**, pp. 223–35.
Chappell, Vere (ed.) (1994) *Cambridge Companion to Locke*. Cambridge: Cambridge University Press.
Clapp, J. G. (1967) 'John Locke', in EEP, vol. 4, pp, 487–503.
E: Locke, John (1975) *An Essay Concerning Human Understanding*. P. H. Nidditch (ed.) Oxford: Clarendon Press.
EHU, EPM: Hume, David (1975) *Enquiry Concerning the Human Understanding* and *Enquiry Concerning the Principles of Morals*. L. A. Selby-Bigge (ed.) Oxford: Oxford University Press.
Flage, Daniel (1990) *David Hume's Theory of Mind*. London: Routledge.
Gaskin, John (1988) *Hume's Philosophy of Religion*. 2nd edn. NY: Macmillan.
Grayling, A. C. (1986) *Berkeley: The Central Arguments*. London: Duckworth.
Hart, W. D. (1988) *The Engines of the Soul*. Cambridge: Cambridge University Press.
Jenkins, John (1983) *Understanding Locke*. Edinburgh: Edinburgh University Press.
Jolley, Nicholas (1984) *Leibniz and Locke*. Oxford: Oxford University Press.
Lennon, Thomas (1993) *The Battle of the Gods and Giants: The Legacies of Descartes and Gassendi 1655–1715*. Princeton, NJ: Princeton University Press.
Lowe, E. J. (1995) *Understanding Locke*. London: Routledge.
McCracken, Charles (1988) 'Berkeley's Cartesian Concept of Mind', in *The Monist*, **71**, pp. 596–611.

MacNabb, D. G. C. (1967) 'David Hume', in EEP, vol. 4, pp. 74–90.
Norton, David (ed.) (1993) *Cambridge Companion to Hume*. Cambridge: Cambridge University Press.
Pears, David (1990) *Hume's System*. Oxford: Oxford University Press.
Pitcher, George (1977) *Berkeley* [Arguments of the Philosophers]. London: Routledge & Kegan Paul.
Stroud, Barry (1977) *Hume* [Arguments of the Philosophers]. London: Routledge & Kegan Paul.
T: Hume, David (1978) *A Treatise of Human Nature*. L. A. Selby-Bigge (ed.) Oxford: Oxford University Press.
Taylor, Charles (1989) *Sources of the Self: The Making of the Modern Identity*. Cambridge: Cambridge University Press.
Tipton, I. C. (1974) *Berkeley: The Philosophy of Immaterialism*. London: Methuen.
Tipton, I. C. (ed.) (1977) *Locke on Human Understanding*. Oxford: Oxford University Press.
Waxman, Wayne (1994) *Hume's Theory of Consciousness*. Cambridge: Cambridge University Press.
WGB: Berkeley, George (1948–57) *The Works*. A. A. Luce & T. E. Jessop (eds.) London: Thomas Nelson.
Winkler, Kenneth (1994) *Berkeley: An Interpretation*. Oxford: Oxford University Press.
Woolhouse, R. S. (1983) *Locke* [Philosophers in Context Series]. London: Harvester Wheatsheaf.
Yolton, John (1984) *Perceptual Acquaintance from Descartes to Reid*. Oxford: Blackwell.
Yolton, John (1985) *Locke: An Introduction*. Oxford: Blackwell.
Yolton, John (1983) *Thinking Matter: Materialism in Eighteenth-Century Britain*. Minneapolis, MN: University of Minnesota Press.

Chapter 8, Section 3

Burnyeat, Myles (1982) 'Idealism and Greek Philosophy: What Descartes Saw and Berkeley Missed', in *Phil. Review*, **91**, pp. 3–40.
Crouzel, Henri (1989) *Origen*. Trans. by A. S. Worrall. Edinburgh: T & T Clark.
Lohr, Charles (1988) 'Metaphysics', in CHRP, pp. 537–638.
MacClintock, Stuart (1967) 'Averroes' and 'Averroism', in EEP, vol. 1, pp. 220–26.
Snell, Bruno (1953) 'Homer's View of Man', in *The Discovery of the Mind*. Trans. by T. G. Rosenmeyer. Oxford: Blackwell, pp. 1–22.
Strasser, Stephen (1977) *The Phenomenology of Feeling*. Robert E. Wood (ed. & intro.). Pittsburgh, PA: Duquesne University Press.
Taylor, Charles (1989) *Sources of the Self: The Making of the Modern Identity*. Cambridge: Cambridge University Press.

Index of Names

This does not include names cited in the footnotes. Principal entries for original authors are in **boldface**.

Abulfaraj, Samuel 237
Accius 80
Achillini, Alessandro 227
Aelred 248
Aetius 27, 77
Afnan, S. H. 169
Agrippa, H. C. 240
Albert the Great 176, **177–84**, 227, 355
Alcmaeon 52
Alexander of Aphrodisias 161, 172, 227–8
Alexander Polyhistor 102
Alfārābī **162–5**, 354
Alghazāla 171
Alkindī 161–2
Allen, Michael 218–21, 225–7
Ambrose, St. 146
Ammonius Saccas 107, 131
Anaxagoras 30, 110
Anaximander 26
Anaximenes 26–8
Annas, Julia 48, 74–5, 77, 79
Anonymous English works 245–62
Arbman, Ernst 13–14
Aristeas 23–4
Aristotle 23–6, 31, 34, **54–71**, 73, 75, 79, 92, 107, 109, 116, 118, 141, 161–3, 166, 171–5, 177–84, 186–91, 191–3, 197–9, 201, 206, 227, 243, 282, 301, 319–20, 330, 353–5, 360–61
Arnobius 135
Armstrong, A. H. 108–9, 114, 120
Arnauld, Antoine 288
Augustine, St. 32, 109, 112, 135, **143–60**, 182, 200, 203, 209, 211, 226, 236, 239, 249, 283, 322, 354, 361
Averroes **170–77**, 179, 182–3, 194, 196, 199, 226–8, 235, 354–5
Avicenna **165–70**, 174, 178–83, 354

Ayers, Michael 334, 336

Bacon, Roger 251
Bailey, Cyril 84
Baker, G. & Morris, K. 285, 289
Barnes, T. D. 138
Bazan, Bernard 186
Bell, David 48, 128, 133
Bennett, Jonathan 291
Berkeley, George **338–43**, 360
Berkouwer, G. C. 105
Biro, John 345, 349
Bloom, Harold 264
Blumenthal, H. J. 121–2
Blund, John 251
Boccacio, G. 209
Boethius 190, 196
Bokenham, Osbern 247
Bolton, D. P. 24
Bonaventure, St. 258
Boyde, Patrick 190–91, 194–5, 198–202
Bremmer, Jan 13–17
Brown, Colin 92, 103
Brown, Peter 146
Browne, Thomas 330–31
Bruno, Giordano 225, **241–3**
Burkert, Walter 40–41, 43, 45
Burnett, John 38
Burnyeat, Miles 54, 70, 357
Bultmann, Rudolf 98–9, 105

Campanella, Tommaso 225, 241
Cardano, Girolamo 241
Carter, Richard 280
Cary, Phillip 160
Cassirer, Ernst 213
Cefalu, Paul 265–6, 275, 277
Celsus 136

387

Cesare of Cremona 176
Chadwick, Henry 93, 113, 124, 130, 137
Chamblin, J. K. 105
Chaucer, Geoffrey 246, 249, 252, 254, 256, 258, 280
de Chauliac, Guy 252, 255, 258
Chrysippus 71–2, 76, 111
Chrysoloras, Manuel 209
Cicero 48, 71, 79–80, 83, 86, 135–7, 144–5, 149, 190, 208–9, 245, 353
Clarke, Samuel 307
Claus, David 12, 15, 17–19, 27–8, 30, 33, 40, 42
Cleanthes 71–2, 76
Clement of Alexandria **129–31**
Collins, Ardis 221–4
Conway, Anne 322
Copenhaver, Brian 212, 215, 230, 233–5, 240–43
Copernicus, Nicolas 242, 326
Corbin, Henry 162, 168
Cottingham, John 283
Crombie, I. M. 37, 46
Crossan, John 105
Crouzel, Henri 133, 353
Cudworth, Ralph 332
Cusanus, Nicholas **212–15**, 240

Danielou, Jean 126–30, 132, 134, 136, 140
Dante 188, **190–204**, 208
Davidson, Herbert 170
Deleuze, Gilles 308
Della Porta, G. B. 241
Descartes, René 1, 18, 22, 112, 168, 207, 216, 265, 277, **279–91**, 295, 304, 307, 312, 315–17, 321–2, 325–31, 333, 336–7, 344, 357
Digby, Kenelm 263, 315, **329–31**
Diogenes Laertius 24, 71, 72
Diogenes of Oenoanda 77–8
Dodds, E. R. 33. 43, 105
Donato, Jerome 227
Ducharme, Leonard 178
Dunn, J. G. 97–100, 106
Dumezil, Georges 16, 80

Eckhart, Meister 203
Eichrodt, Walter 8
Elizabeth, Princess 288
Emilsson, E. 122
Empedocles 31–2, 112

Epicurus 32, 71, **76–80**, 83, 87, 148, 322, 327–8, 353, 361
Euripides 20, 42
Eusebius 131
Everson, Stephen 59

Ficino, Marsilio 190, 207, 213, **217–26**, **231–5**, 239–40, 321–2, 343, 356
Frede, Michael 282–3

Galen 74, 85, 166, 192
Galileo 176, 279, 327
Garber, Daniel 304, 331
Gassendi, Pierre 281, **326–9**
Gatti, Hilary 242–3
Gilson, Etienne 163, 182, 184, 190, 196, 198
Glanvill, Joseph 324
Gower, John 248, 256, 259
Gregory the Great 123
Gregory of Nyssa 136, **140–43**
Granger, Herbert 34, 55–6, 69–70
Grant, Robert 142
Grayling, A. C. 341
Gundry, Robert 97–100, 104–5

Hadot, Pierre 111
Hall, Rupert 325–6
Hawkins, J. D. 213
Henry, John 330
Heraclides Ponticus 24
Heraclitus 24, **28–30**, 361
Herodotus 24, 40, 77
Hesiod 23, 102
Higden, Ranulf 247–8, 254
Hilton, Walter 251, 254, 257–8
Hippocrates 41, 90
Hippolytus 29
Hobbes, Thomas **315–20**, 329, 331, 361
Homer 2, **11–22**, 27, 35, 37, 47, 64, 83, 127, 352
Hume, David **343–9**

Iamblichus 75, 121, 207, 234
Ingegno, Alfonso 241
Innocent VII 235
Irenaeus of Lyon **124–8**, 137
Isidore of Seville 123
Ivry, Alfred 173–5

Jacob, Alexander 322

Index of Names

Jaeger, Werner 33
Jerome, St. 2
Jessop, T. E. 342
Jewett, R. 99
John, St. 95, 103, 201
John of Damascene 123
Johnson, Aubrey 3, 10
Jolivet, J. 174
Jolley, Nicholas 307
Josephus 94–5
Julian the Apostate 121
Justin Martyr 124, 137

Kahn, Charles 29, 33, 66–7
Kempe, Margery 251, 257–8, 260
Kenny, Anthony 185
Kessler, Eckard 207, 277–8
Kirk, G. S. & Raven, J. E. 23, 27, 31
Kosman, L. A. 67–8
Kretzmann, Norman 185, 187
Kristeller, P. O. 208–9, 221, 226

Leibniz, G. W. **300–13**, 322, 360
Lennon, Thomas 337
Levao, R. L. 214
Lloyd, G. E. R. 63–4
Locke, John 306–7, **322–8**, 344, 348
Lohr, Charles 213, 216, 237–40, 356
Lucretius 71, **79–87**, 245, 327, 353
Luke, St. 92, 95–6, 103
Lull, Raymond 176–7, 240
Lydgate, John 251, 256, 260–61
Lys, Daniel 11

MacClintock, Stuart 171, 175, 355
McKirihan, Richard 26, 30
Malebranche, Nicholas 344
Mann, Nicholas 209
Marcus Aurelius 71
Marenbon John 189
Marius Victorinus 144, 146
Mark, St. 96, 103
Markus, R. A. 150, 153
Marti, Raymond 176–7
Mates, Benson 301
Matthew, St. 95–6
de Medici, Cosimo 217, 225, 235, 240
Meuli, Karl 34
Menn, Stephen 109, 116–18, 145–7, 159, 285–7
Mersenne, Marin 329

Michael, Emily 217
Minucius Felix **135–7**
de Mondeville, Henri 202, 258
More, Henry **320–26**, 338

Nadler, Stephen 299
Nardi, Bruno 190
Netton, Ian 164
Newton, Isaac 307, 344
Nibridus 152
Nietzsche, F. 12
Nonus 80
Norton, David 344–5
Nussbaum, Martha 30

O'Connell, Robert 154
O'Daly, Gerard 144, 148–9
Onians, R. B. 12, 15, 17, 22, 29, 52, 80
Origen 107, 115, **131–4**, 142, 149, 188, 237, 353
Orm, Canon 248
Osler, Margaret 327–8
Ostenfeld, E. N. 39, 47, 49, 51

Padel, Ruth 8, 18, 19
Panaetius 71
Paracelsus 240–41
Parmenides 31, 219
Paul, St. 47, 89–90, **97–107**, 122, 132, 142–3, 154, 157–8, 239, 353, 358
Pecock, Reginald 251–2
Petrarch 203, **208–12**, 217
Pherecydes 23
Philo Judaeus 90, 92–4, 102, 123, 143
Pico, G. F. 216, **235–40**, 356
Pitcher, George 339
Plato 24, **37–54**, 59, 68, 79, 92–3, 104, 107–10, 121, 128–9, 136, 138, 141, 143, 146–7, 149, 159–60, 166, 181, 206, 218–20, 235, 271, 283, 320, 324, 337, 353, 356, 361
Plautus 81
Plotinus 47, **107–21**, 131, 134, 143, 147, 150, 154, 157–8, 207, 218, 226, 233, 235, 331, 356
Plutarch 75, 77, 84
Pomponazzi, Pietro **228–30**
Porphyry 107–8, 111, 140, 151, 154–6, 161
Posidonius 71, 111
Proclus 121–3, 161, 207, 219, 226, 237

Protagoras 41
Pseudo-Dionysius 214
Ptolemy II 89
Pythagoras 23–4, 37, 40–41, 43–5, 51, 57, 101, 136, 139, 236, 250, 271, 329

Randall, J. H. 229–30
Rawski, Conrad 210–11
Reizenstein, R. 106
Remigius of Auxerre 246
Rescher, Nicholas 306, 308, 313
Ripley, George 253
Rist, J. M. 108, 112, 117, 151, 157
Robinson, J. A. 98
Robinson, T. M. 37, 39, 40, 46
Rohde, Erwin 12
Rorty, A. O. 60, 291
Russell, Bertrand 185
Russell, L. J. 304
Rutherford, Donald 311–12
Ryle, Gilbert 265–6

Schmitt, Charles 215, 230, 235, 241, 243
Schmitz, Kenneth 187
Schofield, Malcolm 25, 28, 29
Schweizer, E. 90, 95–6, 101–2
Servius 198
Sextus Empiricus 74, 207, 326
Shakespeare, William **264–78**
Shapiro, Marianne 198
Simplicius 24, 31, 122
Smith, Andrew 121
Snell, Bruno 12, 16, 349
Socrates 24, 30, 37, 38–45, 47–52, 68, 124, 219–20, 352
Spenser, Edmund **262–4**, 329
Spinoza, Benedict **291–300**, 337, 347
Stocks, J. L. 48
Strasser, Stephen 351
Synesius 207

Taylor, Charles 337–8
Telesio, Bernardino 241

Tertullian 135, **136–40**
Thales **23–6**, 27, 83
Theophrastus 32
Thomas Aquinas, St. 46, 176, **184–90**, 199, 226, 228, 234, 239, 355
Timaeus 51–2, 92, 110, 118, 140
Tournemine, Father 311
Trevisa, John 246–7, 251–4, 259–61
Trinkhaus, Charles 205, 210, 212

von Uexkull, Jacob 308
Urvoy, Dominique 173, 176

Vailati, Ezio 307
Varro 83, 137, 147
Vergil 82, 136, 198, 208
Vernant, J-P. 21, 119
Vlastos, Gregory 33
Von Fritz, Kurt 18
Voss, Angela 234

Wallis, Richard 113
Walzer, Richard 164
Waszink, J. H. 137, 140
Waxman, Wayne 348
Weeks, Andrew 213
Westermann, Claus 5–10
White, Thomas 317, 329
Whiting, Jennifer 60–62, 64
Wilkes, K. V. 282
Wilson, Catherine 309
Wolfson, H. A. 92, 177
Wood, Robert 351
Wycliffe 246, 250, 253–4, 259

Yahweh 3–6, 9, 12, 127
Yandell, David 288–9
Yates, Frances 242
Yolton, John 336–7, 347–8

Zalmoxis 39–41
Zeno of Citium 71
Zostrianos 113

Index of Subjects

'Mind', 'soul' and 'body' are too common to be usefully indexed.

abstract 2–5, 10, 42, 258, 332, 345, 350
abstraction 165–8, 170–75, 182, 229, 289, 341
active 13–14, 168–70, 172, 181, 285, 294, 297–8, 339–40
activities 65–7, 78, 81, 95, 188
actual, -ity 58, 65–70, 168–70, 173, 181–3, 196, 200, 222–4, 282, 302
Adam 106, 126, 130, 143, 148, 154–7, 236, 262, 354
adequacy 294–6, 332
aether 94, 111, 122, 132, 279–80, 342, 357
agent, -cy 18, 34, 64, 69–70, 79, 116, 165, 171, 222, 293
aggregate 78, 300, 308, 310
aion 13
air 7, 27, 64, 73, 79, 81, 83, 132, 150, 201, 232, 284, 319, 326, 342
aitia 46, 55, 57, 59, 65, 72
alchemy 253, 329
algorithm 302
anger 8, 11, 60, 141, 148, 189
angels 132, 138, 159, 167–8, 185, 188–9, 194, 201, 212, 216, 223, 229, 236, 251, 271, 319, 324, 337
anima 2, 5, 22, 80–87, 125, 139, 144, 154, 180, 183, 185, 220, 223, 245–7, 251, 253–5, 268, 279–80, 283, 293, 327, 349–50, 353, 357
animal 4, 8, 11–12, 22, 25, 32, 46, 53, 59–60, 63–6, 72, 75, 77, 130, 139, 151, 155, 196, 240, 251–2, 259, 271, 283, 293, 299, 302, 304, 306, 308, 327, 335–7, 343, 354
animus 80–87, 139, 144, 220, 223, 245, 253–5, 268, 327

apeiron 26
appearance 75, 97, 112, 302–6
apperception 302, 306
arbitration 184
archē 27, 29, 34, 46, 63, 65, 67, 115, 122, 179
archetype 46, 51, 102, 118, 164, 188, 219, 321
ascent 46–7, 95, 101, 113, 121–2, 131, 133, 145, 158, 200, 219, 225–6, 234, 236, 283, 292, 296, 356
ascesis 94, 115, 131, 236, 353
association 294, 338, 346
astrology 231, 239
astronomy 26, 51, 231, 242, 321
atheism 76, 322–3, 327, 332
atoms 76–7, 83, 85, 102, 242, 292, 301, 328, 330, 335, 337
augoeides 122, 343
automaton 302–3, 317, 360

bark 26, 112, 271
basar 3, 12, 29, 99
beauty 112, 135, 159, 201, 212, 219, 277, 303
behavior, -ism 265, 269, 272
bile 62, 232
bilocation 31
birds 47, 83, 140
birth 32, 72, 91, 148, 220, 306, 310
blessing 6, 33, 38, 104, 133, 187, 295
blood 3, 6, 12, 20, 32–3, 60–63, 84, 95, 100, 192, 232, 247, 271, 284, 318, 349
bones 12, 20, 29, 52, 62–3, 84, 91, 102
brain 6, 52, 63, 73, 170, 174, 192, 232, 252, 254, 258, 268, 290, 318–19, 328, 337
breath 3–4, 7, 11–12, 14–17, 27, 47, 64, 73, 81, 84, 126, 129, 135, 148, 154–6, 200, 232, 254, 262, 271, 279, 349, 353
building 193–4, 202–3, 262–3, 338
bundle 98, 339

butterfly 201

Caballa 236–7, 321
calor 82
caro 125, 138, 157, 248, 359
cause 46, 54–5, 69, 72, 163, 169, 188, 200, 217, 243, 295, 297–8, 301–3, 332, 342, 347–8
caterpillar 202
chain 131, 222, 279, 298, 337, 343
change 55, 60, 63, 65, 138, 153–4, 292, 295, 301
chariot 46–7, 149, 219
charms 39, 121, 231, 233
child 29, 44, 115, 128, 253
Christ 95, 97–8, 101, 104, 124, 127, 131, 135, 139, 142, 150, 215, 237, 247–8, 259, 312, 354
city 47, 154, 163
clothes 32, 93, 103, 106, 122, 132, 146, 169, 200, 248–9, 276
cold 34, 73, 87
communicate, -tion 75, 84, 118, 234
composite 46, 52, 57, 62, 73, 78, 149–50, 178, 186, 193, 198, 224, 234, 285–8, 305, 308, 333, 346, 355
conatus 293, 298–9, 318
concrete 2–3, 5, 8, 10, 18–20, 28, 63, 138, 332, 349–50
configuration 292, 298
conscious, -ness 67–8, 81, 86, 114, 147, 256, 282, 291, 298, 336, 359
consilium 81, 195
contemplate, -tion 81, 112, 117, 120, 167, 215, 220, 237, 247–9, 257, 334, 356
continuum 76, 99, 133, 303, 310
control 27, 52, 63, 245
conversion 143, 190, 203
corporeal 31, 44–6, 50, 52, 78, 82, 100, 104, 116, 122, 132, 138, 174, 183–5, 198, 222, 316, 320, 342–3, 359–60
corpse 60–62, 86, 104, 151
corpus 80, 98, 133, 138, 157, 359–60
cosmos 27, 30, 72, 76, 109, 112, 134, 137, 163, 210, 215, 231, 299, 360–61
create, -tion 7–8, 23, 51, 92, 95, 98, 112, 125, 129, 131, 149, 157, 173, 188, 199, 201, 215, 231, 238, 335, 356

darkness 68, 82, 87, 117, 119, 133, 221, 239, 320, 326

death 3, 6, 8, 13–14, 19–21, 28, 32, 38, 43–4, 76, 83, 86, 90, 96, 102, 131, 144, 148, 156–8, 173, 179, 185, 199, 210, 249, 261, 303, 306, 310, 327, 353–4, 361
definition 55, 58, 61, 65–6, 110, 181, 188, 195, 221, 224, 300
demiurge 51, 110, 127
demon 25, 33, 38, 93, 132, 242, 279, 324, 356
dependent 39, 45, 53–4, 79, 115, 169, 222–5, 289–90, 292, 301, 310, 359
descent 116–19, 168, 217, 220, 236
desire 5, 7, 15, 22, 46, 48–9, 52, 54, 75, 130, 133, 141–2, 184, 189, 192, 255, 258, 298, 350
dianoia 65, 67
dignity 212, 214, 221, 238
discipline 32, 94, 115, 131, 159, 200, 216, 236, 283
disposition 18, 49, 58, 70, 75, 115, 172–4, 186, 255, 276, 334, 343, 351
diversity 132, 169, 179, 214
double (-nature) 32, 115, 144, 156, 200, 249, 262, 354
double (-soul) 19–21, 97, 120, 198, 249–50, 257
doubt 146, 152, 168, 268, 284, 326, 357
dream 13–14, 20, 28, 131, 272, 319
drive 293, 298, 302
drunken, -ness 10, 29, 260
dualism 1, 11, 13, 31, 39, 42, 50, 66, 79, 91, 93, 104–5, 112, 128, 134, 186, 202, 265, 277, 291, 333, 351, 358, 361
dunamis 49–50, 58, 60, 64, 75, 141, 254, 353
dynamic (reality) 239–40, 243, 326, 343, 356

earth 25, 91, 106, 117, 132, 150, 154–5, 200, 232, 280, 321
ecstasy 23, 34, 41, 245, 250, 257, 351
Egyptian 45, 90, 107
eidolon 20–21, 120, 250
eidos 52, 55, 111, 301, 353
element 23, 25–6, 32–3, 57, 60–62, 64, 77–8, 80, 83–5, 117, 135, 137, 139, 179, 232, 292, 330, 339, 351
emanation 94, 119, 129, 164–8, 181, 237
embalming 45
embryo 91, 199, 308
emerge 309, 313

emotions 6–9, 15, 18, 30, 46, 75, 82, 90, 93, 139, 148, 152, 189, 210–11, 245, 254, 258–9, 270–71, 285, 290, 297, 349
endeavor 318
energy 17, 69, 298
ennoia 129
entelechy 58, 65, 67, 300, 304, 310
ergon 49, 254
essence 54, 59–60, 63–4, 110, 163, 178–80, 185, 188, 223–4, 232, 284, 289–90, 295, 300, 316
eternal 96, 103, 174, 221, 292, 295, 335, 354
ether *see* aether
eucharist 312
evil 44, 50, 107, 111, 117, 132, 157, 296
existence 92, 100, 103, 168, 175, 196, 292, 303, 318, 320, 334, 347
experience 75, 78, 285, 289, 300, 313, 332, 346
extension 74, 116, 123, 151–2, 168, 222, 243, 246, 286, 289, 291, 296, 321, 334, 345–6
extra-somatic 24, 31, 33, 80, 98, 250, 326
eyes 39, 49, 52, 58, 61, 68, 86–7, 135, 193, 203, 261, 263, 273

face 155, 166, 172, 193, 293
faculty 67, 75, 172, 183, 216, 282–5, 323, 345
faint *see* swoon
faith 102, 123, 146, 176, 197, 212, 215, 230, 323, 328, 330
fallen 33, 112, 130–31, 134, 140, 143, 153, 158, 188, 248
father 115, 124, 268, 321
fire 20, 26, 28–30, 77, 82, 136–7, 145, 159, 203, 232, 279–81, 325, 327, 342–3, 357
flesh 3, 20, 29, 33, 52, 61, 84, 97–100, 125–7, 132–4, 138, 142, 157–8, 201–2, 248, 251, 258, 353–4, 359
flower 83, 136, 327
food 4, 9, 41, 59, 90, 154–5, 203, 260, 273, 309
force 38, 85, 102, 138, 146, 252, 303–5, 309–10, 335, 343
form 34, 45–8, 51–2, 56, 58–60, 63–71, 110–11, 118, 153, 163, 170, 173, 178–9, 185, 193, 201, 222–3, 229, 234, 301, 310–11, 325, 328, 342, 355
fortune 210–12

free-will 5, 132–4, 158–9, 184, 200, 216, 322–3, 332, 335, 353
function 31, 49, 53–4, 59–61, 65, 70, 72, 77–9, 117, 139, 152, 170, 174, 193, 196, 203, 230, 254, 266, 277, 280–81, 309, 318, 335, 349, 359

garment *see* clothes
genius 52, 80, 115
genos 48, 66, 115, 125
ghost 37, 247–51, 257–9, 316–17, 321, 324
gift 94–6, 102, 126, 132, 175
Glaucus 50, 52, 118
glory 30, 47, 112, 133, 144, 187, 353
goals 59, 63, 65, 184, 194, 196–7, 320, 356
gods 25–6, 30–33, 38, 47, 51, 80, 115, 118, 234, 358
God 91, 93, 95–103, 106, 125–30, 132–60, 198, 200, 210–11, 214–16, 221, 224, 235–40, 257–9, 281, 284, 289, 292–4, 298–9, 301, 306, 310, 316–17, 319–24, 328, 334, 338, 343, 348, 356
going-under 23, 41, 43, 351
good 38, 40–41, 53–4, 76, 113, 115, 212, 223, 228, 248–9, 260, 296, 343
Gnostic 91, 93, 106, 109, 111–14, 117, 123–5, 131, 134, 139–40
growth 62, 120, 135, 140, 142, 152, 182, 188

habit 81, 167, 171, 182, 266, 275, 345
Hades 13, 45, 91, 96
hands 125–7
harmony 33, 52, 193, 217, 304, 311
head 4, 14, 39, 52, 78, 135, 263, 327
heart 8–11, 14–15, 18, 32, 60–62, 73, 78, 82, 101, 141, 170, 192, 203, 232, 246–7, 254, 257, 262, 270, 276, 280, 317–18, 351
heat 20, 26, 34, 64, 73, 81, 83, 136, 159, 187, 203, 239, 280, 342–3
heaven 48–50, 131, 136, 167, 173–5, 197, 200, 212, 220, 249, 328
hēgemonikon 74–5, 129–30, 170, 354
hell 97, 134, 250, 274, 320, 328, 353
heresy 109, 124, 131, 140, 145, 177
hexis 68, 73–4, 140, 292
Hermetic, -ism 207, 218, 220, 233–4, 236–7, 240, 242, 321, 329, 342, 356
hierarchy 114, 134, 167, 173, 185, 292, 308, 321

horses 46–7, 49, 77, 149–50, 218–19, 248
hugros 25, 29
hulē 52, 55, 67, 183
humanism 207–10, 217, 328, 355–6
humanity 155–7, 179, 196, 199, 210, 238, 325, 354
humors 85, 232, 268
hypostasis 56, 114, 144, 157
Hyperborea 23

ideas 77, 92, 201, 285–7, 293–5, 307, 316, 331–2, 338, 345–7
identity 17, 42, 98, 113, 120, 157, 174, 179, 186, 336, 348
ignorance 115, 212, 214, 237, 239, 315, 326
image 16, 20, 90, 110, 119, 125-6, 129, 133, 140, 149, 153, 194, 220–21, 229, 234, 254, 284, 316, 353
imagination 106, 229, 254, 263, 292, 297, 315, 332, 341, 345
immaterial 137, 145–6, 151, 156, 168, 172, 181, 185, 197, 228, 233, 288, 303, 307, 317, 328, 332, 334, 338–41, 347, 352, 355, 358–9
immortal, -ity 12, 23, 41–4, 49, 53, 76, 91–4, 103, 105, 128, 131, 140, 145–6, 153, 156, 175, 183, 186–8, 199, 202, 212, 216, 221, 227–30, 243, 250, 261, 272, 278, 280, 299, 306–7, 319, 323, 327–8, 330, 332, 341, 348, 351, 358
impressions 345–7
impulse 75, 82, 102, 210, 286, 334
incorporeal 31, 50, 52, 92, 103, 115–16, 146, 187, 215, 222–3, 237, 246, 316, 319–20, 355, 359–60
individual 5, 8–10, 13–14, 22, 42, 64, 79, 95, 98, 117, 125, 130, 149, 157, 163, 169, 174–5, 179, 188, 196, 199, 202, 209, 227, 243, 277, 304, 310, 328, 354, 359–60
infinite 31, 241, 291–3, 300, 302, 305, 309–10
initiation 44–5, 106, 236, 243
innate 80, 172, 285–7, 307, 316–17, 332, 353
inner 2–3, 5, 8–10, 13, 19, 94–5, 101, 104, 155, 160, 203, 216, 254, 266, 269, 276–7, 349
intellect 11–12, 15–16, 43–4, 55, 67, 75, 118–20, 129, 142, 162, 171, 174–5, 182–3, 189, 195–6, 199, 227–30, 251, 285, 293, 297, 316, 331–2, 354, 359
Intellect (Agent) 161–8, 171–5, 182–3, 354–5
intelligence 120, 164, 181, 224, 234, 291, 308
intelligible 92, 110, 112–15, 119, 215, 219, 243, 292, 360
intention 7, 102, 172, 182, 189, 270, 276, 282, 293, 333, 351
interaction 286–90, 295, 301, 307, 318, 344
intermediate 51, 103, 121–2, 154, 159, 164, 197, 228, 250
intuition 284–5, 294, 333, 341

journey 80, 145, 191, 211, 214, 336
Judaism 91, 94–5, 97, 127, 143, 237
judgment 9, 163, 181, 195, 268, 286, 297, 323
justice 42, 50, 53

kardia 2, 18, 62, 78, 101, 254
katabasis 41, 43
kephalos 52
kind 39, 47, 54, 58, 83, 93, 125, 138, 147, 169, 174, 184, 310, 350, 359
kinesis 24, 26, 52
knowledge 31, 41, 47, 58, 68–9, 78, 90, 114, 130, 145, 163, 167, 174, 183–5, 194–6, 214–15, 220, 230, 234, 255, 257, 259–60, 284–5, 290, 292–4, 308, 326–7, 334, 340, 346, 357
koinē 90
Koran 165, 175
krasis 51, 111, 144
kratein 27

language 30, 74–5, 294, 316
Lateran Council 227–8
learning 41, 58, 173, 182, 208, 212, 273
leb 2, 6, 8–12, 15, 22, 90, 101
letters 162
level 73, 104, 113, 133, 147, 158–9, 164–5, 185, 222, 251, 294–5, 302
libido 148
life-force 2–6, 8–10, 11–15, 17–20, 22, 34–5, 38, 46, 64, 86, 102, 107, 131, 144, 147, 185, 196, 240, 246–7, 254, 270, 297, 321, 336, 349–52
light 28–9, 67–8, 82, 112, 150, 180, 194, 220, 239, 343, 356

Index of Subjects

likeness 120, 125–6, 129, 153, 200, 206, 215, 247
limbs 81–3, 86, 168, 342
link, -age 180, 242, 284, 292, 298, 301, 312, 343
logic 55–6, 162, 234, 294, 298, 326
logos 16, 24, 28, 48, 54, 58, 61, 77, 92, 124, 128, 143, 179, 233, 360
love 5–6, 9, 32–3, 131, 142, 158, 190–91, 219, 225, 231, 251, 267, 271, 273–4, 295, 299, 321
lungs 14, 18, 284

machine *see* mechanical
madness 232, 260, 268, 274–6, 319, 323
magic 31, 34, 121, 207, 231–44, 277, 325, 351, 356
magnet 24, 26
Manichean 143, 145–6, 158
marrow 52, 62, 83–4, 102, 254
material 17, 25, 31, 42, 52, 54–60, 62–8, 70–71, 76, 82, 87, 110–12, 115, 118, 122, 125, 163, 168–70, 173, 180, 197, 201, 222, 229, 233, 239, 252, 283, 288, 304, 307, 315, 322, 326, 330–31, 334, 345–8, 351, 358–60
meaning 75, 99, 237, 282, 316, 319, 339–40, 349–50
mechanical 59, 74, 151, 280, 283, 286, 303–4, 307, 309, 315, 318, 328, 330–32, 335–7, 356
medical, -cine 8, 42, 72–3, 76, 80, 166, 192, 202, 252, 254, 258, 275, 279, 354, 357
meditate, -tion 118, 166, 263, 279–80
memory 9, 12, 31, 77, 90, 170, 183, 194, 252–7, 260–62, 269, 277, 306, 341, 351
menos 2, 17–18, 245
mens 2, 80–81, 139, 144, 185, 194, 250, 254, 280, 283, 293, 353, 357
microcosm 27, 215, 238, 268
microscope 308–10
might 256–7
milk 62, 77, 128
mirror 224, 243, 254, 256, 305
mixture 1, 31, 33, 42, 51, 72, 83, 111, 144, 149–50, 192, 281, 289–91, 310, 351
mode 292–3, 322, 347
moist, -ness 28–30
monad 300–312, 360
moral, -ity 9, 38, 46, 53, 99, 166, 189, 203, 220, 236, 245, 255, 308, 353

morphē 55
mortal, -ity 20, 22, 29–34, 38, 76, 79–80, 87, 99, 105, 210, 247, 277, 353, 358
motion 46, 78, 82, 84, 195, 222, 240, 284, 292, 296, 315, 318, 325, 334, 348
moving (self-) 12, 22, 24–5, 46, 51–2, 59, 63, 82, 93, 132, 144, 151–2, 166, 181, 183, 193, 222, 252, 293, 321, 325, 349
mystery 106, 133, 149, 187, 236, 326
mystics 32–3, 37, 53, 57, 109, 131, 203, 214, 257
myth 23, 42–4, 46, 50, 137

names, 78, 84, 138, 315–16, 332–3, 338, 342
nature 50, 54, 66, 80, 107, 115, 179–80, 199, 203, 206, 216, 231, 243, 285, 289, 292, 295, 298–9, 303, 317, 324, 342, 353
Neo-Platonism 113, 121, 129, 166, 173, 178, 197, 206, 218, 226, 234, 263, 321, 342, 354–6
nepesh 2–8, 11–12, 15, 22, 29, 90, 129, 155, 253, 349–50
neshama 4, 7–8, 22, 155
noein 16, 22, 65
noema 32
notion 234, 288, 294, 341
nous 2, 16, 18–19, 22, 25, 31, 43–4, 55, 65, 67–8, 73, 77, 92, 100–101, 110, 114, 128–9, 133, 145, 159, 189, 350, 353
nous poetikos 66–8, 118, 164, 175
number 51, 159
numen 135

occult 34, 235, 240, 243, 310, 356
octopus 74
okhēma 121–3, 144, 152, 158, 343
One, the 114, 120, 134, 165, 220
one-ness 149–50, 172–5, 358–9
operations 48, 139, 141, 180, 185, 193–5, 215, 227, 285, 288, 321, 331, 341
oracles 121, 139
order 69, 110, 113, 116, 120, 158, 165, 170, 186, 222, 238, 284, 287–8, 290, 292, 308, 324, 328, 354, 359
organ, -ic 12, 21, 60, 62, 64, 74, 116, 141, 170, 175, 180, 192, 199, 229–30, 280–81, 304, 310–12, 315, 318, 326, 335, 354, 359
origin (of souls) 112, 115–17, 120, 140, 148, 174, 220, 356

Orphic 22, 33, 37, 40, 44–5, 53, 236–7
ostreōdes 122
ousia 46, 48, 57, 60, 65–6, 129, 133, 141, 353
outer 3, 8, 22, 115, 266, 277, 350
oven 203

paideia 128, 171
parallelism 301, 311
part-for-whole 4, 11, 22, 157, 350
particles 81–2, 281, 284, 292, 306, 318, 326, 330, 335
particular 57–8, 117, 173, 175, 187, 243
parts 31, 40, 45–49, 51–3, 57, 61–3, 66, 72–4, 81, 86–7, 103, 105, 116, 125, 128, 131, 139, 144, 154, 157, 222–3, 228, 232, 273, 281, 284–7, 292, 296, 299, 304, 307, 321, 327–8, 343, 346, 353, 358–60
passions 59, 62, 130, 141, 211, 236, 254, 284–5, 290–91, 297, 318, 341
perception 9, 32, 62, 78, 86, 147, 163, 166, 189, 240, 263, 285, 302, 305, 308–9, 338–40, 344–7
perfection 65, 95, 118, 125–7, 130, 159, 166, 170, 186–8, 193, 195–7, 200, 202, 221–3, 234, 240, 246, 285, 295, 298–9
person 6, 11, 60, 90, 99, 104, 106, 149, 151, 158, 169, 200, 264, 295–7, 336, 359
phasma 21
philos, -ia 20, 32, 49
phronesis 32, 162
phrenes 15–18, 47
physical 54–6, 59, 71, 76, 99, 102, 104, 210, 277, 291, 360
Pimander 218, 233
plants 73–4, 140, 166, 199, 231, 251–2, 271, 299, 304, 336, 343
plasma, plasis 125, 130
plenum 93, 301
pleroma 168
plurality 167, 186, 300, 310
pneuma 2, 7, 22, 27, 49, 64, 71–5, 93–5, 101–3, 106–7, 115–16, 122, 125, 130, 133, 144, 155, 199, 232, 250, 320, 353
potential, -ity 58, 60–61, 66–8, 166–7, 172, 183
pollution 44, 276
post-formation 303, 309–10
power 8, 11, 25, 29, 31, 46, 49–50, 53, 66–8, 75, 86, 132, 135, 139, 141, 151–2, 161, 166, 174, 180–82, 188–9, 192–5, 215, 22, 247, 252, 256–7, 260, 282, 293, 318, 333, 338, 346
practice 42, 166, 184, 221, 285
prayer 233, 248
predicate 55–7, 70, 180, 303
pre-exist, -ence 45, 91–2, 103, 131, 133, 148–9, 303, 321, 325, 353, 358
pre-formation 303, 309–10
principium 8, 85, 195, 255
principle 25–7, 34, 57, 63, 68, 85, 114–15, 118, 163, 166, 180, 185, 200, 222–3, 243, 281–2, 288, 293, 304, 321–2, 336, 349, 355
prison 45, 50, 82, 93–4, 107, 111–12, 158, 188, 220, 268, 272
program 301, 305
pronominal 6, 102, 245, 350
property 23, 33, 54–6, 69–70, 83, 133, 302, 316, 333, 351
prophecy 8, 9, 31, 122, 124, 126, 163, 168
providence 76, 92, 112, 135, 137, 197
psychē 2, 11, 12–16, 19–20, 24–6, 28, 30, 33–5, 37, 40, 45–7, 53, 59, 63, 65–6, 69, 73–6, 90, 93–6, 100–102, 106–7, 115, 130, 133, 144, 147, 189, 200, 245, 306, 321, 349–53, 360
purify, -ication 24, 31, 33, 44, 147, 187, 295, 321

qualities 34, 52, 114, 333, 341, 344

ratio 28, 78, 84–5
ravish 250, 257–8, 271
reason 10, 16, 38, 43, 46, 49, 54, 75, 77, 110, 116, 145, 165–8, 172–4, 178–80, 193, 195–6, 202, 212, 215, 230, 251, 256, 261, 268, 294, 302, 306–8, 324, 328, 337, 345
rebirth 31, 37, 45, 106
reduce, -tion 54, 138, 160, 169, 291
reflect, -ion 9–10, 16, 44, 65, 95, 118, 120, 255, 262, 272, 298
resurrect, -ion 92, 97, 100, 103, 124–5, 133, 143, 152, 154, 158, 175, 180, 187, 202, 212, 239, 250, 320, 332, 353
return 13, 44, 53, 93, 120, 134, 145, 174, 193, 200, 215, 226
righteous 41, 91, 94, 133
ruach 2, 7–8, 10, 12, 16, 22, 103
ruling part 72, 74, 78, 129, 180

Index of Subjects

sacrifice 96, 253
salvation 7, 103, 121, 130–31, 134, 149, 158
sarx 29, 97, 99–101, 125, 248, 359
scale 73, 167, 201, 296, 343
science 73, 175–6, 183, 189, 194, 294, 308, 326, 349, 355
Scripture 92, 123–4, 137, 155, 319–21, 325, 328
seat 11–12, 21, 86, 93, 101, 127, 144, 246, 254, 258–9, 270, 327–8, 331, 350
seeds 25, 31, 52, 82–3, 106, 133–6, 201, 308, 310
seems 110, 266, 287
secret 107, 114, 168
self 3, 7, 11, 18, 30, 39–41, 75, 90, 120, 289, 316
self-conscious 296, 308, 336
semen 62, 74, 133, 135, 199, 233
sensation 38, 52, 67, 74, 78, 84, 86, 166, 181, 193, 284, 290, 305, 315
senses 9, 62, 74, 129, 142, 182, 189, 232, 287, 305, 318, 323, 332, 345
separate, -tion 60, 66, 85, 97, 100, 105, 120, 142, 157,172, 229–30, 288–90, 319, 331, 358
Septuagint (LXX) 2, 7, 11, 89, 92, 99, 144, 245
shade *see* double
shadow 188, 222, 224, 320, 325
shaman, -ism 13, 23–4, 31, 34, 40–41, 53, 351
simple 76, 285–8, 303, 306–7, 328, 333
simulacrum 19–20, 61, 120, 198, 215, 250
sin 44, 91, 97, 99, 107, 130, 156, 158–9, 202, 247, 259, 266, 274, 354
skeptic, -ism 74, 143, 207, 240, 282, 322, 326–7, 344–5, 357
skin 31, 63, 93
sleep 28, 38, 58, 64, 67, 94, 175, 256, 272, 306, 339, 349
smoke 16, 44, 86, 148, 232
snake 22
sōma 41, 66, 71, 91, 96–100, 106, 122, 359
sophists 41, 43, 137
spark 67, 131
species 30, 56, 65, 139, 153, 169, 173, 179, 182, 187–8, 194, 201, 233, 300, 325
speculate 195, 221
speech 81, 195, 252, 277, 291

spirit 48, 54, 91, 103–4, 122, 125, 133, 155, 186, 200, 232, 262, 305, 308, 322–4, 330, 340, 342, 353–4
Spirit, Holy 103, 114, 155, 200, 262, 353–4, 358
spirits (vital) 170, 192, 197, 239, 262, 277, 281, 287, 318, 354, 360
spiritus 2, 7, 81, 125, 144, 154–5, 232, 245, 250, 353
stars 47, 52, 73, 106, 112, 136, 232–3, 239, 271
statue 127, 233, 280
Stoics 25, 71–6, 94, 107, 109, 115, 118, 135, 137, 145, 150, 166, 170, 207, 228–9, 236, 245, 283, 308, 353–4, 358
struggle 19, 31, 134, 245, 248, 354
stuff 55, 72, 76, 86, 111, 338
subject 55–7, 181, 187, 303, 317–19, 336
substance 18, 34, 39, 50, 53–9, 62–70, 96, 104, 111, 138, 151, 153, 158, 169, 181–3, 185, 199, 227, 243, 246, 257, 281, 291, 295, 300–305, 310, 317–19, 333–6, 340–41, 346–7, 351, 353–5
suicide 94, 108
sun 49, 72, 119, 136, 221, 321
survival 33, 43, 60, 76, 96, 105, 169, 179, 187, 285, 358
swoon 13, 15, 260, 306

talismans 233–4
tension 72, 75
theory 65–7, 69, 166–7, 285
therapy 39–40, 42, 53, 212
theurgy 121, 127, 219, 233–4
thinking 32, 52, 60, 65, 68, 78, 83, 93, 114, 161, 172, 174, 216, 224, 247, 279–83, 305–6, 308, 316, 331, 334, 341, 347, 351, 357
thumos 15–17, 47–9, 81, 128, 139
tomb 43, 93, 111–12, 127
tomeus 102
touch 63, 86, 110, 168
translation 2, 11, 47–8, 79, 81, 89, 92, 99, 135–7, 144, 177, 189, 206–7, 251, 253, 319, 353, 355
transmigration 32–3, 38, 139–40, 271
Trinity, the 133, 153, 200, 238, 255, 257
truth 38, 68, 114, 137, 173, 176, 194, 212, 214–16, 221, 223, 230, 254, 284, 294, 296, 323–4, 356
tubules 32, 287

two-ness 105, 358, 360

unconscious 13–14, 302, 306
unicity 119, 172–5, 226, 359
uniform 61–4
unify, -ied 17–19, 57, 70, 73, 75, 78, 170, 193, 212, 301, 339, 352, 359
union 82, 99, 131, 150–51, 164, 169, 181, 188, 236, 285, 288, 295, 312, 331, 359
unity, -ed 13, 22, 75, 104, 137, 142, 150–51, 170, 179, 196–7, 222, 286, 288, 302–3, 308, 310–11, 322, 336, 339, 341, 352, 359
universal 56, 161, 166, 175, 189, 230, 316, 359

vapor 20, 82, 84, 200, 232
vegetative 147, 166, 181, 251, 321, 328
vehicle 32, 50, 93, 96, 121–3, 152, 158, 217, 325, 343
ventus 82, 84
vessel 43, 78, 150
vires 139, 254, 304

virtue 194, 240, 254, 256, 258, 351, 355
visible 67–8, 114, 118, 214, 221
vision 112, 118, 138, 144, 147, 168, 187, 214, 221, 226, 273, 354

wax 110, 119, 316
water 24–6, 28–9, 43, 64, 232
whole 39, 54, 57, 63, 81, 85–6, 99, 123, 200, 221, 287, 290–91, 299, 301, 359
will 8, 10–11, 117, 120, 146, 184, 195, 228, 245, 247, 256, 259–60, 285, 339–40, 351
wind 7, 27, 47, 82–4, 255, 279–80, 320, 357
windows 86, 194, 203, 301
wings 46–7, 117, 220, 271
wisdom 9–10, 32, 38, 44, 89, 91, 110, 117, 145, 147, 156, 159, 190, 217, 236, 243, 356
wit 247, 251, 253, 257, 260, 263, 323
world-soul 72, 110, 116–17, 119, 134, 137, 219, 232, 243, 272, 325, 342, 356
worm 201, 276, 300